Microsoft® Exchange Server 2003 Scalability with SP1 and SP2

Microsoft® Exchange Server 2003 Scalability with SP1 and SP2

Pierre Bijaoui

ELSEVIER
DIGITAL
PRESS

Amsterdam · Boston · Heidelberg · London · New York · Oxford
Paris · San Diego · San Francisco · Singapore · Sydney · Tokyo

Elsevier Digital Press
30 Corporate Drive, Suite 400, Burlington, MA 01803, USA
Linacre House, Jordan Hill, Oxford OX2 8DP, UK

∞ Recognizing the importance of preserving what has been written, Elsevier prints its books on acid-free paper whenever possible.

Library of Congress Cataloging-in-Publication Data
Application Submitted.

British Library Cataloguing-in-Publication Data
A catalogue record for this book is available from the British Library.

ISBN-13: 978-1-55558-300-2

ISBN-10: 1-55558-300-8

For information on all Elsevier Digital Press publications visit our Web site at www.books.elsevier.com

Transferred to Digital Printing 2009

To my family

Contents

Foreword

I began using Exchange on servers that had 80486-class CPUs, boasted an amazing 32MB of memory, and offered all of 4GB of disk to hold system and user files. That was just ten years ago, yet it seems that an incredible distance has grown in terms of the hardware that is now available as a platform for Exchange. Over the same period, user expectations and behavior have changed too. In 1996, users did not send as many messages as now, the messages were not as bloated as they are now, and we did not have the many ways that we have to interact with Exchange through the various clients that now exist. Other influences include the appearance of the plague of spam and viruses that afflict all email systems, the growing need for compliance, and the move to Internet protocols. And then you have the fact that email is firmly on the list of mission critical applications for companies, so business continuity and resilience against natural and man-made disasters have to be taken into account. Looking back, the world of Exchange was much simpler in 1996.

Because everything is now so much more complex, it is more than useful to have practical guides available to help answer the difficult questions that any Exchange deployment throws up. Performance and scalability are in this category because, while you can model the performance of Exchange in a lab or test environment, the results that you see through simulation do not always correspond with real life. Simulated users don't behave like real users, test systems are usually set up and managed better than production servers, tests often ignore the fact that other software (like anti-virus) steal CPU cycles on production servers, and the test plan usually focuses on just one client type rather than the mixture of Outlook, mobile, and web clients that Exchange servers support on a daily basis. The bottom line is that you need to do more than just test Exchange in a lab to be able to achieve reliable levels of acceptable performance over a sustained period when servers are used by real-life people.

This book will help you to understand the critical elements in an Exchange 2003 ecosystem that you need to focus on to achieve the desired level of performance. I won't pretend to be an expert in hardware and I don't think that you need to understand the finer details of server or storage hardware to be able to deploy and manage Exchange successfully, but you do need to understand the fundamentals of the interaction between Exchange and its supporting hardware. There are just too many examples of bad deployments due to a lack of knowledge on the part of the administrators, especially in storage configuration, an aspect that is becoming more critical as the amount of data used by Exchange grows.

All we can predict for the future is that technology will continue to change, so while the details of performance tweaking will change for new versions of Exchange, new server technology, and new storage configurations, I think that the fundamentals will remain the same. Pierre has lived Exchange performance for the last decade. His real value is that he approaches the issue in a pragmatic and practical way so that even people who don't want to be in-depth experts in performance can understand the fundamentals of how to keep their server running smoothly.

Tony Redmond

Vice President and Chief Technology Officer

HP Services

Preface

The Albatross
Charles Baudelaire [1821-1867]

Often to pass the time on board, the crew
will catch an albatross, one of those big birds
which nonchalantly chaperone a ship
across the bitter fathoms of the sea.

Tied to the deck, this sovereign of space,
as if embarrassed by its clumsiness,
pitiably lets its great white wings
drag at its sides like a pair of unshipped oars.

How weak and awkward, even comical
this traveler but lately so adroit -
one deckhand sticks a pipestem in its beak,
another mocks the cripple that once flew!

The Poet is like this monarch of the clouds
riding the storm above the marksman's range;
exiled on the ground, hooted and jeered,
he cannot walk because of his great wings.

Charles Baudelaire's albatross is what Microsoft Exchange might have been without the efforts of many of us to propagate knowledge, generate and transmit know-how, and establish best practices for the software.

As we all look forward to the next generation of Microsoft Exchange, called Exchange 2007 (E12), this book might seem a bit outdated to you. In fact, it is not at all so. Not all customers will proceed to ramp-up with Exchange 2007 as fast as Microsoft and possibly other vendors would want. Moreover, the notion of legacy is quite strong in complex IT environments, although I would certainly not yet qualify Exchange 2003 as being "legacy."

Exchange 2007 opens up new ways of deploying Microsoft Exchange, it takes unprecedented advantage of technologies such as 64-bit computing, and it implements storage management functions, such as replication. These were long awaited for the Microsoft Exchange platform, and were only possible with a drastic change of the product.

This said, some things remain, and while you might think that you should focus your research and development on the eventual Exchange 2007 roll-out, you should also consider how you are going to maintain and run your existing environment, based on Exchange 2003 SP2.

This book took an unusual amount of time to be produced. Of course, it is a second edition, and as such, builds upon the first edition. On the other hand, it does discuss areas which were too lightly covered in the opinion of the readers, such as Storage Networks. It also covers newer technologies, such multi-core processing and iSCSI. Best practices have also evolved, as well the whole ecosystem that Microsoft Exchange is part of.

High performance and scalability remain topics of importance, right after the considerations for high availability. They are not so easy to dissociate, but they need to be addressed, and both at the same time. Without a performing environment, you will get mail delays, user connections dropped, and eventually frustration building up amongst your user communities. Like it or not, email is becoming more and more a business-critical application to the enterprise. We have some strong indicators at HP that many customers are moving Exchange (and more generally speaking, mail and messaging) to their Tier-1 application standards. This means that Exchange gets to benefit from business continuity infrastructure components; it also means that it needs to comply with these business continuity components and processes and policies.

Exchange 2003 is still very relevant. I expect many customers will move to Exchange 2007, and I think they will get a lot of value from that transition. But I also believe that many other customers will continue on the

Exchange 2003 technology path for some time, and for many good reasons. I hope this book can be a good resource to help them in dealing with technology change, and in dealing with continuity of their Microsoft Exchange service.

Acknowledgments

This book was written during a special period of both my social and professional life. It could not have been finished without the support of my editor, of my family, and my company.

Many people helped me finish this project. I would like to thank Tony Redmond for giving me the energy and inspiration to get through this work, and for sharing his drive towards excellence. Tony's a great mentor and leader and I feel very lucky being able to work with him.

The people I work with at Hewlett Packard are just fantastic. I have been through two major computing industry mergers. I have seen friends leave, I've made new friends, and I kept some old friends. All through my career at HP, I've worked with very talented people, and I feel very privileged to have done so. I would like to thank my friends Kieran McCorry, Kevin Laahs, and Donald Livengood; being part of the Exchange Academies with my buddies and the rat pack is something that one is lucky to do once in a lifetime. I know that Kevin is embarking on a new journey with Exchange 2007 with a great crew and I wish him and his team good wind!

Beyond the Academy team, the Advanced Technology Group at HP is the collection of some of the most talented people I have ever met. Being a team is more than just being part of the same reporting structure. It is also about helping others do their job, and helping them to succeed. Stan Foster, John Rhoton, and everyone at ATG helped in their own unique way and I'm very grateful to them for that.

I'm based in a relatively small HP facility located in the Southeast of France and you are welcome to visit me. If you come, you will find the site is not exactly small: it is concentrated. It has an incredible quantity of experienced and talented people, with whom taking a coffee break is like going to a two day lecture at the university. In particular, I wish to thank Christophe Dubois for those opinions that he is never short of and for the time he generously spends with my colleagues and I at HP. He's hardly short of anything, as a matter of fact, and is one of the cleverest and kindest people I've ever met.

There are many other people with talent, kindness, and generosity where I work. I would like to thank Denis Cotta for his availability to help; Patrick François, Patricia Darmon, Thierry Carpentier, Armand Zuntini, Didier Lalli, Christophe Bedin, Maria Jordan, and all the people at plateau 1G in Sophia Antipolis. Not only they are talented, they are also fun to work with.

Thanks to modern telecommunications and networking technologies, at HP we really feel close to our colleagues, even when distance and time set us apart. I would like to thank Steve Tramack and his team; they are really the best at getting a server smoking and making sense of performance benchmarking. I think that the HP StorageWorks Customer Focused Testing team is embarking on a tough journey, and will be successful by showing expertise in core technologies and their application to complex customer situations. Mike Good, Rich Gianattasio, and Stephanie Schwartz are leading a great team of technologists, such as Christophe Dubois, Bob Snyder, Mike Rolinson, and Hollis Beal. I'm sure I'm forgetting many here, but none in my heart.

At HP we work hard to turn an individual's knowledge into global know-how. Sharing best practices and customer experience is not an easy task, but HP Services and C&I did embark on that journey a few years ago. As a result, the community of consultants and senior technologists in relation to Microsoft technologies in general and Microsoft Exchange in particular is just second to none in the industry. I'm very proud to be part of them, as they are all valorous brothers in arms: Mike Daugherty, Tim Garrett, Tonino Bruno, Thomas Strasser, Patrice Rondeau, and Jean-François Debuisson are people I've had the honor and pleasure to work with, and who help HP remain the Number One system integrator for Microsoft-based infrastructures. Special thanks to Juergen; he's a great person to learn from, in many aspects, both technical and human.

And then, there are people that I worked with who allowed me to discover my passions and who mentored me, and are no longer with HP. Because the world is so small, perhaps they will come back. In any case, I wish them well.

I would like to thank the customers I have worked with, because they have had something challenging to deal with, and working with them is an everyday learning experience. And finally, I'd like to thank Microsoft and some people in particular, Matt Gossage, Paul Bowden, Robert Quimbey, and Laurion Burchall: they all helped in this project, and also in my everyday work.

Acknowledgements would not be complete without a quick hug to my buddy Franc Gentili-it's funny how souls can meet and then never disband, whatever the distance, the destiny of each, and the time that runs like a mountain water stream.

Finally, I think Theron Shreve, at Elsevier, is an incredible person, and without his tenacity, I would have certainly abandoned this project. Alan Rose and Tim Donar contributed to the production of this book and were professional and flexible to work with. I would also like to extend my respect and sincere gratitude to Jerry Cochran of Microsoft, who helped me all through this project in the technical editing.

I started this section with a reference to my family, and I would like to close with another. Having kids is the most enriching experience I've ever had. I think they are just great; I think they are fun and that they have the one true flame that burns in their heart. I just hope that they'll never lose that genuine love inside them as they grow up and move on. Work has taken me away from them on occasion and I wish to thank them and my wife for their patience in dealing with it.

Family and love work well together.

Pierre Bijaoui.

Exchange 2003 Architecture

1.1 Introduction

For the overall purpose of this book and to better explain the concepts related to Exchange 2003 scalability, this chapter reviews the Exchange 2003 architecture. It identifies the main components and reveals the most critical components used in high-end environments as well as scale-up and scale-out models (many transactions or users per server and many servers in a single Exchange 2003 organization).

Microsoft Exchange 2003 embodies many features of both Microsoft Exchange 5.5 and Microsoft Commercial Internet Services (MCIS): it is a solid database engine for messaging and collaboration information, coupled with a scalable and unique way to deal with that information. The last feature, implemented through the Exchange Installable File System in Exchange 2003, is quite a new way for clients and protocol servers to deal with the storage databases.

Microsoft Exchange, as a product family, has evolved by proposing a client/server–based model (at a time when file-share messaging systems were being deployed, such as cc:Mail or MS-Mail) to a fully scalable high-end platform for enterprise and Internet messaging and collaboration, as it is today.

In fact, Microsoft Exchange is becoming an increasingly important source of information in an enterprise and may very well feed rich applications with information and processes, such as workflow processes.

When Microsoft Exchange 4.0 was released in the first quarter of 1996, the messaging market was vastly disparate, ranging from file-sharing solutions such as MS-Mail, cc:Mail, or GroupWise, to true enterprise-level but niche client/server messaging systems, such as Digital's ALL-IN-1 product.

This initial release was in fact the first milestone in a series of technology steps being taken while Microsoft was learning from the Microsoft Exchange deployments. This happened at a time when enterprises were making increasingly stringent demands of the messaging infrastructure, viewing it as a mission-critical function.

The real improvement introduced at the time was to use not a file share for message repository, but a true transacted database that could contain the messaging information and could also roll transactions back or forward as a result of data insertion or deletion in the database. Not many products at the time were capable of such functions, and while this technique is in fact quite common in the relational database world, it was quite a novelty compared with file-sharing messaging solutions in the Windows environments.

Moving on, Microsoft made a first technology step in the first quarter of 1997, about 12 months after releasing the initial version of the product.

This resulted in a closer relationship with and better support for the Internet protocols. Remember that in 1996, X.400 was the predominant messaging transport, and, quite appropriately, Microsoft Exchange 4.0 was based on that protocol. Nevertheless, as time went on, Simple Mail Transport Protocol (SMTP), which was used primarily to exchange information over the Internet, became more and more popular. However, it was still not sufficiently powerful to meet the X.400 specifications for message transfers (due to lack of delivery and read notifications and of a reliable transfer service required to efficiently cope with the data network reliability).

The common point between those two releases, which was in fact a major scalability limit, was the maximum size of the single mailbox storage you could have on a single server: 16 GB. In 1996, that quantity of information seemed a lot, given that the industry was still shipping 1-GB and 2-GB disk drives. Nevertheless, the push for more data to be stored in Exchange servers for hosting users' collaboration and messaging information forced the introduction of Microsoft Exchange 5.5 in the fourth quarter of 1997, along with support for the unlimited storage in the Enterprise Edition of the product. There was (and still is) a limit for the storage database of 16 TB, but no one in their right mind would deploy a single-file database of 16 TB—even today, when that amount of information could fit in the trunk of the once popular Volkswagen Beetle.

Microsoft Exchange 5.5 arrived on the marketplace and introduced more connectors for use with "legacy" messaging systems, especially those running in the IBM environment—for example, the PROFS (for OfficeVM) and SNADS (for Memo/MVS) connectors.

That time was the beginning of a long period during which Microsoft was in fact preparing for the next major technology step of Exchange, code-named Platinum. In the meantime, most enterprises managed to deploy quite effective organizations and Exchange-based networks, and Exchange rapidly became one of the two leading products for enterprise messaging.

Many designs were based on X.400 connectors and backbones, then thought to be more reliable in adverse networking infrastructures and, in fact, since proven to be.

Use of the Internet as a business communication tool was becoming a major trend, and the Internet features of Exchange that appeared in releases 5.0 and 5.5 became more and more predominant. X.400 was becoming less used, and Microsoft put much of the focus of its development teams on supporting native SMTP out of the store (this is why the Internet Mail Connector of Exchange 4.0 and 5.0 became the Internet Mail Service in Exchange 5.5), as well as Internet client protocols such as IMAP and POP.

Another interesting point that the Microsoft Exchange designs introduced was the notion of specialization of servers, known as "server roles." You could now deploy one server hosting mailboxes, another hosting public folders, two or three dedicated to message switching within the Exchange organization and beyond, and so on. But computing technology evolved and steadily followed Moore's law: doubled capacity every year and doubled computing power every year. Random Access Memory (RAM, also known as the physical memory of the server) prices came down, and that led many customers to realize that deploying many servers was not necessarily the most efficient way to run a messaging system. Microsoft has a service pack and hotfix release schedule that seriously impacts companies' decisions to deploy and maintain several hundreds of servers.

Each of the servers could fail, potentially impacting the overall messaging function, and each required attention. The time and attention required could be mitigated by means of monitoring products, but the multiserver approach still entailed complex administrative structures that were adversely affecting the cost of the overall infrastructure.

Total cost of ownership became a buzzword phrase, and many of the customers and implementers of Exchange started to *consolidate* servers by hosting more users per server (which was facilitated by the unlimited storage capacity introduced in Microsoft Exchange 5.5). This involved increased risk of an adverse effect should a server go down; because more users would be affected, restore times and timely recoverability of data and service became and continues to be a major concern for nearly every

Microsoft Exchange deployment, regardless of the scalability and reliability features of Windows and Exchange 2000.

During the three years between the release of Microsoft Exchange 5.5 and that of Microsoft Exchange 2000, Microsoft, as a software vendor, didn't remain inactive. The firm started to get customers used to the notion of service packs, which initially were aimed at fixing problems but gradually included more and more functionality along with corrective fixes for problems found. There was an attempt to differentiate between service packs intended to fix problems and service packs that introduced new functionality.

From this came the notion of the option pack, introduced by Microsoft for Windows NT, as well as feature packs. In addition to features packs (which are now simply called *service packs*), Microsoft releases tools and add-ons to the base product by the means of Web releases. They are by no means mandatory to deploy; however, they often provide incremental functionality and help in the troubleshooting and maintenance of Microsoft Exchange infrastructures.

Eventually, Microsoft reverted to a single update release scheme for its products by means of service packs, and, while most of them are produced to add more functionality, quite a few remain designed to fix new problems in the product sets. Never underestimate the power of service packs; it would be virtually impossible to ignore the service pack rollout in any Windows or Exchange deployment nowadays.

The third quarter of 2000 was a big milestone in Microsoft's history of messaging and collaboration products. Microsoft Exchange 2000, also known as Platinum, was finally released to meet the demand that emerged from an increased usage of messaging within enterprises and on the Internet.

Exchange 2003 should have been a service pack, too, but the changes incurred in that release required users to run the administrator through a full setup scenario, including schema changes required to support the mobility features built into the product.

To date, Exchange 2003 has two additional services packs (SP1 and SP2), which bring their load of feature adding and bug fixing. None of them, however, changes fundamentality the architecture of Microsoft Exchange. If you are familiar with Exchange 2000, you will have little trouble in migrating to Exchange 2003 and adopting its new functions.

This book focuses on the scalability aspects of Exchange 2003. Much of this book concentrates on the aspects of scaling up the back-end Exchange 2003 servers, which host the users' mailbox information. This particular server role needs a lot of attention, because of the way Exchange 2003 stores information. There can be only one instance of a mailbox active in a Microsoft Exchange network, and, unlike other enterprise collaboration environments, Exchange 2003 does not support the notion of application-level replication when it comes to user mailboxes.

Another aspect of this book focuses on the ability of Microsoft Exchange to handle large quantities of SMTP (message) traffic. The growth of email use in business means that more and larger messages are exchanged on a daily basis. Considering additional traffic resulting from pollution (spam) and virus attacks (worms that automatically send email), you rapidly realize that you need unusual message transfer capabilities and headroom in these capabilities for handling surges in traffic. Microsoft does not stay idle in the way it can combat such "malware" of the twenty-first century, and new features, such as Outlook 2003 Intelligent Message Filtering and Sender ID, were introduced in the Exchange 2003 product family.

The remainder of this chapter aims at providing some background information about the product, relevant to the scalability slant of common deployments, and some additional information about the product's internal functions. The aim is to provide a better understanding of the relevant technologies, the deep interaction with the Windows Server operating system and Active Directory infrastructures, and ways to take most of the product.

1.2   Benefits at a Glance

Microsoft Exchange 5.5 proved to be a very successful product, one quite applicable to most environments. But from the good, Microsoft decided to produce the better (while waiting for the best) by introducing Microsoft Exchange 2000, bringing key benefits to the enterprise and commercial Internet environments (known as service providers). This section aims at describing those benefits; it is assumed that the reader has good background knowledge of Microsoft Exchange's features.

The benefits can be summarized as follows:

- Microsoft Exchange 2000 introduced improved scalability, providing lower total cost of ownership and greater availability by enabling more mailboxes per server while enabling a high level of consolidation.

- Standards are upheld by supporting and enhancing the Internet-based protocols controlled by the Internet Engineering Task Force (IETF), which issues requests for comments (RFCs), the basis for standards in the Internet world. When the standards did not meet the product requirements, Microsoft enhanced these standards. Through a process of feedback, the enhancements were incorporated into the standardization process, and the firm is committed to implementing the standards once they have been validated by the IETF RFC submission process. For example, extensions were brought to the Simple Mail Transfer Protocol (SMTP) implementation in Exchange 2003, allowing a more optimized traffic within a Microsoft Exchange infrastructure, and they are available to the public to be retrofitted in other non-Microsoft components of a messaging infrastructure.

- Microsoft Exchange 2000 is integrated with Windows 2000 and the latest features of the Windows server family—the Volume Shadow-Copy Services introduced by the Whistler code base (Windows XP for the desktop and Windows Server 2003 for the servers), Active Directory, Internet Explorer 5, Internet Information Service 5, and Clustering. These components, part of the Windows Server environment, are utilized by Microsoft Exchange, since Exchange 2000, and onwards with Exchange 2003 and SP2.

- Microsoft Exchange 2000 helps the information worker: we tend to deal with a constant information overflow, increasing volumes of data and traffic, and the need to communicate anytime, anywhere. Exchange 2003 integrates the mobility functions that used to be available from Microsoft Mobile Information Server and deals more efficiently with Microsoft Outlook. Today, you can no longer assume that a client of Microsoft Exchange connects using only Outlook during office hours. There is a necessity for a 24 × 7 availability model, with little or no maintenance window, designed not only for the large enterprise; Small and Medium Businesses (SMB) have similar needs for larger businesses, with, possibly, fewer and less knowledgeable IT personnel.

This list is by no means exhaustive, and the reader can find many valuable sources of information (starting with the Microsoft Exchange Web site at http://www.microsoft.com/exchange) that actually deal with these benefits.

For the focus of this book, I would like to concentrate on the features that make Microsoft Exchange a truly scalable platform for developing messaging services for the most demanding enterprises and Internet commercial services.

1.2.1   The View from 10,000 Feet

The Exchange 2003 component architecture is rich and complex. Presenting the various components in action, along with their mutual relationship, is best done graphically. I shall refer to such graphical views many times in the book, mostly by concentrating on particular areas. Figure 1.1 gives an overview of the Exchange 2003 architecture, leaving out certain parts that will be covered later.

Figure 1.1 shows many components, some of which will be familiar, others not so familiar. As we move on in this chapter and in the rest of this book, you will see the relationships between each of these components.

Figure 1.1
*Exchange 2003
global architecture*

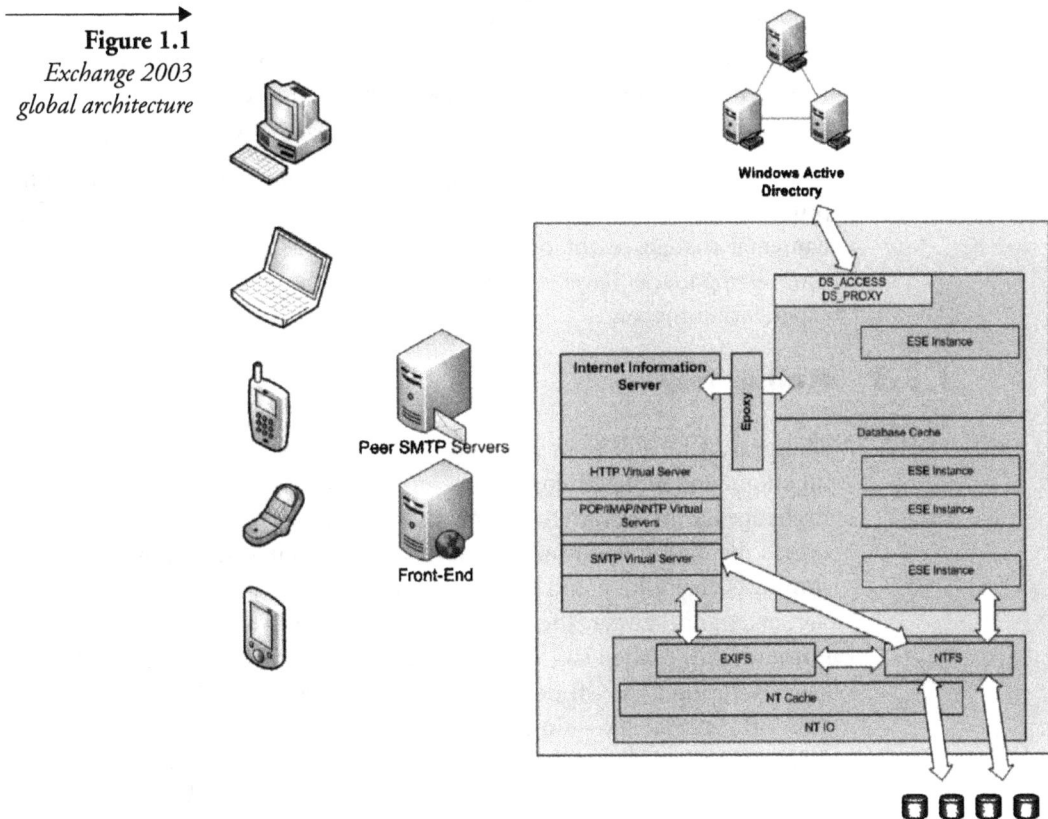

1.3 **RAMS**

RAMS was an abbreviation used by my team when we delivered the very first Exchange 2000 Academy program in September 1999. After spending several months working with the Microsoft engineering team and developing the material, Donald Livengood of Hewlett Packard (HP) came up with the RAMS acronym, which is derived from *reliability, availability, manageability,* and *scalability.* These four key features are well implemented and represented by many key functions of the product.

In fact, since the release of Microsoft Exchange 2000 in late 2000, and later with Exchange 2003, many deployments managed to benefit from the RAMS features of the product, described further in this section. More importantly, Exchange 2003 managed to grow out of the features from the Windows Server 2003 environment, and, for each service pack or major release, improves on the reliability, availability, manageability, and scalability.

Had the journey ended just yet? Definitely not—Microsoft gets to deal with a legacy of Microsoft Exchange rollouts; even for future versions of the product, we will see improvement in each of these areas. Some require fundamental changes at the operating system level, application level, or hardware components level. As each mature, the end solution and user experience improves.

1.3.1 **Reliability**

The goal of reliability in Microsoft Exchange 2003 is to perform service functions under stated conditions within a given time period. Microsoft Exchange has often suffered from database corruption errors that could be caused by faulty hardware or software components, imposing on the administrators a long and painful recovery process involving part or all of the server and, always, the entire corrupted database. When Exchange 5.5 introduced unlimited storage, it also left the door open to unlimited problems: restoring a 16-GB database file takes much less time than restoring a 250-GB database file—time during which the users do not have access to their mail service. Some deployments today have to deal (suffer?) with +1.5-TB Information Stores, which cannot be repaired rapidly and for which backup and recovery are painful.

To the extent possible, Microsoft improved the core database engine utilized in Microsoft Exchange—Extensible Storage Engine (ESE)—to prevent any malformed database pages from being stored on disk. Exchange 4.0 introduced the notion of database pages whose content could be validated by a simple checksum calculated over the 4-KB block making up a database page. If the checksum stored with the page differed from the checksum calculated after reading the page, the database was considered corrupted, and the database was flagged as bad. With Exchange 2003 SP2, the checksum can recover information: a single-bit flip can be recovered by using an error-correcting checksum algorithm (instead of using a simple error detection algorithm).

In a situation with page-level corruption, you have two choices:

1. Run the ESEUTIL tool to remove the invalid pages;
2. Restore the last known good database from backup and play back the intermediate transactions stored in the transaction log files.

In fact, neither of these two solutions is very satisfactory, especially the first, since it could lead to irreversible loss of data—which is impermissible in modern infrastructures.

Microsoft worked hard to reduce the likelihood of software-based corruption. Today, virtually all page corruptions are due to faulty hardware: the component at fault could be a disk, a controller, or an interconnect element, such as a host-bus adapter, or fibre channel link (just like software, hardware and firmware have bugs, too!). Some of these components have their own built-in recovery mechanisms, and with Exchange 2003 SP2, very few page-level corruptions are occurring; this is one thing the Microsoft Exchange administrator does not have to worry about anymore!

In conjunction, hardware manufacturers have vastly improved the reliability of storage infrastructures, especially when these are put under stress load or abnormal activities (for example, a RAID5 volume rebuild). They didn't really wait for Microsoft to do this, but as RAID and multidisks volumes became more utilized, a significant effort and investment was put forth to ensure that volume protection was actually efficient. In addition, the notion of checksum has been extended to the transaction log records (preventing you from playing back a corrupted transaction into the database) and, with SP1, to the streaming store.

Unfortunately, we are still lacking the tools needed to recover data from corrupted transaction log files. This can be an issue because if for some reason your database needs to be recovered and transactions played back, and if the transaction logs are corrupted halfway through the replay, you essentially have lost data. I will remind you several times in this book: protecting the transaction log volume is far more important, in terms of data recoverability, than protecting the main database.

Beyond storage data and information, reliability must be ensured in how the information is actually handled. A good example is the Anti-Virus Application Programming Interface (AVAPI) that Microsoft developed and enhanced to enable high-performance virus scanning, without the need of running interleaved code as part of the Information Store. This allows to create a better isolation between the Microsoft Exchange product base and solutions from Independent Software Vendors (ISV), achieving reliability and stability of the overall solution.

1.3.2   Availability

Availability is of great concern to IT administrators, especially when they attempt to perform server consolidation with Microsoft Exchange and its multiple database model. The most important feature in terms of availability has been the introduction of native clustering support in Exchange 2000. It is not the only feature, though: multiple front-end and bridgehead servers are an important part of Exchange's availability functions.

But the main one remains the support of clustering. Clustering is an important concept in making available solutions in the data centers. Put simply, clustering consists of logically and physically grouping and interconnecting two or more computers to perform a common task. Introduced with Windows NT 4 Enterprise Edition and now available in Windows 2000 Advanced Server and Data Center editions and Windows Server 2003 Enterprise and Data Center Editions, Microsoft Cluster Services (MSCS, also known as *Wolfpack*) provide core services on a group of two to eight computers maximum to allow an application to *failover* from one node to another if the cluster resources that it utilizes and relies upon are made unavailable (a resource can be a network interface, IP address, network name, or a disk).

Clustering has been one of the many strengths of Digital's (now HP's) OpenVMS operating system, and in fact, Microsoft's clustering technology borrows a lot from OpenVMS's concepts, with the exception of shared storage.

Indeed, in a Microsoft cluster, while two or more machines are sharing a storage enclosure, each logical unit (disk, volume, RAID set) can be accessed by only one node at any point in time. If the owning node fails, that logical unit can be brought over to one of the other nodes in the cluster, but it is not possible to see and access securely a single logical disk drive (and therefore a single file or database) simultaneously from more than one node in a cluster.

In short, Microsoft Windows 2000 and 2003 clustering lacks a distributed lock manager, a component that can arbitrate who does what on which block and logical unit number (LUN) in a fully shared clustered environment.

Do not think that clustering solves all the problems. In fact, many more reasons for downtime are not addressed by clustering technology, the main one being system administration mistakes and systems upgrades. For example, have you ever tried to match the mean time between failures (MTBF) of a system administrator with that of any single component of a server, such as a disk drive? That said, clustering does help in performing system maintenance and upgrades (by moving all resources owned by a node to another node in order to service the server), and removing any single point of failure as far as the server component is concerned. This, today, represents the number one reason for using Microsoft Exchange Clustering and is far more interesting than a few years ago, given the frequency at which Microsoft releases service packs for both Windows and Exchange and imposes (strongly recommends) installing security hotfixes.

With Exchange 5.5, the clustering feature was supported by the generic resource management function, which was basically forcing the services to run either on one machine or on the other (active/passive). That caused Microsoft Exchange 5.5 clustering to be considered too weak and expensive by the customer base to gain an anonymous adoption.

With Exchange 2000, all nodes in a cluster can actually run the Exchange 2000 services and functions at the same time and provide messaging services to the end-user community and peer servers and applications. This is also known as active/active clustering and represents a major improvement for Exchange 2000.

With Exchange 2003, the Active/Passive mode of operation is recommended, guaranteeing failover and failback procedures between nodes inside the cluster. What has changed with Windows Server 2003 is the ability to run clusters with up to eight nodes from Enterprise Edition onward, leading to a necessary overhead (passive server) much smaller than in the case of a two-node cluster. For instance, we can observe deployments of five-node or seven-node clusters with only one passive node.

To operate the Exchange components (resources) inside a cluster, Microsoft provides an Exchange-specific resource management library, such that a particular storage group, part of a given Exchange Virtual

Server (EVS), can be served from one node or another, independently of other EVSs. This is a "10,000-feet" overview of clustering. For a better understanding of clustering with Exchange and high availability in general, I highly recommend Jerry Cochran's *Mission-Critical Microsoft Exchange 2003: Designing and Building Reliable Exchange Servers*, November 26, 2003, published by Digital Press Storage Technologies.

In summary, clustering does help in terms of both removing the single point of failure that a server can represent and performing server maintenance, but it will never protect against storage failures, network services failures, major disasters, and operational or procedural failures.

In addition, clustering does not help scalability. As mentioned in the preceding paragraph, clustering helps in bringing redundancy to certain scenarios, but it imposes scalability limits, making it hard to justify full active/active clustering (compounded with the fact that Microsoft strongly recommends running an active/passive configuration instead). In any case, if you do intend to take advantage of clustering, make a careful analysis of your service downtime instances and determine whether clustering does bring real added value.

For example, in our own experience at HP in deploying Microsoft Exchange 2000 and Exchange 2003, we found that the majority of failures, as perceived by the end users, were due either to surrounding network services ((Domain Name System, DNS or active directory servers) or to invalid client configurations—rarely to the servers themselves.

Another availability feature is the ability to separate Internet protocol handling from the main mailbox (also referred to as *back-end*) servers and dedicate one or more servers to act as front-end servers that can be in direct contact with the end users. If a front-end server fails, DNS load balancing enables another front-end server to carry on the processing of users' client protocol commands. Nevertheless, the front-end servers by themselves do not hold any particular piece of information and are pretty much useless if the back-end servers that actually host the users' mailboxes or the public folder hierarchies are down. Therefore, do not assume that using many front-end servers alone will provide great availability absent sufficient care for the back-end servers.

1.3.3 Manageability

One of the big problems with the Microsoft Exchange 5.5 release and prior ones is the administration model. As you know, Microsoft Exchange 5.5 incorporates its own directory, which is linked to the users' account, whether it is located in a SAM database on a Windows NT Domain Controller or in the Active Directory for Windows 2000 environments.

One problem of management with the Exchange 5.5 directory is that in order to make a change in a particular Exchange 5.5 site, you have to connect to a server belonging to that site. There is little chance to make changes that can be replicated to the entire environment from a single seat or a single access point to the Exchange 5.5 directory. This is because the directory is partitioned according to Exchange 5.5 sites (a partition is called a naming context), and servers outside of the site have read-only access.

Microsoft Exchange 2003 does not own the directory of information related to the end users, nor even its configuration in the Microsoft Exchange organization. It relies on the presence of a fully functional and deployed Windows Active Directory forest, which it uses to store configuration information in the configuration naming context as well as user information in the form of additional attributes to the user object. This is enhanced by modifying the schema when you install the first Exchange 2000 server in a Windows Active Directory forest. This operation happens before the server is actually defined in the Exchange 2000 forest, and it can be dissociated from the server installation by running SETUP with the FORESTPREP command switch. Figure 1.2 gives a synoptic view of the main Active Directory naming contexts and objects.

As you can see, information related to Microsoft Exchange is stored in two distinct locations:

1. The configuration naming context, which holds most of Exchange's configuration, including objects and attributes relative to performance tuning;

2. The domain naming context (and there are as many of these as there are of domains in the Windows Active Directory forest), which holds the user objects, which themselves have Exchange 2000–related attributes (e.g., the mail server name, the database name, delivery options, and quotas).

This represents a major manageability improvement. Instead of having to connect to sites (or what are now referred to as administrative groups), you can, from a single domain controller or global catalog server in your forest, perform changes to any object belonging to the Exchange organization.

You can thereby take advantage of the multimaster replication model of the Windows Active Directory, which enables these changes to make

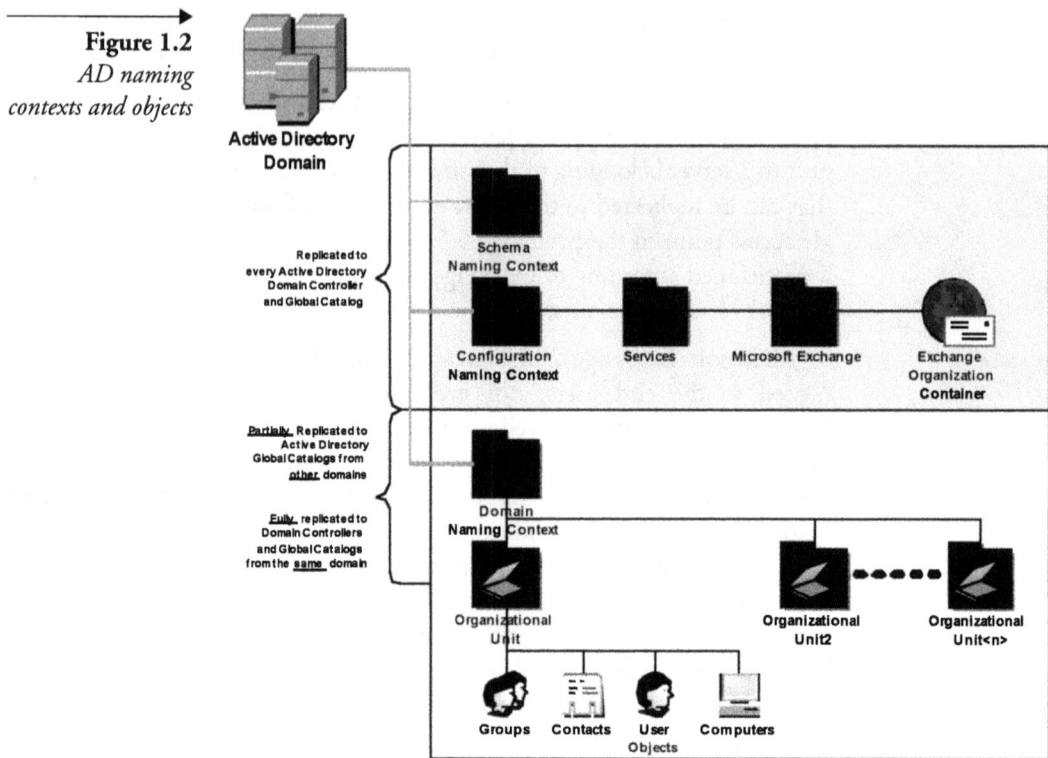

Figure 1.2
AD naming contexts and objects

their way to the Exchange servers. That is a great advantage, but it introduces an inconvenience for certain Microsoft Exchange deployments: the dependency on a sound and efficiently performing Windows Active Directory infrastructure:

1. The replication of the Active Directory has an implicit latency, and while changes you make may appear to have been done in the configuration, they may not be readily available to the designated Microsoft Exchange servers immediately. I've seen many deployments where an end-to-end replication could take as long as three hours, and that is sometimes not appropriate.

2. The absence or lack of connectivity of responsiveness from the Windows Active Directory servers used by Microsoft Exchange (which can be determined from the directory tab in the server properties), as shown in Figure 1.3, renders most (if not all) of the components of Microsoft Exchange inoperative.

Figure 1.3
*Directory servers
used by an
Exchange server*

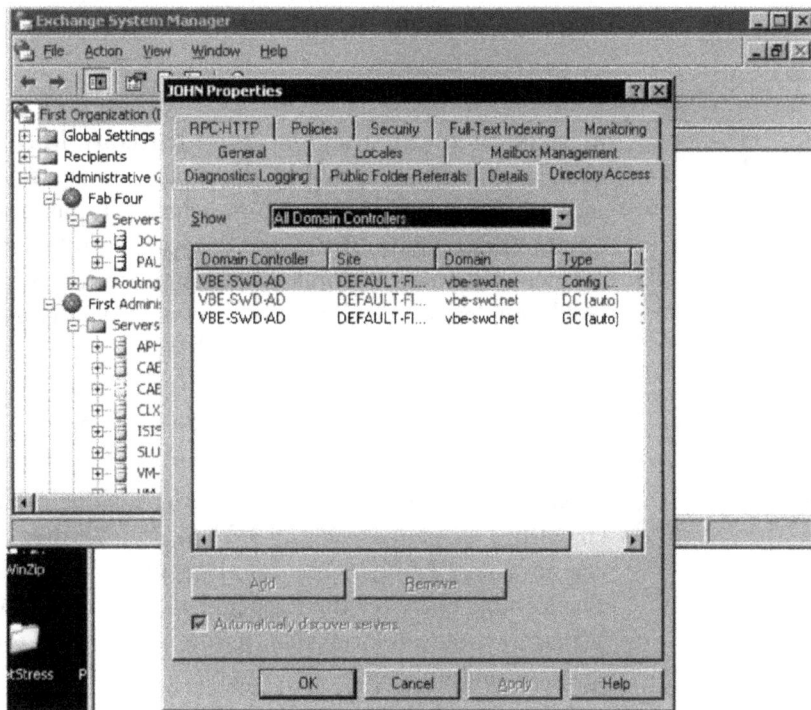

There have been attempts at deploying Microsoft Exchange in such a way that the dependency on the Windows Active Directory is lessened. One scenario is the use of a Microsoft Exchange–dedicated forest. Not only does this have the advantage of creating an administrative and operational distinction from the mainstream Windows Active Directory, it also ensures that the Windows Active Directory servers are used by Microsoft Exchange. The Global Catalog (GC) servers, used for address lookup for message routing, for instance, are assigned to Microsoft Exchange, and any troubleshooting is faster than it would be to deal with multipurpose (e.g., client authentications and message routing) GC servers. We will cover this topic later, but keep in mind that having a dedicated forest for Microsoft Exchange is not such a bad idea, despite the additional burden it might incur.

There is an impact on organizations as they deploy Microsoft Exchange 2000 and 2003 because administrators who used to manage the mailbox information are now called on to utilize the Active Directory to manage the configuration (through the Exchange System Manager snap-in) and to manage the users' messaging and collaboration attributes (through the Windows Active Directory Users and Computers snap-in). This is a simple change in the user interface, and Microsoft Exchange 2000 has been around for sufficient time that now most Windows administrators are comfortable with this type of User Interface (UI).

Snap-Ins

In conjunction with using the Active Directory, Microsoft Exchange 2000 offers a administration tool by the means of a standalone Microsoft Management Console (MMC) snap-in, which can plug into the Active Directory by connecting to the closest domain controller or by connecting to a designated domain controller (this latter option is available only if you build your own MMC snap-in environment). This deals well with the latency-everywhere problem of the Active Directory. The other advantage to using an MMC snap-in for the main management tasks of Exchange 2000 is the ability to provide an interface that is consistent in style and formatting with other management tools in the Windows Server environment.

While Exchange 5.5 administrators definitely have to refresh their knowledge when approaching Exchange 2000, they can also take advantage of a very familiar user interface style of information presentation. The learning curve for the Exchange management tool (Exchange System Manager) is far less steep than if you had to use a totally different management environment.

Figure 1.4 gives an overview look of the Exchange System Manager tool.

Figure 1.4
Exchange System Manager (ESM)

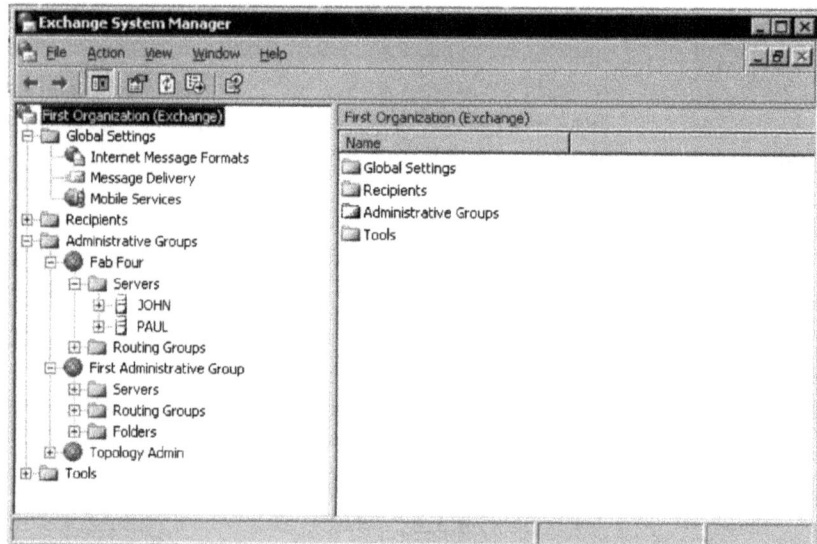

In order to manage the users' Exchange–specific information and create distribution groups (the equivalent of Exchange 5.5 distribution lists) or contacts (the equivalent of Exchange 5.5 custom recipients), you will need to utilize the Active Directory User and Computers snap-in. Note that Exchange 2003 comes with new objects and attributes to support user-level additional functions, such as mobility.

An example of Windows Active Directory is given in Figure 1.5. With Exchange 2003, Microsoft made a big effort to implement task-oriented wizards, such that you configure users not by their attributes, but by what it is you wish to do (e.g., "I want to enable this user for mobility").

Figure 1.5
Active Directory
Users and
Computers

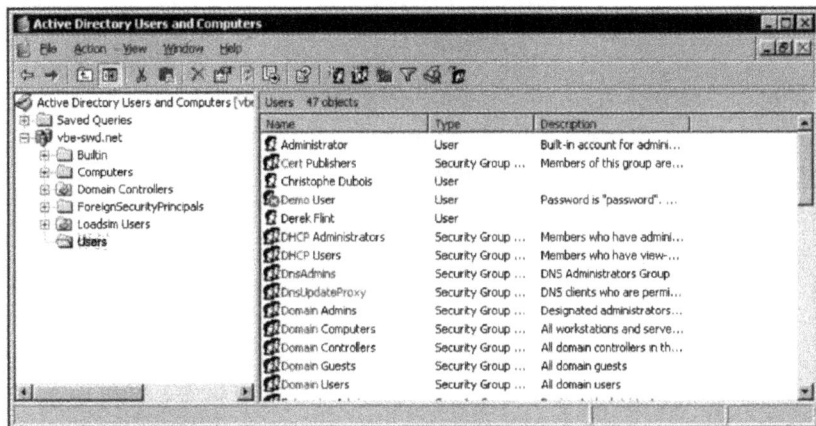

You will probably want to customize these MMC snap-in tools, and the nice thing about them is that they can be tailored to the administrator's actual function. For instance, a help-desk support person may have access to functions such as resetting a user password or unlocking an account but not creating an account or changing mailbox quotas. This is all made possible by means of permissions and role settings as well as by customizing the actual MMC snap-in, and by using facilities such as the MMC Taskpad. I often create a snap-in that gathers Windows Active Directory Users and Computers, Exchange System Manager, and the Windows 2003 Support tool one management console/environment with all tools at hand.

New Administration Models

With Exchange 5.5, a site administrator had to be given permissions that could potentially affect the entire organization (the classic example is an administrator defining a new, bogus Internet mail service with an organizationwide scope). The problem implied by the Exchange 5.5 site model is that sometimes you had to define sites for routing reasons, for network topology reasons, or for directory replication reasons. Indeed, the behavior of the mail flow or the directory replication flow in Exchange 5.5 is very much dependent on the actual site topology.

With Exchange 2000, and today with Exchange 2003, the administration model can have far more granularity by controlling the exact set of rights or permissions that a particular Windows 2000 user (or security principal, which encompasses security groups) can have on a given container or object. Furthermore, servers and services are not arranged anymore by "sites" but rather by administrative and routing groups.

This is a very important concept that got introduced with Exchange 2000, and allowing very flexible deployments. However, as time went on, many deployments went for simplicity in the definition of the administrative groups, possibly due to a simpler administration model, and in some cases, to the definition of a single routing group. The latter enables point-to-point delivery of email within a Microsoft Exchange organization, and is appropriate in consolidated or well-connected environments.

With Exchange 2000 or 2003 in *native* mode, you can get to administration models that allow centralized organizationwide operations and decentralized server and services-specific operations, by outlining a clear separation between administrative groups, routing groups, policies, and public folder hierarchies, as well as server roles, such as:

- Front-end for client connections;
- Bridgehead servers for intra-Exchange SMTP communication;
- Bridgehead servers for communication with other messaging systems;
- Connector servers;
- Mailbox servers;
- Public folder servers.

In fact, the roles you can attribute to a Microsoft Exchange server can serve as the basis for the creation of the administrative group. This carries the advantage of being able to delegate permissions to administer the servers to other groups inside the IT function.

On the other hand, I would suggest trying not to overengineer the resulting administrative group and routing group layout, or you might otherwise spend precious time in search of a server or a connector.

Figure 1.6 shows a sample layout. Notice how the grouping of servers actually occurs. While you can delegate administration of the various administrative groups to particular administrators, possibly local to the server's physical location, you can also gather all the routing information into a particular *topology* administrative group. This group can contain servers (in this example, it contains servers HBEXC01, HBEXC02, and HBEXC03), but also maintains topology information relevant to the entire organization—something the server's administrators will not be able to see or change.

Figure 1.6
Administrative groups and routing groups

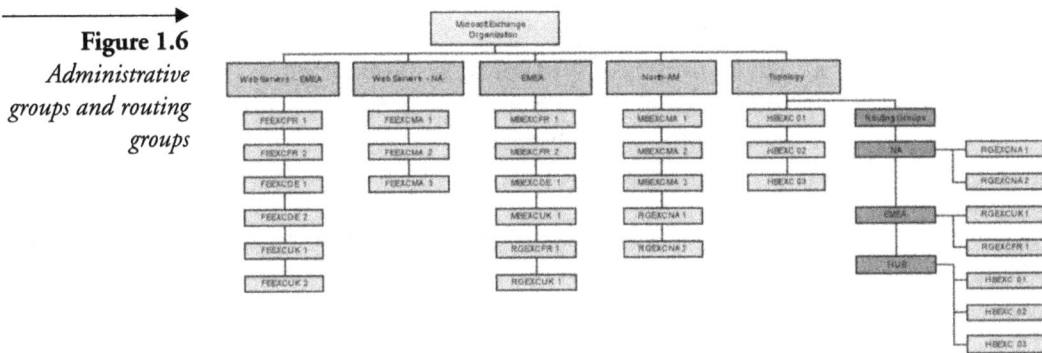

Additional administrative groups, not necessarily related to area-based servers (here, we have two geographical areas, EMEA for Europe, Middle East and Africa, and North America), can be defined to host servers that handle client connections for Web access (by the means of Outlook Web Access), which isn't necessarily part of the administrative group that describes the area. In this model, we can delegate administrative permissions to the servers handling the Web access to Microsoft Exchange while keeping control of the mailbox servers and SMTP routing servers.

As Exchange 2003 gained adoption, many companies matured in the way they were deployed. This created knowledge and best practices—coupled with much better network connectivity, it is not infrequent to find single routing group deployments, where all servers can connect to each other by the means of point-to-point connections.

Scripting

Scripting is a key advantage introduced with Exchange 2000 that goes far beyond what was possible with the product's 5.5 release. With Exchange

2003, this was improved by a greater adoption of Windows Management Instrumentation (WMI), Microsoft's implementation of Web-based enterprise management (WEBEM).

This became possible for several reasons:

- The new ability to store and retrieve information in a relatively "open" location, the Active Directory, by the means of the Active Directory Service Interface (ADSI) or simply LDAP (Lightweight Directory Access Protocol), the standardized protocol for directory access;

- The provisioning of collaboration data objects for exchange management (CDOEXM), which provides methods and properties applicable to the objects that can be retrieved from the Active Directory;

- The availability of WMI providers, which enables the ability to query and sometimes do actions on Microsoft Exchange objects by the means of the WMI abstraction.

With all this combined, customers can now create a number of task automations, often required in high-end environments where administration may not be done by just a discrete set of administrators, but rather by automation and delegation of certain administrative tasks.

The most common automation has been the ability to script users' migration from one server to another in order to resize a particular server or possibly to balance the load across servers. It can be necessary to move users from one database or storage group to another database or storage group, either on the same server or on a different server. Scripting this particular task is relatively easy. It will be much easier with the next major release of Microsoft Exchange (known as Exchange 12), as a new scripting model, Monad, gets adopted.

This is all possible because of the management architecture offered in Exchange 2000 and described in the simplified diagram in Figure 1.7.

In complement to the CDOEXM management objects, Exchange 2003 exposes a large number of functions and objects by the means of WMI. The set of WMI providers that you can now find with Exchange 2003 SP2 is described in Table 1.1. WMI providers typically provide information about the configuration and state of the Microsoft Exchange servers. It might not always be very optimal to use WMI for certain tasks that can be intensive, such as collecting performance information. In such situations, even though

Figure 1.7
*Simplified
management
architecture model*

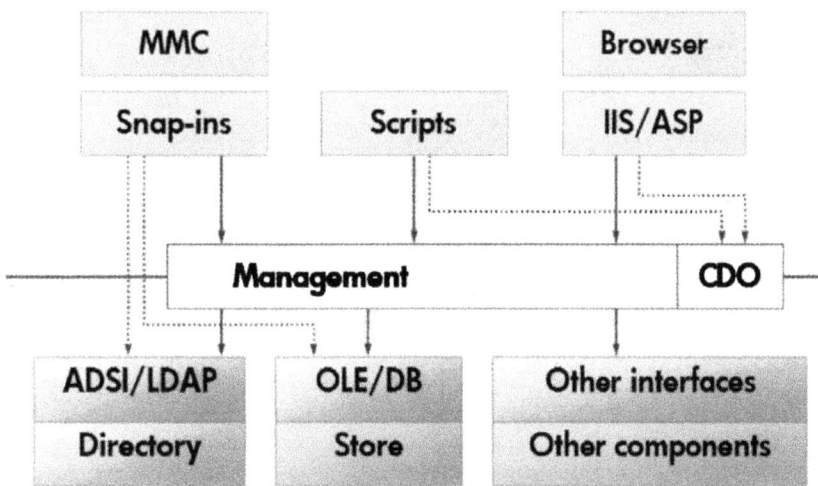

Table 1.1   *SP2 is description*

Provider Name	Description
ExchangeRoutingTableProvider	Provides information about the routing topology and link state for each server connection, and status of connectors
ExchangeQueueProvider	Provides information about the dynamic message queues created to represent the transfer of messages between Microsoft Exchange servers of the same organization
ExchangeClusterProvider	Provides information about the status of resources inside a Microsoft Cluster
ExchangeDsAccessProvider	Provides information about the utilization of Active Directory by Microsoft Exchange (DSACCESS in particular), and which are available for Microsoft Exchange directory lookups
ExchangeMessageTrackingProvider	Enables to track messages and events related to messages during the time they were under the control of a Microsoft Exchange server
ExchangeFolderTreeProvider	Provides information about the public folder and mailbox folder trees

Table 1.1   *SP2 is description (continued)*

Provider Name	Description
ExchangeMapiTableProvider	Provides information about current logons and mailboxes in use on a given server
ExchangePublicFolderProvider	Provides information about the public folders, their properties and replication status
ExchangeQueue2Provider	Provides supplemental and more detailed information about messages queues and connectors
ExchangeServerProvider	Provides functions for Exchange Server property lookup and management

you may have a less rich programming environment (if at all), you may prefer to use Windows or Exchange's native tools to collect information.

Across time, most of the information that Microsoft Exchange displays and manages from Exchange System Manager (ESM) can be accessed by the means of programming interfaces. This lends well to automation, as we mentioned before, and helps to decrease the efforts required to manage larger and larger Microsoft Exchange environments. This simplification will be carried over to the next major release of Microsoft Exchange, by offering a simpler and more powerful set of scripting verbs and interfaces.

If you plan to deploy a large-scale management and monitoring infrastructure, it is recommended that you investigate third-party vendor management products as well as Microsoft's own operations management tool, Microsoft Operations Manager (MOM). Make sure that they can take advantage of WMI, since this is definitely the way to go for organizing the management and monitoring of enterprise-class servers and services. In the largest setups, it is not uncommon to see both the presence of Microsoft MOM and a larger enterprise management framework, such as HP Open-View of IBM Tivoli. The reason is quite simple: Microsoft tends to be very good at its own platforms but fails to operate in multivendor environments. In situations where you have a mixture of operating systems, servers, and storage architectures, you need to have one layer "above" and beyond the Windows and Exchange environments. At the same time, you may chose not to discard MOM at all, because Microsoft has a development policy for the management packs (the application-specific management modules) that demands that application engineering groups write their MOM management pack. For Microsoft Exchange, it is the Exchange developers that write the management pack for MOM—it then becomes hardly possible to obtain better information on how the product behaves, unless you can complement it with best practices and great experience.

1.3.4 Scalability

The last RAMS feature is scalability, and I will not cover much of it in this section, given the particular attention focused on this subject in this book.

Scalability goes far beyond handling many users per server. It is a mixture of being able to scale up server configurations, or sometimes even scale them down, and often scale out the server infrastructure. We cover scalability in Chapter 2 in much greater detail. The principal scalability features found with Exchange 2003 (up to SP2) are as follows:

- The ability to partition and deploy many user or public Information Stores on a single server, using several databases logically grouped in storage groups.

- The ability to deploy dedicated servers to the messaging network, thereby eliminating the burden of deploying an associated directory service for each individual server, as was the case with Exchange 5.5. This reduces the number of directory service instances (decrease of replication traffic) and simplifies the configuration of the Microsoft Exchange servers.

- The ability to process vast quantities of transactions and message transfers by optimizing data paths for Internet protocols. The MAPI-oriented traffic is handled pretty much the same way as in previous releases of the product, but with the capability to take advantage of the multiple storage groups and database models.

- The ability to operate in the most optimized way with Microsoft Outlook. Even if Microsoft made a reference implementation of Internet protocol for client access, the best client for Microsoft Exchange is Microsoft Outlook, and, since Exchange 2003, the best client is Outlook 2003, where a real effort was made to develop optimization of client-server traffic by having both products closely aligned.

1.4   Performance Improvements

From a performance perspective, the Microsoft Exchange 2000 architecture and the Exchange 2003 follow-on release made improvements, sometimes imperceptible to the end user. The improvements are major from Exchange 5.5, although there hasn't been any "apples-to-apples" comparison between the two architectures.

Microsoft Exchange 2003 has better performance in its ability to handle a larger amount of traffic and manage larger quantities of data (which I sometimes refer to as *data sets*). This is made possible by the use of Windows Server 2000, and more importantly Windows Server 2003, which brought key data management benefits such as the Volume ShadowCopy Services.

Starting with the Exchange 2000 release, we saw improvements in the way client communication is offered: you do not necessarily have to use the MAPI Remote Procedure Call (RPC) interface to gain access to a mailbox; in fact, using the HTTP WebDAV interface delivers a much greater scalability, from both Internet browser clients as well as applications. This holds true with POP and IMAP clients, and one specific change in the Exchange architecture was to add a new format for the data stored in a Microsoft Exchange server, located in a database called the Streaming Store.

In this particular spirit, Microsoft Exchange 2000 has been optimized to avoid unnecessary data transfers. In Exchange 5.5, all information stored on the server was in fact located in the main private Information Store, PRIV.EDB, as a collection of MAPI properties. This means that if an SMTP message was received from the Internet, it was parsed, decoded, and stored as MAPI properties. If the client is an Internet client (such as a Web browser or an IMAP or POP client), a second conversion has to occur to convert this MAPI content back into MIME format. This prevents the systematic conversion of information back and forth between MAPI and MIME properties of a message. Note, however, that in pure Microsoft Exchange environments, this conversion is automatically done: Exchange figures that the message is coming from a peer server, that it has a set of MAPI properties transferred in a MIME bodypart—the transport neutral encapsulation format (TNEF)—and automatically converts (we use the terms "promotes" or "upgrades" also) the MIME content into MAPI properties.

Another attempt at optimizing operations—and, in fact, decreasing *unnecessary* operations—is to cache directory information that is often requested. Consider the two main components of Microsoft Exchange 2003—the STORE process and the INETINFO process (IIS). When a message is delivered to an Exchange server by the means of SMTP, this message must be *categorized*—that is, examined to determine whether it should be relayed to another server or delivered locally to one of the many mailbox stores hosted on that particular server.

It would be much better for the directory information fetched for that particular user by INETINFO to be actually cached such that the STORE process could retrieve the data right away from memory and actually expedite the message delivery faster than if it had to request the information again to the Active Directory servers. This led Microsoft to introduce the DS_ACCESS, which is not a service in itself. It runs into the context of the Information Store and caches directory queries to the Windows Active Directory.

As Microsoft Exchange matured through service packs and relatively minor updates, the DS_ACCESS module was rewritten and upgraded to have a cache area of a significant size. This upgrade came when Microsoft could eventually solve virtual memory fragmentation issues. In general, you should not attempt to tamper with the default cache size configured for DS_ACCESS, especially by using settings that were defined for another release of Microsoft Exchange (even across service packs). The ability to use larger cache with DS_ACCESS strongly depends on the ability of the STORE to properly manage the virtual memory, and I have seen cases where growing the directory cache, in the hope of decreasing the query rate on the Windows Active Directory servers, caused the STORE to run out of contiguous memory—an event that is flagged in the Windows Server event viewer and usually the indication of more severe problems (such as client lookout failures, messages delivery failures, and other STORE crashes) to come.

Trust Microsoft for its ability to optimize its environment and make the most of a 32-bit operating system, because that's basically what you have in the Exchange 2003 "generation" product. The industry is very interested in the adoption and the ability for Microsoft Exchange to operate on 64-bit environments, but it is too early at this point to see how fast it will adopt a 64-bit operating system and application.

1.4.1 Native Content

Native content enables the Exchange 2003 ESE to handle data in the native protocol transmissions format. When data comes from the network, it is stored *as is*, which saves on processing time. In fact, you may now be confused, and wonder where the information goes—MAPI format or native format?

The basic answer is that the information is always stored in the last writer's format with one exception (this exception is discussed at the end of this section). To store information natively into Microsoft Exchange, you have to first determine all the types of data transmitted. Clearly, when the information originates from a MAPI client, a MAPI-based connector, or the "old" RPC or X.400 connector, the message consists of MAPI properties.

MAPI properties are nothing but tagged streams of information. This information can be quite long, such as the 70-MB auto-signature that an employee decided to use at one of the sites I had the pleasure to visit, or quite small, when it represents a simple flag such as the sensitivity or the urgency of a message. MAPI properties are primarily stored in the *Property Store*, which is represented by a single database file with the .EDB extension.

So far, there is nothing new compared to Exchange 5.5, which used to have a PRIV.EDB (for mailboxes) and a PUB.EDB (for public folders).

Figure 1.8 gives a quick overview of this information handling.

Figure 1.8
Microsoft Exchange 5.5 databases

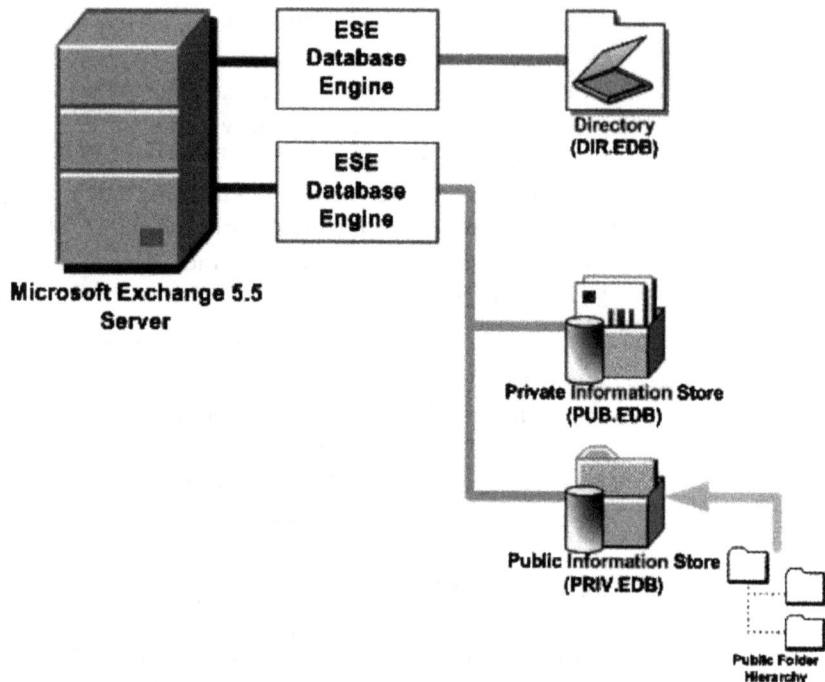

Information was equally stored in the same format for these two files, as is the case with Exchange 2000 and 2003, except that instead of having one PRIV.EDB file, you now can have several of them, as shown in Figure 1.9.

Figure 1.9
*Microsoft Exchange
2003 databases*

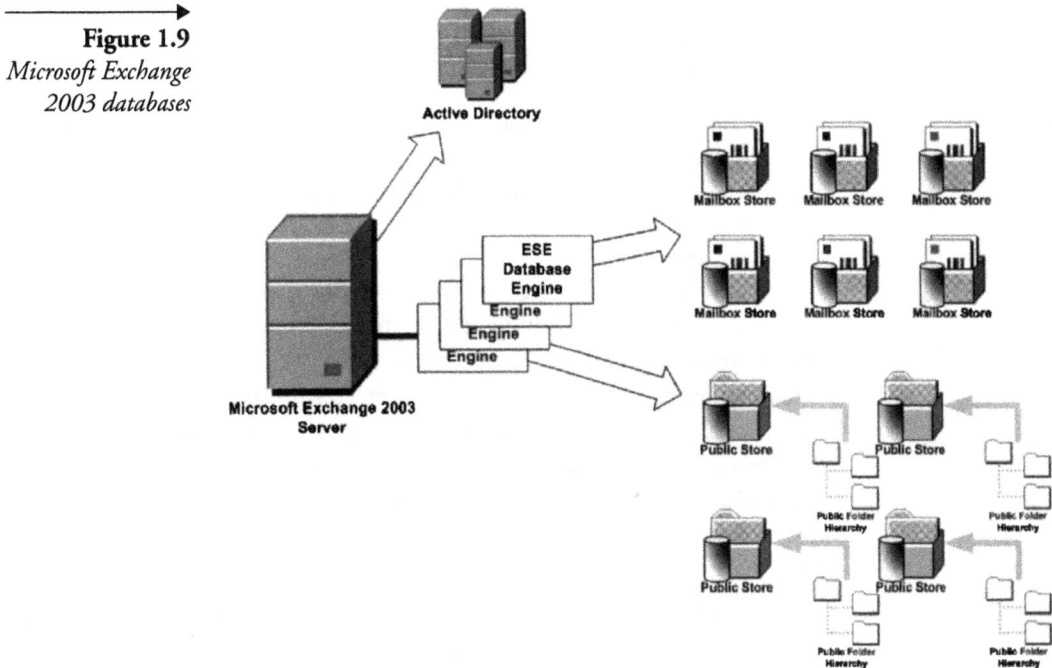

As you can see, you may now have several databases and up to four ESE database engines. Note also that the Microsoft Exchange server no longer carries the directory information, which is being sourced from the Windows Active Directory, making it an *absolute* prerequisite before installing any Microsoft Exchange 2000 or 2003 server on a Windows 2000 server.

I wanted to keep a sort of legacy view of the way you can lay databases and information in Figure 1.9, because there was indeed a goal to enable more than just one public folder database per server. However, Microsoft Outlook can only deal with one public folder hierarchy, which seriously reduces the flexibility you can draw from multiple databases when it comes to public folder information. In reality, it's the whole concept of information sharing that Microsoft revised as it brought to market the Microsoft SharePoint Portal Server and SharePoint Team Services. Public folders tend to be migrated away from Microsoft Exchange, making it a super-specialized messaging system, as we can now enjoy with the Exchange 2003 SP2 function state.

As mentioned earlier, and we will have the opportunity to discuss later, the Microsoft Exchange database has to deal with two types of information flows:

1.   Content from MAPI clients, which is stored in the *Property Store*, a database file with a .EDB extension;

2.   Content from Internet clients/peers, which is stored in the *Streaming Store*, a side database to the Property Store, which contains native content from the client or peer server.

Just like bread and butter, the Property Store and the Streaming Store depend on each other. If you have a corrupted Property Store database, you must restore the Property Store database as well as the corresponding Streaming Store database within the same restore operation. You should always consider that there is one single database, except that now information can be in either one place or another but rarely in two separate places. You could make an analogy to the Schroedinger's Cat experiment, which aims at resolving several microscopic possibilities into a particular macroscopic state.

Put simply, you may consider the relationship between the Property and the Streaming Stores as the same as the relationship between a folder and its contained files. Without the folder, you cannot get to the files. Without the files, you have no data.

Figure 1.10 gives a view of the relationship between the Property Stores and the Streaming Stores. We are stepping through the image with the means of callouts (white numbers in black circles).

1.   When a MAPI client stores or submits information to the Exchange Store, that information gets stored natively in the Property Store. The Streaming Store is untouched.

2.   When a MAPI client wishes to retrieve information located in the Property Store, the data is transmitted natively.

3.   When an Internet client (which also includes an SMTP server) submits information, that information gets stored on the Streaming Store.

4.   Property promotion takes place such that the information stored in the Streaming Store can be browsed and searched by any client

(this can be the subject of the message, the recipient list, or the date the information was created, among other things). Property promotion consists of information duplication for the sake of getting the folders and message rows in the Property Store filled in. If the property itself is very large (a big subject), only a pointer to the Streaming Store offset may be stored.

5. Data is transmitted natively from the Internet client into the Property Store if an Internet client retrieves information.

6. If the information is located in the Property Store, an *on-demand conversion* occurs in order to transform the MAPI properties into Internet content.

7. If a MAPI client retrieves information stored by an Internet client (for example, reading a message received by SMTP from a non–Microsoft Exchange host), a similar on-demand conversion occurs to transform the SMTP/MIME format into MAPI properties.

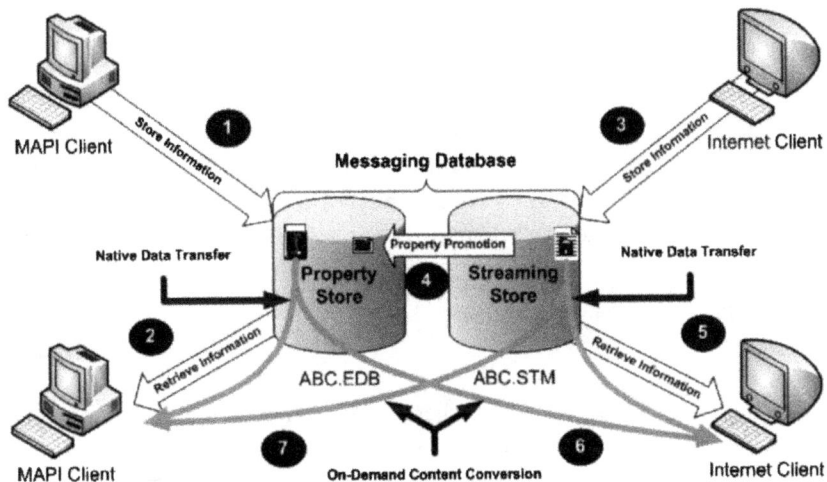

Figure 1.10
Property Stores and Streaming Stores

This mechanism is very efficient and increases the ability of Exchange 2003 to switch and deliver messages rapidly while displacing the systematic conversion that was happening with Exchange 5.5, which now occurs only on an as-needed basis. Granted, this means that data conversion now sits on the critical path of an end-user transaction, but processors' capabilities are such that this additional task is fairly insignificant, making Exchange 2003 an excellent platform for Internet-based protocol access and data transfers.

1.4.2 **DS_ACCESS**

DS_ACCESS is a very critical module to Microsoft Exchange 2003. As a shared component of any service and process that needs access to the directory, DS_ACCESS—along with its companion, DS_PROXY—handles the directory requests necessary to route messages inside the Exchange 2003 organization (also known as *categorization*) and caches directory information such that the load imposed by Microsoft Exchange onto the Windows Active Directory is significantly diminished. In addition, fewer CPU cycles and resources are required to access directory objects. DS_ACCESS is also used to discover appropriate global catalogs for user and group expansion and domain controllers for storing and retrieving *configuration* information.

We have already explained the benefits of DS_ACCESS. You may notice events in your application event log reported by this particular module. They should be taken very seriously; without a proper connection to the Active Directory, you cannot run a high-performance Exchange 2003 server. DS_PROXY is a companion to DS_ACCESS: as you know, Outlook clients make a pre–Exchange 2000 era assumption that the directory server is the same as the Exchange server. When you configure your Microsoft Outlook profile, you have no choice but to enter a single server name. When Microsoft Outlook clients connect to back-end Exchange 2003 servers, they (the servers) determine if the client is able to deal with a separate directory server (as in Outlook 2003) or if any directory queries, such as those generated when the user resolves a name or browses the global address list (GAL), have to be handled through the client-server connection.

This is mimicked by the DS_PROXY component. That component can do two things:

1. If the client is pre–Outlook 2000 (such as Outlook 98 without the latest service release), it will proxy the client requests to the Active Directory GC and act as a kind of broker between the directory service and the user's MAPI client.

2. If the client is Outlook 2000 or later, it will *refer* the client to the Active Directory GC of choice (the choice being made by the Exchange server, not the Outlook client), and the Outlook client will connect directly to the name service provider interface (NSPI), which is the MAPI-like interface for accessing the directory.

Note that it is possible, by the means of registry settings on the client, to force the MAPI client (in this case, Outlook) to connect to a particular GC or to search the GC server by itself. In consolidation scenarios, where the client may actually be closer to a GC server than a Microsoft Exchange server, this setting is appropriate to configure. Ultimately, Outlook 2003 and later are preferably configured in cache mode, i.e., accessing a local replica of the mailbox and of the directory (in an offline GAL) such that the client-Active Directory performance is not too critical for the usability of the messaging client.

1.4.3 Transaction Logging

I won't cover in detail the principles of database transaction logging, but I would like to provide some information about changes made by the database engineering team that reflect Microsoft's desire to take advantage of the best hardware capabilities. As you will see in Chapter 4, storage technologies have evolved in quite an unbalanced manner. Bandwidth (also known as *data rate*) is consistently increasing (from 40 MB/s to 320 MB/s for SCSI, from 100 MB/s to 400 MB/s for fibre channel). However, disk I/O operations (also known as *transfer rates*) haven't greatly improved in the last decade, ranging from 80 to 160 I/O per second in the very best cases (those used for the marketing brochure).

We have the opportunity to discuss more of the storage technology; in high-end storage environments, it is safe to assume that a disk drive can handle 140 I/O per second at 20 ms response time.

Even from the times of the first version of Microsoft Exchange, it was common to write sequentially to disk drives, a far more efficient mode than writing randomly across a large volume. With the actual need for logging transactions to a database to allow a rollback or roll forward of these transactions if needed, the notion of writing the transaction sequentially to a volume came as a real benefit. By issuing sequential transfers to a volume, you diminish the mechanical movements introduced by the disk access and can actually realize quite decent transfer rates (in the order of 1,000 I/O per second at submillisecond response times).

Beyond the pure performance aspects of storage systems, the ability of the application to optimize its disk accesses will only be beneficial: techniques such as I/O coalescing, which can happen at any time in the path from the application to the back-end disk (spindle), has been gradually introduced in successive versions of Microsoft Exchange.

In fact, the I/O coalescing or optimization of sequential write to disks is typically done at the back-end level. Recent Microsoft Exchange deployments tend to use storage arrays connected in networks (storage area networks), and these arrays have significant quantities of cache memory such that they can perform a great deal of optimization. This optimization is such that it does not necessarily require dedicated individual disks (spindles) to the transaction logging of Microsoft Exchange. All it requires is the ability to have a small response time (low latency) for any of the write requests.

1.4.4   Storage Groups

Storage Groups, a long demanded feature, was introduced in Exchange 2000, and they remain relatively the same with Exchange 2003; they represent a great improvement in upward scalability of server configurations, allowing the hosting of many more users and much more data than with Exchange 5.5.

As in all situations, it is necessary to guard against pushing to the extremes. As we will see in Chapter 2, there are tactics for properly choosing the right storage model for your server.

The first thing to consider is the fact that each Storage Group is a database instance that has a significant footprint in the STORE process's virtual address space. This has caused some concern about the early deployments of clusters with Exchange 2000, which was addressed with SP1 and further improved with subsequent releases of the product (the most notable being Exchange 2003 SP1, which helps in scaling out database deployments on Microsoft Exchange servers).

Storage groups can really help to deploy highly scalable solutions by enabling partition of information across manageable databases, by keeping them relatively small.

The other advantage of using storage groups is that you can spread your transactional workload across more back-end units. This is very much in line with the principles of reaching high performance by leveling as many resources as possible, spreading across many units that can operate in parallel. This forms the basis for high-performance technical computing or grid computing. When brought in the perspective of Microsoft Exchange and storage groups and databases, this means using more back-end logical units, across more logical paths, than otherwise possible with a single database system. This particular approach is recommended whenever you have a non-compressible latency, although you have expandable bandwidth: by parallelizing traffic, you improve your overall throughput. For example, if you have four storage groups for 2,000 users, you have to satisfy the workload of 500 users per storage group. This means that the transaction logging results from the workload of 500 users. In an environment where you have only one storage group, the transaction logging is four times more important. When dealing with a fixed latency, and because logging is serialized, a four–storage group configuration will be four times more efficient, will deliver four times more throughput compared to a single storage group configuration.

1.4.5 Content Indexing

Content indexing was introduced as an add-on to Microsoft Exchange 2000 and never really made it. It consumes a fair quantity of back-end processor resources in order to be kept up to date and delivers a relatively mediocre service, compared to the more general desktop indexing solutions that can be used in complement with Outlook, such as the MSN desktop search or Google desktop search.

The story is not over when it comes to content indexing—we enter into an area where we can use indexing technology to rapidly search for information against massive quantities of data, as we daily do when using MSN or Google search engines. This functionality is definitely required inside Microsoft Exchange and needs to be taken advantage of by Outlook in a far more integrated way than what we currently have with the content indexing of Exchange 2003 and Outlook 2003. Expect Microsoft to come up with better technology in future releases of Microsoft Exchange, but be very careful about the rapid adoption of desktop search engines in Microsoft Exchange environments. This type of technology will typically crawl and search for any items it can access and build an index that can be searched against. This is very fine if Outlook 2003 operates in cache mode, but if it is connected to the Microsoft Exchange back-end server in online mode, you quickly end up with a much larger traffic (RPC operations per sec) on your back end than you originally anticipated.

Most corporate deployments tend to lock down the configuration of the desktop clients to prevent such problems from occurring, but they do happen at times. If you are not sure of the policy for desktop engine search in your enterprise, I strongly recommend that you ask users about their practices and recommend the use of cache mode for Outlook 2003. Isn't it ironic that Outlook 2003 implemented the cache to insulate the user from the network and server conditions, yet now we recommend cache mode to

insulate the server from desktop search engine and to use the MAPI interface and hammer the back-end server to build and maintain their indexes!

Such events can happen with no warning and only contribute to a high
back-end utilization, leading to long response time, message queues built
up, and decreased service levels. Microsoft provides tools to analyze MAPI-
RPC traffic per user, such as ExMon, allowing administrators to easily identify abnormal traffic—at least workload that does not correspond to the
behavior of an Outlook client, be it in cache or online mode.

1.5   Exchange Server 2003 Core Architecture

This section covers the deep Exchange 2003 architecture concepts that can
better explain the rest of the recommendations and observations in this
book.

Exchange 2000 revolves around two main components:

1.	The STORE process facilitates mailbox and shared information
	access by means of public folders and allows communications by
	means of MAPI RPC, X.4000, and any MAPI-based connectors
	with outer components of the messaging network. It is the heart
	of Exchange and is the process instance that runs the database
	engines, which allow administrators to store and retrieve informa-
	tion in back-end storage.

2.	The INETINFO (IIS) process handles the Internet protocols ser-
	vices (e.g., SMTP, HTTP-DAV, POP, IMAP, and NNTP).
	INETINFO ships as part of the base Windows Server operating
	system and provides the basic SMTP and NNTP services. How-
	ever, when you install Exchange 2003 on a Windows server, the
	basic services are actually replaced by "Exchange-aware" equiva-
	lent services, which allow SMTP message delivery directly into
	the Information Store databases and NNTP access to the public
	folder stores defined in your infrastructure. In addition, Exchange
	2003 adds increased Internet protocol support for the Windows
	Internet Information Services (IIS), such as IMAP and POP pro-
	tocols for client access to the Exchange-owned mailboxes.

In this section, our attention is focused on these two key components,
and their interaction is described.

1.6 The STORE Process

The STORE process (I often call it the Information Store) is the heart of Microsoft Exchange. It facilitates mailbox and public information storage as well as MAPI RPC connection handling.

Figure 1.11 describes the STORE process from a fairly high-level view.

Figure 1.11
The Store Process

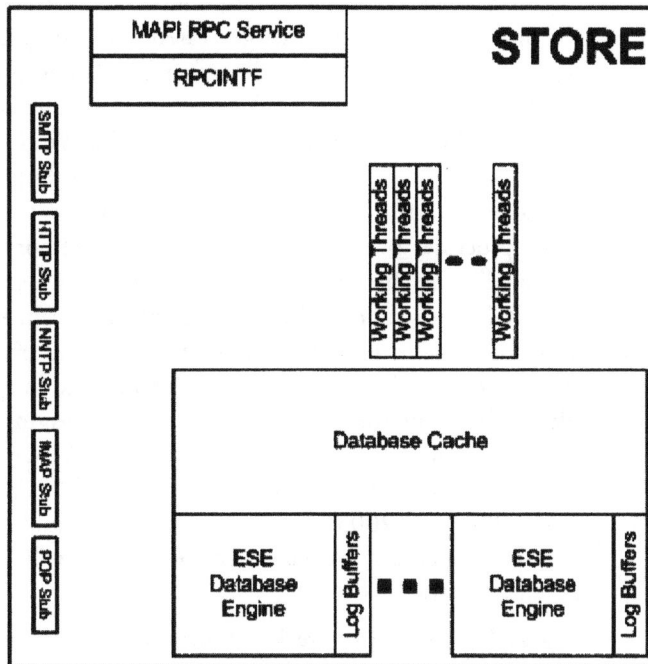

The STORE main components include:

- *Internet protocol stubs* are used to communicate through a shared memory and the asynchronous queue mechanism (called the *Epoxy* layer), along with the INETINFO process, which handles the Internet protocol communications.

- *Working threads* handle the RPC requests generated by the MAPI clients and handed over by the local RPC server. Clients connect *directly* to the STORE to get access to the mailbox and public information storage. The RPC connections are handled by the MAPI RPC service, which itself is built on the RPCINTF interface (a legacy component from previous versions of Exchange) and allows minimal overhead in handling the MAPI RPC requests.

- *Database engines* handle the databases defined on the server. Although designed to handle up to 15 database engines, Exchange 2000 at shipping time supports only 4 database engines running on a given Exchange 2000 server. This restriction was primarily due to limitations of virtual address space in the STORE process. With Exchange 2003 SP2, you can now have a fifth instance, known as the recovery storage group, used to simplify database recovery scenarios.

- *Database cache* is cache pages used in the databases in order to make the most efficient possible usage of RAM. The database cache is managed by the dynamic buffer allocation (DBA) component, which was introduced in Exchange 5.5. The size of the cache will vary, depending upon the available physical RAM on the Windows Server and its utilization. It is very common to have very little physical RAM left available on a running Exchange server (5 MB or so). However, if other processes put a demand on physical memory, the DBA algorithm will trim the size of the cache (based on a Least Recently Used, with Reference count [LRU-K], model) to prevent the STORE process from paging to disk. Therefore, the second observation we can make is that an Exchange 2000 server will seldom page to the page files defined on the servers. There may be paging activity on the server, but this will represent only *soft page faults*, which basically consist of getting and storing memory pages (of 4 KB in size on Windows 2000 and 2003) in the free pages and look-aside lists of the Windows memory manager. By no means will they represent a potential bottleneck.

- *Log buffers* contain the series of outstanding or current transactions that are being issued to any database belonging to the database engines. There is one log buffer per database engine instance. The log buffers can be viewed as a series of contiguous buffers, which are written *sequentially* to the transaction log files, one stream per storage group.

- *Version Store* (not presented in Figure 1.11) is an area of memory reserved to store original pages while transactions are being applied to the current database cache (more on this later in this section).

- *Interface to the DS_ACCESS module* performs all directory lookups on behalf of every Exchange 2000 component local to the server. DS_ACCESS is a module that has been a critical component in the rollout of Microsoft Exchange 2000 and has been further enhanced and corrected for each release of the product (including service packs.

1.6.1 Storage Groups

Storage groups are very important components of the Exchange 2003 Store. They represent the database engines loaded in memory (one storage group corresponds to one database engine). Each storage group can have up to five active databases, which can be mailbox stores or public folder stores. Typically, high-end environments tend to deploy four storage groups per server, although it is frequent to observe deployments with one or two storage groups.

1.6.2 The Database Engine

The ESE database engine is a very interesting component that has developed during the past five years into an extremely reliable engine. It implements the basic features that you would expect from a true transactional and relational database, the main one being transaction logging (covered in the following subsection).

ESE can be tuned in many ways, but most of the deployments should take the values given by default. A lot of information can be gathered by performance counters (see Chapter 6 for more information on these) about the ESE database engine's behavior and resource utilization.

There are also attributes that can be explored using advanced Active Directory tools such as ADSIEDIT, which allows you to control the parameters of ESE. This is in fact an effective way of tuning the ESE engines, since by using scripts that use ADSI you may automate, replicate, and centrally tune the settings for each server profile in your organization.

1.6.3 Transaction Processing

When a modification has to be made to any of the databases handled by ESE, the calling thread will start the transaction and proceed to perform various page modifications. These page modifications are stored in the transaction log buffers, and the corresponding pages are modified in the main, in-memory, database cache (ESE cache). Once all the page modifications have been done, the calling thread will proceed to *commit* the transaction to the database. The rule is simple: either all page modifications are done, or none are done.

Besides, while a transaction is in progress (this could take several minutes if the transaction consists of storing a 10-MB message over a slow link), the other threads must have no knowledge of the transaction in progress and should consider that the database pages that are modified as a result of this transaction are in fact intact. There comes the role of the version store, which is a special area of the virtual address space, in which pages that are being modified by a given transaction in progress have their original content saved, such that other transactions in progress can still access the original page if they need to. Because a complete database transaction can affect several pages, from the other transaction perspective, those pages should be seen as modified only when the transaction that touched them has been completed, and committed. While a transaction is in progress, the pages that it modifies should be seen in their original content by all other threads of the STORE.

The process of committing a transaction simply consists of writing sequentially—and as quickly as possible—the transaction log buffers to the transaction log files. When the commit transaction buffer has been written to the log, the calling thread can assume that the database modification has been done and can resume execution. Therefore, if the process of writing to the transaction log drive is slow, you can expect slow response times and lowered throughput on your Exchange 2003 server.

1.6.4 Logging

The logging process is quite simple in that the buffers are written sequentially into the transaction log file. The notion of log buffer gathering was introduced with Microsoft Exchange 2000, the idea being that if you had to write 10 records of 1 KB each, instead of doing 10 I/O writes to the volume, you might as well do 1 I/O of 10 KB to the volume. This makes Exchange 2000's behavior quite different from its predecessors in that the actual I/O size can vary greatly in size, and in fact could reach 64 KB and above if the traffic demands it; with Exchange 2003 SP2, the maximum I/O size, to either transaction log files or databases, is now 1 MB.

Transaction logging is in itself very useful; because sequential disk access is significantly much faster than random disk access, the disk operations that sit on the critical path of the transaction are only sequential. The process of updating the database back with the modified pages is done as a background activity and is called the checkpoint process. (In other database technologies, this component is called the lazy writer).

There are two very important observations to draw from this behavior:

1.   Never assume that your database on disk contains the most up-to-date information. In fact, as soon as you mount a database in Exchange 2003, that database is considered inconsistent, and the real state of the database—from an end-user perspective, for instance—is reflected in the modified pages in the cache and the pages stored on disk.

2.   If you lose your transaction log files, you run the risk of losing information. Because the transaction commit happens only when the data is stored in the transaction log files, if, from your client, you decide to save a message in a folder, you get confirmation that the message is saved once the transactions have been written to the log files, not when the pages have been modified on disk (they are, of course, modified in the database cache). Should a system failure occur (e.g., abrupt shutdown of the server) and the cache contents are lost, the database, still flagged as being inconsistent, will be reopened when the STORE process starts up again, and recovery steps will be initiated (this can easily be viewed in the application event log of the server), playing back recorded transactions to the database during mount time. The length of transaction playback can greatly vary depending on the storage configuration and the number of outstanding modified pages waiting to be flushed to the databases. This quantity is known as the *checkpoint depth* and is a tunable parameter via the Active Directory object of the storage group (this parameter, along with many others, can be found by looking up the properties of the mailbox/public store object or the parent storage group object in the configuration naming context of the Active Directory forest by using ADSIEDIT). Having a small checkpoint depth helps in recovering faster from a database crash. On the other hand, it requires much more frequent access to the databases and significantly decreases the likelihood of page gathering during the database page updates.

The database I've been referring to so far is the Property Store. You may ask, "What about the Streaming Store then?" Well, the transaction logging in the Streaming Store is quite different. Because the data is stored natively and streamed from the NT cache to the Streaming Store by means of the Exchange Installable File System (ExIFS), which I'll discuss later, the transaction log buffers don't see any of this information, except to the point where the ExIFS consumer (typically an Internet protocol virtual server running as part of INETINFO) decides that the file has been written and closes the file handle. At that very point, the virtual server will provide to the STORE the file handle utilized for that particular session, and the STORE process will *read* back the data from the Streaming Store, in order to generate the transactions.

You may find this pretty inefficient, and in fact it is. Because the process of using the installable file system (IFS) takes advantage of the NT cache, by the time the file handle is passed on to the STORE process via the Epoxy component, there is a great chance that most of the data written to the IFS will be still in the NT cache.

Reading back the file content consists simply of accessing the cache and writing sequentially to the transaction log files, making the overall process very efficient, especially if you have tuned your server to maximize the NT cache (which is rarely the case in most Exchange 2003 deployments).

For this reason, it is common to recommend the utilization of 2-GB kernel space tuning for any server that is not hosting mailboxes, enabling the NT cache to be fully utilized for the Windows NT File System, NTFS. However. However, for mailbox servers, the 3-GB kernel space tuning should be used. We will cover later this particular tuning mode, which is enabled by the means of a boot switch in the boot.ini file of the server.

1.6.5   Checkpoint Process

With all those database pages modified in memory, there comes a time when it is appropriate to flush dirty pages to the database (Property Store). This task is done by the checkpoint operation *asynchronously*, independent of the user's perception of the transaction completion. This operation will simply look at the modified pages and proceed to flush them to the database through random I/Os most of the time. In Exchange 5.5 and earlier, the checkpoint process was happening every 30 seconds and could fire in parallel up to 64 × 4-KB I/O to the database volume. This has caused some grief in low-end storage environments, where every now and then the volume hosting the database would be hammered by 64 write operations. This wouldn't be a problem if the volume could handle write operations efficiently. However, in most deployments employing RAID5 volumes, each of the 64 write batches would translate, in fact, to 256 actual physical disk I/Os, not counting the read operations that result from normal read access to the databases.

Since Exchange 2000, checkpointing has gone through a series of improvements.

First, the database pages are actually flushed, depending on the size of the checkpoint depth. Suppose you have a checkpoint depth of 5 MB; once you have more than 5 MB of information to be flushed, the checkpoint process starts to update modified pages from the cache to the database on an ongoing basis, helping to reduce peak volume access and to iron them out across time.

The second big improvement is that the checkpoint process will attempt to write contiguous pages together in a single I/O write. Hence, instead of writing 64 4-KB pages in 64 I/Os, you could very well be writing those same 4-KB pages in one 256-KB I/O should the pages be contiguous (and there has been a lot of optimization work done to help this out in Exchange 2003 and in the SP2 release of Exchange 2003).

Finally, and with the most recent release of Exchange 2003 (Exchange 2003 SP2), the I/O checkpointing is now done with fewer concurrent I/Os: with pre-SP2 of Exchange 2003, there can be up to 512 outstanding write I/O generated during checkpointing; with SP2, this is limited to 96 I/Os. This is particularly advantageous if you have a large back-end array with many disks to service these I/Os. However, there are situations where any write operation has to be handled with extra processing, such as in replicated storage environments. In such environments, any write must be applied on a remote array, possibly miles or hundreds of miles away.

Simply put, you go more often to disk, yet with less data; you avoid spikes in workload, which would have typically resulted in spikes of response time, not only for write operations, but also for read operations.

1.6.6 The Exchange Installable File System

The ExIFS is a file system installed by Exchange that allows accessing the STORE databases as if they were folders and files.

Exposing the STORE by means of a file system, which in fact provides Win32 file semantics over the data stored in the STORE, is quite efficient and was needed for the Internet protocol virtual servers. Instead of marshaling information into MAPI properties and passing them by some efficient communications device, all the virtual servers have to do, should they wish to deliver a message into the STORE, is to open a file on an Exchange file system and store information there.

The ExIFS used to show up as the M:\ drive on pre-Exchange 2003 servers, but since Exchange 2003, the file system is hidden. Too many attempts were made, voluntarily or not, to use the content of the M:\ drive (e.g., running a backup or a virus-scanning program) and eventually alter items such that they would become unusable.

Storing a message into the M:\ drive is much different from submitting this message through SMTP, for example. Consider Figure 1.12 and observe the two information channels between IIS and the STORE.

Figure 1.12
*ExIFS and the IIS
and STORE
processes*

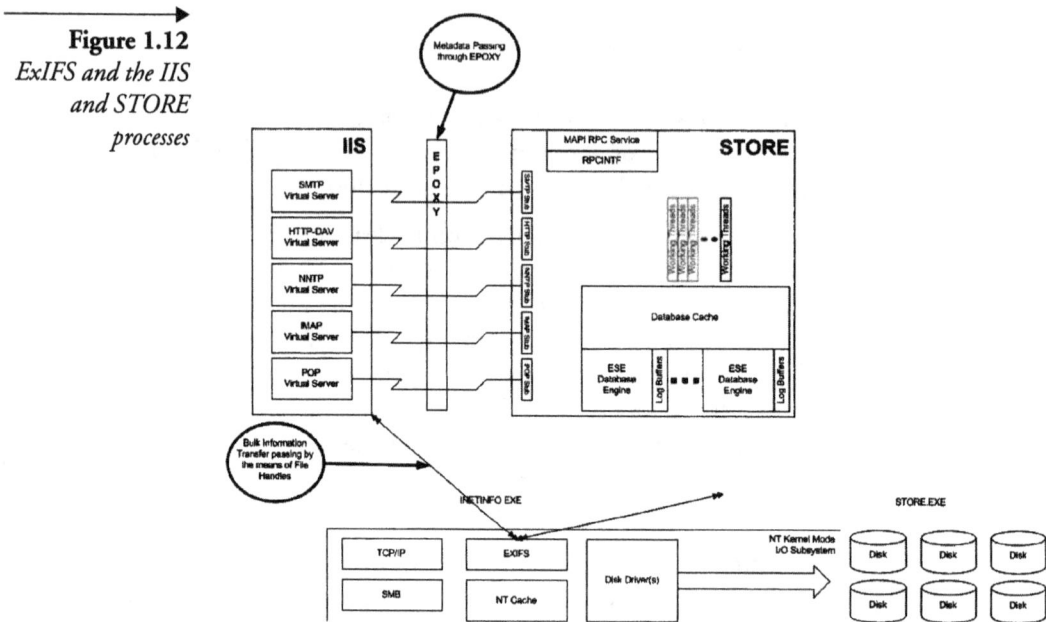

The first channel utilized is the one to the ExIFS; when the IIS virtual server gets inbound information, it opens up a handle and makes a kernel mode call (TransmitFile, described later in this book) that gets data from the TCP/IP stack, transfers it into the NT cache, and instructs the file system to fetch that data from the cache and store it on disk. All of this operation is happening in kernel mode, as shown in Figure 1.13.

As you can see, data comes in from a socket and gets stored in the NT cache; the ExIFS interacts with the STORE process to figure out where in the Streaming Store this data should go. In response, the ExIFS gets the data to the cache and passes it on to the disk drivers, which in turn will proceed to write the data on disk in a simple NTFS file, the Streaming Store database.

At this point you may say, "Yeah right, I know how to pass from user mode to kernel mode, but there is no way that kernel mode code can actually switch back to user mode!" Indeed, once you have a component execut-

Figure 1.13
*Data paths
between TCP/IP
and the
Streaming Store*

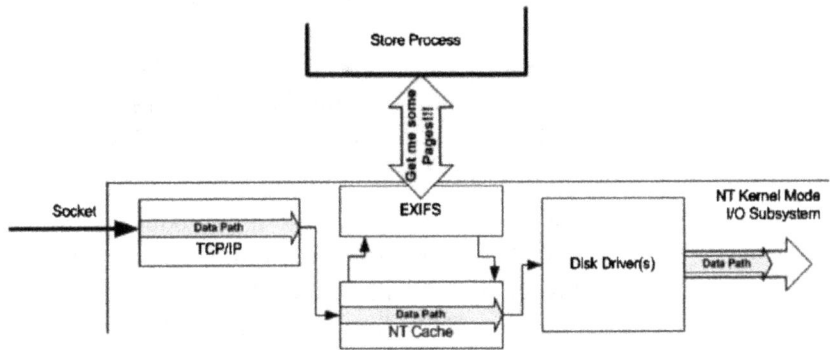

ing in kernel mode, such as a device driver, there is no way to call user mode code. Then comes a clever mechanism used between the ExIFS and the STORE called a *user-mode reflector* (see Figure 1.14).

Figure 1.14
User-mode reflector

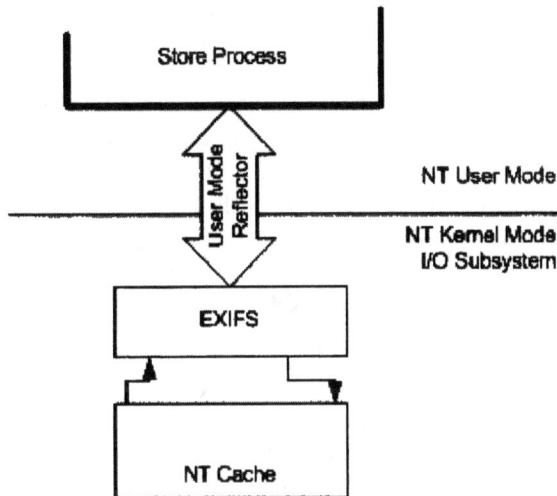

This component is not a Windows Server component per se. The STORE process issues a set of IOCTL commands, which are queued to the ExIFS, and when the ExIFS needs to communicate with the STORE, it completes an IOCTL call and provides information requests in the status buffer. This reminds me of when we used to pass information between device drivers and calling programs with the means of the I/O Status Block (IOSB) data structure in SYS$QIO calls, but that is ancient history (at least for me).

This is a very efficient mechanism; once the write operation has completed, the property promotion can happen as well as storage of the metadata transmitted by the Epoxy layer (which is not really tuned to handle large quantities of data interchanged between IIS and STORE), which contains the famous file handle, such that the STORE can further reference the file by means of ExIFS without having to create a new file handle.

Quite new at the time of its introduction with Exchange 2000, the ExIFS functions perfectly well with Exchange 2003, but you might wonder if this component in Microsoft Exchange is here to stay, given the processing power available in the first half of 2006 from the main chip manufacturers, Intel and AMD, and from server vendors, such as HP, IBM, or Dell. It seems as though this once-bright optimization of data transfer is now not so relevant, due to the increase of bus bandwidth, clock rate, and otherwise improved communication components inside modern Windows servers.

1.6.7   The INETINFO Process (IIS)

IIS plays a big role on an Exchange 2003 server. It is the prime component of any communication using Internet protocols, apart from LDAP (which is activated by the means of DS_ACCESS). I don't think that there is very much to say about IIS now, after all we said about the STORE process and its relationship with IIS, but there are few points that are worth considering.

HTTP-DAV Support and OWA

IIS implements the HTTP virtual service and thereby allows to access an Exchange 2003 server through HTTPDAV (DAV is an acronym for document authoring and versioning), which is used for Outlook Web access (OWA) Exchange ActiveSync (EAS) but can also be utilized for Web folders and any application that figures it's a neat way to get to database information. OWA has made major improvements all along the various releases of Microsoft Exchange, to the point that it is often considered an alternative to Microsoft Outlook in deployments with multivendor clients. Unlike Exchange 5.5, in which OWA was primarily a set of active server pages (ASP) that were issuing collaboration data object (CDO) calls—and in fact, behind the scenes, were establishing MAPI session—OWA in Exchange 2003 is implemented as a much improved ISAPI filter that can handle many more connections out of a single server (4,000 to 5,000 active connections are possible out of a low-to-medium-class OWA Exchange 2003 server) and can fully take advantage of Exchange 2003's native support for XML data transfer. The basic mechanisms are depicted in Figure 1.15 and apply to other protocols, such as EAS, the mobility interface to Microsoft Exchange. The result is a very rich OWA implementation for Web browsers such as Internet Explorer 5.5 and above, although down-level clients have a simpler rendering of information yet can still gain access to the Exchange databases by the means of an extremely efficient and scalable mechanism.

Figure 1.15
Simplified OWA implementation view

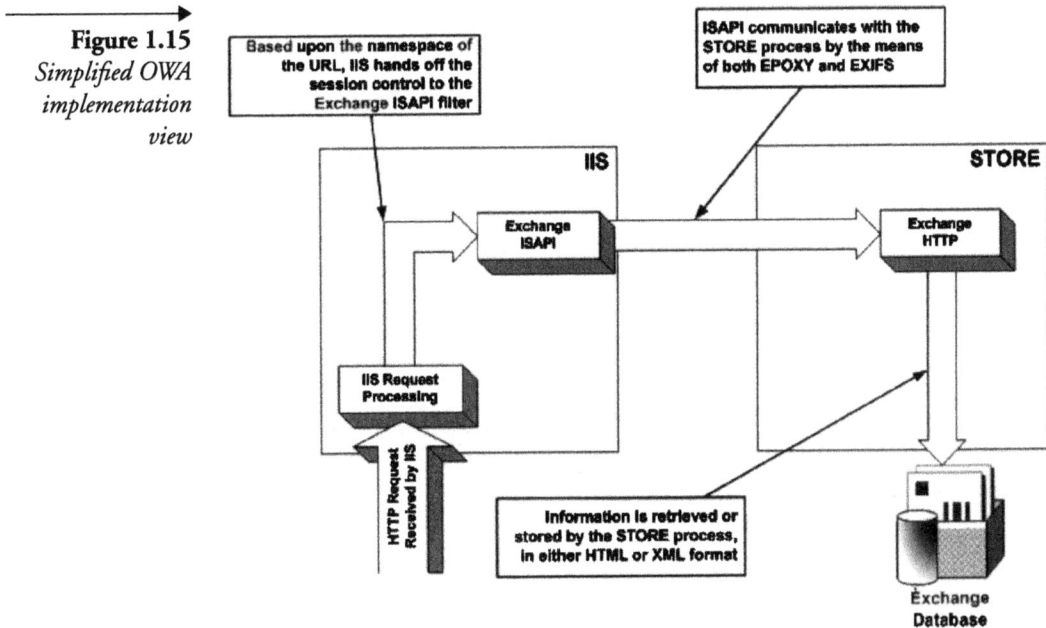

SMTP Protocol Handling

The particular point with the SMTP handling is that when an inbound SMTP message is delivered to an Exchange server, it has to go through several steps, one of them being the *categorization* of the message.

This consists of looking up the Active Directory GC (by means of DS_ACCESS) to determine whether the message should be delivered locally or rerouted. The peculiarity of the current SMTP virtual server implementation in Exchange 2003 is that unless the message is to be delivered to a local recipient, the SMTP virtual server stores transient messages in its own set of NTFS-based folders (Mailroot). By default, this folder structure is located under the Exchange 2003 binaries folder hierarchy and is typically moved to a fast disk array (4–6 spindles) for demanding traffic.

It is only after the categorization step that effective delivery can be made to local recipients through the ExIFS and the Epoxy layer that we described earlier.

Note that the queuing and routing component does not necessarily store transient messages in the Exchange 2003 Information Store but depends on the component for that. It happens that both X.400 MTA and SMTP transports use their own local storage for transient messages, and this is an area that you should not ignore when configuring high-performance switching components in an Exchange 2003 environment. Figure 1.16 shows how you can reach to the properties of the SMTP virtual server of a running Microsoft Exchange server and alter the paths used by the virtual server for storing these temporary messages.

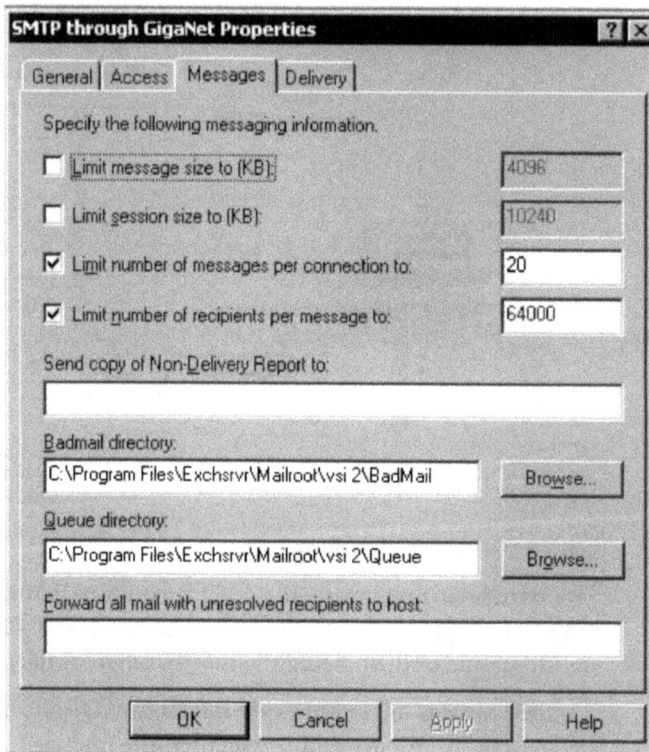

Figure 1.16
Changing the path to SMTP folders

1.7   Exchange Server Futures

Microsoft Exchange 2000 does represent a major technology step forward for the family of messaging and collaboration products produced by Microsoft. That said, technology evolves rapidly, especially on the hardware side of things, with the introduction of 64-bit Intel and AMD machine architectures. Trends of utilization and implementation of mission-critical line-of-business applications also evolve, and Microsoft has shown great dynamism in adapting to the ever-changing needs of the information technology community.

It would be very ambitious to make any kind of predictions of what the IT landscape will look like five years from now. Nevertheless, there are trends happening in all areas that should not be ignored. In fact, you can take significant advantage of these trends to build computing infrastructures that cost less to operate and acquire yet can provide improved services to end users to give an important business advantage to your company.

In the first edition of this book, I spent time on how 64-bit architectures were likely to be adopted, and, eventually, Microsoft was likely to merge two database engine technologies: ESE and SQL Server. The reality is that neither of the two happened, nor will they happen in the foreseeable future. Many plans were put on board then scrapped for Microsoft Exchange (do you remember Kodiak?). Similarly, 64-bit architecture processors from Intel, known as IA-64 (IA is an acronym for Itanium Architecture), did not manage to strike into Microsoft Exchange environments, for an obvious lack of supportability. The resulting servers, built on IA-64, do run Microsoft's Windows Server 2003 operating system, in 64-bit native mode, but not Microsoft Exchange.

Microsoft SQL Server 2005 does operate very well in these environments, yet does not provide a database engine for Exchange 2003 SP2 or the next major release of Microsoft Exchange, code named Exchange 12.

On the other hand, 64-bit processor architectures made their way through the 32-bit world, and AMD led the trend by offering processors with 64-bit capabilities, yet were able to operate in a legacy 32-bit mode and look like any other 32-bit processor to the Windows operating system. The change is coming from that path, and Intel now proposes similar technology (called EM64T, where AMD calls its technology AMD64), with Microsoft providing a version of the Windows Server 2003 operating system for what is known to be x64 machines. It is this particular processor technology and operating system version that will be supported by the 64-bit version of Exchange 12. In fact, Exchange 12 will not ship on 32-bit platforms, except for test purposes.

I personally was pretty dubious when Microsoft first leaked the news through its closest partners. But in reality, you can hardly find a server shipping today that does not implement both 32-bit and 64-bit instruction sets.

More so, the envisaged migration models for Exchange 12 are simplified. There is no in-place upgrade, and you must move mailboxes to a new

64-bit server from your Exchange 2003 "legacy" 32-bit environment. It's quite unclear at this point how this will affect the adoption of Exchange 12. Maybe customers will ramp up rapidly after realizing the benefits of running Exchange in 64-bit mode, with a significantly reduced I/O footprint. Given that the best practice for migrating from Exchange 5.5 to Exchange 2000 and 2003 was to use the "move mailbox" option, there is little risk being taken here.

I think it has been interesting to observe the evolution between Exchange 2000 and Exchange 2003. From a product that was to be at the center of collaboration environments (maybe like Domino was proposed to be four years ago?), Microsoft Exchange has evolved into a super-messaging system, able to deal with a variety of clients, especially mobile ones, out of the box. It becomes simpler to operate by the means of supplementary tools that Microsoft makes available over the Internet. And, finally, Microsoft has realized that there is nothing like a great Outlook client for connecting to Microsoft Exchange (this is possibly why the code-name scheme of Outlook was adopted by the Exchange group). Long gone are the days where you could get to Microsoft Exchange from any kind of client: the best experience in using Microsoft Exchange is to use Outlook, and the best server to Outlook is Microsoft Exchange.

Exchange 12 will come with its batch of new features and has an opportunity to adopt new ways of communication: mobile devices and voice over IP, which are gaining adoption every day. Drawing from this messaging system on steroids to address the strongest and most critical workloads seems like a challenge that Microsoft will not miss.

2

Exchange 2003 Scalability

2.1   Why Would You Want to Scale?

Scalability is the ability of a system or a group of systems to grow in processing and storage capability without architectural modifications. Applied to software engineering and telecommunications, according to wikipedia.org, scalability indicates the capability of a system to increase total throughput under an increased load when resources (typically hardware) are added.

In the Microsoft Exchange environment, scalability has always been a concern to address to cope with the rising use of electronic messaging in commercial or corporate environments.

Today, commercial environments include wireless messaging services or pure Internet messaging services that require the capability to cope with the peak load of activity while at the same time remaining manageable. In corporate environments, scalability needs to be addressed mostly in terms of constantly growing information to store, manage, transmit, and retrieve efficiently.

The basic idea of scalability is to architect solutions that don't require fundamental changes as the transaction load—or, put more simply, the user activity—ramps up and increases across time. User activity may be represented by a volume of transactions (RPC operations per second) or by a volume of data (MB or GB) stored, sent, and received, or simply by the quantity of mailboxes hosted out of a given server.

The ramp-up of activity can be very steep in service provider environments, more than in enterprise environments. The goal is being able to deal with activity ramp-up in a proactive manner so that users don't have to suffer from sluggish server performance if and when they can actually connect to the server and that they can use storage for their needs.

Microsoft Exchange 2003 comes with similar scalability features to Exchange 2000, and in this chapter we discuss the areas of the product that have improved the most compared with Microsoft Exchange 5.5 and Microsoft Exchange 2000. However, it is necessary to guard against not trying to exceed too rapidly Microsoft Exchange's scalability boundaries and to learn how to properly address them. It might even be possible, to build such scalable infrastructure with complementary solutions, e.g., for helping with the data management and growth.

Indeed, Microsoft, in shipping Exchange 2000 during fall of 2000, did address immediate issues perceived by the installed Exchange 5.5 base (e.g., by providing multiple Information Store databases and active/active clustering) and the demand from certain commercial services. Nevertheless, when a barrier is removed, you will always find inventive customers or the most demanding environments that will actually arrive at a new barrier, hopefully in a way and in a time frame such that Microsoft can actually address their concerns in the best manner possible. So with Exchange 2003 and Windows Server 2003 came requirements to deal with even larger quantities of data, larger workloads (sometimes motivated by the change of behavior, users, or user's clients, such as Outlook 2003), and higher availability requirements.

The ability to store information in a partitioned (from a database files perspective) data store led many customers to increase the mailbox quota allocated per user, thereby allowing more data to be managed from Microsoft Exchange: restore times of information database was addressed because you could deal with smaller entities. Yet, an entire server being able to handle several hundreds of gigabytes of information, and possibly a significantly large number of users (5,000 and above), led customers to demand much more availability features, something that clustering can address, to a certain extent.

Even with the most rapid backup and recovery technologies, you may figure that two hours is still too long for recovering a 200-GB Microsoft Exchange database, and you need to address this with different backup techniques, such as VSS-based backups, available from Exchange 2003 and Windows Server 2003 combined.

We are going to study a few areas that require this scalability and explain how you can address them with Microsoft Exchange and Windows Server, assuming that you use the most recent version of both (at least Exchange 2003 SP2 and Windows Server 2003 SP1 and R2).

2.1.1 Service Providers

The concept of the application service provider (ASP) was introduced during the late 1990s: mainly it consists of renting application services to companies that would otherwise run their own application environment. The necessities of ASP become relevant when companies decide to concentrate on their commercial activities and decrease operational costs to the greatest extent possible. Application service providers are now proposing to host business-critical applications, such as enterprise resource planning or electronic messaging, viewed often as a vital means of communication for an enterprise. Across time, many service providers studied and implemented Microsoft Exchange for providing messaging services. They can either be ASPs, Internet service providers or even satellite or cable operators.

It is rather interesting to cover scalability in the case of service provider because of their strong dependency on customer acceptance: unlike a corporation that can deploy Microsoft Exchange on a policy basis, service providers are highly dependent upon customer satisfaction and are unable to impose a messaging system if it does not respond to the users' needs. In addition, service providers have to deliver the service "no matter what." In short, not only do you need strong resilience built into the overall solution, but you also need to have an architecture that can adapt to the demand without having to tear down and rearchitect it. You might compare this to the requirement of exchanging aircraft engines with more powerful ones without landing, while in flight.

Types of Service

In a messaging environment, Internet protocol clients primarily provide the ASP services. IMAP and POP are the main protocols used for accessing mail servers. HTTP is a growing protocol for accessing to mailbox information, either by the means of interactive interfaces (such as Hotmail, Yahoo!, and AOL) or by the means of HTTP-DAV (also known as WebDAV), allowing an office client such as Outlook 2003 to connect to an HTTP server to access mailboxes from a Windows-based user interface.

SMTP is used for sending messages. For customers that desire to utilize the Microsoft Office suite of products—specifically Outlook—terminal services such as those offered from Windows 2000 Advanced Server, are appropriate. Service providers that provide such a computing environment tend to do it on a smaller scale, though. With Outlook 2003 and the RPC/HTTP mode of connectivity, it is becoming quite easy to offer electronic messaging as well as personal information management (e.g., contacts and calendars), as long as the user is using Outlook 2003 in either cache or online modes.

Because of security constraints involved in accessing the Internet and because a company wouldn't want to expose too much of its infrastructure by opening many protocol ports, MAPI is seldom implemented over the Internet. IMAP, POP, and HTTP are protocols that can be relayed by Exchange front-end servers or generic proxy servers, which is an important condition for securely connecting to the Internet. RPC over HTTP is therefore the preferred mode for connecting into Microsoft Exchange servers that are hosted in service providers' data centers.

Modes of Access

How would Windows Server 2003 and Exchange 2003 help in such environments?

The key is that Microsoft Exchange 2003 technology addresses the most needed and requested service for an enterprise that requires uptime, connectivity, and fast delivery—e-mail. But reducing Microsoft Exchange to just interpersonal mail messaging is an inadequate shortcut.

In a completely outsourced situation, an ASP would offer to small enterprises the hosting and the transport of mail messages, which are becoming more and more important for business communications in the twenty-first century.

Instead of acquiring a server and managing this server and associated storage, a company can decide to completely outsource its messaging and collaboration environment to a service provider that would provide a point of access by the means of Internet protocols, such as POP, IMAP, or HTTP (including RPC/HTTP).

The latter protocol is becoming more and more prevalent, and many Internet providers (e.g., Microsoft with its Hotmail service and its newly introduced .NET My Services) provide access by the means of HTTP, which can offer a richer set of functionality by building the necessary HTTP commands to send, retrieve, and store information at the site of the service provider. You can use HTTP with Exchange 2003 in two ways:

1.   OWA: Outlook Web access in Exchange 2003 is stunningly similar to Outlook 2003;

2.   Outlook 2003 in RPC/HTTP mode: in such mode, all you need to establish is an HTTP entry point in your network, most

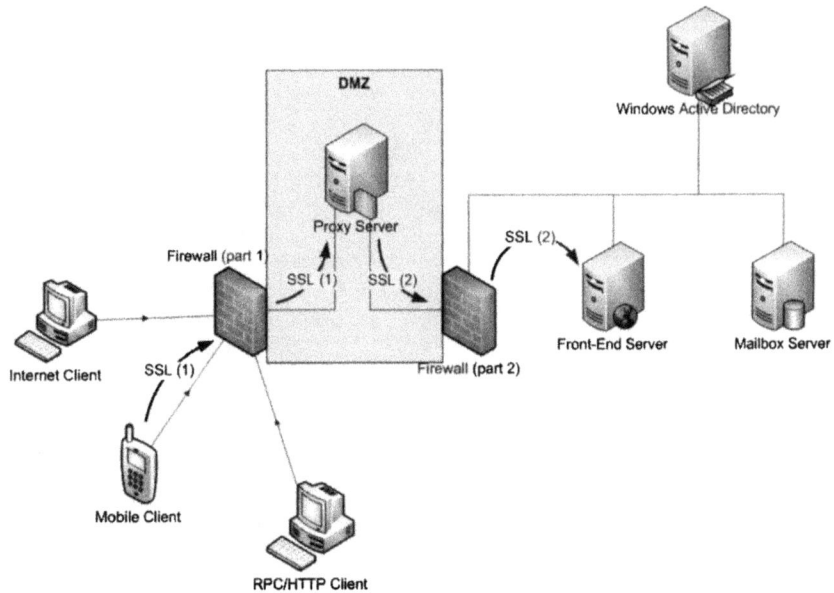

Figure 2.1
*Using Outlook
2003 in RPC/
HTTP mode*

typically configured in a reverse proxy manner, bridging the SSL connection between the outside Internet and the intranet (see (1) and (2) in Figure 2.1).

In addition to Outlook and Microsoft Exchange, service providers also provide web publishing space and possibly file sharing capabilities. The particularity of service provider environments is that they have to combine the high availability required for their business to be viable for end users, with the scalability required for their businesses to be viable, economically speaking. In fact, there is a lot to learn from operations and architectures of data centers found in service providers. They are usually at the cutting edge of advanced computing service provisioning, implementing a pay-per-use model that most corporate IT departments wish they could implement nowadays.

2.1.2 Server Consolidation

The consolidation of servers is a common topic for many enterprise customers with a strong wish to reduce their total cost of ownership. In a large proportion of Exchange 5.5 deployments, it was very common to dedicate particular servers to particular tasks. Servers could be assigned to hosting mailboxes in private Information Stores, or to a public folder in the public Information Store, or to message switching by exercising only

Figure 2.2
*Specialized servers
with Microsoft
Exchange*

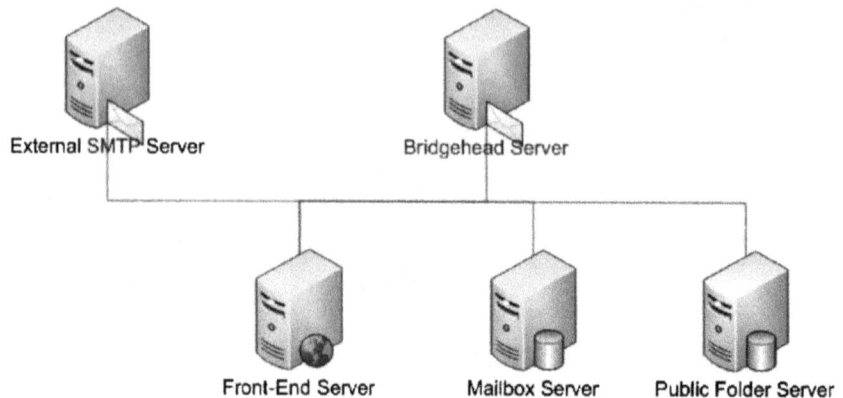

External SMTP Server   Bridgehead Server

Front-End Server   Mailbox Server   Public Folder Server

the message transfer agent component. This last case is designated as a bridgehead server.

Figure 2.2 gives a view of such an infrastructure:

- External SMTP servers are used to communicate with SMTP servers that are outside of the Microsoft Exchange infrastructure. Typically, they are located in the demilitarized zones (DMZ) of a firewall, but not always, such as in environments where you have multiple messaging systems.

- Bridgehead servers are regular SMTP servers, except that they can have additional protocol support by the means of add-ons (e.g., a third party FAX gateway) or X.400 by the means of enabling this option in Microsoft Exchange. In the majority of Exchange 2003 deployments, SMTP is used for intraorganization email exchange.

- Front-end servers are used to accept and route POP, IMAP, HTTP, and RPC/HTTP connections to back-end servers. Front-end servers do not enable a greater quantity of clients to connect to the messaging environment, but instead help in providing a unified namespace. You can perform load balancing across several front-end servers.

- Public folder servers are used to host public folder mail hierarchy. Even though public folders are not the way you would want to share information using Microsoft technology, they are still used with Exchange 2003 for sharing free/busy hours (useful when you book an appointment that comprises resources or other users) and distributing in the organization some system-level information (forms) by the means of replication.

- Mailbox servers are used to host mailbox information. I have listed the mailbox servers last, but they are the most important. From all the server specialization mentioned here, the mailbox server "role" (that term is used for later releases of Microsoft Exchange) is the *only* one that cannot be duplicated in an active way across the infrastructure—hence the reason that much of the energy spent on high availability for Microsoft Exchange focuses on mailbox servers and the storage components required for supporting their implementation.

Segregating the workload on each of the systems allows a better understanding of what is going on, better tuning of the system parameters, and a simpler connectivity and management topology. For instance, a bridgehead server will require little storage capacity, good network connectivity, and good processing capabilities. In some situations, some servers may be dedicated to the execution of applications running against public folder databases.

We have also often seen cases of specialized Exchange servers when dealing with external connectivity. It makes a lot of sense to utilize a bridgehead server to connect to external networks such as the Internet, locate these servers in firewall DMZ areas, and possibly run content filtering and/or antivirus software. This approach has led to many large-scale deployments, some with more than 300 servers, and many customers are looking at Exchange 2003 technology as a means for consolidating the servers.

This is possible because of the increased processing capabilities of computers (enabled with symmetric multiprocessing, hyper-threading, and dual-core technologies), but, most important, the ability of the Exchange store to handle multiple databases, partitioning the Information Store (either private or public) and allowing more users to be handled per server. Several mailbox servers can now be consolidated onto a single high-capacity server while retaining the individual database size—which has always been the scalability limit in Exchange 5.5—to a reasonable level.

A single Exchange 2003 server with multiple databases can easily replace multiple servers with a single database, as shown in Figure 2.3.

The benefits are numerous. First, there is a great deal of optimization for traffic occurring between databases; instead of having to involve routing and message transfer components when sending a message from a mailbox on server A to a mailbox on server B, the delivery remains local to the server, saving network and computing resources. But probably the most

Figure 2.3
*One Exchange
2003 server can
replace several
Exchange
5.5 servers*

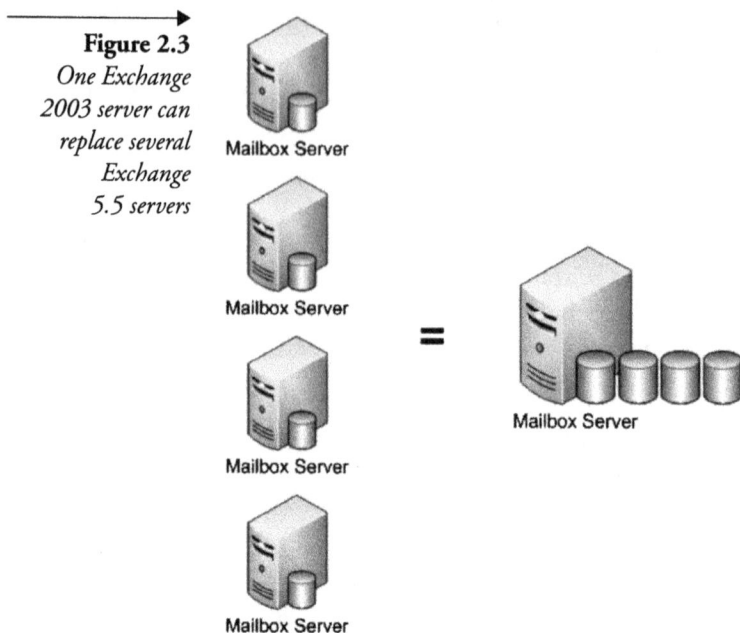

important point is that the number of machines that you have to manage, maintain, and monitor can be reduced by a factor of 75 percent (in this example). You should, however, be aware that server consolidation does reduce the number of servers and units of management, but it generally doesn't reduce the total quantity of data to manage. You end up with one server instead of four, but you still have to care and feed four databases, or the equivalent of four databases.

To gain optimization in this area and decrease the quantity of information that is under the control of a given Microsoft Exchange server, you should aim to utilize archiving tools, supplementary to the Exchange 2003 server software.

As you improve the quality of the storage components that support the Microsoft Exchange server requests, you can increase the number and the size of the databases. Exchange 2003 tends to scale linearly as you add more databases and storage groups. Make sure you use Exchange 2003 SP2, because it contains important virtual address management optimizations that reduce the overhead of running more than one storage group per server.

2.1.3 **Service Consolidation**

The next step to server consolidation is service consolidation. This is a very important approach that you should aim for in reducing and improving your infrastructure services. Today, I am getting customer requests of the likes of: "I want 99.999 percent availability for the authentication service of my 50,000 Windows 2000 users and desktops."

As you can see, little care is given to translating that basic business requirement into a technology-based implementation. Whether you deploy 5 domain controllers or GC servers or 100 of them doesn't really matter, as long as you provide the level of service demanded by your customers (typically the business units, which happen to own budgets for application development and contribute to the infrastructure budgets).

For example, at HP, we centralize the dynamic host configuration protocol (DHCP) service for our offices on a per-area basis (EMEA, Americas, ASIAPAC) when the network infrastructure allows it. What this means, practically, is that there is no DHCP server in each single location where there is an office with a file and print server and the likes of standard network services, but rather a centralized, scalable, and reliable service located in a single place that can serve many locations.

The advantages are twofold: first, you need fewer computing resources. Second, and most important, you need fewer administrators to manage the DHCP service, which, for example, is confined to a Windows 2003 cluster server.

With messaging and Exchange 2003, this is the type of service that you can establish. In corporations that have a long-standing track record of running a successful large-scale messaging infrastructure, the level of service is expressed in terms of availability and workload throughput. As you try to consolidate servers, attempt to have a service consolidation approach through which you can grant certain abilities, such as the following:

- *Availability*: the readiness to accept and carry out functions under varying loads and attempts to deny access;
- *Scalability*: the ability to adapt a solution from the targeted design or implementation to a significantly larger or smaller scale;
- *Security*: the ability to protect information and computer resources from unauthorized use in the most uniform manner possible, regard-

less of which platforms the core business applications are operating from;

- *Reliability*: the ability of a system or a component to perform its required functions under stated conditions for a specified period of time;

- *Performance*: the rate at which an information system such as Exchange 2003 can produce results, including throughput and response time;

- *Usability*: the ease with which a user can learn to operate, prepare inputs for, and interpret outputs of a system or component;

- *Manageability*: the ability to monitor and control the computing environment in the same manner, no matter how many servers and how many different platforms are operating in your environment;

- *Agility*: the ability to extend or modify existing systems to meet new requirements in a seamless manner from both production and end-user perspectives.

Attaining these abilities with Exchange 2003 is possible if you spend enough time understanding end users' requirements and their expectations of the messaging service. In addition, you should be well aware that there is no single technological answer to implement these abilities. Often, you will need to spend time analyzing the infrastructure, the services required, and those provided.

You must define your expectations from each of these services (e.g., what Exchange 2003 needs from the Windows Active Directory service, and not *how* to deploy Exchange 2003 in a given Windows Active Directory environment!) and always be in a position to justify the technology and services required to implement these abilities. That and a solid budget will allow you to move more rapidly to an environment that can create a clear business advantage to your business units and your company as a whole, and allow the company to be more successful in its line of business.

2.1.4   Data Growth

It is unquestionable that data volumes have steadily increased since the introduction of Microsoft Exchange in general and Exchange 2000 in particular. The business needs of messaging are requesting, in addition to lower cost and high availability, higher capabilities in dealing with larger quantities of data. For example, when Exchange 4.0 was introduced in 1996, we started early deployments with mailboxes limited to 20 MB in space. Nowadays, the size of mailboxes, in corporate environments, typically reaches 200 MB, and we are not very far from the days where users obtain 1-GB or 2-GB mailboxes.

There are several reasons for this:

- The rich data environments of multimedia, rich text, and attachments are common nowadays in mail messages. We are not dealing with text anymore. A typical email will contain pictures and graphical themes, automatic signatures with more or less relevant content, and attachments with documents that can exceed 1 or 2 MB in size.

- The use of Personal Store (PST) in Microsoft Outlook has derived from its original purpose, leading to multi-GB PST containers that are typically backed up as single files and located on file servers.

- The need for regulatory compliance, in other words, the business legitimacy of email, led to the need to apply proper archiving and retention policies. Sarbanes-Oxley is a good example of regulations that demand the retention of electronic information related to business needs. The smallest deployments will tend to gather this information in Microsoft Exchange, using the journaling function for instance. Large deployments and companies that need to deal with frequent inquiries tend to use specialized archival software that is certified and that can retrieve individual elements rapidly, using indexing technologies, for instance.

- Mail is business critical. When not mission critical, email is now considered as a business tool, and more and more business processes are making implicit or explicit use of electronic mail for their execution. The result is that there are more mail exchanges in terms of transactions (mail sent and received), but also in terms of overall capacity.

Beyond these reasons, I believe also that we are dealing with a culture change. Indeed, email is the number one business application, omnipresent in companies. More importantly, however, our kids, the teens of the twenty-first century, regularly deal with one form or another of electronic messaging. The use of Short Message Service (SMS) on mobile phones is a good example, although not necessarily to follow to the extreme usage, where we have seen cases of employees being fired by SMS or a teen declaring his crush to another teen by SMS. One way or another, we have a rising generation of individuals that find that electronic communication is natural. This generation represents the business workers of tomorrow, and gradually, we see an increased usage of email, not always for business purposes, and preferably on mobile devices. Mobility, a major theme for Exchange 2003 that introduced protocol extensions that enable Windows Mobile smartphones and personal digital assistants (PDAs) to access an Exchange mailbox. The use of mobility in Exchange deployments kills any backup window or downtime that you might have planned as an Exchange administrator. It also increases the potential number of client devices that can connect on an Exchange server. You may no longer assume that only Outlook clients connect into a server for using Exchange functions. In fact, a typical mobile deployment will demand that you can deal with both a traditional client (desktop machine running Microsoft Outlook) and a mobile device, both at the same time. This increases the pressure put on your Exchange infrastructure such that it can deal with many clients, many more transactions, with a quality of service that must match or exceed those that consumers are used to when using Internet free mail services, such as MSN Hotmail or Google GMail.

The days of information anytime anywhere are here, and Exchange is at the center of it. Now comes the time to properly implement and use technologies of the computing industry to deliver on users and business needs.

2.2 Horizontal vs. Vertical Scalability

Scalability can be expressed using two models:

.

- *Scale-out*: the ability to add computing systems as the workload increases;

- *Scale-up*: the ability to *upgrade* computing systems as the workload increases.

You could be very picky and consider that you may scale out within a particular Exchange 2003 server (by adding more databases, storage groups, and virtual servers). But, essentially, these are the two main models.

We'll focus on the scale-up capability of Exchange 2003 to handle a large number of users or transactions out of a single server, as well as the scale-out capability of Exchange 2003 to function by adding more front-end servers and bridgehead servers and distributing the workload among several computers as opposed to one single monster.

The reality is that today, in the Windows computing environment, 90 percent of the workloads can be achieved by using four-way servers (four CPUs at increasing speed as the technology evolves). It is not often that eight-way servers are used in the Exchange 2003 infrastructure because the nature of the main processing required, typically done by the Information Store process, does not scale very well (i.e., linearly) past four processors. You always have the possibility to go beyond four processors and use affinity: this will assign processors to particular process or tasks. However, that gets into very specific cases and extreme fine-tuning of Exchange 2003, which, although not impossible, is complex and must be done with care.

The front-end/back-end scenario and the ability to host Exchange 2003 Virtual Servers outside of the main mailbox servers is definitely a key advantage for large-scale deployments. Not only can you assign servers with different specifications for handling different protocols and workloads, but you can also easily manage multiple servers by the means of policies and the use of a central administration, the Exchange System Manager snap-in.

You may consider as a local server scale-out activity the process that consists of adding more databases or storage groups, rather than letting the database grow (scale-up). I consider it a best practice not to exceed 30 GB to 40 GB for an individual database size. Using such limits and appropriate backup technologies, you can easily take less than two hours to restore a corrupted database. In scaling an individual server in terms of capacity, for hosting more users, or increasing users' mailboxes quotas, you should always remember to keep the database sizes under control in order to maintain service levels, especially when it comes to restoring databases and possibly entire servers.

A logical step is trying to first fill up an entire storage group before creating a new one. That way, by adding more databases, you minimize the overhead incurred by running several database engine instances, as shown in Figure 2.4 for hosting the database cache (which is shared among all the database engines), but you will find that your server can respond quicker to service shutdown requests if there is a small number of storage groups.

Four steps are involved. Step 1 consists of adding a database to the current storage group. The impact here is minimal, since it is likely that you will host the database on the same volume as the existing databases, and you don't need to create an additional volume for the transaction log of a new storage group. Step 2 consists of adding a new storage group. This requires

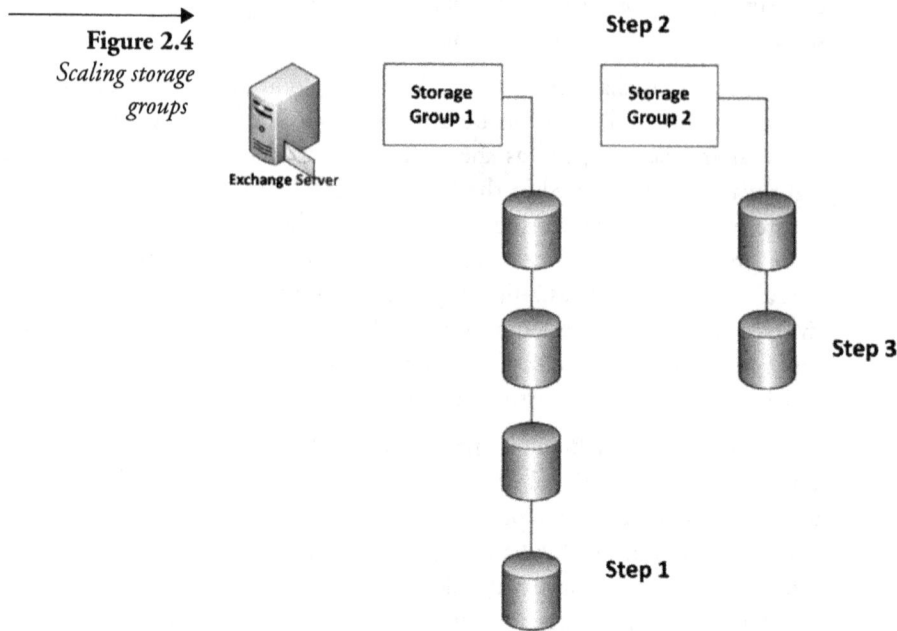

Figure 2.4
Scaling storage groups

significant system changes since you will probably host this second storage group transaction log set on a new volume (although you could reuse the first storage group log volume if it can provide the right performance). Then you can continue to grow the second storage group until you reach the point at which you need to create an additional storage group.

The down side of this approach is the need to create additional volumes as you grow your storage groups, and that may not be such a good thing from an operational standpoint. Remember that a scalable system is a system that can address larger workloads with no modifications but that can also handle or be configured for smaller workloads with no modifications either.

If you intend to deploy Exchange 2003 servers on a large scale (say, 100 or 200 servers), it becomes wiser to predeploy the storage groups, even though there will be an additional overhead (that you will deal with), such that you can grow your server capacity without modifying the server configuration and structure, drive letters, logical unit assignments, and the like.

Figure 2.5 gives an example of a preconfigured server that can handle from 100 to 4,000 users in terms of capacity with no apparent change to the actual server configuration. As you can see, you may fix the drive letters and reference to the operating system (it could be mount points, by the way) and add up to 15 databases with no change to the operating environment.

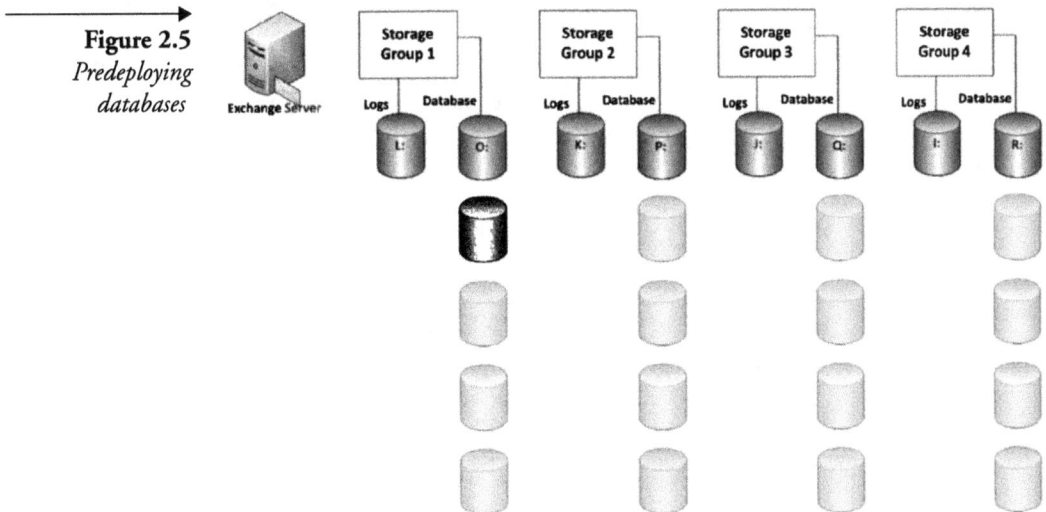

Figure 2.5
*Predeploying
databases*

This is quite appreciable but may require some upfront planning and hardware acquisition—not easy to justify, unless you have trend data that demonstrate that the server, during its lifetime (which can span beyond 36 months), will actually need to accommodate the increased capacity while maintaining service levels when it comes to restoring individual databases.

2.3   Scalable Exchange 2003 Architecture

A scalable architecture for Exchange 2003 is a technology infrastructure that can logically and physically increase in performance and capacity and continue to meet reasonable growth and change over time. Scalability is also an attribute of an architecture that can be scaled down to meet a smaller demand.

Exchange 2003 scales up because it enables hosting large user communities out of a small set of servers managed as one logical entity. Microsoft, during the development of Exchange 2000 and Exchange 2003, incorporated features that permitted this scalability. This section reviews the features of Microsoft Exchange relevant to its scalability, whether applied to a single server or a group of servers forming an Exchange organization.

2.3.1   Front End/Back End

Front-end servers in Exchange 2003 act primarily as relay servers; they proxy protocol commands and do tasks localized to the end-client connection but do not own any form of storage or messaging services. Microsoft designed Exchange 2000 such that Internet protocols can only benefit from such an environment. MAPI clients (those that use the MAPI RPC protocol) still connect directly to the back-end server. The Internet protocols that benefit from front-end/back-end implementations are:

- POP3;
- IMAP4;
- HTTP;
- SMTP;
- NNTP.

Other Internet protocols relevant to messaging, such as LDAP, are serviced directly by the Windows Active Directory. Figure 2.6 gives an example of such a setup.

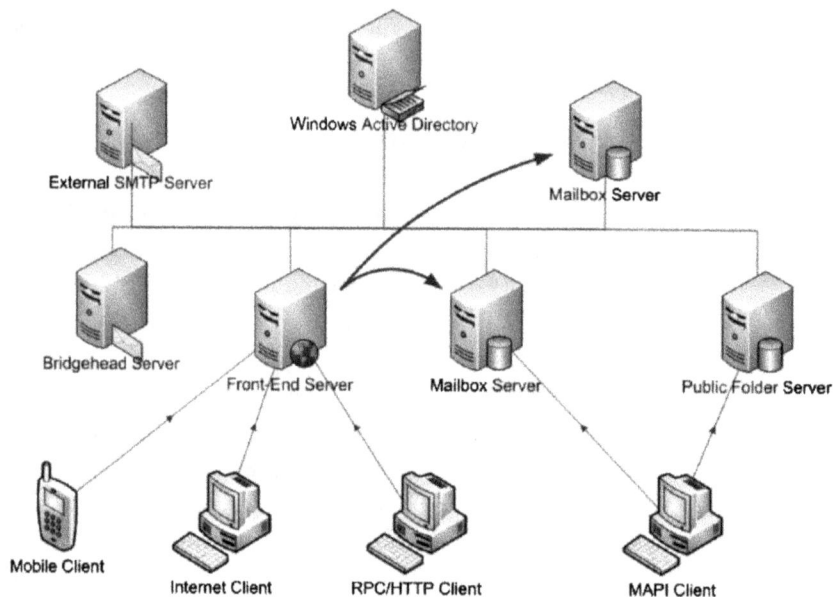

Figure 2.6
Single front-end and back-end setup

The client computer connects only to the front-end server. Upon the incoming connection, the front-end server is responsible for authenticating the user credentials and proxying the protocol commands between the client and the back-end server that hosts the user-requested data. Most of the time, it is the actual mailbox, but it can also be a public folder hosting a discussion or a Web-based application.

The user authentication is done against the Windows Active Directory domain controller or GC server by means of standard LDAP queries. This operation is transparent to the client and could occur on any GC server present in the Active Directory forest. Typically, locality of information is taken into consideration, and the front-end server will connect to a domain controller located in the same site (collection of subnets) as the front-end server.

In addition, the front-end server performs all the tasks of managing and maintaining the end-user connection. This can include secure socket layer (SSL) encryption, which guarantees the confidentiality of the data transmitted between the client and the front-end server. In large-scale environments, however, this function could be implemented using dedicated and specialized hardware that can better deal with the asymmetric encryption algorithms used in the SSL link negotiation.

Exchange 2003 front-end servers do not contribute to the performance of the overall architecture. Indeed, their main function appears to be mainly overhead in transmitting information back and forth between the client and the back-end servers. However, front-end servers do take a load that would otherwise be located on the back-end servers. This load is mainly user authentication, HTML rendition, and spell checking with the most recent version of Exchange 2003.

The main scalability factor remains the back-end servers—i.e., in their ability to handle a large number of concurrent connections, requests, and a large quantity of data.

Front-end servers do remain important, and because they sit in the critical path of any transaction between the client and the back-end server, they should be properly sized. Today, however, any server with 2 GB of RAM and one dual-core processor will deal gracefully with the proposed workload. Note that in Figure 2.6, we show a mobile client, but in reality mobile clients do not connect directly to front-end servers—they usually have to go through an SSL termination bridge located in the DMZ of a firewall, best implemented with Microsoft ISA Server 2004.

The main benefit of using front-end servers is the ability to maintain and refer client computers to a *single namespace.* From an Internet protocol perspective, if you have four Exchange servers hosting mailboxes, you would typically have four IP hosts that can service connections. How would a client know if the back-end server it connects to owns the mailbox information?

This information, also known as the mail drop—a triplet of server name, storage group name, and database name—is located in the Active Directory, a component to which the client application does not have access. As you scale your environment, you may need to move mailboxes from one server to another, or even between databases on the same server.

Unless the client protocol supports and implements referrals, it is not possible to continue servicing the connection from the same server. By connecting to a front-end server first, you in fact decouple the client connection parameters from the actual locality of information. This applies only to Internet protocol clients (IMAP, POP, HTTP, and RPC/HTTP), not to RPC MAPI clients such as pre–Outlook 2003. MAPI clients do support referral but require users to bind directly to the back-end server, as opposed to connecting to the messaging service via a front-end server. The locality of the information depends on the user profile located in the Active Directory or, in the case of public folders, on where the data is actually stored.

This represents a major scalability advantage of Exchange 2003. Indeed, as the number of clients grows, you can continue to add front-end servers and possibly back-end servers, balancing the load between the back-end servers by using judicious data partitioning, and still present this single namespace to the client connection.

The single namespace can of course map to one or more front-end servers, at least to avoid a single point of failure. In that case, the balancing between the two or more front-end servers is done by means of DNS round-robin, network load balancing, or by any other means implemented at the routing layer—for example, Alteon or Cisco routers.

We have found that hardware load balancing was in fact most appropriate for large-scale environments that tend to exceed some of the scalability limits of Windows Network Load Balancing (which can accommodate 32 servers at most).

Figure 2.7 shows how the router component will distribute the load among the front-end servers, thereby maintaining availability and quality of service. The requirements are that the router maintains established connections to the same front-end server in the case of persistent connections, such as POP or IMAP. A stateless protocol such as HTTP can be handled by any of the front-end servers.

Figure 2.7
*Load balancing
across front-end
servers*

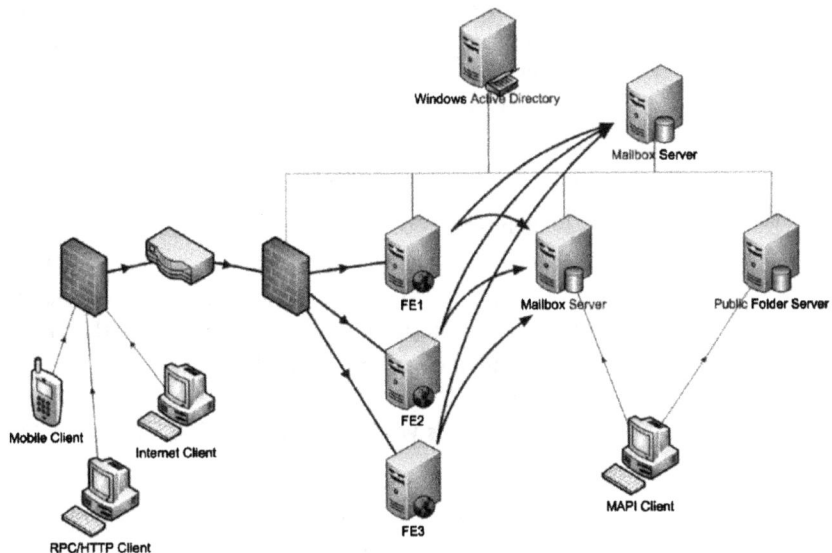

Use of Round-Robin DNS in Scale-Up Scenarios

A company may decide to use mail.company.com as a single namespace and have this fully qualified domain name resolved to mail1.company.com, mail2.company.com, or mail3.company.com. By using DNS round robin, it becomes very simple to instruct the DNS server to resolve the single namespace into any of the three IP addresses that make up the three front-end servers. If a front-end server is not available, the resolution occurs only on the two remaining servers. The failure of one component becomes relatively transparent to the end-user connection that continues to refer to the same namespace, regardless of the underlying infrastructure. The client browser would need, however, to properly reinitiate a transparent authentication in the case of an initial dialogue being interrupted between the client and the front-end server. I believe that round-robin DNS does provide a way to distribute (fan out) connections to multiple servers; however, it has no consideration whatsoever to the actual state (availability, heavy load) of the server.

Use of Load-Balancing Routers

These routers allow you to make a more or less intelligent choice as to which server a connection should be directed to. Their value remains, however, in their ability to properly distribute the load between the front-end servers and to detect the failure of a front-end server. Load-balancing routers are typically scalable, although they are more expensive than regular routers. However, if you anticipate that your workload is going to increase such that you will need to add an unforeseeable number of machines, I strongly recommend using routers of this type. They can perform functions other than load balancing, such as SSL tunneling or bridging, in a more scalable way that independent servers, which, regardless of their running operating system, need to be properly secured.

Depending upon the type of router, you may get a simple and straight-forward load-sharing mechanism (the router balances the connections among the servers), as opposed to a true load balancing, where the router can actually determine which servers respond fast and would favor those servers instead of other servers that exhibit a slower response time.

Using Firewalls with Exchange 2003 Front-End Servers: No-Go

Instead of placing your front-end servers, which can act as protocol proxies, in the DMZ area of a firewall, I suggest that you take advantage of specific Microsoft solutions such as ISA Server 2004, or use a generic proxy service (also known as *reverse proxy server*) that enables the separation between the Internet and the Intranet of a company, can implement load-balancing functions, and, as mentioned before, can handle the SSL connectivity between:

- The client and the proxy server;
- The proxy server and the Microsoft Exchange front-end servers.

This is described in Figure 2.8: the proxy server, for small environments, is best implemented as Microsoft ISA Server 2004; there is a wealth of information available about ISA Server at http://www.isaserver.org.

The reputation of Windows as a secured operating system has vastly improved, especially with Windows Server 2003 SP1, so this does not sound too silly. On the other hand, Microsoft is making life much easier with Microsoft ISA Server 2004, which has publishing functions that simply provide connectivity to the Microsoft Exchange environment from the outside, including to the newest mobility services, which are available over HTTP.

You may be tempted to use IP Security (IPSEC) to create a secure channel between the front-end servers and their back-end and directory servers. The positive side is that you need only to enable ports for the IPSEC protocol. However, on the other end, IPSEC would allow for unauthorized access to the back-end services if someone manages to break into a front-

Figure 2.8
*Using a proxy
server in the DMZ
to proxy and
terminate SSL
connections*

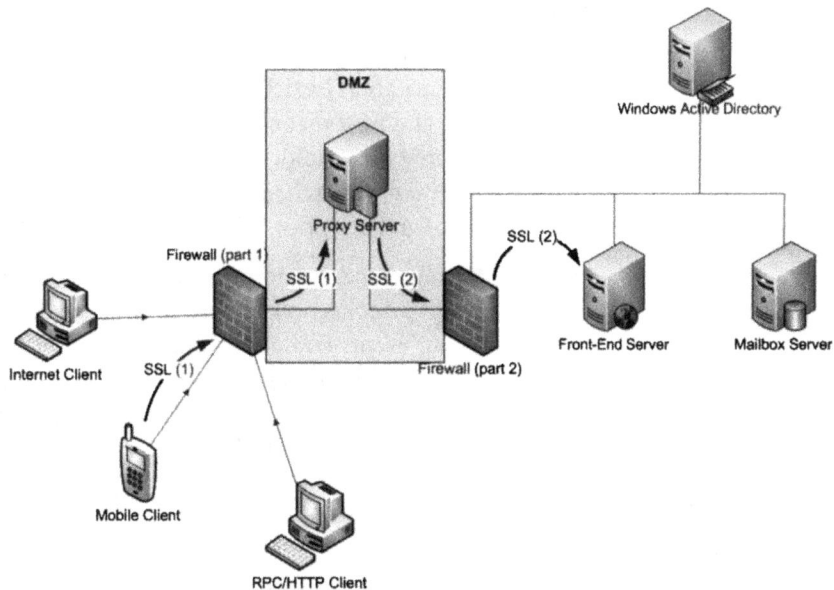

end server. For this reason, IPSEC, although appreciated for protecting traffic between hosts, is rarely used to pass through firewalls.

In the same spirit, rather than tunneling SSL between the client and the front-end server, it is advised to break the SSL connection at the proxy-server level and reestablish connectivity, still secured using SSL, between the proxy server and the front-end server. This has two advantages:

- You can use private certificates (in other words, certificates from your own private certificate authority) for the SSL entry point of the front-end servers.

- You can use a public certificate for *just* the proxy server. Depending upon the identities the proxy server can have, this is much cheaper to acquire from trusted certificate authorities, such as Verisign or Entrust.

- You get a chance to examine the traffic on the proxy server and possibly protect your environment from inappropriate content, rather than accept whatever can come from the client connecting from the Internet.

Don't Forget the Management of the Servers

By placing servers inside an area protected by firewalls, you are essentially blocking communication by defining the source port and host as well as the destination port and host that can traverse the firewall. Firewall administrators tend to be pretty paranoid, and rightly so, because the data and the service hosted by Microsoft Exchange in an enterprise can be extremely critical to the business of an enterprise.

For performing management of the servers, the preferred approach is to have data and event collection servers sitting in the protected area of the firewall, reporting events and alerts by means of the TCP/IP protocol and well-defined ports, enabling free communication among the servers in the DMZ but still allowing consolidation of events in a central monitoring and reporting point by the means of well-known fixed ports.

2.3.2   Public Folders

The use of public folders is gradually being deemphasized by Microsoft, as the company now prefers to promote solutions such as SharePoint portals or team services for dealing with information sharing. We have nonetheless a legacy to deal with and environments where public folders are used for information sharing and sometimes archiving (without necessarily calling it that). In fact, I have found that the need for dealing with large volumes of data was most expressed with public folders environments, with databases exceeding 1.5 TB in size for the maximum and growing!

To deal with a public folder information explosion is no easy task: Microsoft Outlook can only view one public folder hierarchy. You then map this hierarchy to public folder servers that have one copy of the items of the public folder hierarchy, typically replicated. The replication of public folders, initially intended to distribute information throughout a distributed network, is a real savior when it comes to recoverability because even if you have a very large public folder database, you do not need to be very concerned by its size, as you have other Exchange servers with a full replica of this database controlled at the application level.

To deal with the public folder database growth, I typically recommend partitioning the replication of the public folders to several public folder servers, as shown in Figure 2.9, thus decreasing the size of a database, which prevents long recovery delays.

Figure 2.9
*Partitioning a
public folder
hierarchy*

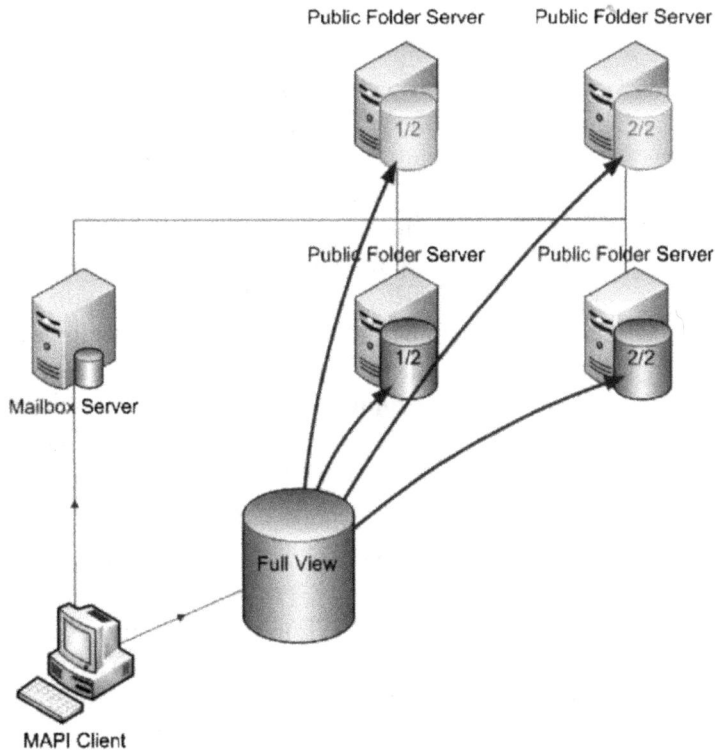

With such an approach, the MAPI client running Outlook will see a full public folder hierarchy that contains many items (e.g., 100 GB), but they are spread across four servers that contain:

- Master data for first 50 GB;
- Replica data for first 50 GB;
- Master data for next 50 GB;
- Replica data for next 50 GB.

The challenge with such an approach is the need for many servers: a single Exchange server (or virtual server in a cluster) may only mount one single public folder database per hierarchy, and since there can only be one single MAPI hierarchy for MAPI clients (a restriction that actually comes from Microsoft Outlook), you need to deploy as many servers as you have of public folder instances. However, you do not need to host the full hierarchy in the replica on each of the servers, attaining the goal of not dealing with large databases for each Exchange server instance.

The use of virtual machines in such an environment is appropriate if you wish to deploy your public folder "farm" on a minimum number of hardware platforms. However, be conscious of the possible impact of virtualization on the I/O traffic. This approach would only be reasonable if you back up your environment outside of the server (e.g., using volume shadowcopy services from Windows Server 2003) and if the traffic is relatively light. Unfortunately, I do not have, at this point, information to share about the maximum number of users that would be supported on a virtual server. This is something you need to work in a lab or on a trial basis in a representative environment. Fortunately, the multimaster replication model used for public folders enables the implementation of additional instances with no major impact to the production.

2.3.3   Mailbox Servers

So far, we've discussed the front-end and the public folder servers; however, much of the scalability necessary to resolve in a Microsoft Exchange organization is on the mailbox servers: they are used to serve the mailbox information for each client and store the mailboxes in the private store databases. We will cut back on the scaling of mailbox servers, but regardless of the number of front-end servers or the size of the public folder hierarchy, the actual problems will arise if your mailbox servers are not properly sized. The growth of data and transactions will directly impact how you configure the mailbox servers. Often, sizing mailbox servers will consist of determining the number of users per server (notion of transaction) and the mailbox quota size of these mailboxes (notion of data volume).

Large Mailboxes or Many Items?

The notion of large mailboxes has always been interesting to address with Exchange, because it is a fundamental need often expressed by the users: "I want a larger mailbox." With the cost per gigabyte ever decreasing, even in managed storage environments, the capacity itself is not problematic to achieve. Disks are shipping in capacities exceeding 500 GB; however, the ability to recover the information and deal with many transactions on these disks varies significantly.

A large mailbox can be a significant burden for the Exchange server, even if the users do not utilize them. With Exchange comes the notion of critical folders (i.e., folders that are accessed often). They are:

- Inbox: The Exchange back-end server needs to access the Inbox to deliver items and execute server-side rules.

- Calendar: The calendar entries are by other users when checking free/busy details.

- Contacts: They contain private contacts that are used for any address lookup when composing email.

- Sent items: They contain items that have been sent and for which a copy was demanded.

The effort (resulting number of I/O to the database) resulting from modifying the contents of any folder largely depends upon the items in the folder: if you have too many (3,500 is currently known as the number of items not to exceed), any operation to the folder might take two or three times more I/O. The actual number will depend upon the indexes that need to be maintained and the views of the folders that the user has defined. Operations such as finds, searches, or sorts happen on the content of the folders. If Outlook is running in cache mode, the effect of a large number of items is diminished from the user viewpoint (because all operations are done against the local cache of the mailbox); however, any replication to the folder back on the mailbox server will cause additional work.

Archiving solutions can decrease the size of mailboxes by pulling content and storing it into an archiving system. They leave behind a stub (redirection link) to the archived content, so the user can access the archived item from the messaging client, typically Outlook. However, they can induce a bad habit of leaving items in the Inbox (critical folder), increasing the total item count and causing extra I/O processing due to extra database transactions required to maintain a large quantity of items. We have found that mailbox servers with archival software were the ones that suffered most from this effect.

Because this is highly dependant upon how the user uses Outlook and how the data is managed, it's very difficult to give anything other than a recommendation to not exceed too large a number of items in the critical folders (i.e., those that must be used by Exchange, regardless of the login to the mailbox). The general rule should be:

Folder	Maximum Recommended Item Count
Inbox	5,000
Calendar	1,000
Contacts	1,000
Sent items	5,000

As a result, even if you accept that your users can have large mailboxes (>500 MB), you should plan to develop a policy to advise users to regularly clean their Inbox by the means of rules. The goal is not to decrease the size of the items, but to move the items away from the critical folders. Creating subfolders in the critical path folders could be considered an option to reduce items counts in the top level of critical folders, as shown in Figure

Figure 2.10
Creating subfolders to diminish the high item count

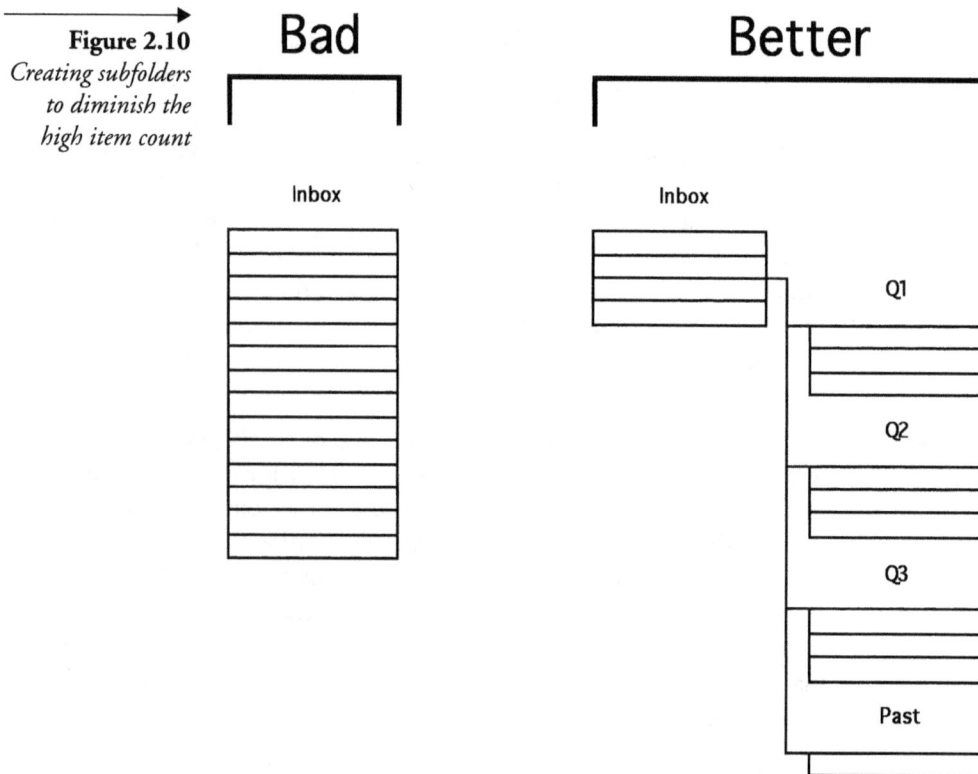

2.10, although this may not always be possible, such as in the case of the Calendar folder.

Other folders, such as "To keep" or "Just in case" (those that you create for archiving items), do not need to be under such a constraint unless the user complains of poor performance when accessing them.

2.3.4 In Summary

Don't be overly excited by the capabilities of front-end servers. From a pure performance perspective, the point of concern remains the back-end server that will actually service the connection and provide data services. The load-balancing features of routers apply only to front-end servers and have no knowledge of the type of load of the back-end servers. Should they have any, it wouldn't help, because the data is located in only a single location; no matter how many front-end servers you deploy, data availability will be only as good as the back-end service availability.

Front-end servers, however, allow the building of an infrastructure that will scale and mask the details of data location at the back end–server level. These are quite appreciable, but note that their use is not mandatory. This will entirely depend on the clients used to connect to the Exchange servers by way of Internet protocols. The lack of support for referral of some Internet clients will orient the choice toward deploying front-end servers, and this will be quite appreciable. If on the other hand you plan on deploying Exchange with Outlook (MAPI) clients, front-end servers will not be relevant; the MAPI protocol handles referrals for both mailbox access and public folder access. If a mailbox is moved from one server to another, the user profile in Outlook will automatically be updated with the server name that actually hosts the mailbox.

Larger mailboxes, a constant scalability aspect of Microsoft Exchange, bring an interesting challenge. Breaking the 1-GB or 2-GB mailbox quota implies certain challenges, regardless of running in cache or online mode. The pressure applied by the Exchange Information Store to the storage subsystem hosting the databases is expressed in two terms:

- Capacity: The overall capacity that you need to provide to the Exchange server for hosting the databases;
- Transaction: The transaction (I/O per second) required by Exchange, which must perform with a reduced latency for satisfactory user response time.

While the capacity can be attained with large drives, the transaction rate is typically addressed with many spindles, which break the mechanical limits of a single disk drive and enable users to have a larger request rate than that of a single disk by arranging several of them together. It is a challenge, because larger drives tend to reduce the spindle count, and more spindles tend to increase the capacity, sometimes exceeding two or three times the capacity needs.

2.4   IIS/Exchange Store

Exchange 2003 goes further than Exchange 5.5 with the support of Internet protocols by tightly integrating the Internet Information Services (IIS) with the Exchange Information Store.

There are several notions present in Exchange 2003 that are not found with Microsoft Exchange 5.5. First, there is this ability to store content in native format; instead of going through a systematic conversion of data into MAPI properties, as was the case with Exchange 5.5, data is stored in the format of the last writer (client, peer server, or MTA). If an IMAP client stores information in the Web store, it will be left in its native format (most likely an RFC-822 header and MIME attachments). If the message is retrieved from an IMAP client, all that will happen to the data is straight (streamed) transmission of information from the Web storage system directly back to the client.

This is possible because of the unique relationship that exists between IIS and the Exchange Information Store. Introduced with Exchange 2000 and carried over with Exchange 2003, the Exchange Installable File System (ExIFS) is a way for IIS to access information located in the Store by means of the Win32 File Access APIs.

2.4.1   ExIFS

I believe that the entire hype once built around the ExIFS is because of the ability, in the Windows Kernel, to stream content between a TCP/IP socket and a file handle. It enables Microsoft Exchange to directly consume and store information coming from the network, using a similar approach to what was once used with Microsoft Commercial Internet Services (MCIS).

When you install Exchange 2000 on a Windows 2000 or 2003 server, you have an additional drive, called M:\ by default, which maps the information located in the Information Store as a file structure. IIS utilizes this mode of access to the Exchange streaming store to, precisely, store and access data as simple files and communicate metadata by means of a component we have previously described, the Epoxy layer, which is a shared memory communication mechanism. Since SP3 of Exchange 2000 (and therefore Exchange 2003), this drive is now hidden: too many customers let antivirus engines run against the drive and cause irreversible damage to the items that were viewed through the filesystem interface.

Figure 2.11 shows the properties of the M:\ drive, which actually corresponds to the Exchange Installable File System. Interestingly enough, beta and release candidates versions of Exchange 2000 were showing the file system type as "ExIFS." With Exchange 2000 SP1, the drive was showing as a regular NTFS volume. The size information for this volume was drawn from the transaction log volumes characteristics (size and available space). Ever since Microsoft SharePoint Portal Server 2001, which uses the Exchange store technology, the M:\ drive is hidden by default, but the object remains present in the NT I/O object database.

Figure 2.11
M:\ drive
properties

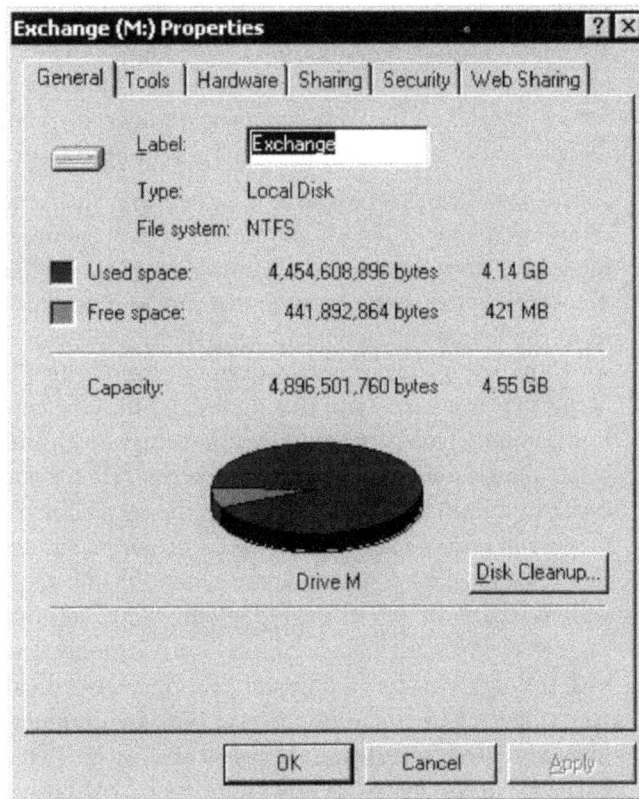

With Exchange 2003 and later, the drive disappeared: too many customers attempted to do special things with the M:\ drive, such as reading information, storing data, or worst of all, running antivirus software.

At the time of design, Microsoft's goal was to take advantage of what MCIS application servers did to store information as one RFC-822 message per NTFS file by enhancing this mechanism to have better scalability than a simple NTFS file system. This makes streaming messages in and out of the message store quite simple:

- Map the client request to a file handle.
- Call TransmitFile() to transmit the message from the remote end of the connection, identified by an open TCP/IP socket.

Now, you may wonder where this TransmitFile comes from. It is a Microsoft-specific extension to the Windows Socket specification, and it allows to transmit, directly from the Windows cache manager, the contents of a file over a connected socket handle. This function provides high-performance transfer of file data, requiring an open file handle (a reference to a file, previously opened) and a Windows connection-oriented socket.

This very same mechanism is carried over in Exchange 2003. To make things even simpler, as we said earlier, content is stored as is by the ExIFS file system, directly into the streaming store (see the following section). The TransmitFile call operates in Kernel mode; it fetches information directly from the Windows Server I/O subsystem cache as it arrives from the network interface and feeds it directly to the file handle. No data transfer occurs between kernel and user mode, and the efficiency of the data transfer is maximum. This particular function brings up an interesting observation: when most Exchange 2003 deployments call for tuning the file system cache to a minimum (by optimizing the server for network applications), they are in fact not helping on this particular means of communication and should be fixed by configuring the system for file and print sharing, which will maximize the size of the file system cache. You may utilize registry settings to override the NT cache size, but I strongly discourage this. Playing with the registry is fine for a single machine, but with a system it can lead to very complicated situations and can, in fact, produce the opposite of the intended effect on the actual machines. Given that the majority of the Exchange deployments are now supporting MAPI users, this might not be a great advantage. Leaving the system in the default memory mapping (2 GB for kernel mode; 2 GB for user mode) for the processes' virtual address space is usually sufficient for giving cache to those servers that need it (i.e., all servers that run operations other than mailbox or public stores, such as bridgehead and front-end servers).

If you intend to facilitate the Internet protocol support of your Exchange 2003 server, it is definitely worthwhile to configure the server for file and print sharing, as opposed to network applications, and give the NT I/O subsystem a chance to perform better than otherwise. Later in this book, we discuss the strategies for the memory tuning of Windows servers running Exchange 2003. For now, let's consider that mailbox servers that primarily deal with MAPI users should have a minimal NT cache so the information store can benefit from user-mode virtual address space. For all other server roles, especially front-end or bridgehead servers, this particular tuning does not apply.

2.4.2   The Streaming Store

Since the introduction of Exchange 2000, and for each service pack and intermediate release of Exchange, the JET database engine has been enhanced. With Exchange 2000 came the notion of two databases representing a messaging database (MDB): the *property store* and the *streaming store*. The property store is the traditional Exchange database (EDB) that we have known since the inception of Exchange. The streaming store (STM) is the database that contains content written through the ExIFS file system. The file system is consumed primarily by Internet clients (to be more precise, by the IIS virtual servers that implement Internet protocols, such as NNTP, HTTP, SMTP, IMAP, or POP).

The underlying structure of the STM database is a simple file with 4-KB database pages, allocated by chunks of 16 pages (up to 64 KB of contiguous information), for enabling a better page coalescing (i.e., gathering) than otherwise observed in the EDB database.

For each of the protocol virtual servers running as part of IIS, information is accessed by means of file handles referenced in the ExIFS namespace. File handles are, in fact, simply regular handles opened by the virtual server, just as it would be on any other file-oriented device, except that it points to the ExIFS and therefore can take advantage of streamed communication. This results in information being stored natively and yielding better performance because of the smaller overhead involved in information processing.

Now, you may ask, "OK, it streams to the streaming store, but what about transaction logging?" The answer is simple; every page written to the streaming store is also logged in the transaction log file. So after you have finished writing to the streaming store by means of the ExIFS, the information store process and the ESE database engine will *read* back the information from the streaming file to log the data that has just been written into its transaction log files. You may think that this operation is expensive, but remember that the NT I/O subsystem cache is used for these operations. Therefore, there is a pretty good chance, unless the data is really big and the server badly configured, that the file was cached in memory, in the file system cache, and that reading this information consists simply of some buffer transfer.

That has led some of my colleagues to observe that even though they were writing constantly to the streaming store, the actual data pattern on the volume hosting the STM database was made of 50 percent reads and 50 percent writes. Half of the writes consist of writing the data and the other half consist of reading the data back from the STM file to create the appropriate log records. Fortunately, many of these reads will directly hit the cache, and the actual overhead is in fact minimal.

2.4.3   Storage Groups

Clearly storage groups and the ability to use multiple databases within each storage group is a major scalability factor introduced with Exchange 2000 and further used with Exchange 2003.

Exchange 5.5 already had the ability to handle two databases from a single database engine—a private Information Store and a public Information Store. With Exchange 2000, this concept was extended to five databases. In addition, as many as four database engine instances can be loaded by the information store process. This results in the ability to have up to 20 databases being handled by a single Exchange server. Each database engine instance is viewed as a storage group and is loaded in the information store process space (in the user-mode virtual address space, to be more precise).

By default, when you install Microsoft Exchange, one storage group is created, with one database for mailbox information and one database for public folder information. It is called "First Storage Group," and you can rename it if you wish.

You may not intend to use public folders for sharing information, but Outlook (MAPI) clients will expect to find at least one public Information Store and a minimal set of system public folders used for hosting the global address list for offline mode, free/busy hours, or organizational forms.

It is an infrequent occurrence to remove this default public store, so at the end of the day you should really account for 19 private mailbox stores maximum on your first server or plan for a dedicated public folder server (see highlight in Figure 2.12). This is often seen in deployments where roles of servers are clearly separated, and it is generally considered a best practice.

Figure 2.12
A dedicated public folder server in a typical multiserver deployment of Exchange 2003

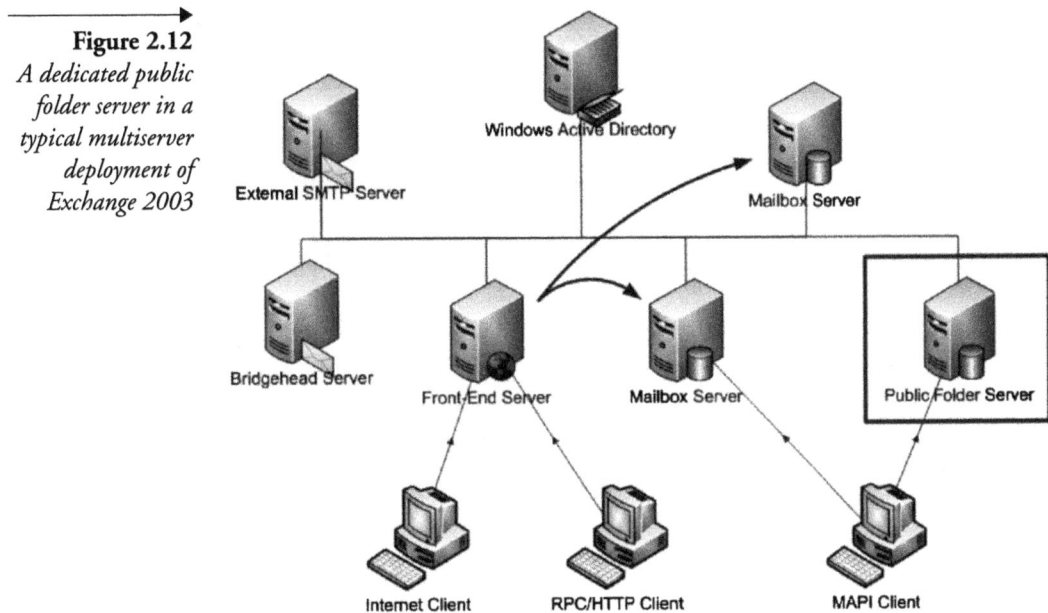

The advantage of a dedicated public folder server is that you can concentrate your efforts on designing servers that deal with a single workload: MAPI clients accessing their mailboxes or servers sharing information. The downside is that you tend to create contention spots. If you reduce the number of public folder servers, you increase the number of client connections made to that particular server. We cover this topic later when discussing the strategies for free/busy information dissemination in consolidated environments.

You can take advantage of multiple storage groups for two key reasons:

- Enabling a multistream backup environment (each stream backing up the databases of each storage group);
- Parallelizing the transaction logging of the database. This is relevant in an environment where the transaction logging speed can be lim-

Figure 2.13
*Parallelizing
transaction traffic
with many
database engines*

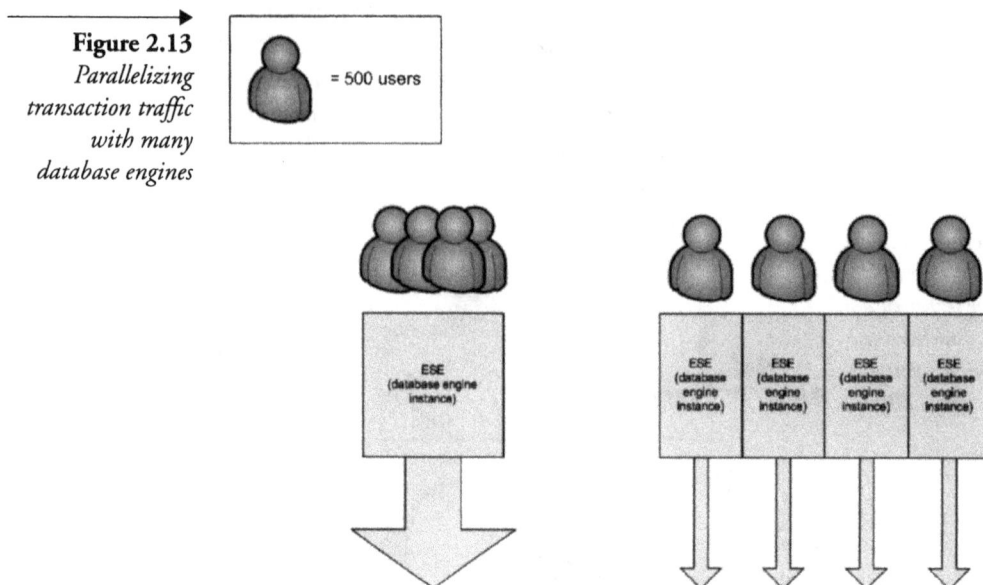

ited, such as in replicated storage networks that insert latency in write operations (Figure 2.13).

Adding storage groups grants you the ability to create more databases than the default five (or four plus a public folder database). You should take advantage of partitioning your overall Exchange store into smaller, more manageable databases. The optimal size of a database depends upon one major factor: the speed at which you can recover the database. Depending upon your backup infrastructure, the range of a "reasonable" database size can span from 20 GB (for when using legacy or entry-level backup solutions) to 400 GB and above (for when using instant recovery solutions).

In practice, I believe that 40 GB is a safe maximum size for a database. It allows for restore of a file in less than 1 hour when using fast backup devices and diminishes the downtime required in case you need to run the database maintenance tool (ESEUTIL, discussed later).

You may dynamically create additional storage groups without shutting down or restarting the store process. The same goes with databases. This of course is a great advantage for maintaining system availability and uptime; you may grow your server capacity for handling information without affecting the Exchange service from the viewpoint of users and peer servers.

Figure 2.14 gives an example of how to create a new storage group on an Exchange 2003 server. This is not something you would do on a day-to-day basis; creating storage groups has a certain impact on an Exchange server.

Figure 2.14
*Creating a new
storage group*

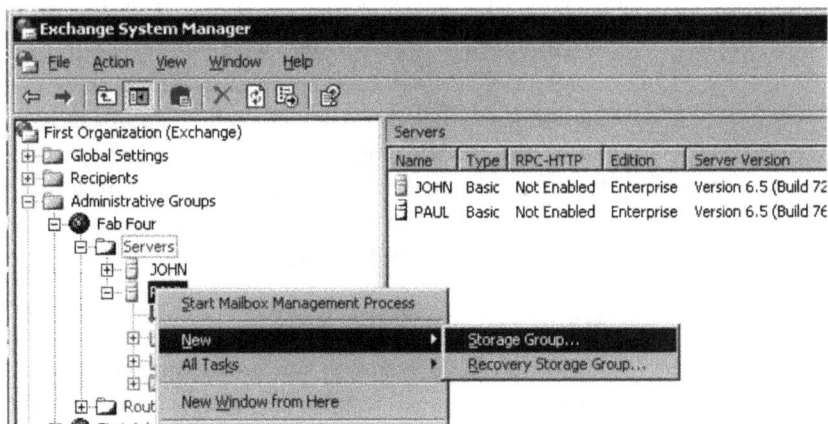

First, you have to carefully consider the storage resources that will be required for hosting the databases. Further, you must keep in mind that the information store process will need to load database instances into the process space. Exchange 2003, being a strict 32-bit application, has a finite amount of space allocated in its virtual address space that it can use for running its application code, depending upon the Windows boot mode:

- 2 GB by default;
- 3 GB if you boot Windows with the /3GB boot switch; this is typically recommended if you have strictly more than 1 GB of RAM on your server.

Even though there is currently a hard limit of 4 storage groups per server, Exchange 2000 was designed to handle up to 16 storage groups. Scalability tests during the beta period of the product led the product group to lower the number of storage groups from 15 to 4.

With Exchange 2003, SP1, and SP2, the recommendation for the deployment of storage groups versus databases changed due to the optimization that Microsoft realized in the handling of multiple database instances and virtual memory utilization inside the information store process.

First, you can create one instance of a special kind: the recovery storage group. There can only be one recovery storage group present per server, but that storage group can run in parallel to the four storage groups that can be created for hosting databases. Second, the overhead of creating a storage group has been almost eliminated with Exchange 2003 SP1. You can create as many storage groups as you wish (with a maximum of four per Exchange server) without impacting the virtual address space occupation of the information store. The downside of such an approach is the increased complexity of the configuration. With each storage group, you need to provide logical disk units for databases and transaction log files. You may decide to share disk units, but this is generally not recommended for data separation purposes and to avoid creating hotspots.

Storage Group Parameters

A storage group requires various parameters to operate. First, there is a unique set of transaction log files that is associated with each storage group. The transaction log files are a set of 5-MB files to which transactions written to any of the databases handled by the storage group are recorded. This means that transactions for different databases are *interleaved* in the current transaction log file. Once 5 MB of transactions have been written to the log file, the current file is renamed as a sequential-number file (known as a log generation), and a new file is created.

To avoid confusion, each storage group has a unique transaction log file prefix (by default E00, E01, and so on). You may change this prefix at the time you create the storage group, but once the storage group has been created, there is no way to change the prefix.

Figure 2.15 shows the Properties dialog box when you create a storage group.

When you click on Apply or OK, you should see the transaction log prefix assigned to this particular storage group, as shown in Figure 2.16.

The resulting transaction log file name is <prefix><generation number in hex> and the extension is LOG.

Figure 2.17 shows a series of transaction log files as you may observe in the transaction log area.

The E00.CHK file is the checkpoint file, which points to the last transaction committed to the database. The E00.LOG is the current transaction log file. Subsequent log files are *generations*, sequentially incremented, and expressed with a hexadecimal 5-digit number (e.g., E000301C.LOG). Note the 5-MB size. Any log file that is *not* 5 MB in size is corrupted, and your

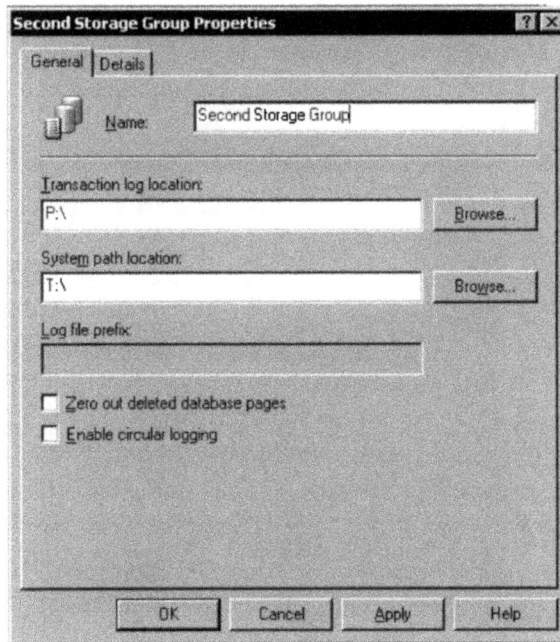

server is subject to data loss unless you can rapidly close your database and run an online backup of the database.

You should carefully plan on how many storage groups you create and where to place files, as this can have a serious impact on the performance and data availability of your Exchange 2003 server. Unlike Exchange 5.5, which was shipping with the Performance Optimizer that could make best guess on file placement, Exchange 2003 leaves it entirely to the administrator to configure the placement of database files. Indeed, you often had to revisit the Exchange 5.5 Performance Optimizer choices based on your storage infrastructure and because you had professional understanding of storage technology. But because that may not always be the case, proper planning and documentation for your Exchange 2003 server setup has to be done before you attempt deployments, with the goal that you will have fairly consistent platform sets to deal with; this will help in reducing your support costs. To assist with the planning and sizing (for performance, primarily) of

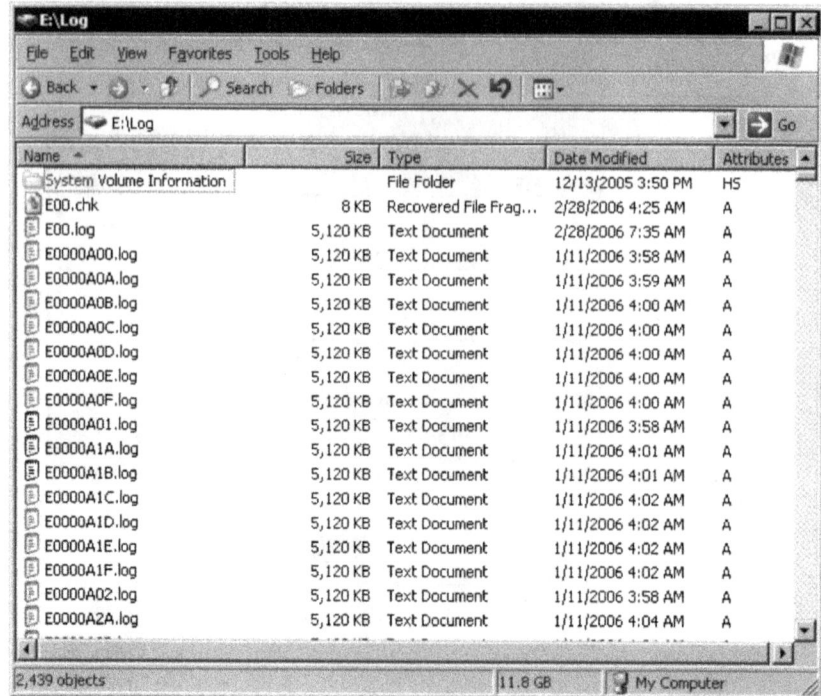

Name ▲	Size	Type	Date Modified	Attributes ▲
System Volume Information		File Folder	12/13/2005 3:50 PM	HS
E00.chk	8 KB	Recovered File Frag...	2/28/2006 4:25 AM	A
E00.log	5,120 KB	Text Document	2/28/2006 7:35 AM	A
E0000A00.log	5,120 KB	Text Document	1/11/2006 3:58 AM	A
E0000A0A.log	5,120 KB	Text Document	1/11/2006 3:59 AM	A
E0000A0B.log	5,120 KB	Text Document	1/11/2006 4:00 AM	A
E0000A0C.log	5,120 KB	Text Document	1/11/2006 4:00 AM	A
E0000A0D.log	5,120 KB	Text Document	1/11/2006 4:00 AM	A
E0000A0E.log	5,120 KB	Text Document	1/11/2006 4:00 AM	A
E0000A0F.log	5,120 KB	Text Document	1/11/2006 4:00 AM	A
E0000A01.log	5,120 KB	Text Document	1/11/2006 3:58 AM	A
E0000A1A.log	5,120 KB	Text Document	1/11/2006 4:01 AM	A
E0000A1B.log	5,120 KB	Text Document	1/11/2006 4:01 AM	A
E0000A1C.log	5,120 KB	Text Document	1/11/2006 4:02 AM	A
E0000A1D.log	5,120 KB	Text Document	1/11/2006 4:02 AM	A
E0000A1E.log	5,120 KB	Text Document	1/11/2006 4:02 AM	A
E0000A1F.log	5,120 KB	Text Document	1/11/2006 4:02 AM	A
E0000A02.log	5,120 KB	Text Document	1/11/2006 3:58 AM	A
E0000A2A.log	5,120 KB	Text Document	1/11/2006 4:04 AM	A

2,439 objects / 11.8 GB / My Computer

the logical units used by Exchange 2003 storage groups, Microsoft created the Jetstress tool, which we discuss in Chapter 6 of this book.

When you create a storage group, you have to complete a couple of text fields that make up the visible properties of the storage group, as shown in Figure 2.15. The most important field is the location of the transaction log. This area must point to a volume, and a folder in that volume will host the transaction log files for the storage group databases. From a purely performance perspective, you want a volume that provides fast, indeed very fast, write access performance (5-ms response time at most) and is extremely reliable.

Transaction Logging

While Exchange 2003 is designed not to lose any single piece of information, if you lose the transaction log volume, you run a big risk of losing information. I strongly recommend that you utilize RAID1 for protecting the volume and that you closely monitor events related to that particular volume.

The size of the volume does not matter much, except that if it fills up, the databases hosted by the storage group that puts its transaction log files on this volume will be taken offline. Again, no transaction will be lost, but service downtime will be recorded. In general, we consider that each user will generate between 0.3 to 1 transaction log file per 8-hour workday. This may vary from one environment to another, and it's a good idea to have an estimate of such a figure for future sizing and capacity planning purposes.

Generally speaking, it is not a good idea to have very large volumes for transaction logging or to let transaction logging accumulate. First, you need to remember that the transaction log files are suppressed when you run a full or incremental backup of *all* the Exchange databases for the storage group. If you accumulate transaction log files, it can be a sign of mail loop, mass mail attack, or (more frequently) failing backups. In such a situation, you must attempt to back up your databases as soon as you can to suppress the log files; do not attempt to remove them manually because in the event of a database failure, you would not be able to recover the most recently completed backup. Second, in the event of a transaction log playback, getting the database to a consistent state from the combination of a previous backup and the playback of the log files can take a significant amount of time. In fact, with recent backup and recovery tape technology, the transaction log playback can take much longer than the recovery from backup tape of the databases.

With Exchange 2003 SP2, the speed of transaction log playback was improved to near 3 seconds per log file. In practice, this can be as high as 1 minute, depending on the complexity of the transactions and the ability of the volume that hosts the databases to take changes rapidly.

The ability to run with a large backlog of transaction logs is a double-edged sword that needs to be carefully manipulated, somewhat like Luke Skywalker's light saber. It's good because in the event of a backup failure, you have some latitude to fix the problem rather than having an emergency; it's bad because if you have to play back thousands of log files, this may require significant downtime. How much is significant? Let's consider the following formula:

Recovery time = Restore time from tape + (n * 10 seconds)

where n is the number of log files required by the information store to bring the database to the most current state from the last backup. For 500 users, in a single work day, let's consider 500 transaction logs per day: that means 5,000 seconds, i.e., 1 hour and 23 minutes (and a few seconds), just for playing back the transaction log files.

The only way to decrease the number of intermediate log files that can be created between any two backups is to run full or incremental backups more frequently or spread users across more storage groups (adding a database in a storage group will not decrease the volume of transactions to process for a given database recovery).

For optimum performance, the recommendation with Exchange 5.5 and Exchange 2000 was to dedicate a single volume (disk unit) for each transaction log set. The rationale is to:

- Establish physical data separation between the database and the transaction log files, such that if you lose the database volume, you can recover the most recent state of the database with the previous backup.
- Prevent concurrent access to the disk, which would degrade performance and cause waiting time when transaction logging is occurring.

In reality, all that is required from the volume hosting the transaction is fast write access and a separate physical location from the databases. With the advent of virtualized storage technology, it is practically impossible to dedicate a pair of disk drives (mirrored for redundancy purposes) for the sole purpose of transaction logging, without wasting large quantities of disk space. With the smallest disk being of 72 GB, it is not reasonable to dedicate two of them for the capacity requirements of a single storage group that will unlikely exceed 10 GB to 15 GB.

I have seen recommendations such as 20 percent of the databases size. This is dead wrong, and I strongly suggest that you ignore such recommendations. The transaction log volume contains transactions to the database. If you have a 200-GB database, but no activity, your transaction log volume will not fill up. On the other hand, depending on policies in your organization, you may have several thousands of users hosted by one or more databases as part of the same storage group with tiny mailbox quotas (e.g., 5 MB, as an ISP would provide for POP3 mailbox access) but lots and lots of transactions.

In either of those two cases, which are real and occur more frequently than you might suppose, you can exceed the 20 percent ratio easily.

So, now you wonder whether the transaction log volume size should be based on the foregoing paragraph. From my own experience, I really believe that the sweet spot of volume configuration is a volume of 20 GB, implemented on RAID1 (mirroring) with underlying disks at spinning at 15 krpm.

You should avoid pointing your log files to a RAID5 volume that has too much of a write performance penalty for the transaction log write operations, unless you are confident in the write throughput of the volume.

Do not forget that transaction logging sits on the critical path of the completion of any transaction to any database in Exchange 2003. The faster you can write, the faster the server will process database changes.

In conclusion, there is nothing wrong with hosting more than one transaction log file set on a single volume, provided that this volume offers sufficiently small (<1 ms) response time for the write operations performed by the Exchange database engine(s). You should also ensure that there is minimal separation between the database and transaction log data areas. Choosing two volumes from separate physical disks in the same disk enclosure is optimal. The worst case is to choose different partitions from the same physical unit.

System Path

The system path location actually points to temporary areas utilized for recovery files. It is very often on the same path (volume and folder) as the database path, and I recommend that you keep it that way. Note the log file prefix. This field is grayed out, which basically means that you cannot choose it. In fact, Exchange 2003 will choose a log file prefix (E00, E01, and up) for this particular transaction log file set associated with the storage group, such that there is no possible confusion with the other transaction log files from other storage groups.

Zero Out Deleted Database Pages

The zero out deleted database pages option gives you the opportunity to zero deleted pages (as opposed to dereferencing them). This is quite helpful, but it can affect performance during backup operations (on a messaging server, a lot of information is simply deleted once viewed by the user) because the pages will actually be filled with zeroes at backup time, which is the one opportunity to traverse all the database pages without much disruption to the production environment. Use sparingly, and do measure the impact of such a change during performance testing or the initial deployment of your Exchange infrastructure. We have seen cases where the backup time was doubled because the disk units hosting the databases had to both read *and* write the pages, causing unnecessary workload at the storage array level. Performing a full backup right after turning on this option takes care of zeroing the deleted pages, and later on you only have the backup to deal with incremental deletions.

Circular Logging

Finally, you have the option of enabling circular logging. The idea behind circular logging is the same as that in Exchange 5.5, so it is not too surprising to see it up to Exchange 2003, because the database engine technology is virtually the same. Instead of creating transaction logs indefinitely (which will get purged only after a full or incremental backup), you can overwrite transaction log files as needed. This option is helpful in two situations:

- You don't really care about the database contents (could be an NNTP feed from the Internet).
- You need to initialize your databases to prepare a Loadsim simulation.

In a production environment, you would never use circular logging. Remember that if you lose the database drive, you can rely only on the database backup, and the intermediate transactions are considered lost. If you lose an intermediate log file, all subsequent transaction log files cannot be processed during a recovery. Loss of information in any modern computing infrastructure is quickly frowned on by upper management. You've been warned; now figure out what's best for your environment.

There is the special case where you wish to make a migration (e.g., "move mailbox" operation), which will generate a majority of write transactions and an unusually large traffic. In such a scenario, do not enable circular logging, but perform frequent (every hour or so, depending on how many mailboxes you move) backups using Windows' NTBACKUP or another backup tool. The objective is to prevent the accumulation of too many transaction log files such that a recovery would take hours or the transaction log volume would fill up. Using backup during a mail migration (normal or incremental) is the safest way to prevent generating too many logs. Often, this topic is overlooked because only the target database sizes are considered.

Databases

Once you have created a storage group on your Exchange, you are ready to create databases that will host your users' mailboxes or public folder trees (hierarchies), as shown in Figure 2.18.

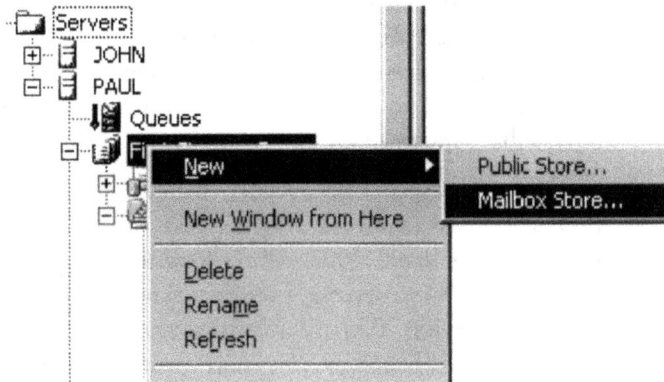

Figure 2.18
Creating a public or mailbox store

Creating a mailbox store will prompt you to fill in the properties for this particular database (see Figure 2.19).

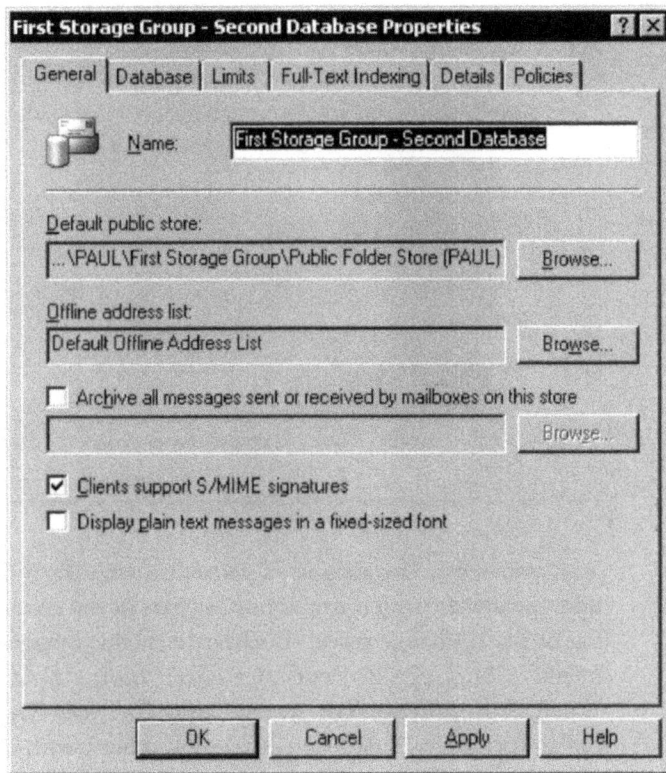

Figure 2.19
Database general properties

I will not go through each database properties page, yet the most important ones remain the actual database name and location. Bear in mind that the database should be placed on a volume that can sustain the workload for this particular database. For example, hosting many users (400 or more) out of a single database will demand enough disks (spindles) to accommodate the random and multithreaded nature of the I/O operations issued by the database engine.

One new aspect to consider with Exchange 2003 compared with Exchange 5.5 is the actual I/O size. Even though the database pages are 4 KB in size, Exchange 2003 will try to write contiguous pages together (this is known as I/O coalescing, such that there is a smaller number of larger I/Os to the device). This is a continuous improvement in each major or minor release of Exchange. The maximum I/O request size to the databases remains 64 KB for Exchange 2003 SP2. Figure 2.20 gives you an idea of the distribution of the I/O size to the databases of a production server. The majority of the events reported an I/O size slightly above 4000 bytes.

Figure 2.20
Repartition of I/O read size (octets per read on X axis) for a database disk

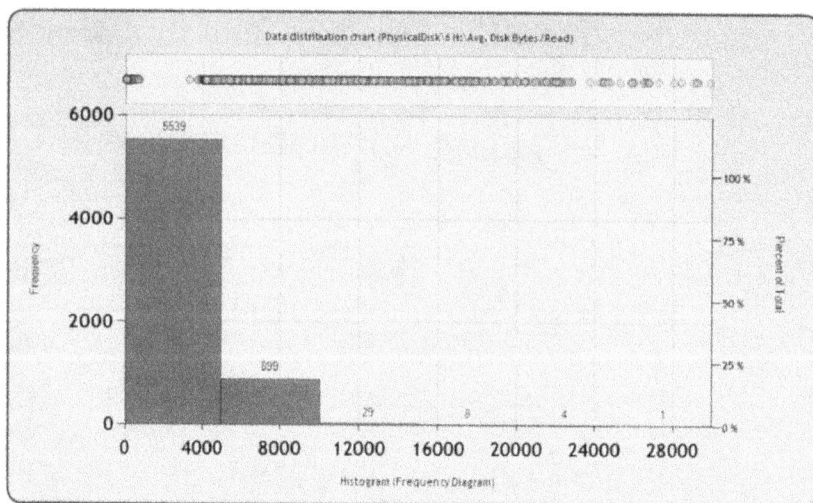

Databases can be assigned a particular time slot for online defragmentation operations, which run nightly as part of the system attendant's sanitizing of the Exchange server. Be aware that this operation can be quite I/O intensive, although it occurs at a lower priority by the information store. When sharing networked storage arrays between several servers in SAN, this low priority cannot be taken into account with other Exchange 2003 servers hosted in the same subsystem, and this can create degradation in the service level of the overall subsystem.

Deploying Storage Groups and Databases Tips

Since Exchange 2003 SP2, there is a clear advantage in deploying many storage groups first and adding databases in each of them. The advantages have been described earlier in this chapter, but in summary, we should remember that multiple storage groups enable us to have multiple transaction log streams. Because logging is a sequential process, you get more out of four parallel threads than one single.

The flip side of this is the necessity to plan for storage units for four storage groups instead of just one. With Windows Server 2003, do make use of mount points, such that you can deploy the volume that hosts the databases and the transaction log files of a given storage group in a coherent manner. Using mount points allows you to have the operating system and the applications access individual logical units by the means of a folder path, as opposed to a drive letter. They do not create any performance overhead; however, they create a parent-child dependency between the logical unit that is mapped to the drive letter and the logical unit that is mapped as a folder:

For example:

Storage Group Name	Transaction Log Files	System Files and Databases
First storage group	F:\Logs (mount point)	F:\ (root folder)
Second storage group	G:\Logs (mount point)	G:\ (root folder)
Third storage group	H:\Logs (mount point)	H:\ (root folder)
Fourth storage group	I:\Logs (mount point)	I:\ (root folder)

The use of volume mount points with Windows Server 2003 can be generalized now that they are supported in Microsoft Cluster (MSCS) environments. The only difficulty is that during monitoring with Perfmon, you might not be able to refer to a mount point by means of its path. Instead, you have to use the logical unit number (LUN). For certain environments that evolved, I have made a habit of using odd LUNs for logs and even LUNs for databases, in a sequenced way. Your habits may differ, especially in environments where you do not really control the allocation of storage logical units.

The most sensible approach we have seen and the one taken at HP for our Exchange 2003 server infrastructure was to always leave one database slot available per storage group and one storage group available per server.

This gives the ability to add databases without needing major changes (such as adding new volumes to host the transaction log files for a new storage group) and possibly to add a storage group when all the precedent storage groups have been maximized in terms of database handling.

Even though there are two files for each messaging database (MDB), you should not try to separate them; this was something envisaged in the earlier versions of Microsoft Exchange, when the STM database portion was introduced, but it does not bring any major advantage. Furthermore, and for simplifying the deployment, I typically recommend allocating, for each storage group, one LUN for the transaction log files and one LUN for ALL the databases of the storage group. Do *not* attempt to use many partitions per LUN because it can otherwise render more complex the online expansion of these volumes. Having a one-to-one mapping between LUN and partitions in Windows greatly simplifies the operation and troubleshooting of the Exchange server, especially if the storage components are managed by a dedicated team.

The first deployments of Exchange 2000 suggested separating the EDB and STM files, given that they have a slightly different access pattern, primarily because of their I/O size. However, in the long run, and because of the strong dependency between the two files (they always have to be at the same revision), it is unwise and overcomplicated to separate STM and EDB databases on an Exchange 2003 server.

In Summary

There is no single answer to the question of how you should create storage groups and databases in Exchange 2003. A lot will actually depend on your operating environment, your storage subsystem capabilities, and the level of capacity and performance required—both from a regular utilization of the Exchange 2003 server and from the backup—and, most important, on the restore capabilities that you wish to attain. I have seen designs that were entirely based on the restore speed for both the database itself and for the speed taken to bring the database to the most recent state by the means of transaction log playback.

As discussed before, the transaction log playback can take a large stake in the actual time required to bring a database back into an operational state, sometimes larger than restoring the database from tape (or disk) media.

2.5   Virtual Servers

The terminology did not do us great justice with the term *virtual server*, which is being used in many places with Microsoft Exchange and can correspond to many different things.

With Exchange 2003, you get to deal with three types of virtual servers:

1.   IIS virtual servers: They run the Internet protocols that Microsoft Exchange uses to communicate with the "outside"—peer servers via SMTP or clients via HTTP, POP, IMAP, and (again, but in a different way) SMTP.

2.   Exchange Virtual Server: You will find them only in clusters, and they represent the instance of a Microsoft Exchange server in a clustered environment.

3.   Windows Virtual Server: Really, this is about running the Windows operating system as a *guest* in a *host* environment that emulates the traditional server hardware. There are two major solutions on the market for virtual server/machine: VMware and Microsoft Virtual Server 2005.

In this section, we are going to discuss these virtual servers from the perspective of the scalability of Microsoft Exchange.

2.5.1   IIS Virtual Servers

Like other aspects of Exchange 2000, the ability to create multiple virtual servers aims at leveraging the abilities of IIS. Multiple virtual servers, even with the same protocol (for example, two IMAP servers), let a single server, perform the same function that would otherwise require multiple servers. This does not represent a scalability factor from a performance standpoint but more from a manageability aspect. Figure 2.21 shows how you can create an additional SMTP virtual server. Doing such will enable you to map different virtual servers to different network interfaces and create a different class of service, such as in a hosted environment. In such an environment, you have a single hardware and software environment that supports different Exchange environments, which although part of the same organization are logically separated by the means of access control.

Figure 2.21
*Creating an SMTP
virtual server*

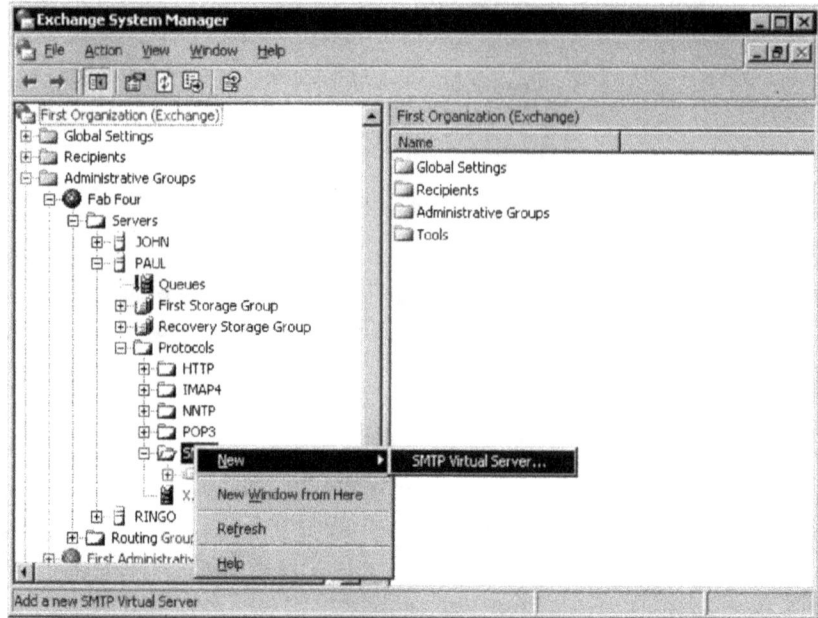

Although this is something that was found in service provider environment, this is seldom the case in corporate environments, where the default configuration of using a single virtual server is amply sufficient.

You may create multiple virtual servers that bind to different TCP/IP addresses, which, in turn, are bound to one or more network adapters. This is quite relevant if you decide that a single host will connect to multiple networks. You may, in that case, segregate traffic per network adapter by defining multiple virtual servers and possibly configure special filters for different SMTP virtual servers, as in Figure 2.22.

When Windows Server does not provide resource partitioning at the I/O subsystem level, features such as multiple virtual servers in IIS for Microsoft Exchange can contribute to create a somewhat static but effective partitioning that allows you to split traffic among controllers and possibly networks.

In ISP environments, or high-end SMTP-based message switching, this is definitely an appealing feature: an ISP may have different circuits connecting on the Internet, with different quality of service for different types of customers. Free accounts access the service by the means of the regular quality circuit, while paying accounts get to access the service by the means of high-quality (redundancy, high-bandwidth, low-latency) circuits.

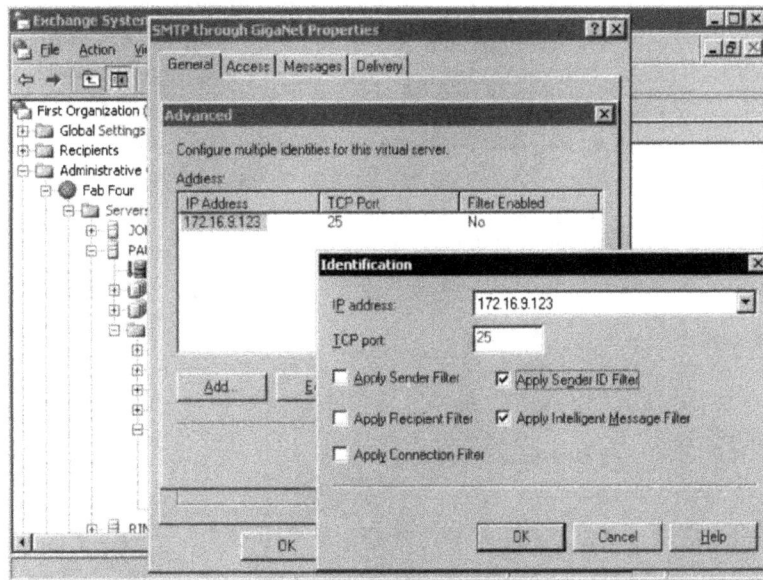

Figure 2.22
*Configuring
SMTP virtual
server*

Scalability and Multiple Virtual Servers

Multiple virtual servers are useful if you wish to scale your environment by using a reduced number of machines for a large number of different network connections. You can present a different identity on the network without necessarily adding different machines. This is one of the key principles of hosted Microsoft Exchange infrastructures (i.e., creating multiple "virtual organizations" on top of a shared infrastructure).

From a throughput viewpoint, we have always found that the default pair of network interface cards (NICs) could deal with the workload. Using a separate card becomes appropriate if you wish to use a particular NIC for a particular set of traffic, such as enabling TCP offload engine for high-performance SMTP traffic.

2.5.2 Exchange Virtual Servers

The Exchange Virtual Server can "move" (failover and failback) from one cluster node to another, along with the resources that it depends upon, such as the disks used for the databases and its network identity (name and IP address); there can be other resources that accompany an Exchange Virtual Server, such as advanced storage management resources that are essential when you deploy Microsoft Exchange in a geographically dispersed and replicated storage environment.

In Figure 2.23, we have a four-node cluster with NodeA, NodeB, NodeC, and NodeD. However, from a Microsoft Exchange viewpoint, these node names (server names to be more precise) will never appear in the Microsoft Exchange topology. Instead, the Exchange Virtual Server will appear, and here in our diagram, these are EVS1, EVS2, and EVS3. The Microsoft Exchange Virtual Servers do not bring any particular scalability feature. They do allow running an instance of a Microsoft Exchange server on one machine or another, as long as they are part of the same cluster.

Figure 2.23
EVS in a four-node cluster environment

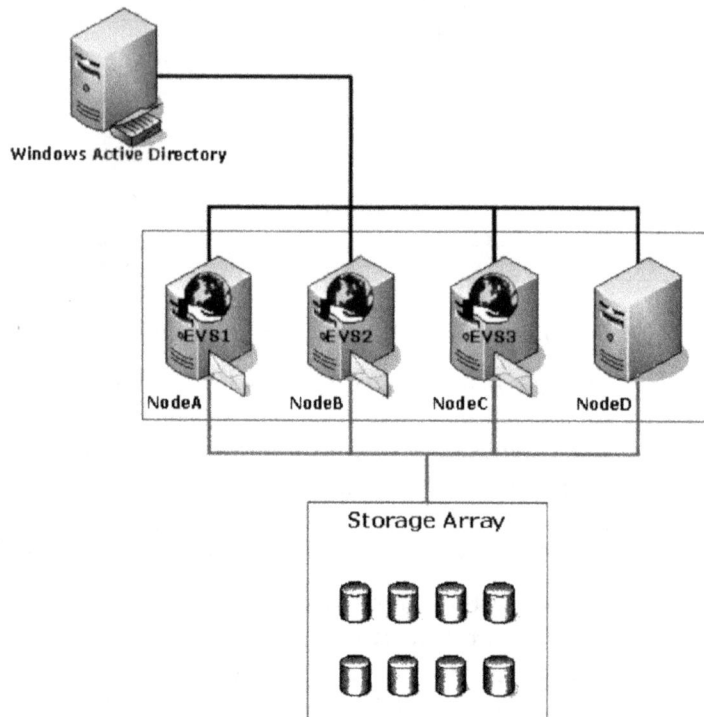

2.5.3 **Windows Virtual Servers**

So the idea of using virtual servers (virtual machines) in the Windows world is to have the ability to run several instances of Windows Server on a shared server hardware environment. With the increased performance from processor vendors such as Intel and AMD, the industry-standard server computing environment is now providing ample CPU capacity for running moderately loaded Microsoft Exchange server instances.

With Exchange 2003 SP2 and Microsoft Virtual Server 2005 R2, Microsoft supports running an instance of Microsoft Exchange in a virtualized environment. If you use another server virtualization technology (e.g., VMware's Workstation, ESX, or GSX server products), you might check with the OEM for support conditions. HP, for instance, supports the end customer in a VMware environment and then gets to work with Microsoft if a problem arises with Windows, Microsoft Exchange, or any other application running in the guest operating system based upon Windows Server.

Opportunities

In the case of a scaled-up environment, there is a great opportunity to consolidate several Microsoft Exchange infrastructures on a minimal set of hardware environment (as shown in Figure 2.24).

Figure 2.24
One physical machine for four different Microsoft Exchange Servers

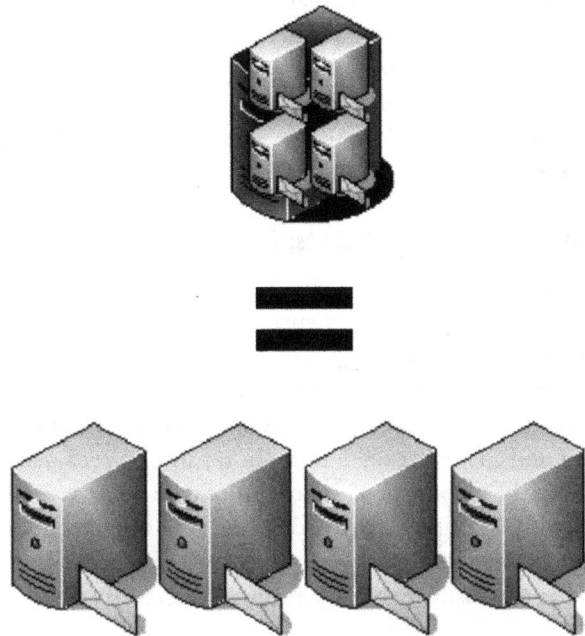

Of course, you are then in a situation where you need to *share* the hardware resources that support the virtualized server environment, and this means you have less CPU and less memory for each server, and you possibly share one component that typically is harder to scale: the I/O subsystem. This said, CPU and RAM can be relatively easily addressed with SMP and systems that are capable of embarking more than 4 GB of physical memory. On the system bus side, it's a different matter, and you may have to physically partition the machine to create some level of isolation in the usage of the I/O interfaces and buses. The problem with the latter approach is that it will add complexity to your environment, and that may become counter-productive. You would typically be interested in this approach in several environments:

- Offering fully separated and relatively small Microsoft Exchange infrastructures from a reduced server hardware environment.
- Testing and lab environments: The use of virtual machines enables you to build a realistic environment that can reproduce the conditions in which you will perform a migration or run a business application.

The challenge with virtual machines and Microsoft Exchange is that the I/O path is actually performed twice: once at the host operating system level and a second time at the guest operating system level. Until we get in a mode where the guest and the host operating system instances agree on how to perform I/O, it is unlikely that we will get the desired scalability for medium- to high-end environments.

One Last Important Consideration

Virtualized server environment are becoming more and more popular in lab, test, and QA environments because they allow you to reproduce a set of servers with minimal hardware resources. They are extremely convenient for hosting server instances that do not have a very high workload on the server environment. So there is a substantial saving in terms of hardware procurement and maintenance but *not* in terms of server management. If the goal of your IT department is to consolidate servers, understand the reasons behind it: using a virtualized server environment does not help to reduce the workload related to managing Windows or any business application such as Microsoft Exchange running atop of it.

2.5.4   In Summary

By means of database partitioning, front-end and back-end configuration, and multiple virtual server creation, Microsoft Exchange 2003 offers a greater level of flexibility compared with Exchange 5.5. Used appropriately, you can take advantage of this flexibility by accommodating scale-up and scale-out scenarios, and increase the ability to handle massive throughput and workloads with appropriate systems configurations. Clearly, the scale-up situation is being enhanced every month as OEMs release faster servers and more efficient storage infrastructures.

Your goal should not be to get the fastest and hottest machine available on the market, but to define and deploy a well-balanced messaging architecture based on Microsoft Exchange and Windows Server. Windows Server 2003 SP1 has significant enhancements related to Microsoft Exchange 2003 and its deployment. Nonetheless, the biggest (scale-up) scalability improvement will not occur until Microsoft Exchange can run native in 64-bit mode and take advantage of physical memory for caching larger quantities of its database in cache, therefore diminishing the frequency of relatively slow I/O access.

Finally, you should always keep in mind that the server and throughput capacity of your design depends largely on the data network. It's a given that nobody has enough bandwidth. Nevertheless, appropriate use of Exchange components and proper tuning of both Microsoft Exchange and Windows Server infrastructures can definitely help you get the most from your environment, not necessarily at the highest cost. As we discuss in Chapter 6, the performance factors in Exchange 2000 can be addressed in many ways, and not necessarily by throwing hardware at application-level problems to solve them. In fact, Microsoft has really improved and listened to the OEM and customer base to make Microsoft Exchange use the computing resources as efficiently as possible and help organizations to deploy high-speed and scalable infrastructures that can be relied on by the most mission-critical applications.

2.6   Components That Scale

In this section, we give further consideration to the scalability aspects of specific components and to the actual scalability limits of these components.

2.6.1   Concurrent Users

The ability to handle a large number of concurrent users is quite relevant in a number of scenarios. Beyond the actual capacity required to host the user information (mailbox storage, public folder space), it is important to determine whether a given server can handle the peak activity gracefully.

Microsoft's performance goal for Exchange 2000 was to be on par for MAPI connections and scale much higher than Exchange 5.5 for Internet Protocols connections (HTTP, POP, and IMAP). Given that machine specifications and processing capacity have significantly increased since 1999 and will continue to increase for who knows how long, it is very difficult to compare previous Exchange server architectures with their current one.

I much prefer to make an abstraction of the current environment and try to aim for the new levels of service that you wish to implement while you deploy Exchange 2003. Quite rightly, you and your management have the right to expect a significant added value in the deployment of Microsoft Exchange, and server/service consolidation can be one of them.

The actual number of concurrent users on a single Exchange 2003 server depends on storage capabilities, with a Windows Server architectural limit that tops at around 5,000 to 6,000 *active* MAPI users per server (four-way, 4 GB of RAM, many disks). The architectural limits were first found on the management of the user-mode virtual address space of the information store process. With the Exchange 2003 SP1 and SP2 releases, major improvements were made by Microsoft to prevent virtual address space fragmentation and waste. However, the other portion of the information store address space, the kernel space, typically 1 GB in size (this is defined by the boot parameters of Windows), is showing signs of weakness in environments where there are many connections made to a server (in excess of 20,000) or the use of large security tokens. The security tokens are used when validating the credentials of a particular network user when accessing a resource, such as another person's mailbox. If the user is part of many security groups, the security token is larger than usual. The problem is that tokens are stored in the kernel space of the information store process, the paged pool, and this is a finite and nontunable memory area. Running out of it has bad consequences, and the only way to deal with it is to reboot the server.

From a pure processing perspective, Exchange 2003 has been shown to scale well beyond four physical processors, but not beyond eight processors, primarily due to the SMP limitations. With the introduction of dual-core and quad-core processors, the SMP limitations (front-side bus saturation and memory access contention) are somewhat overcome.

You can regard the marketing benchmarks published on Microsoft's Exchange Web site (http://www.microsoft.com) as an indication of the system's capability to handle a given workload. How close to this workload is your user population is the key point and certainly the most difficult to address.

The real question is "Is it wise to gather 5,000 users on a single box?" If that server goes down, that means 5,000 users will not be able to use the messaging service. Does it matter to your environment? In an ISP environment, when you have to deal with hundreds of thousands of users, this is actually not a very big deal and you will expect to deal with much larger servers in terms on registered and concurrent users (125,000 or more), but with little storage capacity. In such an environment, the number of concurrent users and active users is actually quite small, in the range of 10 percent to 15 percent of registered users during the peak period (estimated to be between 6 PM and 9 PM).

In corporate (private enterprise) environments, where messaging and collaboration services offered by Exchange 2003 are considered mission critical, I believe that between 2,500 and 4,000 is the upper mark for handling concurrent users on a single server.

Now, concurrent users may not necessarily mean *active* users. A concurrent user is a connected user; an active user (as per Microsoft Exchange's performance counter) is a user that has issued an MAPI RPC request in the last 10 minutes. Most of the time, you can base your server-sizing calculation on the basis that 80 percent of the registered users are connected and 40 percent of those connected users are active users. I found this to be pretty much the case in most environments in which I collected performance information for capacity planning and performance analysis.

What will really guide the number of concurrent users per server lies very much in storage capacity and capabilities. Nowadays, 1 TB of storage can easily fit within a briefcase (in the first edition of this book, I was quoting 1 square meter; I suppose you realize that our briefcase is not 1 square meter in width…). So, in theory, it would be very easy to deploy 1 TB of data to host users' mailboxes. However, backing up—and, more important, restoring—1 TB of data within a reasonable amount of time (you need to define and negotiate this time with your business units and user communities) are not trivial tasks, and we see very often servers deployed with no more than 200 to 400 GB of storage.

Now, how many users can I host on a 200-GB storage space? It depends largely on two factors: the deleted item retention period and the mailbox quota given to your users. Deleted item retention is a hidden cost that can backfire very easily. I estimate that a 7-day retention period requires an additional 20 percent of the estimated storage space (mailbox quota multiplied by the number of users). Fourteen days require 30 percent, and 30 days require 100 percent additional space. Of course, depending on your users' activity, these figures may change. Do observe the deleted item space on your server (performance counter), and watch it vary as you change the time period.

Besides, as discussed before, the users will apply a certain pressure beyond capacity to the storage subsystem in terms of I/O per second. There are variations in how many I/O per second you need to provide per connected user, depending on the user profile, as shown in the following table.

User Profile	I/O per Second per User (Sustained)
Light	0.2
Medium	0.5
Heavy	0.8
Very heavy	1.0–1.2

These figures are pulled from experience in monitoring and analyzing storage performance in production Exchange 2003 SP2 environments. However, they may vary in your environment, in a few aspects:

- The count of items in the critical folders' influence on the I/O per second per user (sometimes, by a factor of 2).

- The I/O per second required is generally expressed in peak and sustained periods: peak I/O per second means that at some point, the request rate to the disks went very high, but for a short period of time. High peaks for short duration is OK because they tend to be worn out by the effect of cache mode in Outlook, for instance. It is advisable to focus on the sustained I/O per second per user and possibly decide how many of those peaks you wish to "satisfy" with a correct response time. In Chapter 6, we explain how to measure both.

- The use of multiple clients (e.g., Outlook and a mobile device) can seriously affect the I/O per second per user requirement, sometimes by a factor of 5 to 10, depending upon the mobility solution, how often it polls the server for new items to synch with the mobile device, and so forth.

At this point, it should be clear to you that there is not a single answer to the right number of users per server. Architectural limits, such as system memory pool exhaustion, currently place the high number of active users to approximately 5,000, but beyond this simple-to-follow guideline, there is a whole spectrum of options that may very well dictate to not exceed more than half of the maximum (2,500) number of users we typically advise for Exchange 2003 SP2 deployments.

2.6.2 Front-End Servers

Front-end servers are interesting components to tune, and they tend to scale quite differently depending on the type of protocol that they proxy. Unlike Microsoft commercial Internet services and other products on the market, adding more front-end servers will not increase your ability to handle the workload. The back-end servers are critical to the actual workload handling.

Microsoft has said that one front-end server could and should be deployed for every four back-end servers. In fact, in view of the deployments we have worked on, this rule applies particularly well.

In very high-end scenarios, you will certainly want to segregate and size your front-end servers by the type of protocol that they proxy. It is very common to isolate one or two servers for handling the SMTP traffic, one or two servers for the HTTP-DAV (or, WebDAV) traffic (which can be generated by a native or customized Outlook Web access application), and one or two servers for POP and IMAP, if they are implemented in your scenario.

HTTP front-end servers tend to scale up pretty high, given the work that they have to perform. Beyond the initial session authentication step, HTTP front-end servers in Exchange also have to deal with the information rendering (transforming the XML data from the back-end servers into HTML commands that can be interpreted by the user's navigator) and implementation of features such as spell checking. They are good candidates for multiprocessing machines and can scale up to four physical processors very easily. The demand on memory, however, is rather small, as is the demand for local storage. Examples of server configurations are given in Chapter 7.

POP and IMAP servers tend to deal with a much more simplified protocol than MAPI or HTTP-DAV servers and are quite predictable. I have observed that POP and IMAP front-end servers would not scale beyond two processors and would not take advantage of more than 1 GB of RAM.

Table 2.1 gives rough guidelines for sizing front-end servers, depending upon the protocols used, and the optional use of SSL (for any of HTTP, IMAP, or POP) and GZIP compression (for HTTP), on Windows Server 2003 with medium user profile (20 mails sent per day, 60 received).

Your mileage may vary depending on the actual user workload, which, while being quite predictable for POP and IMAP users, can be rather different from one scenario to another for HTTP-DAV clients, such as OWA or ActiveSync (which was introduced with Exchange 2003).

Table 2.1 *Front-End Server Sizing Summary*

Protocol	Max Number of CPU	Memory	Ratio to Back End
HTTP (OWA)	2 × physical	2 GB (30 KB per user)	1:4
HTTPS (OWA, SSL)	4 × physical	2 GB (50 KB per user)	1:4
HTTP (ActiveSync)	4 × physical	2 GB	1:4
HTTP (RPC/HTTP)	2 × physical	2 GB	1:4
POP	2 × physical	512 MB	1:5
POPS (SSL)	4 × physical	512 MB	1:5
IMAP	2 × physical	512 MB	1:8
IMAPS (SSL)	4 × physical	1 GB	1:8

Although the data in Table 2.1 is drawn from testing on actual server configurations and scalability information from Microsoft's scalability web site, the evolving technology and the rather static and synthetic nature of the workload may actually differ from the actual workload. The challenge will be for you to properly monitor and size front-end and back-end servers as the activity ramps up, making appropriate adjustments. I know this is not a satisfactory answer, but if it were different, you wouldn't have to perform any kind of tuning and could just acquire specialized configurations drawn from workload input.

Just as we used to do with Exchange 5.5, if you are not too sure of the actual impact that can be brought on your front-end servers and if you really plan to deploy front-end servers that address the three major Internet protocols used by clients along with the additional and inevitable SMTP traffic, you can opt for a specialization of your front-end servers as suggested in Figure 2.25 that will help you to monitor your workload and possibly to adjust machines (adding more resources or simply adding more machines) without affecting the overall architecture. This approach is particularly indicated if you attempt to start enabling a protocol for a preproduction pilot. The dedicated server does not have to be physical; it can be a virtual machine that is then migrated to a physical server when the service is rolled into production.

What the diagram in Figure 2.25 suggests is that if your users' traffic is shifting from POP/IMAP access to HTTP access for OWA, you have the ability to clearly identify this change in workload (by monitoring the num-

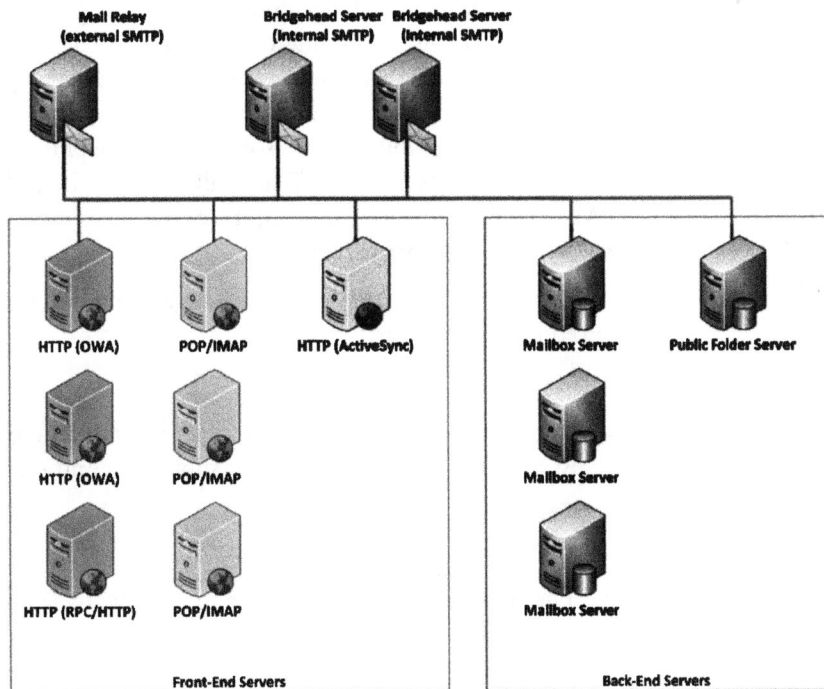

Figure 2.25
Specializing front-end servers

ber of active connections handled by IIS, for example) and to scale out your model by adding more machines. Alternatively, you can scale up your model by bumping the system resources provided by the front-end servers without touching either your back-end infrastructure or your overall system configuration. Eventually, if you get under a certain workload utilization (for example, less than 200 concurrent IMAP connections at any point in time during a working day), you may decide to migrate the IMAP front-end server from a physical to a virtual machine and claim "back" the physical server. This flexibility, mostly available for front-end servers (they can move relatively easily and have light storage requirements), can be automated more or less easily, depending upon the server virtualization software that you utilize.

2.6.3 Message Throughput

Message throughput in Exchange 2003 is optimized for the SMTP traffic. I know that many customers decided to deploy the X.400-based Exchange 5.5 infrastructure because of the reliability of the X.400 protocol and because of the relatively small overhead incurred.

The fact is that Exchange 2003 has been designed to operate at best with Internet protocols, and while this is valid for client connections, it is also valid for back-end communication between peer servers. SMTP is a protocol that has significantly matured during the past three years in terms of performance, reliability, and security. The deployments done since the introduction of Exchange 4.0 have all been revisited to embrace and adopt SMTP as the native transport protocol to switch messages around and outside an Exchange organization.

I have found that the SMTP message throughput was very much influenced by three factors:

- The ability of the volume hosting the transient messages (\MAIL-ROOT) to process I/O quickly (submillisecond response time);
- The ability of the Active Directory to quickly resolve address lookup requests from the SMTP service;
- The ability of the SMTP service to open many simultaneous connections to a remote host.

In fact, this last point does outscore X.400 to a very large extent; you can easily switch more than 120 messages per second (10-KB messages, no network limitations) between several Exchange 2003 servers using the SMTP transport and an adequately configured disk subsystem for the intermediate storage used by the SMTP service.

With the foregoing figures, you must realize that there are many additional factors that can influence the actual switching capacity of a bridgehead server or the capacity of a back-end server to expedite outbound messages to outer parts of the Exchange organization. Network capacity is the first one that comes to mind when you consider the outside environment.

Peer server capacity is also an important point and can actually endanger your messaging infrastructure. The final aspect is proper sizing of the Windows Active Directory service. To come up with the largest traffic and mail categorization operations, investigate the option to deploy Windows Active Directory on Windows Server 2003 x64, which run on a 64-bit environment, can take advantage of caching large portions of the directory information tree (DIT) in their RAM, and provide the throughput of 10 to 15 32-bit equivalent GC servers.

2.6.4 **Backup and Restore**

Scalability in backup and restore technologies depends very much on the technique utilized to back up (i.e., backing up as in duplicating the information) and restore the information back to a state known to be good.

Most of the time, I believe that you should utilize online backup on Exchange 2003. This involves using backup agents that implement the backup API from Exchange and can perform hot backups such that access to the databases by users and connectors or other components is still possible when the backup is in progress.

There are several basic types of backup that can be performed on an Exchange 2003 SP2 server, which are summarized in Table 2.2.

Table 2.2 *Backup Modes*

Backup Type	Resulting Action
Incremental	Copies the transaction log files and *truncates* the log files (deletes them)
Normal	Copies the current database, a small set of current transaction log files, and additional information created while the backup was in progress and truncates the log files
Differential	Copies the transaction log files but does not delete them
Copy	Same as normal, except that the transaction log files are not truncated

The data duplication operation (copy) depends on the mechanism used for the online backup. Since Exchange 2003 on Windows Server 2003, the online backup can either be streamed, as we've known it since day one, or completed through the use of the VSS framework that came with Windows Server 2003.

Depending on the actual volume of information, the strategy for running either differential backups or incremental or full backups can vary. In 90 percent of the cases, I recommend daily full backups. It does mean that you must have sufficient tape storage for storing several hundred gigabytes of information every day. Incremental backups are seldom implemented and typically apply to small environments. The problem with incremental backups is that you have to restore your database to restore the last Normal backup, along with all the intermediate incremental backups. Most advanced backup software will perform these operations automatically if your backup solution knows how to use a large enough tape library (10 slots or more). The real problem, however, is that if there is an intermediate incremental backup that is invalid, you have simply lost information up to the point of the last good incremental backup—not a good situation.

To decrease tape manipulation and simplify the restore process, you could use differential backups in combination with normal backups. If a database restore is required, all you need to restore is the last normal backup and the last differential backup. The problem with this approach is that differential backups do not truncate the log files; therefore, after three or four days of activity, you have to back up three or four days of transaction log files. Worst of all, during a restore operation, you have to wait for the playback of three or four days of transaction log files—an operation that alone can sometimes take more time than any of the actual tape restore operations.

Copy backups are seldom implemented and are good only if you wish to save the current environment without truncating the log files.

Streaming Mode vs. Volume ShadowCopy Services

In general, my recommendations depend on the volume of data, the type of backup device used (tape drives, disk farms, or VSS copy), and the mean time to repair (MTTR) imposed by the service level agreements. The most efficient, simplest, and least error-prone approach is still to perform online normal daily backups to tape drives or disk farms, in streaming mode (Figure 2.26).

Figure 2.26
Backup to tape

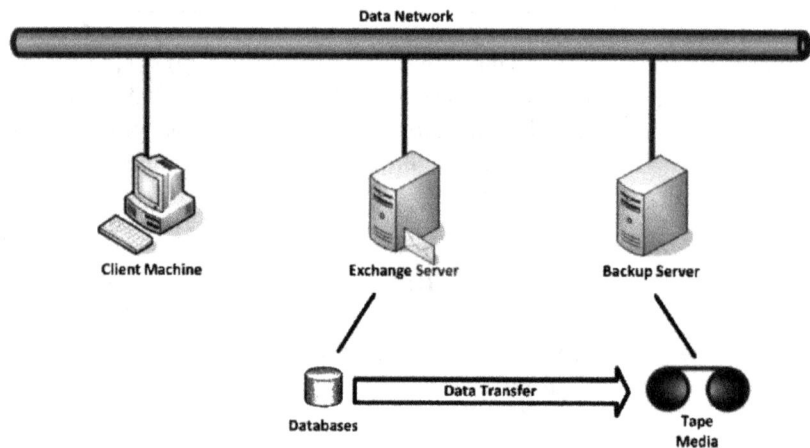

For that particular mode, the target device will definitely matter in terms of speed of execution, for either the backup operation itself or the restore operation. I have seen rates of up to 200 GB per hour when backing up to disk farms; specialized virtual tape libraries, which are no more than a dedicated server connected with many links to a SAN infrastructure, can exceed 600 GB per hour.

Similar or higher rates can be observed when backing up to fast tape drives such as LTO-3. Even if you opt for a backup to a disk farm, which would presumably speed up the restore time, you will still need to archive the disk-based backups to tape media for archiving purposes. So backup to disk can be good, but it is not a complete solution in itself, unless you use a more complete solution such as a virtual library system.

Figure 2.27 describes the simple process of backing up to a disk farm. In a first step, you back up to a simple volume "seen" by the backup agent or backup software (which could be as simple at NTBACKUP), then, in a second step, you "migrate" this backup save-set to the tape library.

Figure 2.27
Backup to disk then to tape

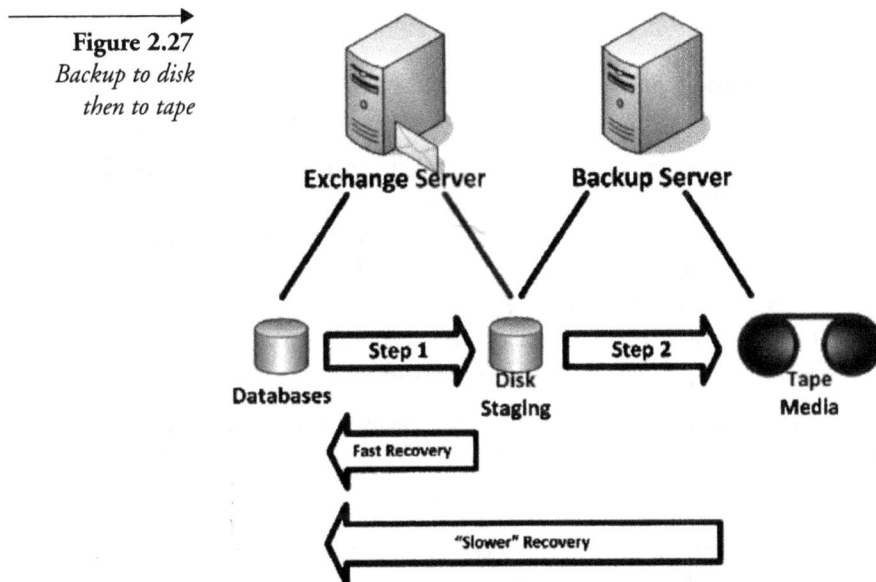

The best tactic to adopt here is to benefit from the actual disk farm by leaving behind one or two backup cycles on disk, even though they are migrated to a tape media. That way, you can restore from disk, even though you have managed to archive your data on somewhat cheaper storage media such as tapes.

Functionally speaking, the VSS backup mode is much better because it enables rapid recovery of the disk units that have been cloned or for which a

Figure 2.28
*Copying the
content of a
shadowcopy*

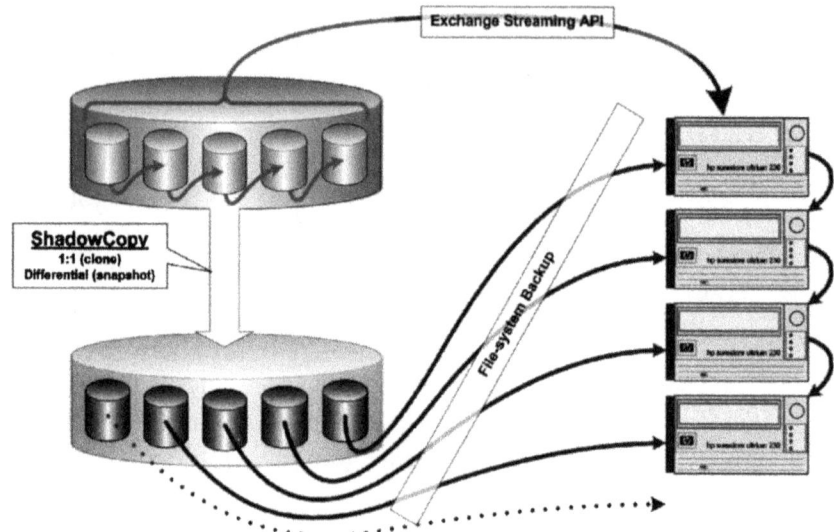

snapshot was taken at some point. It does not suppress the need to copy the data away to tape or other media for archiving purposes (see Figure 2.28).

In terms of pure scalability, what we have observed is that the online backup API from Exchange is a potential bottleneck in terms of data rate (gigabytes per hour). It is quite normal, since part of the backup job in the API is to perform page-level checksum verification (i.e., verify that the page contents are actually what they are supposed to be). It is during this operation that you may discover corrupted databases that contain invalid page checksums, which will force you to return to a previous backup.

If you wish to qualify a particular backup scenario in terms of data rate, I highly recommend you to proceed with the following steps:

1.   Perform a normal file-level backup: dismount a database of a sufficient size (20–30 GB) and proceed to back up this database as if it were a regular file.

2.   Mount the database and perform an online backup of this database.

3.   Compare the data rates obtained; if they are similar, it means that everything is fine and that the Exchange backup API is not getting in the way of the obtained data rate. If the online backup data rate is significantly smaller, that indicates that the Exchange backup API does have an impact on the data rate. You should

examine which system resources (CPU, RAM, others) are being stressed during the online backup process, and you may have the opportunity to correct the problem.

4. Compare the backup rates using various types (RAID0+1, RAID0, and RAID5) of target volumes for your disk farm.

Although losing a disk occurs quite seldom these days, it is always recommended to utilize a minimum of redundancy, the cheapest (from a capacity perspective) being RAID5. As you will discover later in this book, RAID5 imposes a certain penalty on write operations, and unless the controller is particularly smart in dealing with sequential streams of data to RAID5 volumes, you may be forced to back off using RAID0+1, which is obviously more expensive in terms of dollars per gigabyte and may defeat the purpose of backing up to disks.

The foregoing list focuses really on the backup speed: but is it what really matters the most? The simple answer is *no*. Backup time windows are important and must be maintained as the volume of data increases. This is where the rapid recovery capabilities of a VSS backup takes its importance, given the need for a fairly advanced storage subsystem.

In designing performance testing, you should always include a performance test that aims at determining the impact of running an online backup and restore while there is user activity. While this depends a lot on the storage subsystem's capabilities, it is possible to configure an environment such that the user response time and the server throughput and workload capacity handling are not negatively affected by online backups running. This enables you to ease your backup window and feel comfortable in running online backups at any time during the day or the week. This tranquility has a cost (the cost of a high-performance storage subsystem), but has its advantages.

In fact, if the backup speed does not matter most, the real thing that is important is the restore speed. The ability to quickly get back in an operational state for part or all of an Exchange 2003 server is what really matters in backup and restore operations.

The good thing about Exchange 2003 is that although the backup API can represent a bottleneck in extreme environments (>120 GB per hour), the restore process itself is relatively simple, since it primarily consists of restoring the database to its original location just as with any other file, mounting the database in a shadow ESE instance, and playing back the transaction logs. This job is particularly easy with the introduction of the recovery storage group in Exchange 2003.

That in itself represents an interesting challenge when configuring your storage subsystems for the Exchange 2003 server. You may be tempted to provide capacity for the users' mailboxes, and you may be tempted to provide enough spindles/disks to handle the random requests from the database engine, but, unfortunately, the ability to quickly play back the transaction log and to quickly restore a database is often overlooked.

If you take this restore point into account, the database volume characteristics can vary largely and can require the deployment of many more spindles than originally anticipated to sustain the transaction log playback operations. This is why I used to recommend the use of 18.2-GB disk drives for Exchange 2000 deployments, rather than 36-GB or even 72-GB drives, at the expense, granted, of the footprint of the solution and maybe the cost. The funny thing is that these drives are not available anymore, and we are stuck with 72-GB (at minimum), 142-GB (most common), or higher capacity drives, which helps addressing the capacity requirements but not the performance ones. Forward looking, the introduction of small form factor (SFF) serial-attached SCSI (SAS) drives is to be monitored: by providing small disks in volume and capacity, we are now into a mode where putting many spindles at a cost similar to using fewer larger drives is plausible. Besides, SFF SAS drives tend to consume less power and dissipate less heat than their big brothers. A great opportunity for consolidated environments!

2.6.5   Database Maintenance

Exchange 2003 runs a database maintenance operation scheduled by default to occur every night at 4 AM, as shown in Figure 2.29.

The initial screen sets the frequency of the maintenance window. By selecting "customize," you can actually set the duration (the default of two hours is shown in Figure 2.29.

The main goal is to perform online defragmentation of the Exchange 2003 database. Appearing in Exchange 5.5, the online defragmentation is a necessary step that aims at reclaiming empty space in the database and optimizing the contents of the database pages so that further search and allocation of free pages can be done more efficiently.

Not often considered in large environments, this particular operation can take a significant amount of time. A single night (or what you could consider an off-peak period) may not be enough to complete an entire

Figure 2.29
*Schedule for the
maintenance
interval*

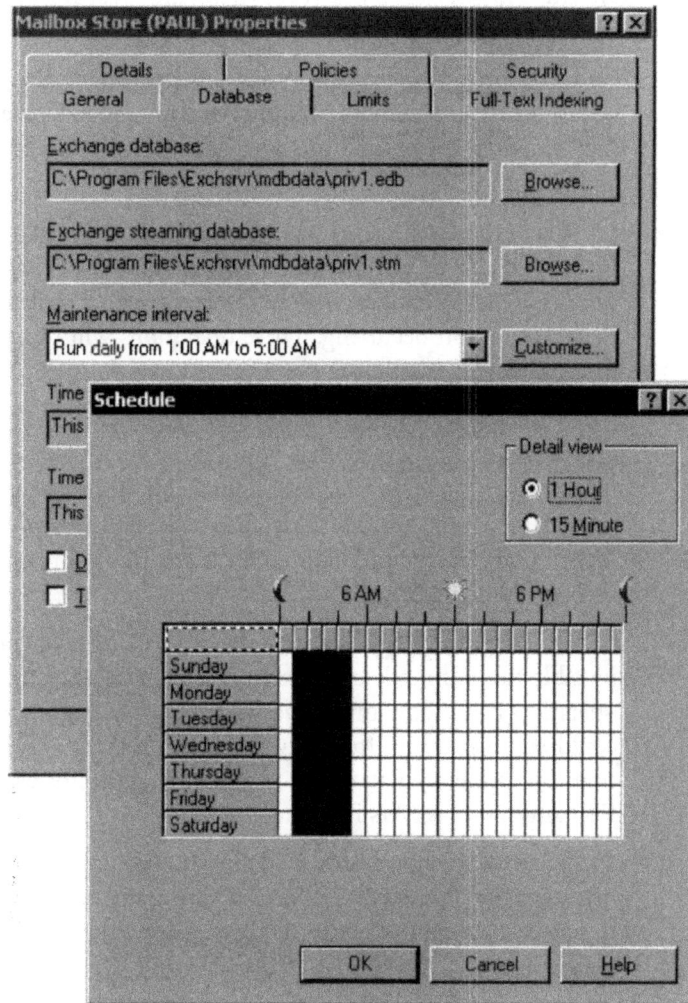

defragmentation on the entire set of databases that an Exchange 2003 server can hold. In such case, the defragmentation will be interrupted and it will resume during the next maintenance interval.

The defragmentation is primarily an I/O-bound operation that aims at going through the binary tree that makes up each Exchange database and rearranging those pages. There is in fact very little CPU processing allocated, and the memory utilization remains within the boundaries of the normal Exchange 2003 information store process. However, fetching each page and rewriting most of them puts a major load on the storage subsystem. This is where you will benefit the most from using multiple spindles and fast RAID arrays for your Exchange 2003 databases.

Nevertheless, do consider that this operation, although necessary, can occur during user activity. If it does, it happens at a lower priority than normal transactions issued from user activity, whether MAPI-based or using another protocol.

Where the clash can come in is if during that off-peak period, you also have the desire to run online backup operations. Things are well designed, however, in Exchange, and an online backup will suspend any online defragmentation occurring. These operations will resume once the backup has completed.

In lab environments, on live data generated out of Microsoft Loadsim activity, I have observed that approximately 30 GB of database could be defragmented in an hour. This is quite a lot, but for servers designed to host up to 300 GB or 400 GB of database, that can span well beyond the entire night or off-peak period and not leave any room for background operations such as online backup.

The proper strategy in such a situation consists of expanding as much as possible the online database maintenance window and letting the backup operation come and interleave with the defragmentation. Note that you could set this setting for every database on every server of your organization, but remember that one of the key scalability elements of managing Exchange 2003 servers is setting policies.

Figure 2.30 shows how to define the policy for the scheduling of the maintenance of a database. After defining the policy, all you need to do is to apply it to one or more databases in your organization, as shown in Figure 2.31.

Applying the policy consists only of setting the configuration attribute in the predetermined Exchange 2003 containers in the Active Directory configuration container. Before your servers will actually pick up the change, you will need to wait for the replication to occur between the domain controllers used by the Exchange 2003 servers for pulling their configuration.

Of course, you may set individual settings on each database, depending on its size, its backup policy, and the type of storage utilized to host the database. When you select the policy item in ESM, you can view which databases are controlled by this policy (Figure 2.32).

Figure 2.30
*Setting the
maintenance
interval in a policy*

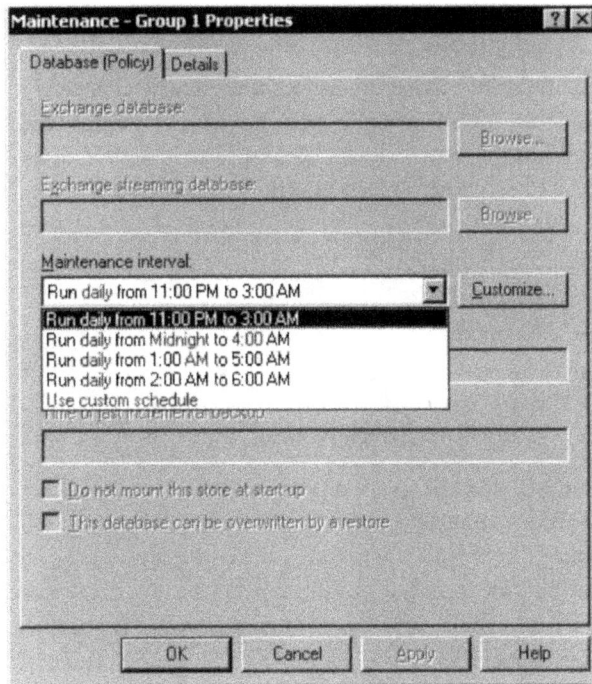

Figure 2.31
*Choosing a
database to put
under the policy*

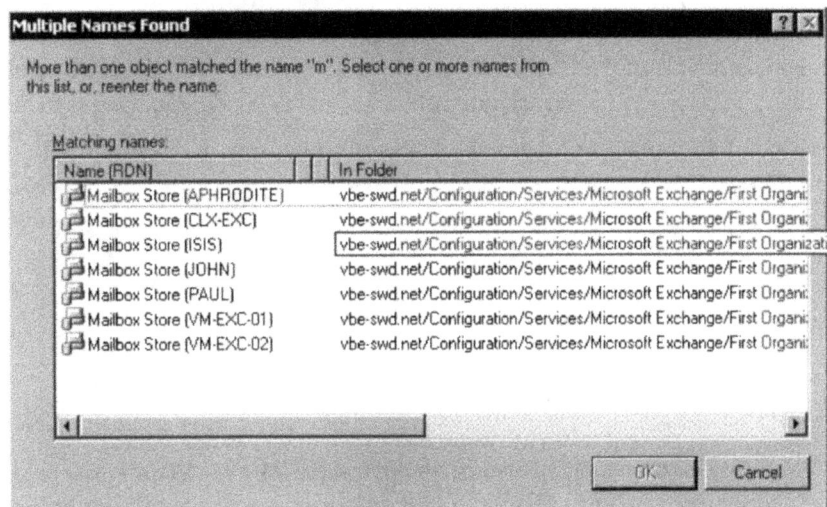

For information that is largely used in read-only mode, defragmentation isn't a very important operation. However, for mailbox stores that receive a lot of traffic during the day, you wouldn't want to skip this operation; oth-

I personally believe that although this operation was useful with Exchange 5.0 and previous releases, the online defragmentation introduced with Exchange 5.5 and carried over with Exchange 2003 does not require any kind of offline defragmentation, with the exception of reclaiming storage space after a mass mailbox migration.

Another reason to use ESEUTIL is to perform a database repair. If for some reason your database became corrupted and was flagged corrupted by Exchange 2003, you can attempt to repair the database using ESEUTIL.

Unfortunately, the repairing process is fairly blunt and consists of throwing away pages that don't verify the checksum and/or that are considered invalid. The result is that you may have a database that is repaired and consistent, but you may also have lost valuable information. For this reason, I never recommend that my customers run ESEUTIL to repair databases unless the restore operation from a previous backup fails for some reason (e.g., bad tapes, missing tapes) and unless the customer is ready to accept data loss.

This maintenance tool should be invoked only under the command and supervision of Microsoft support services to prevent any fatal damage to the database that could cause the loss of part or all of the information contained therein.

ESEFILE is a tool that can be used to perform page-level checksum verification in a database. ESEFILE should be run on any database backed up in offline mode. It is mandatory for VSS backup solutions to ensure that the backup has actually been successful. This is done by dismounting the database, copying it to another volume (or creating a duplicate copy by splitting a clone from the hosting volume), and running the tool against it. This operation is required because the page checksum verification is done only during online backup operations by the online backup API of Exchange 2003. Failing to verify the page checksum may hide database corruption errors, which can range from lost messages or attachments to the loss of a complete mailbox or folders within that mailbox. You may perform a very safe backup, but if that backup saves a corrupted database, it has very little purpose.

Throttling ESEUTIL

The challenge in VSS or offline backups comes from the fact that the clone or snapshot copy of the database is still hosted in the storage array that runs the production database. In such cases, running ESEUTIL for the purpose of verifying the contents of the database requires I/O resources that are drawn from the same storage subsystem as the production databases, resulting in an impact to the performance of the production database.

ESEUTIL is fairly blunt: it will read one page at a time and proceed to verify the checksum. If your system is able to deliver 3,200 read I/O per second, it will consume them, and in the meanwhile it may reach bottlenecks in your infrastructure, such as storage network or controller port bandwidth.

To diminish side effects of ESEUTIL page-level checksum verification, Microsoft introduced in Exchange 2003 SP2 the notion of throttling of ESEUTIL. You have the option to insert a 1-second pause every *n* operation, with *n* being configurable as a switch to the command. The result is that the operation of checking the database may take longer, but the production database performance is not impacted too badly. (Figure 2.33 shows the /p<x> option.)

Figure 2.33 *ESEUTIL checksum option*

```
CHECKSUM:
    DESCRIPTION:  Verifies the checksums of a database, streaming file,
                  checkpoint file, or log file (or set of log files).
         SYNTAX:  ESEUTIL /k <file name> [options]
     PARAMETERS:  <file name> - file name to verify
        OPTIONS:  zero or more of the following switches, separated by a space:
                  /s<file> - set streaming file name (default: NONE)
                  /t<db>   - set temp. database name (default: TEMPCHKSUM*.EDB)
                  /p<x>    - add artificial 1 second pause once every x I/O's
                             (default: no pause)
                  /e       - don't checksum database file
                  /i       - don't checksum streaming file
                  /8       - set 8k database page size (default: auto-detect)
                  /o       - suppress logo
          NOTES:  1) This operation does not run database recovery. If
                     the database file (.edb) is in a "Dirty Shutdown"
                     state it is not possible to verify checksums in the
                     streaming file (.stm).
                  2) If the file is not a database file, the options are
                     ignored.
                  3) If the file is a streaming file, only the header is
                     verified and not the data pages.
                  4) The pause (/p) option is provided as a throttling
                     mechanism. It only applies when verifying checksums
                     of a database file.
```

The best value to use in your environment will depend on several factors:

1. How fast you wish the checksum verification to run;
2. How busy the storage array is and how many resources (disks, controllers, network connection ports, cache) it has;
3. How demanding the production workload is.

By default, ESEUTIL inserts a 1-second pause every 10,000 I/O reads. This is also the maximum value you can use for the switch. If you vary the pause value, you will obtain a varying read throughput for the execution of ESEUTIL. In our lab environments, we tested how fast we could go on an ideal SAN storage array configuration (>100 drives for the database engine, recent generation controllers). Figure 2.34 shows the read throughput of the ESEUTIL command based upon the throttling parameter.

Figure 2.34
ESEUTIL linearity

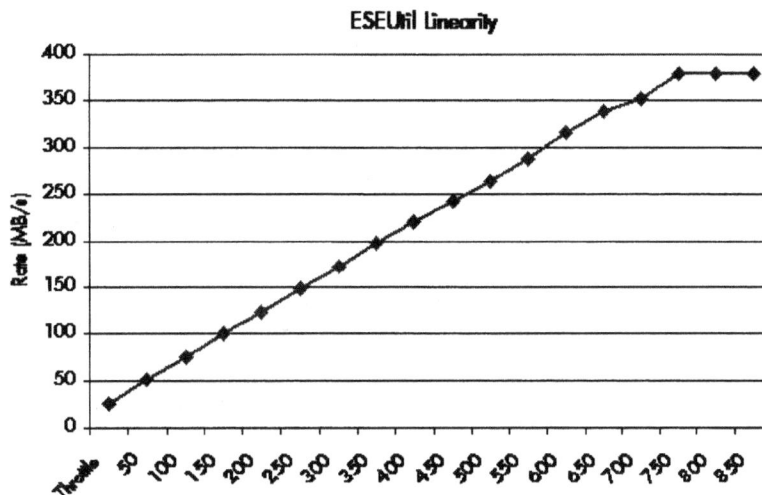

From this, and based upon your storage configuration and the controller capability to support both the production workload and the ESEUTIL checksum workload, you can determine the best throttling value. In our test environment, we figured that the optimal value was 400 (i.e., approximately 200 MB/s of ESEUTIL checksum operation in such a way that it would not affect the production workload).

Use of ESEUTIL throttling is really indicated in VSS backup verification cases; you would not use it otherwise because the stream backup API of Exchange does the page verification. Nonetheless, as we move into more agile storage infrastructures and the ability to perform image copy and recovery of volumes almost instantaneously by using background controller management, this mode of backup is likely to become far more indicated than before.

2.7   In Summary

In this chapter, we have reviewed the scalability aspects of Exchange 2003. I think it should be clear to you that running many users off a single server is not always the best idea, although it may make sense if you have opted for a high service-consolidation scenario. That said, it is at times quite difficult to anticipate the workload that will be applied to your Exchange 2003 infrastructure, and some of its components have limitations in scale-up scenarios that can necessitate scaling out by adding more servers to accommodate the workload and keep user satisfaction at the highest levels.

For your further planning work, attempt to refer to the various scaling models using these terms:

- *Scale up* refers to expanding a solution's capacity by incrementally adding more devices to an existing server, typically by adding CPUs, memory, disks, and NICs to a server. This is also referred to as vertical scaling or vertical growth.

- *Scale out* refers to expanding a solution's capacity by incrementally adding more servers, complete with processors, storage, and bandwidth sharing the user load across these servers. This is also referred to as horizontal scaling or horizontal growth.

Advantages to scaling up are as follows:

- There is only one server to manage multiple services or applications.
- Server capacity can be easily increased in a server with sufficient expansion capability.
- Software licensing costs may be lower since the software is hosted on only one server.

Disadvantages to scaling up are as follows:

- Since one server hosts multiple services, all services will be unavailable if the server is down.
- Availability is limited and dependent on server resources. If server load is maximized or the server fails, the services may be discontinued until the server is replaced with a more capable or operational server.
- Scalability is limited and dependent on server resources. If server capacity is maximized, greater service capacity is not available until the server is replaced with a more capable server.

Advantages to scaling out are as follows:

- Scalable and highly available services can be deployed, allowing capacity improvements without interruptions.

- Servers can be maintained and supported much more easily, since services are not required to go down to add or remove a server for repair or replacement.

- There are linear and predictable costs associated with scaling out an application across multiple servers.

Disadvantages to scaling out are as follows:

- Depending on the application, the cost per server and the cost of hardware load balancing may be higher than the implementation on one server.

- Software licenses may be higher when licenses are sold on a per-server basis.

- Management may increase for each server added to the array if appropriate best practices are not defined for the environment.

3

Microsoft Exchange and Windows Server

3.1   Microsoft Exchange 2003 Requirements

In this chapter, we refer to Windows 2000 and Windows Server 2003 as Windows Server. When topics are specific to either of the versions of the Windows operation system, we will call out the correct version of Windows.

Microsoft Exchange 2003 is integrated with Windows Server and its associated services, and it cannot be deployed correctly without a sound Windows infrastructure and related services. Certainly, the most important component is the Windows Active Directory service, which is used for storing almost all aspects of the Microsoft Exchange configuration, as well as referencing and addressing the recipients, the distribution groups, or other components.

Next, the DNS services are also critical, essentially for mail routing purposes—note that because they are critical to the correct operation of Windows Active Directory, there is little chance that you will encounter an operating Windows Active Directory without a solid DNS infrastructure.

Additional components of Windows are required for hosting and executing Microsoft Exchange services. Internet Information Services (IIS) is one of these components. In fact, Microsoft Exchange will just not install if IIS and the SMTP and NNTP (Network News Transfer Protocol, used for accessing Internet newsgroups) services are not present. It uses IIS to communicate with Internet protocols by the means of IIS virtual servers and borrows from and enhances the default Windows-supplied NNTP and SMTP services

By looking at the Microsoft Exchange 2003 architecture presented previously, it is clear that tight integration into the operating system and its related services is characteristic of Microsoft Exchange. The challenge becomes to properly take advantage of the infrastructure so it can better serve your Microsoft Exchange organization, functions, and overall quality of service.

Beyond directory and network-related services, Microsoft Exchange 2003 does take advantage of multinode clustering in a much better way that Exchange 5.5 did. With Windows Server 2003 and the support of eight-node clustering from the Enterprise Edition onward, we have seen a number of clusters deployed with more than two nodes, with five or six becoming quite common.

Finally, there have been some underlying changes in the Windows Server 2003 storage management that enabled users to take advantage of the massive progress done in the field of networked storage for the past five years. This networked storage is a key enabler of reliable cluster operations and a provider of key resources for a healthy and scalable Microsoft Exchange service.

There are features of Windows Server 2003 that Microsoft Exchange does not exploit directly, such as the encrypted file system or data compression. These are best implemented at the application level for ensuring the best performance required for high-end messaging environments. I think that the most needed, yet not available for this current generation of Microsoft Exchange (i.e., from Microsoft Exchange 2000 to the last release before what is currently known as Exchange 12), is support for 64-bit system architectures.

The lack of a 64-bit Exchange has a significant impact on the scalability of the application, and we shall explain why later in this chapter. For now, let's consider that when Microsoft Exchange did not support the Address Windowing Extensions (AWE) available by the means of Physical Address Extension (PAE) boot mode, this was not much of an issue because Microsoft Exchange had other scalability issues, starting with the storage and the relatively slow instruction processing from CPU. But more recently, and in particular with the shake-up of the CPU industry with AMD and its Opteron processor, there has been a significant increase of processing capability, without even requiring users to operate in a native 64-bit environment. Beyond the improved CPU processing capability—which is partly due to clock increase—bus bandwidth increase, the need for greater storage, and business requirements such as consolidation are all elements that encourage Microsoft Exchange administrators to host more users per server. In addition, the increase of email traffic and the pollution resulting from SPAM (such as unsollicited commercial email) and virus attacks, contribute to the necessity to build a high-performance Microsoft Exchange infrastructure, with a particular focus on servers and their storage components.

Microsoft Exchange 2003, including its most recent release with SP2, is not supported in any other environment than the 32-bit mode of execution of Windows Server 2003 and Windows 2000 Server (regardless of their respective editions). While you can install Exchange 2003 on a 64-bit processor, that is only possible if the processor implements the native 32-bit instruction set and runs in legacy mode (i.e., with a 32-bit operating system and a 32-bit application version).

The next major release of Exchange (Exchange Server 2007) will operate in 64-bit environments only, at least those offered when booting 64-bit Windows on x64 processors (there will be no support initially for the IA-64 architecture, also known as Itanium, from Intel). We will discuss this topic later, but for now we'll have to consider that Microsoft Exchange is still a 32-bit application that must run on a 32-bit operating system instance and, as such, is limited by a virtual address space of 4 GB in total size, split between the kernel execution mode (1 GB at least) and the user execution mode (3 GB at most). The mode of execution delivers a relatively large address space mostly consumed by database page cache, but there are situations in highly consolidated environments where this has proven to be a limit.

For the rest of this section, we are going to review some of the key Microsoft Exchange needs from the operating system, Windows server. I will baseline most of the operating system features on the Windows Server 2003 SP1 release.

3.1.1   The Necessity for a Directory

In a messaging system, you can hardly perform any routing and delivery of information without a directory. The directory serves three purposes in the context of Microsoft Exchange:

1.   It is used to provide at least one GAL, which can be browsed and searched against, and provides a correspondence between a friendly name (e.g., "First Name<space>Last Name" or "Last Name, First Name") and the actual user address and location.

2.   It provides and distributes configuration information—specifically, how the servers are actually linked together and how mail should be routed between servers and delivered to the actual user mailbox. This information is actually located in a precise parti-

tion of the Windows Active Directory service space, the configuration naming context.

3.   It provides delivery information to Microsoft Exchange routing services, such that messages can be routed and delivered to their final destination, either within the Microsoft Exchange organization or outside.

Exchange 5.5 came along with its own directory, which was linked to the security database (the SAM database) of the Windows NT domain by associating each mailbox to a primary Windows NT account.

Figure 3.1 shows the properties of a mailbox and the reference to the Primary Windows NT Account (here, EMEA\provoz). Note that the account does not need to be in the same domain as the Exchange server; the only requirement is that the domain hosting the Exchange server must trust the domain in which the accounts reside. Many Exchange 5.5 deployments are in fact deployed in a model in which all the Exchange servers are located in a resource Windows NT domain, which trusts (one-way) one or more Account domains.

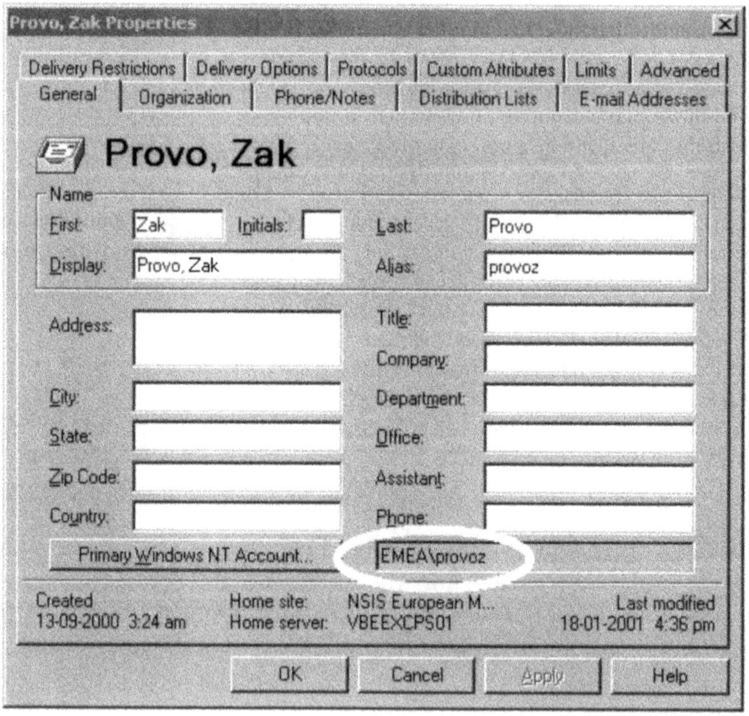

Figure 3.1
Exchange 5.5
mailbox properties.

With Microsoft Exchange 2000 and beyond, the mailbox information is actually stored in the Windows Active Directory, directly in the user account properties. Because the directory doesn't integrate those attributes upfront, Microsoft Exchange 2000, when installing for the first time in the Active Directory, will "enhance" the Active Directory with additional classes and attributes by modifying the schema of the Active Directory. Schema updates are usually of great importance in the context of the Active Directory, and not every administrator is allowed to modify the schema, for two key reasons:

1. Changes to the schema of the Active Directory cannot be undone in Windows 2000 deployments. Windows Server 2003 introduced a mechanism by which schema extensions can be removed, at least from an administrative viewpoint.

2. Schema changes require a redeployment of all directory entries and a selected set of their attributes to GC servers. In early deployments of Microsoft Exchange 2000, Windows 2000 was not deployed to a large extent, and the replication caused by the schema changes was not of a significant impact on the infrastructure. However, as Microsoft built additional features in their Microsoft Exchange product and required additional schema extensions (e.g., for Mobility services), the impact of a schema change began to be quite a big deal, causing several hours or days of replication traffic on fairly large corporate networks.

So while the operation of changing the schema of the Windows Active Directory can be fairly fast on a local domain controller, the impact of replication must be carefully assessed, and it is usually recommended that for the largest deployments, this operation is done during a long weekend break under strict monitoring, ensuring that replication is progressing satisfactorily.

Fortunately, you can deploy schema changes without installing the corresponding version of Microsoft Exchange. This is very helpful in the numerous situations where the Microsoft Exchange administrators are not the same as the Windows Active Directory administrators.

Furthermore, Microsoft did not sit on the issues mentioned previously. The company has made critical changes in the Windows Server 2003 Active Directory, as far as Microsoft Exchange deployment is concerned:

- Schema changes can be undone in Windows Server 2003 directories.

- The replication multivalue attributes is done at the value level rather than at the whole attribute. This eliminates one of the famous restrictions in Windows 2000 and Microsoft Exchange 2000 deployments, where you could not have distribution or security groups with more than 5,000 members. This restriction was in place because the transaction required for replicating all the values of the multivalue attribute was too large. With the introduction of the link value replication (LVR), it now becomes possible to have a large number of values for describing the members of a distribution or security group without endangering the integrity of the database transaction required during replication of the group objects.

- Most importantly, the need for replicating all objects of the Windows Active Directory to the GC servers is diminished to the replication of the partial set of attributes that must be contained in the GC servers. Therefore, the impact of a schema upgrade is much smaller with Windows Server 2003 than it was when changing the schema with Windows 2000.

The other use of Windows the Active Directory by Microsoft Exchange is the configuration storage: in the configuration naming context, which is an area of the Active Directory replicated to all domain controllers of the forest, a container is created for the Exchange services, and all configuration regarding server placement in the topology, storage groups and databases, virtual servers, and so on is located in this naming context. This has serious implications on the requirements that Exchange 2000 can put on a deployed Windows Active Directory forest: you need to place within reasonable reach (LAN-type connectivity) the domain controllers from your Microsoft Exchange servers. An Exchange 200x server that cannot connect to any domain controller (or GC server) is as useless as cheese without bread and wine.

Another point that is quite significant in large deployments is the fact that an Exchange organization cannot span Windows 2000 forests. This is important especially if you plan to have multiple forests for whatever political or technical reasons. There is a direct one-to-one mapping between the Windows 2000 forest and the Exchange organization. Technically speaking, Microsoft could have enabled multiple organizations per forest, but the time constraints, the test case scenarios, and the number of components that would potentially be confused by such a setup discouraged Microsoft from supporting such a configuration option.

3.1.2   Mixed Mode vs. Native Mode Active Directory Domains and Forests

By the time you deploy the Active Directory, you may be in a situation where the Active Directory has to run in mixed mode. More precisely, we refer to domains running in mixed mode; these are domains that combine Windows NT 4 backup domain controllers with Windows 2000 domain controllers and GC servers. Microsoft Exchange does not depend upon the mode in which you run your domains, with the exception of security group status. In a mixed-mode domain, the security groups cannot be universal. That can be a problem if you have used the Exchange 5.5 Distribution List to secure access to public folders. As the public folders are replicated or migrated to Microsoft Exchange, and as the directory is replicated and synchronized with the Windows Active Directory by the means of the Active Directory Connector (ADC), also known as the *light-saber*, Exchange 5.5 distribution lists are transformed into distribution groups by default. Because Microsoft Exchange uses the Windows Security subsystem for securing access to public folders, these distribution groups must be upgraded to security groups, which will carry a security identifier and can be used in access control lists (ACL) that are used for the public folders in the Microsoft Exchange environment. For this operation to happen, the domain hosting the security groups must be in native mode.

With the introduction of Windows Server 2003, the operation of multiple versions of Windows Server domain controllers and GC servers slightly changed names, but remains along the same lines.

Scope	Functionality	Description
Domain	Windows 2000 mixed	The default mode; you can operate domain controllers in Windows NT4, Windows 2000, or Windows Server 2003 versions of the operating system
	Windows 2000 native	All the domain controllers should be running either on Windows 2000 or Windows Server 2003
	Windows Server 2003 Interim	Allows you to comprise NT4 domain controllers and Windows Server 2003 domain controllers

Scope	Functionality	Description
	Windows Server 2003	The most advanced mode of operation of the domain; requires that all domain controller and GC servers be running Windows Server 2003
Forest	Windows 2000 mixed	The default mode of Windows Active Directory; allows you to run NT4, Windows 2000, and Windows Server 2003 domain controllers
	Windows Server 2003 Interim	Allows you to run NT4 and Windows Server 2003 domain controllers
	Windows Server 2003	All domain controllers and GC servers must be running Windows Server 2003

To fully benefit from the LVR and reduced schema replication, it is mandatory that you upgrade all your domain controllers and GC servers to Windows Server 2003. Fortunately, this operation proves to be fairly innocuous and rapid, even in the largest environments. Inside HP, we found that the upgrade of a Windows Active Directory server was less than 30 minutes, with little associated downtime.

Otherwise, you can decide to gradually upgrade the functionality mode of the forest and the domain. The improved Windows Active Directory replication algorithms and LVR will require the forest to be in Windows Server 2003 functionality mode. The GC improvement requires that the two replication partners be running Windows Server 2003, even if the forest is in the Windows 2000 functionality mode.

Getting the Most of Windows Server 2003 Windows Active Directory

I would recommend that you influence the deployment of Windows Active Directory components to Windows Server 2003 at minimum and Windows Server 2003 SP1 at best. The upgrade is relatively simple, and the benefits yielded from this version of Windows Active Directory are quite significant in scaled and high-performance environments.

3.1.3 Single Forest vs. Multiple Forests

Many Microsoft Exchange 2000 deployments have been gated by the design and implementation of the Windows 2000 Active Directory ser-

Feature	Benefit
LVR	Enables users to run larger groups and decrease replication traffic.
Intersite topology generation	Allows users to make much faster calculations in complex deployments that employ a large number of domain controllers, GC servers, and sites.
Automatic load balancing of replication workload across bridgehead servers	Allows you to have a much better balanced workload in hub and spoke deployments with a large number of replication partners: when new connection objects are added to the topology, the Windows Server 2003 domain controller will determine by a random process the replication bridgehead, avoiding the creation of hotspots or performance/replication bottleneck out of a particular Windows Active Directory server.
Improved intrasite replication	With Windows Server 2003, the replication within a site is occurring at a shorter interval of times (15 seconds maximum) and can be as low as 3 seconds when there are several replication partners; some account-level operations, such as account lockouts are replicated immediately.
Partial attribute set replication improvement	This improvement is quite critical if you intend to deploy Exchange 2003 because it requires schema changes that will cause the GC to fully replicate in Windows 2000 Active Directory mode. In Windows Server 2003 mode, only the attributes that are changed in the schema are actually replicated, helping to quickly expedite the schema changes required by upgrading your infrastructure to Exchange 2003.

vices. In my experience, we have found that the time taken to properly deploy an Active Directory was due not to the complexity of the technology itself but mostly to the level of decision as well as to political issues within a given enterprise.

The reason for this is that deploying a single-forest Active Directory affects many portions of the Enterprise and requires the development of an overall design that includes the many business units that make up a large company, all of which will need to buy into the model and actively support it.

With Exchange 2000, you would go with a single-forest environment to deploy a single organization and take advantage of many features that cannot cross organization boundaries, such as public folder replication, advanced security, and a uniform GAL. Microsoft Exchange organizations do not span forests, so many people thought that meant they should approach Exchange 2000 deployments by implementing single-forest Active Directory designs. However, the business reality of mergers and divestitures, as well as political "battles," do not help to achieve such a model on a relatively stable basis.

From a pure Windows perspective, Windows Server 2003 provides cross-forest authentication and authorization, as well as trust between forests. So multiple forests can be good, especially if forestwide operations (e.g., schema updates) or applications (e.g., Exchange 2000) are gradually implemented or are not desired by all business units.

Proper study has to be made of the actual implications of a multiforest deployment; however, this is a step that will help in getting acceptance of Windows Active Directory in very large enterprises, which often are unable to deal rapidly with the deployment of a technology that spans all their business units and functions.

This has the advantage of delegating the management of a well-defined directory service to the Microsoft Exchange administrators without requiring access to other Windows Active Directory forests that are hosting the user accounts. Such a model is particularly useful in a high-end environment with disjointed administration staffs (such as a large industrial group that owns many separate business units and companies), each owning its own Windows Active Directory forest. This model, referred as the "resource forest" deployment model, requires that a trust relationship is in place between the Microsoft Exchange forest and the other forests, and that user accounts in the Microsoft Exchange forest are defined (for the purpose of describing the mailboxes and enabling mail delivery) and authorized to be accessed by the user accounts defined in the trusting forest. This is typically achieved with the use of a directory synchronization tool, such as Microsoft's GALsynch utility that appeared with Exchange 2003, HP's LDAP Directory Synchronization Utility (LDSU), and Microsoft's current directory service solution, Microsoft Identity Integration Server (MIIS). Both enable users to bridge multiforest deployments together.

There are specific scenarios where this will be recommended, such as when you decide to delegate the administration of Microsoft Exchange to a specific group of people, such as in the example of infrastructure outsourcing. By outsourcing Microsoft Exchange, you realize certain business objectives, but, most important, by using a dedicated forest for Microsoft Exchange, you establish a clear boundary that enables a more flexible operations model and a much decreased mutual dependency. The deployment of the dedicated resource forest can then be performed according to Microsoft

Exchange needs, rather having to deal with both the Windows Active Directory needs (user authentication) and the Microsoft Exchange environment.

3.1.4   Internet Services

As described in Chapter 1, Microsoft Exchange makes extensive use of IIS as a vehicle for transporting data over IP. In fact, IIS runs a modified version of the various virtual services, such as SMTP, HTTP, NNTP and POP, and IMAP, which are Exchange aware. These protocol services are updated when you install Microsoft Exchange on a Windows 2000 or Windows 2003 server.

The idea of taking the services off the main platform and utilizing them as part of IIS is part of the process of additional partitioning of the functions, enabling Microsoft Exchange 2000 to be more distributed and potentially to scale higher rather than utilizing its own services. In fact, the first result of having IIS run the virtual services is the ability to configure Microsoft Exchange 2000 in a front-end/back-end environment. In such an environment you can actually dedicate platforms that will act as point of contacts for the connecting clients, while other platforms with different hardware specifications can concentrate on providing high-performance and high-capacity storage services.

When Microsoft Exchange 2000 came with the possibility to run into front-end and back-end environments, it only allowed this mode for Internet clients and protocols. This fact is further reinforced with Exchange 2003 and follow-on service packs, where it becomes mandatory, for security reasons, to deploy mobile messaging functions (which are in fact carried over the HTTP protocol) in a front-end and back-end architecture. Separating the functions enables us to have a much clearer view of the function performed by the front-end and the back-end servers. The introduction of the RPC over HTTP mode of operation with Exchange 2003 and Outlook 2003 (Outlook 11) requires that you enable the RPC over HTTP components, and this is best done on front-end servers, keeping the back-end server configuration as simple as possible.

3.1.5   Core Operating System Requirements

Microsoft Exchange 2003 requires at least Windows 2000 for all of its core features, including the ability to load the installable file system that initially shipped with Exchange 2000 and opens a high-speed access to the Exchange store as well as file-oriented access to components in this storage system. The IIS virtual servers are prime consumers of this particular interface for storing information coming from the Internet protocols. But beyond this particular ability, Microsoft Exchange can leverage other features of Windows 2000 and Windows Server 2003, the most significant of which, for Microsoft Exchange deployments, are the clustering and storage management services.

Although clustering technologies are available from non-Microsoft vendors, such as VERITAS, Microsoft Exchange only supports the Microsoft cluster services that ship with the standard edition of Windows Server 2003.

From a storage management viewpoint, the VSS framework is the key component that enables us to create hot point-in-time copies of Microsoft Exchange databases, enabling us to perform blazingly fast backup and most importantly recoveries, without requiring us to bring down the Microsoft Exchange services. Beyond the VSS framework, Windows Server has come a long way in the handling of networked storage (especially for fibre channel–connected storage) and offers, with Windows Server 2003, the ability to use built-in multipathing and implement a driver model for host-bus adapters, which is more suitable for network storage throughput, turning away from the SCSI miniport implementation to a new implementation called STORport. STORport allows for the much larger throughput (3,000 I/O per second and above) typically found in consolidated and scaled-up Microsoft Exchange environments.

3.2   Windows Server

Windows 2000 Server is the minimum version of the operating system that you can use for Microsoft Exchange. With the introduction of Windows Server 2003, you need at minimum Exchange 2003 for installing on that version of Windows. One simple reason behind this fact is that for security purposes, Microsoft decided to lock-down the default installation of Windows server at installation time. IIS is not installed by default and, even when selected, it misses the components that Microsoft Exchange requires for installing successfully. So while you can enjoy the deployment of Microsoft Exchange 2000 on Windows Server 2003, you cannot deploy Exchange 2003 on any other version of Windows than Windows Server 2003.

For describing the main components of Windows, we shall refer to the Windows Server 2003 features and note when these features significantly differ from Windows 2000.

Windows 2003 comes in various editions and names, as described in the following table:

Edition	Description
Windows XP (Professional, Home, and Media Center Editions)	Windows XP is part of the same code stream (code name: Whistler) as Windows Server 2003. In fact, some services from Windows Server 2003, such as the volume shadow copy services (VSS), are available on Windows XP, only with less feature and flexibility.
Windows Server 2003 Web Edition	This is for deploying the front end of web applications.
Windows Server 2003 Standard Edition	This is for deploying small environments and basic Windows networking services.
Windows Server 2003 Enterprise Edition	This is for deploying high-end servers with the support of 64-bit machine architectures and eight-node clustering.
Windows Server 2003 Data Center Edition	Similar to the Enterprise Edition, the Data Center Edition comes assorted with advanced technical support. Just like with its predecessor with Windows 2000, Data Center is a particular edition: you can't purchase it from the local Microsoft reseller; it can only be made available by OEMs such as HP, Unisys, IBM, or Dell, on precertified platforms.
Windows Server 2003 Compute Cluster Edition	This is for deploying clusters of multiple servers to form large supercomputers and address high-performance technical computing requirements (massive parallelized computing jobs).
Windows Server 2003 Storage Edition	This edition is only available through OEMs and can be purchased with preconfigured network attached storage appliances. It is optimized for file and print sharing, and does not provide supplementary services, such as Active Directory.

The main goal of the Windows Server platforms—to represent a scalable and reliable mission-critical environment for enterprise computing—has been reached by Windows 2000 to a greater extent than any previous release of the product family built on NT technology. With Windows Server 2003, this has been pushed further with native support for 64-bit CPU architectures such as Intel's Itanium processor family, as well as support for 64-bit CPU architecture that natively implements the 32-bit instruction set (x64 extensions). More specifically for Microsoft Exchange, the storage services present in Windows Server 2003 enable greater scalability by rendering the management of large volumes and databases much easier with the utilization of the VSS.

Besides the various versions of Windows servers, if there is one single recommendation I could give to a customer building a Windows Server, it would be to start from a *clean* installation. I know it may require new or additional hardware, but after several months spent visiting customers running large Windows infrastructures with Microsoft Exchange servers, I found that the best reliability was achieved not only with high-quality hardware but also with good management practice and a clean and sound knowledge of what the system does. It is usually OK to directly upgrade Windows 2000 servers to Windows Server 2003. You might run into issues related to special components, such as multipath management software in networked storage environments, which require you to disable the multipath function as you run through the upgrade. With native support of LUN multipath in Windows Server 2003 (MPIO), this type of consideration does not apply to future upgrades to the operating system. MPIO is Multi-Path I/O, a component from the Microsoft Windows Server 2003 operating system that manages the many paths that can be used to reach a particular storage target (primarily, disk units or logical volumes).

But if at all possible, try to build your production servers from scratch, using the latest hardware if your budget permits; there should be no compromise on this.

3.2.1 Key Differences Between the Various Editions of the Windows Server 2003 Operating System

The several editions of Windows Server 2003 are based on the same architecture and code base, the differences being mostly in the hardware architecture supported—the number of processors in an SMP (Symmetric Multi Processing) environment, the number of concurrent network connections, and additional services that come in selected versions of the operating system.

Table 3.1 summarizes those key differences relevant to us in the scope of scaling Microsoft Exchange infrastructures.

Please note that the values listed here are maximum values—they don't always address a pure Microsoft Exchange 2000 or 2003 environment. In fact, using more than 4 GB on a server running such an environment will bring little, if any, benefit. Likewise, a lot depends on the actual hardware certification list from Microsoft and what the server manufacturer can actually provide.

Table 3.1 *Hardware support by the various Windows Server editions*

Version	Processor	Key Differentiator
Windows Server 2003, Web Edition	X86	1–2 processors SMP (Symmetric Multi-Processing) 512-MB–2-GB RAM Cannot be a domain controller
Windows Server 2003, Standard Edition	X86 X86-64	1–4 processors SMP 512-MB–32-GB RAM Windows Active Directory
Windows Server 2003, Enterprise Edition	X86 X86-64 Itanium-2	1–8 processors SMP, NUMA (Non-Uniform Memory Access, an alternate implementation of multi-processing to SMP.) 512-MB–64-GB RAM (x86) 512-MB–1-TB RAM (x64, Itanium-2) Windows Active Directory Cluster service Windows System Resource Manager
Windows Server 2003, Data Center Edition	X86 X86-64 Itanium-2	1–64 processors SMP, NUMA 512-MB–64-GB RAM (x86) 512-MB–1-TB RAM (x64, Itanium-2) Windows Active Directory Cluster service Windows System Resource Manager

Note also that all versions of the Windows Server operating system are available off the shelf, except for the Data Center Edition, which ensures that the OEM has preconfigured a tested and validated hardware and software environment, including proper coordination of the driver, firmware, and BIOS of I/O components.

3.2.2 NTFS Volume Management

Some of the improvements of Windows 2000 in availability and performance have been made in the area of NTFS volume management. A particular point is when an NTFS volume becomes "dirty" after an abrupt system shutdown (e.g., a crash) and needs to be verified again. To this effect, Windows 2000, during boot time, will run a CHKDSK command, whose duration can vary depending on the volume size and, most important, on the number of files and folders located on the volume. For the case of Exchange 2000, the number of files on a particular volume is relatively small. Typically, you would have four or five databases on a database volume and a few hundred files for the transaction log area. The actual number of transaction log files depends on the activity of the system and backup operations schedule and the backup job type and scheduling *not* on the actual database size or number of users. I have seen people configuring Exchange 2000 log volumes based upon the size of the databases (e.g., 10 percent), which are as related as the cruising altitude of an airplane and the age of the captain. Seriously, though, a very active population of users would generate between 5 MB and 10 MB of transaction log data per day per user—but again, do assess your particular environment, even if you have only deployed Exchange 5.5. Much of the MAPI activity will depend upon the client, in spite of the notable changes introduced with Outlook 2003 and Exchange 2003, such as the cache mode and the optimization of the protocols, all of which aim at reducing the network traffic between the client and the server.

Yet you will want to decrease this unavailability as much as possible; one tactic is to use modifiers to the CHKDSK command during boot time, such that minimal time is spent on checking the NTFS volume at boot time so the server can boot as quickly as possible. This is especially interesting in a redundant array of independent servers (RAIS), which provides redundancy using N + 1 servers (see Chapter 4 of this book for a description of this technique as a workaround when clustering is not applicable or not desired).

Featured in Windows NT4 SP4 and Windows 2000 (all editions) are two new switches to the CHKDSK command that can reduce the CHKDSK operation to bare minimum and reduce the downtime. /C and / I are provided to bypass certain checking operations. These switches trim the operations done to verify a volume; you may pass the CHKDSK command successfully with those modifiers yet not obtain a completed accurate and operational NTFS volume.

To better understand the use of the switches, you need to understand what is going on during a CHKDSK command. The command basically goes through four key steps, three of them being mandatory and a fourth being optional:

- During the first phase, CHKDSK verifies metadata about the files present on the NTFS volume. A file record segment (FRS) in the volume's master file table represents each file. Note that this "metadata" is maintained by NTFS using a journaling mechanism. The data itself (the contents of the file) is not protected and is left for the calling application to protect. For Microsoft Exchange databases, this is achieved by transaction logging and checksum of database pages and transaction log file records.

- The second phase consists of verifying the indexes of the NTFS volumes, which are essentially the directory files. CHKDSK makes sure that the directories are consistent and that each FRS has a corresponding directory entry in one or more indexes. It also confirms that each FRS in the indexes actually has an entry into the master file table of the volume. The result of that phase is that there are no "orphaned" files on the volume.

- The third phase consists of verifying the security descriptors associated with each of the files and the directories. It does not verify, though, that the listed users or groups actually exist and that the permissions are appropriate.

- The time taken by these three mandatory phases is usually not dependent on the size of the volume itself, but on how many files and directories are present on the volume. The fourth phase is processed when using the /R switch, which aims at verifying bad sectors in the volume's free space. Sectors that are associated with metadata are read even if this switch is not used. The duration of this CHKDSK pass depends, this time, on the actual volume size.

This is an overview of the main passes; CHKDSK can actually perform additional tests, which generally don't affect the actual completion time. For a 100-GB volume with only two or three files, the CHKDSK completion can actually be quite fast—within seconds. This is not true if there are many files and directories. We have seen volumes of 100 GB, hosting 1 million files, taking as long as 4 hours for a CHKDSK operation. Your mileage will vary, depending upon the volume structure, the number of files, and of course the actual number of disks making up the volume and their speed of execution (latency, mostly).

The /C switch bypasses checks that detect cycles in the directory structure. A cycle is a case where the directory sees itself as an ancestor. Cycles are seldom seen in directory corruption.

The /I switch bypasses the comparison of FRS in the MFT (Master File Table) with the contents of the directory. Thus, the result of skipping this operation is that although the directories are checked for self-consistency, they are not necessarily consistent with the data stored in the corresponding FRS. Using this switch typically trims by 50 to 70 percent the time required to run the CHKDSK operation.

Using the two switches repairs the type of corruption that could result, by a snowball effect, in bigger problems. They do expedite the operation in much less time than a regular CHKDSK operation. While this procedure is useful when time pressure is present, this is only a stop-gap solution. A complete CHKDSK operation at a later time (e.g., during off-peak hours, planned downtime, or system maintenance) should be executed to make the on-disk NTFS structure as clean as possible.

Another tool that was introduced with Windows NT4 SP2 is CHKNTFS, which can be used to disable automatic CHKDSK during boot time or to unschedule a scheduled CHKDSK. This can help to improve the boot time and availability of your service.

In the normal boot procedure of Windows NT, AUTOCHK determines which disks have to be checked. By the means of a registry setting, you can disable specific volumes to be checked at boot time or use modifiers to the CHKDSK command invoked during the boot such that you can speed up the process of boot and run the CHKDSK operation later.

CHKNTFS is a somewhat nicer and less error prone interface to straight registry editing.

Deferring some of the CHKDSK operation can bring some performance advantages. After CHKDSK completion, the Windows 2000 operating system typically has more resources to perform the CHKDSK operation than at boot time, where resources such as RAM are scarce. On the other hand, after boot time, there maybe additional applications loaded that would adversely affect the execution of the command.

My recommendation here is to perform a series of tests to establish a baseline necessary to set the proper expectations in service availability and determine the impact of running the CHKDSK command at boot time, as compared with after boot time. That's an appropriate exercise for a lab environment.

Nevertheless, with Exchange 2000 you should not normally be affected by CHKDSK operations at boot time, since Exchange 2000 uses relatively few files for its normal operations, except in extreme cases with SMTP servers relaying a large number of messages. After all, this is what this book is about: extreme Exchange 2000 implementations, so I felt it would be useful to discuss these techniques.

The NTFS Allocation Unit Size

You might wonder which allocation unit size you should be using for Microsoft Exchange. There have been many comments and much discussion concerning the utilization of partition alignment using diskpar as well as allocation unit size value during the NTFS formatting.

The allocation unit size is important to ensure the minimum quantity of guaranteed contiguous space on an NTFS partition. It does not impact the resulting I/O size. It does impact the alignment of the file in the partition (and the partition alignment is controlled by the utilization of diskpar).

My recommendation would be to configure the allocation unit size to the cache page size. This ensures that you do not trash cache entries if you are not aligned on cache pages.

At HP, the partition alignment was recommended for the EVA-GL (and recommended by other vendors on their respective platforms) because of performance degradation in sequential operations on VRAID5 volumes. There was little impact on VRAID1 volumes and random workload.

At the array level, if you are not aligned on the cache page entry, you will use two cache entries instead of one. This is not a problem, unless you have many misalignments. The value of this setting must be discussed again with your storage vendor for each release of the array model and firmware. For instance, in the case of the EVA-XL array (next generation EVA), known as EVA 4000, 6000, and 8000, the problem was solved by using a variable cache page size, ensuring that there would not be trashed cache pages simply because of misalignment.

So, if you know your I/O size, and if you run the risk of having relatively fragmented files on the volume, you should set the allocation unit size as close as possible to the I/O size.

It does not have to be the same. Remember that there will be a split I/O (a condition you wish to avoid) *only* if you issue an I/O that spans across two noncontiguous allocation units. This split I/O will occur at the NTFS level.

With the volumes that are used by Exchange the most intensively, i.e., the database volumes, the I/O size is generally of 4 KB and the files are quite large: the allocation unit size is unlikely to be of a major concern, and the default use of 4 KB is generally found in most Exchange deployments.

3.2.3 64-Bit Windows

The 64-bit version of Windows is actually shipping in two main editions, depending upon the target 64-bit processor architecture. In the industry and for Microsoft Windows Server operating system, there are two 64-bit implementations available:

1.   Intel's Itanium processor family: the Itanium is the result of collaboration between HP and Intel in producing a 64-bit processor, based on an explicitly parallel instruction computing (EPIC) architecture. The corresponding version of Windows Server was launched in April 2003 (Windows Server 2003 for Itanium-based Systems).

2.   AMD's AMD64 and Intel's EM64T processors: both are 64-bit processors that natively implement the 32-bit x86 instruction set. The processor architecture is generally referred as x86-64. Processors implementing this architecture are the AMD Opteron, AMD Althon 64, Intel 64-bit Xeon, and Intel Pentium with EM64T. Windows Server 2003 x64 Editions support these various processor implementations.

The difference between the two approaches is major. In the first case, you have a new 64-bit architecture that requires your application to be recompiled for taking the full advantage of the processor's increased speed and bandwidth. If you decide to not recompile the application, you can execute it in an emulated 32-bit environment, in the same way that you could run a 16-bit application on Windows 95 in a special Windows-on-Windows environment. But running in emulation does not deliver the throughput that intensive applications such as Microsoft Exchange require.

In the second case, the processor can execute 32-bit instructions and therefore does not require the application to be recompiled. In actual fact, it can even boot a 32-bit operating system and be totally supported by the whole suite of 32-bit applications and drivers for the 32-bit version of Windows. And this is where the advantage for such technology begins: the 32-bit environment takes advantage of a 64-bit infrastructure (twice the bus width, 64-bit instructions, and registers). Depending upon which version of the operating system you decide to boot, you can run in either

- legacy mode: boot 32-bit Windows Server, run with 32-bit drivers and applications;

- compatibility mode: boot 64-bit Windows Server, run with 64-bit drivers, run with 32-bit applications;

- Native mode: boot 64-bit Windows Server, run with 64-bit drivers and applications.

For the case of Exchange 2003 SP2 and earlier, only the legacy mode is supported. However, it will not be long before Microsoft proposes a native 64-bit version of Microsoft Exchange. After all, 64-bit Windows is already running a 64-bit version of the database engine as part of the Windows Active Directory services.

In fact, and for scalability matters, the 64-bit version of Windows server for Windows Active Directory proves to be extremely useful for scale-up purposes: by using very large memory (VLM) systems (>4GB of RAM), you can cache a greater quantity of the Windows Active Directory database in memory and therefore respond faster to a larger number of transactions per second.

From an application viewpoint, moving from a 32-bit to a 64-bit architecture is not an easy and straightforward task. I personally went through the experience as a product developer when the company I worked for at the time, Digital Equipment Corporation, went from VAX-11 32-bit architecture to Alpha 64-bit architecture for OpenVMS. You would be right to argue that the problem at the time was also compounded by the change of processor instruction set! That led to very interesting efforts and initiatives within the company, such as providing emulated environments and translation efforts. Eventually, the only viable approach is to rebuild the application and make sure that regression didn't take place in the process.

Which Benefits?

Using a 64-bit processor and operating system architectures enables users to have more resources, at both the application and kernel level for handling the workload. It means more connections, more database page in a cache, and so forth. Although 64 seems twice 32, in reality, the difference is to be expressed in 32 to the power of 32.

As shown in Table 3.2, the quantity of system and application resources is suddenly increased, largely exceeding the actual values of a computer system (128 GB of nonpaged pool, which is used for kernel memory that is to be kept resident, is largely enough for most computer's RAM capacity).

Table 3.2 *Differences Between Windows 64-bit and 32-bit Processor Systems*

Architectural Component	64-Bit Windows	32-Bit Windows
Virtual memory	16 TB	4 GB
Max paging file size	512 TB	16 TB
Paged pool	128 GB	470 MB
Nonpaged pool	128 GB	256 MB
System cache	1 TB	1 GB
System Page Table Entries (PTEs)	128 GB	660 MB

In the case of Microsoft Exchange, and as we see later on in this book, the need for cache of data is omnipresent to satisfy shortest latency in transactions and queries, augmenting the overall throughput of the system.

The Case for Windows Active Directory

Windows Active Directory is running on Windows Servers, and today you can build and deploy 64-bit domain controllers and GC servers. Because Windows Active Directory uses a database engine that is very similar to Microsoft Exchange, using a 64-bit architecture enables users to grow the engine cache in memory, reduce the time it takes to look up entries in the Windows Active Directory, and increase the number of lookups per minute/second. In short, you can have fewer Windows Active Directory 64-bit servers than 32-bit ones.

The Windows Active Directory can be assimilated as the best business application to embrace 64-bit computing. Why? Because its multimaster replication model allows users to gradually rollout 64-bit servers in a 32-bit environment—with the safety that if something goes wrong on the 64-bit platform, there will be 32-bit servers ready to pick up the load temporarily.

In internal testing at HP, we have found that a 64-bit architecture would improve by 4 to 40 times the request rate and response time for Microsoft Exchange Windows Active Directory lookups. Consider then the following diagram:

32-bit GC servers

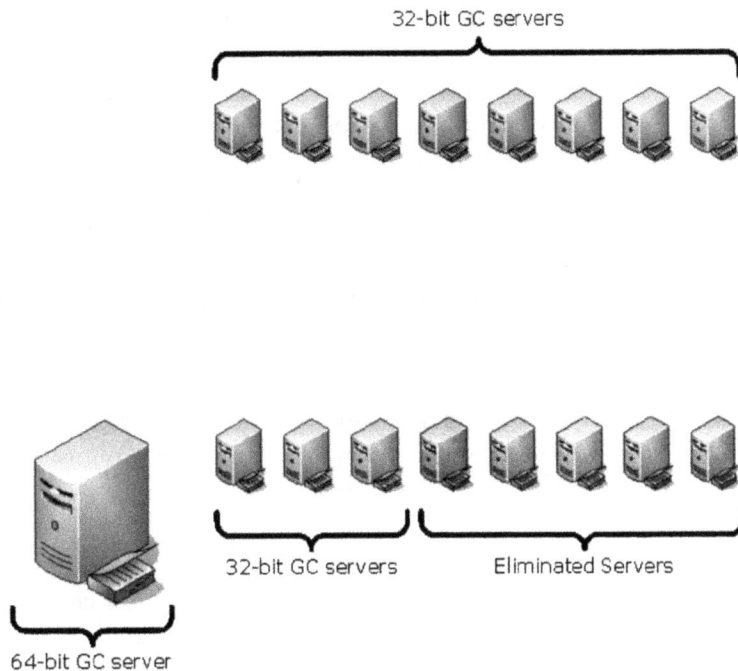

32-bit GC servers   Eliminated Servers

64-bit GC server

In this environment we either deal with 8 × 32–bit GC servers for a consolidated Microsoft Exchange deployment, or ... 4 servers, with 3 × 32–bit servers and one 64-bit server. The second case brings improved overall transaction capacity, with far fewer servers and room for growth. At the same time, the multimaster replication enables users to be resilient in case the 64-bit environment was to run into a problem specific to this processor architecture.

We still need to obtain information from Microsoft on sizing guidelines for 64-bit servers, and these are unlikely to be generally available and understood before there is a 64-bit version of Microsoft Exchange itself. But in the meanwhile, we can conclude that gradually inserting 64-bit machines in a Windows Active Directory environment is a safe and economical step forward for the following reasons:

- You use the same hardware: the difference between a 64-bit Windows Active Directory server and a 32-bit one is essentially in the operating system version. The hardware platform and modern processors equipped with AMD64 or EM64T technologies are strictly the same, whether you operate in a 32-bit or 64-bit environment.

- You can deploy in a fully resilient environment: GC servers are read-only servers, used for address lookups by Microsoft Exchange and connected clients. While the 64-bit machine can handle the load of eight equivalent 64-bit machines (based upon empirical testing we did at HP), the added requirement is just enough RAM to hold the equivalent of the Windows Active Directory database (NTDS.DIT) in RAM. If the 64-bit server dies due to an unforeseen problem, you do not lose any transactions or data, you just observe a temporary increase in Windows Active Directory requests response time to Microsoft Exchange.

- Savings can be measured in hardware acquisition, software licensing, and most importantly server management. Today, in consolidated environments, finding a case for which you can safely reduce from eight servers to four is hardly frequent.

Why Should You Adopt 64-Bit Windows?

I believe the need is very simple. The race for computing processing is on going with key industry players such as Intel, AMD, IBM, and HP to produce faster and faster processors. As I write this book, 3.4-GHz Pentium processors are shipping from Intel, in hyper-threaded and dual-core editions, and by the time you read it, "they" will have probably broken the 4-GHz barrier on the road to higher frequencies achieved by using new chip design and implementation techniques.

How does this relate to the actual addressing capabilities of the processor? It's simple—your high clock frequencies and increasing number of instructions per second are only as good as you have data to give it. Long gone are the days when CPUs were actually busy enough to withstand a slow I/O operation. The increasing processing capability is causing a slight imbalance in the computing systems architecture if data cannot be provided as fast as the CPU demands it. While improvements have been made with PCI (Peripheral Component Interconnect) buses (with the gradual introduction of PCI-X, and now of PCI-eXpress), there are still major latencies incurred by even the fastest disk arrays and network accesses compared with the latency of memory access. So the idea here is to provide lots and lots of memory for those CPUs to have massive quantities of data available for processing, thereby reducing the latency in transactions (by decreasing the number of disk operations) and increasing the overall transaction or operation throughput.

By moving to a 64-bit architecture in Windows Server, you can increase the quantity of RAM available for one or more processors to up to 16 TB, while I would suppose that most implementations will range between 16 and 128 GB of physical memory. What can you do with so much RAM?

- You can run in-memory database applications. When the Altavista search engine was exposed to the Internet in the mid-1990s, it was successful because of its very fast response time and its ability to handle many hits in a single day (several millions). At the time, this was achieved by using Alpha-based computers that could load up a complete Internet index of several gigabytes and thereby virtually eliminate all disk accesses for user transactions. Microsoft Exchange will be a great application for a 64-bit architecture with a database transaction logging that can be processed very quickly by fast disk arrays, controllers, and an in-memory cache that grows well beyond the initial 2.1-GB limit imposed on the product at release time in late 2000. Microsoft SQL Server is another application that can benefit from large RAM. In fact, any database engine that is used in reporting or data warehousing, will benefit from servers with large quantities of RAM, by minimizing slow disk accesses in favor of much faster memory accesses to any (or all!) portion of the database.

- Applications that have complex computational requirements can take advantage of 64-bit instructions that can perform more calculations in fewer cycles compared with a 32-bit architecture.

- Terminal services provide the ability to host many user contexts in terminal service sessions, thereby bringing real the consolidation of application servers and moving the computing requirements imposed on the client side of a client/server communication, back to the server. This turns the client into a more-or-less smart display, yet much simpler and cheaper to administer than a full PC client machine.

- Virtualization is the last and not least of the advantage of 64-bit computing. By offering a wider range of address and memory accessible to virtualization kernels, such as VMware or Microsoft Virtual Server, you can run more instances of an operating system and take better advantage of the CPU and memory utilization by seamlessly loading and unloading virtual machines across one or several 64-bit servers.

You should consider 64-bit Windows Server as only an enabling technology; do not forget that the operating system is present only to support mission-critical applications, and Microsoft Exchange is one of them.

It has a great potential for taking advantage of 64-bit addressing by taking off the original 4-storage group limit, and letting more databases be accessed and cached in the STORE virtual address space and scaled forward. With the version of Microsoft Exchange for 64-bit environments, it is planned to operate in the range of 80–90 databases maximum per server.

Nevertheless, having lots of physical memory and huge virtual address space does not provide the solution to all problems. You need to harmoniously grow your application server, in terms of both physical memory capabilities and processing capabilities. Here 64-bit Windows 2000 does not bring any particular improvement, other than the ability for vendors to develop 4-, 8-, or larger processor platforms. The issues of a well-balanced application design that can take advantage of symmetric multiprocessors (SMP), which allows concurrent operations to occur without overwhelming them with too many context switches resulting in too large concurrent thread execution, still remain. But the future looks good for Microsoft Exchange, and I believe that waiting for a 64-bit version of the application and the operating system rather than implementing a solution based on AWE API was a sound and strategic, though not the best timed, approach.

What Should You Do Now?

I think that your best bet is to proceed by gradually deploying 64-bit servers and operate in two modes:

- 64-bit for Windows Active Directory servers (GC servers and domain controllers). This enables you to insert 64-bit Windows Server management into your operational framework. The multimaster replication lets you mix and match 64-bit and 32-bit GC servers.
- 32-bit legacy mode for Exchange 2003 SP2 and earlier. You operate on a well-supported environment for your mainstream Microsoft Exchange environment.

Then, gradually migrate your 64-bit server into native mode by rolling out upcoming 64-bit versions of Microsoft Exchange. Finally, adopt 64-bit virtualization technology to host instances of 32-bit Windows and Microsoft Exchange.

This entire approach can be achieved with the same processor architecture. In using either of the AMD Opteron or Intel Nocona processor families and their successors, you ensure that your base hardware investment is protected and that your adoption of 64-bit computing is only a matter (not a small one though) of rolling out 64-bit versions of the operating system and applications.

The 32-bit compatibility mode, for obvious supportability issues, should be avoided at best and does not bring any real benefit.

3.3 Volume Shadow Copy Services

Windows Server 2003 came with a new framework for managing storage devices that is of great importance in high-end Microsoft Exchange environments. There are two new components in Windows Server 2003 that relate to the management of storage devices and that were not present in previous version of the operating system:

1.   The volume shadow copy services (VSS);

2.   The virtual disk services (VDS).

Both components create an abstraction layer that allows implementers of storage management functions to be relatively independent of the hardware specifics and of the specifics of the applications that use this storage.

VSS represents a major step forward when it comes to Microsoft Exchange environments and high-end configurations because it eventually enables a supported and well-controlled way to perform "hot" volume clones without requiring administrators to dismount Microsoft Exchange databases or disconnect user sessions.

Exchange 2003 and greater can take advantage of the framework. In the rest of this section, we are going to come back to the new terms introduced and how they all fit together. We primarily focus here on the VSS framework, because it is the one that delivers most of the value to Exchange 2003 deployments.

Shadow Copies

A shadow copy is a logical or physical copy of a volume. Taken at a particular point in time, the shadow copy describes the state and the blocks of a volume. How you implement the shadow copy really depends upon the software and hardware capabilities of your environment. A storage array that creates business continuity volumes will typically clone, block by block, a given volume when you create a shadow copy. You may also decide

Figure 3.2
*The Windows
2003 storage
services*

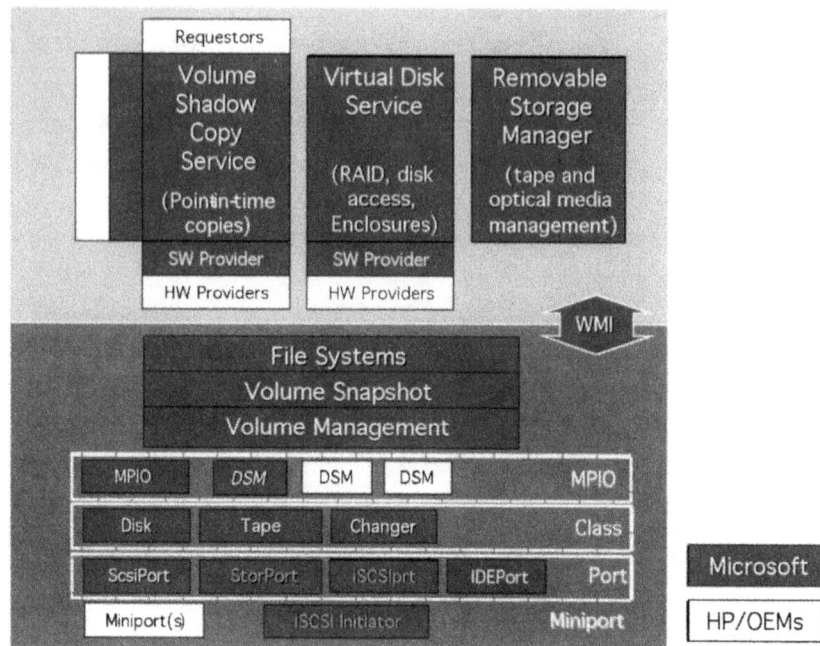

to keep track only of the differences that occurred between the time you take the shadow copy and the current time. This is sometimes referred to as a snapshot or a differential copy. Anyhow, the objective is to be able to take a snapshot of a volume at any point in time and refer to it later—either block by block by streaming it to a backup media, or in its entirety in case the original volume breaks down.

Herein, I'm using the term volume to basically designate an NTFS formatted disk partition. Of course, if you have a physical disk that holds five partitions, and if you make a full copy of that physical copy, you end with five copies of partitions, one for each partition on the disk unit.

Put simply, VSS is an orchestrator. In other words, it ensures that operations that require the cooperation of various elements from different horizons are done in a consistent way. The prime application of VSS is the ability to make a backup of a volume that has files in use by applications. This is known as the *open-file* backup. The challenge of an open-file backup is that you wish to take information at the point of the backup and preferably avoid having half of a modified file on your backup media. In the past, backup applications such as HP's Data Protector or VERITAS's NetBackup were proposing a filter driver that basically stopped I/O operations on files that were in the process of being backed up. But inserting in the I/O stack a filter driver can have nasty consequences in peculiar environments, and they can possibly cause system hangs or crashes.

3.3.1 Introduction to VSS

So, with VSS, the first benefit that you get, out of the box, is the ability for the file system to freeze operations on the volume as far as the backup application is concerned, without impacting the regular applications that do use the volume. This feature is enabled in all editions of the Windows part of the Whistler code stream, including Windows XP. In fact, if you go to a Windows XP client machine and type VSSADMIN at the command prompt, you obtain the following information found in Figure 3.3.

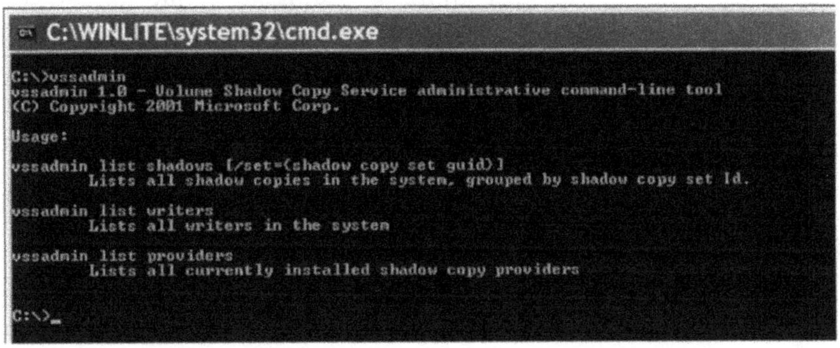

Figure 3.3
VSSADMIN on
Windows XP

This shows initial traces of VSS on a Windows XP Professional machine.

3.3.2 Providers

For VSS to control the storage operations, you need a provider. There are various kinds of providers, depending on which types of the storage volume they are able to control:

- System provider: there is only one system provider, including with Windows, and it controls operations at the file system level. Issue the command VSSADMIN LIST PROVIDERS at the command prompt of your Windows Server or workstation and you will be able to rapidly spot it! This provider is being proposed for basic file-level *copy out*. The two primary functions that are used with this provider are open-file backup and VSS for shared folders. From a data movement perspective, the Windows software provider will copy out entire files in the SYSVOL area of the target volume, under a folder name uniquely identified by a GUID (Globally Unique Identifier) generated when the snapshot was requested. These files are then kept for later retrieval, until the retention period is reached. This method of copy-out is very useful for file shares but does not help in the case of most of Microsoft Exchange data files and databases and OST/PST archives created by Outlook 2003. In this case, a provider that is implemented at the block level carries greater value because it will operate at the physical or logical block level, rather than at the file system object level.

- Software provider: a non-Microsoft software provider that can control the management of shadow copies of a volume at the block level. In other words, you can use these providers to create shadow copies of a drive (as seen by Windows) and place them on disk units. Typically, software providers are provided by companies such as VERITAS or CommVault, and they enable you to create shadow copies on disk units seen by the Windows server operating system.

- Hardware provider: a provider that can control the management of shadow copies at the hardware level. The hardware provider will interface more or less directly with the back-end storage array and instruct the array to perform shadow copy creation, deletion, and so forth. The advantage of operating at the storage array level is that you can eventually obtain units that are completely independent from the operating system: a mirror or a snapshot that can be used for recovery purposes.

For the case of Exchange 2003, there are two reasons why you would want to use VSS framework:

1. To make an open-file backup of the Microsoft Exchange databases;

2. To create a physical or logical copy of a volume that can be used for rapid recovery purposes.

In the first case, the use of a software provider is usually sufficient. In the second case, you will need to use a hardware provider, ensuring that there is a sufficient level of independence to how the data is stored, so you can easily recover in case your production volume fails.

Writers

The writer component in VSS is the application-specific interface that registers the presence of an application to a framework. It can enumerate the disk units used by the application and control the I/O flow to the disk units from an application perspective.

In Figure 3.4, we can see a number of providers, built into the operation system. The examples I provide herein are from Windows XP to prove that this VSS framework and features are designed into the core Whistler code stream; they are, of course, available in all Windows Server 2003 editions.

Figure 3.4
Providers and writers on Windows XP

```
C:\>vssadmin list providers
vssadmin 1.0 - Volume Shadow Copy Service administrative command-line tool
(C) Copyright 2001 Microsoft Corp.

Provider name: 'MS Software Shadow Copy provider 1.0'
Provider type: System
Provider Id: {b5946137-7b9f-4925-af80-51abd60b20d5}
Version: 1.0.0.7


C:\>vssadmin list writers
vssadmin 1.0 - Volume Shadow Copy Service administrative command-line tool
(C) Copyright 2001 Microsoft Corp.

Writer name: 'IIS Metabase Writer'
Writer Id: {59b1f0cf-90ef-465f-9609-6ca8b2938366}
Writer Instance Id: {c30e35f6-f0ac-4954-9556-17168cad77c4}
State: [1] Stable

Writer name: 'WMI Writer'
Writer Id: {a6ad56c2-b509-4e6c-bb19-49d8f43532f0}
Writer Instance Id: {8bdec440-ea43-4786-a5de-9fec6fdfe2bc}
State: [1] Stable

Writer name: 'Microsoft Writer (Bootable State)'
Writer Id: {f2436e37-09f5-41af-9b2a-4ca2435dbfd5}
Writer Instance Id: {525f3042-5871-4d2d-ae29-415648c8e210}
State: [1] Stable

Writer name: 'MSDEWriter'
Writer Id: {f8544ac1-0611-4fa5-b04b-f7ee00b03277}
Writer Instance Id: {782b2a82-4b2b-498d-a18e-5cb85402f62b}
State: [1] Stable

Writer name: 'Microsoft Writer (Service State)'
Writer Id: {e38c2e3c-d4fb-4f4d-9550-fcafda8aae9a}
Writer Instance Id: {50a5da51-6931-4893-ad38-69f66dfedbe7}
State: [1] Stable

C:\>
```

To further illustrate the necessity of a provider, in Figure 3.4, we note the presence of the IIS Metabase Writer. The function of this writer is to enable IIS to perform any operation on the metabase while a shadow copy is being created. In other words, the goal of the writer is to let the application hold its breath while the storage volume is undergoing a modification. That way, you can ensure that the storage shadow copy is relatively consistent, from both an application and a file system perspective.

Requestors

The Requestor is basically driving the creation and use of the shadow copies. It does not interface directly with the application or with the storage array, and it is only with a requestor that you realize the full power of the VSS framework. With no knowledge of an application or a back-end disk array, a requestor can obtain a physically identical point-in-time copy that only took seconds to create (regardless of the volume size), and that copy contains data that is exploitable and consistent vis-à-vis the application.

We generally break down the types of requestors in three categories:

- Category 1: Traditional backup (e.g., Data Protector, NTBACKUP). These requestors will perform the equivalent of open-file backup by creating a shadow copy from which they will read to stream data to a backup media (tape or drive).

- Category 2: Volume transport (e.g., vsnap, VERITAS Storage Foundation). The volumes are duplicated, physically or logically, and presented to another server for backup purposes. Volume transport enables users to offload the backup workload from production servers onto dedicated and fit-for-function backup servers.

- Category 3: Rapid recovery (e.g., HP FRS, EMC SIME, NetApps SnapView). The requestor is used for *both* backup and recovery and is application-aware to a certain extent. In the case of Microsoft Exchange, it knows about databases, logs, and storage groups.

In Summary

The VSS is an important aspect for Microsoft Exchange scalability. Even with the ability to partition a mailbox server into multiple databases, storage remains the prime scalability issue in a transacted world such as Exchange 2003. When storage technology evolves, allowing the implementation of point-in-time backups and restores, Microsoft Exchange needs somehow to integrate these storage technology advantages to allow for flexible operations.

In the case of Microsoft Exchange 2003, this technology simply translates into a supported way to perform an online point-in-time backup. This carries the following advantages over the existing online and offline backup solutions:

■ No need to shut down, and therefore render unavailable, the Exchange databases or services;

■ Ability to save and restore several hundreds of gigabytes of data within minutes and take full advantage of back-end storage technologies;

■ Ability to operate a fully supported solution.

It can justify the migration to this new operating system by helping with the management of ever-growing information databases in Exchange 2000 and other back-end applications. We will come back on the VSS framework and its use with Exchange 2003 when describing machines architectures.

3.4 Windows Clusters

Of all the areas of Windows that evolved in the last three years, clustering is certainly one of the most interesting. The evolution mainly revolves around its adoption and ease of deployment, rather than the core technology that makes up Windows clustering.

In this section, we are not going to cover in great depth the clustering of Windows servers and Microsoft Exchange, primarily because it is targeted at improving the uptime of the Microsoft Exchange service by preventing application and operating system downtime with failover capabilities. However, when you deal with Microsoft Exchange scalability, you have to consider clustering for the simple reason that the more users you concentrate on a platform, the greater the dependency on that platform is, and clustering is one way to get this platform resilient.

In this section, we will discuss clustering in simple principles and explain the key scalability aspects related to Microsoft Exchange deployments.

Windows Clustering Principles

Microsoft's clustering is based on a shared-nothing model. You can group servers that are typically (but not exclusively) located in the same data center and establish a relationship between these servers such that they are under a common monitoring environment (the cluster resource manager).

The shared-nothing model relates to the way storage components are managed. In a Microsoft cluster, each node has exclusive access to the storage units. This means, for Microsoft Exchange, that you may only access a Microsoft Exchange database from one node in the cluster. For this reason, clustering is to be considered not for scale-up of a service on a single machine, but for improving resilience across a farm of servers—each user being tied to a Microsoft Exchange server, physical or virtual.

In Figure 3.5, we can view the main components of a Windows and Microsoft Exchange cluster: four nodes (servers are called nodes in a cluster) are actually four servers running Windows Server, and they require a data network connection between each other and the Windows Active Directory services, along with the clients, and shared storage network connections to a storage array that hosts volumes that can be used by one and exactly one node at any single point in time.

Figure 3.5
Cluster schematics

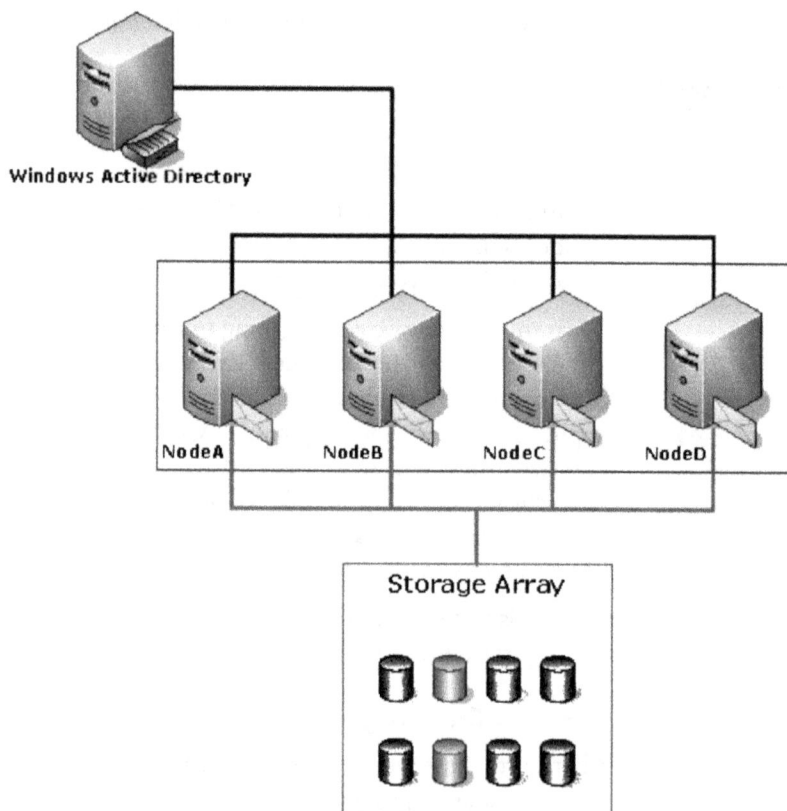

In terms of scalability, there is absolutely no difference in such environment than if the servers were running in standalone mode (i.e., not coupled together in a cluster).

Active/Active vs. Active/Passive

With Microsoft Exchange 2000, the real novelty brought in the space of clustering was the ability to have both nodes of a two-node cluster to run Microsoft Exchange and service user clients. However, during data center certification of Microsoft Exchange, known as stress harness, Microsoft realized that a node running a Microsoft Exchange Virtual Server (i.e., an instance of Exchange on a cluster node) could not failover and failback in all situations—the causes for failures were largely attributed to the lack of contiguous virtual address space in the STORE process.

To cut this long story short, Microsoft came with an (almost) arbitrary recommendation of active/active clustering being supported only if each node was hosting less than 1,900 connections each. So if we consider the case described in Figure 3.6, NODEA and NODEB must have less than 1,900 connections active to guarantee a failover to work from NODEA to NODEB and vice versa.

Figure 3.6
*Two-node active/
active Microsoft
Exchange cluster*

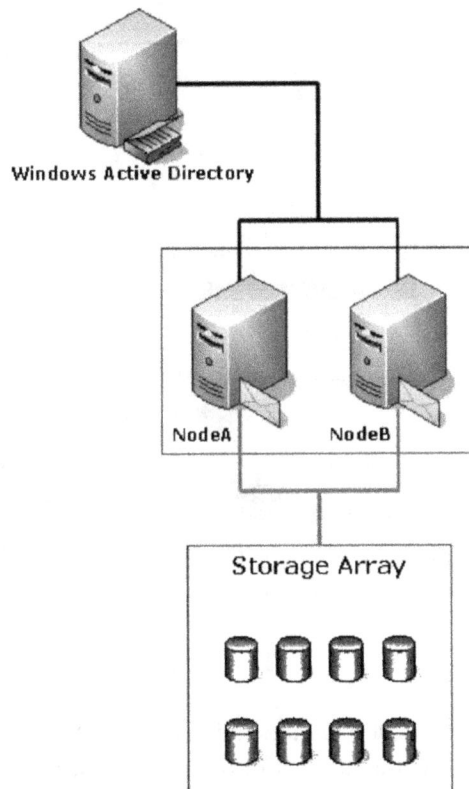

For this reason, and although the initial idea of all nodes of a cluster being active to run Microsoft Exchange was progress, Microsoft customers eventually backed off from the idea of having both nodes in a cluster being active for the simple reason that one could not really guarantee that the server would have less than 1,900 connections open at any point in time, unless you define a significantly lower number of mailboxes for each node of the cluster. For 1,900 connections, you would probably want to define 1,500 mailboxes and take into account the fact that a single client may open several connections to a cluster node for delegation purposes, calendar lookup during free/busy browsing, and so forth. The number of connections open on a given server can be monitored using the MSExchange IS\ Connection Count performance monitor counters, as shown in Figure 3.7.

Figure 3.7
Monitoring the number of open connections on a Microsoft Exchange server

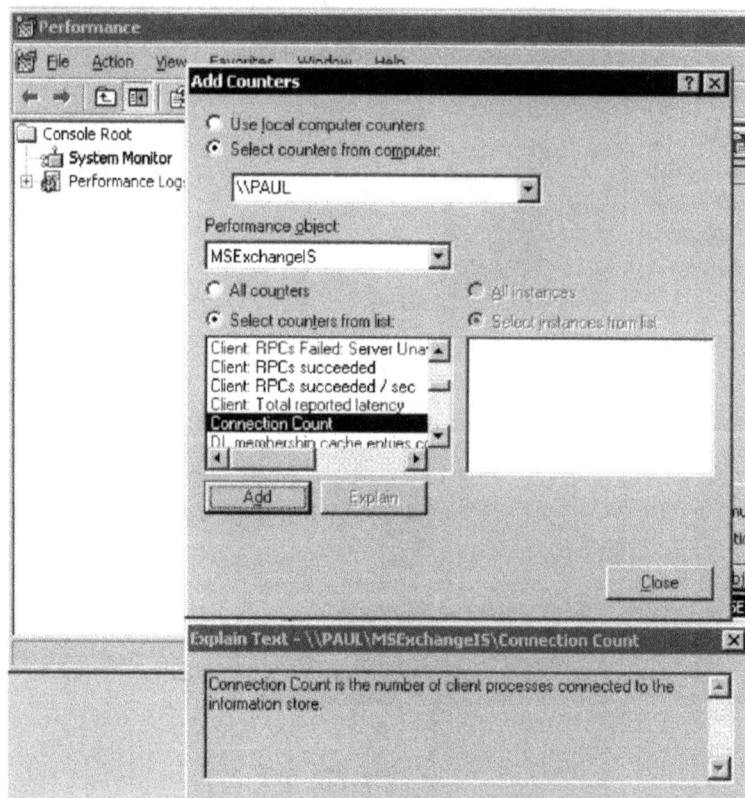

With Exchange 2003 (and included with the SP2 service pack), it is not possible to throttle the number of open connections. So you really have to bring the number of mailboxes well below what is defined on the server to fit the requirement of less than 1,900 connections per server.

Eventually, what our customers decided to do was to deploy an active/passive model for which there is no limit on the number of open connections for the failover and failback operations to satisfactorily happen (Figure 3.8).

Figure 3.8
Active/active and active/passive clusters

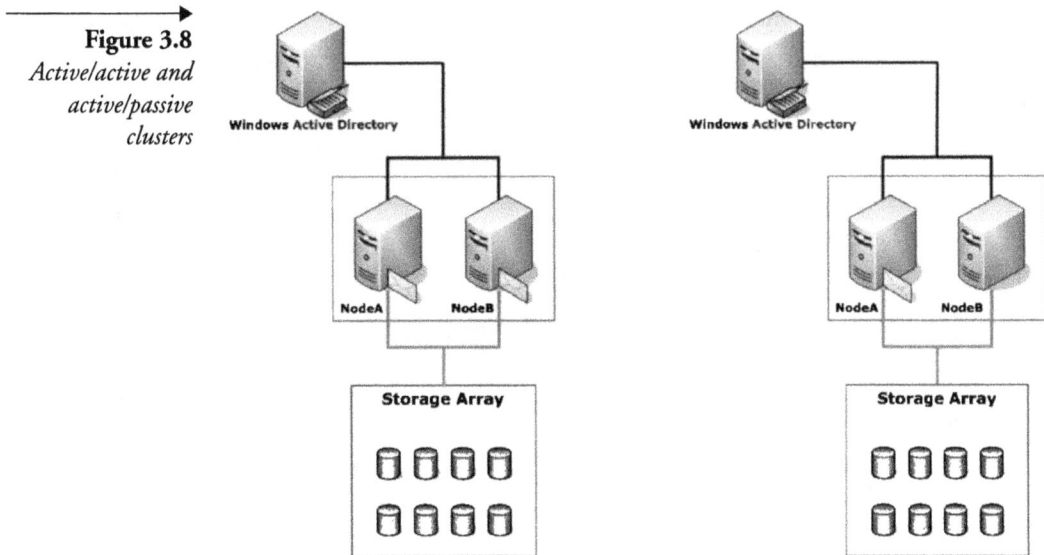

In the case of an active/passive cluster, both nodes have Microsoft Exchange installed, but only one of them is running an actual instance of Microsoft Exchange, often referred to as an Exchange virtual server. This Exchange virtual server is defined in the cluster administrator, by adding a resource of type *system attendant*, and it will take the name specified in the network name resource defined as a mandatory dependence when creating the system attendant resource type. In the following example, we have a three-node cluster, and the name of the virtual server in the Exchange organization is the parameter of the network name.

Windows Server 2003 Clustering

The release of Windows Server 2003 (and subsequent SP1) came with a number of significant features related to the deployment of Microsoft Exchange in scale-up environment. We shall review the main ones in this particular section.

Eight-Node Clustering

With Windows 2000 Advanced Server edition, you were limited to two-node clustering, and had to use the Data Center edition, delivered solely through an OEM such as HP, to be able to use four nodes in a cluster. The advantage of having more than two nodes in a cluster is the ability to operate in an active/passive mode (i.e., with at least one node available to host an Exchange virtual server instance, yet not running one actively) without "wasting" half of your computing resources.

We are now seeing models—typically labeled "N+M"—where N is the number of active nodes (i.e., with Microsoft Exchange installed and running an Exchange virtual server) and M is the number of passive nodes (i.e., with Microsoft Exchange installed but not actively running any Exchange virtual server).

Let's study the example in Figure 3.9:

Figure 3.9
A seven-node cluster

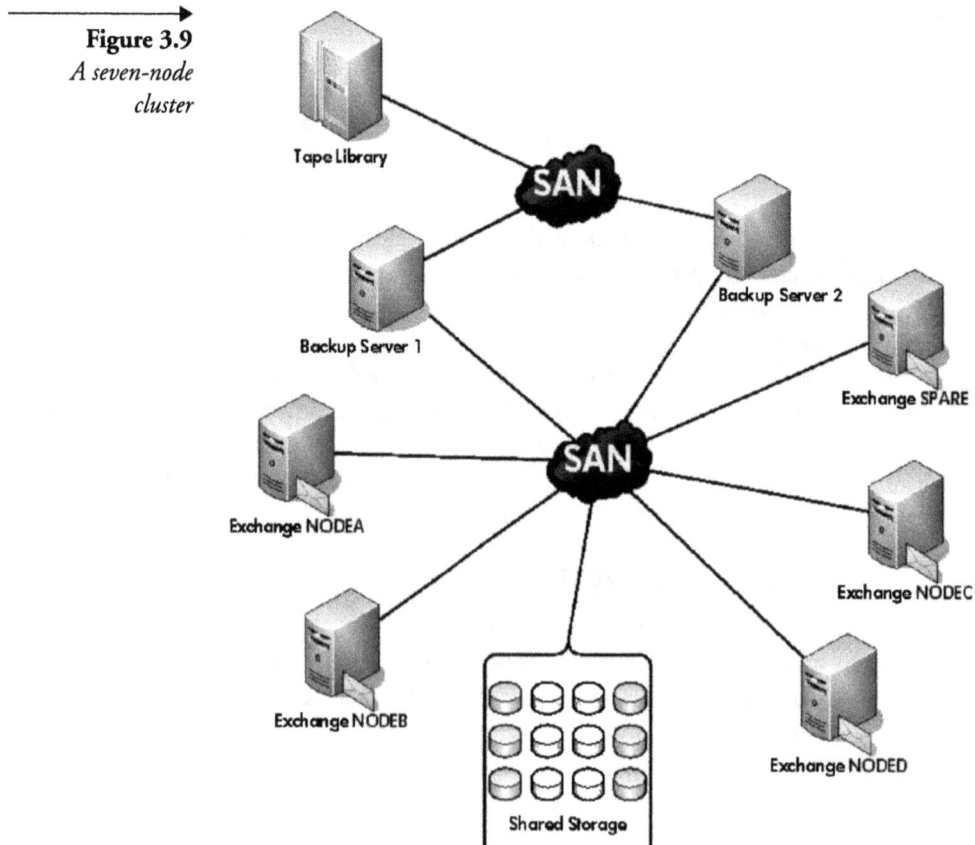

In this example, four nodes are active, and one node is left as spare (passive), ready to pick up the Exchange virtual server hosted on any of NODEA, NODEB, NODEC, or NODED. Two nodes are reserved for moving backup savesets from the cluster nodes up to a tape library. In such an environment, we have a 4+1 Microsoft Exchange cluster, with four active nodes and one passive node. When you think about it, you still have one node that is left inactive (as far as Microsoft Exchange is concerned), but that is only the equivalent of 25 percent of the active nodes, a much better overhead compared to the two-node scenario we discussed before, where you had a 100 percent overhead!

The eight-node clustering is a capability that Windows Server operating system has had for quite some time. I think the reason that Microsoft decided to "enable" it from the Enterprise Edition of Windows Server 2003 onward is that the interconnect technology that is required for connecting the servers to the shared storage enclosure has vastly improved. Five years ago, we were still stuck with bulky SCSI cables with rigid electrical specifications and fibre channel networks that were both expensive and subject to instability. In the meanwhile, this interconnect technology has evolved in two ways:

- Maturity: the fibre channel protocol has not been through any major technology improvements but has gained a lot in adoption from storage vendors, server vendors, and Microsoft, especially with Windows Server 2003 and the new storage driver model, which are much more adapted to fibre channel networks than the legacy ones.

- Affordability: the cost of switched fabric (i.e., fibre channel interconnect based on switching technology) has improved over the past years, while fibre channel infrastructure remains more expensive than equivalent (gigabit Ethernet) data network operations.

With Windows Server 2003, connecting eight nodes in a cluster does not require any particular hardware other than a solid/reliable fibre channel fabric back-end environment and fibre channel host bus adapters, while running the setup configuration of the Microsoft cluster service. A clear change in the adoption of clusters with Windows Server 2003 has been the fact that cluster software is now installed by default with Windows Server and simply needs to be enabled by executing the cluster administrator Create Cluster command, as shown in Figure 3.10.

Figure 3.10
*Creating a cluster
on a Windows
Server 2003 server*

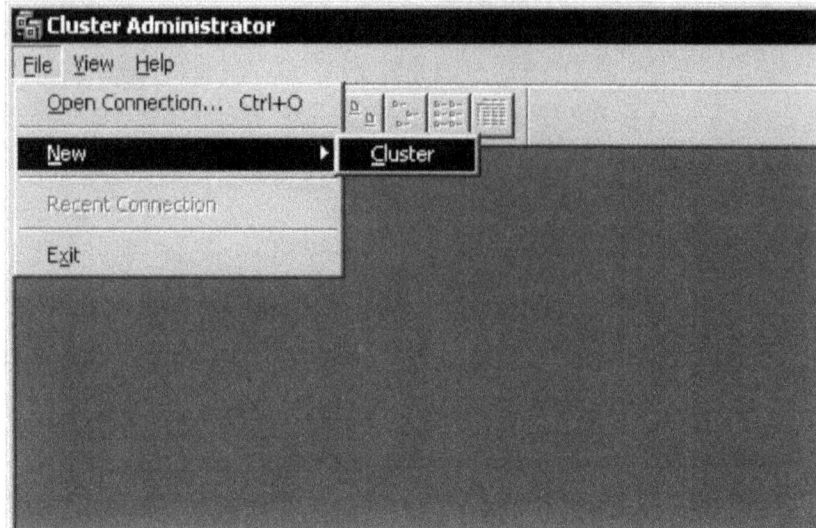

Mount Point Support

Only 24 letters can be allocated to disk drives on a Windows Server. If you wish to expose and uniquely identify a path to more than 24 logical units (A: and B: being reserved to removable drives), you can use mount points. Mount points enable you to "mount" a logical unit in an empty folder on a disk drive. You make the distinction between a regular folder and a mount point by the icons that they represent. From an application perspective, this is transparent and abstracted at the I/O subsystem level in the NT kernel.

The use of mount points in clusters has enabled us to define many more Exchange virtual servers than before, by the simple fact that we can use more logical units and have them uniquely defined in the cluster through the use of mount points.

Local Quorum and Majority Node Set

The addition of two new quorum methods, the local quorum and the majority node set, are quite important when building a highly redundant Microsoft Exchange infrastructure, especially across sites. The quorum, a cluster, is a resource that must be available for the cluster to be declared healthy. With Windows 2000 and earlier, the quorum resource is a disk unit (the quorum disk). With Windows Server 2003, you now have the ability to establish a quorum (i.e., declare the cluster to be healthy and operable in two additional means):

- Local quorum: you just need to have a locally attached disk where quorum information is stored, and that must be present. Local quorum is appropriate for any environment that does not have a storage interconnect. Local quorum is appropriate for lone-wolf clusters—in other words, single-node clusters.

- Majority node set: you need to have a majority of the nodes up and running the Microsoft cluster service for the cluster to be considered healthy and operable. This mode of quorum is only applicable for clusters that have three nodes or more and are appropriate in that you do not need to provision storage resources access to each of the nodes of the cluster. This method is particularly interesting for geographically dispersed clusters.

iSCSI-Based Cluster

This is the newbie in the list of enhancements of the clustering software in Windows Server 2003, which appeared with SP1 of Windows Server 2003. When using the Microsoft iSCSI Software Initiator, you can now build up to eight-node clusters. This is a significant improvement because as data networks evolved, iSCSI is becoming more and more a viable way of connecting a Windows Server to back-end storage networks in block-mode across a simple IP network. Of course, with the I/O workload that is typically demanded from Microsoft Exchange, you might hesitate to deploy storage networks over iSCSI rather than a fibre channel, which has proven itself in terms of high-performance transport.

SAN Boot Support

Although it was possible to build diskless servers in Windows 2000 clusters, the requirement was to use a separate fibre channel path to the boot units from the shared storage disk units. This required users to use 4 (2 × 2) HBA (Host Bus Adapter) for ensuring a redundant path to the data disks (first pair of HBA) and to the system disks (second pair). With Windows Server 2003 and the combined use of STORport drives, it is now possible to build clusters with diskless servers (i.e., servers that boot off the storage area network) and use the same data path for the system disks and the data disks in the cluster.

3.5   Scaling the Active Directory

There are two ways in which the Active Directory can scale: using a scale-up model, where you attempt to store a large number of objects in the Active

Directory, and using a scale-out model, where you try to deploy a large number of Active Directory domain controllers and servers. A combination of the two can be used by corporations that decide to have a global roll-out of the Active Directory, which results in gathering a large number of objects into a single forest (in separate domains, however) and a large number of domain controllers due to the presence of multiple sites.

Scale-Up the Active Directory

The scale-up of the Windows Active Directory service is typically achieved across two dimensions:

- Growing the number of objects in the Windows Active Directory;
- Diminishing the number of domain controllers and GC servers in the infrastructure: a single Windows Active Directory server would serve more client machines/Microsoft Exchange servers.

When I first worked on this book, we looked at growing the number of items in the Windows Active Directory by loading it with the U.S. phone book. It was a simple experience that consisted of adding as many contacts as possible and making observations on the scalability factor of the Windows Active Directory service. That corresponded to approximately 100 million objects stored into the directory. We found interesting things as the result of this experience:

1. The size of the database would grow in a linear fashion. That was of little surprise to us. The Active Directory database engine is a variant of the ESE (discussed in Chapter 1 of this book), which has proved in past versions of Exchange to scale quite well in capacity. The only issue with it is the single-file database model, but for most deployments that shouldn't provide too much of a problem.

2. The response time for a transaction would not grow with the size of the database. This is a very important aspect of the scalability of the Active Directory, and in general of any directory service, based on solid database technology. With 100 million objects, we found that for a given request, more time was spent in rendering the information for the user's browser than actually looking up

the query. Of course, that assumed that sufficient hardware resources were being provided to the directory service.

3. Replication could take a large amount of time. In fact, the replication, even on local connectivity network links (e.g., 100-Mbps Ethernet LAN), could take as many as 45 days of continuous processing to replicate data between two domain controllers.

The replication is, however, a very important feature of the directory because it provides multiple points of access to the authentication and directory lookup service.

The resulting infrastructure of an Active Directory will depend largely on the requirements placed by the environment and on the applications making use of the Directory, such as Microsoft Exchange 2000.

Scaling up an Active Directory server is in fact quite easy, provided you understand the technology implemented for the Active Directory. The main one is the database engine, ESENT. ESENT varies slightly from previous versions of the engine shipping with Exchange 5.5. One of the main differences is the page size, which is 8 KB instead of the usual 4-KB page size found in Exchange 5.5 and Exchange 200x. That doesn't much change the way you should configure the server, especially from a performance perspective. Check the performance section of Chapter 6, which describes the relevant aspects of server and storage configuration for ESE. In particular, it describes the access patterns to the storage volumes, an essential concept to understand for providing adequate services to the Active Directory database engine as well to the Exchange 2000 database engine.

For scaling up an Active Directory domain controller, you have to make sure that you have plenty of RAM available to allow database cache pages to grow significantly. With the roll-out of x64 processors (64-bit processors capable of running 32-bit native code), the best way to load a sufficiently large proportion of the database is to use the 64-bit version of Windows Server 2003 and use RAM based upon the following sizing:

512MB (for operating system + applications) + NTDS.DIT size

The other aspect is the processing power; authenticating a user or looking up entries in the directory can consume a fair amount of CPU resources. We found that L2 cache was definitely helpful for speeding up these operations: the frequency and the similarity of the authentication requests is such that local processor cache is most likely to contain the instructions required for these functions.

Nevertheless, even with the fastest processors, you definitely need to consider having large quantities of RAM (4 GB for a high-end domain controller to start with) to allow the database cache to be exercised as much as possible. Because there are several orders of magnitude in the completion of a transaction, depending on whether it goes to RAM (50–80 ns) or to disk (20 ms), maximizing RAM access is definitely key in speeding up the completion of the transaction.

Another difference from Exchange 5.5's use of the ESE engine for its mail messages is that the Active Directory will mostly read to the database.

We have observed approximately 90 percent read operations in the requests sent to the database volume by a domain controller. Now, you may decide to optimize your environment so those read operations can complete as fast as possible, and, as discussed in Chapter 6, this is achieved by using caching.

Cache everywhere is the key. Although it's relevant to a certain extent at the disk controller level, it is mostly important at the application level, which has a much better understanding of the pages it needs most and accesses them more frequently.

Typical specifications for a domain controller are summarized in Table 3.3.

Table 3.3   *Specifications of a High-End Domain Controller*

CPU	Intel Xeon—dual-3.2 GHz—2-MB L2 cache—800-MHz FSB
Memory	2 GB–4 GB depending upon NTDS.DIT size and workload
Disk 1	RAID1 for operating system
Disk 2	RAID1 for transaction logs
Disk 3	RAID5 array for database (NTDS.DIT)
Network	Dual-redundant 1-Gbps NIC

Given the access patterns of the Active Directory, RAID5 is a totally plausible choice, given that for an equal number of disks, it is as efficient as RAID0 or RAID0+1 for read operations. And since a large proportion of operations consist of READ, access to the NTDS.DIT, RAID5 seems like a natural choice. Of course, you should closely monitor the performance of your domain controllers or GCs to (a) establish a baseline of activity on the system, and (b) determine the trend in resource utilization.

For smaller domain controllers or GCs, you may trim on the L2 cache; try to have a reasonable amount of RAM since this will greatly speed up transaction processing by means of ESE database cache and reduce the number of drives. From a pure recoverability standpoint, it is always recommended to separate the transaction log files from the actual database—here the NTDS.DIT NTFS file. So you may have a lower specification server that fits this type of configuration, as described in Table 3.4.

Table 3.4   *Specifications for Low-End Domain Controllers*

CPU	Intel Xeon—single 3.0 GHz—1-MB L2 cache
Memory	1 GB–2 GB depending upon NTDS.DIT size and workload
Disk 1	RAID1 for operating system
Disk 2	RAID5 array for database (NTDS.DIT)
Network	Dual-redundant 1-Gbps NIC

One of the aspects is recoverability and service continuity, something often put under the general banner of service level agreements in an enterprise. The multimaster model of the Active Directory performs quite well in the most stringent environment that aims for great availability. In fact, it is one common approach to duplicate services for enabling high-availability.

The problem with the Active Directory in a scale-up model is that maintaining the actual synchronization between any two domain controllers, even on the same LAN, must be treated carefully. I believe that for relatively small directories, including less than 100,000 objects, you're probably OK with replication and can have two or three domain controllers continuously kept up to date. For large environments, such as the one we used for the 100-M object Active Directory, the replication employed by the Active Directory is insufficient to maintain service availability, and we had to resort to other techniques for data and service duplication.

First, we used highly protected storage; the databases are located on RAID0+1 volumes, which provide the highest levels of availability and performance (they do have a cost, however); with what we know of high-end storage today, we could have used RAID5 with the tolerance of perhaps slower database fill-up. The operating system and transaction log files are located on the RAID1 volume, all of them handled either by local controller (system volume) or in a storage area network that provides redundancy at all levels (path, controllers, disks, cache memory modules, fans, and, most important, power supply).

Second, because you can't rely on the replication mechanism of the Active Directory, we had to closely maintain the system, especially in the area of backups, and, most important, data recovery. Very often, in large computing environments, the backup window will cause some concern, but it is the speed and the agility of the data recovery that will eventually decide for most configurations.

Finally, we proceeded to perform the load with two domain controllers replicating to each other, such that we wouldn't have to generate a complete replication of the environment.

A point to consider is when replication in a high-end environment is likely to happen. One example is schema update: changing the schema in the Active Directory will generate a complete replication of all objects to all domain controllers and GCs. Because of this, we highly recommend deploying schema changes as early as possible in the deployment of the Windows 2000 forest, or, deploy Windows Server 2003, at least on domain controllers and GC servers.

If you plan to have Exchange 2003 running in your environment, you may hand over and have executed the necessary schema updates by running the Exchange 2003 setup program in Forest Preparation mode (SETUP.EXE /ForestPrep). This will cause the schema updates to be done without installing the actual Exchange 2003 server.

Another reason for doing this is that the schema in an Enterprise Directory is typically controlled by a restricted set of administrators, who are not necessarily the Exchange administrators. So you may let the schema administrators do the updates of the schema and let Exchange administrators do the Exchange 2000 organization and server deployment, without granting them additional rights to manage the schema. In conjunction with Forest-Prep, you will also need to prepare the domains in which Exchange 2003 servers will operate, and this can be done by running the setup program with the /DomainPrep switch.

Now, you may consider that not many organizations or businesses need scale-up Active Directory implementations. Well, I believe that this is a question of when rather than whether. The explosion of the demographics of the Internet, coupled with the connection of two worlds, the Internet and the wireless (mobile phone) worlds, will soon force providers to consider a much more extended user base than before. We already talk with telecommunications providers that require high levels of scalability, well beyond 10 million objects in an Active Directory.

A significant change with Exchange 2003 and Outlook 2003 cached mode suddenly raised the need for a consolidated Windows Active Directory deployment model, where you have *instances* of the Windows Active Directory service present to satisfy the workload demand from consolidated Microsoft Exchange servers. With Outlook 2003 in cached mode, you have the benefit of being relatively shielded from the conditions of the network. Today, many corporations and large deployments aim at consolidation of the Microsoft Exchange servers in two or perhaps three locations worldwide, hosting tens of thousands of mailboxes out of a single data center. In such context, there is opportunity for offering scaled-up Windows Active Directory services by the means of high-performance servers. Eventually, the use of 64-bit Windows Active Directory servers can really help in delivering the best performance with a low quantity of servers.

Scale-Out the Active Directory: Exchange 5.5 Directory Issues

As discussed previously, one of the key scalability issues in Exchange 5.5 was the replication model utilized for the directory service. As the number of sites grew, the number of messages exchanged on the intersite replication would grow as well, consuming precious bandwidth, from both the networking and the message transfer perspectives. The intersite replication in Exchange 5.5 called for two request messages per site: one for the site configuration-naming context and another for the site-naming context. For a 300-site Exchange network, this would result in 600 messages sent over the wire, with an expected 600 responses for these replication requests. The basic content of the request message is "I have a USN (Update Sequence Number) for these objects, give me the objects that have a USN higher than that." Even if there were no change in the object, the requests still had to be sent.

In a hub-and-spoke environment, each site would replicate from the hub site, and the hub site would be flooded by 600 requests each. Say you had 300 sites around the core site. This would turn into 180,000 message requests to be sent to the hub, with an equal number of responses to be sent back. Such a layout is shown, in smaller scale, in Figure 3.11. The advantage is that latency is reduced to its most simple form, a single hop, but the hub server (or servers) at the core site would have to bear the load of requests from multiple requesters. To avoid a sudden storm, one would need to properly schedule the directory replication connectors so that all requests would not come at the same time and that the replication would occur during off-peak hours. This definitely needs analysis and goes beyond

Figure 3.11
*Complete hub and
spoke*

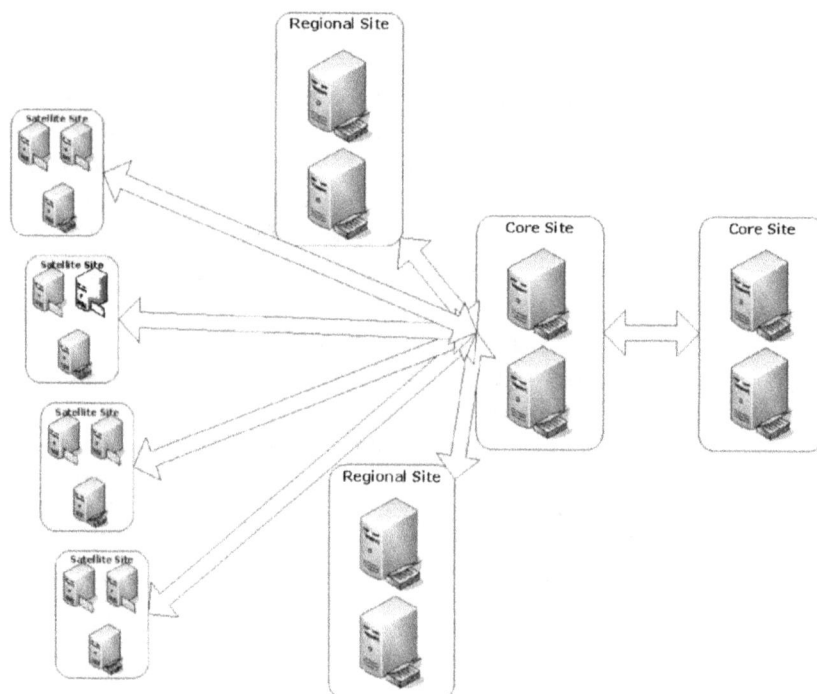

the default settings of the directory replication connector that comes with Exchange 5.5.

So this pushed the design limits of Exchange 5.5 and forced some customers to implement two or three stage models, by which a reduced number of sites would actually communicate with the hub, as shown in Figure 3.12.

Nevertheless, adding these extra layers builds latency into the replication environment, and that is something that may not be desired. Servers in tier 3 are now two hops away from the hub, and as many as four hops may be required to replicate directory information between two tier 3 servers.

Adding additional hops may not be so much of a problem, as long as the customer understands the implications. I have seen situations in which the customer asked for a maximum of three hours replication latency in an Exchange 5.5 environment, and given the number of sites (created from both network topology and political reasons) replication storms were likely to follow, which would result in clogging up the message transfer agent (MTA) machines, which in turned affected the delivery of higher priority messages, such as interpersonal mail messages.

Figure 3.12
Multitiered
replication model

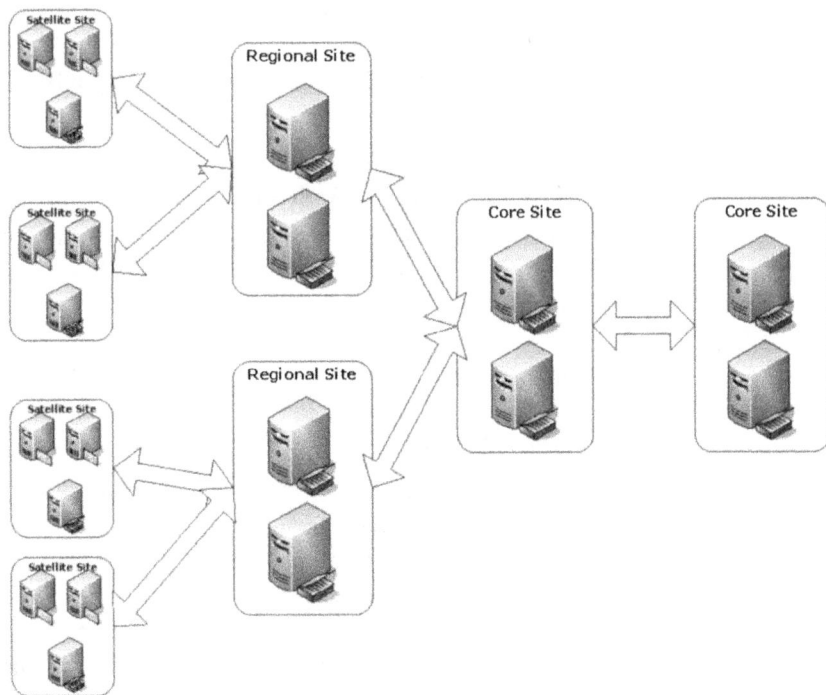

To alleviate these problems in an Exchange 5.5 environment in which mail-based intersite replication can possibly affect the delivery of regular mail messages, it is possible to purge the MTA from directory replication messages (which just means adding more latency in the replication of the directory, not necessarily causing severe inconsistency or corruption). The use of the MTACHECK command on a shutdown MTA was definitely helpful in resolving urgent situations.

Challenges

The challenges associated with the deployment of the Active Directory are very similar to what we used to have with Exchange 5.5 directories, compounded by the fact that you not only deploy a directory service for a messaging application, but, most important, you deliver a crucial portion of a suite of network services for your enterprise, which includes both the authentication and location services.

Active Directory brings a solution to many of the problems faced by administrators of Windows NT domains: trust relationship spaghettis and multiple (often uncontrolled) resource domains appear like mushrooms after a short rainfall in October. These are things that we have often seen, including within HP's own computing environment. Another thing that our company also experienced was the process of company acquisitions and bulk integration of a totally external computing infrastructure into an existing one (often the result being a totally new different infrastructure, which in fact, is not the worst approach).

With the Windows Active Directory, the replication model between sites is more optimized. First, in a general way, replication is attribute based as opposed to object based; it got further improved in Windows Server 2003 with the LVR, which replicates at the value level, useful for multivalue attributes, such as group membership information. So if you change the telephone number for a particular user entry, you don't need to replicate the entire user profile (as is the case in Exchange 5.5), just the particular attribute.

Second, the Active Directory sends request messages or issues RPC (Remote Procedure Call) requests per each naming context, but unlike in Exchange 5.5, the number of naming contexts, and therefore resulting requests, is much smaller. Typically you have to replicate the schema naming context, the configuration naming context, and then the domain naming context, which contains all the information about the user accounts, the computer accounts, and the distribution or security groups. No matter the number of sites in your Windows Active Directory infrastructure, you will need only three requests in a single domain environment for replicating the change.

The issue with Active Directory around the scale-out model is the work required by the knowledge consistency checker for actually doing its job of calculating the replication partners' connections. With Windows 2000, that has shown to be a scalability limit in the number of sites, domain controllers, and GCs that you could actually deploy.

By increasing the number of domains and sites, bridgehead servers, and domain controllers, you render the task of the knowledge consistency checker more difficult in actually determining a proper partner replication layout that is the most efficient. With Windows 2000, you cannot deploy more than 300 sites per domain. With Windows Server 2003, that limit was changed to more than 3,000 sites. Of course, you should ask yourself the question of whether having 3,000 sites is something manageable. In fact, for the Microsoft Exchange environment, the trend of consolidation has been such that this would hardly be the case. However, there are other considerations for the deployment of Windows Active Directory than just Microsoft Exchange, such as the requirements of authentication services, which may justify a large number of sites in highly distributed environments.

The Windows Active Directory replication is very important for Microsoft Exchange 200x; without a proper and usually a low latency–based replication environment, your Microsoft Exchange infrastructure will not work well (a message might be incorrectly routed because recipient information is not consistent for all recipients across the forest), and you will not be able to fully take advantage of the outstanding features of Exchange 2000.

The key thing to remember in deploying and managing Microsoft Exchange 2000 in large environments is that latency is everywhere. Whatever you may identify as a problem in the configuration or the product functionality, make sure that you understand where latency occurs in your environment and, most important, in your Windows Active Directory infrastructure, and be sure to take it into account. Tools from the Windows 2000 Support Tools, such as ADSIEDIT or REPLMON, can be handy to determine replication latency issues and can be used to force replication in emergency situations. In large environments, you may want to take advantage of advanced monitoring and supervision tools, such as Microsoft's MOM or HP's OpenView Operations for Windows (OVO) and the add-in components specific to the Windows Active Directory.

Common Models for Scaled-Out Active Directory Deployments

I would refer to scaled-out Active Directory deployments, those that include either a large (>50) number of sites or domains. The actual number of domain controllers or GCs is generally similar to or smaller than the existing Windows NT 4 Domain environment. But beyond those practical implementation considerations, there are geopolitical implications, such as the multiple administration groups that suddenly need to interact with each other or the highly distributed nature of the company (the classic example being a company with 2,500 branch offices connected over low-bandwidth, high-latency links).

With Windows NT, you could more or less push the model to accommodate these environments (separate domains with little or no trust relationship but limited functionality, especially for roaming users). With Exchange 5.5, you also had the option of the extremes: centralize into a single data center and rely upon network links quality for your quality of service, or distribute many Exchange servers in many locations. However, increasing the number of sites could lead to unbearable replication traffic, or many distant servers in a single site could result in RPC time-outs and failed message deliveries.

I found that most of these issues were actually solved with the Windows Active Directory and that many of our large customers went into implementing a placeholder root domain and one or more child domains, depending mostly on the chosen management model (centralized, decentralized, independent).

The placeholder domain does not need to be very big and typically consists of one or two small, reliable machines that host forestwide flexible single master operation (FSMO) roles, such as the schema master or the infrastructure master, and that's about it. That model works pretty well in a distributed conglomerate of different companies, because it creates a *zone-franche*, where a very small number of administrators have actual control over the full administration rights being delegated to *child* domains, each under a management model and staff and potentially as independent as if they were located in a separate forest.

There are still issues with the Windows Active Directory for forestwide operation, the main one being the schema changes. Changing the schema in the Active Directory is a big deal; it is not a reversible operation unless you operate in a Windows Server 2003 full-functionality mode, and it affects the entire directory (one of the side effects of the schema update is to trigger a complete replication of the directory to all domain controllers and GCs in the forest).

Scaling the Number of Sites

The existence of too many sites can raise the issue of having increased replication traffic between sites. We have found that for most large-scale deployments, the reasonable limit of sites was around 1,000 sites for a single forest, even though the Windows Server 2003 updates for the knowledge consistency checker and intersite topology generator (ITSG). As in Exchange 5.5, the recommendation is merely to avoid extremes and try to either concentrate a large number of small sites into a single data center location or have a reasonable number of sites that the knowledge consistency checker of the Active Directory could deal with.

The issue of a large number of sites lies very much with replication and is a two-edged sword; you need low-latency replication for Exchange configuration information to make sure that any change made can be replicated as fast as possible in order to reach the domain controllers used by the Microsoft Exchange servers. We consider 30 minutes to be about right for latency in a large distributed environment as far as the Exchange replication is concerned. However, there are parts of the Active Directory that do not require low latency, such as the domain-naming contexts that contain users, groups, printers, and computers. You may very well operate in an environment in which the change can take up to 24 hours to replicate to all the domain controllers and GCs of the infrastructure.

The replication of the Active Directory is essentially based on the sites and the naming contexts. The naming contexts themselves replicate differently depending on the target and source domain controller or GC.

The key points to remember are:

- The configuration naming context fully replicates to all domain controllers and GCs of the forest.

- The domain naming context fully replicates to all domain controllers and GCs that belong to the same domain.

- The domain naming context partially replicates to all GCs that belong to other domains.

Therefore to avoid replicating the entire set of attributes for all objects across all the forest, it would be to your advantage to split your forest into multiple domains.

The replication mechanism and its frequency for the Active Directory objects also depends upon the site topology. Within a particular site, the replication is occurring every five minutes (300 seconds); if a change occurs on a domain controller, that server will notify the replication partners (i.e., the other domain controllers and GCs) within the site every 300 seconds, notifying them that changes have occurred. It remains the responsibility of those replication partners to act on this notification and request changes to the notifying domain controller or GC. Three hundred seconds within a site may not sound like much, but it can be a very long period of time in certain environments. For example, with a service provider that provides a user-driven provisioning system, the user, after registering with the service provider, will want to access the newly created account well before the 300 seconds are over. You could always choose to insert the change into a specific domain controller, but that is generally a bad idea because your Exchange and application setup suddenly depend on specific servers or elements of the topology. The net result is to lose the benefits of multimaster replication and introduce single points of failure. If you really need to access the account in less than 300 seconds after its provisioning, you need to act upon the default intrasite notification interval so that the replication occurs much faster and allows the user to use the account well before 300 seconds elapse. An acceptable latency could be within 20 or 30 seconds after activation.

This is possible by changing the replication notification interval on all the domain controllers. This change, however, is not enabled by a user interface element, but rather by a change in the registry setting of the domain controllers and GCs part of the same site. This registry setting is documented in the Microsoft Knowledge Base under article number 214678.

You may wonder what the effect would be of changing this particular attribute to, say, 5 seconds. The challenge of a small change notification interval is that you get more frequent notifications to the domain controllers.

On the other hand, for each notification, you have fewer changes to carry over. In any case, the intrasite topology in Windows 2000 Active Directory *assumes* high-bandwidth, low-latency network connectivity (LAN-type). On the other hand, from a server processing perspective, very little is demanded upon the machine for each replication. From experience, we did not perceive an impact on the servers' performance by decreasing the notification interval from 300 seconds down to 5 seconds. With Windows Server 2003, this interval is decreased from 5 minutes to 15 seconds at most and 3 seconds if there is more than one replication partner in the site. The change suggested earlier therefore does not apply to the Windows Server 2003 environments. This is another example that shows how the improved hardware capabilities have enabled the improvement of the application throughput and the number of operations to be performed for maintaining a loosely consistent environment.

The intersite replication, however, occurs on WAN links, which can have characteristics such that too small an interval would have a negative impact on the bandwidth utilization. The actual utilization of the bandwidth and the impact of a low bandwidth—and possibly of a high latency—mostly depend on the changes made to the objects, the types of changes, and their frequency. The traffic, however, is largely predictable, and Microsoft has provided models that determine the quantity of data exchanged depending on the type of changes for the various types of objects (groups, computers, accounts, and the like).

While intrasite replication does not use compression (based on the assumption that any two domain controllers in the same site are in a LAN-type—100 Mbps, latency less than 10 ms—connectivity realm), intersite replication will compress data to save on the quantity of information exchanged during a replication between any two partners. By default, the intrasite replication will occur every 180 minutes (3 hours), and you may decide to change this replication interval, depending upon the level of change in the Windows Active Directory as well as the network interconnect characteristics between any two sites. Figure 3.13 shows how to change the replication characteristic of a given intersite link. The minimum replication interval is 15 (minutes); the maximum is 10,080 minutes (one week).

Figure 3.13
*Changing the
intersite replication
interval*

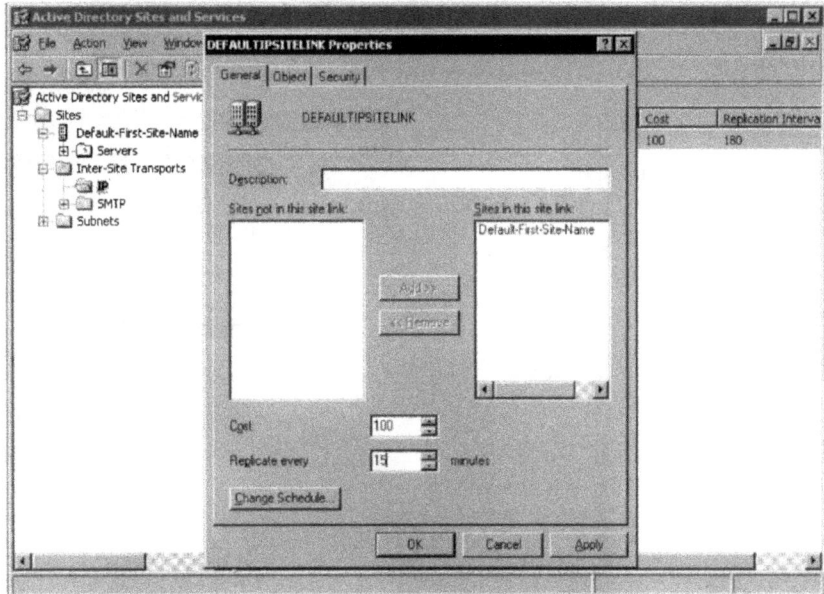

In addition, you may schedule this replication so that it does not occur during sensitive, mission-critical application needs. Still, as it has increasing importance for the infrastructure, the Active Directory should not be considered lightly, and an inconsistent Active Directory can cause many problems and help desk calls.

While you reduce network contention by displacing intersite replication, you also affect the replication of the Microsoft Exchange configuration data, and this can have a serious impact on the operations of the Microsoft Exchange servers, unless you decide to perform changes on remote domain controllers rather than on domain controllers close by the administration console.

By default, the Exchange System Manager snap-in will use a writeable domain controller within the same site of the administration station. However, in a large-scale environment, if you have a central operation center, you may want to define alternative Microsoft Exchange system management environments that directly connect to distant domain controllers close by the remote Microsoft Exchange servers. You can achieve this by creating a custom Exchange MMC console, and, when manually adding the Exchange System Manager snap-in, it will let you decide on the target domain controller, as shown in Figure 3.14.

Figure 3.14
Choosing a domain controller for ESM

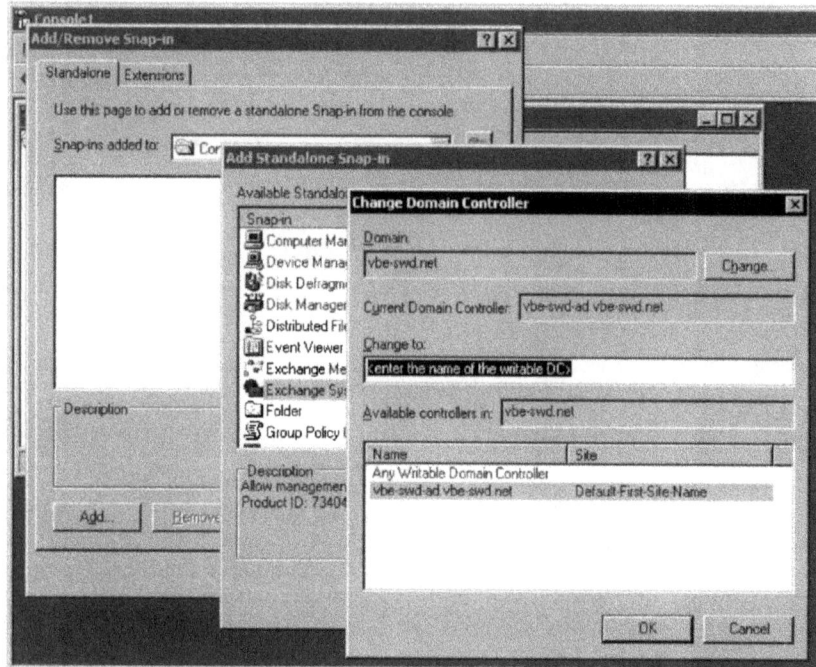

Intersite replication occurs typically over RPC links. It is possible to utilize SMTP transport for the intersite replication, but this will add some protocol overhead compared to the RPC connectivity method. Yet, in highly dissociated environments (e.g., a forest spanning across a WAN with unreliable links or nondirect connectivity—for example, with firewalls in between), SMTP can be a good method for replicating intersite changes.

Just bear in mind that intersite replication is not a complete replication for all objects of the forest; it fully replicates the schema and configuration naming contexts and partially replicates the domain-naming contexts for those domains in which the replication partner is not located.

3.6   Summary

The scalability of the Active Directory can be a very lengthy topic to cover, and in any large environment, it should be considered with care. I hope that now you have a good understanding of what is required to scale up the Active Directory (i.e., add a large number of objects inside a forest) as well as to scale out the Active Directory (i.e., have a large number of sites and domain controllers and GCs).

In any case, carefully plan your Active Directory and its topology in terms of sites. Don't attempt to map domains with sites. Site topology is what decides how complex the Active Directory replication will be and how much overhead it can have on the data network.

I found that those customers migrating from Exchange 5.5 to Windows 2000 and Exchange 2000 have a much better grasp on deciding how to place sites because the Active Directory replication model is quite close in principle (although much improved) to the Exchange 5.5 replication model. The net result can be a one-to-one mapping between Exchange 5.5 sites and future Windows 2000 sites. Moving further, the upgrade to Windows Server 2003 prior to touching to the Microsoft Exchange environment and performing the rollout of Exchange 2003 is considered very important for the features and improvements it brings in the replication of large environments. You can run Exchange 2003 on Windows 2000 infrastructure, and this will probably be OK for small environments but not the big ones.

The scale-up options of Windows Active Directory have significantly changed with the availability of a 64-bit version of Windows Server 2003. The 64-bit Windows did not get much traction when it could only run on Itanium processor family. However, with the general availability of x64 processor architectures (i.e., processors that are built on 64-bit instruction sets, registers, and data paths, yet that implement that 32-bit instruction set), we see a new opportunity for further consolidation of Windows Active Directory services, in harmony with the consolidation of Microsoft Exchange servers (yet with limited scale-up of Microsoft Exchange because it can only run in 32-bit Windows environments).

For a successful deployment of Windows 2000 and its key service, the Active Directory, it is critical to have clear and well-formed communication paths between the Windows architecture and deployment team and the Exchange architecture and deployment team. Failure to do this will result in faulty expectations on both sides and an undesired level of service from the Active Directory to Exchange 2000.

Storage networking has evolved so well that it is almost ubiquitous in any corporate environment. Windows Server 2003 builds upon this by proposing eight-node clustering from its Enterprise Edition. This is not the number of nodes we could have conceived in times where shared storage clustering could only be established with shared SCSI buses and strict electrical and physical limitations. With a revamped storage framework, Microsoft has brought its core operating system on par with storage networking and advanced volume management capabilities, and offers a platform that is ready to be exploited both by business applications, such as Microsoft Exchange, and by operational solutions, such as backup and recovery tools, that we study in subsequent chapters of this book.

4

Technologies for Exchange 2003 Deployments

4.1 Introduction

Data networks are certainly an essential part of the overall operations of an Exchange 2003 organization, but require less attention from Microsoft Exchange standpoint than three other crucial parts. The main one is the storage technologies. The other two relate more to the actual core server technology: the computing power and the physical memory appropriate for your servers.

More and more we are seeing a storage-centric approach to Exchange 2003 deployment, primarily due to the compelling aspect of Exchange 2003—its ability to handle in a more manageable manner (compared to Exchange 5.5) large quantities of data through the use of multiple databases per single server instances. Besides, the constant growth of information in mail environments, as they are used with richer content and more business activities poses a new kind of problem around retention capabilities, as well as managing data sets that often grow 80 percent year-over-year (although a 20 percent growth is a more conservative figure).

As you approach your deployment of Exchange 2003 and beyond, you need to freeze your vision of the technologies offered by the many vendors and make choices. These choices will always be a set of compromises, because nobody has a blank check to acquire hardware and technologies for their deployment, technologies continue to rapidly evolve. This chapter discusses elements that will enable you to make the most appropriate choice for your server components and to a larger scope, for your deployment. You must also realize that the choices that you make will have a certain lifetime: today, as we walk through deploying Exchange 2003, possibly migrating customers from Exchange 5.5, we realize that some choices made 2 or 3 years ago have become obsolete: it's not that they were wrong at the time they were made, just that technology evolution provides options. And I've yet to find a crystal ball or a magic wand that would nullify the efforts necessary for making such choices—avoiding extremes is a nice shortcut to all of them.

Server choice

Servers come in many forms and they may have different roles in an Exchange 2003 deployment. One of the primary goals is to protect your investment so that you don't need to "touch" these servers for a determined period of time, usually 24 to 48 months, as demanded by the business units that will fund your deployment and to whom you must justify the investments required in capital acquisition and operation cost. Nonetheless, nobody can actually develop a view of what will happen two to three years down the road. Microsoft and general IT providers make movements that can render obsolete a lot of the designs put forward. If you are into the mind-set of not tying yourselves to a particular technology (e.g., should I use Intel or AMD processors?), you can take a rather extreme approach to purchase a service (electronic messaging) instead of a server. Which approach is best depends a lot on the business rationale and model used for your IT environment. And one way or another, you will need to buy a server to run the service, whether you're a small, medium, large, or enterprise customer or simply an IT services provider.

Choosing a server involves going through several steps.

- First, you need to ensure that your server infrastructure can actually meet the expected immediate demand. Your growth rate might dictate certain attributes of the server infrastructure, such as scalability (up, out, or down). Often, you will find more appropriate means to meet the initial demand and gradually acquire additional components, with the goal that the hardware acquisition costs typically run down as time goes on.

- Then, you need to build some headroom, so you can accommodate your successful deployment as well as the increased usage of such a mission-critical application as electronic mail or collaboration. This headroom is specifically important for handling surge of the traffic found when a virus outbreak happens, or when your business rapidly grows.

   To do this, you may choose a server than can scale up to four processors but equip it with only one or two processors, thereby minimizing the actual cost of scaling up the server through the simple acquisition of additional processors. This means also to you that you must choose, beyond the platform, a server form-factor that can actually evolve. HP's ProLiant platforms are good examples of servers that can be delivered in two, four, or eight processors. The same holds true for computing platforms from other vendors. So before embarking onto a particular choice of server-based technology, understand the relevant factor and don't hesitate to ask your vendor for upgrade paths, which can rank from simple processor additions to complete server replacement. For instance, HP provides Intel or AMD based servers, scaling up to 32 processors; soft or hard partition enables you to vary the volume of computing power according to the volume of the demand, without increasing the number of servers.

- Finally, you need to determine how you wish to manage your server: we are not necessarily speaking about how to run Microsoft Windows Server, more on how you are going to manage the physical box.

- Determine a form-factor: computing capability can be delivered in many ways:

  - rack-mounted
  - pedestal
  - blade
  - virtual

Not all are appropriate for all scenarios; we shall expand on this topic later in this chapter.

The think time and study efforts can largely vary from one customer to another, but this short introduction shows that many solutions can answer a particular problem.

Typically, you will rank servers by ability to perform high-speed computation (clock speed) and host enough RAM for Microsoft Exchange. In general, large (5,000 mailboxes) back-end Microsoft Exchange servers are deployed with 4GB of RAM and 4 processors, while front-end and communication servers are using cheaper dual processor servers with 2GB of RAM.

Frankly, there will be little difference on that particular matter between one vendors or another. DELL, IBM, HP are examples of server providers that use relatively similar server chipsets and processors. These are known as "Industry Standard Servers," and are simply based on non-proprietary architectures from processor, memory, and interconnect viewpoints. Nonetheless, there can be significant variations that can affect the cost of ownership for a particular case.

4.1.1   Storage choice

This is a major undertaking, one that must not be underestimated. Storage in Microsoft Exchange deployments has to be designed right, because the service quality depends heavily upon it. Choosing storage goes far beyond the technologies that we present here. It ties to the fundamental service level objectives that the IT organization has defined.

For example, you might define a Recovery Time Objective (RTO) of less than 2 hours. This means that if something goes wrong with your service or with your storage, you have to be back up and running within 2 hours.

After your have defined the RTO, you need to identify your RPO (Recovery Point Objective). The RPO will define how old the recovery data should be, in case of the loss of the live storage databases.

In this section, we review storage technologies, and how they have evolved across time.

In the world of computer storage, trends indicate that controller (but not tape drives) transfer rates (MB/s) tend to increase and double every other year. For instance, we rapidly saw an evolution from the narrow SCSI-1 (10Mb/s) all the way to the UltraSCSI (320MBs) in terms of data rate increase for parallel transmissions. This was a plateau for the data rate until the electrical signals were serialized, enabling higher speeds with the SAS (Serial Attached SCSI) norm. This norm also enabled having far better connectors and physical implementations, compared to the bulky SCSI connectors.

Capacity (GB/foot^2) evolved in the same way, witness the current maximum capacity of 3.5 inches drives (500GB) and the capacity available on small form factor drives (60GB and growing). Request rates (I/O per sec), however, lag behind. Unfortunately, this is an area that was not given proper attention until Microsoft and several vendors could educate the customers in what the application demanded and what the storage components could deliver. While comparing two storage solutions between two vendors, you may see one vendor proposing twice as many disks as the other vendor for similar storage capacity. Don't just base your decision on number of drives (i.e., choosing the lowest number of highest capacity drives); that would be a mistake given Exchange 2003's need for fast and parallel transaction rates to the storage subsystem.

Carefully analyze your needs (either planned workloads or existing workloads based on your Exchange 5.5 infrastructure, if you have any), mention them to the hardware vendor, and let the vendor propose and demonstrate a solution to meet your needs.

These are two examples of choices that you will be confronted with, and many others will come up, undoubtedly. This chapter covers some of these critical technologies for Exchange 2003 and provides some useful recommendations. Nevertheless, even in your server and systems architecture model, you will need to justify the need for what you plan to acquire upfront and proactively make sure that you make the best use of the technology that the financial department and the business units let you acquire.

This proactive monitoring can be done by the means of third-party tools or by simply using Windows Server out-of-the-box utilities such as SysMon or PerfMon, and proper analysis of meaningful data. This aspect is covered later on in the book.

4.2 System Processing

Above all, technology has evolved in an unbalanced manner over time. Certainly computing processing is following Moore's law, and doubles almost every 18 months; 2005 brought more on this trend with the introduction of dual-core processors, and we are now looking at quad-core processors being delivered from the key industry players that Intel and AMD are. Exchange 2003 is a great application for taking advantage of processing capabilities, being used with either fast processors or multiple processors, or processors with advanced parallelism.

Among deployments already observed, the sweet spot for Exchange 2003 was in 4-processor systems. Scaling up (i.e., adding more processing capability) often does not help due to the overhead of context switches and contention at the system bus level. From a system processing viewpoint and for Exchange 2003 in particular, I propose you review some of the key system components and attributes, such that you can actually realize which of these technologies matter to Microsoft Exchange.

4.2.1 Systems architectures: Processors and buses

Microsoft Exchange 2003 largely benefits from the increasing speed of processors provided by Intel and other chip manufacturers such as AMD. Across the years, the "megahertz war" transformed into a "gigahertz war." As found often in desktop computing, you will benefit from fast clock rates. However, there are variants in industry standard processor architectures that offer better improvement than just a high core processor clock rate. Today, industry standard processors, provided, for the majority, by Intel and AMD come with varying attributes beyond the simple clock rate (the GHz figure), which include inner components such as cache, hyper-threading, inner and outer clock rates, and addressing/computing capabilities (32-bit vs. 64-bit). One particular advantage of processors that run slower is that they demand less power and as a result, dissipate less heat, significantly decreasing the cooling requirements for the computing platform and environment.

Beyond the processor, which you might consider as a black-box, you need to understand how well does the processor communicate with the outer parts of the core server and motherboard that equips a server. These parts include:

- memory bus
- network and storage interfaces (I/O)
- peer-processor communication

This point is critical to understand, because no matter how fast a processor can execute instructions, if the data does not come in and out fast enough, all you obtain is an idle computing system that keeps on waiting on slow interfaces. The objective, therefore, does not only consist in using powerful computing units, it also aims at providing data fast enough to keep the CPU busy.

For example, processors can operate beyond 3-GHz, based on a system bus architecture that operates four times as fast as the current system buses that normally operate between 400 MHz and 533 MHz. Furthermore, newer system models take advantage of PCI-Express, a serial evolution from the PCI/PCI-X parallel architecture. This brings a new standard for high-speed bus access, joining the more traditional PCI/PCI-X and AGP bus technologies together into a much faster transport, and opening the opportunity to advanced CPU communication, possibly amongst other peer CPU.

Initially co-founded between Intel and Dell, PCI-Express has an opportunity for scaling-up architectures that use PCI-Express serial interconnect for gathering several 2-way or 4-way servers; the catch is how well the underlying operating system can take advantage of this underlying capability, and eventually, the application.

Figure 4.1 shows a flow diagram of data and basic components interaction of an industry standard server. Each of these components can indeed operate at varying clock speeds. Although a single component of the motherboard will actually generate the overall clock, each subcomponent (CPU, Front-Side Bus, System Bus, Memory and PCI/PCI-X bus) will operate at a fraction or a multiple of this motherboard clock rate (a CPU might even operate at varying clock rates, depending on the CPU region). A classic hack for home computing is to rev up the motherboard clock rate, with various side effects, one being to improve the overall system performance, another to get a chance to fry eggs on the computer chips, and eventually burn them.

Figure 4.1
Multiple Clock Rates

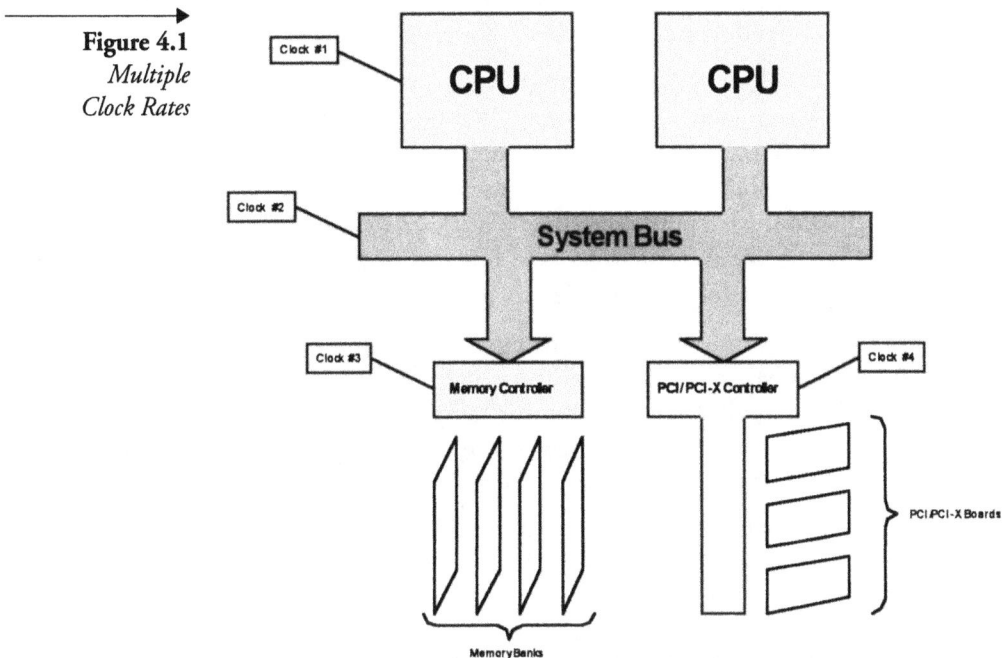

Figure 4.1 tends to show that even if the clock rate of a CPU is very high, if the clock rate of the memory controller or of the PCI/PCI-X controller and interfaces are not "on par," the resulting throughput of system would not necessarily be optimal. Fortunately, vendors balance their configuration such that a 3GHz processor chip does not communicate with a 100-MHz Front-Side Bus. However, there are subtle differences between two 400-MHz and 533-MHz Front-Side Buses that can result in a much improved (15 percent to 20 percent) transaction throughput when considering a Microsoft Exchange workload.

Modern server diagnostic tools will tell you how to identify a potential bottleneck: a bogus PCI adapter may, for instance, saturate the PCI controller with too many interrupts, turning into a higher CPU interrupt rate, and resulting in the CPU being busy servicing the interrupts rather than executing user-mode code (i.e., the application, in our case, Microsoft Exchange).

Basic configuration guidelines aim at using similar clock rates for every component behind a controller: avoid mixing PCI adapters that operate at different clock rates, as the overall PCI controller will downgrade to the lowest capable rate. This holds true for memory banks, although, in the server space, one will tend to use vendor-provided memory cards which are certified and avoid any kind of incompatibility that might lead to significant performance degradation (or even worse: data corruption!).

While this sounds shocking to you, the reader, the objective in your configuration will be to run CPU-bound: a 20 percent CPU utilization is NOT necessarily a good sign of a healthy server. First, it means the processor was idle for 80% of the time. Ask yourself: why was my processor idle? Did it have nothing to do? Was it *waiting* on data to come for being processed? Was it *interrupted* too often, having to switch from execution mode and therefore report little user mode utilization?

It is only by the time that greater quantities of data are available at hand that Microsoft Exchange can benefit from core CPU compute power. Otherwise, all it does is allow for the processor to go faster to an I/O breakpoint that will need response from more or less fast devices (memory, network, disks).

In the monitoring chapter of this book, I will provide you with performance counters that let you determine what the processor is doing, or, more precisely, what it is not doing and why.

4.2.2   Single Core, Hyper-Threading or Dual-Core?

The most notable evolution that will hit server-side computing is the dual-core technology, which, by the time of publication of this book, will become widely available: building upon the wide adoption of Intel's Hyper-Threading, the industry is moving towards providing two processors within one die. I would not be surprised if the "dual-core" processing term was replaced by the "multi-core" term. The dual-core processing principle is very straightforward: instead of using a single processing unit, which could look like two processing units, each processor die contains two physical processors. From a server-vendor perspective, this can be a rather simple move: AMD, for instance, was smart enough to provide their dual-core processors with the same pin count as the single-core processors: the net result is an upgrade path which only requires a BIOS upgrade, not even requiring a server change.

Of course, an interesting point is how this affects the per-processor model of application licensing.

Single Core

If you have been running Microsoft Exchange for quite some time, there is a good chance that you are using a single core processor, composed of:

- a computation unit known as the ALU: Arithmetic Logic Unit

- a variable number of registers (such as the Program Counter that contains the address of the execution being executed) which typically hold 32- or 64-bit of information

- a series of flags that can be used to indicate if/when something important has happened (e.g., an external board wants to communicate buffered data to the processor)

- cache, which is a very fast memory typically embedded in the processor, although the cache now tends to break down into several levels (typically 3, depending on how "far" they are from the processor)

- buses: internal or external, they are used for communication between the processing unit and the outer parts of the system, sometimes not that far away, such as the RAM or ROM, sometimes much farther, such as the network interface card, or perhaps, some other processors

- some optional components, such as floating point units, can be found for assisting the processor in performing its operations. Some very old computers (at least to me) used to have a separate co-processor for floating point operations. Note that Intel did introduce more that just FPU in their x86 processors series, with for instance, the MMX instruction set, which allowed performing multimedia operations. This instruction set is actually relevant for Exchange 2003 SP1.

In a single core processor, there typically is only one instruction being executed at the rate of the lock tick. The executions are actually coming from the operating system which runs each process or threads and the scheduling component that submits them for computation.

The notion of pipelining was introduced in the early 90's for single core processors, and it enables them to start/execute several instructions at the same time, "anticipating" one instruction result to generate the next one. Depending on processor architectures, there can be 2, 4, or even 8 instruction pipelines. The processor clock speed can be slower, yet more work is done at the same time.

The challenge with pipelining at the processor level is that this parallelism only works to a certain extent. Executing a line of code as a series of CPU instruction might require the result of previous instructions—if the previous instruction is in another pipeline, the current pipeline needs to stall and wait for the instruction results it depends upon.

As a short conclusion, single-core processing, even when enhanced with pipelining, does require faster clock rates for faster instruction execution (i.e., the ability to process more instructions per second). A 3-GHz single core processor will be faster than a 2.5-GHz processor. This is in fact quite simple when making a server's CPU choice. However, this is not the end of it, if you read on into this section.

Hyper-Threading

Put simply, hyper-threading was built to bring the level of parallelism of execution back to the operating system: a single core processor would present two CPU architectural states, and Windows, in our case, suddenly sees two processors instead of one. The scheduler, component of the operating system that submits threads for execution, can execute two parallel threads at the same time, instead of one, and this for each processor. Hence, when you enable hyper-threading on a CPU, you obtain twice as many CPUs as are actually implemented on the motherboard. There are several advantages of using hyper-threading with Microsoft Exchange. First, Microsoft Exchange is a threaded application by nature: each connection, RPC requests, client connection is typically handled as a separate thread execution. The ability to compute several threads at the same time is therefore fully exploitable with Microsoft Exchange. Secondly, from a server manufacturer viewpoint, you do not really need to modify your core motherboard and CPU interconnect architecture: in a single-core processor with hyper-threading enable, you still have the same physical topology in terms of bus, memory access, interrupt signals, etc.. The only difference is that while a processor might be only 65 percent busy executing one instruction from one thread, it can now use more of its resources for executing the instructions of two independent scheduled threads from the operating system, yet not requiring twice as much of system bus and bridges and CPU interconnect.

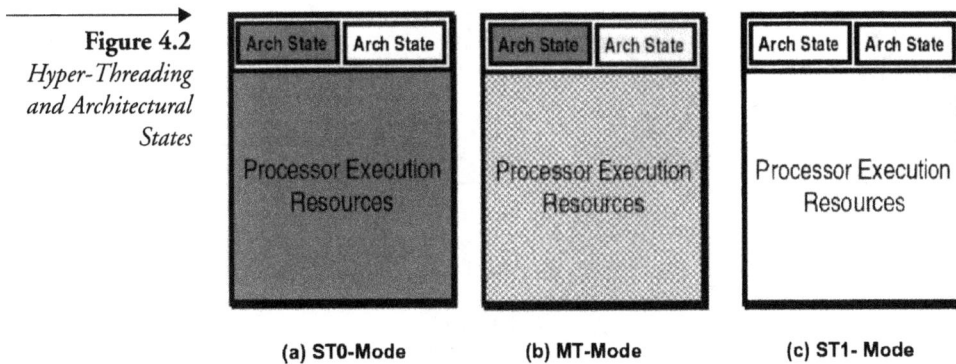

Figure 4.2
Hyper-Threading and Architectural States

(a) ST0-Mode   (b) MT-Mode   (c) ST1- Mode

Figure 4.2 shows how a hyper-threaded processor (b) can share more of its internal resources by presenting the equivalent of two independent processors (a) and (c).

Hyper-threading is typically enabled by a non-volatile BIOS setting at the server level. The challenge becomes in licensing terms when you consider that the Microsoft Windows operating system is limited in terms of processors it can use based upon the edition. While Windows Server 2003 knows the difference between physical and logical processors, Windows 2000 will only grab the first processors it is licensed for, logical or physical. From a licensing viewpoint, this is a significant difference, since not all Microsoft Exchange servers are deployed using Windows Server 2003 Enterprise Edition!

Now, improving the clock speed and the parallelism of instruction execution is not left without consequences. Figure 4.3 shows that if a physical processor now presents twice as many CPU states as before, it must be ready to pump data in and out twice as fast.

If the Front-Side Bus, used for the main external communication of the physical processor, is not fast enough, you might have increased your ability to compute twice as much data, but you run the risk of not having twice as much data to process. In fact, we have found, during benchmarking (therefore rather specific workloads) of Microsoft Exchange, that memory latency was a key factor in the CPU burn rate: in other words, as we strive to turn Microsoft Exchange into a CPU-bound application and deliver a greater transaction throughput at a lower response time, the latency of the memory cards (50ns to 70ns) and the memory bus speed was in fact more important than the processor clock rate!

Benchmarking has shown that hyper-threading could bring 25 percent or more of better CPU utilization in a Microsoft Exchange environment.

Figure 4.3
*Front-Side Bus: A
Possible Point of
Contention?*

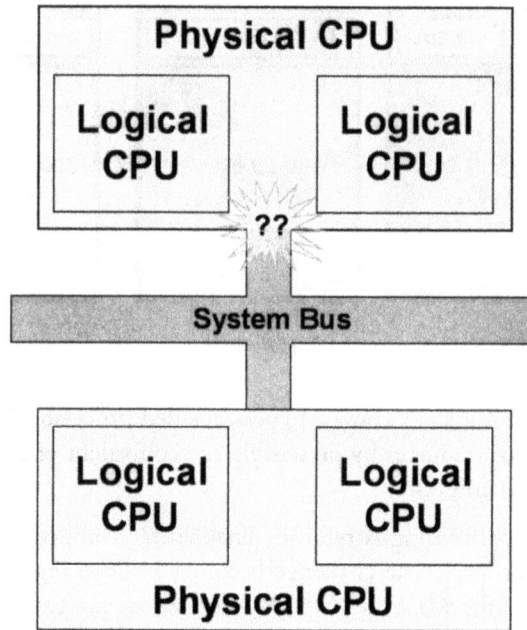

This, however, is not necessarily true for all applications. For instance, an application which does not have many threads to execute in parallel, or which has lots of dependencies between the threads, might not benefit from sharing inner CPU resources. Today, we can safely confirm that Exchange 2003 benefits from enabling hyper-threading—this is the first tuning tip you may actually use for optimizing your server configuration. For the rest, experience and workload characterization in production environment can be the most deterministic approach, although we can expect vendors to benchmarks their servers and report accordingly.

Dual-Core, Multi-Core

When hyper-threading demonstrated that there was efficiency in paralleliz-ing instruction execution by involving (cheating?) the operating system, then came the notion of instead of pretending to be two processors, a CPU could actually embed two processing units, distinct, with (inner-die) com-munication systems yet sharing the same Front-Side Bus and external pro-cessor communication paths, as in hyper-threading. This is the principal of dual-core. AMD, for instance, designed the Opteron processor with the dual-core concept right from the beginning. So the idea is to have a very fast communication path called the HyperTransport inside the die, let the die have the same physical and electrical characteristics as a single processor, and double the experience of the operating system by including two processors on one socket. In fact, although HyperTransport was really designed for multiprocessor communication, it became relevant for dual-core and further on, multi-core. We come back on HyperTransport later in section 4.2.5 when discussing SMP. HP and IBM have developed (separately though!) motherboard and chip architectures that provide close-to dual-core architectures for Itanium machines, by fitting two processors on a single processor socket: the motherboard is the same, yet, the processor unit is composed of two distinct CPUs. In these architectures (HP mx2 processor in the HP Integrity rx4640-8), clock speed has to be decreased for thermal reasons. This latter point is key for new server architectures: to diminish power consumption and cooling requirements, clock rates are now being decreased in favor of multi-core processors. Dual-core and Quad-core processors are just a beginning: expect to see more coming in the next 5 years.

Now What?

The idea I wanted to carry along here is that processor execution speed is not a direct factor of the megacycles or megahertz quoted on the die. In fact, between any two industry-standard vendors' machine configurations, the utilization of hyper-threading, dual-core, or even different processor models (e.g., Xeon vs. XeonMP) does affect the machine's transaction throughput capability. Don't get overly excited by new technology and carefully weigh the total cost of the server, but at this point, it becomes very important for you to not regard the machine with the faster clock as being faster.

A simple analogy can be made: when driving on a motorway subject to a 75 km/h speed limit, you can transport many more cars if you have eight lanes than if you were to drive on a two lane motorway with a 120 km/h speed limit. Now, for this to be true, you need to have many cars to transport. If you only have two cars, they will hardly need the eight lanes. In the case of Microsoft Exchange, we are dealing with jam-like traffic: the multi-threading nature of the application, plus the necessity for computation that even goes beyond Exchange, such as anti-virus checking, does create more traffic. I will come back with this analogy when discussing its limits.

4.2.3 L1, L2, and L3 cache

An important attribute of a CPU is the quantity of cache it can dispose of. Physically different from the cache that is typically used in storage subsystems, the processor cache fulfills a similar function: provides a somewhat smaller area of memory with significantly faster access time and clock rate. L1 is known as the primary cache and is embedded in the processor die (chip). The cache may be used for instructions, data or both; some processors, such as Intel's Celeron, have two separate primary cache areas inside the processor.

Cache is like general RAM: it is dynamic (volatile), yet comes directly attached to the processor and in rather small quantities for the primary (L1), secondary (L2), and tertiary (L3) cache modules. These modules are typically integrated in the processor die, and some server vendors, such as HP or IBM, do propose an additional cache (L4) separate from the die.

The idea is to prevent the processor from reaching to RAM through the Front-Side Bus and memory controllers: this is particularly useful in multi-processor environments (4 to 8 physical processors), such that you can prevent FSB/system bus saturation by having fewer processors that reach out to the common and shared physical memory.

This consideration typically applies to Symmetric Multi-Processing (SMP), and not so much to Non-Uniform Memory Access (NUMA) mechanisms.

Processors with larger cache are more expensive than others, and, while they do bring an advantage after performance benchmarking of Microsoft Exchange, there is no real requirement for using the processors with the largest L1, L2, and L3 cache combination for getting the best scalability: your limits will be reached by other attributes of the server, such as the quantity of data attached to it (disks and databases).

Unlike L1 (primary) cache, L2, and L3 cache vary in size (>2 MB, 32 MB to 64 MB for 64-bit Itanium architectures).

The closer to the CPU, the faster will be the memory access, either by the means of higher clock speed or lower latency or a combination of both; in all cases, these cache modules are faster than the main RAM of the server (see Figure 4.4), primarily because they do not reside on the main system bus.

The objectives of cache modules fit well for Microsoft Exchange; note that you may not "upgrade" a motherboard L2 or L3 cache: this typically requires a processor/server upgrade. While L3 cache tends to replace the legacy definition of the L2 cache, L2 cache itself gets closer to the processor in terms of access speed (core processor clock rate) and bus bandwidth, while L3 cache comes as a last resort before accessing the RAM through the system bus.

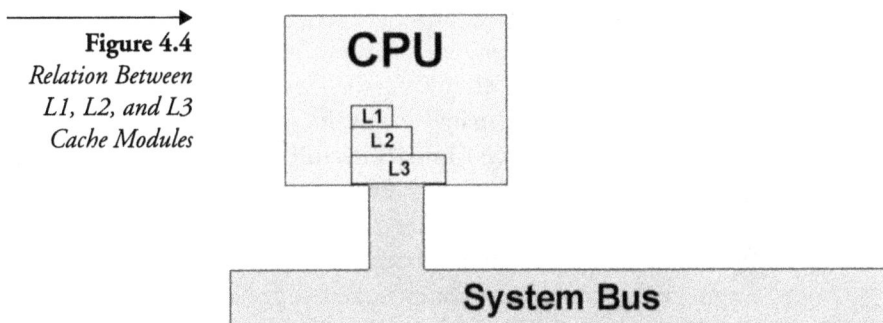

Figure 4.4
*Relation Between
L1, L2, and L3
Cache Modules*

Of course, the benefit of the cache will largely depend upon the likelihood of getting a "cache-hit," i.e., for the processor to execute a cached instruction or use cached data—remember also that a thread execution (context) held at one point by a processor, might be scheduled on another processor for its next quantum of execution: this results in the cache not being as useful because of the general distribution of threads across several processors. In short, the largest is not necessarily delivering the best performance improvement, and probably not in the scale of the additional cost. While large L2/L3 cache is considered valuable for 4-way and above multi-processing architectures, its value decreases for dual-processor servers, and unless you can confine application threads' execution to a defined set of processors (by the means of *processor affinity*), there is little benefit in using the largest cache sizes.

4.2.4 32-bit vs. 64-bit

There is a significant shift happening in the processor architecture with the migration from 32-bit to 64-bit processor and operating systems architectures. The idea behind this shift is simple: instead of using address and registers of 32-bits, the processor uses 64-bits: the address space is largely increased, enabling it to build servers that contain large quantities of RAM, which in turn, can cache part or all of the contents of a database. With data at hand, this is the most likely way that our processors will eventually turn CPU-bound, i.e., not having to wait on I/O for completing application thread execution.

Moving to 64-bit is no easy task for Microsoft Exchange. For simple applications, this means regenerating binary code from source. For more complex applications, and especially in the case of Microsoft Exchange, there is a legacy of components and internetworking that must be validated. Besides, 32-bit processors, so far, have provided ample computing power for most of Microsoft Exchange deployments. But the move to 64-bit is ineluctable, and this is something we will eventually see. In the meanwhile, AMD, and later, Intel, have been touting the idea of building a 64-bit processor architecture that could natively execute 32-bit code. This has the major advantage in adopting a 64-bit architecture and getting early benefits (you double the width of the highway), even if the application is not 64-bit enabled. Running natively is extremely important for performance purposes. When Digital Equipment Corporation introduced the 64-bit Alpha chip, customers that could not recompile their code had the option of running inside an emulator (FX!32) that would not provide the incremental performance that one could hope from such advanced processors.

The same is valid for Intel's 64-bit Itanium Processor Family: to be supported by Microsoft Exchange, it does require the application to be recompiled and the WOW64 mode (Windows on Windows 64-bit) is not supported by Microsoft for a business application such as Microsoft Exchange.

With the Opteron processor, however, AMD provided a way to use the high-speed of the processor and technology advances in SMP, without having to wait for a native 64-bit version of the operating system and of the application. We therefore are confronted nowadays with machines which are 64-bit capable, an operating system that can run either in 32-bit or 64-bit mode and an application that can only run in 32-bit mode. Although the processor architecture is 64-bit, we typically refer to these environments as "x64 extensions" or a variant, depending upon the vendor:

- EM64T (Intel)
- AMD64 (AMD)
- X64 (Microsoft)

You may then execute in three distinct modes:

- legacy mode (32-bit Windows and 32-bit Microsoft Exchange)
- compatibility mode (64-bit Windows and 32-bit Microsoft Exchange)
- native mode (64-bit Windows and 64-bit Microsoft Exchange)

Until Microsoft makes Exchange available in native 64-bit, your option should be to execute in legacy mode, i.e., using 64-bit processors and booting 32-bit Windows Server 2003. Although both Intel and AMD are the main providers of such technology, their implementation differs quite significantly: Intel is staying on a shared memory bus principle, while AMD moved into a NUMA-like architecture, with each processor having memory locally attached (Figure 4.5).

Figure 4.5
NUMA-Like
Memory Access

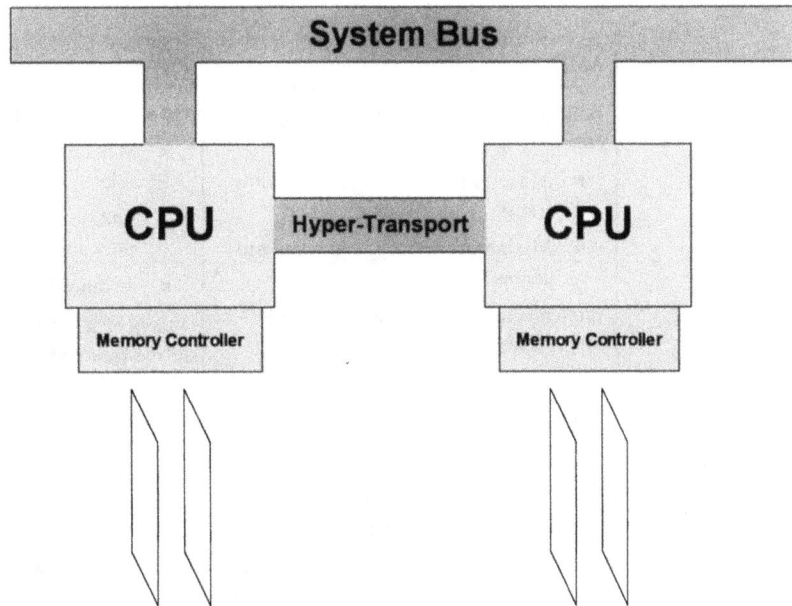

We refer to NUMA-like architecture because memory is not uniformly shared and accessed between all processors: it is locally attached to a single processor, and if one processor needs to address an area of physical memory owned by another processor, it must query and transit through the special communication channel known as "HyperTransport." You might consider that this is creating additional work to the processors compared to a shared memory infrastructure such as in Figure 4.6.

Figure 4.6
Shared
and Uniform
Memory Access

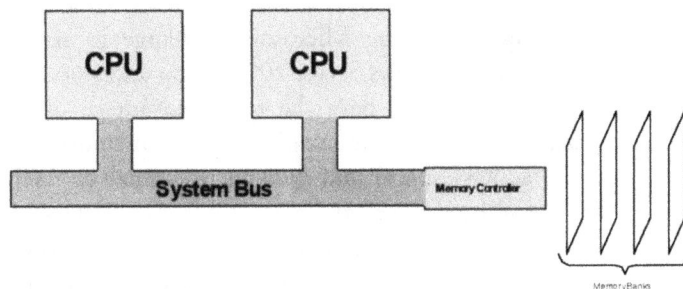

This is correct, however, the HyperTransport operates as core CPU clock speed, while the Memory Controller (also known as the North Bridge) operates at significantly lower speeds (although increasing from 400-MHz to 800-MHz for the newest Intel "Nocona" processors).

The following table provides a small comparison between the two approaches:

AMD	Intel
Built-in memory controller running at core CPU speed ■ AECC is the only High-Availability feature ■ Maximum memory requires all processors installed Implementation of industry-standard HyperTransport	External Northbridge chipset ■ Maximum memory is readily available ■ Additional hops at ASIC (not CPU) clock speed ■ Advanced memory protection Shared FSB limits bandwidth and increases latency

Both have therefore their advantages and inconveniences, depending of the target environment you envisage. For a long time, in 2004, Exchange 2003's best benchmarks were obtained on AMD Opteron's class machine, because of their ability to decrease the physical memory latency. This was not due to the ability of using the 64-bit address space (which is about 18 billion GB), because the tests were run against Windows 2003 32-bit in legacy mode, but just by the low latency and wide system buses that you can find in 64-bit servers.

In reality, both Intel and AMD are making significant steps that will most likely help the large number of 32-bit Windows servers moving painlessly to 64-bit environments: first in legacy mode, and gradually, in native mode—the compatibility mode proposed should be avoided, unless you cannot avoid it, such as in a server that would require both 64-bit native Microsoft Exchange and additional 32-bit components (e.g., monitoring modules).

Naturally, running Microsoft Exchange in native 64-bit mode will require both Windows Server 2003 64-bit and a 64-bit version of Microsoft Exchange. This will have the major advantage of utilizing a flat 64-bit address space, therefore avoiding virtual memory fragmentation (for the virtual address space) and growing the database cache in RAM (for the physical address space): the net result is more data available at hand for the processor to compute, a higher CPU utilization, a lower transaction latency dependency and a somewhat reduced dependency on storage performance, because of the large cache in system memory. In short, there is a lot to expect from a 64-bit Microsoft Exchange, and this is likely to be the platform of choice for high-end environments supporting more than 3,000 active connections.

4.2.5 Symmetric multiprocessing (SMP) and Non-Uniform Memory Access (NUMA)

Symmetric Multi-Processing is an important technology for Microsoft Exchange. It enables us to utilize several processors, physical or logical or both for processing information faster than a single processor. As we have seen in the previous sections in this chapter, you can enable hyper-threading on a single processor server, and obtain two logical processors from the Windows operating system viewpoint. Nowadays most high-end Exchange servers are using 2 or 4 processors. Multi-processing is possible in two ways with industry standard servers: SMP, which uniformly accesses physical memory through a shared memory bus and controller, and NUMA, which dedicates physical memory to configurable groups of processors, and further interconnects by the means of a crossbar switch (high-speed interface) to these very same groups of CPU (Figure 4.7).

With all processors accessing the same physical range of memory through a common bus, you run the risk of contention, and secondary, tertiary or quaternary (L4) cache are present in processor dies to prevent saturation of the system bus. However, this saturation becomes inevitable as you grow the number of processors.

Figure 4.7
NUMA-Based Architecture: 4 Groups of 4 Processors

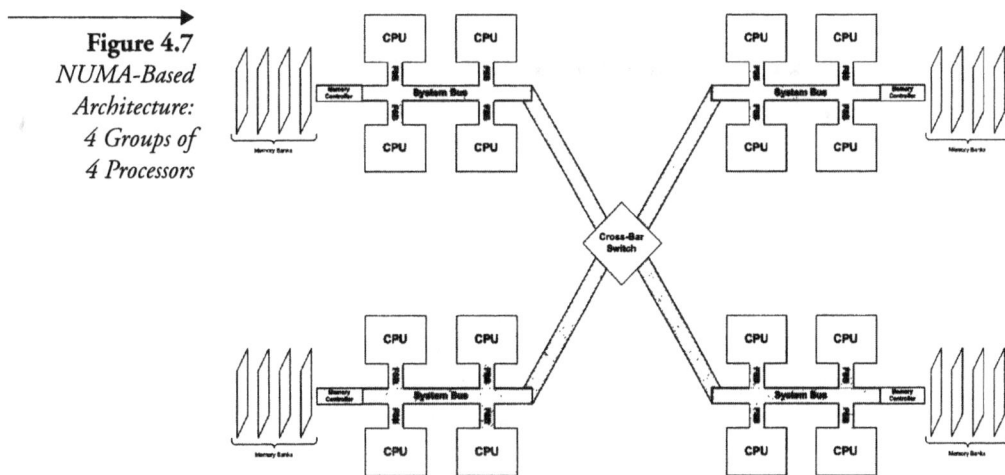

The notion of grouping processors and closely interconnecting them (NUMA) is not new, and in fact, is the basis of high-end multiprocessing computing, using industry standard processors (e.g., ES7000 from Unisys, HP's Integrity and Superdome) or not. The size of each computing "cell" may vary. In traditional 8-way computing, you have two cells of 4 processors closely interconnected by a proprietary chipset (e.g., HP's F8 chipset). However, true NUMA machines typically enable create cells of a single processor or more, and interconnect many of them. They also introduce, from a processor's perspective, the notion of *local* memory, a physical memory area locally attached to the system bus of a cell, and of, *remote* memory, a physical memory area located in another cell.

The challenge introduced by NUMA-based architecture is that components, such as memory or I/O controllers and interfaces (e.g., a Fibre Channel Host-Bus Adapter connected on a PCI-X controller) can be either local or remote—more or less distant from the computing processor, and therefore, adding more or less *latency*. In our efforts to design fast Microsoft Exchange servers, the additional distance (or hop) caused by traversing a cross-bar switch can be causing latency that in fact degrades performance. Check the Microsoft Exchange performance and scalability Web site, and you shall notice that very few servers have shown better results than 4-way servers.

You will value NUMA or 8-processor SMP architecture for the flexibility in server partitioning and reallocation of resources for varying needs: as you can connect computing cells together, you may decide, without changing the hardware configuration, you allocate 8 processors (2 × 4-processor cells) to your server instead of one.

4.2.6   PCI, PCI-X, or PCI-Express?

I believe that much of the improvement you should expect from I/O device is brought by the ability to avoid PCI-bus starvation, should a particular PCI-X adapter require a lot of data transfer (e.g., a Fibre Channel adapter). Based on preliminary testing, an improvement of 25 percent in I/O has been observed compared with traditional PCI technology running at 64-bits on a 66 MHz bus. Keep in mind that to take advantage of the growing CPU processing capability, these CPUs need enough data bandwidth to be fed with data: L2/L3 cache is a way to keep data at hand, but in an environment such as Exchange 2003, most of the data will actually be issued either from RAM, or from network or storage devices or adapters. Being able to quickly feed the processors permits taking better advantage of the processing capability and maximizing the overall processing ability of the system.

Note that this applies certainly to the Intel processor architecture, but is also valid for other architectures such as Alpha, developed by Compaq Computer Corporation. Table 4.1 shows the various bus types observed on Intel-based computer architectures. Clearly, in the server space, we see a predominance of PCI-based buses, so that is the technology you should concentrate on and invest in. Typically, servers operate with one or two (sometimes three for the high-end server models) PCI-X buses that operate at 66 MHz and 33 MHz. What you will need to be careful about is to properly configure the PCI adapters so that you don't place a 33 MHz PCI adapter on a 66 MHz bus; this will cause the bus to operate at 33 MHz, instead of its normal operating frequency. Because servers have several buses, it is necessary to clearly identify the slot placement for the PCI adapters, which typically ranges from RAID Array (for the case of direct attached storage), to network adapters and to Fibre Channel adapters. This last is particularly important since it can be a source of intensive I/O operations during large data transfers found in backup and/or restore operations.

Table 4.1 *Intel-based computer architectures*

Bus Type	I/O bandwidth
ISA	4.77 Mhz or 8.33 Mhz with 8-bit or 16-bit
EISA	8.33 Mhz with 32-bit bus width
PCI 33	33 Mhz with 32-bit or 64-bit bus width
PCI 66 (PCI 2.2)	66 Mhz with 32-bit or 64-bit bus width
PCI-X (and PCI-X 2.0)	133 Mhz (and 266 Mhz and 533 Mhz) with 32-bit or 64-bit bus width
PCIe (PCI Express)	x1 (single lane), x4, x8 and x16, between 2.5 Gbps and 3.7 Gbps data rate

The industry requirements have largely evolved during the past few years and will continue to do so for the forthcoming future. Although pure CPU performance capability has increased by up to 700 percent when you compare a Pentium-II 450 MHz and a 486/66 MHz in the same time frame, the I/O performance change for system buses has grown only by a fraction of the CPU processing, a 200 percent gain in most cases between a 64-bit 66 MHz PCI bus versus a 64-bit 33 MHz bus. As emerging applications require more processing capability, the processing requires better I/O performance to deliver multiple ways of communications (Gigabit Ethernet, Fibre Channel, Ultra SCSI 3, Multi-Ports NICs), being able to provide more slots coupled with lower latency. The improvements in the PCI buses and the upcoming PCI-X generation will be able to help in increasing the communication capabilities of CPU architectures (single or multiple CPUs). PCI-X breaks new ground by introducing 100 MHz and 133 MHz operating frequencies, breaking the 1 GB per second barrier for burst traffic. Designed to support the existing PCI Hot Plug support, PCI-X adapters are able to operate on PCI buses, and PCI-X buses operate with PCI adapters. From a software compatibility perspective (including the operating system), it is mainly transparent; it requires neither operating system modification nor driver modification in Windows Server. With a seamless hardware upgrade, you can get up to eight times the I/O throughput (should that be your concern) with the new PCI-X system and PCI-X adapters.

This versatile approach helps best to protect the existing customer investments and ensure a smooth migration path to the higher data communication patterns required by the I/O–oriented applications, such as Microsoft Exchange 2003. For best performance, however, you should always attempt to group adapter cards by speed and type per bus segment.

PCI-Express (also referred to as PCIe) takes quite a different approach by serializing the transport of data—note that this move is also confirmed in the SCSI and Fibre Channel environment for disk drives. Simply put, using parallel data transfers, you may not increase the clock rate indefinitely: there is a time where presenting information in parallel on several chip pins can cause single bit flip if the clock rate is too high, something you may attribute to electromagnetic alteration or simply a different cable size. To alleviate this problem, you are safer in transmitting information one bit at a time, although at a much higher rate (Figure 4.8).

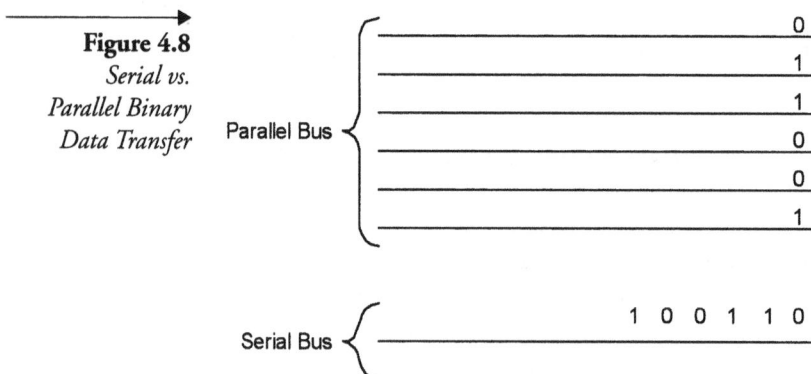

Figure 4.8
*Serial vs.
Parallel Binary
Data Transfer*

Parallel Bus

```
_____ 0
_____ 1
_____ 1
_____ 0
_____ 0
_____ 1
```

Serial Bus

```
                        1  0  0  1  1  0
_____
```

While you simplify the actual electrical implementation, you open up ability to rev up clock rates and transmit information faster in serial implementations compared to parallel ports. A similar move happened for external device connection (USB is a serial bus implementation) in other computing environments, and PCI-Express eventually displaced PCI and PCI-X in modern server architectures. At the desktop machine level, this also happened with PCI-Express slowly deprecating the Advanced Graphic Port (AGP) for graphic adapters that are usually hungry for data to crunch, calculate, and output for intensive graphic applications.

For PCIe, you do not refer to bus bandwidth (because the bus is serial), instead, you refer to the PCIe as a lane. Depending upon the implement, and simply because you have more room for the connectors, you can multiply the lanes, by 4, 8, or 16 (x4, x8, or x16). The basic lane clocking is 2.5 Giga bits per second, however, the signal for a given octet comprises start and stop bits, preventing the receiving board to loose track of the signal. An 8-bit raw data becomes a 10-bit encoded data.

When designing your server's architecture, this is something you will need to take into serious consideration to take better advantage of your system's configuration. But before rushing out and acquiring the latest technology, keep in mind the need to build well-balanced systems with the right mix for processing capability and I/O capability. Up to the adapter card, you will find it fairly easy to build a coherent environment, and your choice will probably be oriented toward upgradeable components and an architecture that can evolve. PCIe (PCI Express) is likely to become a widely adopted standard for new machines, and is certainly a good reason for you to replace existing adapters.

4.2.7 Context switching

Context switching is an activity that occurs on a Windows server when the CPU switches the context of execution of one process's thread to another thread ready for execution. Context switching can be easily measured with the Windows Performance Monitor. Within the same process, context switching is not as expensive as it could be across two processes, because there is less contextual information to save and restore between the switch of context of execution. It is more expensive between processes, and can also be expensive (in terms of privileged execution mode) if the context switching occurs across two different processors, especially if those processors do not sit on the same Front-Side Bus (such as in an 8-way or NUMA-like system architecture)

During this activity, certain operations can be made by the kernel and the symmetric multiprocessing management, such as virtual address space tracking, thread state management, CPU registry content saving, and so on.

These context switches are inevitable, and can result when highly parallel activity occurs on the system. Exchange 2003 and two of its core components, the STORE and the IIS Virtual Servers, are multithreaded. They are a source of a lot of context switching (10,000 context switches per second). The problem is that in SMP environments, beyond two processors, numerous context switches tend to create too much overhead to the server, and while the processor will appear to be utilized, it will in fact spend most of its time in privileged mode, tracking and processing these context switches (up to 40,000 context switches have been observed on an 8-way machine, and peaks at 80,000 or even 100,000 context switches per second have been observed while the privileged time was relatively low, keeping the CPUs busy doing user more, i.e., application-level code execution). At that particular point, adding more processors will not help in increasing the processing capabilities of the machine. If context-switching processing is too intense, you should choose fast system bus architectures (533 MHz and beyond) and probably a lower number of faster processors. By no means will you be able to reduce the context switching, because this happens inherently as result of (a) the parallel workload on the server, but, more important, (b) the design of the application software under stress—in our case, Exchange 2003, its STORE process, and the IIS Virtual Server implementation.

4.2.8 Real or Virtual?

The introduction of virtual server computing with VMware and later, with Microsoft, led many customers to investigate the possibility of using virtual machines in their Microsoft Exchange environment. The typical support question comes in first: if something goes wrong, Microsoft will ask you to reproduce the problem on a physical server, before proceeding further—the reason for such an attitude, which might seem blunt initially, is that the operating system and application are not executing atop certified hardware components, but rather, above a layer which is out of the control of the software manufacturer. From a business applications viewpoint, this is not a significant problem; however, from the operating system, and the inner components executing in kernel mode, such as device drivers, this can be a big difference.

The case for virtual servers grew with the necessity to dedicate servers for a particular application, preventing application-stacking consolidation, and the availability of large computing power with introduction of faster and faster processors and cheaper RAM components.

Ask yourself the question: if something goes wrong, do you want to deal with many vendors (including the virtualization components vendor), or as few as possible? HP, like other partners, offers, for virtualized environment, support contract such that in the even, of an escalation, you have the ability to deal with a single vendor (in this case, HP), and avoid going back and forth with the various solution providers that contribute to a healthy Microsoft Exchange environment.

With time, there is little doubt that Microsoft will proceed to push further their own virtualization solution (Microsoft Virtual Server) by certifying it for certain application; already, Microsoft has documented how to configure and operate Windows Active Directory domain controllers in virtual server environments.

In the immediate, I would strongly advise that you refrain from deploying Microsoft Exchange servers as virtual machines except in a functional testing environment; unless you have a good handle on the I/O path and the expected performance, running back-end servers on virtual machines is not a good idea, both from supportability and performance viewpoints.

Blades or Regular?

On the front of physical servers, there are three different form factors you may choose from:

Blade server: blades servers are computer boards that fit inside a framework which provides external connectivity. Their power requirements are typically smaller than a regular server, and the resulting footprint is impressively reduced: you have 6 times more servers in the same foot-square than of regular servers. The challenges with blade server computing are two-fold:

1.   There is a very simple issue around the kg/m^2 you obtain when using a blade server rack; some environments are just not suitable for having such weight concentrated in a small foot-print— before considering the deployment of blade servers, I therefore recommend you speak with the person running the data center (from a physical viewpoint), and ask for the specifications of the room in terms of weight and heat dissipation and power specifications. More density wreaks havoc on power distribution.

2.   Connectivity and redundancy: Blade servers are optimized for
      density; some of the advanced communication components, such
      as dedicated host-bus adapters for iSCSI or Fibre Channel proto-
      cols just do not fit inside the smallest blade servers—this point,
      however, varies from one vendor to another. It is quite frequent to
      see the availability of at least one PCI-X slot, to which you may
      insert a fully redundant Fibre Channel adapter. In addition, the
      goal for reducing space for the computing platform counterfeits
      in the implementation of advanced resilience mechanisms, such
      as redundant memory; of course, the surrounding enclosure of a
      blade server does contain redundant components, however, the
      server itself is quite exposed to inner failure—how often do they
      occur? Maybe not enough, depending on the environment and
      the availability requirements.

These challenges are addressed in varying ways by manufacturers. First,
the processor makers, AMD and Intel, are now designing multi-core chips
that can run at lower frequencies: this brings down the power and cooling
requirement of the high-density blade environment. Having servers that
run colder augments significantly the lifetime of inner components (controllers, memory banks, disks!).

Redundancy and connectivity are something which are more delicate
within a single blade server, and actually require blade enclosure design
changes, such that the environment made of the computational units is
more "dynamic" and leads to automatic error detection and correction.
This is where most of the progress needs to be made by the manufacturers
in the blade environments.

1.   High-density servers: they are optimized for availability and
      power, yet, provide as little internal storage as possible (typically,
      4 × UltraSCSI disks with on-board disk controller). High-density
      servers are compact without the compromise of resiliency features
      found on dependable platforms, such as redundant fans, power
      supplied, and memory banks. One would typically choose high-
      density servers for back-end Microsoft Exchange environments
      (mailbox or public folder servers) that are dependable for data
      availability and require efficient communication interfaces (e.g.,
      two or more Fibre Channel Host-Bus Adapters).

2. Pedestal servers: they allow you to build servers that can contain 6 to 8 disks, and an additional tape controller. Pedestal servers may also be racked, but the goal is to minimize the external dependencies, and enable the delivery, to a remote office, of servers that just require to be plugged on the AC power and the network. They are ideal for small offices or small environments in a pedestal form factor, and in racked environments, for any server that requires high-speed locally attached storage, such as bridgehead servers.

You should, when choosing your server, consider the manageability options. Having servers with built-in lights-out management interface is critical for central operations of distributed environments. Depending upon the vendors, the lights-out management is more or less easy to implement; HP's ProLiant G4 (G as in Generation) servers now all come with a built-in lights-out management interface, accessible by the means of Ethernet interface, and eventually built-in web portal that lets you monitor all the vital functions of a server, including performing a cold reboot of the machine or booting from a virtual floppy or CD drive, if necessary.

4.2.9 In Summary

Beyond basic computing power and PCI bus architectures and placement, Exchange 2003 makes a lot of use of RAM and disk subsystem. Often considered as an I/O–bound application, a lot of current designs aim at removing "slow" device bottlenecks (network and storage) to turn the I/O–bound application into a CPU–bound application. At that point, you should increase your processing capability if the demand justifies it, and have an overall solution that is well balanced between CPU, RAM, and storage services for the Exchange 2003 server.

Whether Microsoft Exchange will really benefit from such new technologies such as Multi-Core or PCI-Express or X64 execution mode is to be seen: Exchange 2003 and its predecessors are much more I/O oriented than CPU bound. There is a long time before Microsoft Exchange will become a CPU-bound application: until it can actually dispose of all the data it needs without going to disk, this type of computational mode is only available in 64-bit native mode (for both operating system and application) and for wealthy customers that may afford several dozens of GB of RAM in their servers.

Beyond the actual "guts" of a server, you should consider the environmental aspects that will trigger your options. Blade server computing can be a strategy for decreasing cost of operation: it is much faster (and requires fewer skills) to replace a blade server than a high-density server; it may, however, impact your server deployment standards. Think about it when considering the operating model of your environment.

4.3   Networking services

Networking services are of course critical for proper operations of Exchange 200x deployments, including the largest ones. From my deployment experiences, Exchange 2003 relies on the following network services.

4.3.1   Data networks

Data networks establish the connection not only between the Windows infrastructure servers and the Exchange servers, but also between the messaging clients of all kinds (Outlook, Outlook Web Access, or mobile clients) and possibly some back-end storage components when using NAS for Exchange 2003 or iSCSI target devices.

Solid data network services imply redundancy when availability is required as well as sufficient bandwidth and low latency. In highly centralized environments, this becomes even more critical: in the move to concentrate operations and servers and consolidate infrastructure, more accesses are done across wide-area network links, which sometimes can be a cause for slow response time and unavailability. Network aspects can be very straightforward in corporate environments, where every computing resource can connect to each other happily and with no barriers. Nonetheless, Exchange 2003 must sometimes be deployed in environments where firewalls, Virtual Private Networks, and other such advanced networking techniques have to be deployed or are already implemented.

The classic example is the interconnection of two companies that are just merging. In the beginning, you need to establish basic connectivity, which can be as basic and as simple as SMTP protocol handling. In the longer run, however, you need to merge data networks together, often going through the intermediate steps of establishing VPNs and trusted connections, and only later end up in one single WAN that can ease the deployment of Exchange 2003 and related applications.

There are many references in the literature and in customer experiences where such steps are looked into and advice given for how best to implement them. Don't always assume that you can deploy Exchange 2003 in a transparent and straightforward manner as you would in a LAN environment.

Sometimes, indeed, the connectivity is just summarized by mail exchanged and Free/Busy calendaring replication. Microsoft provides tools that can enable multiple organizations to connect together. The Active Directory Connector is one example, and the Exchange 2003 resource kit contains additional utilities; do take the time to study them before making any decision on what you can and will actually implement and deploy.

In many cases, this particular topic is addressed by infrastructure teams, and usually in the course of the planning and design of the key Windows Server services, such as directory and authentication. By the time you approach your Exchange 2003 design, those considerations for networking topologies will have been addressed, to a certain extent.

We have seen many environments, however, where firewalls between islands of wide-area networks are implemented, thus creating disjoint Windows environments and implying disjoint Exchange 2003 environments. In such situations, my advice is to utilize inter-organizational replication tools for the directory services, the calendaring information, and possibly, the public folder replication. SMTP is by far the simplest way to address the exchange of messaging data. Do note that in that case, there are certain aspects of Exchange 2003 that you won't be able to take advantage of, such as a unified management console and some routing topology intelligence built inside the SMTP routing layer of Exchange 2003. Kieran McCorry has written an excellent book on this topic: Microsoft® Exchange Server 2003 Deployment and Migration, First Edition (ISBN: 1555583164).

4.3.2 DNS

The Domain Naming Services provided by (or for) the Windows 200x infrastructure are key for Exchange 2003 to be able to route messages, enable communications, and look up between Exchange 2003 servers.

Don't forget that in a multisite, multidomain Windows 2000 environment, DNS is key for retrieving site topology and appropriate Global Catalog servers and Domain Controllers from the Windows 2000 infrastructure. Unavailability or bogus information in DNS can bring your Exchange 2003 service down, no matter how much effort you put into building robust back-end or front-end services. The challenge with DNS is that very often, customers already have DNS services in place, mostly running on UNIX platforms, and are not necessarily willing to switch completely over to Windows 2000–based DNS services.

However, I have found that in the Windows 2000 environment, the best practice is to "delegate" a DNS sub-tree to Active Directory–enabled DNS and take advantage of dynamic name registration and Active Directory replication. In such situations, Windows 2000 Active Directory and surrounding network services have been found to work really well.

4.3.3   Active Directory

This is key for operations, and Exchange 2003 requires availability of both Domain Controllers for retrieving configuration information. Most important, however, Global Catalog servers provide services for distribution list expansion, user authentication, and mail address resolution. In fact, the last of these places the heaviest load on the Global Catalog servers. Microsoft Exchange 2000 was designed with the idea that several Global Catalogs could be used in parallel to service multiple server requests. Unfortunately, this didn't make it into Exchange 2000 RTM, and only from SP1 onwards (or by the means of intermediate hotfixes and QFEs) do we see Exchange 2003 being able to gracefully fail over if a GC is down. This caused many problems at several levels in the Exchange 2003 server's ability to deliver messages and authenticate users. So Exchange 2000 SP1 is a big win, but you should keep in mind that in terms of scalable architectures of Exchange 2003, Windows 2000 services must be up to par and extremely solid.

As Microsoft Exchange deployments evolved, the notion of multi-forest was found to be inevitable in large enterprises where a single Windows Active Directory forest could not be deployed in time, or was not adequate to the operating model. Let's take the case of the company that decides to outsource their messaging environment, yet retain ownership of Windows Active Directory function, for security reasons, or simply because it is considered a key asset. In such situations the messaging service provider is strictly dependent on how the Windows Active Directory servers (Global Catalog servers and Domain Controllers) are being deployed, with the golden rule that there is always a Global Catalog server in nearby connectivity (read: LAN) to the Microsoft Exchange server.

In fact, this rule has been confirmed on several occasions, not only during validation tests but also (and more painfully) in production environments. The key consideration to remember is that without Windows Active Directory, Microsoft Exchange is lost. If you wish to have a certain level of independence between the messaging function and the authentication and user registration viewpoints, your only alternative is to implement a multi-forest deployment scenario, where Microsoft Exchange has its own forest, and where the authentication function is implemented in another forest.

You encounter new challenges in such an environment, because Microsoft Exchange was not initially designed by Microsoft for operating according to such topology rules, but I know of many customers that went through this route, and once they had proper directory synchronization tools in place, found they had the ideal solution to their environment.

This said, you should try to avoid this approach as much as possible, because it is far easier to deploy and operate Microsoft Exchange in the same forest as the user accounts.

4.4   Scale out and scale up

In scaling any Exchange 2003 server deployment, and choosing between a scale-out model that involves many small servers and a scale-up model that involves a reduced quantity of large servers, the storage services provided to these systems are adequate. They should not necessarily be oversized, but should be open and flexible enough so that you can take advantage of new technologies and evolve your architecture without the need to rework it.

In scale-out models, which require the deployment of many small servers, you must ensure that you provide sufficient capacity and performance so that you don't have to revisit those servers in the next 18 to 24 months. This is generally the life cycle of a server, although one can observe longer life cycles of over 48 or 60 months! This is a hard prediction to make from an IT manager or architect perspective, so it's basically a question of setting a high enough watermark on your server's characteristics.

Reworking the servers in a scale-out model should be avoided as much as possible: most of the time, because the actual cost of the hardware upgrade will in fact be a fraction of the overall cost, which is mainly incurred by labor and system downtime.

In scale-up models, the technology to be used must match not only the overall user load model (e.g., IMAP, POP, or MAPI workload), but must also evolve, as technology can be extremely relevant on those monster servers' deployments. I don't believe that much of the problem with the scale-up model involves the CPU sizing and scaling up. We will see, for another long period of time, most of the large Exchange 2003 servers (handling 5,000 or more concurrent users and perhaps twice as many mailboxes) being deployed on 4 or 8 physical processor servers (four being considered the sweet-spot configuration, even in future evolutions of Windows 2003 and Exchange 2003 using the 64-bit Itanium architecture).

But the most crucial point, in my opinion, is not the sheer need for computing power, which can be addressed by technology, but the ability to easily maintain and manage large quantities of data, often found in consolidation scenarios—how new technologies in that area can best be leveraged, based on current system designs and their evolution characteristics. One of the peculiarities of Microsoft Exchange is how a particular database, and therefore user's mailbox can be tied to a given server: you do not have the ability to mount and enable mailboxes on any given Microsoft Exchange, at least, not "out-of-the-box." Users' mailboxes are referenced by the name of the server, the storage group and the database name, and this information is located in the Active Directory. Unless you actually go and patch the user's Windows Active Directory entry, you do not have the ability to redirect user mailboxes on least busy servers in a data center farm environment. We shall discuss this topic later, but this is a point that is important to keep in mind.

4.4.1   Building an agile infrastructure

In any deployment involving a large number of servers, you will need to study carefully how you can maintain an environment that can take advantage of new technologies as they are released, while simplifying the task of supporting the new environment.

Processes

The issue that must be dealt with is the frequent update necessary for the operating environment. Windows Server gets one or two service packs per year, and so does Exchange 2003, not counting the numerous mandatory security hotfixes and Web release components.

You may of course decide not to deploy these service packs, but most of the time, aside from the quantity of bug fixes included in a service pack, new features are made available which may be relevant for your environment. For example, Windows Server 2003 includes the ability to load the Active Directory contents from media (CD-ROM, tape, file) instead of waiting for replication of the necessary elements to a domain controller or a Global Catalog.

In a scaled-out environment, where servers can be fairly distant and connected with relatively slow links (64 kbps and below), that feature is mostly attractive, to enable the directory to be kept up-to-date, and to save on network bandwidth: shipping a CD with the Active Directory snapshot can certainly be more efficient rather than clogging up the network link for this replication to happen. So it would make sense that far-reaching sites hosting Global Catalog servers get deployed with Windows Server 2003, taking advantage of this feature. In the same vein, because Exchange 2003 introduced a schema change that typically requires a rebuild of all Global Catalog server content, many customers did wait to deploy their Windows Active Directory infrastructure to Windows Server 2003, and to take advantage of optimized replication to Global Catalog servers, therefore avoiding the so-feared replication storm.

You then need a process that can roll back changes brought to the operating environment to the actual production environment, while maintaining zero regression in the compatibility of the environment, be it hardware, firmware and BIOS, and applications.

It is important to define a process to rollout updates in a seamless manner, such that the infrastructure is stable, while it takes advantage of new features of corrective code.

This process requires three key items:

1. The necessity to define and test support platform builds.

2. The ability to roll-out updates and build new servers according to the new operating environment standard.

3. The ability to feedback installation of hotfixes and QFE (Quick Fix Engineering) from the base Microsoft products—note that this process is also valid for the enterprise applications, and spans way beyond the actual Microsoft-software environment.

As you can see from Figure 4.9, several organizations are required to validate and process build updates. How these updates are eventually carried out on the servers is purposely not addressed here. The Microsoft Operations Framework (MOF) based upon a series of standardized IT processes that can be consulted out of the IT Information Library (ITIL) can be a good start to defining the IT process in your environment if it does not exist. You can also validate these processes, either by the book, or by contracting Services organizations that have many years of collective experience on IT Service Management and Optimization.

The Windows Software Update Service is a private version of the Windows Update tool, which enables servers to download and install updates specific to their environment. Distributed as a free patch management tool, it enables network administrators to distribute patches (and security

Figure 4.9
*Server Build
Process*

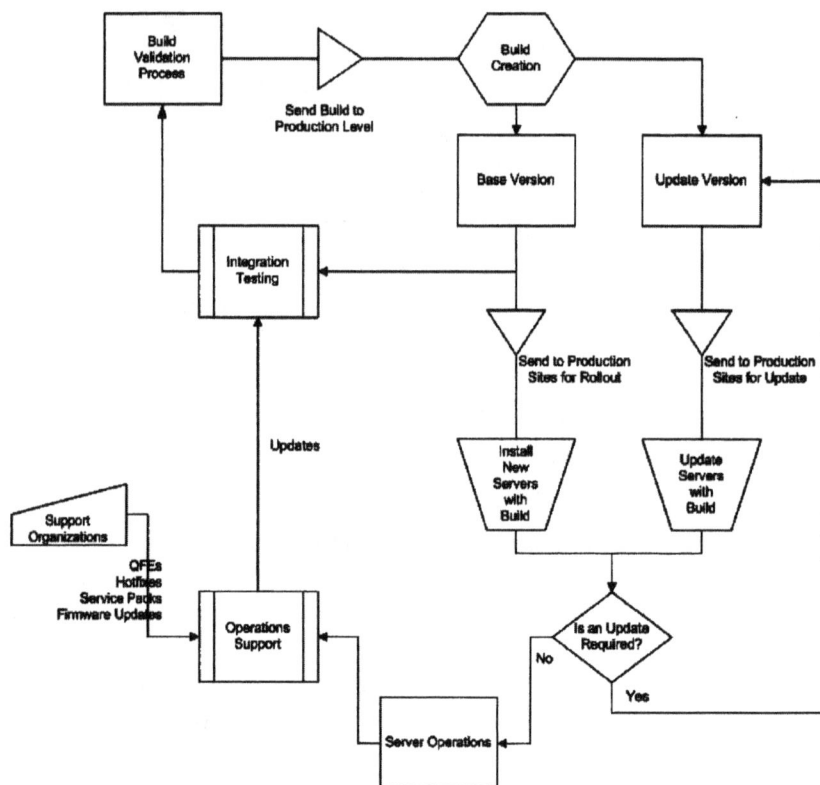

patches in particular) more easily. Microsoft SUS sits between Microsoft Update and the corporate network and can act as a filter for making sure that you get to deploy only the fixes that you need. SUS has some shortcomings, such as the inability to "push" updates to server and to handle multiple platforms—in some multi-vendor data center environments, customers might want to adopt a wider solution, such as HP's Radia or Altiris' Rapid Deployment Pack.

Take the example of a server that has a particular problem, and is instructed, by Microsoft's support organization to install a hotfix. You then face a dilemma: should you install this particular hotfix on all similar platforms (say, Exchange 2003 servers), or should you wait for a similar problem to happen before rolling out the hotfix? Consider that only a few weeks after the release of SP2 of Windows 2000, over 230 hotfixes were available from Microsoft's Web site: not all of them are mandatory; in fact, Microsoft only imposes the immediate roll-out of security-related hotfixes.

Consider that for Exchange 2003 SP1, only a couple of weeks after this version was released, already three hotfixes were available that were correcting functional problems. Microsoft prefers their customers to rollout hotfixes as needed (i.e., when the problem occurs). In large environments with a strong wish to decrease operational costs, you will probably want to avoid having to handle a problem that can cause service downtime, and bring this downtime as shortly as possible in order to re-establish the service. The identification of the cause of failures, as well as the rollout of the hotfix and testing of possible regression caused by this hot fix, can reduce the service downtime to an acceptable level.

So, while Microsoft's recommendation makes sense in order to prevent unnecessary updates to machines running perfectly fine, it is necessary for you to review the hotfixes available, by consulting the support services from Microsoft, and then proactively proceed to systematic updates of your machines, rather than waiting for problems to happen.

What next?

To implement agile infrastructures, you need to define your processes. The process definition is helpful to map the IT processes to actual labor and IT assets, such as servers, storage or network. After the process definition is complete, you will probably be asked to decrease costs. Costs in IT environment can be decreased in three ways:

- Reduce IT assets: this is about consolidation
- Reduce Labor costs: this is about employing offshore resources for those processes that can deal with such operation mode
- Reduce Labor: this is the novelty and where you will need to spend time in the future: labor reduction means automation, means that you can deliver your processes faster, most likely through complex automation engines that are tightly coupled with the IT infrastructure components and can model the needs of the business or the applications.

This new form of process management is going to be the challenge of the small, medium, and large data centers in the coming years. You can get prepared by simply attempting to automate as much as you can simple processes such as the installation of a new server in your environment. But as you have a clearer definition of your environment and of your processes, you will be able to make the most progress and savings.

4.4.2   The difference between service packs, hotfixes, and QFEs

The basic difference between these updates lies in the fact that Service Packs have undergone regression testing, both within Microsoft's testing labs, and at sites of customers participating in beta programs. Hotfixes and QFEs, on the other hand, are one-shot fixes, tested to fix the customer problem, but they have not undergone any regression testing. Security hotfixes are mandatory updates from Microsoft and you are generally asked to deploy these fixes as they are officially made available. Don't take a chance here, and of course, because security hotfixes tend to be rather frequent, the automation of the rollout of these fixes (as mentioned in the previous section) is a key winning component to consistently and rapidly deploy your hotfixes.

4.4.3   Prevent or correct?

In any business-critical environment where Exchange 2003 is taking a more and more important role, you can just wait for a problem to happen before correcting it; as you know, preventive actions are much preferred over reactive actions, which can sometimes lead to catastrophic failures (a hotfix is installed that causes a third-party product to fail, which in turn can cause unavailability of data, or even worse, loss of data).

Microsoft's position is clear: you may install a hotfix or a QFE only after the problem has been detected. Service Packs, on the other hand, are strongly recommended for rollout. In my opinion, neither of the two approaches will prevent you from performing regression testing of your platform builds. Even if a Service Pack has been tested to avoid any regression and "bad" interaction between hotfixes, you have no guarantee that your environment—which includes Microsoft's own software along with additional software such as monitoring tools, anti-virus detection packages, and custom-built applications—will not be negatively impacted.

I agree that building a lab of all the configurations spread throughout an organization is a costly and complex effort; nevertheless, I believe that you can alleviate this particular problem by:

- Standardizing the hardware platform: choose at most two or three server models to be rolled out. Most modern servers can both scale up and scale down to accommodate and better satisfy the anticipated workload.

- Maintain a representative set of machines in a pre-testing lab environment that can replicate the vital business applications, and define a set of regression test criteria that can help to validate the insertion and wide adoption of a service pack, hotfix, or QFE throughout the entire environment. The wide adoption of Virtual Machine/Server computing easily enables such an approach for any non-kernel validation (drivers and specific HBA would require, of course, the most fidelity platform). It is common to implement such pre-testing environment in a virtual server environment, based upon VMware or Microsoft Virtual Server.

  If you adopt such an approach, you can restrict the utilization of the main server roles and components (such as connectors) and representative data sets (directories).

- Acquire an automated build and software installation package that can help to deploy, update, and maintain the software standards within your organization and track appropriate changes. Apart from SUS, Microsoft proposes SMS or you may seek multi-vendor tools if you intend to adopt a wider range of servers and application services.

4.4.4 In summary

I believe that it should be clear that for either mission-critical environments or scaled-out environments, you need to properly weigh the pros and cons for the adoption of hotfixes, service packs, or QFEs in your environment.

The problem is that sometimes you have little choice—for example, when you need to apply hotfixes that deal with security issues, particularly in an eCommerce or mission-critical environment, you can hardly skimp on this type of update.

Starting with ten servers or more, I strongly recommend a scale-down test lab environment, as well as a solid build validation process that involves the many organizations that deal with the day-to-day server support and administration.

You should lock down the security policies in your environment to prevent users from installing additional software that could cause "noise" in your infrastructure, and this can be done by proper utilization of Security templates and Group Policy Objects in Windows Server.

Finally, the technology landscape evolves at a very rapid pace, and it is very easy to get seduced by cool marketing messages that call for rolling out new features and new operating systems, either on the desktop or in the server environments. My basic advice is to stay away from the technology hype and be sure to properly maintain your environment. Your support costs will decrease, which your Chief Information Officer will greatly appreciate.

Remember, the battle for lowering the Total Cost of Ownership (TCO) is happening at the support and administration levels mostly; this is where you can save the most, while taking advantage of new software updates and features.

This said, at HP, we determined that most support calls were related to the desktop environment rather than to the server environment. This proposed process should also be applicable to your desktop environment, which ultimately represents the user-visible window of your computing infrastructure and services.

My strong advice is to give certain abilities to your infrastructure that will make it so dependable that you will have little trouble justifying and receiving additional budget and authorization for rolling up advanced technologies.

These abilities include:

- *Scalability.* This gives you the ability to grow your environment in terms of users, transaction volume, and data volume without dumping your current environment and re-architecting your infrastructure every 12 months.

- *Reliability.* Make sure that your infrastructure gets the highest levels of reliability, not necessarily from a server's perspective (it is very easy to **observe** a 99.999 percent availability on a standalone Windows 2003 server), but more from a service perspective. Be able to demonstrate that 99 percent of your e-mail messages got delivered within five minutes throughout your organization.

- *Manageability.* Ensure that you have the proper tools to proactively manage your environment, and determine the level of service provided by your infrastructure before anyone can notice a failure of one component.

- *Availability.* Take considered advantage of availability processes and technologies, and keep in mind that if the sole answer to availability were technology, this would be a well-known fact in the IT landscape. Instead, aim at creating redundancy where it is necessary while avoiding bottlenecks and single points of failure.

- *Supportability.* When deploying an Exchange 2003 infrastructure, make sure that each and every component is easily supportable. This includes the ability to track errors in a meaningful way. (I've seen backup software reporting an error during backup in the most simple terms "Backup has failed." How can you find out *why* the backup failed, and how can you correct the problem?) You must have strong support contracts with your hardware vendors and your software vendors. A strong support contract includes the ability to have a fast turnaround time (negotiable, can be for instance a maximum of four hours for resolution, 24x7), and knowledgeable support interlocutors—for example, make sure that your support contact knows how to operate the software element in your particular environment.

- *Expandability.* I don't know of any computing environment that does not evolve. The evolution of this computing environment should *not* depend upon the technology changes. If it does, you are running an IT shop driven by technology and sooner or later you will be hitting a wall—that is, proprietary solutions that do not integrate. Your life jacket has STANDARDS written all over it. Going for a standard-based infrastructure will ensure expandability. Microsoft showed its understanding of this fact when it introduced Windows Active Directory and the native support of LDAP and Kerberos for directory and authentication services. DNS is much favored compared to WINS in the Windows 2000 environments. Microsoft, as the credible industry contributor that it is, is still maintaining the two environments to ensure backward compatibility, but the way forward is wide open to standards. For example, numerous Windows Active Directory deployments are based on QIP or BIND for DNS services, as opposed to Microsoft's own DNS services.

  Exchange 2003 goes far beyond Exchange 5.5 in terms of standards support, by enabling external and internal communication using SMTP, enhancing those protocols at times with proprietary extensions that are immediately rolled back in the standard process for wide industry adoption. WMI and WBEM are also two prime examples of standards and implementations supported by Exchange 2003 and enhanced throughout the life cycle of the products provided by Microsoft, including Windows Server. Finally, to close on this particular topic, the mode of operation of today's companies is much different than that of 10 or 20 years ago; spin-offs, acquisitions, and joint ventures are just a way of life in contemporary enterprises. When a company decides to grow its business, it will not try to hire and retain qualified staff; it will research the market for the best players and attempt either a strategic partnership to build a joint venture and achieve a particular initiative, or simply acquire and merge the two companies to create a stronger, more capable conglomerate. From an IT manager's perspective, this work involves integrating servers, organizations, assets and application processes, and only standards can help to ease this particular job. Your ability to present these abilities and to demonstrate them in action can help you in getting support for further investments and create a real business advantage that your CIO will be proud to present to his CEO and Chief Financial Office (CFO).

4.5   Leveraging storage technologies

The trend for Exchange storage is one of continuous growth, even though many companies attempt to control the size of the information by enforcing quotas and maintaining user mailboxes by removing unwanted messages.

As companies strive to reduce their infrastructure and operational costs, they are moving to server consolidation and centralization, aiming at reducing the number of servers that they have to manage.

You may take the problem one way or another, but you should always keep in mind that in any consolidation scenario, data remains; typically it doesn't reduce in size and will quite probably increase in terms of availability requirements. As you were planning to redeploy a computing infrastructure to reduce costs, you have to increase your investment in the area of storage, so important for the mission-critical applications such as messaging.

As companies evolved into creating large data centers that host massive quantities of computing power and are built around high-speed networking accesses, the concentration of data has to be addressed in three perspectives—cost, performance, and availability. Apart from these three criteria that should shape your final technology solution and strategy, the manageability of this information is growing important. Today you can build a server that serves 1 TB or even 1 PB of data, but making this data manageable is another problem. This was first addressed with Microsoft Exchange 2000 by allowing for a single Exchange server to serve more than one mailbox store: instead of gathering a large quantity of information into a single file database, you can now create more than one of these databases, all managed and processed by a single server.

This is a serious scalability advantage of Exchange 2003 and a big improvement compared with Exchange 5.5, one that can lead to more flexible designs that take advantage of new technologies.

When building any Exchange 2003 server, you must first determine how much space you should plan for hosting the user mailboxes and optionally, shared information (public folders). In short, you will have to build storage solutions that implement to various degrees the following attributes:

- Capacity
- Availability
- Performance
- Manageability
- Cost (affordability)

Throughout this chapter, we will return to those key aspects, because they represent the roots for any storage design decisions you make. As we cover the storage technologies you can (and you cannot) use with Microsoft Exchange, you will quickly realize that there is an advantage in having a sound storage strategy for your enterprise, both from a management perspective and from a storage platform acquisition standpoint.

It is generally a good idea to appoint as part of your administration staff a storage administrator who will be responsible for looking up these issues, not only across your Exchange 2003 environment but also across your Windows Server environment (including file and print services), and probably beyond the Windows Server platform by including such environments as UNIX or other high-end operating systems (not that Windows Server is not a high-end operating system).

I mentioned earlier how storage embraced the networking paradigm: do project yourselves into the past and think about how networking was introduced in IT infrastructures, how it evolved and how it is run today. With Storage, you will find the same pattern of server specific components, which then get deployed in an interconnected way. Then you need to address the redundancy and performance and security of the interconnecting components and links. Finally, you will need to address a level of multi-vendor interoperability, which is best addressed by standards implementation.

For the remainder of this section, we are going to cover three key storage approaches:

1.   Direct-Attached Storage: this is really about local disks in servers. They are present today, and the networking and high-performance interfaces still do not allow building diskless servers for all solutions. In some cases, this is appropriate and this is something we cover later in this book. Interestingly enough, when much emphasis was brought on networking functions (see below), direct-attached storage technologies evolved more recently and get a new fame for Microsoft Exchange deployments today and for the near future.

2.   Storage Area Networks: built using a standardized protocol, Fibre Channel, these networks are designed for high-performance block-mode access to raw devices. There is no sense of file system for devices attached to a SAN, this is a notion that remains at the operating system. After being placed in complex and high-end infrastructures, SAN are now making their way in the smaller SMB market. Much of the upcoming challenge of the storage industry is to propose simple ways of managing relatively complex storage components.

3.   Network Attached Storage: the fundamental of NAS is the utilization of a data network protocol, IP (and more precisely, TCP/IP) to carry two kinds of protocols: file-share protocol or block-mode protocol. NAS made their ways from file-sharing appliances, which rapidly evolved into mature storage components. I purposely place iSCSI (which is really block-mode over IP) and CIFS in the NAS "basket," because they address the same goal of using IP networks to provide storage to servers.

It would be a narrow-minded exercise to compare these technologies and claim that one is better than the other. In fact, you will find that each of these storage approaches have pros and cons, which all depend upon the objectives you are pursuing, the revision of Microsoft Exchange and Windows Server that you intend to use, and your operating model. So my primary goal is to cover these technologies as they are present in 2005, and indicate areas of improvement, bearing in mind that storage is a moving target, that constantly changes—as a customer and implementer of Microsoft Exchange, you will be astonished by the type of problems you encounter for deploying a mission-critical and probably one of the most demanding applications on the market when it comes to storage.

My secondary goal, only second by order of citation, is to educate you on the favorite sport in France: getting good wine at a fair price, but for storage. It's very easy to get an excellent wine at € 1,000 ($1,000) a bottle—It is very difficult to find a pleasant wine that perfectly fits to your palate and your meal at a fraction of this price. For storage, the situation is more difficult: it's not obvious that you get the best storage solution for your Microsoft Exchange environment if you pay for the most expensive one. In fact, it is rarely the case.

4.5.1 Direct-Attached Storage (DAS)

The most common way to provide storage to a Windows Server is to use a locally attached storage device controller. In fact, many servers today come with onboard controllers, directly integrated in the motherboard. You may utilize backplane controllers (named after their position in the server) and connect using PCI, PCI-X or PCI-Express. From these controllers, you can connect one or more drives, at least one (for the smallest servers, such as "blades"), more often two or four, and sometimes a dozen.

The storage capacity and performance offered by these locally connected devices is owned privately to the server—you may share some of this capacity by the means of file sharing protocols, but really, the disks are to be used by this server and not another. This storage is directly attached because it has no intermediate networking components, other than the RAID controller and the electrical wires that connect to the disk electronics which control the drive rotation and head movements. We will cover RAID later on to the extent that you can really determine their relevance to Exchange 2003.

Onboard controllers are now predominant because operating systems that run on industry-standard serves typically require a local boot device. Windows Server 2003 makes certain assumptions to this boot device and to the fact that there is a direct path which is always available for memory dump operations after a system crash. Typically, the boot device contains the operating system components and pagefile (swap space for virtual memory management). Further components, such as Microsoft Exchange databases and transaction log files are assigned to additional disks, for performance, management and redundancy purposes, but not always.

With Windows Server 2003, it is possible to boot over a networked storage device, however, there are still recommendations on using local disks for memory paging activities. Later on, we cover these concepts of network boot and address the notion of SAN-based boot devices.

You may go as far as using PCI-based disk controllers to store the Exchange 2003 databases, and this is in fact a very reasonable choice in small and medium environments, where the user workload, capacity and recovery requirements are not very significant to address. I consider that for less than 500 users, direct-attached storage with network backup and recovery is a very appropriate and cost-effective solution. Some of our customers have considered using direct-attached storage for larger capacity (2,000 users per server and more), however rapidly failed back to network storage for manageability and recoverability purposes.

Local Connections: SCSI or ATA? Serial or Parallel?

With direct-attached storage, you do not have a single approach anymore. Before 2003, it was almost automatic to associate parallel SCSI (SCSI as in transport) with direct-attached storage, and in fact, it represented the majority of disk interconnects (80 percent).

Figure 4.10
SCSI Cables

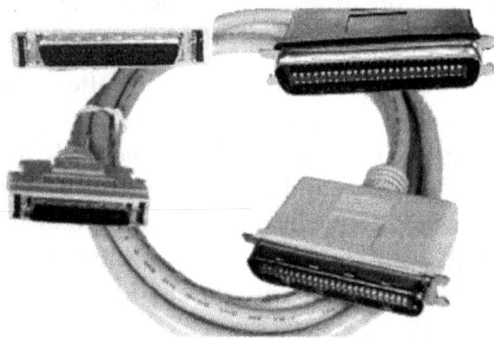

Naturally, SCSI protocol was used to access the block-mode devices connected to the SCSI bus.

Alternatively, and commonly used for desktop PCs, the ATA protocol (ATA: Advanced Technology Attachment) is now proposed for entry-level servers.

By applying serialization of electrical signals to both SCSI and ATA disk access protocols, two disk access specifications emerged:

1.   SATA: Serial ATA, positioned for the entry-level servers and low-cost ($/GB) and high-capacity, low-performance disks

2. SAS: Serial Attached SCSI, positioned for high-performance disks, with relatively smaller capacity

In the future, both of these interfaces will be predominant on the server market, and address some of the problems initially found with parallel SCSI, such as limitations in the number of devices attached to the bus, arbitration of access to the disks and cable length restrictions. In SAS enclosures, you are now able to plug both SATA and SAS drives. This helps you in building storage solutions that have high-performance for part and high-capacity at reduced cost for another part.

In other words, in the same way that information in your Microsoft Exchange infrastructure has varying values, you are able to align this information storage on varying components which fit best the criticality of the information and its access rate, as shown in Figure 4.11.

Figure 4.11
Mixing Drive Capacity and Access Mode

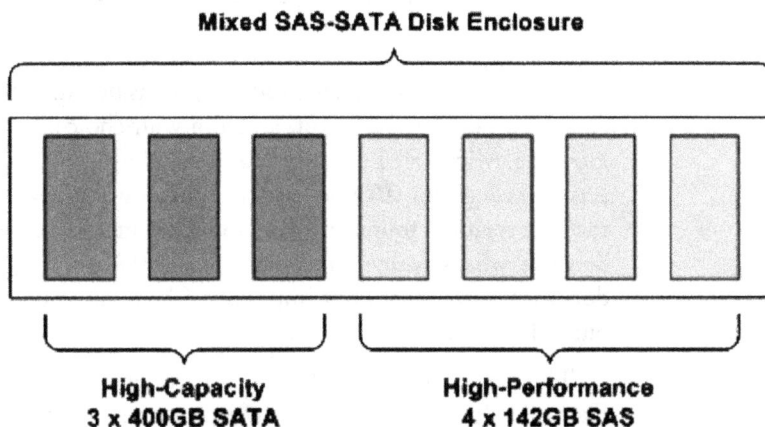

Mixed SAS-SATA Disk Enclosure

High-Capacity
3 x 400GB SATA

High-Performance
4 x 142GB SAS

In this example, you have 1.2 TB raw storage in three drives, compared with 560 GB raw storage in four drives. Of course, the resulting capacity will depend upon the type of RAID level you use for these disks and how you decide to assemble them together. The net result is that at a lower cost and space, you can store massive amounts of information, however not at the same throughput (I/O per sec).

While there are similarities in terms of electrical signaling between SAS and SATA, the major differences can be summarized as follow:

- SATA drives are less expensive (30–40 percent cheaper for similar capacity)

- SATA drives use the ATA command set

- SAS drives are dual-ported, use faster rotation speed and lower latency, and can be configured using variable sector size

- SATA backplane cannot host SAS drives (but the inverse is true: SAS enclosures can host SATA drives—as in other examples, such as PCI buses, using devices with varying response times may result in degrading the overall performance)

- SAS drives are responding to stricter specifications than SATA drives, resulting in greater MTBF (Mean Time Between Failure) and duty cycles: 1,500,000 hours with a duty cycle of 100% for SCSI drives versus 500,000 hours at a duty cycle of 20 percent for the SATA drives (see http://h18006.www1.hp.com/products/quick-specs/11945_div/11945_div.html for reference).

Which to choose then? You may consider that SATA drives provide greater capacity at lower cost, and aim your choice towards this technology. However, Microsoft Exchange is a demanding application in terms of transaction throughput (I/O per sec) and this is not likely to decrease. Secondly, the data typically found in Microsoft Exchange cannot easily be partitioned between what's really important (3-months worth of mailbox or shared document) and what's not important (the mails you exchanged for 2 years, but that you keep, just in case).

The net result is that there is a requirement for hosting the Microsoft Exchange databases to fulfill the capacity requirement at the same time as transaction throughput, and while the SATA drives appear to be very cost effective for capacity, they do not offer the same level of transfer rate and reliability that is often demanded for Microsoft Exchange, even the smallest environments (200 users or more).

Therefore, you should investigate the use of SATA drives for hosting backups or shadow copy images of production volumes, which should be hosted on SCSI or SAS drives. This modus operandi enables greater availability and performance for the production volumes (online databases), while the sheer capacity delivered by the SATA drives is used for storing backups, and therefore are less subject to utilization than the SCSI drives. Furthermore, because the direct-attached drives are actually components of more advanced solutions, such as in Network Storage Servers (NAS) or small to medium SAN arrays, you should extend to this recommendation when using these components.

But one of the problems with direct-attached storage is the inability to scale up to the demands of both capacity and performance requirements. As your user base grows and the demand increases, by taking advantage of Exchange 2003's ability to use multiple databases, you will quickly get into a situation where you may not be able to add units and where the expansion of existing units can be problematic and require significant down time. For example, it is not possible to dynamically expand a volume using direct-attached storage technology without bringing the server to a halt. You may envisage this type of operation during planned downtime of your servers.

While the lack of expandability on a particular bus-attached controller can be noticed, you may argue that you can add additional controllers to the PCI bus. This is true, but the current host I/O bus technology and the way Windows Server handles it is such that by adding more controllers, you will introduce more interruptions in the processing of the server and in fact decrease the server's performance—its ability to perform optimally. Furthermore, lower-priority bus addresses and requestors can quickly become starved as higher-priority entities (network cards or others storage controllers) grab the bus bandwidth. Slow response time on certain devices can have an overall negative effect on the computing capability of the server, and worst of all, the response time of user transactions.

Performance scaling can also be a concern for bus-attached storage controllers. In Wide SCSI, you typically can connect up to 15 drives per bus. However, the SCSI multi-device operation will depend on the SCSI bus arbitration sequence that determines which device has the right to make data transfers. Because the arbitration is based on bus addresses, this means that low-priority devices have to wait a relatively long time before their attempt to control the bus is not overtaken by a higher priority device or the controller itself. Low-priority devices on the SCSI bus become starved and prevent the feeding of high-speed modern processors with data to process.

This said, direct-attached storage is an excellent strategy for small to medium-sized servers that do not require immediate expansion. PCI-based RAID controllers are becoming faster and faster, and although they are often pointed out as a single point of failure, they have proved to be reliable to the point that you can deploy them with confidence, provided that you accompany this type of deployment with advanced data management and fast backup and recovery. With these controllers you can use advanced storage optimization techniques such as RAID5 or RAID0+1, and, most important, write caching, which will boost performance for the response time of your transaction log traffic and your database accesses.

Servers can ship in high-expansion models, by which drive cage and bays are prepared in the server enclosure. This carries great advantages for expandability reasons, but it shouldn't be assumed that new high-capacity drives will be supported in these existing configurations. Some manufacturers, such as HP, have made the effort, however, to build drives around the same form factor and plug characteristics, thereby enabling you to interchangeably use disks between servers of various models, and even external storage shelves.

This is certainly a step in the right direction, one that helps in protecting the company's investment.

Given this, many deployments I've seen are really targeted to last for a minimum of 2 to 3 years. The cost of hardware upgrade is certainly considered, but, most important, the cost of downtime and the cost of servicing typically prohibits from "touching" to already deployed servers. So came to the storage market new ways of providing storage to clients and servers, almost on demand, and built around architecture will allow easy expansion, easy management and monitoring, and provide an "on-demand" storage service to both clients, and applications servers. This leads to two storage-related technologies: Storage Area Networks (SAN), and Network Attached Storage (NAS), which shift from bus-oriented storage to network oriented storage: the network paradigm is applied to storage components, coming with incurred flexibility, yet with more complexity and more choices to chose from: which becomes then a significant equation to solve, and can only be made if you have clearly identified your requirements.

4.5.2   Storage Area Networks

SANs basically represent a paradigm shift in the storage world by applying the best concepts of networking to storage. Note that this is also true for NAS, but NAS has a separate and not competitive place in the Exchange 2000 data centers. However, for the most part, SANs rapidly became a predominant technology in high-end Exchange 2003 environment, because of its several virtues:

- Scalability
- Flexibility

- Performance
- Consolidation
- Manageability
- Availability

You have certainly heard about SANs if you have to manage a large-scale environment and if you've been attentive to developments within the storage industry. Given that storage represents approximately 60 percent of IT spending, administrators certainly have had to care about it. For IT directors, data storage should have a strategic orientation, and CIOs just want it to work while the company carries on its business without worrying about details and shortcomings of one implementation or another.

The important thing, really, is that when we build those large Microsoft Exchange infrastructures for hosting massive quantities of data, the servers are of much less concern to us than the storage.

In the past 5 years, we moved from a host-centric approach to a storage-centric approach: evaluating the storage capacity as well as its performance became the key decision criteria for the architects. When using SAN technology, we have to bring additional considerations beyond the disk and RAID systems, by including the networking components, which typically consist of Fibre Channel switches and hubs and Host-Bus Adapters (HBA), special controllers that enable the server to enumerate and access the logical units defined on the back-end SAN controllers, as shown in Figure 4.12.

The exercise must consist of establishing a solid and reliable connectivity between the servers and the SAN array controllers, building controllers that can support the peak and aggregated workloads anticipated, and then issue servers that will run the Microsoft Exchange services and access the units over the Storage Area Network. These units are accessed independently between servers, and cooperatively between servers which are part of a Microsoft Cluster.

Figure 4.13 illustrates the approach to a server-centric design, where client computers connect to servers by the means of a network infrastructure (typically LAN, but can be expanded to a WAN in highly centralized environments) and application servers are provided by servers each having their own server-tethered storage. With Exchange 5.5, this type of deployment was extremely frequent, because of lack of SAN maturation. The application itself is confined to the realm of resources, processor, memory, but, most important, storage, all of which are available on the server.

Figure 4.12
*SAN in a Microsoft
Exchange Network*

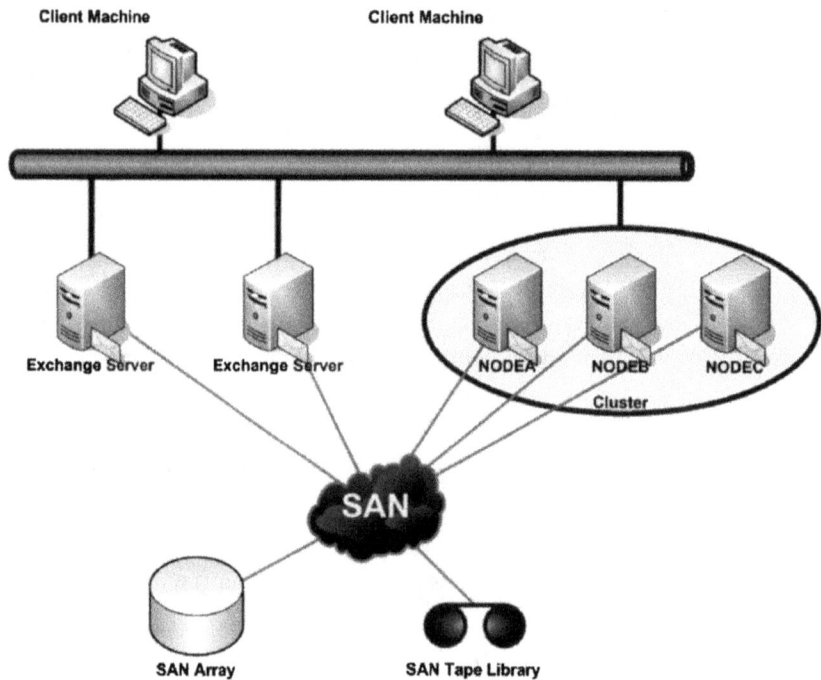

Figure 4.13
*Server Centric
Approach*

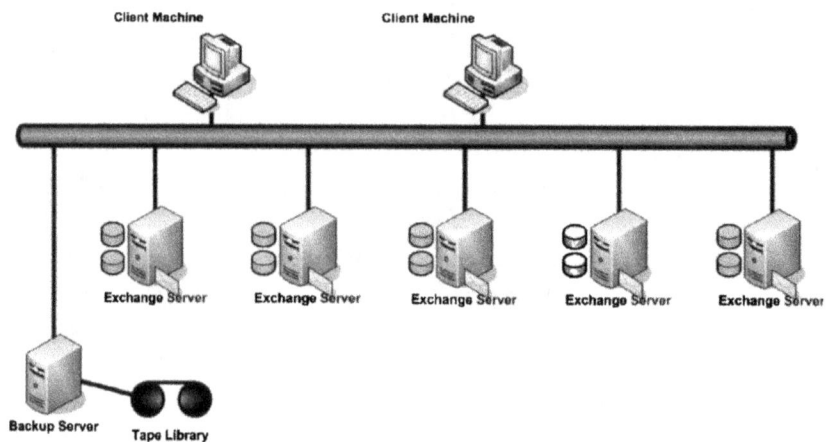

By contrast, Figure 4.13 exhibits a storage-centric approach, where servers have minimal local storage resources and share one or more common storage cabinets to access mainstream data required by the application.

Some deployments can even go as far as using diskless servers that can boot directly from the SAN infrastructure. We are in this case building a redundant array of independent servers (RAIS), a proposal that is quite attractive when clustering of Exchange 2003 does not comply with the customer's requirements. Servers are becoming almost "throwaway" items; if one breaks down, another can replace the broken server. These configurations are sometimes called "N+1" configurations, where N servers are active, and 1 server is kept as a cold-standby server. This may be implemented in many ways. Clearly, the ability for a SAN adapter to boot into a SAN greatly simplifies the process of replacing the existing failed server with a new server. All that is needed is granting access to the boot and data volumes to the new server (this can be done usually at the storage cabinet level, by enabling access to the volumes to the host-id of the host-bus adapter of the recovery server).

Storage Area Networks enable you to do the same things as you did before, only differently and with greater flexibility. It would be a mistake to buy a SAN solution for its performance, unless you need the performance of high-end storage cabinets. In that case, you will concentrate on deploying an *island* of SAN, which is, admittedly, a common practice at the moment. SAN is an enabling technology, which will improve on certain aspects of data storage operations, such as:

- *Backup and restore*—the ability to localize the bulk of the backup and restore data transfer to the SAN, without the need to build a separate high-speed LAN or use-dedicated, locally attached tape drives, while keeping the same levels of performance. Remember that SAN are typically Gigabit networks (200 MB/s and more for the years to come) that are perfect for backup applications that can take advantage of such a large bandwidth.

- *Advanced disaster tolerance*— the ability to implement distant mirrors or clones or snapshots of individual volumes much more easily than with direct-attached storage. In fact, with DAS, it's almost impossible to build such solutions, unless aiming for a software-based solution, which does not always address the strict requirements of data consistency and performance required by an application such as Exchange 2003. Disaster tolerance, or what we could simply reduce to availability is important, and if you ask anybody, the basic requirement will fall to 7×24×forever, no matter what.

- *Easy growth*—SAN storage cabinets can usually grow beyond several terabytes, not that it would be a wise thing to build 1 TB logical unit or volume; this can have a severe impact on the manageability of the volume (see subsequent discussion of RAID volumes and how large they should or can be). Local storage capacity to servers is typically limited by physical space, and sometimes connectivity.

The important concern in storage growth is not always capacity; often it's the requirement to maintain the same levels of performance and availability, especially when adding third party applications such as anti-virus or other mobility enabling solutions such as RIM's BlackBerry Enterprise Server.

- *Cost Recovery*—the ability to serve storage to many servers helps to reduce the somewhat incremental cost of a SAN-based solution; you can make economies of scale by sharing advanced features of the SAN, such as data replication for disaster tolerance and recovery purposes.

- *Ability to deploy disk-less server farms*—also known as Redundant Array of Independent Servers or RAIS. This is accomplished by enabling a boot device to be located in the shared storage area network.

Cost recovery is a key factor for most IT directors, since you will find many environments in which established shared-storage vendors will attempt to offer their storage services to the Exchange 2003 servers, thereby reducing the overall cost of the storage solution. This aspect of sharing is quite important. As you invest tens of thousands of dollars in a storage solution, it will provide certain availability features that you won't find on PCI-based RAID controllers, such as cache mirroring, bus redundancy, or controller redundancy. Coming into play also is the benefit of tape automation, disk hot spares, and emergency access to temporary storage—for example, making a 100 GB volume available to several servers for database off-line defragmentation or maintenance operation or debugging.

Finally, the notion of online growth and expansion without taking down the service is particularly important when building Microsoft Exchange networks. For any storage design for Microsoft Exchange, you will want to build in your design enough capacity for growth: this growth, estimated between 20 percent and 50 percent per annum, depends upon your business. Your company can (will) grow, either organically or by acquisition. The quantity of data also grows, both in terms of quantity of messages processed per day and per employee and in terms of individual size, by using rich documents, media, digitized information, etc....

Just like any consumer, ask yourself the three following questions:

1. How much ($ or €) was a GB last year?

2. How much is it today?

3. How much will it be in 1 year down the road?

I think you will find that the trend of an ever decreasing cost of storage, combined with improved footprint (and therefore required infrastructure) and somewhat improved performance, implies that the storage infrastructures of today will be different in 3 years from now. The modern IT infrastructures are therefore designed to adapt, and use only what they need: this is the concept of "On Demand" that can be applied to storage components or even application services. You pay for what you use, period.

Note that this model does not apply to all companies, either because of the technology (lack of) readiness or of the culture or other parameters. However, you should keep this model in mind, and understand that SANs are key enablers for building such flexible infrastructures: adding a server on a SAN is far less costly than building a server with it's own server-tethered storage, simply because you can build on existing practices (processes) and staff and technologies, instead of adding additional units.

Again, I wish to stress herein that SAN is not a unique solution to all environments, it's just that it benefits most of them, with, granted, a somewhat increased cost—this cost increment is basically the value you obtain with such technologies.

The concept of sharing can also be extended to an entire RAID volume, where you would define a 10-disk array, partitioned into several independent Logical Units (LUNs) of reduced capacity. The advantage is that you get an incremental performance by using a volume with many disks that can handle a large quantity of transactions. The disadvantage, and you should be aware of this, is that in most implementations, the LUNs are accessed without any cooperation between each other. What happens if you share a single large volume between several Exchange 2003 servers, and suddenly you need to perform a database integrity check on one of the databases of one server? The other servers will suddenly get "polluted" by the sheer transaction rate of the server performing the integrity check and may have their performance severely impacted. Sharing in a SAN is a good concept and can be extended to volumes, but you must make sure that you have sufficient capacity so that individual servers can effectively maintain their workload.

4.5.3   Fibre Channel: The basis for SAN

Fibre Channel (as a protocol) provides high levels of bandwidth, connectivity, and flexibility. Today's SAN are deployed using multiport switches that can provide nonblocking 200 MB/s (that is Mega-Byte, not Mega-Bit) per port with any-to-any connectivity. Although early implementations were seen on copper (serial cable type interface), Fibre Channel moved very quickly to optical fiber, which provides a flexible approach to connectivity, including long-range connectivity (up to 100 km and above), appropriate when building secondary disaster recovery sites. But this is not all; Fibre Channel will soon get to 4 to 8 GB/s and is projected to grow to 10 GB/s real soon. Most implementations are based on switch deployments and sometimes combine switches together, in rings or cascade. Be warned, however, that although switches from different vendors can have the same origin (e.g., Brocade switches are OEM'ed by many vendors), differences in the firmware may appear and cause incompatibility.

Today, simple SANs are built on low-cost (small number of ports, 8 or 16) switches with a single array, designed to serve a handful of servers.

Figure 4.14
*Simple SAN
with Two
Redundant
Switches*

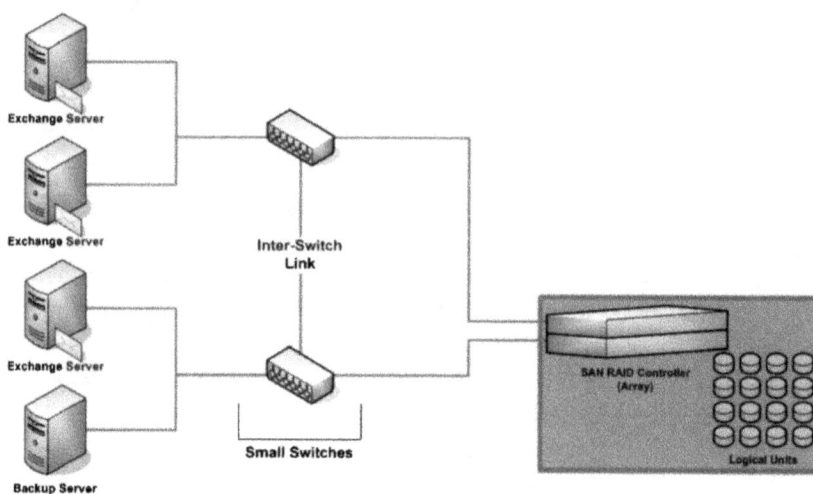

The switches are connected together by the means of an ISL: Inter-Switch Link. If a switch breaks, the path to the Storage array is still available to the other switch. The problem with this approach is that the more switches you add, the more ISLs you need to guarantee path availability and performance. Adding an ISL to a switch is basically wasting two ports: one for each switch.

With ports being a scarce resource in SAN environment, because switches are relatively expensive, a new approach has been considered in the past couple of years by utilizing a series of switches at the center (core) of the Fibre Channel fabric, and another series of switches for connecting to this core, at the edge of the fabric. Core switches can scale up in ports and performance and run multiple protocols (particularly interesting for consolidation of networking infrastructures for mixed iSCSI and SAN deployments).

Known as a Core-Edge SAN infrastructure, this type of approach is schematized in Figure 4.15.

Figure 4.15
Simple Core-Edge
SAN Design

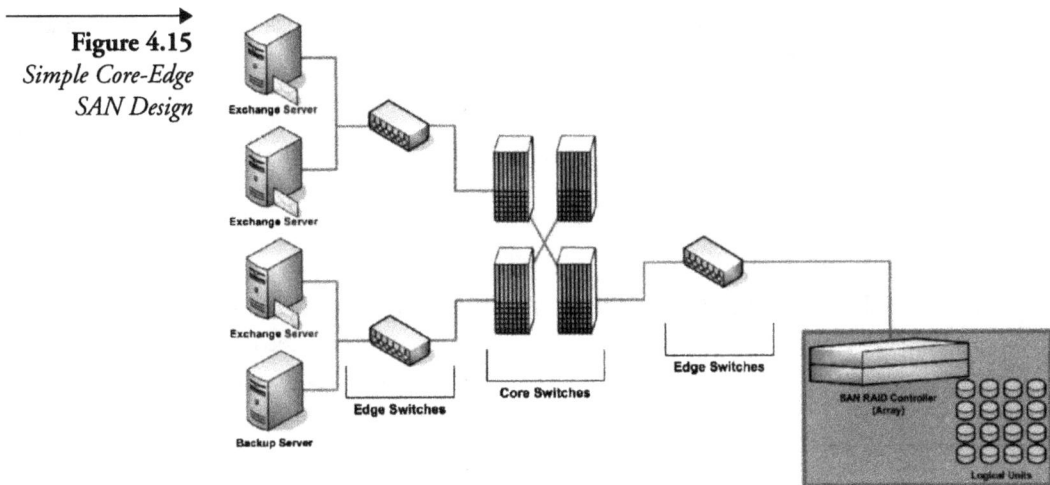

Core-Edge SAN designs are now well established in high-end SAN environments because they enable some level of separation between servers (particularly useful in mixed-vendor server environments) and also between back-end storage components. Besides, the mesh at the core can connect to remote switches, i.e., connect over a long distance by the means of multimode, single-mode optical fibers and possibly Fibre Channel extenders. Deciding when to move to a core-edge infrastructure really depends upon the number of ports available on your switches. In the past, switches would not scale in footprint and performance beyond 32 or 64 ports. Therefore, in order to accommodate 500 or 600 port access, you had to multiply these switches, multiply the ISL, have many ports wasted and finally, many resources wasted. Cascading the switches is a possibility, but only if you can keep the number of hops rather minimal (3 hops is considered to be a maximum for within a data center: one edge, one core, one edge).

With such an approach and the combined usage of zoning, you also have the possibility to create a protocol-level isolation, which carries the advantage of avoiding servers being annoyed at each other (Microsoft clusters, for instance, use SCSI commands with the SCSI miniport driver which can be disruptive to other servers, even if they are not running a Windows server). Although fabrics are migrated in the goal of merging SAN islands, the core-edge approach enables us to bridge islands, sometimes continents (because they are so large), together, and enjoy a common physical infrastructure for manageability and cost recovery perspectives. Eventually, the variations are too immense to describe in this book.

We've seen two basic approaches, but then, as a Microsoft Exchange administrator, you will be confronted with two approaches:

1. Build your own SAN and control it—in that case, depending upon your budget, you might consider core-edge scenarios, but generally, a simple dual-switch approach will work well for a small number of servers (less than a dozen)

2. Use (reuse?) the corporate SAN infrastructure, typically built in a core-edge approach, and in that case, you become a subscriber to a storage network service, and you will need to face the same advantages and problems as a customer to the service: ensuring you have full and reliable access, dealing with congestion, etc.... In such approach, defining clear and measurable service levels is essential to determine if the SAN delivers the throughput required at an acceptable latency. Without SLA (Service Level Agreements), an Exchange administrator is vulnerable to SAN service quality fluctuations, with little possibility to make changes.

This is a just a quick browse, but as you can notice, the network paradigm applied to storage, as I mentioned earlier, comes with its problems. They are not unsolvable—it's just that in Microsoft Exchange environments, we have not always been accustomed to these notions, especially when we grew out of server-tethered storage. In the longer run, you shall be surprised to see how Microsoft Exchange can hammer the storage back-end, and this becomes particularly relevant in shared and virtualized infrastructures, where your art will consist of getting the right quantities of resources for dealing with the majority of your workload, and ensuring you have some headroom for peak periods (high traffic due to business or external reasons) without over engineering the solution.

4.5.4   SAN boot: can I use my SAN to host my boot volumes?

SAN Boot is a convenient way to create a redundant server infrastructure without having to implement Microsoft Clustering Services (MSCS). The idea is to build upon the notion of Redundant Array of Independent Servers (RAIS) and to place the boot volume of one or more servers in a SAN environment in order to enable error-free and semi-automated server failover. Of course, because the server depends upon the SAN for both its data and boot volumes, any storage failure directly impacts the server operations. In this section, I describe a handful of best practices to keep in mind when you want to implement Windows servers with boot volumes located in SAN environments.

Background

Figure 4.16 shows the principles of RAIS and SAN boot. Servers are configured with no local disk, and use their Host-Bus Adapters (HBA) to communicate with a storage array on a SAN, using SAN-based LUN (Logical Units) as boot volumes.

Figure 4.16
*SAN Boot
Principles*

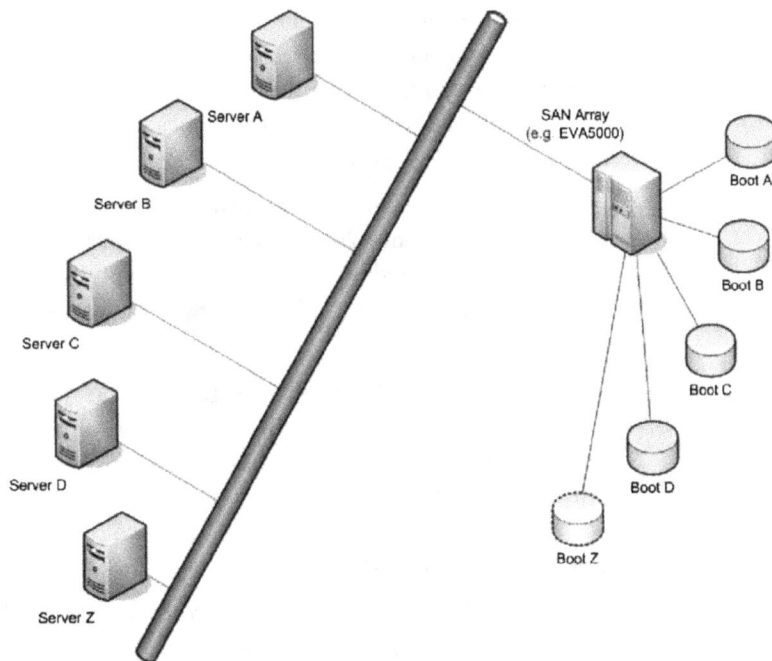

In this example, we have four production servers (A, B, C and D) and one standby server (Z); each has boot volumes hosted in a SAN array (Boot A, B, C, D, and Z). We will see later why you should use a boot volume for server Z (the standby server).

How does it work?

SAN booting is typically enabled on Intel servers by programming the HBA BIOS to lookup a logical unit on a SAN as a boot device. This assumes that:

- You have programmed the server's own BIOS to enable HBA boots
- You have selected the correct LUN in the HBA BIOS configuration

HP has published a very comprehensive white paper describing how to enable a SAN boot in HP storage environments: "Booting 32-bit Windows Systems from a Storage Area Network—Application Notes," that you can access through this link: ftp://ftp.compaq.com/pub/products/storageworks/techdoc/san/AA-RS2UF-TE.pdf.

You should read and understand this document and ALL of its terms prior to deploying your infrastructure into production. In here, I assume that you are familiar with the basic operations required to configure the server to operate with a boot volume located on a SAN array.

Microsoft has published an article on SAN boot considerations available at http://download.microsoft.com/download/f/9/7/f9775acc-baa6-45cc-9dec-b82983705620/Boot%20from%20SAN%20in%20Windows.doc. This article gives a pretty good overview on the pros and cons for SAN boot for Windows server, as well as providing some generic server and HBA configuration guidelines.

As IP SAN (iSCSI-based storage networks) technology develops, the same principle will be applicable in such environments. For now, and until the technology matures, the majority of SAN boot environments are using Fibre Channel SAN.

The Crash Dump issue

The downside of boot volumes located on a SAN is the crash dump analysis: when executing a STOP instruction, Windows Server expects to generate a memory dump on the system partition volume. When booting from a SAN volume, a crash dump stack is created based on the Fibre

Channel path used to locate the boot volume on the SAN. If, for some reason, this path is not available at the time of a STOP error, the crash dump stack will be unable to locate the boot device and a memory dump will not be created.

You can ensure that memory dumps can be created in your environment using the Ctrl-Scroll Lock-Scroll Lock key sequence, which is enabled as documented at: http://support.microsoft.com/default.aspx?scid=KB;EN-US;244139. One might argue that you will rarely want to perform server debugging using a crash dump analysis, but there are cases where this has been requested by Microsoft support during complex troubleshooting.

Using RDP or Altiris eXpress

The HP ProLiant Essentials Rapid Deployment Pack can be used to install Windows on your servers. RDP has a minimal license fee and the tool provides immense value for consistently configuring server farms. This deployment solution is equivalent for most of the Windows server vendors. In here, I discuss of the technology by referring directly to RDP, because that is a solution that I routinely use.

RDP can be useful to successively install common images of the Windows operating system. It can also be used for capturing a SAN boot volume image that can be reused on a local disk (see Figure 4.17).

This can be useful in instances where you want to exclude the SAN topology from a debugging/support exercise.

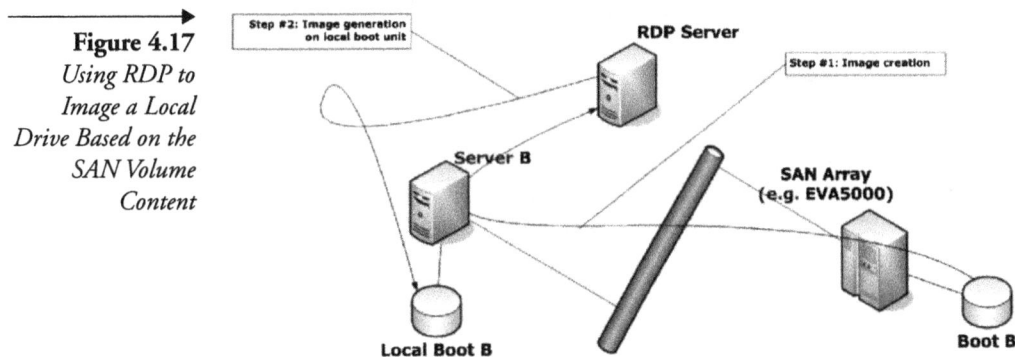

Figure 4.17
Using RDP to Image a Local Drive Based on the SAN Volume Content

You might want to keep (and maintain) the local boot image on the production server (here, Server B) on an on-going basis, and decide by the means of the boot priority order whether you should be booting off the SAN or locally.

There are alternatives to RDP for imaging a server boot device, but the relatively low cost of a single server RDP license is negligible compared to the advantages of deploying such a solution. http://h18004.www1.hp.com/products/servers/management/rdp/index.html has good information about HP RDP.

Note that RDP can be used as an overall server failover/management automation framework that can assist you in the management of the LUN presentation. Also, opportunities exist for coupling RDP deployment jobs with array management command scripting utilities (such as SSSU in HP StorageWorks EVA environments).

Typical usage

Note that a SAN boot can be used without standby servers, for example, in a disaster tolerant environment where the boot volumes are replicated in real-time to a remote site hosting a mirrored hardware configuration. In the case of a site failover, you only need to break the replication link, then present the LUNs to the remote servers and start them.

Standby servers are useful when recovering from a server hardware error; however, if you have a software problem (at the application, operating system, or file system levels), using a standby machine will probably not solve your problem. When you design such an environment, you should always plan on using advanced server monitoring tools that can report and diagnose problems on the physical server. Note that this is the principal weakness of such an approach. MSCS, for example, provides a Cluster Resource Manager that can monitor and move resources between nodes in a cluster.

Failover process

For this knowledge brief, "failover" is defined as the process of using a standby server in place of a production server. This term is borrowed from Microsoft clustering terminology. A typical failover process would consist of:

- Verifying the production server LUNs, which comprise the boot and most likely the database or application specific volumes
- Shutting down both the production and standby servers
- Masking the production LUN from the production server
- Presenting the production LUN to the standby server
- Powering on the standby server

All of these operations can be executed remotely by means of RILO or iLO boards and via the SAN Management Appliance when masking and presenting LUNs. (RILO and iLO boards typically ship by default in HP ProLiant servers and enable remote power on and off of the server.)

Caveats and things you should not forget about

From the field experience viewpoint, it is paramount to completely master the whole environment. Many components depend on each other. In particular, any operations staff that work with the servers and the hardware and key operating system features should have knowledge of:

- The SAN management framework that typically provides a user interface and automation facility for managing the SAN back-end array

- The SAN back-end array and the fabric topology (including zoning information, which is typically defined at the Fibre Channel switch level)

- Host-Bus Adapters, server boot BIOS, SAN fabric and path definition and SAN boot in general

- The host operating system (in our case, Windows Server) and any critical applications

- Last, but not least, all these management interfaces are generally deployed with their own security identification mechanism. For example, a remote console management board inside a Windows server typically requires a user name and password, as does the SAN Management appliance and the Fibre Channel switches. This is required in addition to operating system-level credentials. Make sure you have all of this information in hand before you start implementing/troubleshooting your solution.

The next step is creating a boot volume for the standby server. You may create a small (4GB) LUN for the standby server, ensuring that the machine is present on the network and can be managed. That way, you can monitor the standby server's hardware components, flash BIOS and ROMs, and possibly use the machine for testing purposes. Of course, you need to give priority to the production server's work, but it is always good to be sure that the standby server, seldom used in failover scenarios, can indeed be failed over.

Given that the standby server will be used in the network for monitoring purposes, remember to include it in your software and hardware maintenance processes, for example, Service Pack upgrades, hotfixes and security conformance. On that very same standby server, you will have to pre-configure the HBAs allowing it to impersonate a production server that fails to operate properly. For this "impersonation" to happen, you need to boot the standby machine on the boot LUN used by the now-defunct server. This means that standby server Z must be capable of booting off the boot volume of server A, B, C, or D.

For each of the A, B, C, and D servers, you will typically point the HBA BIOS to boot from one LUN (referenced by the controller's World Wide Port Name and LUN).

Figure 4.18
Selecting a Boot LUN in the HBA BIOS

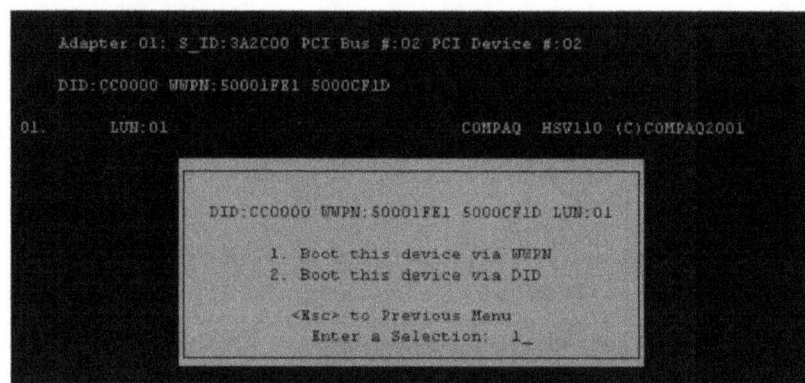

In Figure 4.18, we select LUN 01 on the controller's port "50001FE1 5000CF1D." This port is defined at the controller level, similar to a NIC MAC address. In the case of an EVA storage array, the controller's host port can be viewed from the SAN Management Appliance, as shown in Figure 4.18.

Alternatively, given that the HBA BIOS needs the WWPN of the host controller interface as well as the boot logical unit number, you can simplify this definition process by always using the same LU number (1, for example; don't use 0—this is reserved for controller commands) for each of the boot volumes. This minimizes the BIOS configuration as you only need to register the SAN array WWPN.

Figure 4.20 shows how different servers can use a volume presented with the same LU number (#1 in this case). This is achieved by virtue of the presentation (masking) of the LUN from the SAN array. No conflict will occur as long as you keep the LUN presentation consistent across the servers (and

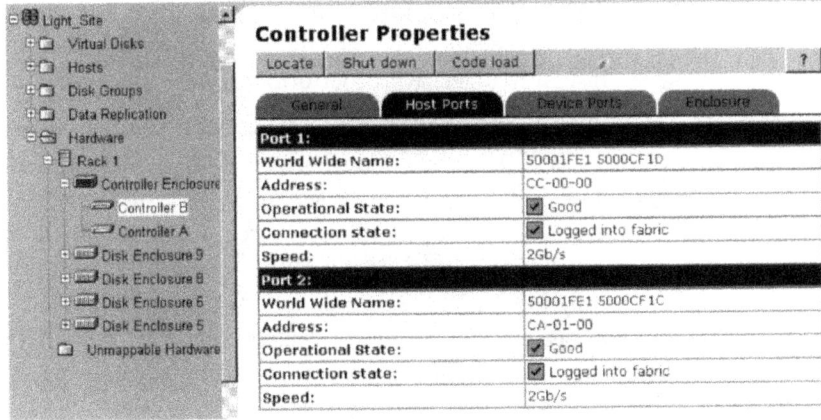

Figure 4.19
*Selecting a Boot
LUN in the
HBA BIOS*

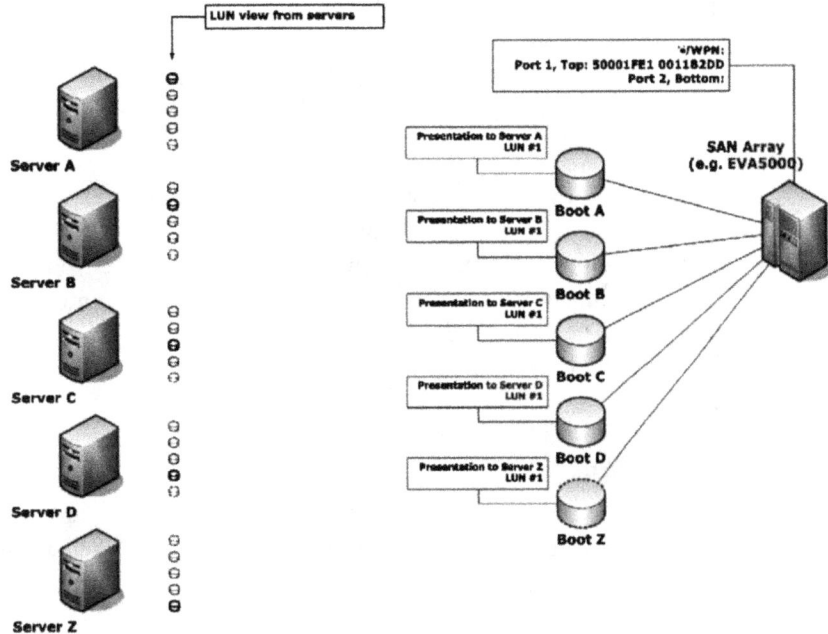

Figure 4.20
*LUNS "as Seen" by
the Servers*

therefore avoid presenting the same LUN to more than one server, unless you operate in clustered environments).

To ensure connectivity and continuous operations, you should make sure that the Fabric Zoning (partitioning used for a Fibre Channel infrastructure to create virtual islands) does not get in the way of the failover process.

Unlike an MSCS environment, there is no process or technology provided with Windows Server that enables you to monitor your server and its applications and make educated decisions for the failover process. You should therefore take advantage of the HP ProLiant tools, for example, Insight Manager when performing hardware monitoring, ensuring that you can predict or be sure that a server failover will indeed solve your problem.

BCV (Business Continuity Volumes) or Clones represent a physical duplicate of a volume. They are typically used for hosting business critical data that must be rapidly recovered, such as databases. If you decide to host your boot volumes on a SAN, it is appropriate to create a block-by-block copy (do NOT use snapshots) of a boot volume, to allow for fast recovery in case the boot volume becomes physically or logically corrupted. This has happened previously in a customer environment, where the only option was to perform a bare-bones recovery of the operating system. Of course, depending on the backup and recovery product you use, this operation can be more, or less, complex. However, it is not as simple as presenting a LUN to the server.

Another use of the SAN array capabilities is to create a snapshot copy (read-only) that is then used to generate an RDP image that can be flashed later on.

By booting a standby server from a cloned volume, you keep the production system disk intact. If, in the process of recovery, you need to install critical operating system or application updates you have a "safety net" that allows you to rollback to the original boot volume if things turn sour. This is an example of how you can take advantage of SAN abilities in your server farm environment.

One last but very important point!

Use a local pagefile volume in replicated environments. A pagefile usually contains transient information that is not required after a reboot. If you operate in a replicated environment where each volume is replicated by means of a DR Group (EVA terminology), it is not necessary to carry paging operations across to the remote site. If there is a site failover, the information will be of no value. While you can still host your pagefile volume on the boot volume or another volume on the SAN, make sure that you do not pollute the inter-site link with paging operations.

Paging over the SAN is not necessarily a bad thing; for a server that pages excessively, you should use a local volume. But then, you should probably fix the paging "problem" first. Microsoft documents how to track possible problems when using SAN-hosted pagefile volumes in Microsoft Knowledge Base article 305547.

In Summary

SAN boot is a great approach for ensuring business continuity with reduced complexity. You should take advantage of the technology, but always remember what your goals are. Using RAIS with SAN boot is not a one-to-one replacement of Microsoft clustering for Windows servers. In fact, some of the operations listed here can be quite complex, even more so than MSCS.

You should keep in mind that this type of approach is not a replacement for any slack in operations and administration; while it can deliver value in well maintained environments, this approach is completely counter-productive if you do not have best-in-class operation processes (such as backup and recovery) and if you haven't thoroughly reviewed the architecture and failover processes.

Remember that technology alone does not solve all the problems and that your processes and operations staff are the key success factors for such an implementation—do not neglect process and training!

4.5.5 RAIS: Redundant arrays of independent servers

Redundant Array of Independent Servers is an approach that can be taken to achieve highly available computing platforms, especially with Windows Server. In April 2001, Microsoft announced a set of restrictions for the support of clustering in Exchange 2000, which would be rolled out and enforced with the release of Service Pack 1. These restrictions strongly recommended Active/Passive clustering as opposed to the much acclaimed Active/Active clustering feature in the initial product release. Eventually, these changes still apply for the most recent version of Microsoft Exchange 2003, including SP2.

While this left a bitter taste, customers have been thinking about ways to scale out clustered deployments, as well as increasing availability. As an alternative to clustering, RAIS can be utilized while providing a reasonable level of redundancy functionality.

RAIS is based on a cold-standby approach: any number of computers can operate to offer a service, such as Microsoft Exchange. Should one of the servers fail, it is replaced by a similar server (in this context, a similar server means that the same hardware and firmware configuration exists for all the system's components, such as the CPU, motherboard and PCI adapters) so this server can resume operations and take over the tasks previously handled by the failed server.

You don't necessarily need advanced technology to build a RAIS. However, you must ensure that when you decide to replace an existing server with a cold standby server, that you perform the necessary tasks required for that standby server to operate in the original server's environment.

A simple RAIS implementation can be accomplished by manually moving the disks from the failed server to the cold standby server (this was an effective solution adopted of a production banking environment). Another approach consists in re-imaging the server boot volumes from a server deployment infrastructure, e.g., using an automated PXE boot that can be served by a server which then downloads (or uploads) the boot disk contents to the server.

The most flexible approach is to boot servers into a common SAN infrastructure that then enables the cold standby server to boot off the system volume of the failing server, as described in section 4.5.4.

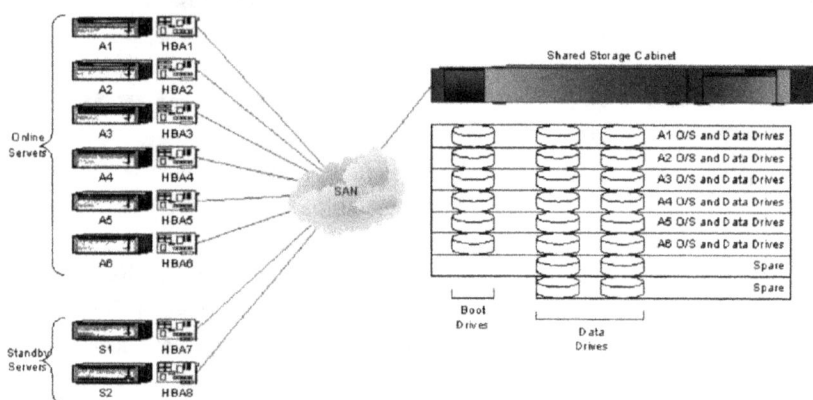

Figure 4.21
Example of a RAIS Using SAN Technology

One of the great benefits of RAIS, is its ability to run standalone Windows servers: you do not need extra Windows administration and operations skilled personnel to operate the servers, and all the third-party products have been developed, tested, and supported on standalone machines.

The most important point to consider when you make your decision is whether you decide that the management of the application resources (such as services and volumes) is under the control of the Microsoft Cluster Services resource manager, or part of an external process (such as Insight Manager's monitoring tools). The actual task of changing servers might in fact be manual, although this is not optimal as it inserts human intervention in the process (something you just cannot achieve even with Remote Insight Management Boards as alluded to in the previous section).

Table 4.2   *RAIS at a glance*

RAIS	Pros	Cons
Technology used to deploy standby servers (typically turned off) in a similar configuration that can replace a failing server. This is best implemented with diskless server technology that instructs the server to boot off volumes hosted in a Storage Area Network. You may also boot servers off the network with Windows Server 2003.	Low cost solution	Supportability issues may arise from Microsoft (see articles Q305547 and Q304415)
	Scalability: you are not limited by the number of servers that can be replaced by one or two cold stand-by servers	Manual or scriptable resource monitoring
	Standard Windows and applications' setup	Microsoft prefers that the system page file is located on the boot drive for recording memory dumps resulting from BSOD*. Page file can be located on the local system's disk enclosure though.
	No integration work required for implementing non-cluster aware applications	The decision to take a system down must be done manually, or requires advanced monitoring tasks
	Guaranteed to fall in 99 percent of the technical calls that technical support personnel usually handle	The failover and fail-back procedures must be scripted to prevent errors during recovery
	Works well with Data Replication Manager to create a mirrored and up-to-date secondary site for disaster recovery purposes	Does not address rolling upgrades

* BSOD: Blue Screen resulting from a Windows operating system crash that requires a complete system restart.

So what to do?

There is no clear cut winner when it comes to deciding on the optimum approach to attain high availability in a Windows environment. The ultimate decision depends upon your customer's requirements. Clustering is an appealing solution if cost is not an issue, especially in Windows 2003 Data Center environments.

With Windows Server 2003 Enterprise edition clustering, you can have up to eight members in a cluster. Even if your application can only operate in active/passive mode, you can multiply by seven your return on investment, having seven active machines versus one passive one.

Table 4.3	*Clustering at a glance*

Clustering	Pros	Cons
Technology that enables two (Windows 2000 Advanced Server) or up to eight (Windows Server 2003 Enterprise and Data Center editions) servers to share a common set of disk resources (typically located on a SAN), and to have an application executing on either or all of the nodes of the cluster managed by a cluster resource manager which monitors the application activity. The cluster resource manager can decide to perform a failover, which consists of moving all the resources related to an application component from one physical node to another.	Cluster Resource Management that can monitor if a resource dies and decide when to perform a failover	Number of nodes is limited to two in Windows 2000 Advanced Server, four in Windows 2000 Data Center (often considered as a cost-prohibited solution), eight in Windows Server 2003 Enterprise and Data Center editions.
	Rolling upgrade which enables you to apply hotfixes, service packs, etc.... with minimal service disruption	Limitation on the number of volumes (22) and the number of Exchange Virtual Servers you can operate across the overall cluster
	Can be utilized with DRM to form a geographically spread cluster across multiple meters or miles (GeoCluster). See Microsoft's HCL for the most recent supported configuration (http://www.microsoft.com/hcl)	Failover can be lengthy, sometimes never end, and exceed the target Service Level Agreements
	Does not prevent booting the servers off the storage area network	Cost factor in customer's mindset when speaking about active/passive scenarios
	Network boot and operations remains to be qualified for Windows Server 2003	Added complexity for operations (requires cluster-aware operations staff)
		Added complexity for 3rd party solutions which are first designed to operate in standalone environments
		Supportability is not always guaranteed from software vendors (ensure that the support person you speak with has ever seen a cluster, especially for 3rd party software)

On the other hand, RAIS is an approach that can accommodate scaled-out deployments using SAN technology, at a lower cost compared to clustering. In both cases, be sure to take the time to discuss exactly what the customer requires in terms of Service Level Agreements, uptime, overall sys-

tem resilience and application support before making a decision on which
technology to recommend.

4.5.6   Storage Replication with SAN

On March 15th 2005, Microsoft published a knowledge base article (Article ID: 895847; Multi-Site Data Replication Support for Exchange 2003
and Exchange 2000) explaining the supportability boundaries of data replication solutions for Microsoft Exchange. As time goes on, the support state-
ments can evolve depending upon the solutions that were explicitly tested
by Microsoft.

In this section, we discuss replication technologies in the context of
Microsoft Exchange deployments and decipher some of the terms and
requirements listed in Microsoft's knowledge base article. Additionally, it
provides guidelines on which replication mode to use with Exchange 2003
(valid until SP2).

Why Replication?

Microsoft Exchange uses the ESE database engine for storing mailbox and
shared documents (a.k.a. Public Folders). In the case of deployments that
need to address efficient disaster recovery, disaster tolerance, or simple site-
level failover, you must ensure that production data can be "replicated"
(copied and made available for recovery purposes) to a spare physical site.
While Microsoft's clustering technology addresses server failures, storage
components are still considered a single point of failure. If you lose the storage components, you lose the data and service availability.

While servers can be easily replaced when they fail, storage typically
requires a recovery from duplicated information, either local or remote.
With shared public folders, this duplication is ensured using application-
based replication. Simplistically, Microsoft Exchange can ensure that a public folder database is replicated to another server instance, without the intervention of any kind of advanced storage technologies.

With mailbox databases, this is not currently the case. Microsoft
Exchange stores mailbox information in a single place (the database referenced by the mailbox attributes of the Windows Active Directory user
account). Further, this database cannot be replicated by the application
itself; therefore, if you need to maintain a second copy of the database for
recovery purposes, you must use storage replication solutions. This can
either be implemented at the host (server) level (typically by means of filter

[1] drivers), or implemented in the back-end storage array (at the RAID controller level).

Basic Principle

The notion of data replication as implemented in host-based or storage-based solution is relatively straightforward:

- Two (or more) copies of a volume/logical unit contents are generated across two different infrastructures connected by a replication link (often referred to as an "Inter-Switch Link, ISL")

- One copy is known as the source or local copy (essentially local to the production application server to which the clients or peer servers connect to)

- Another copy is known as the target or remote copy (remote to the production server, yet local to the recovery server)

- When the application server (in our case, Microsoft Exchange) makes a change to its local copy, that change is also replicated to the remote copy

- The application server reads data from the local copy, if available

- If the local copy is lost, the remote copy can be used, as it contains a replica of the lost local copy.

In such an environment, the production site is also known as the local site, and the recovery site is known as the remote site. Sites must be connected together by a logical link, typically implemented by a set of redundant physical links. We discuss link considerations later on.

Replication and Clustering

You might consider that in addition to maintaining two copies of a data set in two separate sites, you should also have the corresponding servers for providing the final application service to the end-users. In such cases, you have two possible approaches:

1.   Provide a set of mission critical recovery servers on a remote site that can handle the replicated data set

2.   Build a "stretched" Microsoft Cluster solution, where nodes in the solution are spread across both sites

Both solutions are viable with Microsoft Exchange, with a preference for stretch clustering, which provides a suitable framework for monitoring and instrumentation application service and resources failover and "failback."

Host-Based Replication

The purpose of host-based replication is to install a software solution, such as NSI Double Take or equivalent. It can trap any change made to a local volume and send it to a remote server that holds a peer copy of the data. Copying the entire dataset would be subject to significant latencies (as a database is composed of two NTFS files that can exceed 10 GB or 20 GB), however, only the differences will be handled with the exception of the initial copy installation which requires a full resynchronization.

Fortunately, the host-based solution is clever enough to read data locally on the site: any read operation is performed locally to the requesting host, avoiding lengthy inter-site I/O traffic. Write operations are performed locally and replicated remotely, typically in asynchronous mode to avoid penalizing the response time of the write request.

Controller-Based Replication

For server configuration simplicity, the back-end SAN storage controllers can perform the replica change and maintenance without requiring any particular software component on the servers. In that case, any write I/O performed by the Microsoft Exchange server to the storage back-end is performed as well to the remote peer storage back-end. The majority of SAN vendors, such as HP, EMC, or HDS do provide replication functions out of their storage arrays, known as Continuous Access at HP, and SRDF at EMC.

Schematically speaking, Figure 4.22 shows a typical setup for such an environment:

Site A holds production servers and databases and Site B holds a replica of this data with recovery servers that can pick up the services run by the production servers if Site A becomes unavailable to the clients. Although shown separately the replication link and the data network are not necessarily implemented in separate physical infrastructures. In fact, they are very often sharing a dual and redundant multi-protocol link.

Figure 4.22
Typical Replicated
Environment with
Microsoft Exchange

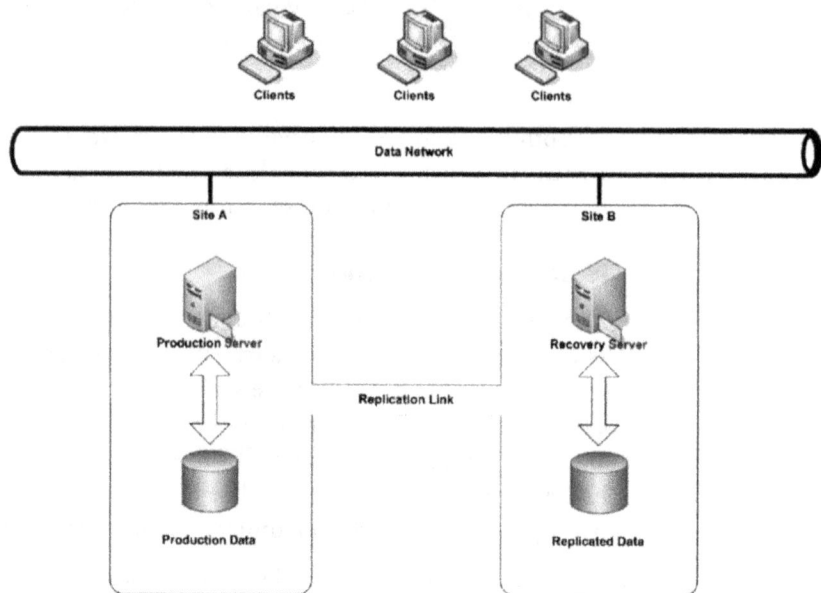

Figure 4.22
Typical Replicated Environment with Microsoft Exchange

Data replication is carried over by the replication link. The responsibility of the replication link is to ensure that changes made locally are replicated remotely. Also, the replication link is used for ensuring that each site can see the other. This dialog between the sites happens at different levels depending on whether you use a host-based solution or a back-end storage-based solution.

The replication link can be quite complex as it is made of hops and more or less redundancy. Typically, you will require a small latency and high bandwidth with (very) high resiliency. These requirements depend on the replication method; asynchronous/synchronous, normal/failsafe.

Note that a "replication link" is not necessarily a piece of wire or fiber. In fact, the replication link is typically made of several physical and logical connections; the number basically depends on the physical and logical infrastructure.

Synchronous vs. Asynchronous

In such an environment, regardless of the replication solution, you must first make a decision about the fidelity of the replica data set. Should it be copied real-time or can you bear a little delay?

The decision is important in a replicated environment because it basically requires that every single octet changed on the local site is also changed at the remote site. The change is either performed in the background or in real-time as the application demands the change, and before acknowledging the change back to the application.

In the latter case, the response time of the query is directly dependent upon the time taken to transmit the information from one site to another.

So in summary:

- Asynchronous mode aims at decoupling the response time of the I/O write operation from the time taken to transfer data over and being acknowledged.

- Synchronous mode ensures that data is safely acknowledged at BOTH sides before acknowledging the change back to the application.

What goes on the link

Typically, one round-trip is made, but in certain situations, two round-trips are necessary; especially if the storage array strictly implements block-mode SCSI commands. See below for a graphical explanation:

Figure 4.23
One or Two Round-Trips

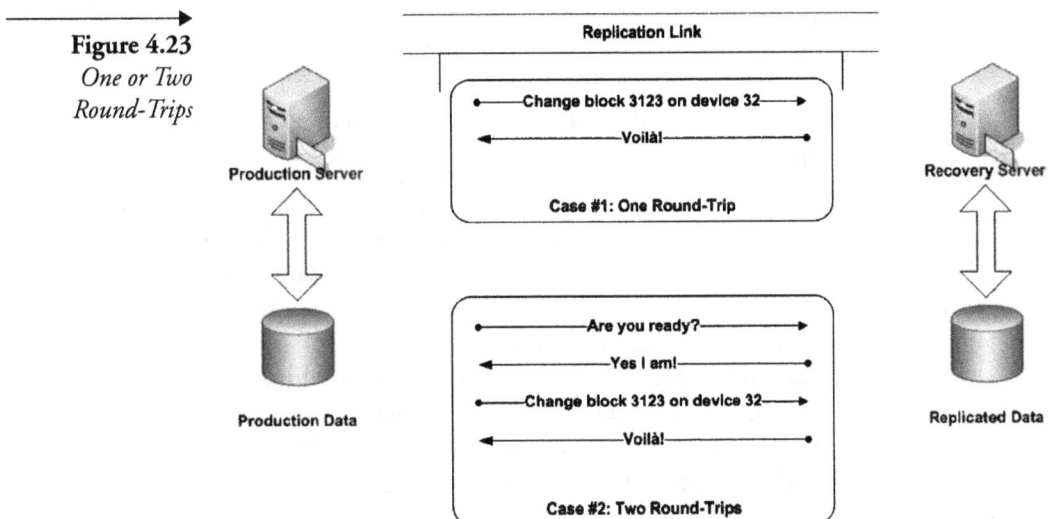

In Case #1, shown in Figure 4.23, the local site sends the data change right away and expects a response from the remote site. In Case #2, the local site first checks that the remote site is ready (handshake), and then proceeds to send the data change across.

There are many ways by which the changed data can be sent from the local site to the remote site. In host-based replication mode, this is typically done across a data network connection (IP-based) using either straight SCSI commands (as one could conceive in an iSCSI deployment) or a proprietary protocol.

In storage-based replication, this change can be sent by any network connection mode supported by the array. Typically, it will be a combination of Fibre Channel and possibly IP protocols carrying over SCSI protocols or using a custom and optimized data transfer protocol (for instance, one that would avoid Case #2 in Figure 4.23).

Going synchronous or asynchronous really depends upon your environment. Obviously, synchronous is best from a data fidelity viewpoint, however, it means that each and every write issued by the Microsoft Exchange production server must go down the replication link, and maybe therefore suffer from latency (which might not be too much of a pain in the case of an optical fiber link of a few hundred meters). Asynchronous, on the other hand, should be considered carefully as it can be a timebomb. There are times when the data must be transferred similar to synchronous mode. If you were to choose an asynchronous replication method, and undersize the link (or oversubscribe it), there will be times when the local site storage component will stop buffering and switch back to synchronous mode. In addition, it will flush the asynchronous data set, and this is NOT a good thing during the day with Microsoft Exchange.

In the most extreme cases, the local storage might just stop replicating. The remote end status becomes unusable, and in the condition where the delta of information to be replicated is very large, the local array might decide to resynchronize the entire volume, block by block, instead of just sending the changes as they were logged locally. This full volume resynchronization will then saturate (or make a good utilization) of the inter-switch link, and this can cause impact to normal and concurrent traffic. Until the target volume is synchronized, you are basically in an unrecoverable situation if a disaster occurs on the local storage site.

Link Requirements

There are fairly stringent requirements for the inter-switch (inter-site) link put in place between any two distant sites. Microsoft Exchange is very sensitive to the transaction logging I/O response time; you must ensure that the link round-trip latency is kept to a minimum.

We consider, in Microsoft Exchange deployments, that a round-trip of less than 10 ms is satisfactory for medium workloads (user, quantity of users). But based on your business requirements and on the workload pattern, that requirement may either be ten times higher or lower. To decide, you have no other option than to carry out testing using some of Microsoft's test tools, such as LoadSim, ESP, or Jetstress, that we discuss later in this book. Microsoft has a comprehensive Web site that gathers these performance testing and evaluation tools: http://www.microsoft.com/ technet/prodtechnol/exchange/2003/stresstool.mspx.

In high-end environments, the link is typically made of optical fiber. The latency caused by the speed of light is actually quite negligible for distances of less than 100 km (you still need to be able to afford the optical link).

When optical fiber connections are not available, because of distance or simply geographical restrictions, links can be IP-based, and certain companies provide "SCSI over Fibre Channel over IP" gateways (OSG: Open System Gateways). There are no good or bad solutions in such environments, just solutions that meet requirements. A 300-user server may very well be satisfactory with synchronous replication across the link with 100 ms of round-trip delay—simply because users may be operating in Outlook 2003 cache mode and their workload is not large.

In high-latency links, however, the mode of operation might have to be asynchronous for the reasons exposed in the previous section. You then have to warn the customer about the potential risk of losing data during a site failover. It will only take one incident for the customer to decide to accept the terms of synchronous replication.

Because replication is a key component of the overall solution, you have to make sure that the link has the following attributes:

- Low latency (discussed earlier)
- High bandwidth (to expedite volume synchronization or full copy)
- Resiliency (to prevent the solution from going down the tube if a physical component is unavailable [2])
- Security (to prevent eavesdropping of data packets, particularly important when dealing with governmental defense or intelligence

departments. The encryption of the traffic CAN incur request and/or data rate limitations).

- Manageability (because it has to be)

- Isolation (to prevent Microsoft Exchange going into a crawl if/when another business application makes full copy synchronization across the replication link)

When the link goes down: normal vs. failsafe

Here is a bit of a dilemma: If the link goes down (or, in other words, if the remote site is NOT available), you need to make a decision on whether you allow the application to run locally, or whether you stop the application from making any changes to the local volume. At HP, we use the terms NORMAL and FAILSAFE to describe the mode of operation of the array:

In FAILSAFE mode, the local storage components will stop operating. For the Microsoft Exchange server, this will appear as if the local volume is unavailable and typically results in the database engines being shutdown as cleanly as possible.

In NORMAL mode, the local storage components will continue to accept changes from the local server. It will keep these changes in a journal, so that they can be applied to the remote copy, when it's available again.

So, in FAILSAFE mode, you basically ensure that the remote copy is always synchronized with the local copy. Hence, you have the highest level of fidelity and need not worry about lost transactions. In NORMAL mode, you are in fact more tolerant to a link failure. If the remote copy is not available for any reason (link down, site down, remote controller/server down, etc.), you continue to accept local changes, thus, increasing your *availability*.

So we hit a paradox, where replicated storage solutions are typically thought of as being high-availability, but then, can be a cause of downtime too. This is a normal law of MTBF (Mean Time Between Failures); the more components and complexity in a solution, the higher the chance for downtime!

Write-Ordering

Replication technologies are typically designed to respect write-ordering, which is a mandatory requirement for a storage solution to be accepted/certified by Microsoft in Exchange 200x deployments. The idea behind write-ordering is that changes made in a certain order to a set of logical units must be performed in that very same order to the copies of the logical units.

Based upon the storage array and replication technology and configuration options, there are different ways to achieve this. There are different circumstances when write-ordering is, precisely, not respected.

In Microsoft Exchange, this can have very nasty consequences. If a database page is written to the database file before its corresponding transaction change was written in the transaction log files, the database engine will consider that the page is "too new" and therefore, the database is corrupted.

Also, Microsoft Exchange can write the same page several times. You might consider that what counts is the most recent page, but still, you run the risk of an outdated transaction record (ESE checks time stamps between the database page and the transaction log record)—the page might be considered "too old."

In summary, a transaction happens on a page referenced by a number, which has a time stamp. Time stamps must match for the transaction to be played against the database, such as in recovery scenarios. Mismatch is basically a database corruption by Microsoft Exchange. In such a corruption scenario, you either have the choice to discard the page (but the consequences can be the loss of attachments, messages, folders, mailboxes, or the entire database), or return to your backup and make a full restore. In all cases, you are in a situation where the remote replica (and the entire infrastructure it requires) served NO PURPOSE.

However, if you were to ensure write-ordering against all units used by a particular server, you could introduce a serialization of data transmission that could be counter productive to the response time to the local server. The basic recommendation is therefore to ensure write-ordering for a given database or transaction log LUN, as well as between LUNs that are used within the same Microsoft Exchange Storage Group.

It's all about writes

Yes. This is because read operations are done on the local site and do not depend upon the availability or the performance of the remote site volumes. Therefore, identify your critical write transactions. In Microsoft Exchange, you typically have:

1. Database writes. They are done in the background when cache flush occur. Using Exchange 2003 SP1 and SP2, you get an

improved I/O pattern (more flat, less spikes), so consider upgrading if you have not done so already. In particular, the SP2 release of Exchange 2003 limits to 64 is the maximum number of outstanding write operations (compared to the default 512 in previous releases), which prevents flooding the inter-site link with write operations.

2.   Transaction logging. The writes to the logs are not necessarily big (between 512 bytes and 4 KB), and on the critical path of the transaction, they also contain the most recent changes to the database. If you miss a log record, you basically lose information.

3.   SMTP messages. When a message is transferred from a peer SMTP server, the Microsoft Exchange server will first write it into a local NTFS folder before passing it onto the categorizer for local or remote delivery. Although these writes are assisted by the NT Kernel cache, the faster the writes, the faster the message delivery rate and the lower queuing will occur. You must replicate this storage area, otherwise you run the risk of losing data during a site failover.

Because Microsoft Exchange depends upon the link latency as well as the fact that you can get GB/s links quite cheaply, you should try to parallelize data flow that sits on the critical path of a transaction in such a way that you can take advantage of the bandwidth more versus being impacted by the link latency.

With Microsoft Exchange, this means creating as many Storage Groups as possible. If you have a production server with ten databases, it is better to run with four storage groups than just two (in simplistic terms, you split the transaction logging traffic in two per LUN). Pre-Exchange 2003 SP1 servers should be handled with care as this can generate undesired Virtual Memory fragmentation in the Microsoft Exchange Information Store Virtual Address space.

And then, at the application level, there is so much you can do to parallelize traffic. Eventually, you are going to be challenged with two arrays trying to communicate. The source side of a storage-based replication solution is typically limited in the number of outstanding packets between the local and the remote arrays. Therefore, it is far more efficient to use two medium-size arrays per site rather than one large array per site (in a strict replication context). In a Greenfield deployment, it would be flawed to omit this option.

Instead of using SAN boot solutions, investigate first the feasibility of running a stretched cluster. They do have restrictions (the maximum latency between the two sites is 500ms, for the heart-beat communication between nodes, all nodes of a cluster need to be in the same subnet, quorum disk must be carefully considered unless you use a majority node set quorum approach) however, the instrumentation and full consistency between all these moving parts (servers, services, network addresses, storage units) delivered by the Microsoft cluster resource manager and complementary extensions to the cluster resource manager are key for simplifying the operations of the environment and avoiding real disasters.

You might otherwise consider SAN boot solutions and then get into a realm of more flexibility in terms of server provisioning and disaster recovery.

Your next step is to ensure suitable testing, especially in high-end modes (many users), where you have worked on a consolidated infrastructure that gathers many thousands of users in a single site that requires a disaster tolerant environment. Make sure that the overall solution suits the anticipated workload. A solution that incurs too much delay in the replicated environment can lead to serious customer dissatisfaction in terms of client response times and message queuing.

I would also like to advise about not getting distracted by the technologies involved in the solution. Focus on clearly defining the service levels of the overall Microsoft Exchange solution. You might find you do not need replicated storage after all. We have cases of companies using Microsoft Exchange for MISSION critical processes that do not even run Microsoft clustering services!

Or, you might want to offload Microsoft Exchange from past data using archiving and/or data management solutions on platforms more suited for site failover (e.g., RISS and its replication mode).

Once you get the business stakeholders to buy into the service levels, you will have little trouble in justifying the exorbitant (includes to acquire, operate, and support) solution. Examples of service levels demanded by our customers in Microsoft Exchange environments:

- recovery within 5mn with no loss of information
- recovery within 15mn with minimal loss of information
- recovery within 4 hours with a maximum of 1 business day of information loss

- recovery within 8 hours for complete site destruction, 20mn for simple site failover—1 day of information loss maximum

- No downtime (99.999 percent availability)

- No more than 4 hours downtime, once a month (99.7 percent availability)

Other Approaches: log shipping and out-of-band replication, storage virtualization

The principle of replication is to transport data to a remote site and keep it in sync, as much as possible, with the "live" production copy. There are other principles that are present in other database environments, which could eventually be found in future releases of Microsoft Exchange.

The first approach is log shipping. Instead of transmitting write operations as they occur, a background process takes care of "shipping" (really, it can be just a safe file copy operation) each log file as they are generated (except from the current log file, of course). At the remote end, you may use the log file and play it against the Microsoft Exchange database (for instance, using the ESEUTIL command line tool).

You might challenge yourself into this type of approach which carries many benefits. There is no need for high-end replicated storage, nor for high-speed/low-latency links, etc.... However, this mode of operation is quite limited in terms of support. Microsoft will be more than happy to support the database and the logs, but will inevitably let you down for debugging the log file shipment as well as the verification of the file integrity. So while this approach has benefits, you might only consider it when it becomes a true option of the base product. Today, Microsoft does not provide log shipping as part of Exchange 2003. However, you might investigate third party solutions that provide continuous backup solutions based upon the principle of saving transaction log files and playing them against a database. XOsoft's DataRewinder is an example of such a solution (with no particular endorsement at this point). More simply, you might want to script the operation.

The alternative to log shipping is to use a loose replication mode (asynchronous normal). Instead of having the replication being done on the production volumes, play the transaction log files against a differential or full copy of the production volume, yet fully consistent. This copy can be created using the Windows Server 2003 VSS framework and Exchange 2003's writer, as shown in Figure 4.24.

Figure 4.24
Out of Band
Replication

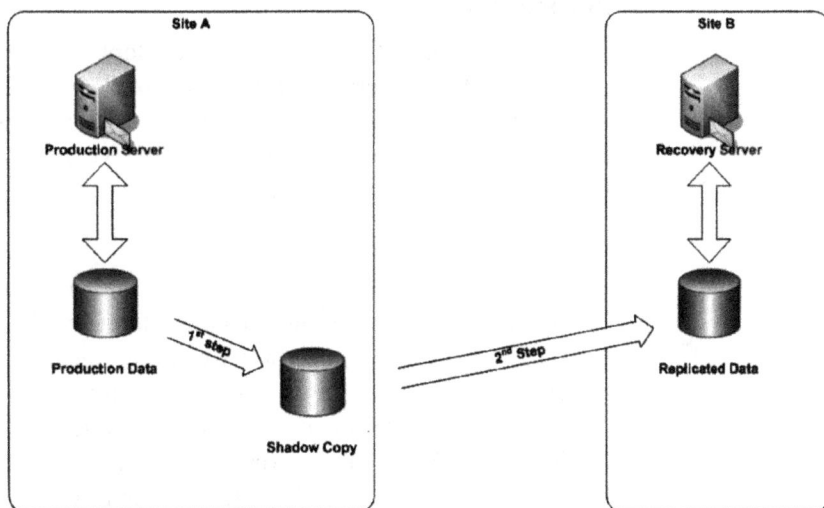

Of course, this brings a specific dependency on the version of Microsoft Exchange and Windows Server. It allows you to have checkpoints of the database sent over links for which the performance is of secondary importance (e.g., it could be a coast-to-coast IP link). The replication of the shadow copy does not impact the production server response time, which is performed in the background. In the case of a site failover, however, you lose the data generated between the time the shadow copy was made and the time at which the failover was executed. The great advantage of such approach is to perform the replication out-of-band of the Exchange application—there is no impact to the production workload, whatever the replication distance and round trip delay can be.

Storage virtualization can lead to multi-site replication; either at the storage components or at the storage interconnects levels. Consider the solutions with all the care that needs to be brought into the supportability and effectiveness of the solution. You really do not want any support trouble when a disaster strikes.

Additionally, consider giving your Microsoft Exchange server a chance to deal with less data. There are proven tests that show the larger a mailbox, the higher the workload on the storage components. Data management solutions can be liberating to a heavily loaded (both from a transaction and data volume perspective) Microsoft Exchange infrastructure. This helps in making it more agile, flexible, and requiring less components at a more affordable cost to the customer.

In Summary

For deciding which solution you should adopt, try first to understand your business needs, and turn them into functional requirements that will motivate the technology employed. There is not a clear decision tree, because of the varying requirements that can arise in a Microsoft Exchange project. I would rather share some examples:

- Use synchronous short (<100 km) distance replication if you must have an exact mirror of the database volumes, and prevent any chance of data loss: short distance allow you to implement optical fiber connections that make the distant site look like a local site to Exchange servers. I have been involved in a couple of designs where the replication is across a manufacturing campus, and the optical fiber media does not add a measurable delay to the transfer of the data.

- Use asynchronous short distance replication if moderate loss (<15 mn) is acceptable and if the workload is particularly high (>2,000 active users) for the inter-switch link.

- Use asynchronous software solution if the inter-site distance and link is not qualified for storage-based replication; ensure full supportability by the means of strong support contract with Microsoft and third party vendors if appropriate.

- Asynchronous storage-based replication on database ShadowCopies is appropriate for a long distance replication that requires fast recovery with a loss of transactions between 1 and 8 hours. This approach, however, assumes your storage back-end is suitably sized for such frequent operations.

  In all cases:

- Favor automated (yet not automatic) recovery procedures

- Perform regular fire drills

- Investigate processes and staff skills such that fire drills can be conducted easily

- Prefer solutions that enable you to verify the integrity of the remote data set without impacting the production service. For example, you might consider having test servers that regularly attempt to mount the databases and verify their content.

- Use, if available, cluster extensions that establish a dialog between the cluster and the storage infrastructure: they make sure that the storage units presented to an Exchange server at any point in time are clean and coherent from a replication perspective.

Microsoft has provided their "opinion" about replicated scenarios, and this is of value to HP's system designers and solution architects. However, each customer scenario is different and some might not fit into the strict supportability realm. To this effect, if you choose to deviate from the proposed synchronous failsafe modes, contact the local Microsoft office with the customer to discuss the technical feasibility of the solution to ensure that the customer has a fully supported Microsoft or HP solution, or both. In any case, even if the solution is supported, this does not save the effort of performing minimal qualifications. There is so much that can happen in lab and quality assurance environments just as there is so much that really happens in customer environments.

Remember the 4-P rule: Process, Policy, People, and Products. Technology is only a fourth of the solution—do not neglect the rest. Disaster often happens after an (initially) innocuous event gets mishandled and is the consequence of many small missteps.

4.6   Network-attached storage

In this section, what we refer to as a NAS is voluntarily restricted to file-share protocol access over IP to a storage device. Block mode over IP, that we see implemented with the iSCSI standard is not assimilated as NAS, instead, we refer to it as IP SAN (or SAN over IP), because of the way storage is provided, in a very similar way as that in Fibre Channel SAN environments.

NAS is a way to provide simple storage services to client-based applications that require access to back-end storage by the means of file sharing networking protocols (NFS, CIFS). They use TCP/IP as the underlying transport, and this is a good thing for versatility and ease of deployment, but TCP/IP as a transport protocol was designed with something else in mind than the data transfer and hyper-fast LAN connectivity required for Microsoft Exchange. NAS devices are typically designed to be optimized for file-sharing modes. Often available as appliances that you connect to your network and manage by the means of a Web browser, NAS appliances do not need to run a generalized operating system such as Windows, on industry standard processors, such as Intel Xeon for instance. This said, HP, for instance, does sell NAS devices (under the name of ProLiant Storage Servers), which are typically based on Windows Server 2003 Storage Edition, i.e., a Windows operating system especially fitted for file sharing. Other vendors, such as NetApps, use their own proprietary kernels that are fitted for the purpose of their use.

NAS devices are often found in simple or complex infrastructures because they fulfill a function that everybody needs: file sharing.

Initially, you may find it interesting to use IP for accessing storage networks, because it is omnipresent in the infrastructure: from clients to servers, from network bridges to interfaces, every device today can communicate over IP, and more specifically, TCP/IP. This versatility is an advantage, but IP carries with it some legacy in the implementation of the protocol, such as the assumption that the underlying media is not so reliable. So the protocol implements packet error detection and reordering, something which is not necessary with Fibre Channel SAN, which on the contrary, was designed with the assumption that the underlying transport is reliable. There is some level of checking, and retransmission will occur if an error is found, but the reliability of the media is considered as high as 99.99999 percent of the time. This allows for less overhead in packet checking and makes the case of a packet resent, less frequent so more tolerable.

The other aspect to consider with NAS is the use of TCP/IP at the Microsoft Exchange server level. TCP/IP stack processing will consume resources, even though we find network adapters that can offload this type of work by the means of TCP Offload Engines (also known as multi-function adapters). You run the risk of shifting a traditional bottleneck at the storage level to a CPU bottleneck. Not that this is difficult to address, but it is definitely something you need to be aware of, because on an application server, there will be other resources than TCP/IP stack processing that will need this processing power. With the advent of faster and Dual-Core CPU, this might not be much of a concern. In fact, I ran some tests in an IP-based networked storage using iSCSI block-mode and I could get as high as 30 percent CPU utilization for over 100 MB/s data rate which is what you would demand from a first generation Fibre Channel SAN link.

In this context Microsoft Exchange, using NAS (and more precisely, file-share protocols over IP) has traditionally been problematic because Microsoft would not support it. The main reason is that NAS-based solutions haven't been tested with Exchange 2003, and while they would in theory and in practice operate with NAS-based storage, Microsoft wouldn't handle calls related to NAS-based implementations. This is a big issue, because data storage is so crucial to the core of Exchange 2003. It is also the area that requires the most attention and can be the most painful to recover. In addition, the Exchange Installable File System (ExIFS), used for streaming content from the Internet to the streaming store, operates in kernel mode and has a certain understanding of what the storage database is made of, and upon which type of device.

Nevertheless, NAS provides great service to client workstations and also to Web application services, because they enable a way to share an entire file system (as opposed to a volume or storage enclosure in a SAN) and have applications take advantage of these storage media. Also, NAS servers now offer the versatility of a networked storage infrastructure at a much reduced cost, both from a back-end storage perspective as well as infrastructure: indeed, there is no need to deploy specific and dedicated high-performance networks for your environment anymore.

All in all, the advantages of NAS (especially in an appliance mode) led Microsoft to be more tolerant with the support of such storage for Microsoft Exchange. With Exchange 5.5, Microsoft has loosened its strict supportability scenarios in respect to NAS storage by enabling the use of mapped drives (see Microsoft Knowledge Base article 317172). However, restrictions remain in effect with Exchange 200x, which does not mount databases hosted on shared drives.

On April 5th 2004, Microsoft announced the Windows Storage Server 2003 Feature Pack, otherwise known as "Thunderclap." This add-on to Windows-powered NAS (Network-Attached Storage) and Microsoft Exchange Server 2003 enables Exchange databases on NAS servers. This approach is applicable to small and medium environments as well as branch office deployments.

The benefit of this Feature Pack is the ability to place Exchange 2003 databases on Windows Storage Server 2003-based NAS servers. Windows Storage Server 2003 is the customized version of Windows Server 2003 for NAS head/server deployments. HP NAS servers with this free Feature Pack shipped a bit later.

NAS was originally introduced for appliances with specialized operating systems and file systems, and two approaches quickly emerged:

1.   The use of Windows 2000 Server as an operating system. In addition, vendors could install the Server Appliance Kit to tune the Windows server for file sharing purposes and offer shared management interfaces and functions.

2.   The use of SAN-attached storage instead of Direct-Attached Storage (DAS). The DAS approach enables NAS servers that have no other dependency (they are autonomous units, a.k.a. appliances), to reduce the NAS to a file sharing server. Using back-end SAN storage enabled customers to build on existing SAN infrastructures and their associated abilities, such as advanced volume management (like clones and snapshots) and a potentially much larger disk pool.

Approach #2 reduces the NAS-specific solution to a simple server with back-end SAN storage, and it is generally referred to as a NAS head (see Figure 4.25).

Figure 4.25
NAS and
NAS Heads

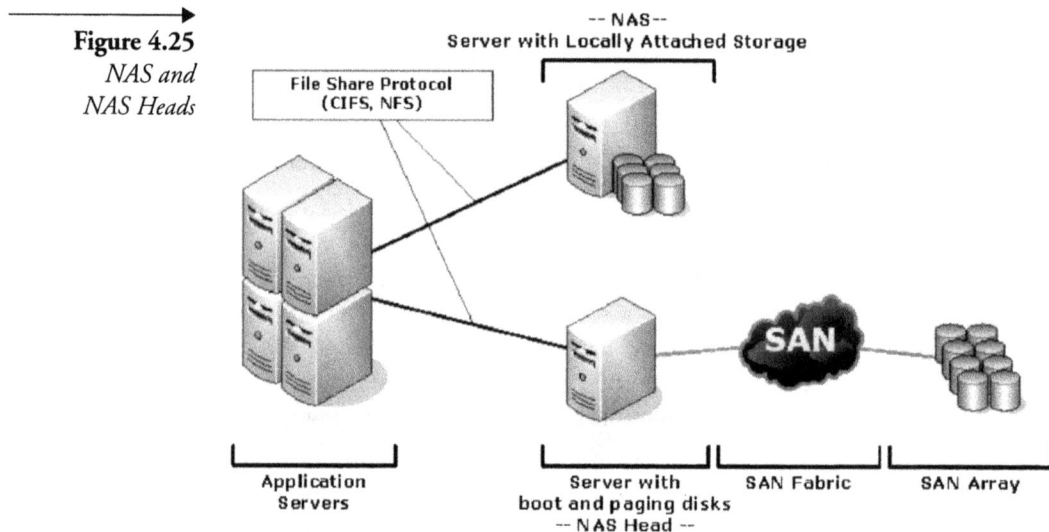

By rolling out NAS-heads in your environment, you can build optimized file-sharing servers, instead of using a general purpose Windows Server. Note that deploying a NAS head does not prevent you from using proper management and operations practices. You are still rolling out a new server instance and it can be integrated into your Active Directory infrastructure to take advantage of a deployed common security and policy framework.

4.6.1 Windows Storage Server 2003 Feature Pack

The main objective of the Windows Storage Server 2003 Feature Pack is to allow Exchange 2003 databases and transaction log files to be hosted on a Windows Storage Server 2003-based NAS server. The Feature Pack creates a local DFS root on the Exchange server that can be used to link to the NAS SMB share; it does not require a block-mode device driver. If DFS is not installed, or if the DFS root is already in use, the installation of the Exchange server Feature Pack components fails. Windows 2000 Server and Windows Server 2003 Standard Edition only support one DFS root per server.

Additionally, the Feature Pack provides the necessary safeguards for ensuring the presence of the DFS root and links prior to the startup of the Exchange Information Store process. This is achieved by setting service dependencies.

Using NAS for back-end servers is generally not recommended in high-end transactional database environments with demanding request (I/O per second) and data (MB per second) rates. However, it is convenient when you wish to benefit from a consolidated storage environment without carrying the cost of a SAN infrastructure. Even today, the cost of a Fibre Channel Host-Bus Adapter is significantly higher than the cost of a 1-Gb Network Interface Card, which are both typically purchased or delivered in pairs in enterprise servers.

Microsoft recommends the use of NAS back-end storage in the following scenarios:

- No more than 1,500 Microsoft Exchange users per NAS server

- Maximum of 2 × Exchange servers per NAS (which means an average of 750 users per Exchange server)

- No support for NAS clusters

- No mailbox level restore (at the NAS level); a Recovery Storage Group is supported

- No remote snapshot/shadow-copy capability

Of course, you should ensure that the NAS server is on the Microsoft Hardware Compatibility List and that the configuration is certified for support by Microsoft.

Deployment Procedures for Exchange on NAS

You first need to install the Feature Pack on the Windows Storage Server 2003-based NAS server, unless it is already pre-installed, as it is on newer NAS solutions. Once installed, you are provided with new options for creating file shares for hosting Exchange databases and transaction log files. In addition, you must install specific components on the Exchange servers that will use the NAS for storing their data.

After installation of the Feature Pack, the necessary setup files for the Exchange servers are located in:

```
%program files%\Windows Storage Server\Exchange
```

You can share this folder out of the NAS to ease the deployment of the Exchange add-ons. These add-ons mainly consist of a service and COM interface for scripting database management functions and an extension to the Exchange System Manager snap-in for performing database move operations out of the Exchange System Manager.

Once you have completed the Feature Pack installation, the NAS web administration provides new options when creating a share and for specifically creating an SMB share for Exchange databases and log files, as highlighted in Figure 4.26.

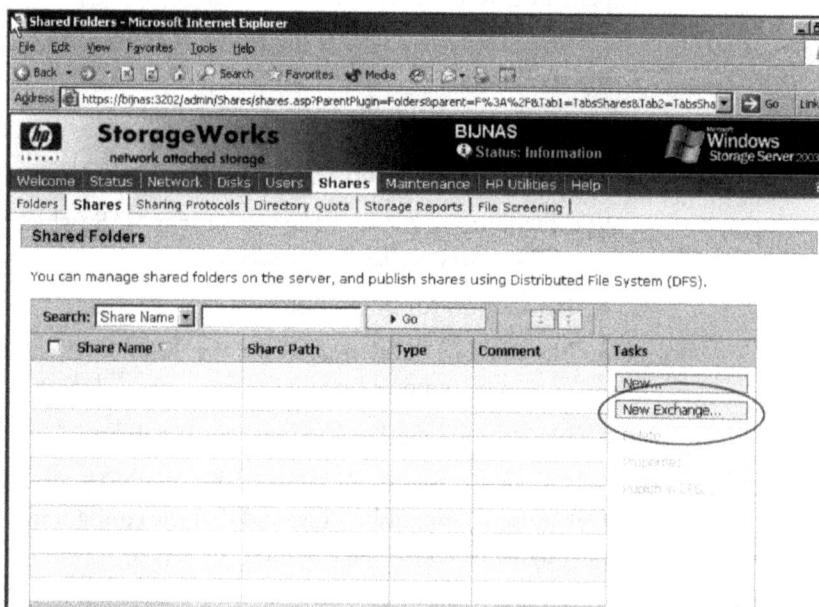

Figure 4.26
New Exchange Share Option in the Web Administration Interface

Even though you have a local administrator account for your NAS server, you should configure it such that it is part of the domain/forest where Exchange is installed: this is important later when granting administrative rights to the accounts used to administer Exchange, and for granting permission to the Exchange 2003 machine account to allow access to the SMB share.

When you select this option, a screen similar to that shown in Figure 4.27 is displayed. This is where you specify the share name and properties.

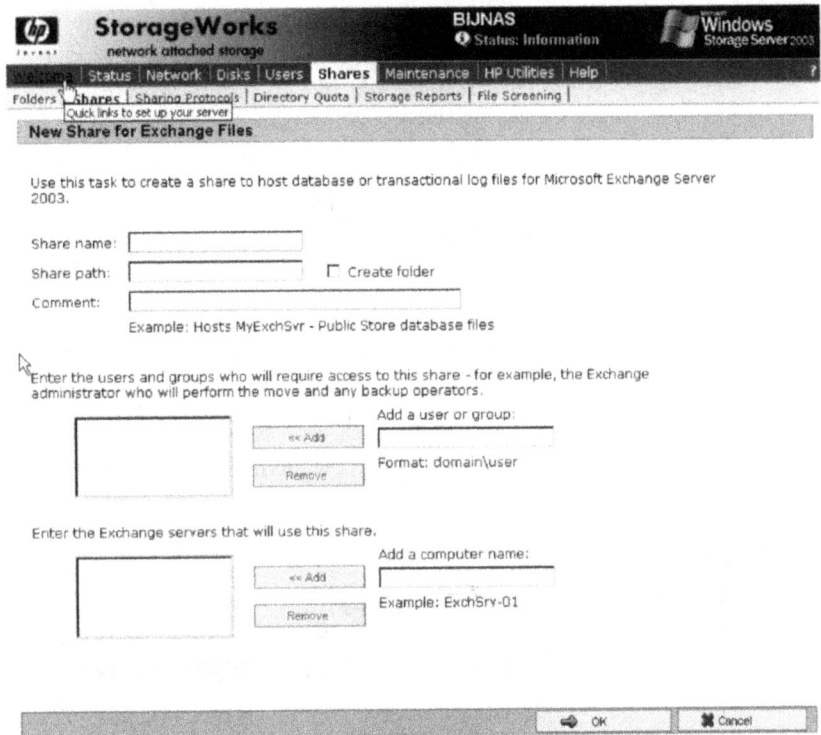

The result of this operation for a single Exchange server should be at least two shares: one of the databases and one for the transaction log files (Figure 4.28).

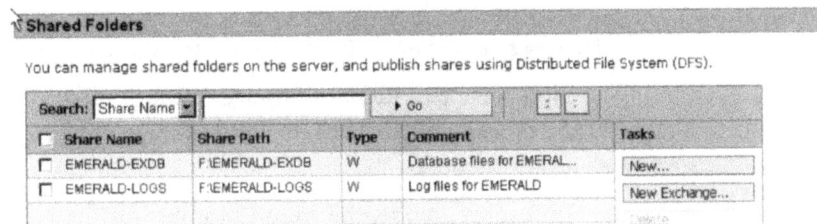

Note that you can bypass the NAS Web administrator and create the network shares directly on Windows Explorer.

Depending on the NAS Server volumes, you might prefer to locate the transaction log files and databases on separate NAS volumes. If so, ensure that you grant Full Control permissions to the Exchange administrators and backup operators, and to the Exchange server account for the share and its subfolders (if any). Finally, the share will not appear as an "Exchange Share" from the Web Administration user interface if created via Explorer. In this case, it just looks like an ordinary share.

Microsoft Exchange Server Components

Running the Setup program on the Exchange server is a very straightforward operation—you just need to specify the location of the binaries. By default, the files are installed as follows under the Exchange server:

```
%Program Files%\Windows Storage Server\Exchange
```

When you right-click on a storage group in the Exchange System Manager a new task is shown, as demonstrated in Figure 4.29

Figure 4.29
Remote Storage
Wizard Task

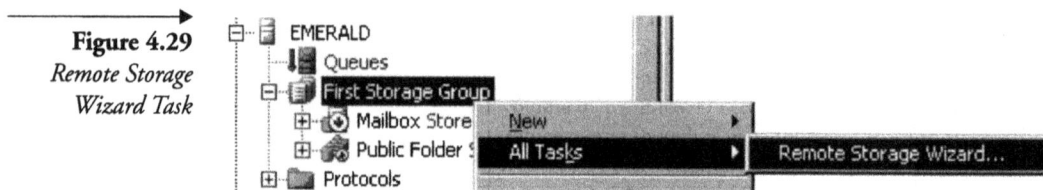

The Remote Storage Wizard allows you to copy databases to or from the Windows Storage Server 2003-based NAS. The process of moving files to the NAS can be performed from the wizard or carried out separately: in the latter case, the wizard is only required to change the configuration in the Active Directory. You do not have the option of placing the databases directly on the NAS server during the creation of the storage group and databases, and should use the wizard to relocate them.

Note that the Remote Storage Wizard allows you to copy files to a NAS, or copy them back to local storage, which is useful for troubleshooting purposes.

In "export" mode, the wizard prompts for the NAS server to which the files should be copied, and then proceeds to inventory the storage group and present the file components to be moved over the NAS (in the case of a move operation):

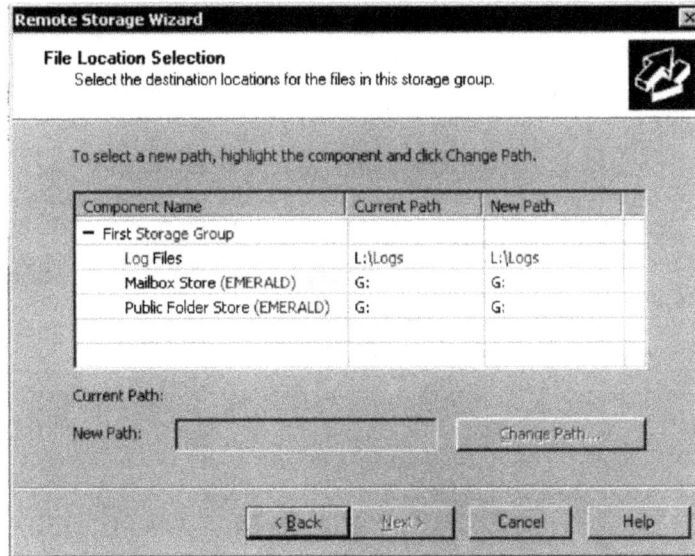

Select a component (e.g., the mailbox store) and click on "Change Path." This provides a list of shares and share subfolders available on the target NAS:

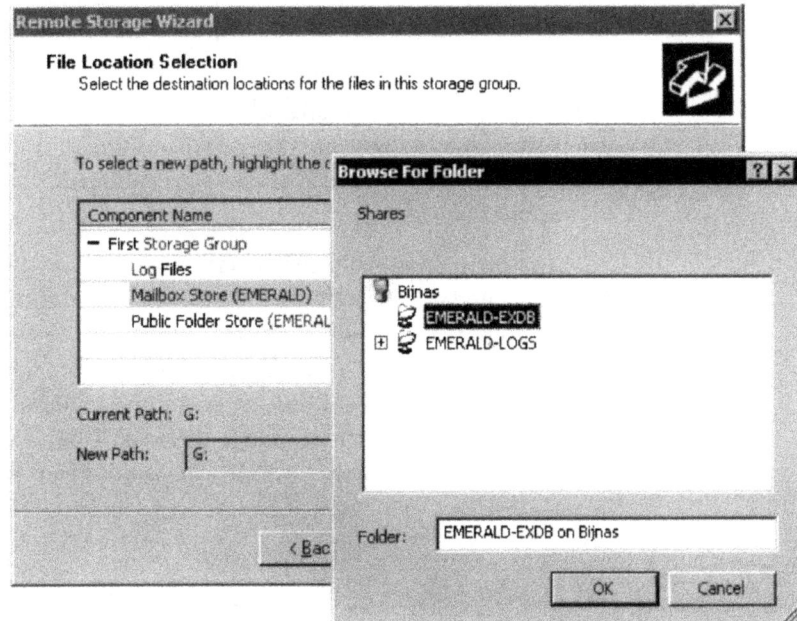

Once you have selected all the files (see below), the wizard moves them and changes the Active Directory configuration.

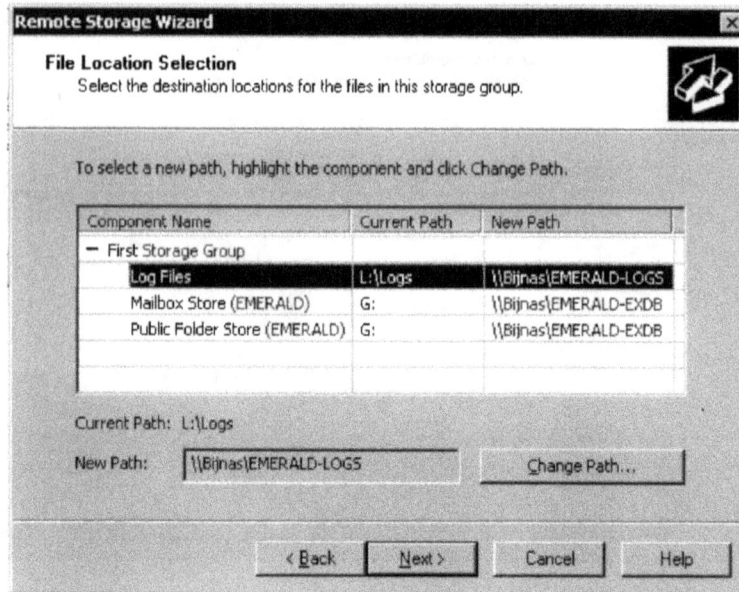

Note that the databases are represented as a single entity (see above): the wizard will not let you move the EDB and STM portions of an Exchange database individually. This is a minor point, given that most deployments usually locate the EDB and STM files on the same volume/partition.

The wizard then dismounts the database and creates a local DFS drive with links to the SMB shares selected as Remote Storage for the Exchange databases. The databases are transferred and the Active Directory configuration update takes place. If the stores were mounted prior to the execution of the wizard, they are mounted again.

Running the wizard in configuration mode allows you to create the DFS links and update the Active Directory configuration without transferring data. This is useful if you have another method for placing the database files and logs on the NAS or if you are restoring a server. For example, if the data is available on the NAS, the paths to the databases and logs must be restored, created, or verified. Once the wizard has executed, the path and reference to the Exchange databases in the Active Directory changes: the new path is now represented by the drive letter S:\ followed by the NAS name and an ordinal number.

You can view the change by checking the properties of the database using the Remote Storage Wizard:

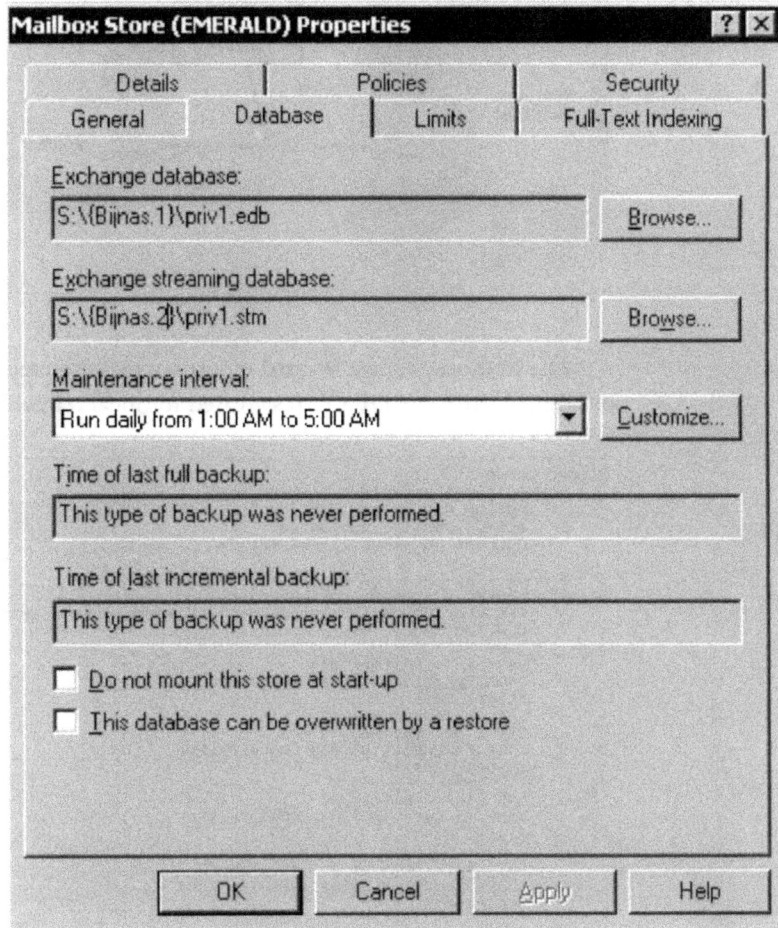

S:\ drive?

Prior to Microsoft Exchange 2003, the M:\ drive letter was assigned to the Exchange Installable File System (and now we have a new pre-assigned letter, S:\ used for referencing the databases and logs. Note that the S:\ drive is not displayed in the Disk Management MMC snap-in: it is a DFS root, used as an interface between Exchange and the SMB shares located on the NAS.

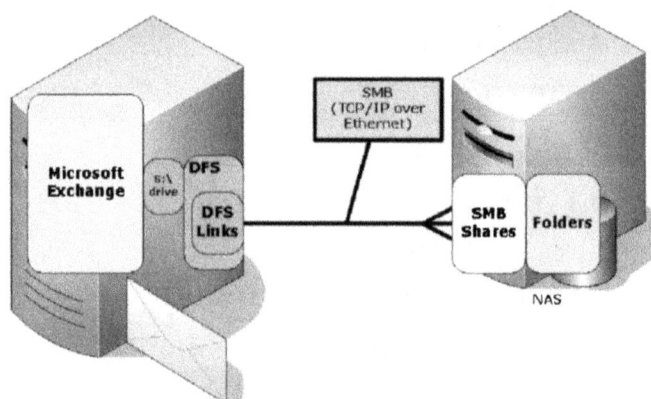

NAS

The Remote Storage Wizard report contains references to the DFS Root Name (S$) and the DFS Links created for local reference.

```
---------------------------------------------------------------------
Mapped Drive
        Original Location: \\EMERALD\S$
        Action Requested: None
        Action Result: Succeeded
        Current Location: \\EMERALD\S$

---------------------------------------------------------------------
Distributed File System Configuration
        DFS Root Folder: C:\Program Files\Windows Storage Server\Exchange\DFS
        DFS Root Name: S$

        DFS Link: {Bijnas.0}
        Link Target: \\Bijnas\EMERALD-LOGS
        State: Pass

        DFS Link: {Bijnas.1}
        Link Target: \\Bijnas\EMERALD-EXDB
        State: Pass

        DFS Link: {Bijnas.2}
        Link Target: \\Bijnas\EMERALD-EXDB
        State: Pass

        DFS Link: {Bijnas.3}
        Link Target: \\Bijnas\EMERALD-EXDB
        State: Pass|

        DFS Link: {Bijnas.4}
        Link Target: \\Bijnas\EMERALD-EXDB
        State: Pass

---------------------------------------------------------------------
WSSExchMapSvc
        Current Status: Stopped
        Run Mode: Automatic
```

You can view the DFS root entries in the DFS MMC snap-in, available from the Administrative Tool program group.

Note that even if you have only two SMB shares to host your server databases and logs, a DFS link is created for each data file. In the example above, there is one link for the transaction log files, one link for the mailbox

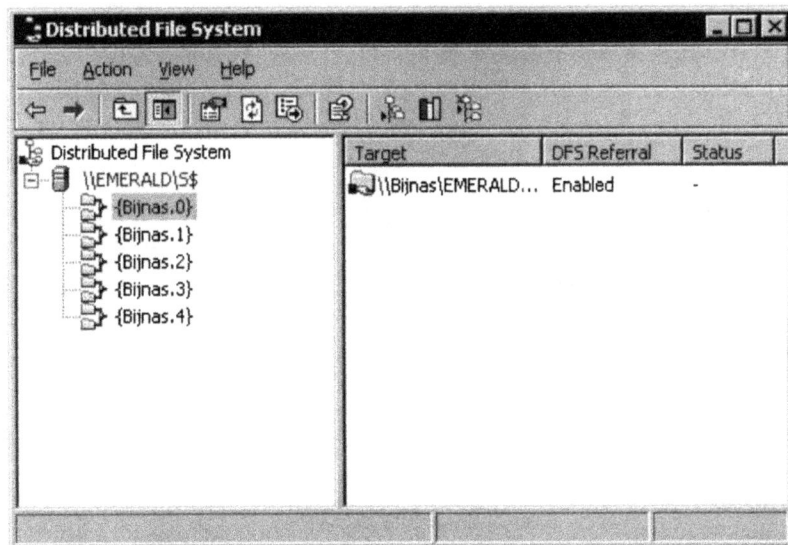

store EDB file, one for the mailbox store STM file, and one each for the public store EDB and STM files.

Backup Operations

You can use any online backup agent, however, be aware that NTBACKUP uses the administrative share of the base volume for restore operations (S$ in our case), which is why the DFS root name is S$. Note that this requirement may not necessarily apply for other backup agents. As always, check, validate, and double-check! When using an NAS server for your Exchange environment, you need to update your backup and recovery plans to include the NAS components, in addition to the Exchange components.

The Volume ShadowCopy Services (VSS) framework in Windows Server 2003 allows the implementation of point-in-time backups and instant volume recovery of NTFS volumes. With Windows Storage Server 2003, you can manage either software or hardware based shadow copies. Although this function is available at the NAS level, you need a VSS provider on the Exchange 2003 server that can communicate and control shadow copy creation on the Windows Storage Server 2003 powered NAS.

Network Design

Exposing back-end database traffic on an Ethernet segment can pose a serious threat to security in that any computer connected on the segment would have the ability to "sniff" Ethernet data packets. In addition, you must make sure that the Ethernet link used between the Exchange server and the NAS head/server does not suffer from network performance congestion—this could result in severely degraded performance. Windows-powered NAS from HP ships with a network teaming driver installed, which can protect against failures of a single network interface.

One possible option is to deploy NAS servers and Exchange servers on an independent Gigabit Ethernet segment. This independent segment can be as simple as a cross-over cable between the Exchange and the NAS servers, or a simple Gigabit Ethernet switch (see Figure 4.37).

Figure 4.37
Separating
Network Traffic

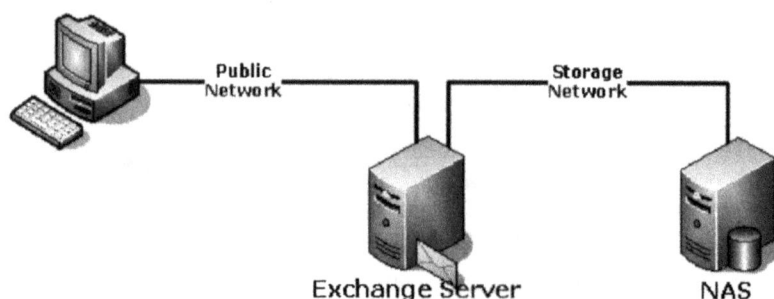

Depending on the environment, a simple Ethernet switch or a dedicated and redundant infrastructure can be the most appropriate solution for this type of connectivity; you certainly wouldn't want to use a cross-over cable between the Exchange server and the NAS server, even if they were in close proximity, as this would create a single point of failure. Creating a separate network topology (see the Storage Network in Figure 4.37) that it is relatively unaffected by client traffic, but most importantly, it prevents "eavesdropping" in a simple way, meaning that you don't have to implement encryption techniques that could further impact the throughput of the storage units.

Alternatively, you could use IPSec, as shown in Figure 4.38.

Consider this option only if you are familiar with IPSec and the Exchange I/O workload anticipated does not exceed the capability of each component. While the NAS may be accessible in the "clear" from client machines, the connection between the Exchange back-end and the SMB shares used for the databases is protected with IPSec encryption.

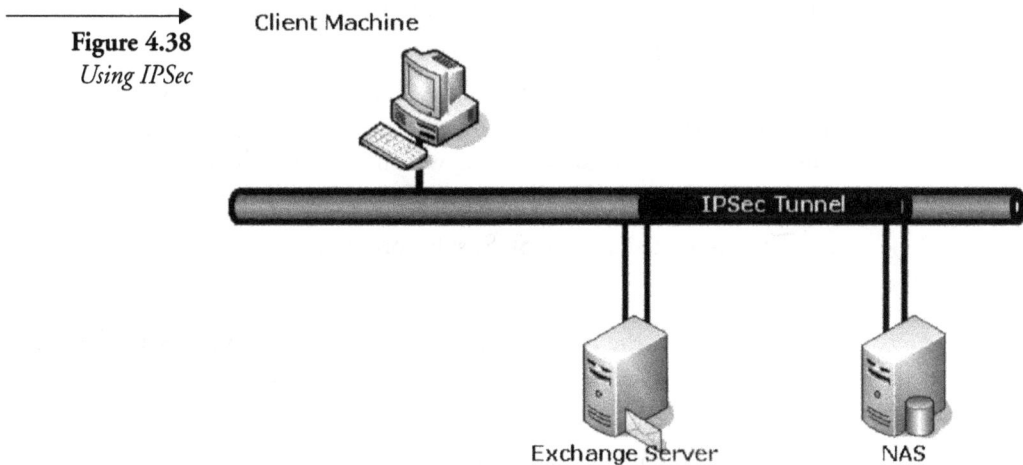

Figure 4.38
Using IPSec

4.6.2   In Summary

The supportability limits, combined with the adoption of the iSCSI did not leave much room for the feature pack to be widely deployed and adopted. It was an intermediate solution for using Exchange 2003 on top of IP networks that eventually showed that there was a customer demand for moderate storage workload over networked storage. Even if the Feature Pack was an interesting approach from Microsoft, it was quickly let down in favor of iSCSI, which we cover in the next section.

4.7   Emerging Technologies: iSCSI or IP SAN

Storage over IP or Ethernet networks enables cost-effective SANs to be deployed over a broad market. Because IP storage runs over the existing Ethernet infrastructure, it retains all of the existing networking, interoperability, manageability, compatibility, and cost advantages that have made Ethernet so successful. Customers are now able to use inexpensive, readily available Ethernet switches, hubs, and cables to implement low-cost, low-risk IP storage-based SANs. In addition, IP storage leverages future advances in Ethernet and IP performance and features, such as 10 Gigabit Ethernet. When NAS proposed a file sharing access mode over the IP network, iSCSI Networks (a.k.a. IP SAN) offered a block-mode access over the IP network, thereby eliminating the overhead of a file share protocol and integrating in the host operating system, in our case, Windows, as transparently as Fibre Channel SANs. iSCSI is in fact a protocol that was ratified by the industry in February 2003, and which rapidly replaced vendor-specific block-mode access to storage devices over IP (such as NetApps's LVD protocol).

Without a doubt, iSCSI is the key storage technology growth for Exchange 200x environments for the coming years. For reasons we discussed earlier, file-sharing mode was never something that was fit for Exchange, of the few file-share recalcitrant Windows application.

The components of an iSCSI solution are at minimum:

- iSCSI target: the representation of a logical unit, addressable by the means of a IP address and port
- iSCSI initiator: the bridge interface between the local host operating system block-mode I/O stack and the iSCSI target.

In addition, the iSCSI infrastructure can also benefit from a iSNS (iSCSI Name Service). The basic principle for iSCSI is to encapsulate SCSI frames inside TCP/IP packets. When concern was brought to the use of TCP/IP for its overhead in NAS environments, the media speed (1Gbps) as well as processor speed and host-bus adapters really enables this type of infrastructure for a majority of the Microsoft Exchange deployments.

4.7.1   IP SAN topologies

An IP SAN topology is always based on IP over Ethernet, and is comprised of hosts, networking infrastructure components, and target devices. The target device is seen by the host as a logical unit, in the same ways as a Fibre Channel SAN Logical Unit is seen. To connect to the networking infrastructure, you just need Ethernet connectivity, something that comes by default in virtually all modern computing environments. Typically, the server has a dual Network Interface Card (NIC) that allows for the client-server traffic over IP. Those same NIC interfaces can also be used for accessing the iSCSI targets located "somewhere" on the IP network, or you can choose to use dedicated adapters that implement network protocol optimization functions, such as TCP Offload Engines.

To connect to the IP-based storage network, the Windows server needs a special driver, known as the iSCSI initiator that enables mapping the IP target in the storage namespace of Windows. Storage arrays or file/storage servers can present their units as iSCSI targets. Between those two parts, you just deal with a common or dedicated IP networking infrastructure, typically based on Gigabit Ethernet. Figure 4.39 gives an overall view.

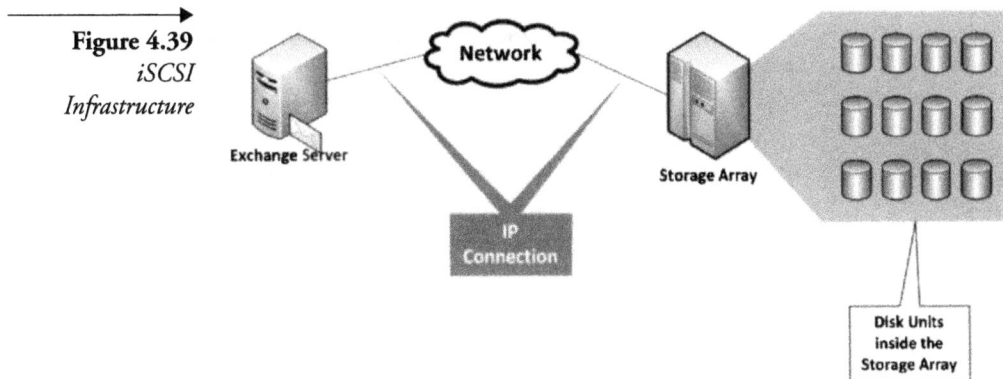

Figure 4.39
iSCSI
Infrastructure

In such an infrastructure, the Exchange Server components run on the initiator side of the iSCSI connection and the Storage Array hosts one or more targets and the network component can be dedicated, and as complex or simple as you require.

You may very well decide to create a physical separation between the client-server traffic and the storage traffic. This is particularly indicated for security reasons, unless you encrypt the storage traffic. Let's look at the following topology in Figure 4.40.

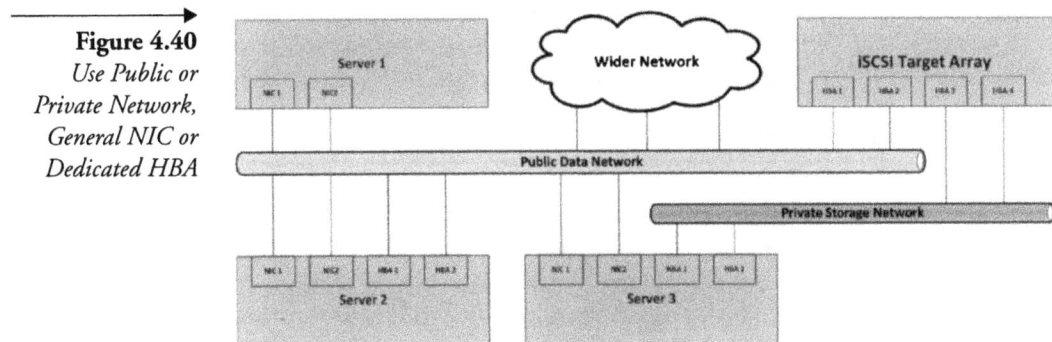

Figure 4.40
Use Public or
Private Network,
General NIC or
Dedicated HBA

- Server 1 is a simple server that has a set of redundant NIC adapters. It uses both of them for connecting to the Public Data Network which is also connecting to the iSCSI Target Array.

- Server 2 has a similar approach in terms of infrastructure use, however, it uses dedicated host-bus adapters for connecting into the public data network. The advantage of using dedicated adapters is that you can use advanced processing functions for the IP and SCSI protocols.

- Server 3 has a configuration that is very similar to what you would end up with a Fibre Channel SAN, with a dedicated pair of adapters connecting to the public data network for client-server traffic and a dedicated pair of specialized adapters connecting to a physically separate IP network. In a Fibre Channel SAN, this Private Storage Network would simply be a Fibre Channel fabric with its own media (optical fiber most likely) and topology.

The advantage of iSCSI is the flexibility and the ability to cheaply build infrastructures that achieve the benefits of storage networks without requiring the complexity or know-how that is often required with Fibre Channel based Storage Area Networks.

The disadvantages of iSCSI are the consolidation of another protocol (SCSI) onto an infrastructure that is already in use for client-server traffic. While sharing is great because it enables economies of scale, it implies possibly unforeseen congestion problems that would be harder to troubleshoot because of the many reasons for failures. To prevent this, you will want to run your iSCSI infrastructure on a separate network infrastructure, and possibly use dedicated host-bust adapters that can optimize the traffic exchange between the iSCSI initiators and targets. The result does not necessarily gain you much simplicity in your deployment, and for this reason, I believe that Fibre Channel SANs have still some future, even though iSCSI and its versatility has a good potential for greater adoption.

4.7.2   iSCSI Initiator

The Initiator component is the part of the iSCSI SAN (or, IP SAN) that runs on the server that will eventually use the units for the Exchange databases and other components that require storage. Microsoft makes the iSCSI initiator available as a free download from their Storage portal web site (consult http://www.microsoft.com/storage). Using the Microsoft iSCSI Software Initiator is probably the simplest (not necessarily the most performant) way to get started with IP SAN. You can install the Initiator on Windows Server 2003 servers and Windows XP SP1 clients (or any greater of these versions).

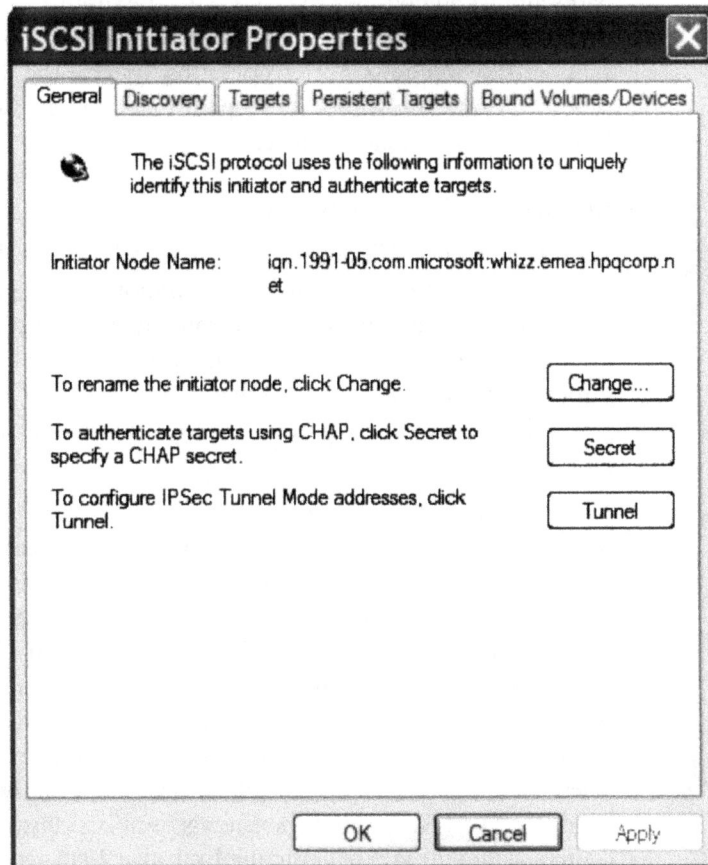

iSCSI Initiator Properties ☒

| General | Discovery | Targets | Persistent Targets | Bound Volumes/Devices |

The iSCSI protocol uses the following information to uniquely identify this initiator and authenticate targets.

Initiator Node Name: iqn.1991-05.com.microsoft:whizz.emea.hpqcorp.net

To rename the initiator node, click Change. [Change...]

To authenticate targets using CHAP, click Secret to specify a CHAP secret. [Secret]

To configure IPSec Tunnel Mode addresses, click Tunnel. [Tunnel]

[OK] [Cancel] [Apply]

If you use a dedicated HBA for your iSCSI connection, such as those offered by Adaptec, Intel, or QLogic, you have to make sure that you use their iSCSI stack, in a similar way than if you were using a Fibre Channel HBA with specific drivers.

Multipathing with iSCSI

Multipath is an important function when you connect your server to a storage network. It allows your server to use one path or another (typically, you use two paths) connect to the back-end array. Using Windows Server 2003, you can benefit from the overall MPIO framework, and use a Device Specific Module (DSM) that is related to the iSCS target and HBAs. The Microsoft iSCSI software initiator uses a software DSM supplied with the kit that lets you define several ways to attain the iSCSI target. Not all iSCSI targets support an MPIO DSM for handling multiple paths and it's a good idea to check with the supplier of the iSCSI solution on the availability of such a module to fit inside MPIO. With earlier versions of the Windows Server operating system, the iSCSI target vendor should provide you with a multi-path management solution that ensures load balancing and path failover.

Configuring iSCSI in clusters

It is possible with Windows Server 2003 SP1 to use the Microsoft iSCSI software initiator in a clustered configuration. Although this simplifies the infrastructure requirements when constructing clusters, you should not assume that you can build clusters wherever iSCSI can take you. For instance, even if IP is a protocol that can be used over a wide-area network, I would not recommend you to deploy a cluster that spans beyond a local area network.

Nonetheless, the perspective of using iSCSI for clusters is interesting because it significantly lowers the entry price of Exchange 2003 clusters. Microsoft is constantly evolving the recommendations and certification of iSCSI topologies for clustered environments. The important point to consider is that the Cluster Resource Manager has a SCSI LUN reservation and reset arbitration mechanism to prevent split-brain situations in disk quorum based clusters. Put simply, it can do nasty things on the iSCSI network and for this reason, it is recommended to create logical and physical separation when building iSCSI clusters. Please refer to http://www.microsoft.com/windowsserver2003/technologies/storage/iscsi/iscsicluster.mspx if you are contemplating the idea of clustering Exchange 2003 over iSCSI.

Generally speaking, Microsoft will impose (recommend strongly) that each node in a cluster has at least 2 NIC adapters for the private and public cluster traffic. With iSCSI clusters, you need an additional third NIC for the SAN traffic, as Microsoft does not support sharing either of the previously mentioned NICs for iSCSI storage traffic. If we refer back to Figure 9, only Server 3 would be suitable to be part of a cluster.

There are additional requirements for the configuration of the iSCSI interconnect (which, functionally speaking, is simply a Gigabit Ethernet LAN) in order to guarantee that the iSCSI traffic is as immune as possible from other sources of pollution, such as:

- use a VLAN (Virtual Local Area Network)
- use a physically separate network (with its own switches)

- use non-blocking switches to prevent the network switch from being a point of contention

- use of Gigabit Ethernet speed (at least) and take advantage of jumbo frames (up to 9,000 bytes payload) and large MTU (TCP/IP parameter that specifies the largest payload in a TCP packet)

Finally, suffice it to say that you need to ensure proper security, and notably prevent two clusters from clashing into each other when discovering iSCSI targets. One easy way to achieve this is to force authentication when logging into a target (CHAP, Challenge Handshake Authentication Protocol is a minimum, mutual CHAP or IPsec is recommended).

Figure 4.42
Required iSCSI
Cluster
Infrastructure

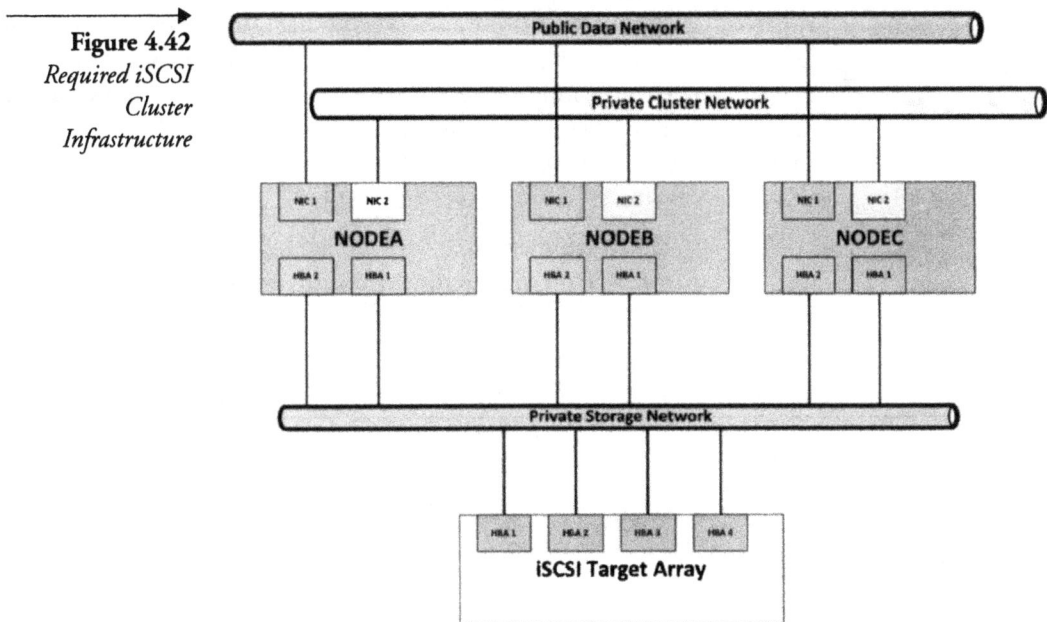

As you can see from Figure 4.42, it is not obvious that an iSCSI cluster is something much simpler than a SAN—and in fact, I think that the addition of a layer of a networking protocol (not originally designed for a storage protocol such as SCSI-3) brings additional complexity. As we are looking to simplify storage networks, it is not obvious that the consolidation proposed by iSCSI can be applied in all cases, at least not in the case of multi-node shared storage clusters with Exchange 2003 SP2 and Windows Server 2003 SP1.

Booting over iSCSI?

Of course, you might wonder if you can boot over iSCSI, thereby simplifying your server deployment setup. iSCSI boot is typically possible if you use dedicated and specialized iSCSI host-bus adapters. If you use the iSCSI software initiator from Windows Server 2003, you will not benefit from such a feature, although it is planned with the next major release of Windows, code-named Longhorn. In that case, the HBA vendor must provide the necessary support for such a configuration, in a similar way as with Fibre Channel storage networks.

4.7.3   iSCSI Target

An iSCSI target can be of many kinds. Initially, we saw NAS appliances being enhanced with another protocol, besides the CIFS or NFS traditional file sharing protocols. Then, network equipment vendors such as Cisco came to market with bridges that would interface between Fibre Channel SANs and Ethernet network (multi-protocol routers). Finally, we are now seeing most of the high-end arrays being equipped with Ethernet interfaces and support for the iSCSI protocol.

Besides specialized equipments, some companies are proposing an iSCSI target protocol stack for Windows or even Linux (http://iscsitarget.source-force.net).

In Figure 4.43, we can see how several application servers can connect into a local area network and "see" iSCSI targets exposed by the iSCSI gateway. The actual implementation of the iSCSI target is residing in the Storage Array, in the form of Fibre Channel LUN. To the array, the iSCSI gateway is another Fibre Channel node.

4.7.4   In Summary

For low-cost deployments of Exchange, iSCSI represents a fairly good approach. But you must understand that a low-cost approach is likely to yield some disadvantages that we have described earlier on. Nonetheless, if you do not have a SAN infrastructure already in place, it is a good way to benefit from advanced storage management functions, such as mirroring or snapshotting, which would otherwise not be available with direct attached storage. Another advantage of iSCSI is that it can be used to provide the necessary shared storage for building Microsoft clusters. With Windows Server 2003 SP1, it is possible to build up to 8-node clusters using the Microsoft iSCSI initiator.

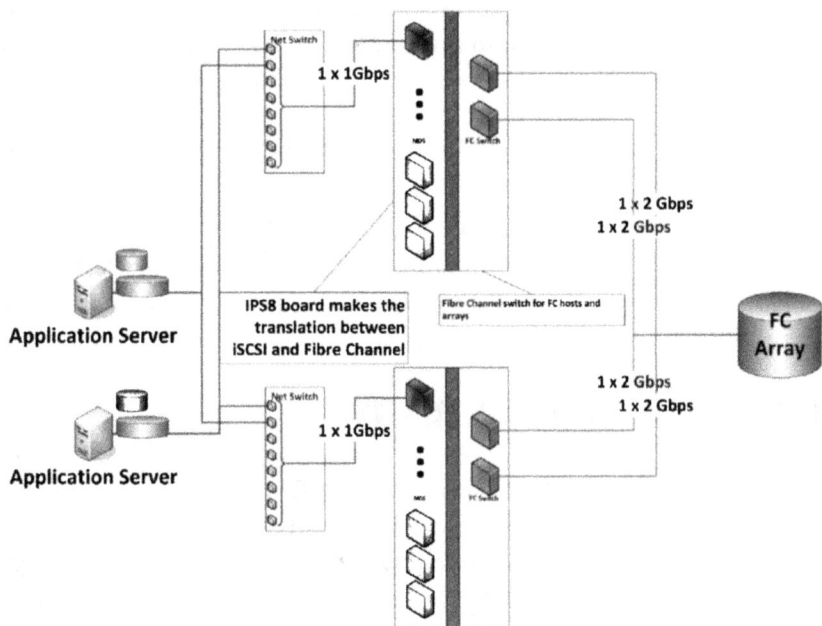

Figure 4.43
*Using an iSCSI
Gateway to Front-
End a Fibre
Channel SAN*

If you decide to deploy iSCSI, pay special attention to the possibility of eavesdropping on the Ethernet network, and plan for some level of separation. Encryption of traffic is possible, just like with NAS devices, with the use of IPsec for instance, but this can have a certain impact on the performance of the host server, which is typically busy. I use a guideline to reserve, for peak workloads, approximately 20 percent of CPU burn rate for IP frame processing at up to 100 MB/s (which is a data rate unlikely to be demanded with Exchange production workload).

iSCSI is not to be completely dismissed for Exchange. Note that we did not touch on performance issues, for the simple reason that the speed of the media (Gigabit Ethernet or 10 Gigabit Ethernet) is not something of great influence for Exchange 2003. So I would not compare iSCSI targets and Fibre Channel SAN controllers, for the simple reason that each can have its performance problems if they are badly configured. Nonetheless, there is a space when traditional Fibre Channel SAN has an advantage and that is in the experience and maturity that has been built into such infrastructures. I would certainly agree with you if you were to respond that Fibre Channel SANs are complex to manage, and I believe that it is up to the vendors to simplify their infrastructures for the administrators, rather than the administrators having to raise their level of know-how (not that it is a bad thing in itself). Microsoft has quite understood that problem with their Simple SAN approach and kicked off with Windows Server 2003 R2: the idea is to bring together vendors under the Windows Storage Management framework (VSS and VDS as discussed in Chapter 3), and produce tools that can control the storage infrastructure components without having the deep knowledge of the tools necessary to manage a multi-vendor "by nature" infrastructure.

In summary, I really think that iSCSI infrastructures are designed to live in parallel with SAN infrastructures for a while, providing the "Toyota [3]" transport for storage, while Fibre Channel SAN offers the "Aston Martin [4]" kind of transport.

4.8   The value of RAID

RAID, originally stood for Redundant Array of Inexpensive Disks and got later used for Redundant Array of Independent Disks, is a technique that combines several independent disk drives into a single logical volume; it presents improved characteristics as if it used only a single disk. These characteristics are as follows:

- *Availability.* By building redundancy in the array, you can sustain the loss of an individual member in a RAID set

- *Performance.* By combining several disks, you can get increased throughput in terms of both data rate (MB per second) and transfer rate (I/O per second)

- *Size.* The resulting volume can be made larger than a single disk drive, quite suitable for environments in which the data cannot be broken down, such as an Exchange 2003 database. Note that this was even more relevant with Exchange 5.5

- *Cost.* It has to be for any given US Dollar or Euro, you get a certain quantity of usable storage space. Depending upon the requirements, you can get factors of 10 or 20 between any two configurations. Cheap configurations typically have a small level of redundancy and do not perform very fast; but do you need high-speed storage after all?

RAID comes in many levels, the base levels ranging from 0 to 5. Additional levels have been developed, such as 10, 0+1, and 6 or 7. It is common to combine RAID volumes into stripes, and append the individual volumes of RAID level with a 0 (e.g., RAID50 for a stripe of RAID5 volumes, RAID10 for a stripe of mirrors, etc....).

Some of these levels have value in an Exchange 200x environment, whereas the storage manufacturers seldom implement others. In the case of Microsoft Exchange 2003 and BackOffice applications such as SQL Server, RAID5, RAID1, and RAID0+1 (a.k.a RAID10) are the most relevant because they combine data redundancy with increased performance levels, in different terms, and that's what makes the choice relevant. The discussion now examines the most common RAID levels and briefly states their advantages and inconveniences; we will then proceed to compare them.

4.8.1   RAID0

The basis of RAID0 is *disk striping*. The idea is to combine several disks into a logical volume, the resulting size of which is the sum of the size of each disk making up the volume. In RAID0, all the disks must have the same capacity and geometry. Depending upon the controllers, you may mix drives of varying size (geometry), but the lowest common denominator will always be used.

The advantages of RAID0 are to obtain the maximum quantity of storage (the sum of the capacity of each drive), and the maximum level of performance (the sum of the request rates of each individual drives). For instance, five 72 GB disks combined in a RAID0 array will yield a total raw capacity of 5×72 GB = 360 GB and the ability to sustain up to 650 random I/O per second (if you consider that each single disk drive can handle 130 I/O per second), no matter whether the I/O request is a read operation or a write operation (that difference between the type of the I/O is important with other RAID levels). Depending on the I/O size and on the low-level formatting of the array (mainly the chunk size) you may get a little less, but you get the overall idea. Later in this chapter we take up the necessity to properly configure the chunk size, if that is at all possible on your controller.

The main disadvantage of RAID0 is the lack of data redundancy. If you lose a single member of the RAID0 set, you loose the entire content of the volume and get an opportunity to check how good your last backup was.

Figure 4.44 describes the layout of data blocks in a RAID0 disk subsystem.

The correspondence between the virtual volume blocks and the actual disk blocks is done by a component of the RAID controller called the Array

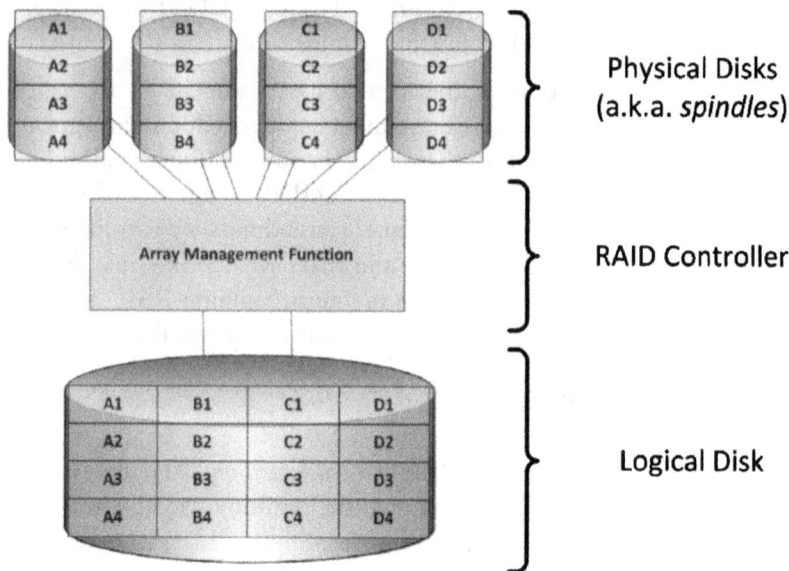

Figure 4.44
RAID0 Disk
Structure

Management Function. Consider the logical disk obtained from the RAID0 disk array described in Figure 4.44.

A single "layer" of blocks at the same level (e.g., A1, B1, C1, and D1) is called a stripe. The size of each block is called the stripe depth, also known as the chunk size. Chunk size carries a lot of importance in performance optimization, depending on the I/O size. More on this subject is covered later in this chapter. The size of a stripe is determined by the number of members multiplied by the size of each chunk or stripe depth.

RAID0 is implemented at times in benchmarking environments to avoid the storage subsystem's presenting itself as a bottleneck. This is an arguable tactic; although it gives the best results, it can indicate a great performance in a configuration that wouldn't be suitable for a production environment, given the hassle of having to resort to restore operations and the negative impact it has on service availability.

4.8.2   RAID 1

RAID1 is another fundamental RAID level, which keeps and maintains the exact same content of a disk drive on one or more additional disks. RAID1 is often referred to as disk mirroring, and carries the great advantage of duplicating the contents of a given disk drive onto another drive. Should the initial drive fail (or any member of the RAID1 set), operations can still continue by getting data on other valid members of the RAID1 set.

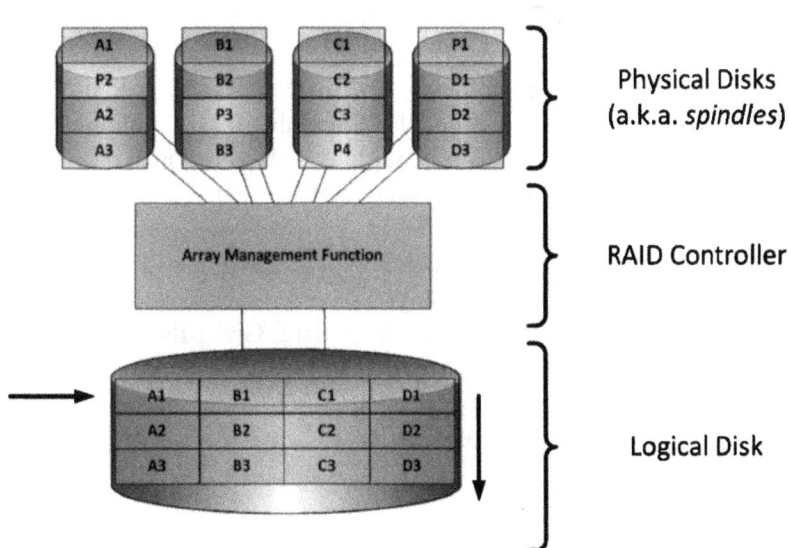

Figure 4.45
RAID1 Disk
Structure

The advantage of RAID1 is the high level of data redundancy and availability.

In fact, it carries other advantages, especially in the area of point-in-time backup operations, which is discussed later. The disadvantage of RAID1 is that you lose capacity. If you combine two 72 GB disk drives in a RAID1 array, the resulting raw capacity is 72 G. You've just lost the capacity of the mirroring drive. The same thing applies if you arrange three drives together: the resulting capacity is still the size of one disk.

From a request rate perspective, the deal is somewhat different depending on whether you mostly read from the volume or write to it. In read operations, the RAID controller can read from either of the two volumes (in a two volume RAID1 set) and yield a performance level of 200 I/O per second, given that your individual disk drives can sustain 100 I/O per second.

When it comes to write operations, the data has to be written to both volumes at the same time, and in some cases, the resulting response time is dependent upon the slowest drive to complete the operation. Therefore, a two-disk RAID1 set has a write performance of 100 I/O per second. This is the first instance in which we see that the read/write ratio gathers importance in the actual performance of the volume. When we compare the RAID levels, you will see that the R/W ratio can have a significant weight in choosing the most appropriate level for your environment.

Figure 4.38 describes the block layout of a RAID1 volume. Notice that for two disks, the contents are the same. I have mentioned earlier that you could combine more than two drives in a RAID1 set. No, this is not for paranoids, although a 3-member RAID1 volume can handle the loss of two disk drives (you would be really out of luck on that day if you were to lose two drives in a 3-disk RAID1 set). The other advantage is that you can "break" the mirror (without necessarily affecting the current operation of the drive, although it's best to do this with a "quiesced" volume), and in a matter of seconds you have a duplicate copy of your original volume. This is a fast way to back up data. Given the decreasing price of storage these days (in terms of $/MB), this can be an interesting approach, and we'll see that in high-end environments, this becomes a sound data duplication strategy for backups.

4.8.3 RAID5

I'm skipping RAID 2, 3, and 4, because not only do they carry little advantage in terms of performance and availability, but they are seldom implemented in modern controllers. RAID5 is by far the most popular RAID level in a production environment, sometimes rightly, sometimes wrongly. You'll see why shortly.

Figure 4.46
RAID5 Disk Structure

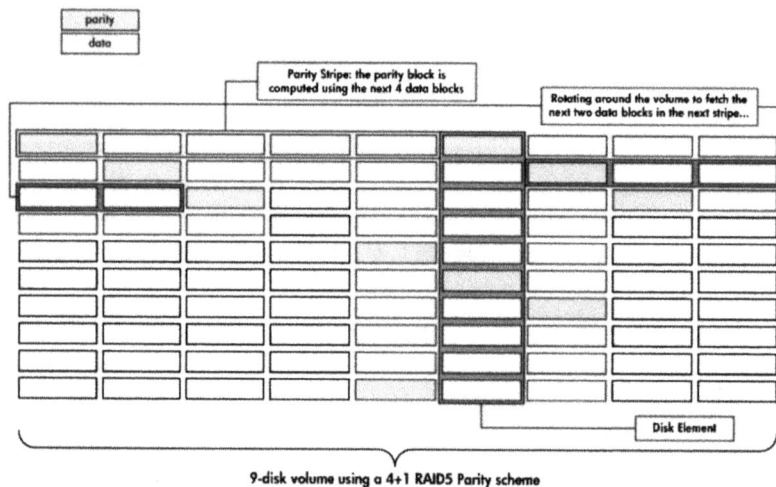

9-disk volume using a 4+1 RAID5 Parity scheme

RAID5 builds upon the notion of disk stripping. But unlike RAID0 where there is no data redundancy, RAID5 introduces the notion of extraneous parity information, which can be utilized should a member of a RAID set fail. The parity information is *distributed* across all members of the RAID set and is a simple logical XOR of each data block of each volume. This parity information is stored in place of data in a member of a RAID5 set. Whereas RAID3 dedicates a drive for storing parity, RAID5 distributes the parity across all members of a disk. Locating the parity on a single drive can quickly turn that drive into a hot spot where time is spent waiting for the total write operation to complete.

When data must be read from a RAID5 volume, the performance and access pattern of the disk drive is similar to a regular stripe set (RAID0).

The big difference comes when data must be written or updated to the volume, and the parity information must be maintained.

An application write to a RAID5 volume consists of updating the parity information from the stripe set and updating the data block supposed to hold the data. First, consider the structure of a RAID5 volume—it is composed of a set of stripes. Within each stripe, for N drives, there are N-1 stripe chunks, and one parity chunk. As the data is written to the stripe chunks, the parity information is computed by an XOR operation between all the N-1 stripe chunks and stored in the parity chunk, as described in Figure 4.46.

In the example shown, P3 is the stripe parity chunk, calculated from A3, B3, and D3. The calculation is done the following way:

$$P3 = A3 \oplus B3 \oplus D3$$

If the disk that holds B3 gets lost for some reason, B3 can be computed from:

$$B3 = A3 \oplus P3 \oplus D3$$

The XOR calculation is very straightforward. In hardware RAID implementations, it can be as simple as implementing it in a dedicated integrated circuit that calculates the parity data as it is transferred. In software RAID, this operation is usually left up to the processor, which is not the best way to use your CPU cycles (the disadvantages of software-based implementations of RAID are discussed later), and it carries some risks because of the write-hole problem (see below).

The value of the parity information is present only if you maintain it as data gets updated. Writing on block A3, in our example, will involve first "subtracting" the knowledge of A3 to the parity block P3, and then proceeding to generate a new parity. For writing to a RAID5 subsystem, you need to read the data block, read the parity block, update the parity block, and write back both the data block and the parity block. This is what I usually call a compound write operation, which can seem innocent at first; however, notice that to maintain the integrity of the overall stripe, you need to write two blocks of data at once. First the parity block must be written back, and then the data block. Typically, the controller will return a successful status when both operations are complete.

4.8.4   RAID5 write-hole

What if the controller has a problem right between those two write operations? You get an inconsistent volume: the parity block is out of sync with the corresponding data blocks. This is known as the RAID5 *write-hole*, and is addressed differently depending on the storage vendor and controller model.

This write-hole can be quite dangerous—if you're lucky, you will get a volume corruption straight away. You will need to address it, but it will not go unnoticed. However, if the controller does not flag this error, you will most likely get a volume corruption by the time the data is actually needed.

I have observed this at a customer site, and the process is quite painful to recover (basically, you need to restore the entire volume).

To prevent this, RAID controllers have implemented various techniques as they evolved. First, we saw models of controllers that would, after a system crash, regenerate the parity blocks for all the volume. This can be annoying, since the volume is unavailable, in fact, for the controller that was implementing this feature; the entire system was not available because this operation was happening at boot time.

Other controllers verify parity information every now and then, as a non-disruptive background task. Finally, high-end controllers will keep an area of their cache for multi-disk I/Os, and even if you operate in write-through mode, will still keep track of the disk I/Os that must absolutely be done. But since this last feature is using cache memory in the controller, you must make sure that before the volume is online, the cache battery is fully charged. Modern controllers will prevent bringing a unit online before the cache battery is fully charged. So a good idea is before planning any operation on the RAID volume, to power the RAID array in advance so the batteries can go through a full charge cycle. This is a classic occurrence when you ship a test environment to a production site and the batteries have discharged in the meantime.

In software-based implementations, you can hardly guarantee that the two write operations will be successful. If you write a parity block, you must write the data block that is "contained" on the parity block, otherwise you lose consistency. Even if the I/O is effectively reported as not done by the operating system, you can have unmatched parity and data blocks for a given stripe, should a system crash occur at a bad time (is there any good time for a system crash anyway?) during the write operation. Some operating systems, such as HP's OpenVMS, go as far as using 6-disk I/Os for the parity and data block updates, instead of the traditional 4-disk I/Os.

4.8.5 Impact of the number of disks in a RAID5 volume

RAID5 comes in a minimum of three disks. Typical large RAID5 volumes can grow up to 14 disks and beyond, but there are downsides to building large RAID5 volumes. For instance, if you lose a member in a RAID5 array, you need to replace that member. Typically, the controller will do this operation automatically (hot swap feature). However, during the rebuild of the volume, every single data block of each member of the RAID5 set has to be read, for the regeneration of the data and of the parity. For large volumes, that can be a lengthy operation (several hours). Furthermore, during this operation you have no more redundancy in the volume. In the unlikely event of a disk loss during volume rebuild, you would lose the entire volume and have to use your backups to restore the volume. Because there are a large number of disks, the backup duration may tend to be long, and therefore, the overall downtime of the application and/or its data hosted on the volume is greater than what it should normally be. So, although theory implies that you could have 30 or 40 disks in a RAID5 volume, practical implementation rarely goes beyond 14 or 15 disks, which is an acceptable limit in most cases.

Another approach is to logically group disks in a RAID5 volume by a certain number decided at the initialization time of the array, or simply part of the array architecture (this is the case for HP's StorageWorks EVA and XP SAN arrays). Using 4 or 5 disks, you can make up a RAID5 set, even though the total number of disks can be much larger. The result is an increase of performance (because of a large number of drives) without the risk of getting too often in a volume repair mode (because of the small number of drives making up the RAID5). The parity arrangement can cycle across disks, it's just that the parity is calculated on a smaller number of blocks than the number of blocks making up a stripe (minus one, of course).

As an example, let's study the grouping on a 4+1 basis (4 data disks and 1 parity disk) without restricting the maximum number of members in a RAID5 volume to five (distribution of data may occur on several "groups" of 4+1 disks), as shown in Figure 4.47. Reducing the number of members reduces the stripe length. The smaller the stripe length, the greater the chance of updating an entire RAID5 stripe and avoiding the RAID5 write penalty.

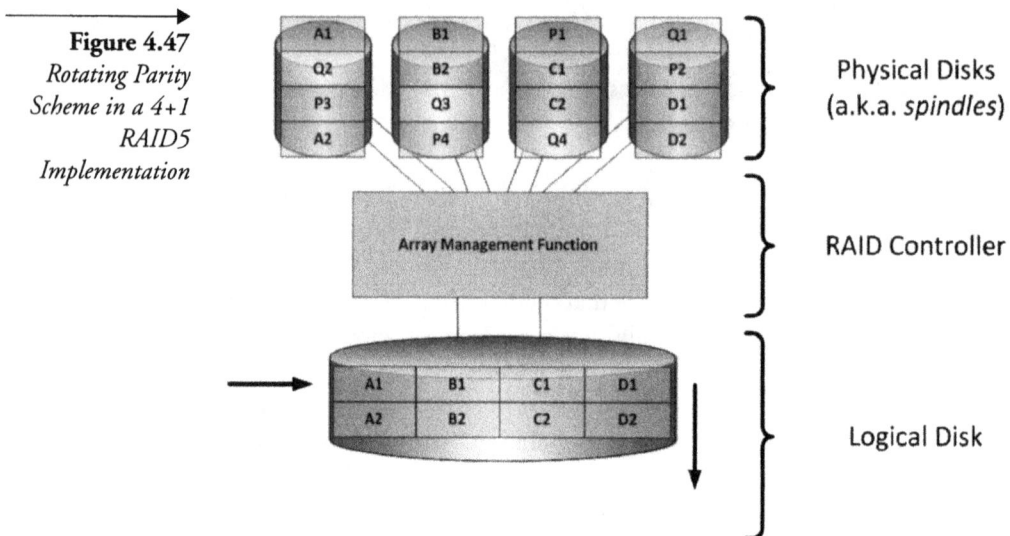

Figure 4.47
Rotating Parity Scheme in a 4+1 RAID5 Implementation

The disadvantage of this approach is the straight loss of capacity (20 percent when using a 4+1 scheme; 25 percent in a 3+1 scheme), no matter the number of disks.

The major advantage is the decreased dependency on the number of disks used to achieve a full stripe update: because the data portion of a parity stripe is 4 chunks, if your chunk size is 8 KB, you only need 32 KB in a write (aggregated or not) operation in order to bypass the parity update, and avoid the write penalty.

For all implementations, the minimum number of drives comprising a RAID5 array is three. This is necessary for generating parity information, which can be used to recover a lost member.

For all implementations, there is no read penalty. For this reason, and given the vendor-specific optimizations for handling the parity updates and RAID5 write-hole, RAID5 (or RAID-S) volumes are commonly used when the transactional access pattern is read only, even if batch mode operations use write transactions. Data archiving and data mining are common examples of processes that suit RAID5 deployments. User transactions are typically read operations, and write operations are performed in batch mode in a non-interactive manner, and with a flow of data that large controller cache modules (32 GB and above) can deal with efficiently.

4.8.6 RAID6

Another approach is the one used in RAID6, seldomly implemented by manufacturers, which provides two levels of parity (instead of one as in RAID5) distributed on two separate member sets, and can sustain the loss of two disk drives at the same time or the loss of a single disk drive during volume reconstruction. This extra security increases the time needed for write operations, since you now need to maintain two parity blocks instead of one.

HP, on the Smart Array controller, implements RAID6, called Advanced Data Guarding (ADG). The block parity layout is actually shown in Figure 4.48.

With HP's implementation of the Smart Array 6400 (which is a PCI-based controller), you can use up to 56 disks in a RAID array. By using ADG, you decrease the impact of an unlikely second disk failure during reconstruct time. However, by using lots of disks in the array, the reconstructing time will be quite significant, and although it is running at a lower priority than normal data traffic, it can be inconvenient. The likelihood of a disk failure within a given module will tend to increase as you increase the number of drives in that volume; if you have a 20 percent chance of losing a disk in a 4-disk volume, you have a 40 percent chance of losing a disk in an 8-disk volume.

4.8.7 Hybrid models: RAID0+1 or RAID10

Because RAID1 gives the most redundancy and RAID0 gives the best performance, the idea came to combine the two RAID levels into one, RAID0+1. RAID0+1 consists of striping (RAID0) mirrors (RAID1) together. The resulting volume has good capacity (half of the overall disk capacity thrown in the volume) and splendid performance (up to N x 100 I/O per second for N drives). RAID0+1 is costly to implement, yet gains popularity because of the low cost of disk drives these days, the high density of storage, and the ability of modern controllers to handle a large number of disks.

Figure 4.48
*RAID6 (Also
Called Advanced
Data Guarding)
Principle*

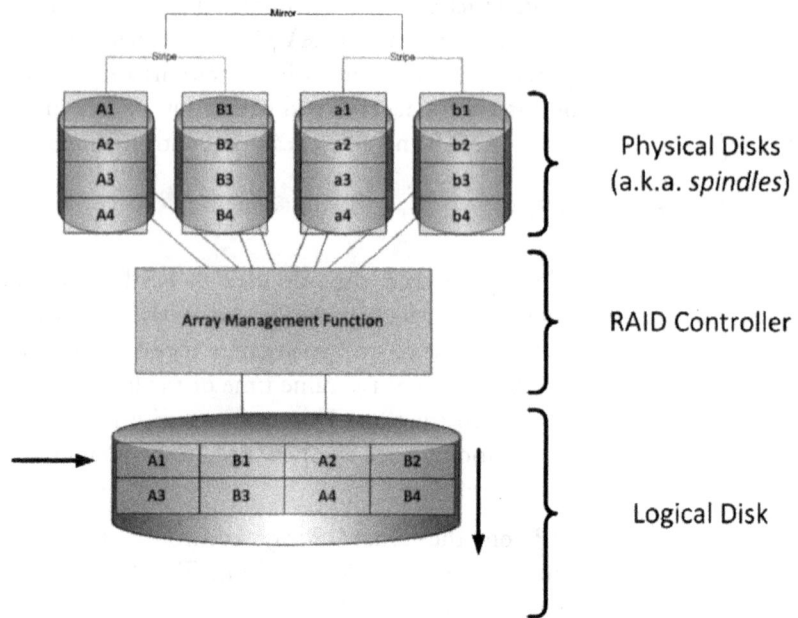

Figure 4.49
*RAID0+1:
Mirroring Stripes*

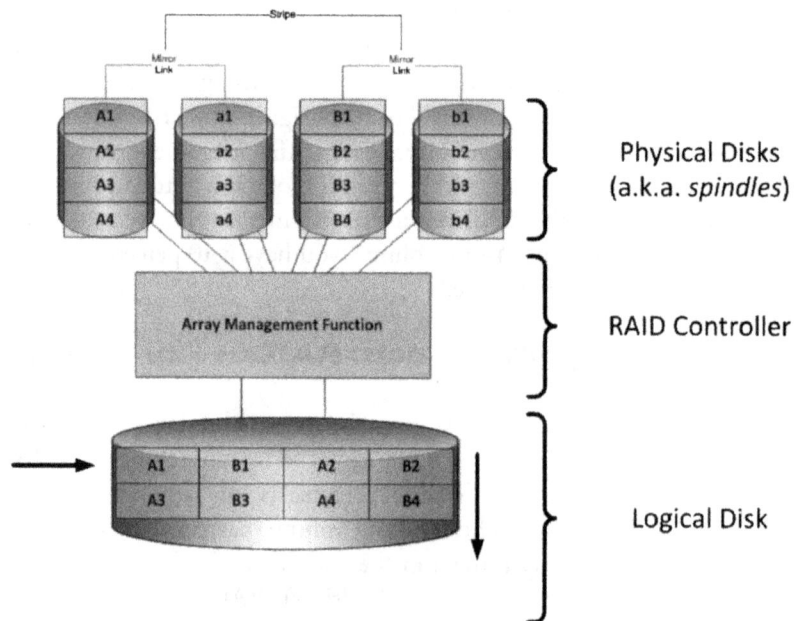

Figure 4.49 shows a RAID0+1 disk structure. Here, we see a 4-disk RAID0+1 volume, where two disks are being mirrored and then striped.

Note that you could do the reverse—stripe two disks and mirror them. This is what is also referred to as RAID10. There is little difference between the two approaches from a performance and capacity perspective. Your I/O throughput is theoretically equivalent to:

```
Total I/O = (read %)*(Total number of disks)+(write %)*(Total
number of disks/2)
```

Yet, from a management and operations, perspective, there are differences that may force or incline you to choose between one and the other.

Let's look at a small visual comparison, and we'll discuss on that basis. Figure 4.50 describes the mirroring of two stripes. From the RAID controller perspective, you have to deal with three units: two stripes and one overall mirror of these two stripes. If we were to arrange the same number of disks in RAID0+1, we would obtain what is described in Figure 4.50.

Figure 4.50
RAID10, Stripping RAID1 Members

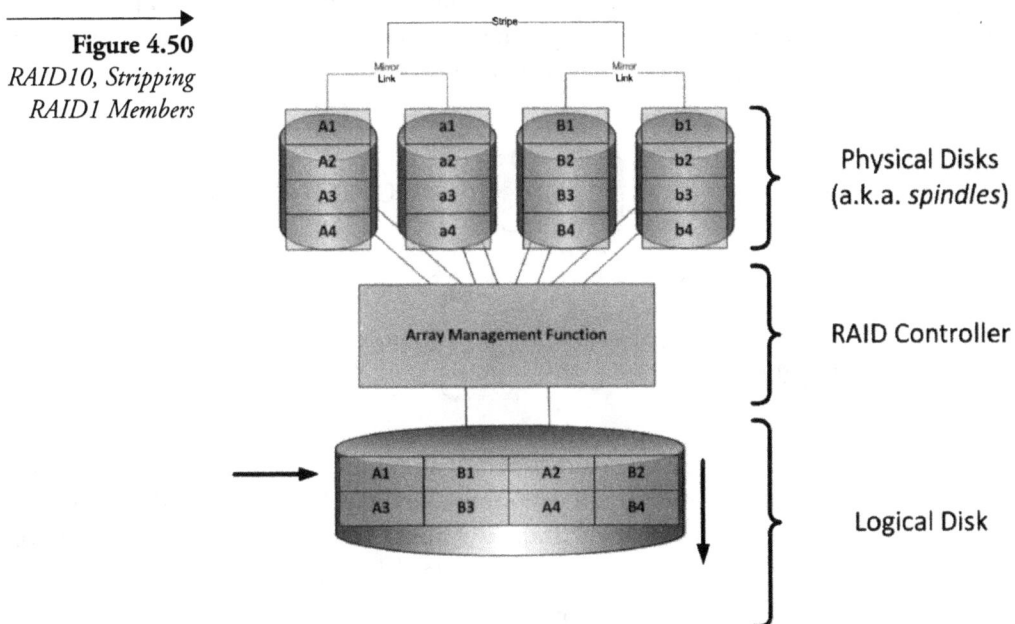

The downside of RAID10 is how gracefully can the controller handle a disk failure. In the case of RAID0+1, if a disk drive fails, the controller will tap into the hot spare pool of disks, and proceed to rebuild a single mirror. In the case of RAID10, if a disk goes wrong, it is the entire stripe that needs to be rebuilt. The consequences, notably the rebuild time, as well as the overall tolerance to disk failure are much different between the two techniques.

Another issue is redundancy. A RAID10 volume can sustain the loss of one drive, perhaps more if the subsequently failing device is part of the same stripe as the original failing drive. A RAID0+1 volume made of N disks can handle the loss of N/2 disks only if these failures are impacting each mirror and never twice the same mirror. Failures can be of several orders, from a regular disk burnout, to an entire back-end bus failure, which has been observed before at several of my customer sites.

4.8.8   Concatenation is **NOT** Striping

There is a fundamental difference between concatenation of disks (also known as drive spanning) of volumes and striping. With concatenation, you collate volumes together. As you traverse the volume through each of the logical blocks, you hit the first member, then the next member, etc.... until you reach the end of the volume. Concatenation is often proposed in array architecture for expansion of volumes and is really interesting for capacity purposes, not performance.

Figure 4.51
Concatenating 5 Disks and Filling Them at 40 Percent

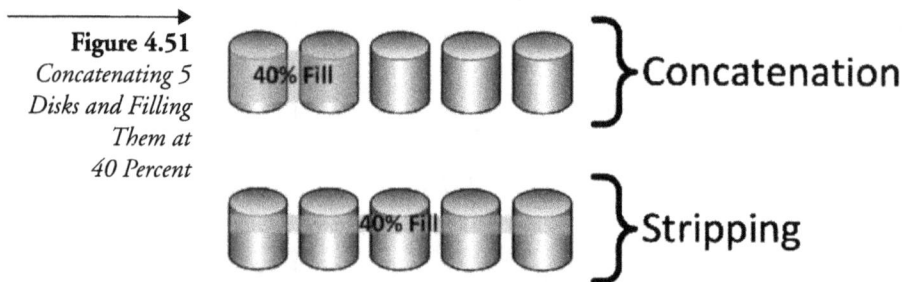

When studying Figure 4.51, if you fill up at 40 percent a concatenated volume, you only access data from two disks. If you fill up 40 percent of a stripe, you access data from five disks. The difference is important for Microsoft Exchange database workload because of the sensitivity on the response time and throughput of random I/O. Because I/Os to the database are random, you can reasonably plan on the fill space being accessed almost uniformly. But if you leave spare space, the disks hosting that spare space will not be used in a concatenated volume, whereas in a stripe, all disks will participate in the I/O, no matter the fill ratio.

4.8.9   **Comparing RAID levels**

There are many ways to compare RAID levels depending very much on your prime requirement. First, is availability a priority? If this is the case, RAID0 is not good for you. Do you need capacity? In this case, RAID1 can be seen as a costly implementation, especially compared with RAID0, which yields the most capacity, and RAID5, which grants the most capacity while keeping redundancy. Finally, maybe performance is more important?

In that situation, RAID0 is excellent, and so is RAID1 or RAID0+1; RAID5 comes in last, unless you have a majority of read operations. (Even in an Exchange 2003 environment this can be the case. For example, ISPs want the maximum level of performance for their POP users, which, when they retrieve their mails, only read to the database!) The key thing to remember is that there is no free lunch in the world of storage, and you will always have to make a compromise between

- Availability
- Performance
- Cost

Figure 4.52 quickly summarizes the comparison.

JBOD stands for Just a Bunch Of Disks, which is not covered because it is of little interest in the context of Exchange 2003. As you can see, the compromise solution here lies with RAID5, which gives a good cost figure (in terms of capacity), good availability (it can sustain the loss of one member of the volume), and a reasonable performance, provided you don't spend your time writing to the volume.

What's more important, because it may have a significant financial impact on the resulting solution, especially in high-end environments, you need to determine your priorities up front and stick with them. For example, you wish to build a volume that hosts 360 GB. Table 4.4 summarizes how many drives are involved and the resulting cost and performance levels that would be obtained. This table assumes a $200 cost for a 72 GB disk drive and 100 random I/O per second at 20 ms response time, which is a good worst-case scenario.

The RAID0+1 solution is quite appealing from a performance perspective, but not from a cost perspective; it is quite understandably more expen-

Figure 4.52
Comparing
RAID Levels

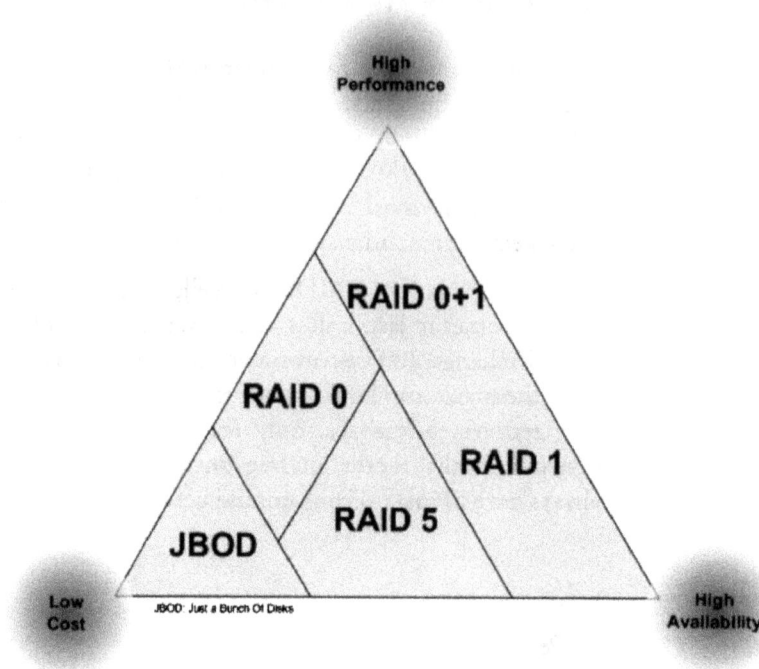

High
Performance

RAID 0+1

RAID 0

RAID 1

RAID 5

JBOD

JBOD: Just a Bunch Of Disks

Low
Cost

High
Availability

Table 4.4   *360 GB Volume Characteristics*

	RAID0	RAID0+1	RAID5	RAID6 (ADG)
# of 72GB disks	5	10	6	7
Request Rate	600	1,200	558	630
Cost	$1,000	$2,000	$1,200	$1,400
Price per GB	$2.77	$5.55	$3.33	$3.88
Price per I/O	$1.66	$1.96	$2.15	$2.22

sive than RAID0 and significantly more expensive than RAID5. Beyond
the pure capacity requirement, you then have to decide whether you wish
this volume to be protected, to offer performance, and more important,
whether you actually can afford the volume.

Notice that to obtain the request rate, we chose a 70 percent read, 30
percent write ratio. If we were to have a majority of read operations, RAID5
would rapidly become an appealing solution, because the overhead resulting from the write I/O does not get in the way too often, and that makes it

acceptable. This carries a lot of importance, and I will take the opportunity, once again, to reinforce the great advantage, if you've been running an Exchange 5.5 environment, of capturing performance counter information and establishing a baseline, a pattern of behavior of Exchange in your particular environment.

As you can see, it's not black or white, red or blue, love or hate: it's all a question of determining, in your own particular environment, what the load looks like, because that may turn out to be a massive cost savings given that the most performance is needed when you do read accesses. In the majority of the servers I've had the opportunity to diagnose, the read/write ratio of the Exchange ESE database with Exchange 2003 SP2 is around 70/30 (60 percent read, 40 percent write); while the ratio for the transaction log volume is a clear 100 percent write (during operations). This has evolved most notably since Exchange 2003, and during the follow-on Service Packs (SP1 and SP2) as Microsoft worked hard to reduce the I/O footprint and flow of the database engine, helping notably in storage replicated environments.

Based on this preliminary information (preliminary because there is much more to include in the picture such as cache optimization), it is definitely appropriate to separate the transaction log files from the database files, not only from a pure data recovery perspective but also because the I/O pattern is so radically different that it's easier to tune two separate volumes that are in line with the workload generated by the Exchange 2003 database engine(s).

There is another way to compare RAID levels, and that is from a pure cost perspective (your financial manager will love this). First, you must determine whether your concern is space or performance. Given the massive processor scalability that the industry in general, and Intel in particular, has given us, it would be a pity to hook a 3800 hp engine on a 4-wheel drive vehicle with all the brakes on. In other words, you may bring all the processing power of the world, it will be relevant only if you can bring the data to process at a fast enough speed. My goal, when I step into a customer site is to tune the systems from a performance perspective. That is what will matter most to your end users, including the CEO and the CIO, who will find hardly acceptable that a $100,000 solution does not respond when *they* decide to (this is the whole deal of tuning a system for transactional access compared to tuning a system for batch execution).

When you study the relative cost per GB for each of the RAID levels of interest, RAID0, RAID0+1, RAID5, and RAID6, you should note that the cost of RAID0+1 does not vary: it's always twice as much as the cost of

The value of RAID

RAID0, simply because we need twice as many disks than in RAID0 to
build up the redundancy. The cost for RAID5 will always be closer to the
cost of RAID0 because of the smaller number of disks required to achieve
the target capacity requirements. Then comes RAID6 and then RAID0+1.
Depending upon the array technology, the distributed parity of RAID5 and
RAID6 may be up against a fixed number of disks (between four and five)
and result in a net overhead of 25 percent or 20 percent, regardless of the
number of disks that make the array.

The other way to compare RAID levels is in terms of request rate or I/O
throughput (I'm not referring here to data rates—that is, MB per second—
but to I/O per second). The write performance penalty of RAID5 does not
play in its favor, quite clearly. Four-disk I/Os being required for any application write creates a lot of overhead, which will have a direct impact on the
response time of the individual I/O and on the overall request rate capacity
of the disk subsystem. Now, keep in mind that the parity overhead in
RAID5 occurs only for write operations. If you know that the majority of
your I/Os are going to be read operations, RAID5 carries a lot of value for
the redundancy it brings in the subsystem as well as the cost per MB that
we have just reviewed. It is even worse with RAID6 (6 disk I/O for each
write operation), however, this brings additional redundancy and resiliency,
such as the ability to lose two members in a RAID6 volume.

For Exchange 2003, we have observed a read/write ratio varying from
50/50 (50 percent read and 50 percent write) in benchmark environment
using the MMB2 workload, to 70/30 in a production environment. In
fact, this ratio can vary not only between environments but between periods of the day. If your users are only reading information from the
Exchange database (as in the case of POP users in an ISP scenario), then
you're mostly interested in getting the highest levels of read performance.
If, on the other hand, your users are reading and writing to the database
(as in MAPI, OWA, or some IMAP environments), then you require a
good level of performance and drive request rate capacity in both read
and write operations.

In a production environment, you will never see RAID0 because of the
lack of data protection. Nevertheless, if your prime requirement is to obtain
a satisfactory request rate from your disk subsystem, then RAID0+1 is a
better, more economical choice than RAID5.

The other comment I'd like to make is that when you see a benchmark
result using RAID0 as the main storage for Exchange 2003 and you plan
to build an equivalent production environment, do not rush to double the
storage by transforming RAID0 drives into RAID0+1. This approach

works only in a pure 100 percent write environment, and that is not always the case in Exchange 2003; even if you continuously write to the database, you will never get 100 percent writes. Because it uses a transaction-based model for the database engine to update its database pages, it will first need to read the page, execute the page modification in memory, record the page modification in the log buffer, flush the log buffer when the transaction (consisting of several page of modifications) is committed, and update *asynchronously* the dirty (modified) data page located in the cache memory back to disk.

A 50 percent read/write ratio is generally used when sizing and choosing RAID levels for Exchange 2003, although there is a trend of a 3:1 read/write ratio observed with Exchange 2003 SP1 and SP2.

4.8.10 Software-based implementation vs. hardware-based implementation

Windows Server Dynamic Disks allows the building of software-based stripe sets, which could include distributed parity (RAID5) or mirror sets that protect the volume by duplicating data between any two dynamic disks.

Furthermore, you can utilize this technology across many disks and partitions, thereby creating load balancing at the system level as opposed to the storage subsystem level. This is especially important if you wish to take advantage of multiple independent controllers that would otherwise present independent logical units (and therefore partitions and drives).

By default, any new device discovered by Windows Server is defined as a basic disk. You need to upgrade the basic disk to a "dynamic" disk in order to use the advanced volume management tools available from the Disk Management MMC snap-in. You may access the disk management snap-in by right-clicking on the My Computer desktop item and selecting the Manage option. From there, you can select the Disk Management component under the Storage container. Figure 4.46 shows how to upgrade a basic disk to a dynamic disk.

Then you may create your host-based RAID implementation using the Disk Management MMC snap-in from Windows (see Figure 4.54). Volume P: is a software based RAID5 volume.

The issue concerning software-based RAID implementations is of two orders. First, you are soliciting the CPU of the system to perform tasks around block device management (striping of disks can be addressed with low overhead, but striping with distributed parity requires CPU cycles to

Figure 4.53
Converting a Disk to Dynamic Disk

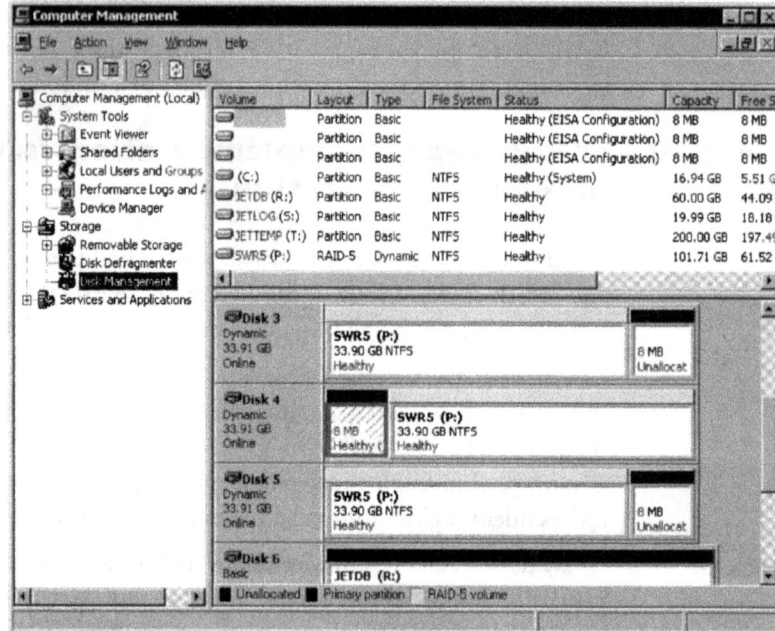

Figure 4.54
Dynamic Disks and Host-Based RAID with Windows

compute the parity blocks). Second, the recovery steps required should a dynamic disk fail, are more complex, manual, and typically prone to operation mistakes. This action typically requires unavailability and service downtime, which are not in line with the goal of increasing volume and data availability by the means of RAID. To this effect, the majority, if not all, of the deployments of Exchange 2003, utilize hardware RAID, which can be implemented with added features such as hot-swap and hot-spare device management, independently and transparently from the operation system and the application.

There are situations where host-based stripping provides an effective advantage, such as in the example where your target storage array has limited stripping capabilities (e.g., HP's XP1024 array), in favor of high availability and resiliency. While this approach generates a little more complexity, the return is the benefit for a super-scaling solution that can deal with the highest workloads, provided you have done a good job at leveling the resource utilization, comprising of the host port interface, cache, and back-end disk buses and units.

All in all, you should take advantage of RAID and the volume management functions offered by PCI-based RAID controllers, as well as the external, possibly shared, storage enclosures that will offload the CPU resources from the parity calculation and disk block management and offer advanced features. The lowering prices of entry-level PCI-based RAID arrays should definitely convince you to go that way. Note also that this practice is becoming more and more common; some computer vendors (e.g., HP) are embedding on their motherboard design a RAID-on-Chip logic (ROC) that provides basic RAID management (mirroring, read cache, no write-back cache), without the need to utilize a PCI slot for a back-plane RAID controller. This is a common practice in high-density server environments, where 1-U servers, such as the HP ProLiant DL360G3, include this ROC chipset and allow building a RAID1 mirror set for the system disk volumes at no additional hardware cost.

4.9   Fundamentals of storage performance

Now that you have been introduced to the notions of RAID, I'd like to step back and present a couple of diagrams that Jerry Bäcklin designed at Compaq Computer Corporation, and which I use quite often in presentations about storage. Note that there is nothing here specific to Microsoft Exchange; you may use this in all environments, including File Services and SQL server environments. Nevertheless, we will relate this to Microsoft Exchange because that is our main concern in this book.

Consider the response time of a general disk subsystem—do you bring much attention to the scales: they will change as technology evolves. As you reach saturation in the system, the response time increases, in an exponential fashion, as shown in Figure 4.55.

Notice how the response time is relatively good when the Request Rate is below 40 or 60 I/O per second. As the Request Rate augments, the response time increases exponentially. This is because of queuing. As each I/O has to wait more and more to be completed and as the queue grows, the completion time augments to the point saturation is reached and the response time becomes unbearable from an operational perspective (typically, users are waiting for their transactions to complete, when that trans-

Figure 4.55
Response Time and
Throughput

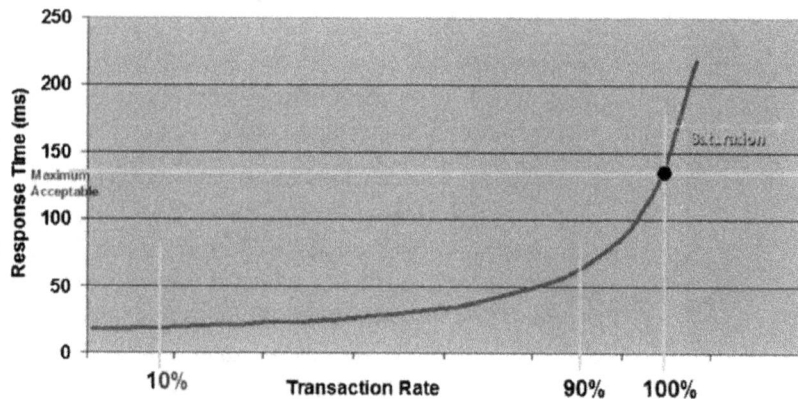

action is tied to storage operation completion). Anyway, as you can see, the response time is a factor. Now, given this curve, there are two things you may consider:

1.   Decrease the Response Time (get the curve closer to the *X* axis)

2.   Increase the Request Rate (get the curve as far on the right as possible)

Two fundamentals techniques can be used in either of these circumstances. To decrease the response time (i.e., not necessarily to increase the disk subsystem's ability to handle a large number of I/Os but to get completion time as short as possible), you must use cache. Adding more drives to a disk subsystem will not improve the completion time. cache comes in many form factors and functionalities, and that is discussed shortly. For now, I wish to cover the second aspect—increasing the Request Rate. If you wish to increase the subsystem's ability to handle a large number of I/Os, you will need to use RAID, and augment the number of disks in the RAID set supporting the volume.

Combined, these two techniques will deliver the best performance in all situations. Yet you need first to understand what's most relevant to your environment, and to Microsoft Exchange's. For instance, in the case of transaction log files, you know that the I/O pattern is synchronous and single threaded; the database engine will not issue another write before the previous one has been completed. In this situation, caching interests you because it's the only technique that will reduce the response time of the I/O, which sits on the critical path of the overall transaction response time. On the other hand, in the case of database drives (and SMTP folder trees used for transient message store), you know that the calling application is multithreaded and will attempt to issue many requests at the same time.

Although you may be interested in getting a fast completion time, your main interest will be to increase the ability of the disk drive to handle many I/Os at the same time.

In conclusion, adding more disks to the transaction log volume is about as effective as a bandage on a wooden leg; it doesn't help, because it doesn't address the basic need to get the transaction log flush to occur as quickly as possible. On the other hand, caching will not only help the transaction log throughput, it will also help the database accesses and that will benefit across the board, including the completion of transactions that need access to the database (e.g., a message read operation). To this extent, caching is definitely important for the Exchange environment, as well as others, and we will spend some time discussing the various areas where caching can be implemented.

The second aspect of storage performance is the relevance of the bus bandwidth (Data Rate). Figure 4.56 describes the evolution of the Data Rate as the Request Rate increases.

Figure 4.56
Measuring the Data Rate vs. the Request Rate

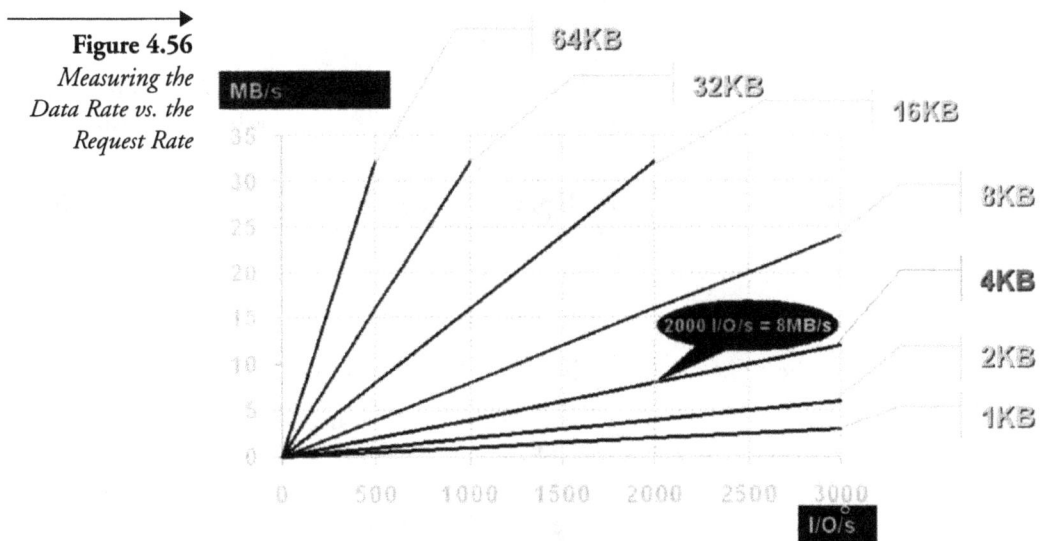

As you can see, a lot depends on the actual I/O size. Considering a 2,000 I/O per second Request Rate, the equivalent bandwidth is of less than 10 MB per second, less than what a narrow SCSI bus can actually handle. This small data rate is not due to media overhead, but to the limited quantity of data pumped in and out the storage volume in small numbers of transactions.

What you should determine from this graph is that the Data Rate, a feature often used by storage manufacturers as a performance-selling factor for Fibre Channel (100-400 MB/s) or UltraSCSI 320, is not so relevant when you deal with a small quantity of I/O per second. Indeed, the actual influencing factor is most likely to be the number of disk drives that can actually pump in and out those 2,000 I/O per second (20 drives at minimum). So don't rush to acquire Fibre Channel storage ONLY because of the accrued performance unless you know you will need this data rate.

In the case of Exchange 2003, you get small I/O size to the EDB database—varying between 4 KB and 64 KB, but for the majority of 4 KB and 8 KB. To get to the property store, the STM database, however, Exchange 2003 will use large I/Os, as large as 64 KB (the actual size depends on the network buffer size of the IIS Virtual Server or on the I/O size of the ExIFS consumer). In any situation, unless you know you will use large I/Os, data rate will not matter that much.

In the IT environment, there are two main applications that will issue large I/Os (beyond 32 KB):

- *Video on demand.* The I/O size here will be 64 KB or more, and clearly your bus architecture must be able to handle the corresponding load.
- *Backup and restore.* Typically, backup applications use large 64 KB and above I/Os.

On top of those two applications comes Exchange 2003 with its accesses to the STM database, which can be done at a maximum of 64 KB.

Although the pages in the STM database are 4 KB in size, they are actually allocated and accessed by chunks of up to 16 pages, helping to reduce the amount of I/O needed to get in and out a certain quantity of data. This makes Exchange 2003 one of the first general-purpose applications that will actually take advantage of large bus bandwidths—that is, of course, if you know that the use of Exchange 2003 in your environment will mainly access information to the STM database, the streaming store.

4.9.1 Software-based caching

The NTFS File System brings its own cache, the size of which can be tuned depending on the setup of the server. Using the /3GB boot switch can have some effect on the space reserved for the file system cache. Another setting, which is not so obvious, determines whether the server can be configured for optimal file service or optimal network applications. You will find this setting under the properties of the File and Print Service under the configuration of the Network Adapter.

The best way to cache is at the application level. After all, when data is written to disk drives or to the file system, these two have very little knowledge of what is really important to cache and which data gets used more often. I find that storage-level cache is good for write operations and for read-ahead operations, but in the case of Exchange 2003, it carries little benefit because of the random nature of read operations to the disk subsystem.

Therefore, you should always try to maximize application-level cache, which, in the case of Exchange 2003, is implemented as part of the database engine's cache, while relying on write-back cache and read-ahead (preferably using an adaptive read-ahead mechanism) to speed operations.

4.9.2 Controller-based caching

Cache comes in various sizes depending on the model of the controller and offers considerable advantages when used in an Exchange 2003 environment.

The idea behind controller-based cache is as follows:

- *For write operations*—to decouple the physical I/O from the completion time of the application I/O

- *For read operations*—to return data from the cache (sub-millisecond response time), instead of accessing the disk drive. In addition to saving on the actual retrieve time from the disk, you realize a subsequent savings by letting the drive be available for other I/Os (in fact, you increase the overall request rate of the disk subsystem).

The nature of I/O in an Exchange environment depends very much on the actual component doing the operation. For the database drives, the I/O is random in nature, and the benefit of cache for read operations is not so important. However, the benefit of caching write operations is immense

Figure 4.57
*Improving the
Response Time of
Write Operations
Using Cache*

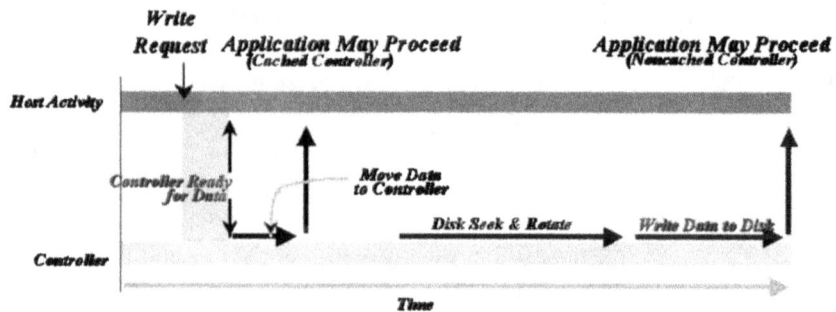

and provides several orders of magnitude of improved response time, in the best cases.

Figure 4.57 gives the logical steps involved in performing a write operation, and compares the sequence of events between cached write operations and non-cached (a.k.a write-through) operations.

4.9.3 Write-back cache

As explained previously, the write-back decouples the I/O completion from the actual physical operation. This is beneficial in the case of Exchange 2000, especially for the transaction log files. The caveat is that in a certain sense, the controller lies to the application and operating system by confirming a successful write operation, even though the data is not actually on disk but resides in memory. Writing to memory is extremely fast compared with writing to disk (especially if the write operation to the disk subsystem is a compound operation as in RAID5 and to a lesser extent as in RAID1 and RAID0+1). The problem with memory is that it is volatile. If you loose power or if you lose the content of the cache memory and the data has not been written to disk, you face database corruption. In the case of Exchange 2003, this will lead you to restoring your best backup—hopefully the last you did—and incur a significant amount of downtime, something that is not good from an administrator's and end-user's perspective.

To alleviate this problem, storage manufacturers propose to protect the actual cache memory. There are several techniques, which, combined, can give you a certain confidence in implementing write-back cache.

Parity checking

Each byte of information stored in the cache is enhanced with an additional parity bit. The parity bit is typically computed by a simple bit-wise XOR operation on each bit of the octet. With parity checking, the controller can detect that the information has been somewhat corrupted. This is helpful up to a point, but it still can't determine which bit got corrupted and how to fix it. The only action the controller can take is to disable the write-back cache, switch to write-through mode, and maybe raise an alert, but the data has been corrupted and almost certainly the database as well. Parity checking is now seldom implemented; ECC is more often used.

Error correcting checksum (ECC)

This can determine whether a bit in a sequence of information (typically an octet) is incorrect and can recover which bit got corrupted and fix it. You can consider ECC as a kind of RAID5 implementation for RAM. ECC is implemented in almost all controllers. The calculation of the checksum can be done with minimal effort by the use of specialized chips that will do the calculation on the fly. This case of data corruption on the cache is in fact very infrequent. The majority of cache corruptions occur when the overall content of the cache is lost, either because of a power failure or because of a controller crash.

To alleviate the volatility aspects of RAM, the storage manufacturers have implemented battery backup to refresh the RAM used for the controller cache should the server lose its power. This is implemented in almost all controllers, and in different specifications. For PCI-based RAID controllers the quantity of RAM is rather small (in the order of 64 MB). The controller board includes a battery that can refresh the contents of the memory.

This battery can generally last for 8 or 10 hours, a time sufficient to swap the controller or reboot the server or reestablish the server's power supply.

Some high-end controllers include batteries that can last for up to several hundred hours. This is not always mentioned by the storage manufacturer and introduces a significant constraint on how fast you need to service your computer.

There is, however, a problem with rechargeable batteries: they wear out. You may have experienced this with your kids' toys; batteries can last only a limited amount of time, after which they lose their original power characteristics. Generally, the batteries used in RAID controllers (PCI-based or in shared storage enclosures) have a lifetime of two years. You must include in your maintenance plans the servicing of those batteries, which can become an expensive process (the cost of the battery is minimal, the expensive side of the service is getting someone to come and service the battery in a secure fashion, the most secure way to change a controller battery being to set the volumes to write-through mode, shutdown the computer or the RAID array and service the battery). Furthermore, while you service your batteries, the systems may become unavailable, which will affect your uptime and ability to attain your availability objectives.

Cache module flexibility

You may argue that even if you protect your cache with batteries, an entire controller crash (dead board) can make you lose the content of the cache memory. This is true in some implementations, but some vendors propose to locate the cache memory and its accompanying battery on a detachable board. If the controller board should fail, you may extract the cache module, keep it "alive" because it has got a battery attached to it that refreshes its contents, and place this cache module on a spare controller. It's a neat feature, but as mentioned before, do keep in mind the limited lifetime of batteries.

You should definitely urge the replacement of the controller board (in fact, having one spare wouldn't be a bad idea) before the battery is discharged and you lose the contents of your cache and therefore the integrity of your database from an application perspective.

The ultimate protection comes from combining the foregoing features and using two separate boards for storing the information; this is known as cache mirroring. For most of the high-end products, cache mirroring is a quite common feature.

I hope that you feel more confident about using write-back cache in an Exchange 2003 environment, given the effort that the manufacturers are investing to protect this key component in RAID controllers' implementation.

Beyond the decoupling of I/O completion, write-back cache provides additional services, which are implemented to some extent, depending on the manufacturer.

One very interesting feature is write-gathering. The idea is that there is a sequential flow of information, and if the data is cached into memory, instead of proceeding with I/O size similar to that originally requested by the server, you can combine these I/Os into one large I/O, and proceed to significantly augment the actual I/O throughput of your target device. This is highly significant in the case of Exchange 2003 and transaction log files; the I/O pattern is definitely sequential and is composed of typically small I/Os (between 1 KB and 4 KB). Taking advantage of write-gathering will decouple the ability of the volume to handle these I/Os with the expected response time of a cached I/O (i.e., 1 ms or less).

This is right on target for great performance using Exchange 2003. The transaction logging of the ESE database engine is on the critical path of a transaction commit and therefore on the actual completion time of the overall transaction, typically led by a user. Not only can you augment the capacity of a single drive to process more I/Os, but you also significantly decrease the response time of the I/Os. The write-gathering feature is not always implemented across all RAID controllers; it is best to check with the vendor about whether and in what way it is being implemented. You may view it as the pendant to the read-ahead function of the cache for read operations.

Another advantage that write-back cache can bring comes with distributed parity stripe arrays (RAID5). You know that RAID5's write function involves updating the parity block, which requires two read operations to be able to "remove" the parity information of the block to be modified from the parity block. However, in the case of a large I/O or a sequential stream of write operations to the RAID5 array, you may need to write an entire stripe to the RAID5 array (i.e., all the blocks within a stripe have to be written). To increase the likelihood of writing an entire stripe, some vendors have deliberately reduced the maximum number of drives used in a parity calculation. With HP's StorageWorks EVA storage, this is limited to five drives. With the XP storage from HP, this is fixed to four drives. This means that the overhead of RAID5, from a capacity viewpoint, is set to 20 percent or 25 percent, and if you have many more drives, the redundancy pattern is reproduced across the next five or four drives. The implementation details vary according to the line of storage, but the net result is that a reasonably sized cache for write (512 MB or above) will tend to optimize the write operations to disk. Indeed, if the controller, by caching these requests, figures that the whole stripe must be written, it will not spend time reading the parity block to update it; it will simply overwrite it and yield greater performance results than if the individual blocks of the stripe had to be written. This last advantage of write-back cache is mostly interesting when it comes to restore operations, where you need to restore large databases by writing sequential blocks of information.

4.9.4   **Read cache**

Read cache can come in two ways—one good and another not so good, or should I say, not so appropriate for Exchange 2003. The goal of read cache is to let blocks of data that have been read from disks by the controller be placed into a memory area, in the hopes that if a subsequent application read requests the same block of data, the completion time will be much shorter (less than a ms versus 10–14 ms). Some controllers even go as far as performing read-ahead caching. The deal here is that should the application request 4 KB of data, the controller will go and fetch those 4 KB, and a bit more behind, the actual quantity of data depending upon the controller's data fetch method (64 KB or even as high as 256 KB). Should the application request the next block of data, then you get a cache hit and great response time; you have made up for the extra time spent in fetching this additional data by getting a great response time on subsequent sequential I/O.

This method works well for file servers and for when you know that the I/O will be sequential. Unfortunately, this is not always the case with Exchange 2003; in fact, it is never the case in normal operations, only in two exceptional situations:

- Transaction log file replay
- Database backup

So it's unfortunate to incur a response time penalty for normal database operations by enabling read-ahead cache. However, things aren't so bad in this ever-evolving environment. During the past few years, we have started to see the introduction of adaptive read-ahead—the controller will go off and pre-fetch data only when it detects a sequential flow of read requests. In this particular situation, random operations are easily handled, and when the time comes to reply to the log files or to perform the backup, the controller will advantageously use the cache memory to pre-fetch information, and obtain great data rates for the application.

Read cache does not represent a real danger from a data integrity perspective; too much can adversely affect the performance, so it'll be important that you properly assess the actual need from the application.

4.9.5 The relevance of the data fetch method

I briefly touched on this topic in the previous section. It is, however, extremely important, because the fetch method can cancel out other advantages advertised by some storage manufacturers.

When an I/O READ is requested of the RAID controller, the controller will proceed to fetch data from the disk set. This can involve more than one disk (called a split I/O—see the later section on chunk size). Within the disk itself, it can involve reading a single track, or for some implementations, reading an entire cylinder (i.e., tracks from each platter making up the disk drive). This can force the controller to fetch much more data than what was actually requested; some implementations will collect a minimum 256 KB of data, whatever the actual requested I/O size. The controller will store this fetched data into cache memory (hence it will tend to require more cache than otherwise optimized controllers) and hope that this data will be used in subsequent operations. In that case, big caches are good and useful. But in the case of Exchange 2003, the data size to the EDB database is 4 KB and random in nature! This means that the 256 KB of data fetched for a 4 KB I/O will only serve the purpose of wasting the cache—trashing it, more precisely—and wasting precious time in transferring a larger quantity of data than what is actually needed.

To alleviate this problem, one approach consists of using larger quantities of cache, in the order of 8 GB and more. Typically, this cache size comes in shared storage enclosures (EMC, Hitachi Data System, HP), which share the cache use among several host connections, and several volumes. By comparison, typical back-plane controllers offer 56 MB to 128 MB of RAM, serve a lesser number of volumes, and are local to the system PCI bus. For a given situation, say, a 2,000-users server with 100 GB of database storage, the back-plane controller cache may be as effective as a shared-storage cache and may in fact yield better performance.

4.9.6 Configuring RAID volumes

I hope that you now have a good understanding of the RAID levels and have the information on which to base a sound decision. As you configure the RAID volumes on your controllers, there are a couple of parameters that are of importance. One is the cache setting, the other is the chunk size (also known as the stripe depth or, incorrectly, as the stripe size). These two can really influence how well optimized your RAID volume is for the type of load that Exchange 2003 will apply. Finally, the actual number of disks you can put in a volume can vary depending on the controller's ability to handle many disks, the size of the disks, and the actual capacity and request rate requirements from Microsoft Exchange.

Chunk size

Tuning chunk size will generally give you a 10 percent to 20 percent performance improvement, which is rather small compared with the 1000 percent improvements you can get with properly sized and tuned controller cache. Nevertheless, you should make sure that you get the most appropriately tuned solution.

First a definition: according to the RAID Advisory Board (http://www.raid-advisory.com), the chunk size is ".." In fact, depending on the chunk size and the I/O size, you will be in a situation where you will have *split I/Os*. Although split I/Os are not necessarily a bad thing, in the case of Exchange 2003, they are.

Figure 4.58
*Split I/O in a
RAID0 Stripe*

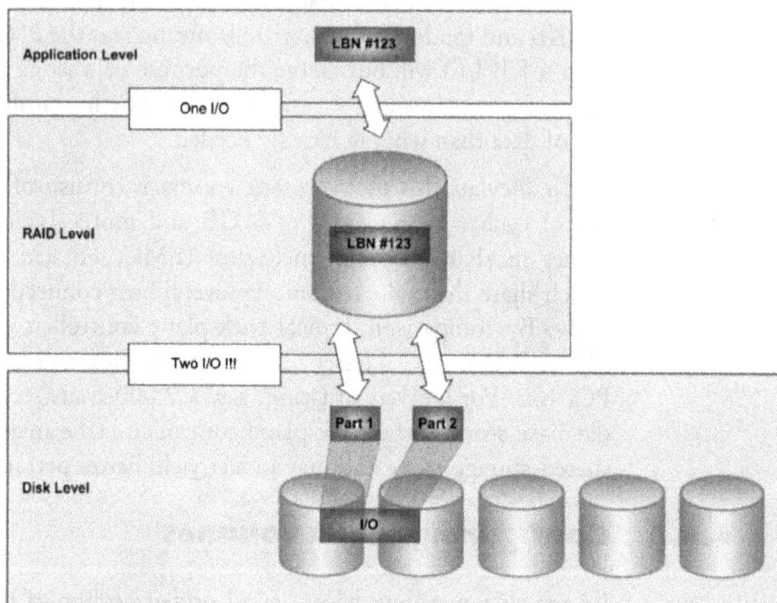

Figure 4.58 shows a split I/O in action. The situation is simple: the application requests a piece of data and it happens that the offset and the size of this data causes its location to be partly on one member chunk (Part 1), and partly on the next member chunk (Part 2). This leads to an interesting situation: for one single I/O, you need two spindles. In a situation where you only have split I/Os, you potentially decrease by two the request rate capability of your volume. Nevertheless, because two disks are in action for servicing an I/O, you could assume that you have twice as much disk transfer happening for the I/O: disk A and disk B can now both transmit data. If they were placed on separate buses (as it is often the recommendation when configuring RAID volumes), the data transfer could occur in parallel and the response time would be improved.

So here we are in a situation where the split I/O can be bad if the data transfer is small, and good if the data transfer is large and the disks are placed on separate buses. This is best explained in Figure 4.59.

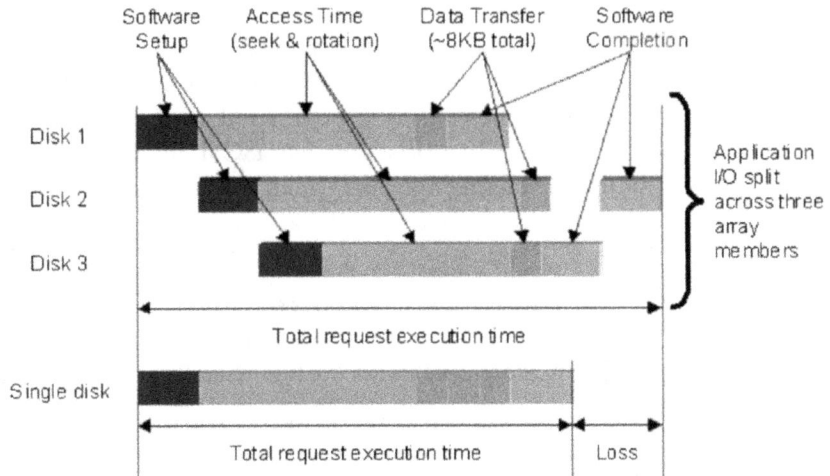

Figure 4.59
Relevance of Chunk Size for Small I/O

As you can see, for a large I/O (typically 32 KB or 64 KB), if the disks that make up the stripe are placed on separate buses, there can be a significant gain for the split I/O in terms of response time. In terms of request rate, the situation is slightly different, because you get more spindles busy performing an application I/O with too small a chunk size than if you were using a larger chunk size (see Figure 4.60).

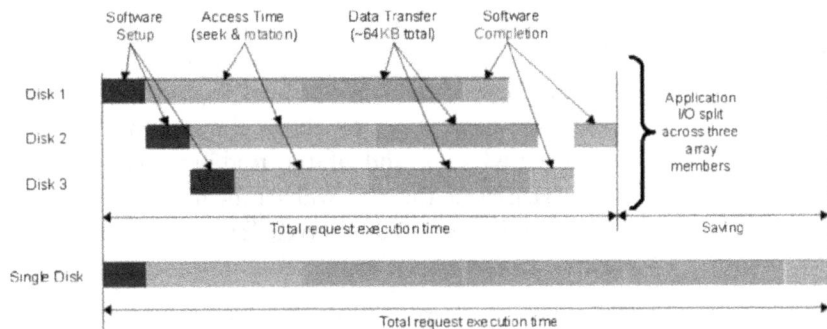

Figure 4.60
Relevance of Chunk Size for Large I/O (Greater Than Chunk Size)

Putting ourselves back in the context of Exchange 2003, we know that we are dealing with small I/Os for most of the data store and retrieve, except for the case of accessing the streaming store (.STM) and the transaction log files (.LOG). Numerous benchmarks and real-life cases have also shown that the request rate was really important compared to the data rate. The RAID book comes with the following recommendation: use a large chunk size if you know that your I/O size is small (<8 KB). A large chunk size can be anywhere between 10 and 20 times the average I/O size. You will ensure that there will be few split I/Os and that the theoretical request rate capability of your volume (e.g., a 10-disk RAID0 should allow for at least 1,000 I/O per second) can be matched when using live data. The back-end buses tend to be so rapid nowadays (100–400 MB/s with Fibre Channel, 320 MB/s with UltraSCSI and Serial Attached SCSI) that the option of using a smaller chunk size to spread the data transfer across back-end disks which are on separate buses is not attractive anymore.

I would suggest staying away from those implementations and checking with the storage manufacturer on how the chunk size and the default transfer size are handled. And by the way, disregard what I call marketing benchmark data that typically shows the best results on the vendor's configuration.

Some manufacturers' products come with a default chunk size of 128 KB up to 2 MB (HP StorageWorks EVA). Still others come with an 8 KB chunk size, which is way too small for Exchange 2003, and for other purposes where the request rate capabilities of the disk subsystem is of any importance.

Ultimately, you should do your own validation, and tools such as IOmeter from Intel can provide a good start in characterizing your volume configuration. IOmeter is discussed at length in the performance measurement section of this book.

Cache

We've dealt with the issue of cache in more generic terms previously. To make a long story short, I strongly believe that in the case of Exchange 2000, cache should be utilized because the ultimate performance of Exchange depends so much on the response time of the transaction log write transaction, and of the read transaction. Moreover, it is by using writeback cache that you will get the most benefit of your environment. For a typical Exchange 2003 server, Table 4.5 shows how I would configure the cache settings for the various roles given to disk volumes.

The cache setting depends very much on the I/O pattern and on the actual application use of the data. For Exchange 2003, you should know by now that very little paging is observed, because of the adaptive use of memory by the database engine(s). Therefore, the pagefile disk (if isolated) does not need any cache memory at all.

Table 4.5 *Cache Settings*

Volume	Cache (%R/%W)	Comment
System disk	0% write/100% read)	Adaptive read-ahead is OK
Pagefile	0% write/100% read)	
SMTP Folders	50% write/50% read	Read cache is usually done at the host level
Transaction logs	100% write	For benefiting of write-gathering
Database	100% write	For benefiting of write gathering and multiple updates per page

The SMTP folders, which contain the root directory and subdirectory for transient message store handled by the SMTP MTA (this is also true for the X.400 MTA, EMSMTA), does 50 percent read and 50 percent write I/O, with a relatively small (below 8 KB) size, and will most likely benefit from some read cache (as a message gets in and written to the directory, it can be re-fetched to be routed or delivered to its final destination). If you observe the read-write ratio at your controller level, you might notice a majority of write operations, because the SMTP agent is clever enough to read back only after restart of the queues, and because these operations are done at the file-system level, which benefits from the generic operating system cache.

The transaction log disks (there can be many if you choose to dedicate drives to the log areas of the Exchange 2003 databases) are 100 percent write for normal operations. There is only one situation in which read access is done to the transaction log volume, and that is when log replay is in progress (after an abrupt system shutdown).

The database disks are typically 70 percent read and 30 percent write. However, although in an MMB3 benchmark environment, I have observed 45 percent read and 55 percent write, and I've seen on production servers ratios of 35 percent read and 65 percent write when journaling was enabled. In any case, write performance is significant, and enabling write-back cache will speed up the write operations. In the case of read operations, the use of controller-based cache is arguable. Controller-based cache can improve on read operations, but the Exchange 2003 EDB database stores pages in a balanced tree, and access pattern can truly become random. Why waste precious cache memory when you know that there is little chance that the next page to read is in the cache?

Speaking of cache, remember that the ESE database engine has its own buffer cache in RAM, and if a recent page has to be fetched, it is more likely to be fetched from the application-level cache that sits in RAM than from the controller-level cache that sits, at best, on the PCI bus and, at worst, behind a host-bus adapter and one of several switches or hubs. My point here is that you should take advantage and rely on the efficiency of the in-memory cache for read operations and favor controller-based cache for write operations. Hence, I recommend setting to 100 percent write-back the cache for the setting of the database volume. On the other hand, the performance requirements for your environment will probably be split into three situations:

- *Operational performance*, where you wish to favor normal accesses to the database.

- *Backup performance*, where, given the growing quantity of data to be managed and the shortened time window for maintenance operations, you wish your backups to be running as fast as possible. In this particular situation, the use of adaptive read-ahead cache can be quite good, enabling the controller to pre-fetch data for sequential read operations, and increasing the data rate for large sequential read operations, which are observed during backup operations.

- *Restore performance*, where you wish to be able to restore data as quickly as possible to your target volume. Write-back cache here has little significance from the perspective of the response time of a single I/O, but it has many advantages when it comes to calculating parity information in a RAID5 array. For some controllers, caching an entire stripe of data makes it possible to overwrite the parity information if the controller knows that it has to write a complete stripe of data; the performance becomes then very close to a RAID0 performance, and the RAID5 write penalty usually observed in transaction access becomes almost unnoticed.

Now, as soon as you attempt to enable write-back cache in an Exchange 2003 environment (and as a matter of fact, in any database transaction environment), you must make sure that the cache is sufficiently protected, and that the controller provides features that protect the cache in the majority of situations.

Number of disks

The number of disks is probably the main criteria when configuring your RAID array. For best performance, aim at using a large number of disks, regardless of the capacity provided. Unfortunately, this has been overlooked far too many times, and caused support issues for both Microsoft and the storage vendors (such as HP and EMC). The rule of thumb is not so easy to create, because of the strong dependency on the number of users, their level of activity, the type of client they use and the array architecture. I have collated the various factors and provided explanations of the dependencies in the following table.

Attribute	Rationale
Number of users	If you have a relatively small number of users per storage group or database, you do not need to deploy many disks for each of the logical units. However, while you create some isolation in spreading the workload across many units, you also create separation between these disks, and do not benefit from the aggregated performance they could bring together. Some array technologies, such as HP's EVA, have demonstrated that grouping many drives (100 and more) together enables to them get excellent peak transfer rates, while maintaining good overall performance.
Activity	The client activity will depend upon the client used to connect to the messaging environment. Using Outlook 2003 in cache mode not only insulates the user from network conditions but also from temporary system delays that might result from overload system and storage components. Using mobile devices tends to add more workload because of the extra processing that the third party mobile device server tends to bring on the server, for monitoring changes on the mailbox of the mobile user and transmitting them to the user device.
Array architecture	Some arrays are cache centric, i.e., each and every I/O is first issued to a cache and then staged off the cache to back-end disks. In such an environment, the number of disks is not so important, except that with Exchange 2003, the I/O workload is so random across such a large seek range that the cache is exercised and stressed, resulting in a poor number of cache hits and high back-end memory consumption. Using more disks also helps in such environments and is advised.

Attribute	Rationale
Disk geometry and speed	Disks come in various sizes (up to 500 GB) and have various rotation speeds (typically between 5,400 rpm for SATA drives to 15,000 rpm for high-performance SCSI and Fibre Channel disks). The rotation speed is by far the most influential factor, and you should aim to use high rotation speed for disks that will host databases and transaction log files. For disks that you use for relatively sequential traffic, using a low rotation speed (5,400 rpm) is acceptable, and often employed for disks that are used for backup and recovery.
	High capacity disks come with a denser storage of data and therefore random access is improved, yet often at the expense of the rotation speed. Always favor the latter in your choice of high performance disk drives.

The number of disks in a RAID set will have a considerable effect on the ability of the volume to handle concurrent I/Os. A too large number of disks can adversely affect rebuild time for the volume, which can be a lengthy operation, depending on the RAID volume. A RAID5 rebuild (or reconstruction) will require reading every block from every disk of the volume and generating the corresponding data or parity.

Although this operation can be prioritized, be careful not to affect dramatically the performance of your Exchange 2003 server should a rebuild occur.

On the other hand, during a RAID5 rebuild, the entire volume is at risk. In a RAID0+1 environment, a disk loss only requires rebuilding the affected mirror set. This can be quite short (20 mn or so, depending upon the volume size), and during that time, the volume can handle loss of disks belonging to other mirrors making up the RAID0+1 volume.

Another consideration for how many disks you wish to create in a RAID volume is the net capacity required. When I compared the RAID volumes, I discussed the impact of data redundancy in the net available space. RAID5 is the clear winner, while RAID1 and RAID0+1 provide the least efficient method to provide capacity but still the best method to provide performance (at an equal rate of read and write operations).

One caveat regarding Exchange 5.5 was the single-file database. This forced many customers to create large volumes to handle large databases, because you could have only one database for your mailboxes per server, and that database was made up of only one volume. To a certain extent, this forced many implementers in many good decisions of gathering large volumes together, increasing the number of spindles per volume, and therefore favoring the number of I/Os per second that could be handled by this volume.

Exchange 2003 provides two key capabilities:

- The ability to create multiple databases to effectively partition the mailbox store into several smaller databases.

- The use of a stand-by database to the main EDB database, the streaming store (STM database), and the ability to possibly locate this database separately from the EDB. What is the advantage of that? Consider an environment in which you know that the STM store is going to be accessed (primarily when making extensive use of Internet protocols to access the Exchange store); because you know that the I/O size is different from the EDB (4 KB for the EDB database, up to 64 KB for the STM database), you can split the files; create smaller, more manageable volumes; and tune these volumes to accommodate the I/O pattern difference (e.g., small chunk size for the STM database and large chunk size for the EDB database).

Consequently, I prefer to consider them as a whole and keep them in the same location.

Right now, it is safe to say that Exchange 2003 brings enough flexibility with multiple mailbox stores. As an extreme case, you might create one volume for each mailbox store. But like any extreme, this can have disadvantages. Consider a situation in which you have determined that 10 databases of 20 GB each would be sufficient for your (quite high-end) Exchange 2003 server that should support 5,000 users with a 40 MB quota. This is a very rough calculation that doesn't take into account single-instance store or, more important, deleted item retention.

You can decide to implement these ten databases in several ways.

- You can decide to split the ten databases amongst two storage groups and locate them all on one volume. The result, from a storage perspective, is the requirement to implement 360 GB (plus a bit more, because it is quite bad to plan for more than 70 percent fill-up of a storage device), which should handle the resulting I/O request rate from 5,000 users.

- You may decide to use two storage groups and locate each database on a separate volume. The result is the same requirement to deploy 360 GB of storage, but across 10 units of 36 GB each (or a bit more).

Those two cases represent extremes, and extremes are generally not desirable in Exchange 2003 deployments.

One 400 GB volume will require lots of spindles (good thing from a performance perspective) but will have an adverse impact if this volume suddenly becomes unavailable and has to have its contents restored. Ten 36 GB volumes will require probably as many spindles as a 360GB volume, but they are split, separated into individual volumes. You may even be tempted to locate each database on a 72 GB RAID1 mirror set, composed of two 72 GB disks. This is good from a recovery perspective, because you have built such independence between the volumes that if you lose one volume, you can continue to operate with the other databases. From a performance perspective, this is not desirable, because you have dramatically reduced the ability to handle peak I/O loads (up to 150 I/Os per second at 50 percent read).

Finally, you may decide to use small disks to increase the I/O request rate capability of each of your volumes, but you will then encounter constraints such as physical space and whether the controller can handle a large number of disks and a large number of volumes. There are limitations in the controllers, so you should check with the storage manufacturer of choice the exact capabilities of the controller that will provide storage before committing to a particular solution.

The proper solution should consist of a compromise for which you know each of the components (size, capacity, performance). When sizing the storage device that will host your Exchange databases, you will need to be concerned with:

- The reconstruct time.

- The request rate (I/O per second) capacity of the volume, according to the read/write ratio (I suggest you start with a 50 percent read ratio, although this may vary). Note that if you have been running an Exchange 5.5 environment for quite some time, it wouldn't be a bad idea to collect some performance data in your own production environment to estimate the read/write ratio from production use. If you don't have such a production environment, you can always run a benchmark or load simulation using the Microsoft supplied load simulation tools, such as ESP or Loadsim.

- The effect on your operations of losing one volume.
- Conflicting volume usage in a shared, hardware partitioned subsystem.

Chapter 7 describes a number of sample configurations with pros and cons, but you do need to raise your objections to your storage vendor so that the best solution that matches your needs and budget can be built.

4.10 In Summary

Servers and storage for Microsoft Exchange are moving targets: you will need to make a call by the time that you engage into your deployment, and possible envisage the technologies that match your deployment requirements and lifetime, and those that are too expensive, and later outdated by the upcoming version of the operating system or the application, Microsoft Exchange.

With Longhorn and Exchange 2007 on the horizon, complex SAN solutions are not mandatory for the small deployments that can accommodate from application or host-based storage management functions. Large environments, on the other hand, may accommodate upcoming functionality in Exchange 2007, but definitely require strong infrastructure components to support them.

From the viewpoint of servers, the race between AMD and Intel is not only on the clock rate (GHz), but also on the number of cores a particular processor implements. Multi-core processors deliver high performance with a reduced clock rate, and therefore, power consumption and cooling requirements are significantly reduced. All modern processors now support the x86 instruction set in both 32-bit and 64-bit modes. This means that the adoption of Windows Server 2003 in 64-bit mode will largely depend upon the readiness of the environment to support this version of the operating system, such as processes, tools, and third-party solutions.

From the viewpoint of storage, iSCSI is the new kid on the block and may displace Fibre Channel in storage networks of relatively small importance. Don't be too hung up about the necessary adoption of one or either of these protocols. They have requirements and deliver benefits that are specific to each other. With Exchange 2003, the dependency on storage performance is such that Fibre Channel is often found in a scaled up environment. With future versions of Exchange, this may not be true any longer, and suggests that iSCSI networks provide the necessary throughput, while enabling economies of infrastructure components and interconnects.

Furthermore with storage, the serialization of protocols such as SCSI and ATA lead to interesting possibilities in terms of density and combination of low-cost high capacity disks (SATA), with high-performance disks (SAS) in server and storage subsystem infrastructures. This gives you the possibility to define and use premium storage for your production workload and secondary storage for your backup and archiving, leading to using the right storage at the right price for the right purpose.

4.11   Endnotes

1.   A filter driver is a stackable component in the NT I/O subsystem that allows vendors to add additional function in the code path used when performing I/O operations. A filter driver is a stackable component in the NT I/O subsystem that allows vendors to add additional functions in the code path used when performing I/O operations.

2.   There is the classic illustration of the Caterpillar that digs a road and eventually breaks an optical fiber. I know of one customer where this happened. They had a single optical fiber link and replication storage with Microsoft Exchange in which they were operating in synchronous failsafe mode. The construction 10 km away from their production site brought the Microsoft Exchange service down. Of course, there is absolutely no connection between the digging company and your operations staff, which renders fault detection and resolution quite difficult.

3.   You may replace with your favorite low-cost car brand....

4.   You may replace with your favorite luxury car brand....

5

Optimizing Exchange 2003

5.1   Introduction to Exchange 2003 Optimization

As you deploy Exchange 2003 in an enterprise, you have to make considerations for the consolidation opportunities and the necessity to place servers in close proximity to the end users. With the introduction of cached mode in Outlook 2003, the ability to centralize Microsoft Exchange servers has been significantly increased, and we now see deployments for large multinational companies that are confined to one or two data centers.

In the case where cached mode is not appropriate, online mode through either Outlook or by the means of Outlook Web Access will require relatively good network connectivity, providing both sufficient bandwidth and relatively low latency.

In either of these two deployment approaches, you must work on how to best optimize server resource utilization and the Microsoft Exchange software configuration, in addition to server components such as CPU, memory, and I/O (both storage and network related). The optimization strategy, however, varies depending upon the type of deployment—whether you adopt a scale-up solution that aims at gathering as high of a workload on as small number of servers or decide to distribute the workload on a number of servers. This latter approach is referred to as scale-out and calls for the ability of the software components of Microsoft Exchange to properly distribute their operations.

Each approach is valid and may be mixed, depending upon the server role. For instance, mailbox servers tend to scale up and host many users per Windows server, while bridgehead servers can be easily scaled out, utilizing less powerful machines (two processors, 2-GB RAM) but in several instances, for helping on availability and easily scaling up if demand rises.

Each of these deployments requires a different type of hardware and software configuration, which is discussed in this chapter.

Some of the optimizations must be done regardless of the client type, server role, and topology but more inline with the actual server hardware configuration.

For example, the use of clustering and the need for fast and reliable failover requires necessary certain modifications in the Exchange 2003 STORE configuration that are not present by default.

Optimization and tuning in Microsoft Exchange is typically done either by means of a Windows Active Directory parameter change in the configuration naming context and Exchange service container or using the server registry. There is a clear advantage in using Windows Active Directory–based configuration settings, as they can be done centrally, replicated throughout the enterprise network, and picked up by the server next time the Microsoft Exchange services are restarted. Some of these settings include most of the optimization required for storage groups and database engines.

The optimization technique will not only depend upon the server role, as we explained earlier, but also upon the mode of utilization of Microsoft Exchange. If you use X.400 transport for connecting into legacy Exchange 5.5 servers or foreign mail systems, you will require some setting optimization, which would not apply if you were to use native SMTP communication across the network.

Although this distinction was quite necessary as Exchange 2000 was introduced, you will find that most deployments are now using the default SMTP transport, and we should be focusing on this transport for optimization: in that case, the communication layer between the Internet information service process and the STORE process should be as optimized as possible, as well as any data processing that might be required, such as content conversion, SPAM fighting, and virus detection/prevention.

Finally, some deployments require very specific optimization, such as in service providers' environments, in which a large concentration of users is gathered, with small activity during most of the day, except for peak access hours. The utilization of POP or IMAP clients can be improved with Exchange 2003, saving precious CPU cycles used for handling connections during peak periods. Another example is the optimization of the Windows Active Directory topology such that minimal replication latency is found between the servers used for provisioning and the Microsoft Exchange servers themselves. Backup and recovery tend to be fairly critical in these environments, although we must accept the fact that messaging is now considered by most enterprises as a mission-critical solution used in many business processes, either implicitly or explicitly.

In this chapter, we discuss possible optimization for the key system resources and dependency resources used by Exchange 2003:

- *CPU*: What are the ways to enable Exchange 2003 to take advantage of the CPU processing capabilities, expressed in the CPU core clock speed and the number of processors in the server? CPUs also come with varying L1, L2, and L3 caches, which allow us to decrease the front-side bus utilization and improve repeated instructions speed. However, throwing the latest and greatest hardware in a Microsoft Exchange mailbox server deployment might not necessarily help, and we have found that it was important to *prioritize* the relevance of processor features between core speed, front-size bus, multiprocessors, processing setting, and secondary cache size.

- *Memory*: The RAM available on a server may be used in full by Exchange 2003, or it can be partitioned across several processes and allocated to accommodate the needs of each component running on a particular server. Most of the time, Exchange 2003 will make the best utilization of the physical memory up to 3.5 GB of RAM. You may add more physical memory, but the core Microsoft Exchange services, and the STORE process in particular, will not use the extra RAM. With the decreasing cost of RAM, most servers today are deployed using 4 GB of physical memory for mailbox servers and 2 GB of memory for bridgehead servers. Using more than 4 GB of RAM on a mailbox server has actually shown negative impact on the performance of the server.

- *Network interfaces*: The network is vital for an Exchange 2003 server, but it is hardly the bottleneck, unless caused by invalid drivers, bad optimization of the network adapter and subsequent layer, or inappropriate usage for data transmission, such as in backup and recovery. We will discuss the ability to define processor affinities for handling the network adapter interrupts per processor, but otherwise there is little to optimize for network cards, other than, of course, using dual redundant adapters to avoid creating single points of failure.

- *Storage subsystem*: Exchange 2003, along with its predecessors (including Exchange 4.0, 5.0, and 5.5), is a real database application that has evolved over time but basically behaves in the same manner as any enterprise-level database application.

Transaction logging, roll forward, rollback of transactions, online backups, and disk latency are all aspects that require significant attention in order to have a STORE process that can fetch and store information rapidly, providing fast message transfer throughput and good user interaction. Exchange 2003 brings numerous improvements, reinforced by service packs, Web releases, or other hotfixes for optimizing and strengthening the storage of data elements, which is crucial for high-quality service. This is certainly the area where you can make the largest increments in performance and reliability with little effort if you have a good understanding of (1) the Exchange 2003 architecture, described in Chapter 2, and (2) the technologies relevant to Exchange 2003 as discussed in Chapter 4.

- *Network services*: They go beyond the simple transport of data as we know it with TCP/IP or X.400 and include authentication services and directory services. They are also important for the performance and the optimization of an Exchange 2003 server. You can invest a considerable amount of time and money in optimizing a single Exchange 2003 server to host, say, 5,000 active users, but this is of little use if the underlying network services, such as DNS and the Active Directory, are not on par with your server configuration. In Chapter 3, we discussed the relevance of such services, and we shall review in this chapter how to optimize the placement and configuration of your Active Directory and DNS servers—not only to enable a reliable Exchange 2003 environment, but also satisfy the needs for a high transaction throughput, whether it is the ability to authenticate many clients in a short period of time or to switch and route messages in the organization with little overhead on the actual server.

- *Application*: Last, but not least, there are application settings that can be improved, based upon your environment. Much of the design principles for Exchange 2003 onward are to fit the widest array of configurations and usage of Microsoft Exchange. However, there are times where a little change can make a big difference.

An overarching goal for your deployment should be to implement as few tuning changes as possible and as many as required.

In other words, it is not necessary to implement registry changes across all servers in a deployment, regardless of their roles. Some will apply to some servers and not to others. Do not try to systematically implement tuning tips that might deliver 3 to 4 percent improvement in service throughput or response time. What is critical is to get the right settings for the right servers and track these changes: as mentioned before, it is a goal for Microsoft to continuously improve the usability of Microsoft Exchange across a wide variety of servers, and many tuning changes that were applicable with Exchange 2003 are now deprecated. Keeping track of changes allows you to make sure that your servers are not running with incorrect settings, which would eventually be counter-productive to the desired effect.

The information provided here originates from many sources, one being the series of technical articles published by Microsoft about Microsoft Exchange, and Exchange 2003 in particular. The other main sources are my own personal involvement in analyzing high-end configurations and the feedback and advice received from the consulting and performance organizations of Hewlett Packard, which has to date the broadest experience concerning the deployment and the architecture of complex Exchange 2003 infrastructures.

Because of the continuous nature of improvements brought to Microsoft Exchange and Windows Server releases as well as the new hardware improvements at all levels, I strongly encourage you to regularly consult the Microsoft Exchange Web site (http://www.microsoft.com/exchange) and refer to articles published there, in the Microsoft Knowledge Base (http://support.microsoft.com), or in the TechNet (http://www.microsoft.com/technet), all of which are some of the best sources of information when it comes to deploying and tuning Microsoft Exchange servers.

Hewlett Packard makes its contribution to the IT world of Microsoft Exchange by means of the ActiveAnswers Web service (go to http://www.hp.com and search for "ActiveAnswers"). I recommend that you to visit this site regularly, even if you are not using HP hardware. Many of the findings from the various consulting, server, and storage architecture groups are published in that space, and, if you can read well enough between the lines, you can apply a lot of our findings to other manufacturers' configurations and setups. I do personally consult a number of HP's competitor's knowledge sites, server or storage vendors, as they always have an interesting view on how to deploy Microsoft Exchange on their own environment. Microsoft has put forth a lot of effort in making sure that the information published was accurate, and they have completed their knowledge sharing with much more than just support articles that can be hard to find.

5.2   System Optimization for Exchange 2003

In this section, we discuss the system and server technologies that are important to Microsoft Exchange 2003. You may consider your server as a black box and buy the latest and greatest server configuration. This approach is perfectly valid for the immediate future but should be factored in the expected lifetime of the server. I have seen cases where server hardware was being deployed and expected to satisfy the ever-increasing workload for the next 36 to 48 months.

In this case, you should plan for some headroom, based on your track record of workload increase and how you anticipate the utilization of the Exchange 2003 service. Note that you should be careful how you plan for future growth, considering the decreasing cost of components such as storage subsystems: four years down the road, there is a good chance that the cost of a gigabyte will be a fraction of its current cost. Thus, if you acquire storage for the next 5 years, and wish to deal with a 20% annual growth upfront, you will have a fair quantity of storage that will not be used initially, and that you will have paid at a higher cost than if you had acquired it later, as you needed it. While it's good to plan for growth, the reality of today's economics is such you should probably favor an adaptive environment more than a scaled-up environment from the beginning.

There are interesting elements to consider in the server architecture itself. Servers are more or less industry standards (based on Intel Xeon or AMD Opteron processors). However, throwing as much hardware as possible into a server configuration does not always increase the response time or the volume of transactions handled in a given time slot. In a given customer case, I had to study the workload of the server and how it could be changed by varying the system resources. We figured that the servers could very well cope with the transaction work load with "only" 2 GB of RAM instead of 4 GB of RAM. While is certainly a relatively small difference of cost for a single server, it can represent a big difference when such a server configuration is deployed 200 times throughout one of the largest computing infrastructures. The same applied with the storage infrastructure: SAN storage does not bring any real benefit to bridgehead servers, which are traditionally requiring temporary storage, sometimes tuned in a high-performance way to expedite message transfers, yet not requiring very high capacity.

Beyond all these options and choices, we are going to concentrate first on the actual server configuration, the basic elements that constitute a server platform.

First, your server architecture could be based on single processors or multiple processors. The Microsoft Exchange 2003 STORE process, the heart of any persistent transaction, makes the best use of resources on quad-processor architectures. By using proper partitioning of CPU resources, you might use more processors in the server, but the sweet spot has been and still is four processors per server.

I think that most high-end deployments actually happen on four-way or eight-way CPU architectures, the sensitive factor in Exchange 2003 being the I/O transaction throughput and response time, both from a network access and a storage subsystem perspective. From that matter, the bus and server chipset architecture is more prevalent than the sheer number of processors.

5.2.1   Typical Machine Architecture

Modern servers are still based on the same principles, which consist of assembling CPU, RAM, and I/O interface on a motherboard. There can be several CPUs on the motherboard, and the way to access the memory may be more or less convoluted, but in principle, there is hardly more that you need to consider when looking at core server components. Each of them can be an area of interest for Microsoft Exchange server optimization and can influence the ability of Exchange to deal with the intended workload.

In Figure 5.1, there are processors (here, Xeon processors) that communicate together by the means of a front-side bus, itself a connection to a central hub that can interface to the memory banks, the various PCI bridges, and additional on-board components such as a remote management board (here shown as the iLO component) and video interface.

For the remainder of this section, we are going to study how these basic building blocks can be useful for Microsoft Exchange and which consideration you should have when selecting and comparing hardware server vendors. We will voluntarily omit other server subcomponents such as ROM or low-end interfaces (e.g., USB, serial).

Being widely adopted in 2004, the 64-bit extension of Windows Server 2003 enables a 32-bit instance of Windows Server 2003 to run on a 64-bit machine architecture that implements natively the 32-bit instruction set of the Intel Xeon processor. This is available today with the utilization of AMD Opteron or Intel's Nocona processors, known as the Intel Extended Memory 64 Technology (EM64T) on Xeon processors. These processors have yet to be standardized in corporate deployments of Microsoft Exchange, but since the beginning of 2006, most shipping servers will be

Figure 5.1
*Dual-processor
server architecture
(source: HP)*

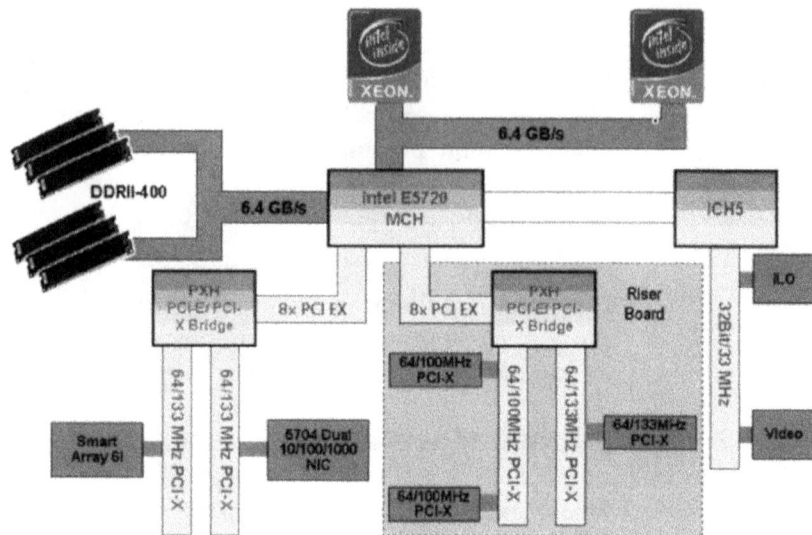

equipped with such capable processors, therefore paving the way for 64-bit computing for Windows and Microsoft Exchange environments.

5.2.2   Multiple-Processor Systems

Symmetric multiprocessing (SMP) is a technique that enables multiprocessors to execute instructions in parallel and offer great upward scalability for applications, including Exchange 2003.

Many vendors base their SMP models around the Intel multiprocessor chipset that scales up to four processors, and some expand it by using a joint model that can actually scale up to eight processors and beyond. This is the case for most eight-processor architectures, which basically gather two groups of four processors around a fast interconnect. Other manufacturers, such as ServerNet, provide multiprocessing chipsets. Late in 2003 and in 2004, we saw the generalized usage of hyper-threading in addition to SMP architectures.

Hyper-Threading

Supported with Windows 2000 and later with Windows Server 2003, Intel Xeon processors now provide support for hyper-threading: this technique is based upon the observation from Intel that during the execution of an instruction, more than 35 percent of the processor resources were left utilized. So the idea of hyper-threading is for the processor to present two machine states to the operating system: suddenly, each physical processor becomes two logical processors to the operating system and applications. There is no preference or notion of a primary or secondary processor, but instead the operating system has the ability to schedule two parallel streams of execution through a single processor die, as shown with the MT-mode presented in Figure 5.2.

Figure 5.2
How two architectural states can be merged on the same physical processor

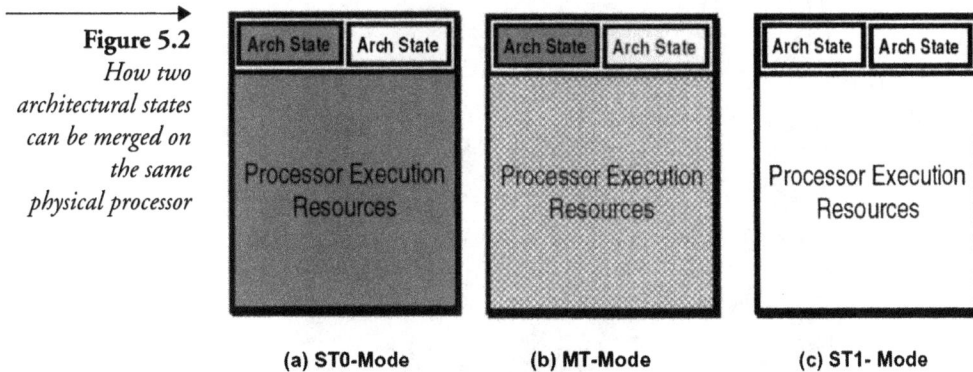

(a) ST0-Mode   (b) MT-Mode   (c) ST1- Mode

Hyper-threading is typically enabled by the means of the server BIOS, and HP has identified that up to 30 percent performance improvement was noticed just by changing this server setting. Setting the hyper-threading on a server will require you to bring the server down, and you might run into licensing issues if you run Windows 2000: indeed, some editions of Windows are limited to the number of processors; while Windows Server 2003 makes the licensing limitations based upon the actual number of physical processors, regardless of the hyper-threading state, Windows 2000 shipped before hyper-threading was implemented by Intel and therefore does not make the distinction between logical and physical processors.

In fact, parallel execution of instructions inside a processor (also known as *execution pipeline*) is something that has been implemented for a long time. However, with hyper-threading, the parallel execution does not only apply at the instruction level, but also at the thread level, by elevating this parallelism capability at the operating-system level.

While hyper-threading is definitely applicable to Microsoft Exchange environments, it does not necessarily help all business applications. For instance Microsoft SQL Server does not benefit from hyper-threading as much as Microsoft Exchange does. Depending upon the applications that use SQL server, if the processors are already saturated in their processing of transactions, the use of hyper-threading will actually decrease the throughput of the SQL server (see Microsoft support article 322385).

But, with Microsoft Exchange, using hyper-threading will always bring a performance benefit.

The following figure shows how you may enable hyper-threading on an HP ProLiant server.

Figure 5.3
Enabling Intel processor hyper-threading in the server BIOS

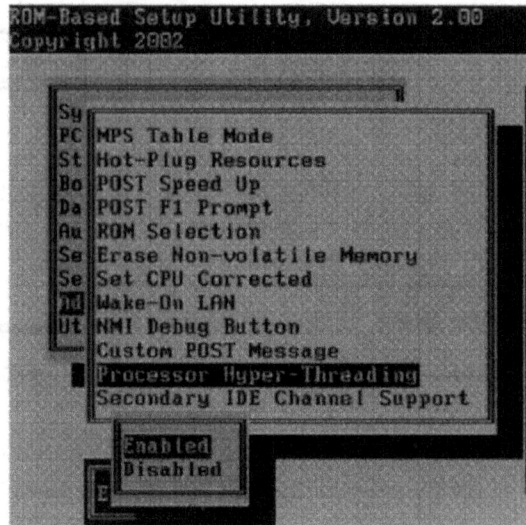

SMP Considerations

Processors in SMP share a common system bus that interconnects to the memory and controllers through a chipset called the northbridge (because, as you might guess, there is also a southbridge).

Northbridge is an Intel chipset that communicates with the computer processor and controls interaction with memory, the peripheral component interconnect (PCI) bus, level 2 cache, and all accelerated graphics port (AGP) activities. Northbridge communicates with the processor using the front-side bus (FSB). Northbridge is one part of a two-part chipset called northbridge/southbridge. Southbridge handles the input/output (I/O) functions of the chipset.

The Intel Hub Architecture (IHA) has replaced the northbridge/south-bridge chipset. The IHA chipset also has two parts: the graphics and AGP memory controller hub (GMCH) and the I/O controller hub (ICH). The IHA architecture is used in Intel's 800 series chipsets, which is the first chipset architecture to move away from the northbridge/southbridge design.

Past the northbridge, processors uniformly (i.e., all processors see the same physical memory) access the memory, itself controlled by a controller.

The northbridge can quickly become a point of contention, as processors have increasing core clock speeds that expedite instruction execution: if too many processors access the same area of memory, the lower the memory response time (and therefore intermediate components), and the better the execution capability of the server is. If too many processors (e.g., eight) attempt to access this common physical memory area, there can be a point of contention that basically will cause latencies that will hinder the throughput and response time of the overall application.

There are ways to mitigate the effect of system bus congestion; one of them is to use a large L2 cache, a fast-access memory module located in the processor. Figure 5.3 shows a sample implementation of a quad-processor system, which utilizes a system bus that enables communication between each of the processors and the memory controller for one part, and the PCI (and PCI-X) buses for the other parts by means of controller chipsets. How efficient such an architecture can be for Exchange 2003 depends a great deal on the availability of the secondary cache. It is much faster for the processor to address the secondary cache, embedded in the chip by means of a back-end bus, than to go over the system bus.

Figure 5.4
SMP implementation using four processors (source: HP)

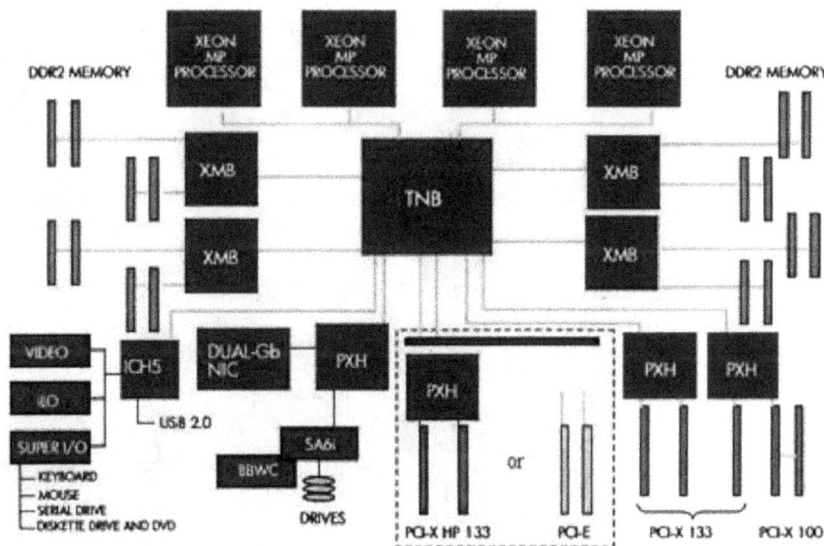

Figure 5.4 shows the relationship between the inner CPU cache modules (L1 and L2 caches and L3 out-of-die cache), and the system bus. By means of two separate buses, the processor can actually either access cached information in L1/L2 cache or fetch the information from the main memory or the I/O controllers by means of the system bus. It is

worth keeping in mind that the cost of switching the context of execution of a particular thread from one CPU to another can be significant because of the L2 cache invalidation and transfer of information between processors by means of the system bus. Eight-way SMP implementations vary from one manufacturer to another. At HP, the basic idea for eight-way Intel Xeon implementations is to gather two four-way CPU implementations around a joint chipset (called Profusion or F8, depending upon the Intel processor architecture), which enables cross-communication between the memory controller modules and two independent system buses, each handling four processors.

Figure 5.5 shows how two four-way CPU system buses are actually coupled by means of the central chipset on an HP platform. Note the presence of the TNB (northbridge) communication block that connects processors, memory controllers (XMB), and PCI and I/O bridges and controllers.

In addition to coupling processors, the central chipset F8 architecture protects against memory bank failure by introducing a dedicated parity bank, which can help the recovery of a single failing memory bank (this approach can be regarded as RAID3 for memory).

Figure 5.5
SMP implemention on eight-way system (source: HP)

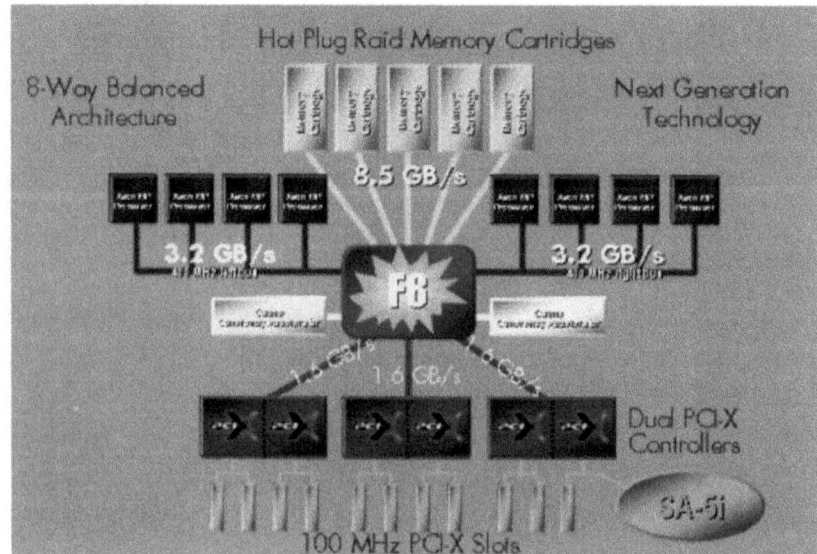

The main question is whether you would benefit from SMP with Exchange 2003. Several indicators say that you should definitely take advantage of SMP on quad-processor machines. Check out the performance benchmarks from vendors on Microsoft's Exchange performance

Web site; you will notice that it is possible to scale up by increasing the number of processors and taking advantage of them. However, remember also that Exchange 2003 is multithreaded by nature and does not necessarily take advantage of more than eight processors: the communication required by the eight processors for concurrently accessing the single physical memory (SMP mode) generates additional points of contention and interprocessor communication that can quickly create overhead, unless you can confine a particular processor/thread execution to a defined group of well-connected processors.

If you increase the application workload (by supporting more users per server), you will increase the number of concurrent threads executed by the Exchange 2003 STORE process and run the risk of having the system spend precious privileged time in context-switching mode. Context switching is not bad in itself; it has to happen whenever a thread has used all of its execution time, when it has to wait for an external operation to complete (network or storage I/O are the most frequent causes), or when the processor is otherwise interrupted by an external source, such as an interrupt from a network adapter.

Machine architectures and implementation from various industry-standard server manufacturers, such as HP, IBM, or DELL, will actually differ from their ability to handle a large number of context switches. On a four-way machine, we consider that anything close to 80,000 context switches per second is a possible area of improvement. Note that the ability of the processors to perform a large number varies upon the processor architecture and motherboard implementation, and therefore this is a topic that you need to revisit every six months, given the rate of release of processor improvements from Intel and corresponding industry-standard servers from server vendors.

Of course, the more the context switches there are, the more time processors will spend in overhead and privileged (or, kernel) mode execution. This time will be taken at the expense of the user-mode execution (i.e., the application code): the overall system performance can suddenly degrade, causing an increase in transaction response time and decrease in throughput, noticeable by high RPC latencies (from the Microsoft Exchange STORE viewpoint) as well as message queues building up.

Sometimes, there is just nothing you can do about a high number of context switches on a server, simply because of the I/O-intensive nature of the Microsoft Exchange workload. You need to determine eventually if it is perhaps preferable to displace workload (by moving very busy users) from one machine to another. Figure 5.6 displays how the number of context

Figure 5.6
*System context
switches and
percentage of
privileged time
relationship*

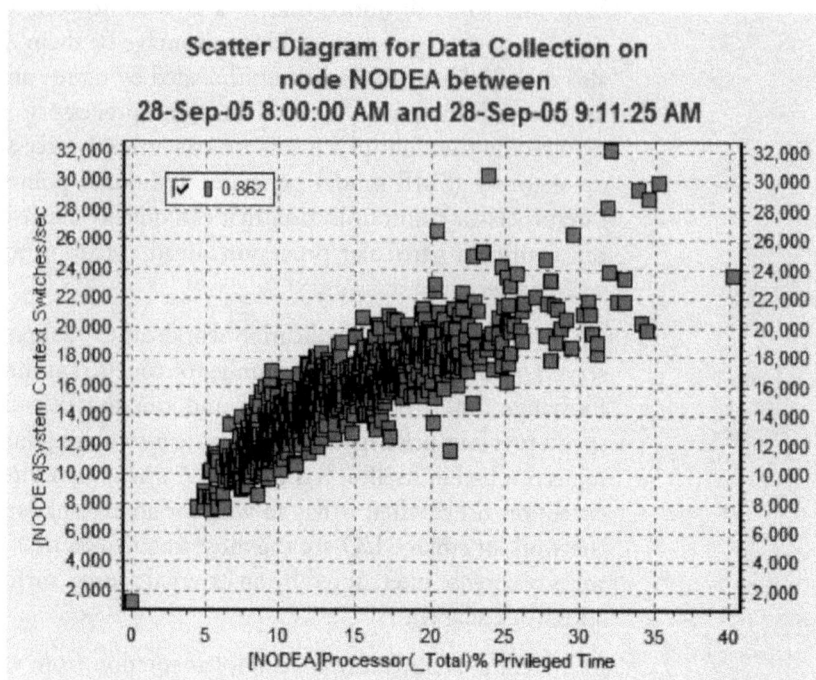

switches are related to the percentage of utilization of the processors in privileged time.

In such cases, there is little to do other than to decrease the workload by reducing the number of context switches per second. When the context switches increase past 20,000 per second, the processors are spending a significant amount of time in privileged mode: this mode is reserved for kernel execution, not for application execution. Thus, less of the application gets executed and the RPC throughput and response are impacted.

NUMA-cc Considerations

Another approach is brought by nonuniform memory architecture (NUMA) multiprocessing architectures as introduced by the AMD Opteron processor chipset. With NUMA, each processor (or group of processors, known as a cell) has its own portion of the physical memory. If it needs to access physical memory that it does not own, it will communicate with another cell to obtain the memory contents. This extra communication is the reason for the "nonuniform" term in the acronym: the memory is accessed in different ways, depending on whether the memory is locally attached to the processor or its cell or it is in a foreign cell.

The cross-cell communication is typically enabled by the means of a cross-bar switch that allows for point-to-point communications. NUMA architectures are often implemented with a cache-coherency (the -cc in NUMA-cc) feature that ensures that the on-die processor cache is coherent with respect to the contents of the local memory.

Figure 5.7
*NUMA-cc
diagram*

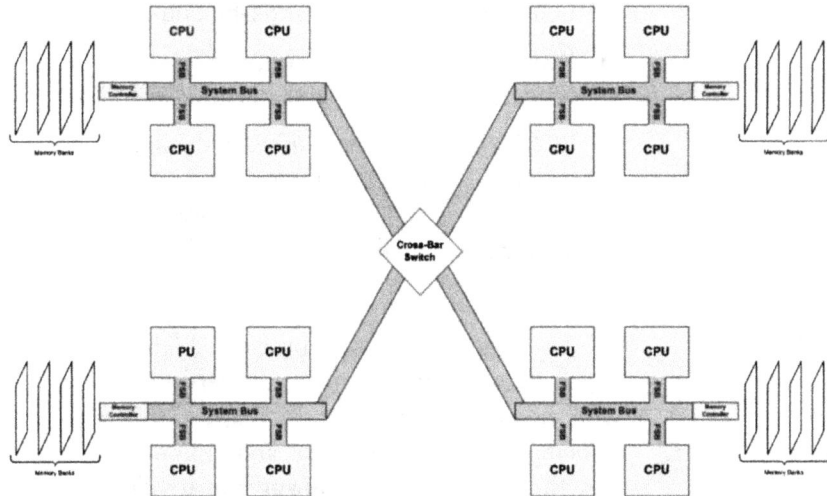

Such implementation is seen (although not specifically called NUMA) in the AMD Opteron processor implementation: it enables processor-to-processor communication by means of a hyper-transport that operates at the core CPU clock speed, unlike a traditional cross-bar switch. The advantage of NUMA is that it scales up to 64 (and above) processors for a given physical machine, as seen with the HP SuperDome or Unisys ES7000.

Why should you care about this with Microsoft Exchange? The challenge with Exchange is that execution might occur on various processors, in a rather unpredictable manner, unless you have defined affinity for processes to execute on certain processors. For this reason, and because cross-bar memory access tends to be significantly slower, most NUMA-based machines are typically *partitioned* in several submachines to avoid too many interprocessor (and overhead) communications. Therefore, a 64-processor ES7000 will be partitioned into 4 × 8-processor instances—leaving you wondering why, in the first place, you would want to use such a large machine for Microsoft Exchange workload.

PCI, PCI-X, and PCI Express Bus Considerations

Initially, PCI and PCI-X buses were implemented at either 66-MHz or 33-MHz clock speed. On high-end and modern servers, we now see the general availability of additional generations of PCI interfaces:

- PCI-X bus that operates at 64-bit and 100- or 133-MHz clock rates;

- PCI-X 2.0 bus that can operate at clock speeds of 266- and 533-MHz and offer backward compatibility to legacy PCI adapters;

- PCI-Express bus that offers scalability and performance for the upcoming processor and systems architectures. PCI-Express (also referred to as PCI-E) brings improved clock rates and bus bandwidth, aiming at eventually displacing both PCI-X and AGP buses.

There can be multiple buses on high-end servers, with a mixture of clock rates. As you configure the server and plan for the adapter layout, you should make sure that the adapter clock speed matches the PCI bus it is being placed on; otherwise, and to honor the adapter clock rate capability, the whole bus will downgrade its clock rate, resulting in possibly underutilized adapters. During the power-on self-test (POST) boot process, the server will typically signal if you have incorrectly placed an adapter in your server (resulting in a mismatch of clock rates or use of an unsupported combination).

When building your server and planning for your I/O (and other) adapters, you should always check with the vendor's supportability matrix, including the ability to combine the use of PCI-E with hyper-threading. Normally, server vendors do have such a matrix; however, adapter vendors (e.g., Emulex or QLogic for fibre-channel host-bus adapter) might propose models that are not part of such a matrix, and you will therefore need to undergo qualification tests, either within your own IT department or with the vendor of either the server or the adapter.

Failure to be compliant with the server PCI compatibility matrix can lead to hazardous results, including data corruption, which is always problematic to deal with in a Microsoft Exchange environment.

Front-Side Bus

The processors communicate with the "outside" (memory banks and I/O controllers, peer processors) by means of the front-side buses. For helping in the performance of the Microsoft Exchange server, you will want to have processors that operate at a high enough bus speed. But just the bus speed is not enough. The width (i.e., the number of bits presented on the bus at each clock tick) is also important. A simple analogy can be made with motorways and cars (see Figure 5.8).

Figure 5.8
The 32-bit vs.
64-bit bus

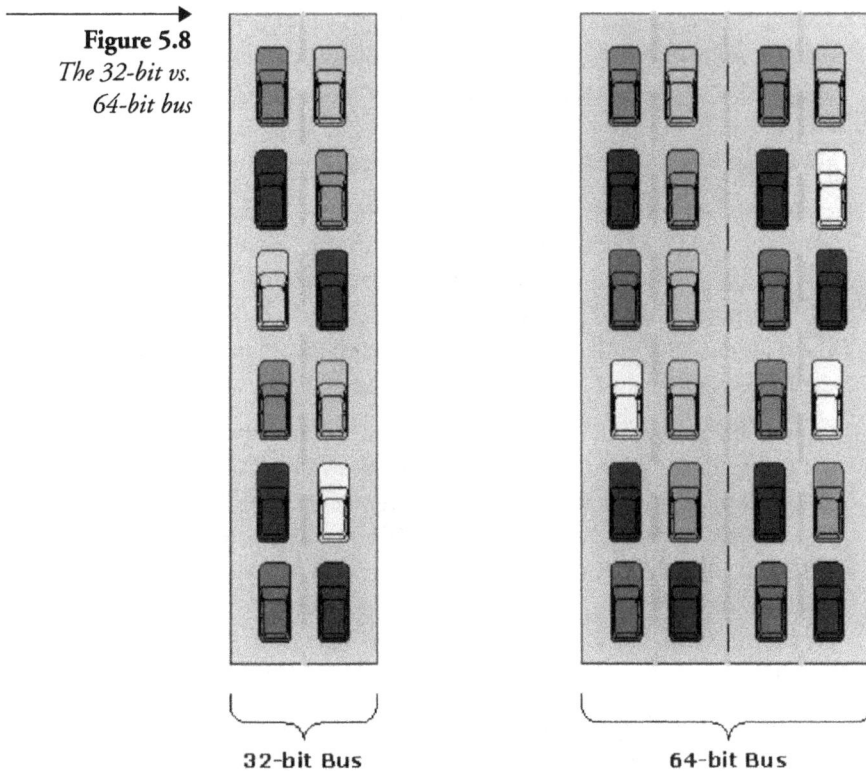

32-bit Bus   64-bit Bus

When you consider the bus speed as the speed imposed on the motorway, you see that you can naturally transfer many more cars within a period of time if you have four lanes than you could if you have two lanes only. The same goes with the bus exiting from the processor and accessing the various components.

We have found, in our benchmark testing at HP, that bus bandwidth was important as the processors were becoming faster and more numerous on the system.

For a Microsoft Exchange server, we generally see servers with:

- 100 Mhz for single-, dual-, quad-, and octo-processor machines;

- 400 Mhz to 533 Mhz for single-, dual-, and quad-processor machines;

- 800 Mhz for single-, dual-, and quad-processor machines.

Ideally, try to select a server and CPU chipset that operates at 800 Mhz. The bus width is typically 64-bit, especially with the more recent x64 processors that implement both 32-bit and 64-bit instruction sets and registers.

CPU Workload: Concurrent RPC Operations

Since the beginning of this chapter, we referred a lot to the need for the processors to deal with many concurrent threads from the Exchange 2003 STORE. In this section, I would like to come back to the fundamentals of RPC operations with Microsoft Exchange, given that they typically relate to the requirements for fast processing, fast front-side bus and memory access, as well as optimized multiprocessing implementation.

The Exchange 2003 STORE can communicate with several types of clients, directly or indirectly. Internet clients using POP, SMTP, HTTP, or IMAP connect to an Exchange 2003 server via the INETINFO process (the IIS), which in turn communicates with the Exchange STORE via the EPOXY component and the exchange installable file system (EXIFS) designated as the M:\ drive on pre-Exchange 2003 server, eventually hidden on Exchange 2003 (see article 821836 in the Microsoft Knowledge Base for specific change of behavior).

For any MAPI clients (which still represent the majority of mail clients in enterprise environments), the client-server connection is primarily by means of remote procedure calls (RPCs), which themselves bind deeply into the STORE process by means of the RPCINTF interface. Note that the RPC/HTTP mode of operation in Outlook 2003 and Exchange 2003 slightly changes this interface by encapsulating the RPC traffic into HTTP command frames. However, from the server component viewpoint, it still ends up as an RPC binding to the STORE process.

With Exchange 2000 RTM, the maximum number of concurrent RPC operations handled by the STORE process was set to 20. After the Windows RPC server starts, the Microsoft Exchange STORE process will proceed to register its RPC service and use the default number of concurrent threads (20). This is a very little known fact; performance degradation can result should the server handle a large quantity of user transactions at a single point in time (e.g., when all the users log in in the morning). To accommodate this workload, which you can't really throttle or control, Exchange

2000 SP1 introduced a setting in the Active Directory that can let the STORE handle more concurrent RPC requests at a single point in time (the default number of RPC threads was increased to 100 at the same time). Do not attempt to modify the default behavior if your server has not reached this limit. Increasing the concurrent RPC operations value to too large a value can result in wasted virtual memory and possibly excessive memory consumption leading to virtual memory fragmentation. Microsoft Knowledge Base article 274766 discusses this particular setting.

Note that there is a possibility that the number of concurrent RPC operations is low because the STORE process cannot process the RPC operations fast enough. This value is likely to hide another performance problem—typically a CPU processing issue, a transaction log storage issue (high latency), or a database read storage issue (high latency, again). Don't forget that database writes are performed asynchronously from the user transactions, unlike database reads and log buffer flushes on a transaction hard commit.

Microsoft Knowledge Base article 274766 documents how to change this particular value. I recommend that you first closely monitor this counter and then make the decision to bump the value, generally to 25 percent more than that maximum observed value. Increasing the value by increments of five seems a reasonable approach while keeping track of the server workload and handling from the STORE process. Furthermore, too many RPC operations in progress can cause excessive thread creation, which in turn can cause excessive context switching, privileged processor time, and little user processor time to perform the actual operations. We figured that the default setting of 100 for Exchange 2003 and later is quite acceptable for most high-end workloads, and in fact, the Windows server itself will indicate signs of failure past 35–40 outstanding RPC requests.

As mentioned previously, you should always take into account the actual reasons for excessive concurrent activity. Is it due to a high number of user transactions or to insufficient resources to complete user transactions fast enough that concurrent activity has fewer spikes?

In Chapter 6, we review the performance and monitoring of Exchange 2003 and provide information to determine whether a high concurrent activity is the result of a high demand (which is totally normal) or the result of a resource bottleneck that prevents operations to complete satisfactorily.

The Need for Speed

To alleviate the problem of increasing throughput in a multithreaded environment such as Exchange 2003, a first approach consists of using fewer but faster processors or using processor affinity, which enables you to control the processors eligible to run a particular process and its threads.

This is called soft affinity and is commonly implemented in large data centers involving more than eight processors (e.g., on the ES7000 Unisys solution). Specifically, with Windows 2000 Data Center Edition and Windows Server 2003 Data Center, it is possible, using the job control process, to set the processor affinity such that you can perform some form of logical partition of your system's CPU resources.

In most deployments, I strongly believe that a safe tactic is to use four-way servers that have shown scaling past the 7,000-MMB2 user workload (and, nowadays, above 8,000 MMB3 users).

This indicates that the server can handle, from a CPU perspective, a 7,000-MMB2 user workload generated by Microsoft Loadsim.

For several reasons it is debatable whether this showing is actually of any significance to your environment. First, MMB2 benchmarks apply to a closed, single-server environment. This means that the system under test is running Exchange 2003 and also acts as the Active Directory GC server, much required for the message routing and recipient resolution. Further, the MMB2 workload does not take into account the additional processing that can take place on an Exchange server. For example, clients very often configure rules on their mailboxes that automatically process the messages. This means that when a message is delivered, additional processing must be done—either transferring the message to another folder or automatically replying to the message or other task, which is not simulated by the MMB2 workload. Finally, MAPI protocol semantics are much richer than those of any Internet protocol such as POP or IMAP, and trying to simulate all of them would create either a meaningless workload or too much of a task for the workload machine to accomplish.

Beyond the CPU clock speed, we also found that the front-side bus was becoming increasingly important, as it could expedite the memory access latency issues: 70 ns is now considered too long for a page access, and any front-side bus contention can be to the detriment of the overall application throughput. You should therefore consider improving your front-side bus speed if you intend to renew your server (hacking a server for revving up the FSB speed is not a good idea!).

For decreasing the physical memory access latency, SMP is far more suitable than NUMA, with the exception of AMD Opteron's multiprocessing implementation that enable core CPU speed access. In benchmarks done with Exchange 2003, this was reflecting, showing that a dual-core Opteron server is faster than a quad-processor SMP server.

A final way to improve your memory speed is to prevent general RAM access by using larger on-die or close-by secondary processor cache (i.e., L1, L2, and L3 caches).

5.2.3   Co-Hosting Scenarios

Don't forget that you should reconsider your server configuration approach if you ever decide to co-host applications on Exchange 2003 servers. Generally, co-hosting is found on small sites, in order to perform sufficient consolidation of server and services. Therefore, an Exchange 2003 server will also act as a print server and a Windows Server 2003 domain controller, and possibly a DHCP server. In such situations, the number of users and the resulting workload is rather small, and the CPU is unlikely to be a performance bottleneck.

Hardware Partitioning

There are other situations in which customers acquiring high-end servers (e.g., with more than eight processors) will want to consolidate their applications. The key here is to use resource partitioning. Hardware-based partitioning is, in my opinion, not desirable. Turning very expensive 32-way machine architectures into four 8-way systems by means of hardware partitions is a real waste of assets, considering that this partitioning is very static and changing the partitions involves significant downtime and reconfiguration of the hosted operating systems.

Soft Partitioning: Resource Management and Affinity

If you have a real desire to operate more than eight processors, by using 16- or 32-way machine architectures, I recommend using software-based partitioning. Here, one single copy of the operating system (it should be Windows Server 2003 Data Center Edition) runs across all 16 or 32 processors, and by using processor affinity and memory allocation control, you indeed perform soft partitions that you can accommodate as application workload increases (hopefully not all applications at the same time). The job control process, described in Chapter 3, is an appropriate tool, but there are other equivalents from computer vendors.

Be sure, however, that Exchange 2003 is optimally configured to deal with a software resource partitioning system. From a CPU affinity perspective, you will see little problem in setting affinities for the STORE and INETINFO processes, the two core components of Exchange 2003.

From a memory perspective, Exchange 2003 has its own way of dealing with memory, some of which has been improved in SP1 by the means of the dynamic buffer allocation scheme, and it will unlikely play well with a resource-partitioning manager, including the job control MMC snap-in from Windows Server 2003 2000 Data Center Edition.

Soft Partitioning: Virtual Servers/Machines

Finally, and currently an approach that is gradually used in enterprise environments, you can perform soft-partitioning of your machine by the means of *virtual servers* or *virtual machines*. The technique is to use a hosting environment that can be a Linux core (such as with VMware ESX edition) or a Windows host computing environment and run Virtual machine or server instances on the physical servers.

The big advantage of virtual machines, even though there is an added overhead compared to the previous approach based upon affinity and resource management, is that you create independency between the Windows server instances, therefore bypassing potential trouble you could run into if you were to deploy a SharePoint Portal server on a Microsoft Exchange server with a particular version of Microsoft SQL Server.

Be careful: while virtual server computing is often considered in physical consolidation scenarios, it does not solve the administrative overhead of managing the logical Windows server instances—you still need to maintain proper inventory and patch management! Nonetheless, and beyond test and demonstration environments, virtual machine or server computing is becoming more and more of a trend, as computer vendors are releasing server architectures that are faster and faster and have ample free cycles for two or more instances of Windows Server 2003 editions.

In Summary

I found that the sweet-spot configuration for Exchange 2003 is *still* a four-way server, on which the relatively low number of processors does not require utilizing the L2 cache at its maximum (1 MB is usually sufficient).

This configuration can represent a significant savings in the server acquisition process; there can be many hundreds of dollars price difference between a Pentium Xeon 1-MB L2 cache and a Pentium Xeon 2-MB L2 cache. On the other hand, it is commonly accepted that in eight-way and beyond, the use of L2 cache is more important because it can decrease the likelihood of a system bus saturation. My general recommendation is to make sure that you use fast processors, or, in simpler terms, that the processor speed meets your actual demand.

One thing is certain: you will not gain a proportional capacity gain by doubling the number of processors on your system. You will not gain very much either by using 2-MB L2 cache if your number of processors is less than or equal to four.

In gaining order, you should therefore consider using:

1. Fast front-side bus with low-latency memory access;

2. Faster core CPU clock speed;

3. Increased secondary cache (L2 and/or L3).

This recommendation applies to the current design of Exchange 2003 SP1 release and earlier. However, as the technology evolves and as your company's typical workload evolves, the landscape may change for proper CPU configuration applicable to Exchange 2003.

It is likely that 64-bit versions of Microsoft Exchange will come to reality and change the requirements for the server computing, RAM sizing, and multiprocessing architectures.

5.2.4 Load Balancing Services

When you deploy a front-end/back-end Exchange 2003 solution, you will want to take advantage of dynamic load balancing between the front-end servers, such that the load is spread across the front-end machines, which will proxy the Internet protocols commands to the back-end servers. Note that although you can use load balancing for back-end servers, it would bring absolutely no advantage, given that the user mailbox is hosted on one single server. This is not necessarily true for accessing public folder information, which can be replicated between servers and for which Microsoft Exchange already includes a way to failover to another public folder server to access this shared and replicated information space.

Load balancing is available out of the box with various Windows Server editions, under the network load balancing (NLB) services. The great advantage of this technology is that it does not require any specific hardware, and it is bundled with the operating system. The main disadvantage is the lack of scalability; a single NLB "cluster" cannot handle more than 32 front-end servers. Therefore, you have two choices:

1.   If you plan to grow your environment, and if your workload is going to grow beyond the processing capabilities of your front-end servers, you should plan for a more scalable, albeit more expensive, hardware-based solution.

2.   If you believe that you will not grow beyond 32 servers, you may safely use NLB to get started with the current and forecasted workload.

Note that a workload increase (i.e., a service provider service ramping up) does not necessarily mean adding more servers. I have found that upward scalability with front-end servers works quite well in an Exchange 200x environment. This was based on lab testing in a closed environment and, of course, will depend entirely on the workload imposed by the users' transactions and activities. Only careful monitoring and trend analysis can help you determine how the front-end systems behave under stress.

The workload will depend largely on the design of the front-end server's application. For instance, you may choose to deploy the default Outlook Web Access (OWA) application from Exchange 2003. Although this is suitable for a private, corporate environment, this interface is not acceptable for commercial services. Such services would require a specific branding, and probably reduced functionality from the original client specifications (also referred to as client segmentation).

Fortunately, OWA in Exchange 2003 offers many ways to customize the front-end applications and make available a richer interface to the end user, leading to a satisfactory experience that will cut down on customer churning and raise the popularity of the service.

Figure 5.9 shows how a set of front-end servers would be positioned with a hardware-based load balancing solution. As you can see, the Active Directory services (logically represented by a single server) and the back-end servers are totally isolated from the front-end server traffic. For clarity, Figure 5.9 shows a typical implementation for a private enterprise environment. Nevertheless, if you were to deploy Exchange 2003 as a service

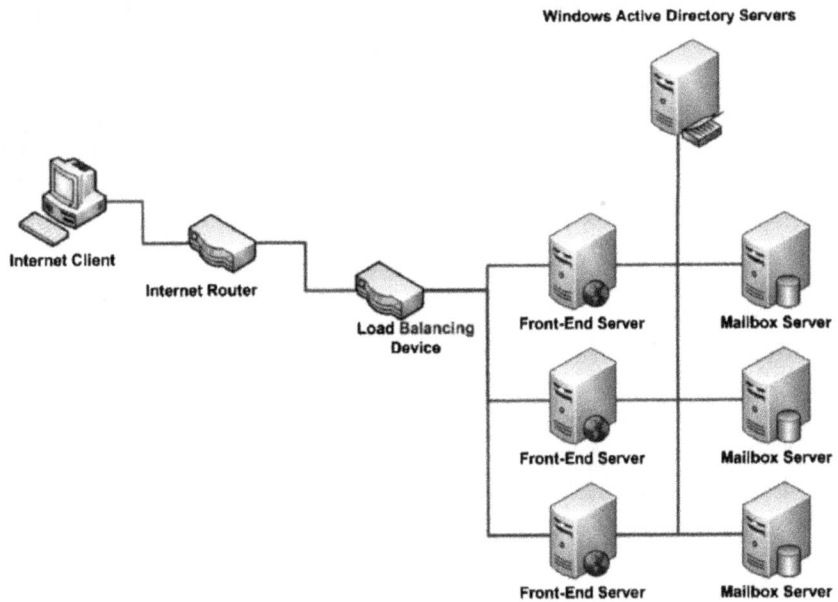

Figure 5.9
Front-end servers controlled by a hardware-bvased load balancing solution

provider on the Internet, you would need to properly isolate the various layers by means of firewalls.

5.2.5 SSL Acceleration for Front-End Servers

Whenever you deploy front-end servers for Exchange 2003, the question arises whether you should deploy SSL for securing the connections to the Web service, the main one being OWA. SSL is very common in the world of Internet applications. Implemented in all Internet browsers (software-based implementation), it can provide a significant load on the hosting CPU because of the encryption calculations—the main one being the RSA private key decryption required to establish a secure session. That operation alone can take up to a second on the fastest processors, which is not something that your front-end server will like. The reason is that the asymmetric private/public key operation requires a 1024-bit key length, and that can result in millions of CPU instructions to perform.

To alleviate this problem, many vendors propose SSL accelerator boards (e.g., HP's AXL600 PCI Accelerator), which bring a significant advantage in CPU consumption while increasing the ability of the front-end server to handle multiple connections at a single point in time. This is because such boards utilize chip-based asymmetric encryption and decryption, which is much more powerful than computed operations done by 32-bit or 64-bit processing chips. Note that the SSL acceleration boards optimize the asymmetric key required when the SSL session is established. Once the public key/private key ciphering has been processed, the follow-on encryption (typically, single to triple DES (Data Encryption Standard, a standardized and commonly used encryption algorithm designed by IBM in the early 1970's, and still in use in many encryption scenarios) is done by the server, but this is far less expensive than the asymmetric key handling.

Figure 5.10

Using an external SSL encryption unit to offload front-end servers

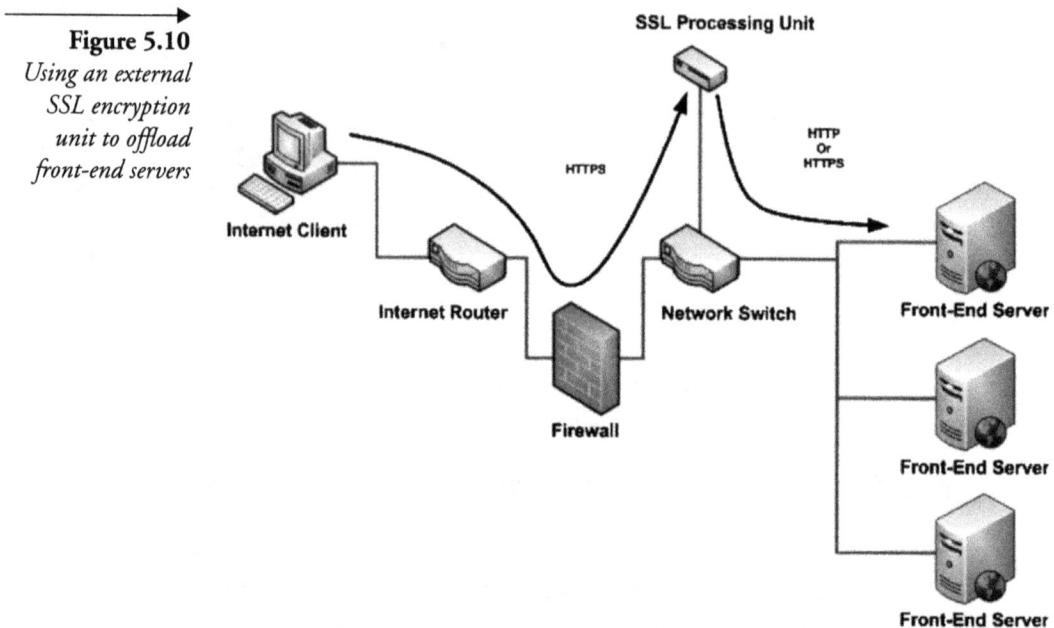

Figure 5.10 shows the benefits of using a single AXL accelerator card on a front-end server handling SSL connections. Up to eight cards can be installed on a particular server with linear scalability. A note of caution is in order. You will most likely deploy your front-end servers on U-type servers, which typically provide only one PCI slot; therefore, you need to factor in the other needs you may have for the PCI slot available. These will include SSL encryption, as well as a remote management board. A vendor that can provide an integrated solution for management can thereby benefit your deployment. The AXL accelerator card is a good complement for software-based load balancing implementation.

Another alternative to host-based SSL encryption is using a separate component, as shown in Figure 5.10. These SSL appliances are significantly more expensive to deploy but are generally part of a wider scope of Internet connectivity and security services infrastructure for a large corporation. SonicWALL SSL-R or SSL-RX offloaders are examples of such offloaders.

Combined with network or Web switches, it can concentrate the SSL session initialization on one separate component, making it unnecessary for you to revisit your front-end servers' configuration (nonintrusive approach). With this approach, you in fact defer SSL management and work to the network infrastructure, which may be a sensible thing to do, especially if your network edge is under the control of another organization inside your IT department, therefore providing, to the Microsoft Exchange infrastructure, a network connectivity and security service (part of DMZ, proxy services, and SSL bridging or tunneling).

In most deployments that would require SSL encryption only for Exchange 2003; this setup will seldom be used. However, if the Exchange 2003 service is bundled into a wider set of Internet-based services, having a global solution and approach to traffic security is very efficient, from both an economical and a management perspective. Furthermore, manufacturers are bringing to market combinations of load balancing services and SSL encryption services, providing a certain economy of scale, and, of course, a scalable implementation that can be used across a variety of platforms as front-end servers (Windows 2000, UNIX, and others).

Note that these benefits can equally be applied in Microsoft ISA server 200x deployments, where the ISA server is used to public and (reverse) proxy the common protocols and services provided by Exchange 2003.

5.3 Memory Optimization for Exchange 2003

The real challenge with memory usage in Exchange 2003 is that the main consumer, the STORE process, will utilize only what is being made available and hardly cause any paging on the server. It is possible to limit the quantity of memory used by Exchange 2003, which is necessary if the server is shared with other applications, as in a data center configuration. The way to limit memory usage is by acting on the dynamic buffering allocation (DBA) scheme parameters accessible from the configuration naming context related to the server. It has no user interface other than ADSIEDIT, and it is quite a risky operation to perform. However, it can lead to very satisfactory levels of performance.

Two key components of the Microsoft Exchange need physical memory for caching purposes:

- The STORE, which we'll discuss at length in this section;

- The ExIFS, the installable file system, that uses the NT file cache for caching file handles and possibly contents whenever network data streaming takes places through the ExIFS consumers, primarily, the IIS virtual servers (SMTP, HTTP, POP, IMAP, and NNTP).

Based upon the server role, you will need to make sure that the optimal settings for Microsoft Exchange are utilized, for back-end mailbox servers, SMTP bridgeheads, or HTTP front-end servers.

5.3.1   Physical Memory Utilization

In almost all situations, one will want to use as much physical memory as possible to store and "cache" data, as opposed to performing disk access. Data rates obtained through disk subsystems can be in the order of 20 MB/s to 40 MB/s, while in-memory access goes well above 6 GB/s and keeps growing with the rapid advances in the world of memory components. Besides, a single disk access is typically on the order of 1 ms to 20 ms (depending upon cache and queuing on the target/source disks), while a page access is on the order of 50 ns to 70 ns. This is quite a difference that you will want to take advantage of.

Microsoft Exchange can be viewed, for most back-end implementations, as a database application, which benefits from performing as many operations as possible in RAM. As discussed in the Exchange 2003 architecture, this is effectively the case. The larger the amounts of RAM made available to Exchange and its STORE process, the less likely the database engines will need to access the disk subsystems, which are several orders of magnitude slower.

The number of storage groups defined on the server and the activity of those storage groups condition the demand on memory, both virtual and physical, of the STORE process. In previous versions of Exchange 2003 SP1, each storage group was estimated to consume 100 MB of memory, plus an additional 30 MB for each database defined in the storage group. The first database defined in a storage group will consume more memory than subsequent databases. If you are conservative about memory utilization, it is more appropriate to create as many databases as possible in a storage group (five), and add more storage groups as you need more databases.

The memory consumption was improved with Exchange 2003 SP1, and the overhead is now negligible with Exchange 2003 SP2.

In addition to these memory requirements, which are due to in-memory loading of the ESE instances, active databases (i.e., databases that have user activity) will consume memory for storing both the database pages (application-level read cache) and the version store, an area of memory designed to hold pages that are in the process of being modified, as part of the execution of a transaction.

Finally, the STORE process will also utilize its virtual memory for holding temporary data for its threads (typically the thread stack size and various memory blocks used by the application code).

With Exchange 2000 SP1 Data Center certification and later, we started to notice instances of virtual memory fragmentation: the user mode virtual memory used by the STORE would be allocated in such a way that further queries for contiguous amount of virtual memory (e.g., during an Exchange virtual server failover in a multinode cluster) would fail due to a lack of contiguous space (and not necessarily for virtual memory exhaustion caused, for instance, by a memory leak).

With these points in mind, there are certain actions you can take to optimize Microsoft Exchange utilization of virtual memory, which is somewhat independent from the actual physical memory in use.

5.3.2 Virtual Memory Utilization

It is preferable when using Exchange 2003 to allocate as much application virtual address space as possible. Introduced with Windows NT Enterprise Edition and supported in Windows 2000 Advanced Server and Windows 2000, Data Center is the option to boot the operating system by allowing 3 GB of application virtual address space.

The 4-GB virtual address space is the hard limit in Windows 2000 and Windows Server 2003 32-bit editions, because it is a 32-bit operating system based on the Intel x86 architecture.

Intel realized the limitation of its processor architecture and released something of a kluge while developing its 64-bit Intel architectures (64EMT and Itanium). With the Pentium, Intel introduced the physical address extensions (PAE) implemented as 36-bit page size extensions (64 GB of addressable physical memory). In comparison, the AMD Opteron uses a 40-bit extended addressing, yet uses 64-bit and 32-bit instruction sets as well as 64-bit registers.

These represent attempts to allow applications to address more than 4 GB of virtual space and to take advantage of very large memory (VLM) systems. During the development of Windows 2000, Intel introduced the 450NX chipset that lets x86 processors go beyond the 4-GB physical limit. Microsoft, for its part, implemented a set of APIs—the AWEs, which enable applications to utilize more physical memory than the 3-GB virtual address space would allow. Therefore, an application can load a 6-GB database entirely into memory if the need arises, the server has sufficient RAM available, and you are running a proper version of Windows 2000 (Advanced Server scales to 8 GB of RAM; Data Center scales to 64 GB of RAM).

Microsoft Exchange 2003 does not implement the AWE. Earlier in the development cycle, the decision was made to implement large memory utilization on the upcoming 64-bit version of Windows 2000. This is the main reason the development team had to withdraw support for 15 storage groups and limit it to 4 instead. However, it can benefit from reasonably large memory servers (1 GB or more, but less than or equal to 4 GB) by means of the /3GB boot switch.

Virtual Address Space Available in Windows Server 32-Bit

On Windows Server 2003 (and earlier), for any given process, there is a 32-bit virtual address space (4 GB) that is typically split in 2 GB of user mode (application addressable space) and 2 GB of system space. Leaving 2 GB for the operating system can have some benefits, such as running a larger file system cache. In MAPI operations, however, Exchange 2003 makes little use of the file system cache. All the I/O operations issued by the STORE process to the EDB (the MAPI property database used for most of the Exchange mailbox contents) are issued in write-through mode (at the operating system level), bypassing the NT I/O subsystem cache.

On the other hand, IIS virtual servers (SMTP, HTTP-DAV, NNTP, and IMAP and POP) take advantage of the ExIFS. This file system uses (and, in fact, shares) cache memory in the Windows 2000 I/O subsystem to expedite data transmission between IP sockets and file handles by means of the TransmitFile Win32 API.

Generally speaking, applications can greatly benefit from a performance perspective by utilizing memory—preferably, physical memory. Exchange 2003 makes extensive use of both virtual and physical memory by using two types of memory management techniques: buffering and caching.

The fundamental difference between buffering and caching is that, in the case of buffering, the data doesn't exist anywhere else. In the case of caching, the data is present somewhere else, except for dirty pages (i.e., pages that have been modified and are kept in memory, but haven't been flushed yet to disk). We discuss in this section the need of Exchange 2003 for memory in these two cases and how to best optimize this need.

Buffering

Buffering in Exchange 2003 consists of staging information into memory to avoid frequent disk access. Primarily, the buffering done in the Exchange 2003 store is at the transaction log level, where each page modification that makes up a transaction is first buffered, then flushed to disk when the transaction requires a hard commit (which is the case in 99 percent of the transactions issued by the Store on behalf of the client and services connections).

By default, Exchange 2003 allocates 512 buffers for transaction logging. Historically, Exchange 2000 was initially allocating 84 buffers, and by Exchange 2000 SP1, Microsoft recommended increasing this virtual memory space to 9,000 buffers to avoid too frequent disk access to the log device. Later on, Microsoft recognized that 9,000 buffers were a bit too high, and this precious virtual memory could better be used elsewhere in the STORE virtual address space. Eventually, with Exchange 2003 SP1 and SP2, the recommendation has been to reset these log buffers to 9,000 this was made possible with the memory utilization improvements made as part of the SP2 release. Not only will it help in the general processing of transaction-intensive environments (2,000 active users and more), but it also expedites the processing of transaction logging during a (soft or hard) recovery of a database after a restore.

While this increases the consumption of memory, it certainly helps in high-end scenarios with many connected users (more than 5,000 users). Now, what will be the percentage of Exchange 2003 servers that run more than 5,000 connected users? It is fairly small, and keep in mind that with a small transaction log buffer size, your server will continue to operate fairly well if you have a good enough transaction log volume (that is, with a small response time for sequential write operations, below 1 ms).

I have found that performance testing using the default parameters provided with Exchange 2003 was definitely adequate without changing the size of the log buffer space. Use this setting very wisely, and always attempt to measure its actual impact on the server operations. Even if you raise the number of log buffers handled by the STORE, you will still have to flush these transactions to the log area.

My recommendation is to make sure that the log area on disk is fast enough that frequent disk accesses can be done in the most optimal manner (see the section on storage optimization).

Microsoft Exchange's use of buffering has vastly improved over time and has been notably enhanced in relation to the ability to flush contiguous log buffers to disk. With Exchange 5.5, buffers were written individually, typically as 1–2 KB I/O. Starting with Exchange 2000 SP1, the log flush algorithm was such that transactions that are written contiguously can be gathered together into a smaller number of larger I/O—fitting perfectly well-replicated storage scenarios and taking advantage of increasing disk transfer speeds (320 MB/s is now quite common for back-end SCSI drives) and saving on the spindle limitations in processing I/O.

This can have some disadvantages, especially if your storage subsystem is not tuned to handle large I/O requests (>32 KB). With Exchange 2000 (RTM release), it has also been observed that under certain stress conditions, the Windows 2000 kernel would be required to extend the log file and may issue a warning message indicating that it is out of resources because of missing page table entries (PTEs). This log file extension is typically done by means of a large I/O issued by the log buffer processing of the STORE. With Exchange 2000 SP1 onward, the STORE (more precisely, the ESE database engine) will retry the file extension with a smaller value (down to 4 KB) in order to proceed with the I/O. This has the negative impact of using smaller I/O, but because the log drive is dedicated to a single set of spindles (typically mirrored), in most high-end servers two subsequent sequential operations will tend to complete fairly rapidly (below 5 ms if write-back cache is disabled and below 1ms if write-back cache is enabled).

Caching

Caching is an action that consists of keeping data in memory, with the expectation that this memory will be accessed again—this is quite different from the log buffering we just covered in the previous section.

If a page is modified by a transaction, the action is done in memory first, and the page gets flushed to disk, preferably aggregated with contiguous pages. In Exchange 2000, up to two contiguous pages could be written with one single I/O (8 KB instead of a single page I/O of 4 KB). With Exchange 2000 SP1 and beyond, and today with Exchange 2003 SP2, more contiguous pages can be written as a single I/O of a maximum size of 64 KB.

Note that while the STORE process will load as many ESE database engines as there are storage groups defined for your server, these engines share a common pool of database page cache memory for caching frequently accessed databases, for holding copies of databases while transactions are in progress, and for keeping modified database pages in memory while waiting for these pages to be flushed in the background, by a component often called the lazy writer in the database world.

The database cache in Exchange 2003 is extremely important; a failure to allocate cache memory for the database engines will result in a STORE crash in the best case and databases corruptions in the worst case. More generally, if the cache is undersized compared to the frequent accesses made to the databases, there will be an increased quantity of disk accesses, which will tend to overload the server and slow down operations. So, keeping data in cache represents a significant savings from the point of view of system resources utilization (CPU cycles and low latency). In the case of the Microsoft Exchange STORE process, you will find that the DBA, which handles the cache size and the management of the database pages held in memory, is far more intelligent in knowing which data it needs, compared to back-end storage array cache implementations. For this reason, you should never expect a lot of improvement from cache-centric arrays, at least not from random read requests to the database, which typically represent 70 percent of the I/O workload done by Microsoft Exchange to its storage subsystem and LUNs.

Tuning the Database Cache Size

Exchange 2003 uses a default limit of 900 MB for its database buffer cache, which is shared among *all* the storage groups and databases defined on the local server. If your server has ample physical RAM available (usually beyond 1 GB), you may want to override this default setting to increase the size of the cache. More cache means less database access, but not necessarily better performance if the storage subsystem cannot handle database page flushes gracefully.

The 900-MB limit has been imposed to ensure that the STORE has ample virtual address space; it prevents a memory allocation failure that could be fatal to the calling thread of the entire STORE process. Microsoft Knowledge Base article 266096 documents settings regarding the virtual address space in Exchange 2003.

Prior to making any modifications, you should attempt to qualify your current setting with a good load simulation (see Chapter 6 for more information on this topic). Increasing this value beyond 1.2 GB can cause instability in the STORE process, so you should be extremely careful when tuning this particular value. Many factors are involved in deciding how much virtual address space will be used by the STORE process. They include the following:

- Initial start-up allocation;

- Number of storage groups defined on the server;

- Number of databases defined for each storage group;

- Number of active threads (which depends largely on your user and transaction workload);

- Size of the STORE database cache;

- Presence of a third-party antivirus solution running in the STORE process space.

Prior to increasing this value, you should make sure that your store process doesn't attempt to allocate more memory than it can actually use. If you are booting your server with the /3GB switch, the Virtual Bytes performance counter for the STORE instance of the Process object should be below 2.8 GB. If it is not, you should leave the default maximum database buffer cache size untouched. If, however, the value is much lower, because of a relatively small concurrent activity, you can safely increase the maximum database buffer cache size. This can be done using ADSIEDIT, and by navigating to the following area:

```
Configuration Container | CN=Information Store,
CN=<server>, CN=Servers, CN=<servers>, CN=Administrative
Groups, CN=<admingroup>,CN=Microsoft Exchange,
CN=Services, CN=Configuration.
```

Each value is expressed in page count (each page being 4 KB in size). To disable the DBA, and thereby force Exchange 2003 to use a fixed cache size, set the two attributes to the same value.

By right-clicking on the Information Store property, you can select the property called msExchESEParamCacheSizeMax—whose default value should be 230,400 pages of 4 KB (approximately 900 MB)—and increase it to a maximum of 307,200 (1.2 GB).

For the STORE process to take into account this value, you must wait for the change to be replicated to the domain controller used by the Exchange server for its configuration (you can view which domain controller is used by checking out the properties of the server from the Exchange System Manager MMC snap-in); then restart the Information Store service.

Each server that requires such a change will need to be updated. The change can be performed locally, and I strongly recommend that you build a script that traverses the Exchange configuration naming context and identifies the back-end servers that require such a change (here, proper naming conventions can be very helpful). Then automatically roll out the changes and *keep track* of them.

Microsoft Knowledge Base article 815372 provides a comprehensive overview of the handling of virtual memory in the STORE process and gives additional details on configuring the parameter in conjunction with other parameters (such as tuning the heap decommit free block, a parameter that triggers the decommit of virtual memory previously allocated based upon its available size).

The size of these areas is automatically tuned as part of the DBA scheme, introduced in the earlier Exchange 5.5 and carried over in Exchange 2003. Prior to Exchange 2003 SP1, the DBA algorithm would start trimming the working set and the database buffer space if the available amount of free bytes of physical RAM fell below 4 MB. Experience has shown that this is insufficient: the resulting low memory utilization could starve the kernel from page table entries, causing network connection failures or drop and eventually user service interruption.

At the 4-MB threshold, there could be situations in which the database buffer cache would actually be paged by Windows, causing major bottlenecks and wreaking havoc in the STORE performance, which expects fast access to the database buffers and certainly needs access to the pagefile to retrieve database pages. With the introduction of Exchange 2000 SP1, this throttling mechanism is now triggered when 4.5 MB of memory remains free in RAM. While this attempt is certainly useful, this issue will likely be addressed in the future with more flexibility. It is certainly not unreasonable to consider that the STORE should start trimming its working set and database buffer areas before only 4.5 MB of physical memory are left.

Prior to the release of Exchange 5.5, the performance optimizer determined the actual quantity of memory utilized by Exchange. Based on the amount of physical memory and the anticipated load, the performance optimizer calculated the amount of virtual memory (buffers of 4 KB) to be used to cache database pages, and the thresholds after which the ESE database engine was to flush dirty pages to disk or discard pages that were not accessed. This was done based on a least recently used scheme, modified to accommodate the reference count of the pages (LRU-K). The least recently used pages are flushed from memory unless they are often accessed by the database engine.

There really are so many advantages to running several databases and several storage groups that tuning the memory for Exchange 2003 should just be a matter of adding more RAM to the server, letting the STORE process decide on the memory utilization, and using the dynamic buffer allocation scheme.

Most of the time, you should refrain, however, from creating too many storage groups; instead, favor database creation and then add additional storage groups. Just like with any rule, there are exceptions to this:

- The requirement for concurrent backup operations, which may require having multiple storage groups enable multiple concurrent backup streams: with Exchange 2003, there can only be one online backup stream active per storage group. All the databases within that particular storage group are backed up in sequence. With two or more storage groups, you have the ability to start two or more online backup sessions that will back up the databases in serial mode within each storage group. You now have the ability to execute parallel streams of data to your backup media. If you have a multiple tape-drive library, you can use them all at the same time, and that can certainly help in decreasing your overall backup window. Note that there is backup software that allows users to stream to multiple tape drives or media from a single source stream, known as redundant array of independent tapes (RAITs), but I strongly recommend that you apply a method where each backup stream has its own target media for ease of recovery.

- The need to have more transaction logging streams than otherwise possible in replicated environments: because storage replication adds a significant burden on the low-level implementation of the storage array, it is sometimes beneficial to implement parallel streams to avoid much of the latency of an interswitch link between any two synchronized arrays across a given distance.

After Microsoft released the initial version of Exchange 2000, certain scenarios and configurations failed to operate in as reliable a manner as possible because of virtual memory fragmentation. In the SP1 release of Exchange 2000, a lot of effort was put into configuring the memory management components of the Exchange STORE so that memory is used more wisely. These efforts consist primarily of the following:

- Reducing the stack size of individual threads from 1 MB to 512 KB;

- Eliminating memory and thread leaks;

- Optimizing memory allocations when mounting databases from different storage groups (documented in Microsoft Knowledge Base article 277999);

- Providing performance counters that can determine the level of fragmentation of virtual memory.

The Microsoft Knowledge Base article 296073 documents the new performance counters that should be monitored, especially in the case of clustered configurations.

Configuring the File System Cache Size

The Exchange installable file system and its relation with the Internet protocol virtual servers represent a considerable improvement within Exchange 2000, which is not always well grasped by implementers of Exchange. Many people will be tempted to configure their servers to optimize network applications.

However, if the majority of the data transfers is using Internet protocols and therefore transmitting data mostly by means of the ExIFS, it is quite advantageous to configure the Windows 2000 server for optimal file and printer sharing services, which permit the NT I/O subsystem cache grow to approximately 400 MB.

The Server Optimization tab in the File and Printer Sharing for Microsoft Networks Properties dialog box can be used to control memory buffer allocation for network connections and the size of the file system cache working set. Note that you can force this particular setting by setting a particular registry key (LargeMemoryCache) in the CurrentControlSet of HKLM, but I would discourage tweaking this particular area of the registry.

I have found that after applying Exchange 2000 SP1, some registry settings were reset to their original default values, which is not desirable. This type of setting is mostly valid for implementations that favor Internet protocols. Otherwise, it is recommended to optimize the file system cache for network applications, thereby reducing its size to a smaller value than otherwise defined with the previous setting. Therefore, depending on the server role and the type of clients, you may have different settings, and this is something often overlooked by implementers of Exchange 2003.

For MAPI-accessed servers, it is preferable to optimize the server for network applications. For all other server types, optimize the server for file and print sharing, and take advantage of the file system cache for fast information transfer between the IIS virtual servers and the Exchange 2003 streaming store databases.

The /3GB Switch

In memory configurations exceeding 1 GB, you should boot the server using the /3GB switch. To do so, you should edit the boot.ini file (located on the root folder of your boot partition), and add the /3GB command switch to the operating system load command:

```
[boot loader]
timeout=10
default=multi(0)disk(0)rdisk(0)partition(2)\WINNT
[operating systems]
multi(0)disk(0)rdisk(0)partition(2)\WINNT="Windows 2000
Advanced Server" /3GB
multi(0)disk(0)rdisk(0)partition(2)\WINNT="Windows 2000
Advanced Server" /fastdetect
/debug /debugport=com1 /baudrate=57600
C:\CMDCONS\BOOTSECT.DAT="Microsoft Windows 2000 Recovery
Console" /cmdcons
```

This enables the STORE process to utilize more than 2 GB of memory. Restricting the STORE process's virtual memory can have unfortunate consequences on the operations of the STORE as well on its overall performance: with less virtual memory (and corresponding physical memory) for its database cache, the STORE process will have to get to disk more often, causing an impact on the device utilization and resulting in longer times to complete transactions. From an end-user perspective, this means an hourglass appearing more often on the client interface; from an overall system perspective, this means increasing queue lengths, which result in increased time to deliver messages to a point where the system is so busy servicing user requests that messages do not have the time to be delivered, and local send and receive queues to the Information Store database increase until the user load decreases. The time taken to deliver a message is getting exponential, and the overall system is completely saturated.

When memory allocation fails in the STORE process, it is necessary to restart it, which has a negative impact on the availability of the service.

Remember that the PAE boot switch and the /3GB boot switch (also known as 4GT mode enabler) are two different (yet not mutually exclusive) things. The PAE boot enables the server to operate according to a very large memory model but needs the application to be aware of how to use this extra memory. The /3GB switch, as we have seen, affects only the virtual address of the processes by allocating 1 GB for the kernel and 3 GB for the user mode code. You can use the /3GB switch with the /PAE switch, and you can also use the /3GB switch on servers with less than 1 GB of RAM, but we have noticed in our deployments that this carried very little advantage.

In fact, if you use the /3GB boot switch, you restrict the kernel to 1 GB of address space, and some side effects, such as running out of page table entries or the inability to issue large I/Os, have been observed with the initial release of Exchange 2000. Some of these problems have been addressed in Exchange 2003 SP1, but if you have frequent (once a week or more) occurrences of the Windows 2000 kernel running out of resources, you may consider *not* using the /3GB switch and letting Windows 2000 enjoy more resources (check articles Q287935 and Q298064 of the Microsoft Knowledge Base).

The PAE Switch

There have been significant changes to Exchange 2003's recommended Boot.ini configuration settings. You should revisit this topic before you decide on the rollout of boot options. With Exchange 2003 SP1 and later, the following recommendations apply:

- Initially, Microsoft would not recommend running Exchange 2003 on Windows Server 2003 for the simple fact that Exchange 2003 does not take advantage of upper memory (above 4 GB) and that limited testing occurred with the PAE kernel. With the release of Windows Server 2003 SP1, the PAE kernel issues were addressed (even though a hotfix was made available to address specific issues prior to Windows Server 2003 SP1), and for Exchange 2003 to take advantage of the data execution prevention (DEP) features of the kernel, you have to boot with the PAE option to load the PAE kernel.

- New PCI Express–based server chipsets require PAE to take advantage of all the memory installed on a system (4GB). Some of the physical address space on server systems is used to provide memory mapping of I/O resources on the server chipset. This memory mapped I/O (MMIO) space is typically provided below the 4-GB address boundary, but if the server has 4 GB of physical memory, this MMIO space pushes a section of physical memory *above* the 4-GB address boundary. If the software running on the server supports only 32-bit physical addressing, it will not look for memory over the 4-GB boundary. This results in the Windows not providing access to all 4 GB of physical memory (so Exchange 2003 gets to use a little less than the 4 GB). The amount of "hidden" memory is equal to the address space taken up by the MMIO. PCI Express confounds this problem by providing extended PCI configuration space to support such features as advanced error reporting (AER). This means the size of MMIO space required to map the chipset I/O resources gets larger. Some early PCI Express chipsets confound the issue further by providing coarse granularity for this mapping, which results in a range of 512 MB being carved out for MMIO. This results in customers reporting hidden memory of 512 MB to 768 MB on servers using such chipsets.

The Exchange Product Group tested Exchange 2003 SP1/SP2 on Windows 2003 (/w 834628) with the PAE kernel and on Windows 2003 SP1 with PAE and DEP enabled, and did not find issues related to the PAE kernel or with DEP enabled at either or both the software and hardware level.

Pagefile Settings

So you may wonder what size your pagefile should be and where you should locate it. I found that on pure Exchange 2003 servers and in normal operations, the pagefile is seldom used, and it is perfectly OK to locate the pagefile on the local system disk, which is the default location used by Windows 2000. Unless you have other applications that can cause paging—in which case the proper strategy would be to place several pagefiles of equal size on separate volumes—the DBA scheme in Exchange 2003 will take care of trimming the STORE process working set, which is by far the largest consumer of physical memory, such that no paging activity is caused by Exchange 2003. This is not the first mention of the DBA scheme, and you realize by now that this is an area that deserves attention for proper tuning of the memory usage of Exchange 2003. In 99 percent of the deployments, I recommend letting the DBA do its job of allocating physical memory and expanding the STORE working set (i.e., the number of pages owned by this process in physical memory at any single point in time), as opposed to setting fixed values for the database cache by changing the attributes of the Information Store object located in the Active Directory.

When other applications are running that consume RAM and require pages to be present in physical memory, the DBA will closely monitor the available free bytes in Windows 2000 and trim the database buffer cache to let Windows 2000, in turn, trim the STORE working set and make physical memory available to other applications.

You will be tempted to monitor the memory performance object—more specifically, the pages/sec performance counter. Although this counter gives an indication of paging activity, it does not necessarily represent the pages actually read or written to the pagefile; rather, it represents the pages that needed to be moved in and out of the processes' working sets (for access to a look-aside list of free pages). Therefore, you can expect to have a fairly high page-fault rate on an Exchange server, but very little absent actual pagefile activity: this is because a process may experience a soft page fault (i.e., requesting a page not present in its working set, but not necessarily needing to get this page from the pagefile). As explained in Chapter 6, you should in fact monitor the page reads/sec and page writes/sec counters that do represent the physical disk accesses and can cause memory trashing and low system performance.

Theory calls for setting the size of a pagefile to twice the quantity of RAM available on the server. This setting is valid for small servers running less than 1 GB of RAM but is not correct for large memory servers—at least for servers hosting 4 GB of RAM or more. I recommend setting the pagefile size to at least the amount of RAM that you have available and let Windows 2000 decide to expand the pagefile. To this effect and to avoid filling up the system disk drive, you may allocate an 8-GB software partition to hold the pagefile, located on the system drive, which is typically local to the server.

The RAID level for this partition is not important, but typical deployments will locate the pagefile on the same volume as the boot partition and therefore be hosted on a RAID1 volume.

It is certainly wise to set an initial minimum value to what you think will be the largest quantity of space utilized by the pagefile. You can track the pagefile utilization using performance monitor counters, such as the Paging File\% Usage Peak counter, but that is only useful once you have a running system. You should make sure, however, that the servers are not configured with pagefiles that are too small, which would require them to be extended without your intervention. From a performance viewpoint, this can be a small hit, although quite an infrequent one. Note that you should not attempt to allocate space to the detriment of other system storage requirements, such as the event log. Therefore, careful partitioning of the local system drives is required to allow events to be generated and *never* overwritten (you may lose valuable information related to the events occurring on your server), and, at the same time, to let the pagefile grow to the value needed by the Exchange servers. Creating additional partitions does not necessarily mean locating them on separate physical disks or volumes. In fact, when most servers are now shipping with 36-GB disk drives, there is enough space to create several logical partitions and assign to each partition a particular area of the operating system, such as the log files or the pagefile. Chapter 7, which discusses best practices, gives a sample configuration of partitioning of storage space.

5.3.3   Dealing with Virtual Memory Fragmentation Issues

For the purpose of the Exchange 2000 SP1 Data Center certification, testing was performed by various vendors and Microsoft. Eventually came a problem that never surfaced in the Exchange 5.5 environment: the virtual memory fragmentation.

A high virtual memory fragmentation in an active/active cluster scenario can prevent one cluster node from failing over the Exchange 2003 resources (i.e., the Exchange Virtual Server) to the other active node. Furthermore, the virtual memory can be so fragmented that a STORE virtual memory allocation may fail, causing abrupt termination of the current transaction/thread.

For a better understanding of the level of fragmentation of the virtual address space, four new key counters have been added to the MSExchangeIS performance object; these describe the level of memory fragmentation and are checked and generated every 60 minutes. Note that these counters should also be monitored in standalone server configurations, given that contiguous virtual memory exhaustion has also been noticed in such environments and not necessarily with the Exchange 2003 STORE being at fault.

They are as follows:

- *VM largest block size*: Indicates the size of the largest free memory block. If this size falls below 32 MB, a warning message is generated, and the STORE process is at risk for performing failover operations.

This counter is a line that slopes down as virtual memory is consumed. When this counter drops below 32 MB, Exchange 2003 logs a warning in the event log (Event ID = 9582) and logs an error if this drops below 16 MB. It is important to monitor this counter to ensure that it stays above 32 MB.

- *VM total free blocks*: Indicates the total number of free 4-KB blocks in the STORE process virtual address space. A decrease of the free blocks along with a value narrowing to zero indicates possible subsequent failures. It is then necessary to stop and restart the STORE process (dismounting the databases is not sufficient), or to failover the current node Exchange resource to the other node in the cluster, and failback these same resources after a while. This line forms a pyramid as you monitor it. It starts with one block of virtual memory greater than 16 MB and progresses to smaller blocks greater than 16 MB.

  Monitoring the trend on this counter should allow a system administrator to predict when the number of 16-MB blocks is likely to drop below three, at which point restarting all the services on the node is recommended.

- *VM total 16-MB free blocks*: Indicates the number of 16-MB free blocks. This counter is important because during a failover condition the node to which the Exchange resources are targeted should be able to allocate contiguous memory blocks. This line forms a pyramid as you monitor it. This counter can be used to measure the degree to which available virtual memory is being fragmented. The average block size is the Process\Virtual Bytes\STORE instance divided by MSExchangeIS\VM Total Free Blocks.

- *VM total 16-MB free block bytes*: Indicates the total number of bytes available as chunks of 16 MB. This line slopes down as memory is consumed.

In summary, these counters should be monitored in all cases (and especially in active/active cluster scenarios) to ensure that the failover can happen as reliably as possible. To prevent a failover failure, you must ensure that there are sufficient contiguous memory buffers available to allow the hosting of the resources being failed over.

For example, a failover of one storage group will require, on the other active node:

- One 10-MB contiguous virtual memory chunk;

- Two 8-MB contiguous virtual memory chunks;

- One 5-MB contiguous virtual memory chunk;

- Several 2-MB contiguous virtual memory chunks.

These memory chunks are required to hold critical sections of code and database structures. Failing to allocate these blocks would result in failing to mount databases within the storage group.

In an effort to decrease the likelihood of virtual memory fragmentation, Microsoft worked hard on reducing the possible cause and giving a chance to the Microsoft Exchange STORE but also to the Exchange administrator to gracefully recover from these conditions. In Exchange 2000 SP1, there was an additional buffer that reserved 10 MB of contiguous virtual memory to decrease the possibility of a storage group or database mount failure. However, problems could still occur if the memory was extremely fragmented. With Exchange 2003, there is a mechanism that automatically detects the instance of a 9582 Warning Event and releases a single chunk of 64 MB of contiguous virtual memory previously allocated to the ESE database cache.

This gives some "air" to the STORE process and should provide enough time for the administrator to restart the STORE process for clearing up the virtual memory utilization problems.

In summary, you should keep an eye on these counters and monitor 9582 Warning and Error Events, which indicate that the maximum contiguous virtual address space available is less than 32 MB. A warning should cause the administrator to restart the STORE process as early as convenient (e.g., during off-peak hours). An error would require a restart at once, since users would start noticing message delivery failures or inbound connections dropping.

Note that with Exchange 2003 and Outlook 2003, the effect of restarting the STORE process or of failing over an Exchange Virtual Server from one cluster node to another would be mitigated by the local cache access: only the online connection (foreground) would get dropped, and the users might be minimally impacted, still being able to read, respond to, and delete messages. The impact would typically be seen in delegated environments, as well as nonreplicated public folder access.

5.3.4 **What You Should Remember**

Caching will rely on the data being present "somewhere else" (most likely on disk) and can therefore be "lost" with no catastrophic consequence to the integrity of the data set, regardless of whether it is a file or, in our case, the Exchange 2003 databases. Using a large cache will help the database engine in going less often to the database file, thereby increasing the latency-sensitive read operations and transactions.

Buffering will contain information that is "buffered" into memory, in the hopes of reducing the frequency of access to "slow" I/O devices, such as network or storage devices. The goal is to perform a lower number of larger I/O, which can take advantage of the ever-increasing bandwidth on these I/O devices without stressing the somewhat stable transaction rate capability of the target device, especially in the case of disk drives or logical volumes that are spread over several disk drives.

The Exchange 2003 STORE is not the only consumer of physical memory on a server. The NT cache, part of the I/O subsystem, is extensively used by IIS virtual servers that stream data in and out of Microsoft Exchange. In scenarios where the server performs a lot of file-level operations, you should ensure that the NT cache is properly sized.

5.4 **Network Optimization for Exchange 2003**

This section discusses two types of optimization for Exchange 2003:

- First, there are basic optimizations to be done at the actual, physical network interface card level.

- Second, there are optimizations necessary at the network services level, mostly involving DNS and the Active Directory.

In Chapter 3, we discussed at length the issues of deploying large-scale Active Directories and how best to optimize these deployments. It would be foolish for me to try to cover large-scale Windows Active Directory deployments, since this would probably require two volumes as large as this one. Instead, you should grasp the key principles of your network services and understand how to best adapt your deployment to match these principles.

5.4.1 Network Interface Optimizations: Interrupts

There is not much to be done on the network side of things, other than making sure that data flows in and out of the server easily. Some network adapters will cause many interrupts, which can be disruptive to the overall performance. During a network-intensive period, some adapters will batch interrupts together, which optimizes system performance. However, whenever the adapter doesn't implement that feature, it may be appropriate, in an SMP environment, to dedicate a processor for handling those interrupts.

This technique is called *interrupt-affinity* and can be enabled using the interrupt-affinity filter called Intfltr.exe from Microsoft. This tool binds selected device interrupts to one or more chosen processors and helps performance as well as scalability and partitioning on large computers.

You will have probably noticed that resource partitioning tools from Microsoft and partner companies mainly deal with CPU and memory partitioning, but not at the I/O level. This is quite a missing piece; however, you can do fairly static partitioning by binding interrupts to certain processors, which would have to be the same processors handling the process that needs to deal with these interrupts. In Exchange 2003, the deal is simple: if you use CPU affinity on the INETINFO process, you need to use interrupt affinity on the same processors as INETINFO. Be careful, however; failing to do so would result in an overhead of context switching between processors, decreasing the overall ability of the server to run user mode, and thus having it run in privileged mode, which bears no advantage for delivering messages and processing user transactions.

Aside from binding network card interrupts to particular processors, you also have the ability with Exchange 2003 to bind IIS virtual servers to particular IP addresses, which in turn are bound to particular network interface cards. This is a great advantage in Internet service provider–type deployments, such that you may consolidate your services (IMAP, POP, SMTP), yet be able to scale up by tunneling traffic and interrupt handling to particular processors.

You may be thinking as you read those lines, "How much of this do I have to do in reality?" Not much, believe me. Most deployments that support fewer than 10,000 users per machine do not need any of this obscure tweaking. You are much better off with simple configurations that can be easily maintained rather than complex configurations that are not known to all of your support staff.

Badly handled, such setups could cause havoc, service downtime, and user frustration.

5.4.2 Bandwidth and Latency Optimization

Of course, in any kind of scalable Exchange 2003 implementation, network bandwidth plays a large role in determining how many users can be hosted on a large server farm. In centralized implementations of Exchange 2003, you will need to determine the bandwidth utilized by your users. Many figures have been given for the required bandwidth, which depends on the type of Exchange client in use. Overall, between 2 Kb/s and 4 Kb/s is what's required per active user with a medium user load. But what is a medium user load, and how well does it match your environment?

Ideally, you should track your user profile patterns and attempt to categorize them; after close monitoring of the server's activities, you should be able to define the most appropriate configurations. I know this is not an easy task, and I know that very often we are confined to basic facts or guesstimates for determining the best configuration. Don't assume, for instance, that HTTP traffic is lighter than MAPI traffic. I have found that MAPI clients behave much better than HTTP clients in terms of bandwidth usage with pre-Exchange 2003 releases. In fact, a combination of the Exchange 2003 and Outlook 2003 release will deliver quite a lot of savings in the way data transfers back and forth between the server and in terms of user interaction, given that the Outlook 2003 cache mode will insulate the user from network conditions in most situations.

With Exchange 2003 and Outlook Web Access, and the support of GZIP (the HTTP compression option for data streams, well hidden behind the enabling of forms-based authentication), you may significantly reduce your traffic, even though the Outlook Web Access interface of Exchange 2003 is very close to the rich user experience of Outlook 2003.

On the other hand, the openness of the Exchange 2003 architecture—and more specifically of the Exchange store—gives you ample opportunities to define new interfaces to your Exchange 2003 service for a bandwidth-constrained environment. These can range from mobile clients that you use from PDAs over cellular communication links to enhanced clients that can be used within the comfortable areas of local connectivity in your enterprise offices.

Don't forget, however, that bandwidth is not everything; latency can be a real killer. Take the example of a petroleum company, which does not choose where oil is to be found. The companies sometimes have to search in the wildest environments, and even though you can get a fairly good satellite link at 128 Kb/s and above, the latency incurred by the satellite link (which can exceed 2 sec) can be a killer for certain types of clients.

Don't bury MAPI RPC just yet; with the advent of Exchange 2003 RPC/HTTP mode usable with Outlook 2003 and the cache mode introduced with that very same release of Microsoft Outlook, great mobility and consolidation can be realized without the expense of high latencies.

Some clients will definitely work well in such environments because parallelizing data transfer is possible, something that is not always feasible with straight TCP/IP traffic using HTTP, IMAP, or POP.

Server Bandwidth

To increase your server bandwidth capacity, you can use several network adapters. Then, you can either partition your service by binding the virtual server to each adapter, or you can *team* the adapters together to create a single virtual adapter using several network interface cards. I found that network adapter teaming is a good solution—one that provides a transparent and reliable means of scaling the network capacity of a server. Be careful, however, of the compatibility requirements as well as of the actual server and operating system's interactions.

Nevertheless, even a 100-Mb/s link is quite enough to bear the load of 5,000 very active users, which is plenty to locate on a single server. Ultimately, the bandwidth issue comes up certainly not at the actual server level but more at the client level, and that can vary from implementation to implementation.

With the rollout of network-attached storage in the Windows infrastructure, you should also consider that it is not only the clients that communicate with the server over the data network. Utilization of NAS's SMB shares or iSCSI targets for Microsoft Exchange storage (possible, respectively, with Exchange 2003 and Windows Storage Server 2003 Feature Pack) puts a new burden on the data network, sometimes in such a way that you will need to further optimize your data network infrastructure for proper throughput and security.

5.4.3   Network Services Optimization: DNS

DNS is queried frequently to resolve host names for routing messages inside and outside an Exchange 2003 organization. Typically, although the DNS services are co-hosted on Windows Active Directory domain controllers and GC servers, access to these services can be configured such that there is a primary and a secondary DNS server used to resolve network names. You can define additional DNS servers, but the simplification of your infrastructure should aim at having one primary, local DNS server to the Exchange 2003 server, and a central secondary DNS server to resolve names that could not be resolved by the primary DNS server. The secondary server can be used when the primary server is unavailable. Note that if the primary DNS server is down, there is a good chance that other services will be affected, including the Active Directory service and the network services used by the client computers of the local site. Consequently, you should ensure monitoring and availability by using high-quality hardware to help the resolution.

In some situations, DNS is not implemented as part of the Windows infrastructure but on other platforms (UNIX is very common), because DNS represents core networking services that span way beyond the actual Windows 2000 infrastructure. Deploying Exchange 2003 and Windows 2000 on non-Microsoft DNSs is a fairly easy and common task. This is bound to work, provided that the DNS service can support servers to dynamically register themselves to DNS (dynamic updates), can use service records (SRV records), and support zones that start with the underscore character.

For certain configurations, such as front-end servers sitting in DMZs of firewall configurations, it may be appropriate to use a local hosts file that defines the key Active Directory servers and Exchange 2000 servers with which the front-end servers will need to interact. In such situations, the DNS service proposed in the DMZ (and exposed to the Internet) contains only a subset of the hosts defined in an enterprise (to avoid revealing the internal infrastructure of the enterprise).

Front-end servers directly exposed to the Internet have a reduced number of hosts defined in their local hosts configuration file (which is a simple ASCII file that contains mappings between fully qualified domain names and IP addresses). The alternative is to use a split-brain DNS approach, where the DNS server hosts the infrastructure names separately from the general Internet naming.

5.4.4 Network Services Optimization: Active Directory

Active Directory servers can either be domain controllers or GC servers. Microsoft Exchange 2003 expects local connectivity to a domain controller in order to retrieve its configuration information located in the configuration naming context of the Active Directory, and local connectivity to one or more GC servers for resolving user addresses and for determining the user's home server, represented as a combination of a server name, a storage group name, and a database name.

I attempted to deploy an Exchange 2003 server with WAN connectivity to GCs inside HP's network, and the result was pitiful. Any network glitch or unavailability of the GC could result in messages not being able to be delivered and client computers unable to resolve their mailbox locations and/or to resolve names and browse from the Global Address List that was provided by the GCs. With the introduction of Outlook 2003 in cached mode, and the ability to upload offline versions of the address book, it now becomes possible to deploy domain controllers and GC servers in close proximity of the Microsoft Exchange servers and not necessarily close to the client machines. This, however, does put a fairly big dependency upon the data network, from a user authentication viewpoint. In a Microsoft Exchange infrastructure consolidation, however, you will need the Windows Active Directory infrastructure to be in close connectivity to the Microsoft Exchange servers and not necessarily to the end users.

In all situations using an Exchange 2003 server, you should try to collocate on the same LAN one or more GCs from the Active Directory. Also ensure that replication of the Active Directory (and of the group policy objects, which perform by means of the file replications services of the SYSVOL [SYSVOL is a pre-defined system area used by Windows services, in particular the Active Directory] share) is solid and working perfectly. Until this is the case, you can be sure that you will be finding all sorts of problems, ranging from undeliverable mail messages, to stuck Exchange 2003 MTA (both X.400 and SMTP MTAs), and user frustration, which is the last thing you want when introducing a new technology such as Exchange 2003.

How Many Global Catalog Servers per Microsoft Exchange Server?

There has been, since the introduction of Exchange 2000, a general rule of deploying GC servers on a 1:4 ratio with Microsoft Exchange servers (i.e., one GC server for four Exchange servers).

This rule typically works when the servers are of the same capacity/architecture (e.g., dual processors). However, with the general adoption of four-processor servers for Microsoft Exchange on one hand, and the scale-out capability of Windows Active Directory on the other hand, I have seen some unbalance and some incoherencies on how to properly supply Windows Active Directory service to Microsoft Exchange.

First, it is important to realize that while the Windows Active Directory can perform a lot of functions in a Windows infrastructure, it is essentially to the well being of Microsoft Exchange. A customer of mine once mentioned that "when Windows Active Directory sneezes, Microsoft Exchange coughs," and this is about right. A slight glitch in Active Directory (replication, unavailability, incorrect topology) can cause Microsoft Exchange to simply stop functioning, and debugging this type of problems is quite painful.

Second, in the high-end (data center) deployments, Microsoft Exchange servers tend to be deployed on four-way servers and GC servers on two-way. Don't ask me why; this is what we typically find.

Third, the actual throughput (call it MegaFLOPS, MIPS, or whichever way you wish to describe how fast a CPU goes) of a server does not linearly depend upon the clock speed. In other words, a 3-GHz Xeon processor is not necessarily twice as fast as a 1.5-GHz XeonMP. The instruction execution capability of a processor goes a long way beyond the megacycles you can find. Eventually, the gradual adoption of 64-bit capable servers in the Windows Server 2003 infrastructures, and Windows Active Directory in particular, will render obsolete such a requirement, due to the massive scalability improvements brought by 64-bit computing mode of Windows Active Directory servers.

Because of these points, some have been tempted to apply the 1:4 rule not only to the processors, but also to the megacycles available. I think this is very incorrect. It might be useful as an initial estimate, but it bears no credible or reliable scientific value for proper sizing of Windows Active Directory services for Microsoft Exchange.

With this in mind, you should be very careful when you deploy Windows Active Directory for Microsoft Exchange, especially when sizing servers: there have been improvements between Exchange 2000 and Exchange 2003 SP1 that cause different pattern of access modes between the two environments. Furthermore, the role of the Microsoft Exchange server can largely vary the assigned workload. Most of the accesses will be done by the Exchange categorizer (looking up where a message should be delivered) on one hand, and from the clients on the other hand, unless … they use Outlook 2003 in cached mode, where GAL lookups are typically done against the OAB (the Exchange Offline Address Book).

In short, there is no ground rule, no magic, no straight line—rather, a fine line and a clear understanding that must be set between the Microsoft Exchange and the Windows Active Directory operations staffs such that in case they point to different groups, there is an effective collaboration and mutual understanding of each other's requirements.

DSACCESS Optimization

DSACCESS is a systemwide shared component that performs Active Directory lookups and modifications. DSACCESS is utilized by many services, including the INETINFO process that hosts the Exchange 2003 Virtual Server running Internet protocols and the STORE process that performs local message delivery and handling. Microsoft Knowledge Base article 298879 describes the interesting behavior of the Exchange 2003 server trying to access the forest PDC (Primary Domain Controller) emulator. The PDC emulator is a forestwide role and should not be utilized by Exchange 2003 for directory lookups. Exchange 2003 SP1 introduces a new registry setting that lets you define the number of alternative domain controllers that should be used to retrieve configuration information before hitting the PDC emulator in the forest.

This is certainly not the smallest issue. DSACCESS was designed to be able to load balance requests across as many as seven GCs. Experience has shown that with the initial release of Microsoft Exchange 2000, if one GC was responding fast enough (within five seconds), this server was constantly hammered by the Exchange server, causing a potential bottleneck for message delivery and proxy GAL lookups.

With Exchange 2000 SP1, this interval has been reduced from five seconds to two seconds, thereby making more GCs available to service synchronous LDAP requests for routing and delivering mail messages, increasing the overall transaction throughput within Microsoft Exchange and especially the SMTP MTA Categorizer. Later on, with Exchange 2000 SP2, the DSACCESS module was entirely reviewed and optimized, and much more flexibility is allowed between Microsoft Exchange and the Windows Active Directory services. The improvements, implemented up to the Exchange 2003 SP1 release, include the following:

- Use of a user-entry cache size of 140 MB (changed from the default 25 MB). This cache size should hold approximately 80,000 entries.

- Use of a configuration cache size of 5 MB (changed from the default 25 MB).

- Ability to connect to up to 200 GC servers.

■ Exposure of Windows Active Directory usage from Exchange System Manager.

It is possible to tune the DSACCESS cache by means of the registry settings; however, you should understand that growing the cache will "eat" on the STORE virtual memory, subject to fragmentation. We have experienced one case where changing the cache size of the DSACCESS module on a Microsoft Exchange server immediately caused virtual memory fragmentation issues to occur: the consequences are much worse in that case than slow Windows Active Directory response time.

In short, I strongly recommend that you deploy GCs within LAN connectivity (>10 Mb/s, less than 10 ms latency) to your Exchange 2003 servers. In hub sites that concentrate message routing, more than one GC should be defined, and each of these GCs should be tuned to serve requests as fast as possible.

Fast Global Catalog Service

Designing a reliable GC service to Exchange 2003 is a fairly trivial task because of multimaster replication of the Active Directory. Designing a high-performance GC service is another ball game. You basically have to make sure that the Active Directory server has ample CPU and memory to be able to cache the Active Directory database (which uses ESENT, a variant of Exchange's core database engine for its storage groups).

Now, because Windows Active Directory servers use the ESENT database engine, they will benefit from the very same improvement when running of servers with 2-GB RAM and booted with the /3GB switch: the database cache can grow and end up to be very efficient, given that approximately 90 percent of the workload to an NTDS.DIT Active Directory database is read operations. This is an example of very simple optimization (ensuring 2 GB of RAM in the server and adding the /3GB boot switch) that can decrease to 20 to 30 percent the I/O workload on the Active Directory database, therefore improving the overall LDAP query response time.

I highly recommend equipping two or three GC servers with 2 GB or more for servicing a population of 10,000 users and locating the NTDS.DIT Active Directory database file on a multiple spindle RAID0+1 volume, such that many random concurrent I/O to the Active Directory database can be performed in parallel with minimal response time.

The CPU should be rather fast (2 GHz or higher); the L2 cache, important for small CPU, should be set to 1 MB or 2 MB, although this is not a prime prerequisite. A 256-KB or 512-KB L2 cache used by a 1-GHz or more CPU would be totally acceptable to perform directory lookups and validation of user credentials. Do not try to scale up your Windows Active Directory servers unless you have particular requirements on limiting the number of GC servers. If this is the case, using Windows Server 2003 64-bit Edition on Itanium platforms and 8 GB to 16 GB of RAM can prove to be quite useful; however, I do not have cost/transaction benefit information to share with you at this point. Just keep in mind that this is a possibility.

A one-million-users ISP-type service—with 10 percent of the users connecting during peak hours—can fully utilize a 12-disk RAID0+1 volume to bear the load applied on the NTDS.DIT Active Directory database. Your mileage may vary, because other background services can come into play—for example, the replication of the Active Directory, which does not take precedence over the authentication requests but must happen at some point in time. This background activity should not disturb the more important and user-visible transactions (e.g., the credentials validation and the user's mail drop lookup). Looking up the Active Directory for switching messages around is not so much of an issue but should not be overlooked. Don't forget that as an Exchange administrator, you will need to maintain a certain level of service and the ability to quickly deliver messages; although this is not directly visible from the end users (except maybe by the paranoid types who use delivery receipt notifications), it is a serious service concern that you must be able to report on. Most important, you must be able to guarantee that level to your business units if you intend to give a business advantage to your company by running a sleek messaging network.

In Summary

Sizing Windows Active Directory for Microsoft Exchange has many facets, and there is no single answer to each situation. You should refer to Chapter 7 for best practices and sample configurations of high-end environments. The key rule to remember is that Microsoft Exchange is significantly dependant upon the Windows Active Directory. At the same time, its workload against the GC servers (for the most cases) is not innocuous, and you should seriously think about proper provisioning of Windows Active Directory services to Microsoft Exchange servers. Avoid at all costs (!) the provisioning of Windows Active Directory services across the WAN: if you are short on servers at a remote branch office where you need to place a lightly loaded Microsoft Exchange server, consider a co-hosting scenario, using the same machine for both services, either in the same operating system instance or having the Windows Active Directory server running as part of a virtual server.

The most complex environments where I have seen the best Windows Active Directory service provided have been where the Windows Active Directory architecture, administration, and operations staff was either the same or sitting closely to the Microsoft Exchange infrastructure team. However, in some scenarios, such as the burning topic of IT outsourcing, an company might want to outsource its Microsoft Exchange environment while keeping the ownership of the Windows Active Directory environment. This is by far the most complex case to deal with, and, as an outsourcer (or a customer), you should seriously envisage the utilization of a dedicated resource forest for Microsoft Exchange, ensuring that the Exchange infrastructure has ample control over the Windows Active Directory deployment and minimizing the dependencies. This is not the simplest system to design and implement, but it has been done before, it works, and it can deliver the value you can expect for most kinds of Microsoft Exchange deployments: rock-solid and never-failing Windows Active Directory service for Exchange components!

5.5 Storage Optimization for Exchange 2003

Optimizing the storage in Exchange 2003 will yield noticeable benefits quite rapidly. Storage tuning has always been one of my favorite part-time fun activities because it deals with very simple elements that haven't greatly evolved during the past few years. Given the improvements in CPU processing and the cheap cost of such components as network adapters and memory, storage, an ever-growing asset to any company, is not the most obvious matter to address if you intend to provide the highest levels of performance at the most reasonable price, let alone the utmost availability and protection.

With Microsoft Exchange 4.0, disks were 2.1 GB in size, and the maximum number of production users you could host on a particular server was severely limited by the size of the Information Store—16 GB; approximately 300 to 500 was the upper limit on the number of users you would host on a single Microsoft Exchange server, with mailboxes hardly reaching out beyond 20 MB. With Exchange 5.0 and subsequent releases, the store database could grow virtually unlimited, and so could your maintenance tasks and troubles if you were not careful enough. While hosting more that 300 users per server was in fact seldom observed, it contributed to the multiplication (proliferation by today's standards?) of Exchange servers in Microsoft Exchange Organizations.

Today, in 2006, disks are becoming denser. You can store several terabytes of data within a cubic meter, but is it the quantity or the actual performance that should be your concern?

When disk vendors announce a 470-GB disk drive, do you think that this disk drive would perform as well as a 15,000-rpm 36-GB drive? The answer is *no* because of the drive mechanics and magnetic encoding of data. That has led me to recommend to my customers that they use configurations that favor the number of spindles over the actual storage capacity.

Customers have deployed 146-GB disk drives and have seen their benchmarks and performance tests fail miserably because of the inability of the system to cope with the high request rate, known as I/O per second (IOPS), imposed by many concurrent users issuing a growing number of transactions, with each of these transactions containing a growing amount of information.

Ultimately, you should tune your storage subsystem such that you can turn an I/O-bound application, like Exchange 2003, into a CPU-bound application. In short, you remove storage bottlenecks and move them to other components—generally, CPU or network. Tests performed in labs have shown—in a configuration in which system, memory, and network bottlenecks had been eliminated—that storage optimization was showing a *direct* impact on the overall Exchange 2003 performance.

This is the most critical component to tune for Exchange 2003. Bearing in mind that performance is only one part of the equation, this can lead to many choices, many options, and, often, tradeoffs in terms of performance, availability, and of course, cost.

In this section, we are going to look into the topics that matter, those that will make a difference as you design your server, with a constant focus on business requirements. Availability (i.e., the ability to recover large quantities of data within the best time frame) is a common need. Granted, the Microsoft VSS from the Windows Server 2003 storage framework greatly helps in these recovery situations, although this is not necessarily the only or best or most cost-effective approach.

5.5.1 Windows Partitions Design Guidelines

When providing storage resources for Exchange 2003, you ultimately need to create Windows partitions, using Logical Disk Manager, DISKPART, or any other volume management tool, such that the partition can be formatted using the NTFS file system and later on used by Microsoft Exchange.

There is no real mandatory requirement for Exchange 2003 to use NTFS: if you wish, you may use another file system (e.g., VERITAS Filesystem for Windows, part of its Storage Foundation suite of products), provided you are confident with it and that it delivers notable difference from NTFS.

The fact is that in case of a data recovery situation, and possible escalation to Microsoft, the simpler your storage infrastructure, the easier and faster the call handling and resolution will be. For this reason, it is quite common to promote the use of NTFS partitions created from Windows basic disks instead of using host-based volume management, be it from Windows or third-party providers such as VERITAS.

There is, once you have made the call on using NTFS, little that needs to be tuned. Two parameters are somewhat relevant:

- Allocation unit size: This defines the quantity of bytes that are allocated at minimum when creating or extending a file on NTFS. The allocation unit default size is 4 KB, and many server deployments have been done with this setting, with little notable impact to performance. Some storage vendors, such as EMC, might require you to format the partition accordingly with low-level disk sector parameters (e.g., 32 KB). I don't think it's much of an influence, given that very little extents are built for Microsoft Exchange databases once you get the database size to stabilize over time.

- Partition offset: A Windows partition typically starts at 63 KB from the beginning of the physical; these 63 KB are used for the master boot record (MBR) of the physical disk unit. Because Microsoft Exchange databases' I/O are multiples of 4 KB (the database page size), there can be an advantage in aligning the Windows partition to the sector boundaries of the underlying disk subsystem: you can use DISKPAR (without the "T") from the Windows resource kit to create a partition that is exactly aligned to a pleasant offset from the storage subsystem viewpoint, such as 64 KB (or 128 KB if you wish). You basically want to make the offset a 4-KB multiple.

These particular settings matter only for those arrays and workloads where a sector change can be a performance difference. We have found that sequential workloads are the ones that benefit the most from these configuration aspects. In the case of Microsoft Exchange, this concerns primarily backup and recovery operations. The purely random access to the databases and the varying I/O size to the sequential logging do not get any major performance boost. You may verify this using storage performance optimization tools (see Chapter 6).

Changing the allocation unit size and the partition offset is data destructive: therefore, if you plan to modify existing deployments, you will have a good opportunity to actually exercise your backup and recovery plans. Otherwise, it's a good practice to include these changes in the new server builds, though, without expecting any *major* impact to the performance of the system.

Always consult your storage provider before choosing a particular allocation unit size and partition offset. You will find that default settings have worked so far, and there is little that proves that they wouldn't continue to work for most deployments. Only extreme high-performance and scaled up cases need this kind of consideration.

Windows Server 2003 SP1 will include the partition alignment functionality in DISKPART. Prior to this version of Windows, you will find DISKPART shipping with Windows Server 2003 (using the VDS framework) and part of the resource kit for Windows 2000. DISKPAR, on the other hand, ships part of the resource kit with all versions of Windows (pre–2003 SP1).

Figure 5.11
Using DISKPAR

```
C:\Documents and Settings\bijaoui>diskpar -s
Usage: diskpar [ -i | -s ] DriveNumber
   -i: query drive layout and partition information
   -s: set partition information (only used on raw drive please)

C:\Documents and Settings\bijaoui>diskpar -s 3
Set partition can only be done on a raw drive.
You can use Disk Manager to delete all existing partitions
Are you sure drive 3 is a raw device without any partition? (Y/N) y

----- Drive 3 Geometry Infomation -----
Cylinders = 2610
TracksPerCylinder = 255
SectorsPerTrack = 63
BytesPerSector = 512
DiskSize = 21467980800 (Bytes) = 20473 (MB)

We are going to set the new disk partition.
All data on this drive will be lost. continue (Y/N)? y

Please specify starting offset (in sectors): 64
Please specify partition length (in MB) (Max = 20473): 20473

Done setting partition.
----- New Partition information -----
StatringOffset = 32768
PartitionLength = 21467496448
HiddenSectors = 64
PartitionNumber = 1
PartitionType = 7

You now should use Disk Manager to format this partition

C:\Documents and Settings\bijaoui>_
```

Letters or Mount Points?

Introduced with Windows 2000, it is possible to overcome the limitations of 24 drive letters for general storage units (A:\ and B:\ being reserved for floppy drives for historical reasons) by "attaching" logical units to empty folders. These are known as the *mount points*. This feature is particularly important in an environment where you decide to handle many small logical units. Unfortunately, mount points were not supported in Windows 2000 clusters—this support only got introduced with Windows Server 2003. Further dependencies can exist when using storage management software such as the following:

- Volume management;

- Path management;

- VSS providers and requestors.

I am not very found of mount points just for the sake of it. Apart from the need to use many LUNs (more than 24, which is to be justified on its own), there is a clear advantage in using mount points in the context of scale-up and scale-down deployments. If you were to expect that *all* your servers would have the same drive and folder arrangement, regardless of whether they host 50, 500, or 5,000 users, you could conceive the following scheme (this was implemented to some customers):

- 50 user servers: With two storage groups, use drive D: for storage group 1 logs and drive E: for storage group 1 databases; create databases in folders database1, databases2, and so forth.

- 500 user servers: With two storage groups, use drive D: for storage group 1 logs and drive E: for storage group 1 databases; create database in *folder* database1 and *mount point* database2. Each mount point actually points to the same LUN (a LUN may be accessed by several paths).

- 5,000 user servers: With two storage groups, use drive D: for storage group 1 logs and drive E: for storage group 1 databases; create database in *mount point* database1 and *mount point* database2. Each mount point points to two separate LUNs.

Repeat the operation for each storage group! The net result is that storage group 1 logs are *always* on drive D: and databases are *always* on drive E:, regardless of the I/O per second and capacity requirements. In the 50-user server, this is supported by two drives (D:\ and E:\). In the 500-user server, this is supported by three drives (D:\, E:\, and E:\database1 & E:\database2). In the 5,000-user server, this is supported by four drives (D:\, E:\, E:\database1, and E:\database2). Although the folder structure looks exactly the same, the underlying logical unit used, and possibly the physical implementation, largely differ!

In Summary

Use basic disk partitions for each of the volumes that you present to host Microsoft Exchange data (storage groups in particular): any recovery or maintenance operation will be largely improved; besides there is little requirement with modern storage arrays to perform host-based mirroring or stripping.

From these basic disks (in the Windows Server terminology sense), align partitions on 64-KB offsets for new servers and leave existing servers alone. There is little benefit in reworking existing servers, generating downtime and possible instability. If you do create new partitions, use an allocation unit size of 4 KB, unless instructed otherwise by your storage vendor. Mount points are nice, but they must be used with care for preventing confusion to your operations staff and avoiding possible conflicts with third-party storage management applications.

5.5.2   Storage Groups

Microsoft has addressed the rapid growth of data by proposing to host large amounts of information partitioned in manageable chunks—the storage groups.

While deploying large Microsoft Exchange infrastructures, we quickly realized that particular care had to be brought to the storage component of Microsoft Exchange—more specifically, to the database store. The store is composed, in Exchange 5.5, of a monolithic database, which enables storage optimization by means of the single instance store but uncovers serious operations issues when it comes to growing the information located in Exchange (which typically doubles every year) and managing a single multi-hundred gigabytes file. There are such instances of Exchange 5.5 and Exchange 2000 databases, and while Microsoft unlimited the size of the database, they also unlimited the amount of pain you would have to go through in any kind of recovery or database maintenance operation.

We covered storage groups at length while describing the Microsoft Exchange 200x architecture in Chapters 1 and 2. Deploying storage groups is an issue that administrators have to deal with in Exchange 2000 and Exchange 2003, whereas Exchange 5.5 administrators and architects didn't have to worry too much about the actual database, other than its maximum size.

Before creating a new storage group, administrators have to realize the actual implications: the loss of single instance store can potentially increase the overall space required and the need to manage an additional set of transaction logs required for the additional ESE instance loaded by the store. On the other hand, the ability to split the Information Store into multiple databases gives better control over maintaining the individual database sizes. The ability to split multiple streams of transaction logging across several LUNs, presumably located on separate physical elements, can be appropriate in, for example, replicated scenarios.

The "Wunsch method" (named after an Exchange administrator at one of my customer sites) is based on the determination that users were allocated to databases based on their mailbox quota. As the user mailbox quota requirement grows, the Wunsch method commands the moving of the user to a database that allows for larger quotas. To maintain the size of the database, the number of users with larger quotas will be inferior to the number of users with smaller quotas on another database. This method does not help the single instance ratio, but it does keep the individual database sizes under control. This is a very valid approach, when there is no real rationale for dispatching users' mailboxes on several databases, because it focuses on the operational aspects of the end result rather than trying to group users that work together on their own databases and possibly running into unbalanced configurations (from both capacity and transaction rate capabilities).

This method carries further importance when you consider that even though the maximum database size is virtually unlimited with the Enterprise Edition of Microsoft Exchange, the practical limit nowadays is around 80 GB to 100 GB, regardless of the instant recovery capabilities brought by the Windows Server 2003 VSS framework and Exchange 2003's specific support for this framework.

You may also decide to separate users across databases based on the journaling requirements: because journaling is enabled or disabled at the database level, if you wish to have a group of users' email handled using

Microsoft Exchange's journaling method, the best approach is to group these users into a given database, designed for journaling purposes. The actual recipient of the journaling does not need to be hosted on the same database or server. In fact, in high-end environments, journaling is best implemented on dedicated servers.

There are several aspects to consider when you want to optimize your storage. First, you need to know the I/O pattern that the application generates.

In the case of Exchange 2003, it can be several kinds of these patterns at a single point in time. Next, you tune the storage volumes according to the I/O pattern to best service the requesting component. In other words, you will want to keep up with the workload imposed on the storage backend and provide, beyond a high request (I/O) or data (MB) rate, a good response time for these operations to the disk media.

Transaction Log Files and Databases

As you configure your storage groups, you need to take care of two key storage areas for your databases:

- The location of the transaction log files;
- The location of the databases.

In this example, Microsoft Exchange JOHN has one storage group, with one drive for logs (E:\) and one drive for all databases in that storage group (F:\). In addition, we define a particular drive for the SMTP mailroot temporary files (S:\). The same is defined for PAUL (it is usually a good idea, in any kind of deployment, to use a consistent drive assignation across *all* servers, whether they are small-, medium-, or high-capacity servers).

As explained previously, introducing storage groups in Exchange 2000 has brought a lot of new options and flexibility in configuring high-end servers that are intended to serve a large quantity of data, but these extra options can also lead to bad choices.

In this section, we focus on the transaction log files. Transaction logs, as explained in Chapter 1, which deals with Microsoft Exchange 200x architectures, contain the modifications made to the database pages, which are 4 KB in size.

Does it mean that a transaction is 4 KB in size? Not necessarily; it can actually be as small as 512 bytes if the data to be modified is small enough

Figure 5.12
*Exchange and
main storage
locations*

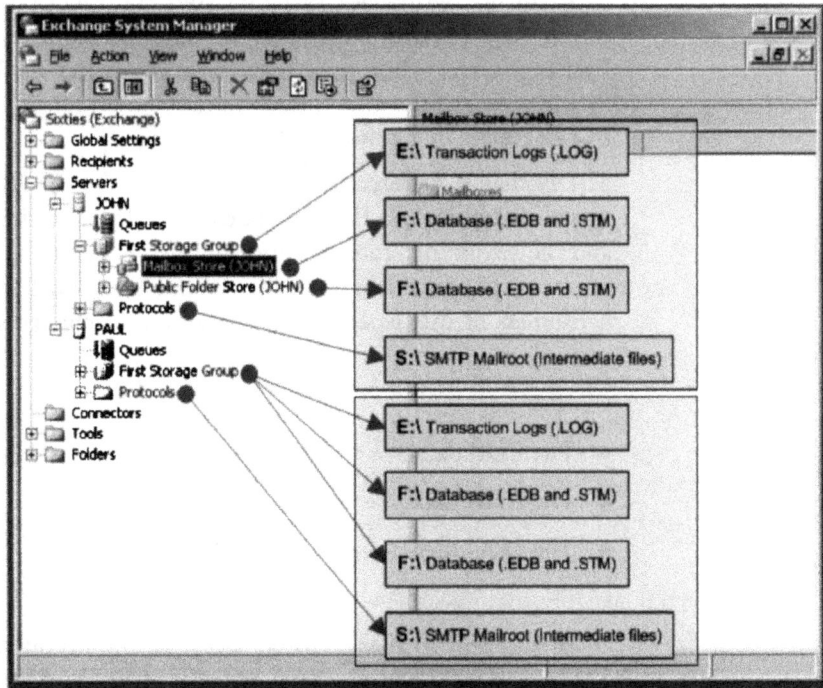

(for instance, incrementing the unread counter in a folder table). The 512-bytes figure is picked from the default sector size of a disk drive. It could have been larger, and it might be increased in a further release of Microsoft Exchange, but if you just want to delete a particular page from a database, you will not have an awful lot of data information to transmit.

Because writing to the transaction log file directly sits on the critical path of a user (or back-end) transaction, if this operation should be abnormally slow (I'll return later to how fast it can or should be), the overall system throughput and response time perception will be affected. To this effect, and since the first days of Microsoft Exchange, it has been a generally well-accepted practice to locate the transaction log files on a separate volume, thereby focusing single-threaded, sequential I/O traffic on a single volume, helping to reduce the response time of the transaction. And this approach does work; whereas a regular disk drive will issue a random I/O of between 12 ms and 15 ms (20 ms is considered an acceptable response time as you reach toward the capability of a single disk drive—i.e., 180 I/O per second), a sequential I/O transfer will actually result in response between 5 ms and 6 ms.

If you use write-back cache on your controller (and you should), you can achieve beyond 1-ms response time for sequential I/O, which your Exchange server—but, most important, your users—will greatly appreciate.

I/O Patterns in Exchange 2003

The Exchange architecture revolves around the STORE and side components, which use the JET database engine for accessing the property store and the streaming store. Additionally, access to the STORE is possible by means of the installable file system, and IIS virtual servers are the prime consumers of this particular interface. The Exchange store uses three distinct file areas:

- The EDB database (property store);
- The STM database (streaming store);
- The LOG files (transaction logs).

In addition to the Exchange store, an important source of I/O is the SMTP server. When messages are relayed by the SMTP engine, they are first stored on disk in an NTFS folder and can quickly become a bottleneck or point of possible improvement. This storage is for a very small period of time while messages are in transit, yet it can become relevant in the case of important interserver message traffic. This traffic can be assimilated to file-share operations for several reasons. First, it originates from the network. When data is obtained from the network packet, it transits through the NT I/O cache. When it has to be written to disk, the data is indeed written directly (i.e., there is no host-based caching mechanism), but it is retained in the cache; the file handle—and, if at all possible, the file content—is kept in NT kernel cache memory. When the SMTP server transfers information further, either for local or remote delivery after the categorization process, it will read the file back from the NT cache: from the point of view of the disk volume hosting the SMTP NTFS queue, there is no particular I/O done at this point.

The type of load on the disk subsystem depends very much on whether the STORE is writing or reading. When information is stored to Microsoft Exchange, it has to be written in the form of transactions in the current transaction log file. Transaction records are processed sequentially, and there is only one current transaction log file per storage group. Even if you have multiple databases inside a given storage group, there will always be one thread that will write sequentially to the log file, with possibly interleaved transactions (to different databases of that storage group) in the stream of records. There is one exception to this process, and that is when data is received from the IIS virtual servers: the information is written in the form of a simple file in the Exchange IFS, and when the transaction is actually committed, that file is read back from the IFS (and it most likely already resides in the NT cache) and logged in the transaction log file(s).

The flush of transaction records happens when a particular calling thread in the store is committing changes into the database or when there are not enough free log buffers. Don't forget that while you may increase the buffer size to very large values, a point will come when the user transactions will require being committed into the database, and that operation occurs synchronously (i.e., the user has an hourglass instead of an arrow pointer). If your storage subsystem is too slow, whatever the size of the buffer space, and if the time to flush the transactions is too long, users will perceive low system response time and will start complaining.

The database buffer space plays an important role in any transaction performed. This space is divided into three major areas. First, there is a main database cache area, which contains pages that have been read recently and modified pages resulting from transactions. Second, there is the transaction log buffer area, where the page modifications, which make up a transaction, are stored. There is one log buffer per database instance. Third, there is the version store. It contains the original version of pages that are in the process of being modified as part of a transaction. Why do you need a version store? Well, if your transaction doesn't complete for some reason, you may want to revert to the state of the database as it was before the transaction started. In essence, you want a certain level of "atomicity" in your database.

Pages could be modified in the version store and then applied in main memory. However, since transactions complete 99.999 percent of the time, it is more efficient to make the modifications in the main cache area (because that is where the modification will eventually end up) and to keep track of the original page in a specific area of the database buffer cache—the version store.

When a modification is made to the database, the following happens in sequence:

- The calling thread starts the transaction, which is made of one or more page modifications.

- The first page to be modified is done in main memory (the original is saved in version store).

- The first modification gets written to the transaction log buffer.

- The second page is modified in main memory (the original is saved in version store).

- The second modification is written to the transaction log buffer.

- . . . <more page modifications>.

- The calling thread commits (wait).

- Transaction log buffers are written to the log file sequentially, one after the other.

- The calling thread resumes execution (the commit is accepted).

- The version store is purged from original pages. Modified pages are flushed later by the lazy writer.

Prior to Exchange 2000, the lazy writer was running every 30 seconds or so. That could result in a burst of activity, which multispindle volumes can handle, but it can badly hurt the performance of synchronous read operations, each being requested by a client and, therefore, a user. With Exchange 2003, the modified pages are flushed as the checkpoint advances, which depends mostly on the number of outstanding transactions and the checkpoint depth. Having a large checkpoint depth helps in having less frequent access to the database; however, too many outstanding dirty pages can cause a long time for an Exchange Virtual Server failover or for shutting down the STORE process or dismounting a database.

There is no such thing as a time interval for flushing dirty database pages. The notion of checkpoint depth is introduced with Exchange 2000 and can be tuned by setting the Active Directory attribute for each storage group located underneath the information store object of your server in the configuration naming context, as shown in Figure 5.13. A value of 20 MB is what usually is found in most cases. Introduced with the SP1 release of Exchange 2000 for Windows 2000 Data Center certification, it was recommended to tune the checkpoint to 5 MB—in reality, even with standalone mailbox servers, this recommendation might avoid too many outstanding dirty pages to be written to a single LUN. This is something appropriate in replicated storage environments, where write requests are to be preferably written synchronously to both sides of a replication link, therefore adding delay to the

Figure 5.13
*Setting the
checkpoint depth
(Storage Group
attribute).*

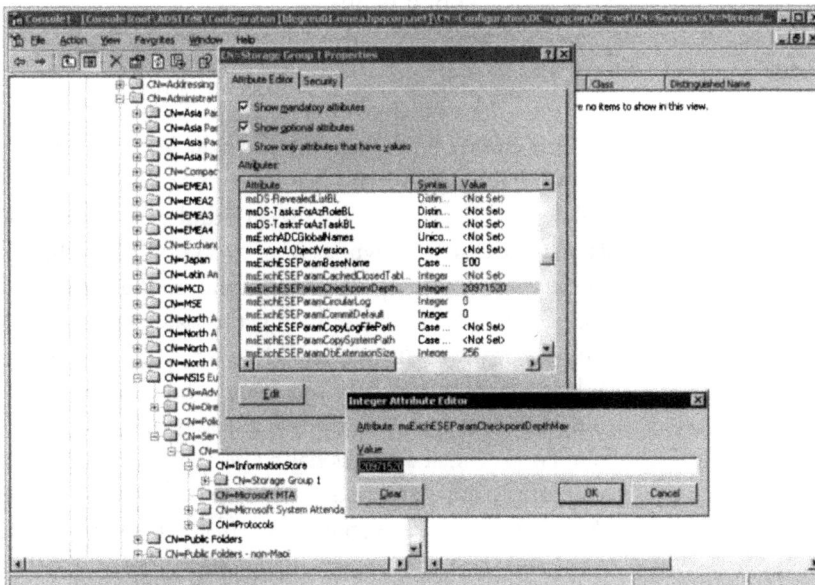

completion of a write operation that would otherwise complete rapidly once committed on back-end storage cache or disk.

In summary, patterns with the database engine are quite specific. First, anything that goes to the transaction log file is written sequentially. Second, anything that goes in the property store is written randomly across the entire database seek range. Therefore, you should assume that if your database is 30 GB in size, any area of the database could be solicited for completing a transaction and flushing dirty database pages. This last point is not innocuous: when some database technologies allow you to define index and data areas, where access pattern and I/O size can be different, Microsoft Exchange forces you to deal with the obligation to perform fast random I/O across a large set of virtual blocks.

Recommended Optimization for Microsoft Exchange

Thankfully, each release of Microsoft Exchange brings a set of automatic tuning that in fact limits the options for additional optimization: most of the settings, out of the box, from Microsoft Exchange are in fact optimal. The only consideration to be brought forward when it comes to storage group design concerns the two parameters that influence the way the database engine deals with back-end storage:

- The checkpoint depth;
- The log buffer size.

In a cluster environment, you will want to favor the speed for failing over an Exchange Virtual Server from one cluster node to another, and this will depend largely on the current number of outstanding dirty pages in the database cache (known as the checkpoint depth). You can control the checkpoint depth by modifying the configuration of the storage group using ADSIEDIT and reducing the `msExchESEParamCheckpointDepthMax` property from its default 20 MB to 5 MB. This will cause more frequent disk accesses but will help to advance the checkpoint of logged transactions, to the effect that shutting down a storage group will be faster. The increased frequency of disk accesses has to be properly assessed. If your storage infrastructure is not particularly responsive (database I/O operations are above 18 ms), this can have an adverse effect. In short, you cannot have both the bread and the butter. I personally believe that the default value is definitely adequate for standalone servers and that in clustered configuration the checkpoint depth should be set to 5 MB to help improve the failover delay, should a failover occur.

The ideal location for the database file—and, in fact, any files in a high-end Exchange 2003 server—varies depending on the type and role of this server inside the organization. Hereunder, you will find general guidelines, which actually may vary and may require additional analysis and tuning depending on the actual workload of the server and therefore its role in the Microsoft Exchange infrastructure/organization.

For transaction logging to happen correctly, you might have to change the number of transaction log buffers allocated to the database engines for recording transactions during their execution and flushing them to disk once they commit.

Check the Microsoft Knowledge Base article 815372 before proceeding on your servers, as it contains up to date and important background information, as well as instructions. See figure 5.14 a example of such a change.

Proper Database File Placement for Mailbox Servers

Mailbox servers, which host users' mailboxes and generate inbound and outbound traffic, should see each storage transaction log file on an individual volume—or, put in a simpler form, on a volume that has fast (<1 ms) sequential write capability for any I/O between 1 KB and 64 KB. A very straightforward approach would be to dedicate a mirrored disk pair

Figure 5.14
*Using ADSIEDIT
to set the number of
log buffers to 9,000*

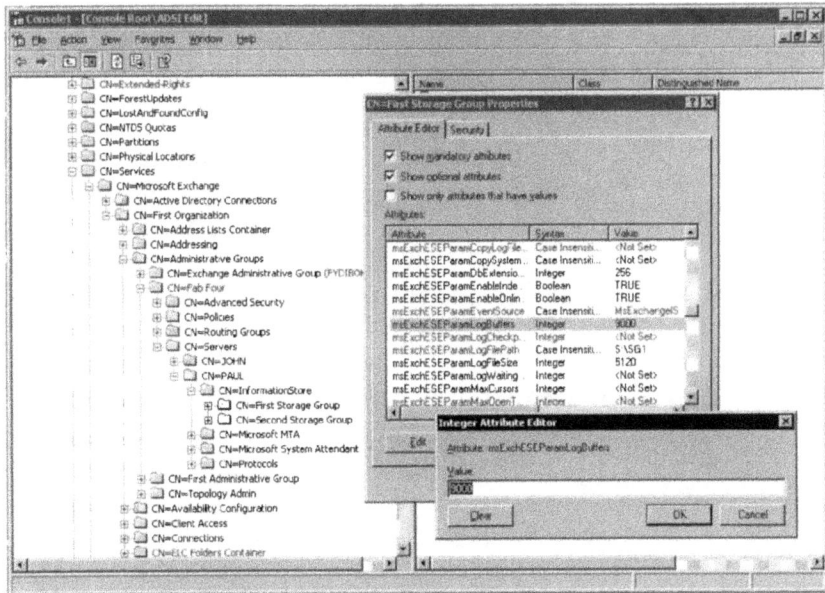

(RAID1) for each transaction log file set, but that is not necessarily the only solution. As you approach a virtualized storage environment, you will not have the choice but to *share* back-end disk spindles among several other applications. The general rule that seems to apply to most cases is to put *like I/O* on the same target disks (e.g., transaction logging) and avoid mixing Microsoft Exchange workload with other applications.

The users' mailboxes hosted by the EDB/STM file pair need to reside on fast read/write volumes that can handle a large number of concurrent transactions. How much is the big question and is a point of debate that has been going for the last four years. When I worked on the first edition of this book, back in 1999–2000, it was common to assign 200 users per spindle pair in a RAID0+1 configuration. Therefore, if you had a 1,000-user server, you needed:

$$5 \times \text{2-disk (RAID1)} = 10 \text{ RAID0+1 disks}$$

That only served as a general rule because this can vary greatly depending on the user's activity profiling and, eventually, mailbox size. This is where monitoring and baseline analysis takes on vital importance in right-sizing your storage subsystem. In addition, with the advent of virtualized and shared back-end storage array, with more or less important cache functions, you may not directly relate the number of users to a spindle count. It is therefore necessary to get back to basic calculations for which a request rate has to be satisfied from the Microsoft Exchange server to the storage back-end components, regardless of whether they are locally, networked, or SAN attached.

A more modern and accurate approach consists of evaluating the I/O workload generated by a possibly representative user set and working out, using simple arithmetic, the needed spindle count. In the monitoring chapter, we describe which parameters to monitor and how to determine proper values, but for this particular section, let's assume the following case:

- 1 × server with 2,000 users;
- 1,800 I/O per sec have been observed during peak hours of utilization.

Note: peak hours are typically a Monday morning 9 AM to 11 AM period, but it could vary based upon the user type, the company type, and the client used. The resulting I/O per user is therefore:

1,800 / 2,000 = 0.9

The characterization shown here may be performed on Microsoft Exchange 2000 and even Exchange 5.5; the basics of the database engine have not significantly changed, although some optimization did occur across time.

If you plan to design storage for your Microsoft Exchange infrastructure and if you do not already run any version of Microsoft Exchange, you may very well start with a "ballpark" estimate of 0.8 I/O per second per connected user for the initial sizing.

At this point, when performing your storage design, you will aim at ensuring, from the Windows operating system viewpoint, that the target workload (e.g., 1,800 I/O per second) can be met with an *appropriate* response time. In the monitoring chapter, we document acceptable values for storage transactions, but they should rarely exceed 20 ms for read and 10 ms for write operations. This may mean certain basic guidelines in the design of the storage components.

Across time and with experience, we have realized that the individual file handled by the Microsoft Exchange server need not be separated, except from the logs, to be put on a separate physical disk volume from the databases for simple data recovery capabilities. If you lose the database, you don't lose the logs, and you may recover operations; if you lose the logs, you do not lose the databases and may recover them and resume operations after correcting the problem.

Microsoft Exchange database files are created with extents of 16 MB (see Microsoft Knowledge Base article 283691); log files are created with a basic size of 5 MB; however, during the initial creation of the log file, there will be a 1-MB I/O to create the file. It seems that for every 5 MB of overall transaction volume, you will see a 1-MB I/O going to the log drive; this should not cause a problem to most high-end arrays and can generally be dealt with in most environments.

In summary, you should understand by now that the Microsoft Exchange I/O workload for mailbox (and public folder) servers is of two kinds:

- Random access to the database (70 percent read):
  - The randomness is across the entire database seek range; you will rarely see "hot" areas for a given database. Therefore, the volume should be designed such that I/O performance for the first logical blocks is the same as the one for the last logical blocks used by the database.
  - The I/O size varies between 4 KB and 8 KB for writes for 90 percent of the time, and 4 KB for reads for the majority of the I/O.
- Sequential access to the transaction log (100 percent write):
  - There will never be more than one outstanding I/O per transaction log stream (i.e., storage group). The throughput of the transaction logging will therefore depend upon the response time of the write operation. If you are operating in high-latency environments, such as in replicated storage, you should consider using more storage groups (therefore, more log streams), each with fewer throughput requirements.

Based upon the remarks herein, a general recommendation is to allocate, per each storage group, one logical unit for logs and one logical unit for all databases of that storage group. You may wish to split storage group databases into separate volumes (e.g., to have smaller volumes to deal with). In that case, try to keep the EDB and STM files for a given database on the same volume. Even though the workload pattern to the STM file is slightly different than to the EDB, the overall pattern does not justify trying to isolate the I/O.

Proper Database File Placement for Mail-Switching Servers

These servers essentially commute messages between servers. Some like to call them bridge head servers; others, mail relays. Your decision depends primarily on your IT background. Servers used to route messages will need transient storage for storing inbound messages on disks and then redelivering them through another route to another server or performing local mail delivery.

By default, the SMTP virtual server will locate these files under a subfolder of the Exchange 2003 installation folder. While this is OK for most deployments and for local servers, it is not a bad idea to relocate the mailroot folder to a separate partition on a separate volume that has particularly fast characteristics. This is where my friend, Donald Livengood, saw an opportunity for the once-famous solid state disks, disk drives that have as much cache memory as storage. The performances of these drives are truly incredible compared with the fastest mechanical drives available in the industry, but they have their problems: they come in small sizes (2 GB or less), and they are quite expensive. But if the business criticality of your Exchange 2003 setup demands such a high throughput, it is well worth the investment.

The actual procedure to modify the location of the mailroot folder for the SMTP server depends upon your version of Microsoft Exchange. Introduced with Exchange 2003, it is possible to change the path to these data areas from Exchange System Manager.

You may also use ADSIEDIT to modify the path of the various mail files described in the following attributes:

```
msExchSmtpBadMailDirectory
msExchSmtpPickupDirectory
msExchSmtpQueueDirectory
```

of the "CN=1" object located in the following container:

```
Configuration Container |
CN=1,CN=SMTP,CN=Protocols,CN=<server>,CN=Servers,
CN=<admin
group>,CN=AdministrativeGroups,CN=<organization>,CN=Microsoft
Exchange,CN=Services,CN=Configuration
```

Figure 5.15
*Changing the path
of the queue
directory for the
SMTP service*

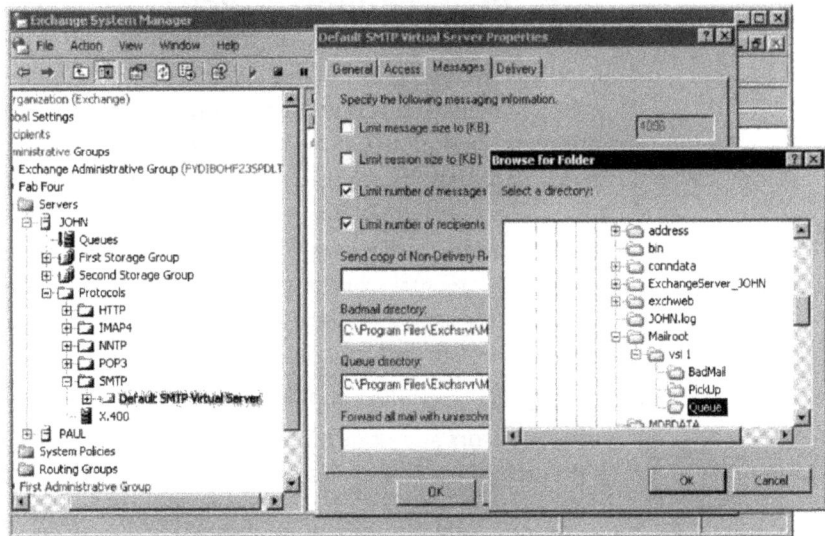

Note that the X.400 MTA has similar restrictions in terms of the number of concurrent sessions that can be handled at a single point in time. Instead of file handles, the throttling is defined by the number of concurrent threads utilized for communication between the MTA process (EMSMTA) and the STORE process.

The MTA database itself is located as a subfolder to the main Exchange server installation (Program Files\Exchsrvr\mtadata), and significant performance increase can be seen when you relocate this directory to a fast volume (RAID0+1, preferably).

This can be achieved by modifying the following registry settings (remember that the EMSMTA is a "legacy" component of Exchange 2003 and most of its inner settings are still based on the local server registry):

```
HKEY_LOCAL_MACHINE\System\CurrentControlSet\Services\
MSExchangeMTA\Parameters\MTA Database Path
```

This is an important step to follow if you are configuring your server as a bridgehead server.

Note that to avoid having to relocate those database paths and create unusual system configurations that could be problematic to manage, your best bet is to install Exchange 2003 in a folder located on a fast volume, such that both the MTA and the SMTP routing and delivery engines can benefit from this fast volume. Refer to Chapter 3 for how to optimize storage.

5.5.3   Backup and Maintenance Operations

Now you are going to build a system according to your requirements that provides a satisfactory level of performance to your end users. This is good, and most vendors will provide you with canned configurations, marketing benchmarks, and powerful system and storage combinations to meet your objectives. Users are happy, and so are you as an Exchange administrator, designer, and service owner. The rubber hits the road when you need to factor in supplemental work in your Exchange 2003 setup. Backups are a typical example, although they are not so difficult to address. Why is that? Because they are typically planned operations!

You allocate a time window and set proper expectations for your storage administrators and users such that you can utilize system resources for running backup operations without adversely affecting end users' productivity.

Restore operations are the most difficult—they never occur at the right time. Typically, they happen during the daytime, when someone actually notices the problem, or, if you're really unlucky, at quarter closure or something similar. Pressure builds up and you need to restore the messaging service—and potentially data—as rapidly as possible.

Consider the situation in which an entire server suffers the outage. To a certain extent, you are in a disaster situation that you need to address, and you will probably have set expectations in your service level agreements such that the outage has a well-defined and expected duration.

An even worse situation is to have to perform a partial restore operation (e.g., restore of a single database out of a storage group of four databases).

Some users are impacted because the database is not available at all, and others are impacted because shared resources, instead of being used for normal execution, are being used for a restore operation. How can you best address this scenario? SANs, which carry so much value in providing a flexible, agile environment, have to be properly sized to match not only performance needs for day-to-day work, but also performance needs for the exceptional, after you have determined how much your infrastructure and end users would suffer from a repair or restore operation.

High-end environments are not likely to suffer from lack of availability, but it can't be assumed that they will never suffer a performance penalty.

With Microsoft Exchange 2003, I believe that two key operations can be resource consuming:

1.   Online maintenance;

2.   Backup/recovery.

Online Maintenance

The Exchange 2003 System Attendant will perform online maintenance to check the validity of the mailboxes defined on the server and will perform an online defragmentation of your database. The online maintenance windows can be adjusted, typically during off-peak hours. But then, when you deploy Exchange 2003 as a service provider on the Internet, there is no such thing as off-peak hours. This may well force you to define the characteristics of your server so it can cope with a moderate user transaction volume, and at the same time perform its tidy-up operations, such as the System Attendant maintenance.

Checking the mailboxes against the Active Directory will generate a high and short load on the GCs. For this particular reason, you should aim to have the Active Directory GCs hosting the NTDS.DIT file on a multi-spindle volume.

What technology is best for this database file? First, you must realize that the database engine used for Windows Active Directory is of the same family as that of Microsoft Exchange. In other words, it uses optimization techniques such as booting with /3GB in the boot.ini file of the GC server, when having more than 1 GB is likely to bring a great improvement.

The one particular difference between the Windows Active Directory and the Microsoft Exchange database engines is the read/write ratio. For the NTDS.DIT database file, we have found from our deployments that 90 percent to 95 percent of the I/O done to the volume hosting the NTDS.DIT consisted of read operations. Here comes a great recommendation for a large (5–10 spindle) RAID5 volume. I recommend sizing the volume to match the request rate, not the storage space required.

Online defragmentation can be the killer background activity on your server and storage subsystem. The idea of online defragmentation is to rearrange the database pages so that more contiguous free space can be made available in the database and so that those 4-KB databases pages are optimally used. On high-end deployments, online defragmentation is a must; you cannot do without it. Failing to run the online defragmentation on a daily basis will slowly degrade server performance because more steps will be required to find free space in the database, which could cause the database to artificially grow.

On the other hand, if you run the online defragmentation on a daily basis, you will enjoy the Exchange 2003 server performance at its best, provided that the system is configured in harmony with the forecasted workload.

I have figured that online defragmentation on a decently sized I/O subsystem (2 × 14 disks in RAID0+1) could take as long as 30 GB per hour. This seems quite good, but because during my study the customer was planning to host more than 400 GB of data, this poses a slight problem—defragmentation would have required more than ten hours to execute. Typically, therefore, online defragmentation occurs at night, as does your database backup job. I do not know of any 20-hour nights, except maybe in Lapland during the winter. Fortunately, Microsoft has done a good job in this particular instance; if the online defragmentation is in progress when a backup is started, the defragmentation will be suspended and will resume once the backup job has completed. So your strategy should be to define a sufficiently large time window for the System Attendant maintenance operations, which includes the backup time window. For example, let online defragmentation kick in at 6 PM, let backup interfere and suspend the online defragmentation between 11 PM and 4 AM, and keep the maintenance window open until 8 AM in the morning. That way, you leave ample time for your online maintenance to occur, even though the backup will suspend it temporarily. You can also decide not to have the two operations overlap; let backup start first and have the online defragmentation complete later in the morning.

Because the defragmentation process occurs at a lower priority than actual user transactions, there is a good chance that even though the users will log on and browse their inboxes in the morning, the defragmentation process will continue to run in the least disruptive manner possible.

So should you care about online defragmentation? Not if you are using local storage or using storage dedicated to your Exchange servers. However, when the System Attendant triggers the online defragmentation, the I/O subsystems hosting the databases are blasted with read and write operations, all happening at the same time, in parallel, on all databases. It is true, though, that these operations can occur with user activity and are *prioritized* such that user transactions are processed in priority compared with background defragmentation.

This is valid at a local system level. But don't forget that we're in the era of shared storage infrastructure, and some other application may actually *share* the storage subsystem with your Exchange server and have no awareness that an online defragmentation is taking place and, above all, have no control over the prioritization of the I/O handled by the shared storage infrastructure.

Offline defragmentation, which used to be a recommended step for pre–Exchange 5.5 servers, should not be done on a regular basis. From Exchange 5.5 onward, the database engine and the online defragmentation process have been tuned such that you should *never* have to run offline database defragmentation except if you wish to reclaim the space utilized by the database yet logically removed from the database (e.g., moving a lot of users or deleting large amounts of information after an archiving process). Even though disk space is cheap, removing empty pages of a database will serve the purpose of reducing backup and recovery times, especially in streaming mode.

Fast Backups

Backing up and restoring an Exchange 2003 storage environment requires speed of data transfer, otherwise called data rate, which is measured in megabytes per second. Often I have explained that, in Exchange, the need for a high data rate was not so important because of the relatively small I/O size. That has held true for quite some time and will continue to be the case in the foreseeable future. However, as you justify your storage investments for providing the right levels of capacity, availability, and performance for operational use of Exchange 2003, you must not forget about the backup and restore operation, and you must define the requirements in this area. How sad it would be to build a 200-GB data storage subsystem for Microsoft Exchange and then realize that one night is just not enough time to back up the environment.

Data rate limitations in storage subsystems are typically due to:

- *Controllers*: They run chipsets and microprocessors and can have limited system buses. Although controllers can interface to fibre channel or ultrawide SCSI environments, they have inherent limitations that are not always advertised by the vendors. If you can get 80 MB/s out of one controller or a pair of controllers, that will be good, yet you wouldn't have saturated your fibre channel media.

- *Disks*: Although they are typically used in combination, the sequential nature of a backup or restore operation can be quite demanding on the disk drives. Faster disk drives are usually equipped with either a fibre channel (100 MB/s) or an ultrawide SCSI-3 (160 MB/s or 320MB/s) interface, yet they might not deliver at these data rates.

- *Transfer media*: This is the important item, because data being transferred from the disk subsystems to the backup devices and vice versa need to traverse one or more media and one or more servers, and each of these can become a bottleneck.

- *Tape drives*: Finally, tape drives have always represented the slow component of a backup infrastructure, although recent media have been measured at speeds approaching 20 MB/s, which is not bad at all. However, in a number of situations, tape drives still represent a bottleneck. This has led vendors and customers designing high-end solutions to envisage tapeless backup and restore environments, based on BCVs or disk dumps.

With Windows Server 2003 and Exchange 2003, the introduction of VSS-based backups does help to address the shortcomings of stream backups, and although they don't represent the majority of deployments, VSS backups are now used with very large Microsoft Exchange data volumes (500 GB to 1 TB) with tight recovery windows.

Online vs. Offline vs. VSS-Based Backups

There have been several schools of thought regarding the way to back up Exchange 2003, and concepts of *online* (or *hot*) backups have been compared with *offline* backups. The difference is important, and both solutions carry their advantages and disadvantages. In a high-performance, high-volume environment, neither of the two is a clear winner, and you must determine your priorities before adopting one strategy or the other.

Online backup in Exchange allows backing up the contents of the database while users are connected and transactions are being performed to the database. The advantage of this is that you can aim for higher availability; as you run your backups, users remain connected and have access to the service. There may be a performance degradation, but this is easily measurable by means of appropriate testing and qualification of the solution. The degradation can be addressed by increasing available resources across the board—CPU, memory, network, and storage—although the exact combination depends very much on the backup software and the backup method).

Offline backups, on the other hand, back up the Exchange 2003 databases as regular files. Because these files are open and active during normal operations, it is necessary to close those databases when you perform the offline backup. A database in Exchange 2003 is closed by *dismounting* the database, or, more simply, by stopping the STORE process. This was how it was done with Exchange 5.5, which didn't provide any way to dismount a public or private store while it kept running and servicing the other database.

The following is a sample script that dismounts a particular Exchange 2000 database:

```
' Script retrieving the list of properties available from the CDOEXM
object'
' MailStoreDB (without fields collection values) '
' '
' Version 1.00 - Alain Lissoir '
' Compaq Computer Corporation - Professional Services - Belgium - '
' '
' Any comments or questions: EMail:alain.lissoir@compaq.com '
Option Explicit
Dim WNetwork
Dim strComputerName
Dim objServer
Dim objStorageGroup
Dim urlStorageGroup
Dim objMailboxStoreDB
Dim urlMailboxStoreDB
Dim objField
' By default this script expects to run on the local Exchange server.
Set WNetwork = Wscript.CreateObject("Wscript.Network")
strComputerName = WNetwork.ComputerName
Wscript.DisconnectObject (WNetwork)
Set WNetwork = Nothing
Set objServer = CreateObject("CDOEXM.ExchangeServer")
Set objStorageGroup = CreateObject("CDOEXM.StorageGroup")
Set objMailboxStoreDB = CreateObject("CDOEXM.MailBoxStoreDB")
objServer.DataSource.Open (strComputerName)
For Each urlStorageGroup in objServer.StorageGroups
objStorageGroup.DataSource.Open (urlStorageGroup)
wscript.echo objStorageGroup.Name
For Each urlMailboxStoreDB In objStorageGroup.MailboxStoreDBs
wscript.echo " urlMailboxStoreDB=" & urlMailboxStoreDB
objMailboxStoreDB.DataSource.Open (urlMailboxStoreDB)
WScript.Echo " * Dismounting '" & objMailboxStoreDB.Name & "'"
objMailboxStoreDB.Dismount
WScript.Echo " '" & objMailboxStoreDB.Name & "' dismounted."
WScript.Echo " * Pausing 10 sec before mounting '" &
```

```
objMailboxStoreDB.Name & "'"
WScript.Sleep (10000)
WScript.Echo " * Mounting '" & objMailboxStoreDB.Name & "'"
objMailboxStoreDB.Mount
WScript.Echo " '" & objMailboxStoreDB.Name & "' mounted."
Next
Next
WScript.DisconnectObject objMailboxStoreDB
Set objMailboxStoreDB = Nothing
WScript.DisconnectObject objStorageGroup
Set objStorageGroup = Nothing
WScript.DisconnectObject objServer
Set objServer = Nothing
```

The most optimal alternative to online backups (we refer to them also as stream backups) is the VSS backup: this technology allows you to take advantage of the advanced storage management functions that you have available in modern networked storage array, with proper synchronization with both the operating system and the application.

There are two key differences between online and offline backups:

- Service interruption;
- Database checksum verification;
- Transaction log file management and truncation.

Service Interruption

With online backups, users can still access their mailboxes, and messages can be delivered to the database. With offline backups, the service will just look as though it is down from an end-user perspective. This situation is not desirable in high-end environments, where typically a large number of users depend on the availability of a database, or in business environments, where working hours are used to calculate salaries; when employees work after hours or simply in different time zones. Availability requirements 24 × 7 is by no means a myth in Exchange 2003 environments. For this reason, many customers are reluctant to utilize offline backups for Exchange 2003, except in situations in which the downtime is planned as part of maintenance operations (e.g., system upgrade or storage rebuild).

Database Checksum Verification

During the online database backup, the API basically provides a way for an agent or a backup program to fetch pages from the databases to be backed up. In fact, these pages are not taken one by one; up to 64 KB of data can be requested from the calling program of the backup API. During that process, the API will verify that the contents of each page are what they are supposed to be—each page in Exchange 2003 has a checksum associated with it. During an online backup, the Exchange backup API will perform page-level checksum verification, and will log an −1018 error in the application event log if the contents of a page don't match the page checksum. Two things should be considered. First, it is not a facility provided by the backup program; every vendor will have to go through the page checksum, and, in a way, this is a good thing. Second, you have to have capacity and time to recover a proper database and play back all intermediate transactions, from the last known good backup to the most current transaction.

Transaction Log File Management

The transaction log files on a Microsoft Exchange server are truncated once a full or incremental backup has been successfully performed. To prevent any potential loss of data, Microsoft Exchange will not remove transaction log files until it "knows" that the backup has been performed and that the content of the data on the backup media are correct. This verification of the data is made through the database checksum verification, and the backup application is responsible for notifying the database engine that the backup went fine. In an offline backup mode, there is no way to report to Microsoft Exchange that the backup was fine. In online mode, Microsoft Exchange will perform the log file management automatically. In offline mode, you have to remove the transaction log files manually and possibly run into unsupported conditions. It is considered a bad practice to just remove all the files in the transaction log area—at best, you should leave behind the generations that the database will require for proper recovery. You can obtain the list of generations of log files by dumping the database header using ESEUTIL, as shown in Figure 5.16.

In this example, the database has never been backed up and cleanly shutdown: the log generations required are therefore inexistent.

This has led to dramatic situations: online backups are performed on a server, and suddenly the administrator realizes that the backup has generated page checksum errors for three consecutive days. The database is corrupted, and, depending upon the page, this can have greater or lesser impact from a usability standpoint. To address such a situation, you have

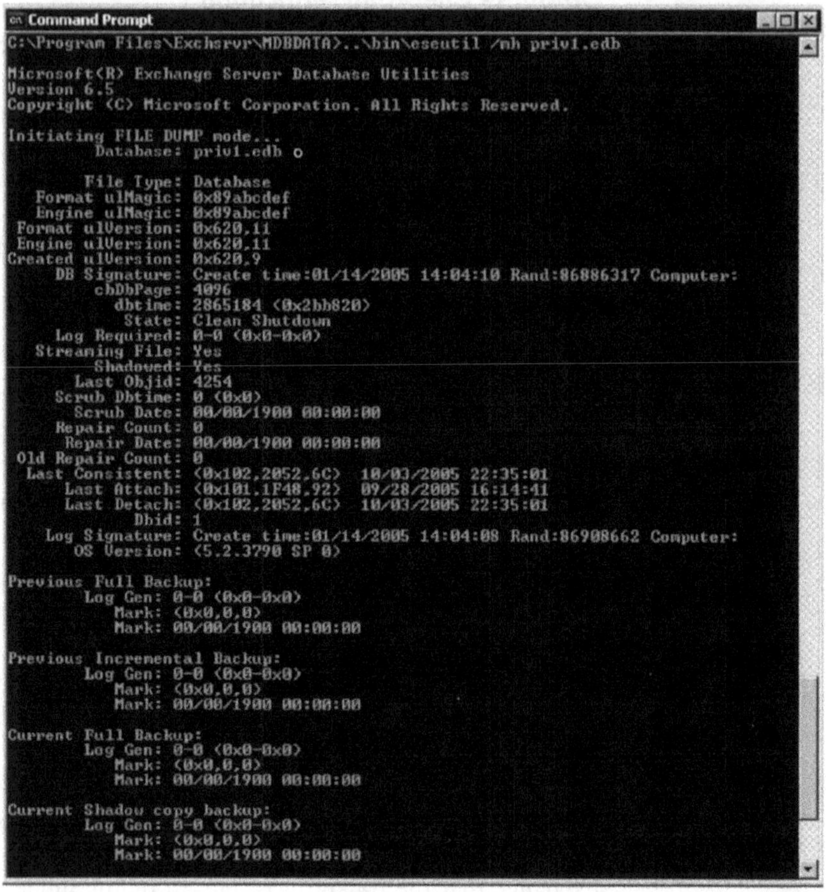

Figure 5.16
*Dumping a
database file
header using
ESEUTIL /MH*

two choices. You can run ESEUTIL to discard the page. But discarding a
page without really knowing what it relates to can have dramatic impact on
the logical arrangement of the database and its contents (lost messages,
folders, mailboxes). This type of repair operation is typically instructed by
Microsoft PSS (support) and only performed when the database may not be
recovered from previous backups. Prior to repairing the database, you will,
of course, perform a backup in case the result, which is hardly predictable,
renders the database unusable.

The alternative is to restore the database and play back the transaction
logs from the past days until you get to the most current status of the
database. This is fine if you still have the intermediate transaction log
files—which, by the way, you should have. However, you are now obliged
to process 4 GB or more of transaction log files. How long does it take to
play back log files? That can vary, but typically it takes between 30 seconds

and 1 minute per log files with a pre-SP1 version of Exchange 2003, and this has been improved to an overall estimate of 10 seconds per log in Exchange 2003 SP1 and later. Note that there is a strong dependency on the underlying hardware capability, and you might have much greater results in your environment.

Logs of 4 GB, generally obtained after a hard day's work on the part of 1,000 users, represent 800 log files. It takes 400 minutes (6 hours, 40 minutes) at minimum to play back those logs into a good database, which is not wonderful for your SLA and your 99.9 percent availability target.

Let me give a word of advice at this point, before you get into an embarrassing situation: check your backups, and make sure you don't get your log volumes filled up with many log files. It is not good to run out of disk space on a log volume, but it is not good either to have to play several gigabytes of transactions into a database, especially if you have designed a super-fast backup environment that in the end logs will have reduced the time to repair your server. You may have a 70-GB/hr restore capability (which is quite good in fact), but that serves little purpose if you have two or three hours of log playback to perform.

One good way of verifying database integrity and recoverability is to use the Exchange 2003 Recovery Storage Group. Using this feature requires little effort to actually restore a backup database on a server. Be careful, however, of the side effects of the recovery workload.

All of this page-level checksum verification is not done during an offline backup. This is a bad situation. Since Exchange 5.5 SP2, with vendors trying to implement offline backup solutions at customers' sites, the utility called ESEFILE has arrived; it allows performing page-level checksum verification on a database. In any scenario involving offline backups, it is highly recommended to have a pass at the database with ESEFILE. Since Exchange 2003, ESEFILE has actually been folded into ESEUTIL as a separate switch (/V).

So why should you bother with offline backups? Offline backups are used typically in point-in-time backup environments. Storage subsystems and architectures allow you either to take a snapshot of a volume or to clone a particular volume in order to make either a logical copy or a physical copy. This topic is addressed further in this section.

Local Tape Backups

Local backups to tape are often used in high-performance environments because they utilize the least amount of resources possible and transfer data as fast as possible. They do, however, impose an important cost and management burden because they require that each server holding data be connected directly, by means of a PCI-based SCSI controller, to one or more tape drive. Typically, you will use one tape drive. In a small environment a DAT drive and in a larger environment an SDLT or LTO-2 drive provides both the data rate (10–30 MB/s) and the capacity (>200 GB).

Most of the time, the tape drive will be the performance bottleneck for data rate transfers. To address this, some vendors propose building RAIT drives and permitting the building of RAIT0 (no parity information) or RAIT5 (distribute parity) tape systems, so you can benefit from the aggregate speed of multiple tape drives. This approach held true for Exchange 5.5 and before because of the single file database and the possibility of obtaining only one stream of data at a time via the Exchange 2000 backup API.

LAN-Based Backups

The most common scenario we have seen so far in a backup environment is based on a client/server architecture; an Exchange 2003 server will host an agent and software client that can communicate over the network to a central server, hooked to a tape library. LAN-based backups are great because they realize an economy of scale. Rather than having a local tape drive device on each of your servers, you can concentrate them all in one location and utilize the budget to acquire a tape automation device, such as a tape library or jukebox, that will greatly help in both the management of the tapes themselves and in the handling of tapes for restore operations when multiple tapes need to be utilized.

Another advantage of LAN-based backups is that they can easily integrate into an existing, heterogeneous systems environment, where backup agents can reside on Windows NT, Windows 2000, and most flavors of UNIX, and where the backup server can even run on a UNIX platform. To this extent, that offers a great advantage, but it is also available in other environments, such as SAN-based backups.

The downside of LAN-based backups is the use of the LAN infrastructure for transporting data. LANs were not originally designed for the transfer of large data blocks, although they are catching up, with the introduction of jumbo frames in gigabit Ethernet protocols, for example. Another problem is that sharing the LAN with the client infrastructure for running the backups is not a great approach due to the risk of saturating the client-level LAN setup.

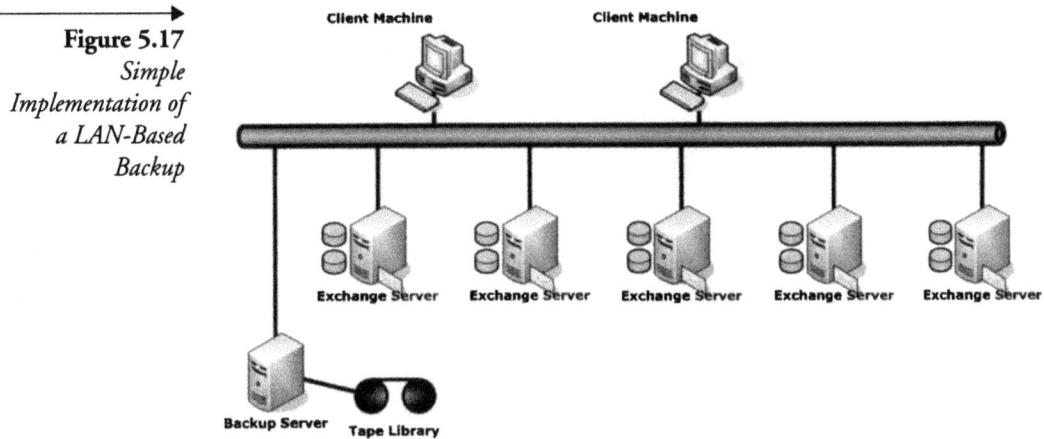

Figure 5.17
Simple Implementation of a LAN-Based Backup

Figure 5.17 shows a simple implementation of a LAN-based backup solution in which servers are all connected onto a local area network as well as the backup server, which is connected directly to a tape library. This diagram assumes that the Exchange 2003 databases are "local" to the servers: they could be located on a SAN, but they could also be located on direct-attached storage, and that wouldn't make a big difference. Clients can also connect on the same LAN infrastructure, and that is not necessarily a good thing during backups. Backups usually have defined time windows, which can be adjusted depending on client usage, traffic, and the expectations of the users. The real issue comes when you have to do a restore, for which you generally don't decide the timing. It mostly comes at the worst times—for example, after a long holiday when all the users try to get access to the resources, and you have a database corruption. The user dissatisfaction level goes high, as there is a group of users who can't get to their mail store and other users who can get to their mail store but find decreased response time from what they are used to.

To alleviate this problem, a relatively cheap solution consists of setting up a separate backup-dedicated LAN that would provide appropriate levels of performance and at the same time alleviate any impact on the end users.

Figure 5.18 shows such an example. As you can see, the difference shown in the upper diagram lies in the supplemental LAN adapters for each of the servers and possibly the LAN infrastructure (switch, most probably). This is not very expensive and is seen in many Exchange 2003 environments.

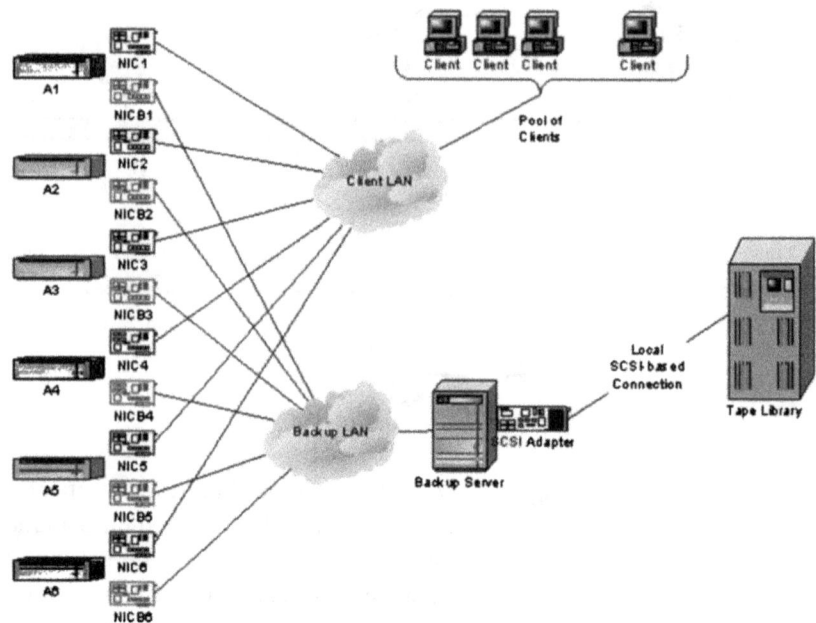

Figure 5.18
*Dedicated
LAN
Backup*

SAN-Based Backups

Now, you realize that you may have to dedicate a networking infrastructure to support the transmission of backup and restore data to your servers.

While the designs presented previously are good for either small or large environments, they introduce the need to have a separate infrastructure. If your servers, by any chance, are connecting to a storage area network for accessing their databases, you have an opportunity to reutilize the SAN for your backup and restore data transfer, while keeping the LAN connectivity free of any major load. All that is required is for the servers to connect on the SAN, for the tape library to also connect on the SAN, and, in most situations, for the backup server to connect on the SAN.

However, the backup server in that situation will most likely act as a resource broker between the servers and will not transfer data to the tape drive; this is another great advantage of SAN-based backups, which allow you to enable direct information flow between the servers and the tape library without the need of a powerful backup server. Other tasks performed by the backup server include the maintenance of the backup catalogs and indexes required to perform restore operations to determine which tape(s) have to be utilized to restore the missing database or server component.

If you already have a SAN infrastructure, the incremental cost remains minimal, because all you need to do is to acquire bridges that can connect to the fibre channel fabric on the one end and the SCSI-based tape drives and automation devices on the other end. As Figure 5.19 shows, the main transfer media for data is the SAN. Fibre channel comes in 100 MB/s (gigabit networking), and while the diagram in Figure 5.19 represents a logical connection, the fabric will be made up of a pair (at least) of fibre channel switches and all server and storage connections will be doubled (redundant path). The connection to the tape library, however, will be single-path.

Figure 5.19
SAN-Based
Backup

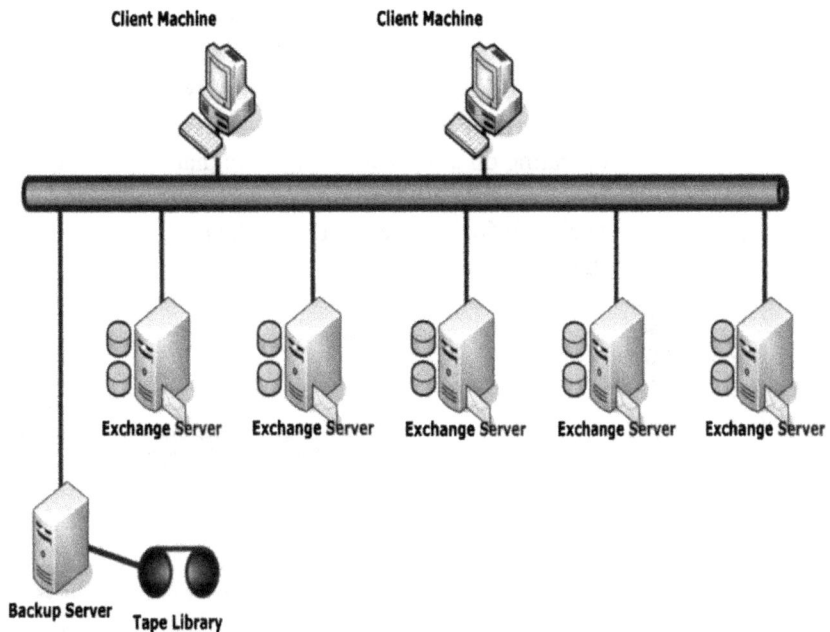

The backup server will be responsible for scheduling backups, allocating tape drive resources (viewed as units on the fibre channel fabric) to the servers, and triggering server-side agents, which perform online backup of Exchange 2003 database stores, pulling data from the storage enclosure and sending it over to the tape library. You may argue that data is transmitted twice on the fibre channel fabric—once to the server, and then back to the tape storage library. Still, that's probably the only downside of this solution.

A word of advice here: when you plan on deploying a SAN-based solution, make sure you have a fully supported configuration at *all* levels: server vendor, SAN vendor, storage vendor, backup solution vendor. You could literally be spending nights and days in a computer room trying to make these components sing and dance to the same tune (the author speaks here from experience). Ideally, a packaged solution from a single vendor will be your best bet, but it may backfire on your multivendor SAN/server strategy or on your plans to address storage needs with multiple sources of storage acquisition. This is a perfect example of why you may end up building a SAN island in your storage infrastructure.

Some customers that already have deployed backup SAN may very well decide to attach their Exchange servers to a separate, dedicated SAN in addition to the SAN utilized for the main Exchange databases. This is a fairly good approach in the sense that it realizes a certain economy of scale for the backup infrastructure (which is typically very expensive); it takes advantage of existing operations, while keeping the main storage SAN untouched and almost "unpolluted" by backup traffic. One of my customers has taken this approach quite successfully: the backup environment is operating on a dedicated SAN; the main backup server is a Sun server running Veritas's NETBACKUP. and they all seamlessly integrate into the Exchange environment without the need to certify their backup solution in the main storage SAN.

Figure 5.20
Dedicated SAN-based backup

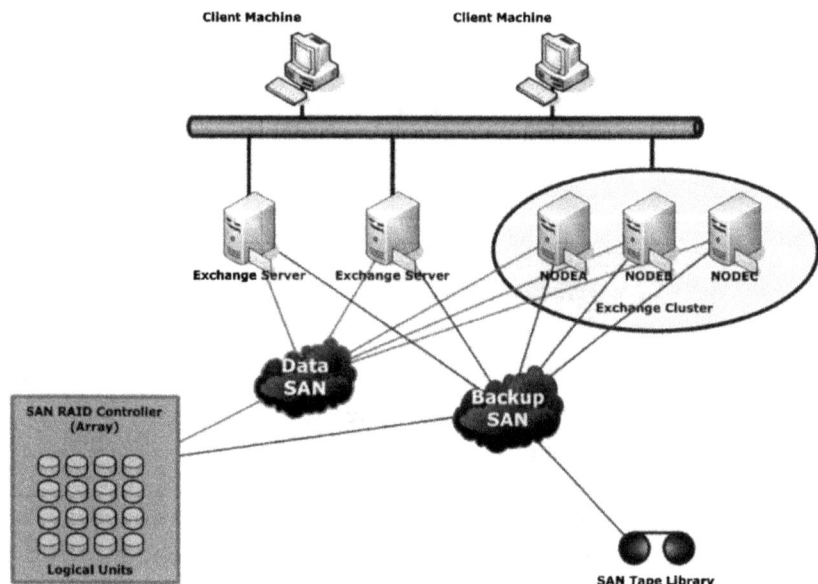

Figure 5.20 shows such an environment. You need an additional host-bus adapter to tap into the backup SAN, but, beyond that, nothing more is needed than running the backup software agent, controlled by the backup

server, typically over the LAN. The data stream consists of fetching the data from the storage subsystems to the Exchange server running the agent, which, in turn, can stream this data directly via the separate backup SAN to the tape library. Complementarily, isolating the tape library from the production SAN helped in stabilizing the SAN and prevented storage arrays from being notified of tape drive and jukebox notification messages. We have observed excellent performance results, such as DLT7000 tape drives running at their full speed (8 MB/s).

Tapeless Backups

Tape drives are difficult to deal with because of the relatively low data rate they provide. DLT is usually at 5–6 MB/s; SuperDLT is higher (11 MB/s). Some point solutions can go as high as 20 MB/s. As always, be very careful when reviewing these data, since they are usually demonstrated in very specific environments, aimed at pleasing the marketing organizations of the storage vendor. Nevertheless, the rate of growth of data rate from tape devices hasn't been outstanding in terms of storage density, and neither have the storage requirements in the enterprise.

Different methods of performing backups are being used in the industry, and it's definitely worthwhile for any environment that operates with large (>50-GB) data quantities to investigate alternative solutions. There are two main solutions to consider:

1.   Backup to disk farms;

2.   VSS backups.

Backup to Disk Farms

Aside from using fast tape streamers (which yields >70 GB per hour uncompressed data rates), one technique is to back up the databases to disk farms. This results in both fast backups and, most important, fast restore operations should one or more database be recovered.

Backing up to disk farms carries some disadvantages, one being the additional maintenance procedure required to move the disk-based backups to tape libraries for offline storage. Also, depending on the target disk volume, the gain may not be that big compared to modern tape drives. However, if you already have a backup infrastructure and wish to take advantage of it while being able to quickly restore databases, this can be a good approach; it is the one utilized by Microsoft ITG for internal Exchange deployment on the Redmond, WA, campus.

VSS Backups: Making a Point-in-Time Copy

The actual process of generating the duplicate volume can be very short (a few seconds). But during that time, no activity can occur on the database, which must be in as consistent a state as possible. In Exchange 2000, to get a consistent database you have to dismount it. With Exchange 5.5, you have to stop the STORE service. In this case, you typically don't care about the transaction log files, because you know that after a database dismount all committed transactions will have been applied to the database pages. So the database itself is fully consistent, and can be reutilized, as shown in Figure 5.21 (the primary access and secondary access shown there are logical connections; physically, everything goes through the SAN and the storage cabinet).

Figure 5.21
Accessing a cloned volume.

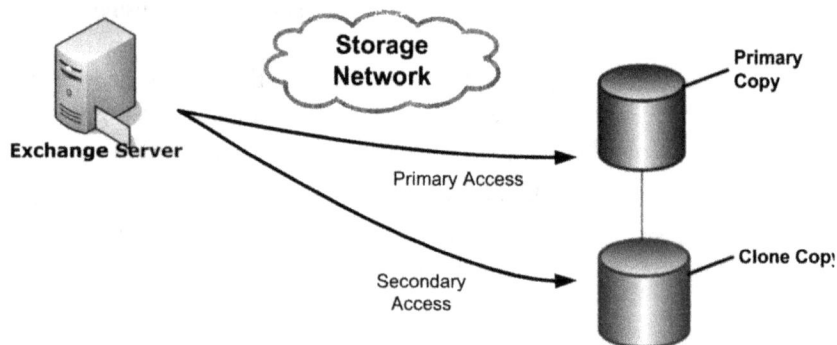

The issue is how "dirty" your volume (and the database it contains) is at the time that you do the split of the clone or the snapshot operation. In an Exchange 2003 environment, we have mostly concentrated on trying to get a clean (i.e., consistent) database. This can be achieved in two ways, which are more or less disruptive to the users:

1. You can shut down the entire store process and obtain consistent databases, which you can copy or do with whatever you wish; this is what is typically called an offline backup. The impact is that all the users hosted on that Exchange server cannot access the messaging and collaboration service provided by the Exchange 2003 server.

2. You can *dismount* one or more databases hosted on the volume that you intend to snap or split. You still end up with a consistent database, but the impact is less important because you

could have users hosted on other databases, possibly in other storage groups, still running and using the Exchange services. Additionally, most of the users in Outlook 2003 cache mode would not notice the momentarily absence of the store because their access to the mailbox is done to the local cache, and the cache is synchronized in background.

The transaction playback will occur at service startup; to ensure that all transactions are played back to the offline-restored database, you must get rid of the EDB.CHK file, which checkpoints the last transaction in the database such that the recovery steps, when missing the checkpoint file, can actually process all the transaction logs. That can be a lengthy operation, so before selling the solution as a wonderful, faster way of doing backups, make sure that you have actually measured the impact of playing back 9 or 10 GB of logs (which is what you can expect on large and busy servers).

The thing that we seem to have forgotten about is the NTFS volume itself: you could, after a split operation, end up with a dirty NTFS volume. Is this a major issue? Not really, because NTFS is based on a transaction logging scheme and can recover from an abrupt system shutdown, which is essentially what you are doing if you try to split or snap a volume at the storage subsystem level. The ideal would be to ensure that the NTFS file system on that volume is clean, and there are hacks that allow to "sync" the NT I/O subsystem cache such that your volume is clean.

You may say, "OK, I can split my volume, and, in essence, I have a 'crash-consistent' volume and transaction logging in NTFS. In Exchange, that would be taken care of by the crash recovery features of both NTFS and the ESE database engine." In this instance, you would be right. Nevertheless, it's better to ensure that everything is clean.

To achieve this, you need some interaction with the NT I/O subsystem and the application. This is where Windows Server 2003 delivers a useful feature—the VSS, which is a service implemented by a dual-sided (provider and consumer) API.

In short, the VSS *provider* side expects the application to perform clean-up operations and suspend transactions (through an application-specific component, the *writer*), while the consumer side (known as a *requestor*) can instruct the freeze and consistency resolution, snap or split the volume, and instruct the VSS to resume (thaw) operations, which in turn calls the provider side to perform application-specific tasks. This is clearly a promising way of performing backups and data duplication for large environments, but that particular mode of operation requires specific back-end storage features, as well as maturing at all levels (VSS provider, requestor, writer, and supporting back-end array).

So this feature makes for fast backups, but, more important, it makes for extremely fast restores. If the database volume should fail, all you need to do is to surface it to the Exchange 2003 server volume hosting the shadow copy of the database, mount it again, and, after a few transactions are played in the target database, you are back online. The size of the database—it could 100 GB or more—does not matter for most shadowcopy implementations. Storage area networks are very much indicated for this type of environment. Implemented with high-end storage enclosures, they can quickly switch two LUNs and provide a full, consistent volume with a clean database very quickly.

5.6   Mail Transport Optimization

The mail transport in Exchange 2003 operates over SMTP by default. It is still possible to utilize an existing X.400 backbone and RPC communication for intrasite communications within a mixed-vintage Exchange 5.5/ Exchange 2003 site, since it is the only guaranteed transport available on Exchange 5.5. Nevertheless, when you deploy Exchange 2003, the best way to approach mail transport and interchange between Exchange 2003 servers is by means of SMTP, which has a proven track record of reliability and has been extended by Microsoft to support advanced transport features (e.g., the bulk transfer of mail data and the exchange of link state information). When it comes to a particular Exchange 2003 server and when you wish to expedite the transfer of inbound and outbound mail messages originating from SMTP, you have to ensure two things:

1.   The folder hosting the transient SMTP messages must be on a performing disk subsystem.

2.   The communication between the SMTP virtual server and the Exchange 2003 STORE, involved when local delivery has to take place, must be optimized to allow fast data transfer from the virtual server to the STORE. In Exchange 2003, this transfer is done primarily by means of the ExIFS, the streaming of data between the TCP/IP socket used for the SMTP connection, and the file handle used to access the streaming store, in kernel mode, by reusing the NT I/O file system cache.

In particularly stressed environments, such as an SMTP relay for an ISP or for a large enterprise, the optimization can be done at the hardware level by using fast storage mechanisms for the mailroot folder of the SMTP service.

For highly stressed environments, you may hit an upper limit in terms of concurrently opened file handles by the SMTP server. Post–Exchange 2000 SP1 update, this maximum number of file handles is calculated from the physical amount of memory using the following formula:

MaxFileHandles = 1,000 + 1,000 per 256-MB blocks of physical RAM

This value is maxed out at 16,000. Should you encounter a problem resulting from insufficient file handles, you may decide to increase this value by means of the system registry.

But before jumping on and tweaking registry drop ins, I would strongly advise you to determine whether the need for additional file handles is because the STORE is unable to accept incoming messages (which may indicate a sluggish performance of the volume hosting the streaming store) or because of high traffic. I would discourage you from trying to bump the limit, since it can have serious consequences on the additional kernel resources required to handle these file handles. This may incur additional processing and, at worst, render the system unresponsive if the kernel should run out of memory. That, in turn, would call for a reboot, and this is not a very good practice in Enterprise computing environments.

A wiser solution would be to load balance and distribute the SMTP mail traffic between two or more SMTP servers, instead of having one single SMTP server handling all the data. In addition to a greater throughput, you will build redundancy into your message routing environment.

If an SMTP virtual server version that lacks open file handles is running on a back-end server, this manifests in the form of high throughput of inbound messages to the local STORE (for any of the databases), and failure to expedite mail messages is probably due to bad file placement for the streaming store and the mailroot folders. Chapter 4 provides background information on storage technologies that is helpful for understanding the necessary device criteria for fast file access. Chapter 7 gives sample configurations of how best to configure high-end mail routing servers and back-end servers that require fast message delivery. In most deployments, you will find that Microsoft's calculation is very well adapted to your environment, and you should not attempt to modify settings that can have an impact on another system's components.

5.7   In Summary

I would like to close this chapter by making some key recommendations dealing with Exchange 2003 server optimization. Granted, I have focused here on the core Exchange services. Additional applications, such as anti-SPAM or antivirus engines might add additional workload.

What I really want you to understand is that the actual process of optimizing Exchange 2003 is based on some simple key principles:

- Don't underestimate Exchange 2003's need for network services from Windows, such as the Active Directory and the DNS services. Most of the time, problems we have experienced in our own in-house deployment were due to surrounding services failures, not to failure of the core product itself.

- Be assured that technology will progress, but some elements will not evolve at the same pace as others. Storage subsystems, for example, will continue to evolve in terms of data bandwidth (what I like to call the *data rate*), but not in terms of transactions (*request rate*). You may decide to deploy complex setups and configurations, but if your environment is a mixture of scaled-up servers and scaled-out organizations, unusual settings are likely to cause some problems if they are not properly tracked and if they are not reported and clearly documented in such a way that a service pack update or a hotfix does not trash your service by surprise.

- Most of the Exchange optimization can be done by adequately configuring the storage subsystem. I can never repeat it enough: Exchange 2003 is a database application, and, like any database application, it needs to process large quantities of data. You, as an Exchange administrator, have to take the utmost care in protecting this data, which, after all, represents a key asset of your company.

- Always make educated choices for tuning one parameter or another of the Exchange service, especially when it comes to the STORE process, the real core of this wonderful application. Making a change to optimize a server is good, and you should understand why this change is important. But being able to measure the effect of that change is infinitely more important and puts you in control of what is going on.

- Some optimizations given in this chapter are available in Microsoft's series of technical articles on Exchange 2003. They are really applicable to the 15 percent of server deployments that need to meet particular transaction workloads. I foresee that most of the server deployments will work out of the box, and I want to thank Microsoft for making such a product that can autotune itself and keep administrators from shooting themselves in the foot by making changes that are not always clearly documented. Study carefully the effect of a particular change to your server, and determine if it is really worth doing. For example, an X.400 MTA running out of concurrent sessions to the STORE that is addressed by a registry setting could only make the problem worse. The real problem could very well be that the STORE itself does not process fast enough the X.400 connections. Increasing the number of gateway in and out thread counts will alleviate the problem for a little while, but not resolve a more fundamental performance issue related to the STORE process. In short, be careful; make one change at a time, measure the effect, and decide when to implement that change.

Script every change you make. This is a basic rule for Internet service provider administrators and a very good practice in my opinion. It ensures that a single change can be repeated in a *consistent* fashion and repeated yet again, with no errors, should a service pack update override the particular settings. This is particularly valid for any change made inside the Exchange configuration naming context and for any change made to the server's registry.

The actual implementation of these optimization practices is materialized in Chapter 7, which describes best practices and gives a set of sample configurations, most of which are drawn from actual customer deployments and have been proven to work. I don't advocate any particular vendor hardware; just keep in mind that solid high-quality hardware will grant you tranquility and keep you from being sleepless in whichever town you happen to live.

6

Performance and Monitoring

6.1   The Challenge

Performance testing for a product such as Microsoft Exchange is focused on two distinct evaluation criteria. One is to estimate the capacity of a given server, storage subsystem, and overall combination of hardware and software to handle a certain workload with a satisfactory response time. The other is to evaluate the features of the product being tested that you believe your environment will exercise most and to determine what the benchmark or load simulation results reveal about those features, how the proposed solution reacts to the stress testing, and how it can evolve in the future. This evolution study is frequently referred to as *capacity planning*. Whatever tests are carried out, they will always occur in a closed, sanitized environment. Microsoft provides a very good set of tools for evaluating the envelope of a solution and for stressing this solution with fairly realistic transactions; however, each and every Microsoft Exchange deployment has a different set of users, each with their own work pattern and requirements.

The best strategy is first to understand the load generated and the response of the server. Second, as you begin your deployment, closely monitor the performance of your servers, observe their sweet spots, and note how far or close you are from the benchmark environment. You can then proceed to some corrective actions (e.g., more disks, better CPU, more RAM) to arrive at the solution that matches your expectations.

In the past few years, the sizing of Microsoft Exchange servers has largely been helped by several factors, the first being that Microsoft Exchange runs in most production environments that are ready to be migrated: as you size for Exchange 2003 (and possibly for upcoming versions of Exchange), you can get a pretty good understanding of the workload applied by network clients such as Microsoft Outlook and therefore relate this to benchmarking information if available.

Regardless of the version of Microsoft Exchange, you can determine how many transactions are issued by the clients, determine the workload pattern, find the peak or idle hours, and then measure the corresponding system impact on far better information than pure simulation: production data from production workload. Eventually, you will also want to have very close monitoring of the platform as you start the rollout and then proceed to refine your model and possibly change it if you didn't get it right the first time.

Fortunately, there are tools and methods that allow most deployments to work on their first rollout. Unfortunately, some deployments experience unexpected workload that results in adjustments in the middle or after the rollout of Microsoft Exchange. In this case, you are confronted with a problem of tuning a production environment, with no budget for an increase of hardware and the pressure of the business users who need a production service that works "fine" real soon. Eventually, missing the necessary period of reaching stability in pilot, and failing to maintain it during production rollout, can result in nasty consequences for everybody in the organization. Do not underestimate growth and do not underestimate the necessary study. The goal of this chapter is to open you to the possibilities of performance testing and monitoring that exist with Microsoft Exchange and that can later save time and money to you and anybody involved in the Microsoft Exchange rollout.

As I studied Exchange deployments, I found that applying the consolidation concepts to large corporations could lead to interesting considerations that you would not have in decentralized scenarios. For example, how do you deal with database maintenance in a 24 × 7 deployment that groups, in a single data center, users from all over the world? How can you ensure that your backups do not impact production users? In a shared storage environment (which really is the fundamental benefit of storage networks), how can you prevent servers from impacting each other, apart from dedicating and physically separating resources?

In order to answer all these questions, you must understand first what Exchange demands from the infrastructure components and how it can accommodate with varying workload. This will allow you to design the right solution—instead of overengineering or undersizing the configuration—and get past undesired situations of budget constraints or user dissatisfaction.

6.1.1 Representative Performance Testing

For application service providers, and Internet service providers, it is not practicable to qualify a scalable solution for 5 million users. Often, the benchmark or load characterization has to focus on a representative part of the target environment (often referred to as a building block). It will require skills to extrapolate the results into the target solution and decide whether the results and observations are satisfactory.

Too often, the rate that commercial services on the Internet will actually be accessed depends on their success, which is not always predictable. In fact, many ISPs will forecast for a given growth and later review that projection, if they are indeed successful. The goal in creating a scalable and adaptable architecture is to enable ISPs to address the increased workload, even at its peak, without modifying the fundamental architecture of their data centers and operations. Proceeding by building blocks allows them to gradually grow the infrastructure in a predictive manner.

In corporate or enterprise environments, the case for performance testing of an Exchange 2003 server or infrastructure happens when you need to qualify new platforms based on new technology (shared storage networks, multicore processors) and possibly new ways of accessing and using the information located in an Exchange 2003 infrastructure, such as the use of Outlook 2003 in cached mode or the adoption of the new storage network infrastructure based upon iSCSI protocol over Ethernet.

There is indeed a challenge in configuring and sizing a system, storage subsystem, network, or an infrastructure hub such that its life cycle can span more than 18 to 24 months; this challenge is also compounded by the necessity to handle a given workload, either current or future. You may be tempted to raise the bar a little higher compared with what you think is your current messaging system utilization, and that is a good thing in itself (add a "fluff factor," quite interesting to justify to the purchasing department). You may also consider that you probably don't want to acquire all the necessary storage you'll need for the next five years of operations at day one of your deployment, on the basis that it is far more expensive than what it will be when you will actually need it. In fact, what many large-scale deployments require is a combination of stability, evolvability, and affordability of the target infrastructure. This combination varies depending upon customers and target environments. Some will plan for and acquire a solution that comprises a 20 percent annual growth for the next five years, while others will start small and implement processes and building blocks that can grow along with the workload. In either case, you have to be careful how you engineer your resulting solution while compromising with the hardware and software limitations, budget constraints, and service level objectives (SLOs). These SLOs should be your driving factors, as opposed to the technology itself, which is only there to serve a purpose.

One way of maximizing your chances of hitting the right configuration from day one and thereafter is to perform adequate performance assessment and testing. Nowadays, there is more space left for performance testing in Microsoft Exchange projects than before, probably due to the track record of the product in production environments and the increased importance of electronic messaging in modern business processes. Besides, Microsoft has published a lot of information since Exchange 2003 RTM to help customers properly assess and size their target environments, with a particular focus on storage, a topic that can be too easily overlooked.

Each Exchange migration or deployment project can comprise the necessary architecture and design phases, and they are often complemented with a performance testing phase, which can stress individual components or the entire solution. This was not the case of earlier deployments of Microsoft Exchange, but the footprint required by performance testing added to the ability to monitor a legacy environment to better define your final goal, justify the necessary hardware resources, and enjoy a working solution. Once gone into production, it can prove very difficult to backpedal on a given configuration (imagine changing the engines of a jet airplane while in flight).

Besides, as an IT manager, you will find it terribly difficult to go to your financial administrator for additional budgeting for hardware (most organizations strive to reduce these costs) only six months after deployment. Basically, you need to ensure the life cycle of your infrastructure. In addition, you need to figure out how to get the best of your environment at the lowest cost, bearing in mind that some qualities of your infrastructure—reliability, availability, and scalability—don't come free. They have a cost, which is acceptable as long as you have the data to justify investments. Even though you may have run a Microsoft Exchange 5.5 or 2000 environment for the past two years, your Microsoft Exchange 2003–based infrastructure might look much different from what you had previously. In the process of reducing IT infrastructure costs, many enterprises are aiming for server or service consolidation, thereby augmenting the density of users, data, and activity per server. This changes the rules of the game for sizing Exchange servers and can lead to catastrophic results if you have not properly sized your machine or estimated the workload for the near and medium term. In the past, Microsoft Exchange 5.5 and 2000 servers seldom scaled up because of some of the storage limitations that prevented the rapid restore of massive quantities of information. Across time, the storage technologies have evolved, along with Windows Server and Microsoft Exchange, enabling you to build Microsoft Exchange back-end mailbox servers that can easily host 5,000 users, all connected at the same time. This quickly exposed the product and the underlying solution to new areas of stretching, and unless you have a good legacy and solid performance test plan, you're almost guaranteed to have "bad" surprises—to experience downtime—and so would your users.

I believe nowadays that we have sufficient knowledge and know-how to help our customers deploy systems architectures that will last for several years; I would be hesitant to acquire it all at once, unless there is a strong desire to freeze the infrastructure design; evidence shows that whatever your growth plans, the actual growth will be much larger and quicker to happen.

This chapter deals mostly with what you can do and what you should do to ensure proactive maintenance of your environment, raise end-user satisfaction, and improve productivity by providing an adequately sized environment that can bear both the current and the anticipated transaction load. It is difficult, however, to simulate or qualify an entire infrastructure in a controlled environment in which you have several areas of measurement and to determine the resource utilization as a function of the transaction workload. To alleviate this problem, I generally advise customers to pick up a representative chunk of the infrastructure, including Windows Server services such as DNS, which could be hosted in other environments (e.g., UNIX) and, most important, the Active Directory. For Microsoft Exchange, a lot of this representative chunk will depend on your target environment. If you are aiming at an enterprise deployment, try to locate representative sites (in terms of load and number of users) and attempt to model its workload for sizing your systems configuration (servers, network services such as Active Directory, and, of course, storage). This may require one or two servers under test, but have several Active Directory domain controllers and/or GCs around to sustain the load that Exchange 2003 puts on the Active Directory.

6.1.2 Industry Benchmark Information

You can access industry benchmarks from either the OEM's performance resource page on the company Web site or from Microsoft Exchange's performance and scalability Web site (http://www.microsoft.com/exchange/evaluation/performance/default.mspx). There, vendors reported quite high rates of concurrent MAPI Messaging Benchmark 3 (MMB3) users on their target platforms (10,000 and above). Microsoft has set definitive rules for how these benchmarks should operate, what software configuration should be used, and how to make sure that the workload is really accurate. You should be careful in reading through these reports, as they are only useful for comparing machines (CPU and motherboard) and do not have representative storage configurations, nor do they exercise all or part of the Microsoft Exchange product functions, such as Internet clients, mobility services, or public folder replication, to name a few. To help as a basis of comparison, Microsoft requires each vendor to document any changes (tweaks) made to the Windows and Exchange products (typically a handful of registry settings) as well as the description of the machine under test.

Standard Data Reporting

The standard data reporting that Microsoft demands must include key configuration elements and basic system resource utilization indicators, such as the CPU utilization, the response time of the storage device, and the overall transaction volume (e.g., number of messages sent and delivered). It is highly dangerous to transpose this into a production environment, something I never recommend.

Clearly, a benchmark environment is quite different from a production environment. Unless you've put benchmarking activities (with proven results) in the bid requirements for your project, you will need to read between the lines of the industry-standard benchmarking reports to decide whether the results boasted by a given vendor are appropriate for your environment.

Most often, the machines used for benchmarking are closer to Formula One automobiles (suitable for speed, but not for production) than for powerful but comfortable cars like the Mercedes Benz[1] E class.

You can quickly identify the production level of the solution by looking at the storage subsystem characteristics and focusing on:

- Type of storage used——DAS or SAN;
- Number of paths used to the enclosure;
- Number of disks used for hosting the databases and message transport folder (usually hundreds of disks, which is not realistic in production environments unless performance is an absolute must);

---

1.   Insert here the brand of your choice. I must specify that I get no incentive in quoting car brands.

- The RAID level used (typically RAID0);
- Controller cache size and protection.

When considering those storage attributes, your goal should be to maintain data availability, while getting the best response time (ms per I/O) for each storage area stressed by Exchange, such as the SMTP MTA NTFS queues, the database volumes, and the transaction log volumes (the former being one of the most critical elements for fast response times).

The use of standard add-ons, such as antivirus products, can indicate how realistic the benchmark was. With Exchange 2000 and the implementation of synchronous events, a simple application that makes use of these events may bring an entire server down due to bad programming practice.

Recall the Exchange 5.5 performance results. In the early days, I saw some vendors using RAID5 for their subsystem, which was proof of two key points:

- Vendors generally benchmark what they want to sell to their customers.
- Vendors don't try to hide the performance impact of a RAID5 implementation.

This is a very important factor: vendors that benchmark production-level configurations are presenting platforms that can address both the performance and the availability requirements of a production Exchange 2003 system.

Of course, there may be other reasons for selecting a particular vendor other than performance and benchmark results. This is especially important when you deal with scale-up and scale-out models, the ability to roll out consistent platforms in a global architecture, and the ability to contract additional services in managing the environment. These can range from purely business-critical services that enable customers to obtain a guaranteed service uptime to complete outsourcing solutions, such that customers need to worry only about their businesses, not their infrastructures.

This last point is a delicate one to address and involves the determination of whether or not the infrastructure and computing services are part of the core company assets. The nature of e-mail communication in an e-business environment makes most of the Microsoft Exchange deployments business critical; four hours without messaging can affect the actual enterprise operations. It can entail a nonnegligible cost that cannot be ignored and should be used to value and finance advanced infrastructures (e.g., clustering, redundant machines and networks, safe storage).

Sample Report 1

Table 6.1 shows a sample report of one of the top system configuration that can handle the largest quantity of concurrent users with Exchange 2003.

Table 6.1   *HP DL 585 Performance Benchmark with Exchange 2003*

Hewlett Packard	
Server	HP ProLiant DL585
Test Results	
MMB3 score	12,000
Response time	279 milliseconds (ms)
CPU utilization	55.9 percent
Average queue	81
Messages submitted	517,757 (4-hour steady state period)
Messages delivered	1,286,202 (4-hour steady state period)
Messages sent	517,709 (4-hour steady state period)
Server Configuration	
CPU	Dual-core AMD Opteron 2.4-GHz/1-GHz Hyper-Transport
CPU count	4 physical
RAM	8 GB
Secondary cache	1-MB L2 cache per core
Operating system	Microsoft Windows Server 2003 Enterprise Edition
Storage	320 36.4-GB 15K Information Store databases (EVA 5000)
	56 36.4-GB 15K transaction log files (MSA 1500)
	2 36.4-GB 15K operating system, Exchange files, and Active Directory

Table 6.1 *HP DL 585 Performance Benchmark with Exchange 2003 (continued)*

Controller	Integrated HP Smart Array 5i Plus controller
	Dual-port fibre channel card (2 Gb)
NIC	Dual-port NC7782

Note a few interesting points:

- The processor clock speed is not very high (2.4 GHz); however, the processors have dual cores (i.e., two processors in a single die), which means that they can achieve a lot of work with low frequency. In return, you get less heat generation and fewer cooling requirements. Multicore processors really outshine with Microsoft Exchange's workload! The processor utilization is not 100 percent: the performance bottleneck, present because we would have otherwise achieved more users per server, is not due to a CPU shortage. So what has the processor been doing during this 44.1 percent of the time? Probably waiting on slow devices: network and, most importantly, disk. In general, a high CPU utilization is an indication that the processor has plenty of work and data at hand. Low processor utilization (less than 75 percent on average) indicates that the processor is either not very busy or spends time waiting on I/O.

- A total of 8 GB of RAM was configured on this machine, and this is due to the AMD processor architecture. Because the memory controller is embedded in the processor, you must provide enough RAM to each of the processors—in this example, 2 GB were attached to each of the four processors. In reality or with a different processor architecture (such as Intel's), you would not need such a large quantity of RAM.

- There is a huge quantity of drives utilized for the private databases (320). This figure gives a pretty good indication of the type of resources needed to support more than 10,000 MMB3 users on a single machine.

- The type of RAID controller used is important. This configuration is using a SAN storage controller, which is a good indication of how you can reuse the configuration data. Note that two different array architectures are used: this is necessary in order to achieve the high throughput for a benchmark environment. In general, you will tend to deploy databases and transaction log files on the same back-end storage array. The advantage of the test proposed here is to get relatively closer to production environments, using a full-blown SAN back-end environment. The relatively low CPU utilization might indicate, as mentioned before, that the SAN interaction is not necessarily delivering as good a throughput as we might have desired, in order to saturate the processors, by approaching 70 percent or 80 percent utilization.

- The LoadSim score is 279. The MMB2 OEM benchmark standards call for accepting tests that have a score less than 1,000. You might think that this particular vendor added a few more clients to bump up the top figure. However, the system performance here is very close to the actual saturation point, and adding another 10 percent of clients could blow the score above 1,000 because of queuing, excessive privileged processor time, and other things.

Sample Report 2

Table 6.2 shows another sample report of the system configuration from, this time using an Intel processor architecture.

Table 6.2   *Fujitsu-Siemens PRIMERGY BX630 Performance Benchmark with Exchange 2003*

PRIMERGY BX630 Server Blade—Single Server	
Test Results	
MMB3 score	13500
Response time	225 milliseconds (ms)
CPU utilization	79.5
Average queue	87
Messages submitted	564259 (4-hour steady state period)
Messages delivered	1398452 (4-hour steady state period)
Messages sent	564184 (4-hour steady state period)
Server Configuration	
CPU	Intel Xeon 5160 dual-core 3.0 GHz
CPU count	Two (four cores)
RAM	4 GB
L1 cache	

Table 6.2 *Fujitsu-Siemens PRIMERGY BX630 Performance Benchmark with Exchange 2003*

L2 cache	4 MB
L3 cache	
Operating system	Microsoft Windows 2003 Enterprise Edition
Storage	2 36-GB disks for operating system and system log files
	570 36-GB disks for Exchange files
Controller	1 LSI Adapter SAS 3000 series
	1 QLogic QLA2340 PCI fibre channel adapter
NIC	Broadcom BCM5708S NetXtreme II GigE

Similar observations can be made for this vendor configuration:

- The number of processors is … 2! These are dual-core 3.0 processors, with 2 MB of cache each (for a total of 4 MB of L2 cache).

- There is a relatively high CPU utilization (79.5 percent) during the reference period, which suggests that the benchmark reached its objectives in saturating the processing capacity of the server, albeit with the relatively small quantity of data at hand (4 GB of RAM).

- The RAM quantity is 4 GB again, 2 GB per physical dual-core processor.

- There is a high number of drives, and these drives are small (36 GB)—smaller than what you typically consider for a production deployment. Although the rpm (rotation speed) of the drives is not reported, there is a good chance that they are 15 krpm.

- There is only a single Qlogic host-bus adapter, something you would not do in production: it shows, however, that a single HBA might be able to deal with the workload for Microsoft Exchange. In general you will use more than one HBA for path redundancy and for possibly load balancing the I/O requests to more than one path in the SAN fabric and, more importantly, at the back-end SAN array level. The test does not disclose the detailed storage configuration. From the data made available, we can consider that the number of disks (570) might have been the key scalability factor (from a performance viewpoint only!).

In Summary

By no means, do I wish to compare Hewlett-Packard with any other company in this book. Microsoft has ensured that results could be reported with minimal information and disclosure of any particular tuning tip (which basically gets summarized to Exchange memory tuning). All vendors play the same game, and that game has nothing to do with building production servers; they do serve as interesting comparison points for processor and server architectures.

Personally, I believe these results have very limited value and must be handled with a lot of care. Such information can be misused, set wrong expectations, and lead to catastrophic results in a large Exchange 2003 project (that does exist). For that reason, I strongly recommend spending some time in conducting your own performance testing if you intend to right-size your environment (i.e., for current and forecasted workloads). The following section discusses what that really means for you and your organization.

6.1.3   What's in a Performance Test?

Just like in a music studio, you can spend weeks and months in performance testing of the various aspects of Exchange 2003 and its dependency components (such as the Active Directory) and not obtain tangible results that can be reused in production deployment. Sometimes, you may have to run through several iterations of the same performance test because of software and/or hardware adjustments made in the testing environment.

I have found it to be useful to run performance testing, not only to determine how many users can be handled by a single server, but also to determine core service levels (e.g., how long it takes for a backup to restore). There are many other activities beyond simple user load that can be undertaken in a performance lab. For example, it is a good opportunity to perform *integrated* testing of all the components running in an Exchange 2003 infrastructure. These typically include antivirus software, backup software, and sometimes hardware-based SSL acceleration boards or multifunction network interface cards.

The list can be long, and precious time and money can be spent in such activity. Accordingly, always try to run such tests so that they gather valuable results that can be used to set IT directors' as well as end users' expectations.

A good example is how long it takes to restore a single database, a single storage group, or an entire Exchange 2003 server. Based on this data, you can very easily justify additional spending for a highly redundant (by eliminating single points of failure) storage subsystems to decrease the likelihood of four to eight hours of downtime because you need to restore your environment. Users will appreciate it, and business units that typically own the budget approval for part or all of the infrastructure can decide whether eight hours of downtime is critical for their activities or not. If they are, you should present them with several options and associated costs, and the budget approval can be quickly expedited.

Dealing with a Transactional System

Traditionally speaking, a transaction system such as Microsoft Exchange 2003 must deal with client requests and message transfers that represent an overall transaction workload to be processed by the various components of an Exchange 2003 server—primarily the information store process, the IIS process, and the SMTP routing engine. What is really required from a transactional system is to provide a satisfactory response time and message throughput that matches the service levels expected by the end users and the messaging service manager. Whether you can handle tens of thousands of clients is irrelevant if your system does not satisfy client requests, usually initiated by the end users. Therefore, knowing the end-user community and its behavior is extremely important in any sizing of computing resources (primarily the CPU, RAM, network, and storage resources). If you have an existing Exchange environment, you are probably already aware of much data that you can collect that enables you to perform an appropriate sizing exercise.

Nevertheless, because Exchange 2003 is so different from Exchange 5.5, you may need to run benchmark testing that can establish a baseline of how a computing platform can actually meet the transaction workload at its peak or close to its peak. We will therefore often refer to the resource utilization in terms of percentile (i.e., the percentage of time that the machine performed a certain volume of transaction with satisfactory levels). This is preferable to using averages, which dangerously hide peak values while end users are usually exposed and generate these peak values and transaction workloads. If you consider a client interface such as Outlook, the users do not particularly care if the system was idle 5 minutes or 1 hour ago; they need a fast response when they need it. Before rushing to your production servers to collect performance data, you can perform some preliminary research, simply based on your company habits. For instance, the Monday morning peak between 9 AM and 10 AM is often seen for office users. For service providers, you would have a peak toward the end of the day for a couple of hours while users are in their home office connecting to their mailboxes. In banking environments, I often found peaks of mail transfer activity in the second half of the Friday afternoon, showing reports being sent off, either by users or by mail-enabled applications.

Rather than collecting and analyzing data for full working days, try to concentrate your performance analysis during these peak hours. Sizing for the peaks will ensure that not only can you deliver performance during idle times, but also when the systems are busiest—for any application that deals with end users, that's the way to ensure good user response time, and Exchange makes no exception to this.

Latency vs. Throughput

A transaction processing system can be characterized by two key elements: the latency (i.e., the time needed to complete a particular transaction) and the throughput (i.e., the ability to process a certain volume of transaction during a given period of time). In high-performance Exchange messaging environments, your focus is on obtaining a low latency for user-initiated actions; users feel that a responsive server is processing their actions (e.g., browsing a folder or searching for an element). As far as volume is concerned, focus your attention on the ability of the messaging system to switch, deliver, and send messages between the messaging servers globally and, most important, within your service levels (for example, delivering 99 percent of the messages within five minutes). Addressing the latency and throughput issues can result in different actions, depending mostly on the server's role and the placement of the server in the computing infrastructure (e.g., across a WAN or on a LAN).

The goal of making a high-performance system is to quantify the transaction volume and the latency, to be able to decompose these transactions into system resource requirements in order to analyze the level of utilization of these resources and to optimize the resources sitting on the critical path of a transaction completion (e.g., the transaction log volume, the database volume for read operations, or, more simply, the network infrastructure).

Exchange Server Roles

As you architect your Exchange 2003 infrastructure, you will be confronted with the need to specialize servers to perform certain roles. You may need to do this because of network boundaries (e.g., front-end servers sitting in front of firewalls for Internet access) or simply because the type of server required differs depending, precisely, on the server's role. In most deployments, we identify the following roles for Exchange 2003 servers:

- *Mailbox servers.* These servers host the user mailboxes and can be accessed directly by means of the MAPI RPC client used by Outlook, by means of HTTP-DAV clients (Internet browsers), or by a combination of HTTP and RPC (RPC over HTTP), which is often assimilated to simple RPC workload. Because there can be only one location for a user mailbox, your aim is to make these mailbox servers as robust as possible, even by using clustering technology, and to equip them with sufficient storage capacity, both in terms of gigabytes and transaction volume (I/O per second, megabytes per second). This is typically where we see monster servers connected to scalable storage area networks.

- *Public folder servers.* For large deployments, you may dedicate servers to share public folders. There are two types of public folders that need attention: the general public folder MAPI tree, which is used to share information between users, and the system public folders, which are used to store and replicate organizational forms or publish free/busy information from the users calendaring. Do not neglect public folders in consolidated environments, where many users might be fighting for a small number of public folder instances to look up free/busy information, especially if you use resource mailboxes to describe meeting resources such as video-projectors or meeting rooms.

- *Front-end server.* These are often present to establish protocol proxying between the client and the back-end or mailbox server when operating across network boundaries imposed by firewalls. Even without a firewall, in a private network environment, front-end servers are useful to provide a simple namespace (e.g., http://exchange.company.com) for any user in the Exchange organization. Front-end servers tend to be loaded by some components of the HTTP interface to Exchange (Outlook Web access) and are sometimes necessary for the deployment of certain functions, such as Exchange ActiveSync.

- *Bridgehead servers.* These are typically designed to switch messages between peer bridgehead servers or mailbox servers. Bridgehead servers will typically host routing group connectors (pure SMTP relay inside or outside the Exchange organization, MAPI-based connectors, such as Fax, and real-time scan of messages for viruses and possibly content). They do not necessarily need a lot of storage, but when they do, that storage is mostly qualified by its ability to deliver a high transaction rate (I/O per second) with a very low latency. Typically, bridgehead servers are less often used than mailbox servers.

They are redundant (i.e., two bridgehead servers can be used to connect a particular site to another) and rely on the network performance to achieve a satisfactory throughput. Bear in mind that if you plan to deploy real-time antivirus software on your bridgehead servers, there can be an incremental load on the CPU resources. If you are not sure of the added consumption, you might aim for a platform that can scale up (i.e., start with a two-processors machine that can be easily upgraded with another two processors) to accommodate the peak workload.

Benefits of Bake-Off Testing

There are multiple benefits of a bake-off in an Exchange 2003 project:

- You get the opportunity to validate a complete, integrated solution, not only from a performance but also from a functional standpoint.

- You have a chance to define acceptance criteria for the overall solution. A basic criterion is the score value obtained from a load simulation. The score, in that case, represents a 95th percentile of the weighted average response time of multiple client operations.

- You can determine, given a defined workload, the areas of the solution that are stressed and understand the headroom for future growth. This provides a proactive approach to long-term capacity planning.

- You can determine the scalability properties of the proposed solution (which component can be acted upon to increase capacity).

- You get a chance to refine your hardware configuration and save many thousands of dollars on unnecessary hardware components. For example, in one instance, reducing the server RAM capacity from 4 GB to 2 GB helped a customer to save $1 million on deployment costs. This is not an advantage to the OEM from a revenue standpoint, but you have management's trust—and this is clearly a long-term investment!

- You understand the effect and load on surrounding components in an Exchange 2003 server infrastructure—for example, Windows Active Directory domain controllers and GC servers.

- You can run tests across multiple servers, exercising server-to-server data transfer, something not usually measured during industry benchmark tests.

- You can fine-tune your storage deployment and allocation model, add or remove storage groups, add or remove databases, and change the layout of the underlying storage volumes, among other things. This can carry a great deal of value. We often may want to deploy several storage groups but wonder whether they should really have a dedicated log volume or whether the log volume could be shared by means of hardware partitioning. This can result in savings in footprint and in cost, but it can also hide some pitfalls—for example, the influence of a log replay on a partition to the other partition during nominal workload.

- You can set service level agreements upfront, based on your testing. But that's not the end of the story. In many cases, you will want to define how well your server behaves under a realistic workload, but you also have an opportunity to determine the impact of exceptional activity on your infrastructure, which is described next.

Take a simple example of an Exchange 2003 server that uses a volume for four databases belonging to the same storage group. The initial approach consists of determining whether the hosting volume provides the necessary request bandwidth to accommodate the load. This is quite straightforward to address. You choose a volume design strategy (RAID5, RAID0+1, with a large spindle count) that addresses the user workload and provides a satisfactory response time (again, the response time can be summarized by the score of the load simulation software). Now that you have sized a disk resource to address a nominal workload, how can you be sure that this resource will be able to cope with an exceptional load? For example:

- *Concurrent restore of a single database.* During a restore operation, you have a stress situation in which users of the database being restored are out of service, and you also run the risk that users on other databases sharing the same resource will be affected by the additional workload.

- *Time needed to perform a global restore of a server that spans beyond the Exchange 2003 server (e.g., the Active Directory servers).* No matter what the raw performance figures are for your backup environment state, only a complete restore allows the IT administrator to define realistic expectations in measuring the mean time to repair. Complete restores can be an entire server recovery or the entire set of databases restored on the server.

- *Single-mailbox restore solutions.* To address a common problem in Exchange 2003, backup vendors propose the option of backing up the Exchange 2003 stores such that you can restore an individual mailbox. Currently, most of these solutions are based on MAPI access to the STORE, and they are resource consuming and may not fit into the required backup time frame. It would seem wiser to me to get to the STORE by the means of HTTP-DAV (WebDAV), which provides a much more efficient access to the Exchange store than MAPI; remember that a lot of effort put in the Exchange 2003 design was to optimize access for Internet protocols, not for the MAPI protocol, where the goal was to be on par with the Exchange 5.5 performance characteristics. Alternatives have to be explored, but you first need to qualify the solution in your own production environment.

- *Antivirus database checking.* If your system is overwhelmed by a worm-like virus (for example, ILOVEYOU), what is the impact on operations if you have to run a database virus scan on your server? How will your users be affected? Also, consider the technologies used by the ISVs (e.g., Sybari or Trend Micro) and determine the incremental workload of running these products.

- *Online defragmentation.* This has to be done on a daily basis or you run the risk of serious performance degradation. How fast does an online defragmentation complete? I have seen cases in which an online defragmentation for a server with 2,500 users would exceed 10 hours. Online defragmentation runs as a background, low-priority task, but what is the impact on the response time of the server if the online defragmentation time window overlaps with the users' main activities? What is the collateral damage caused to servers sharing the storage resources (as commonly found in SAN deployments)?

- *Deleted item retention.* Determine, based on a given workload, the net effect of enabling the deleted item retention period as well as the effect of, for example, moving it from 14 days to 30 days (this can be time consuming, but is a great learning experience). For example, one of my customers determined that a 14-day retention period raised the database size by 30 percent, and a 30-day retention period raised the database size by 100 percent. That's OK, but it might have an impact on your storage planning.

- *Content indexing.* This feature introduced with Exchange 2000 is seldom used with Exchange 2003. It can be very expensive in terms of CPU and disk resources. I have seen an increase of 20 percent to 40 percent CPU utilization when content indexing was turned on. You might want to make sure that your server can handle this incremental load, which is never used in official platform benchmarks and not very often considered in planning for Exchange 2003 server capacity. Implementing content indexing as an afterthought can have an extremely negative impact on the actual server performance. While working in a performance benchmark environment, I figured that turning on content indexing and requesting a full index generation was in fact consuming so much CPU (disk accesses were easily handled) that the STORE kept on growing its send and receive queues—this resulted in message not being delivered in a satisfactory amount of time (i.e., less then 5 mn in a single server environment).

- *Global server optimization.* The Exchange 5.5 performance optimizer no longer exists; how can you tune your Exchange 2003 server and what are the effects? Knowing which knob to turn is a good thing; knowing why the knob has an effect is even better.

- *Applications.* You may be tempted to deploy mail-enabled applications against your production environment: how can you be certain that they are not going to impact the regular interoffice messaging and calendaring functions of Exchange? For instance, we have seen mobility applications that extend the reach of Exchange to fit-for-function mobile devices generating the equivalent of five times the load of a single mailbox for each device. As you adopt new applications, installing them against your infrastructure is just not going to be without effect; there is opportunity, for instance, to dedicate specially tuned servers to deal with such demanding applications.

- *Global Data Center certification and validation.* Going beyond the vendor's certification, you'll feel a lot safer if you have burnt in your production configuration with some performance testing prior to allowing production traffic.

Two possible strategies are available for handling exceptional activity:

- Include some flexibility in your service level agreements; state that server response time is guaranteed under normal operations and that some negative impact may occur under exceptional operational conditions. How much of an impact remains to be determined, and a good performance and integration plan can help in calculating this.

- Size the target resource (apart from the storage subsystem, remember that the CPU can also be a factor) to be able to accommodate not only the nominal charge but also exceptional operations. This is where you need to spend extra time in your performance lab studying the various scenarios and possibly putting in some additional margin (fluff factor?).

In either case, you can help IT administrators take a proactive approach to capacity management. There are many areas that need to be explored beyond the performance benchmarks provided by vendors.

By choosing not to run such activities, you risk deploying an infrastructure based on assumptions and will be exposed to "bad" surprises when exceptional events are to be handled. Granted, it is usually easy to plan for backup time windows and accept a possible impact, but how your environment will handle a restore situation, which does not always occur under the best conditions, is another matter. There are many environments that can deal with the matter without extensive testing, but in the majority of data center and high-end deployments, it is a pretty risky attitude to take, and the consequences of poorly handled exceptions can turn into real nightmares involving downtime, user frustration, and more.

How Long Should It Take? How Much Will It Cost Me?

You will find that running performance tests in a customer environment can be extremely demanding of time, money, and resources. It's like playing in a rock band and getting into a music studio; you can spend a lot of time trying things or tweaking chords or rhythms and end up after a jam session with no tangible result. This is to be avoided in any engagement proposed to customers. To this effect, I often recommend defining a clear set of deliverables and determining how they will be factored in during the customer rollout.

Quite frankly, the answer to "How many users can I host in a server?" is by far the simplest question to address. More difficult questions include, "If I build a 200-GB volume to hold four databases for my mailboxes, how long will it take to back up the databases? How long will it take to restore one database? How long will it take to restore two databases? Can I restore more than one database (on the same or different storage groups) at a single point in time?"

The answers to these questions depend on many factors and will also help in sizing the most appropriate solution for your backup and restore infrastructure, whether it is LAN based, SAN based, clone based, or disk based. For example, based on its infrastructure design, Microsoft OTG decided to use disk-based backups to increase throughput and maintain a reasonable time window for maintenance operations. Nonetheless, modern tape libraries or virtual tape libraries can exceed disk throughput when configured and used correctly.

You must be careful to present the exercise in a positive way to your management. It is not that OEMs need a lot of time on their platforms to design a solution. Rather, each customer environment is different, and each Exchange 2003 configuration is becoming increasingly complex because of add-on components (e.g., antivirus and backup/restore products). Accordingly, there is no single answer to performance questions.

The exercise can also have a serious impact on the choice of technology; it's always good to provide an idea of the possible impact on the infrastructure design as a deliverable of the performance and integration-testing project. Sometimes it will save money and sometimes not, but at least you have hard data, factual information that justifies any incremental investments that are deemed necessary for your environment.

Defining the scope of testing, which allows you to cost the proposal in your project budget, is an important aspect, and you must work hard with your service provider or OEM to come up with a good cost estimate. Table 6.3 provides estimates of the time you will spend on this activity. The parallel running of certain operations can affect the time estimates given here. For instance, a full Microsoft Loadsim run takes about 8 hours, giving you 16 more hours in your day to perform activities such as testing the online defragmentation and testing backups. Consider the tasks to be performed and how to best implement these tasks in your schedule, especially when working in teams.

Table 6.3   *Time Estimates for Performance Testing*

Activity	Duration
3,000-user MAPI benchmark	Four to five days. This assumes that the hardware is in place and that you know your way around Loadsim. An actual run typically takes 6 to 8 hours, but the data analysis and the client setup required to make sure that the workload is properly generated takes preparation time. Also, never base your results on a single test; try to obtain consistent and repeatable tests. If you run these tests at night, don't forget to turn off online database maintenance.

Table 6.3   *Time Estimates for Performance Testing (continued)*

Activity	Duration
10,000-user IMAP/POP/SMTP benchmark	Five days. This assumes that hardware is in place and that you are familiar with the workload generator, ESP (also known as Medusa).
Storage stress and "burnout"	Five to ten days (elapsed). This activity can be quite short if you are proficient with the Microsoft tools, such as Jetstress and Perfmon, and have seasoned analysis methods.
Backup performance	Three days. This assumes that the hardware is in place and the backup software is functional. You need source databases, but you can reuse the benchmark databases.
Defragmentation performance	One day. Quite straightforward, but careful system performance analysis is required during and after the defragmentation
Antivirus performance	Two days. The actual duration may vary if you want to determine the incremental load of an antivirus solution on the messaging servers and possibly compare solutions.
Combined user-load/restore/offline defragmentation/ESEUTIL/volume rebuild/redundant component handling	Two to three days. This can be one of the most revealing tests—how does the system behave when things go wrong? IT administrators can never thank you enough if you perform this exercise and help them handle those stressful situations with proper management and an end-user expectations set.
Active Directory resilience and scalability	Five days. Make sure that Exchange reacts correctly to the Active Directory hiccups, such as a GC failure, and study how you can handle a large number of directory service queries from Microsoft Exchange, possibly using a large memory model (64-bit Windows).

Table 6.3   *Time Estimates for Performance Testing (continued)*

Activity	Duration
Data analysis and report authoring	Three to ten days. It depends on how many activities were performed and how comprehensive you need to present the data. Obviously, methods and tools are key factors in helping to expedite this activity. Remember that there is little point in doing performance testing if you cannot communicate the results in a way that enables for a better design.

The incremental cost of hardware can vary greatly depending on the route you take. In most situations, the system under test and the surrounding components (SAN, tape library, Active Directory domain controllers and GCs) must be present. Software licenses have to be handled too, but that is less important. Most of the time, an ISV will provide you with a 30-day evaluation version of the firm's application, which is sufficient.

Many tools can be used for generating workload, but the most common are as follows:

- Microsoft LoadSim for simulating Outlook MAPI clients;

- Microsoft Jetstress for simulating I/O using dummy instances of the Exchange database engine;

- Microsoft Exchange Stress and Performance (ESP), an Internet protocol workload on a target server (LDAP, SMTP, IMAP, POP, and HTTP-DAV).

A complementary tool is IOmeter, an OpenSource program originating from Intel, that can be found at: http://www.iometer.org. This is useful for determining the performance baseline of your storage volumes and architecture. All the tools mentioned here are free of charge and relatively simple to use.

Additional costs can also come from the infrastructure (dedicated network switches, lab room), and, most important, the loading clients. An Intel Pentium-4 1.7 GHz with 512 MB of RAM will approximately handle the simulation of 600 to 700 MMB3 MAPI users. The same class of machine will generate beyond 2,000 ESP users (because this depends on the Internet protocol workload, this is a gross approximation). You don't need to build a whole wall of desktops or clients.

I found that a rack of 1-U servers with a keyboard/video-monitor switch was adequate. Don't forget to put the switch, screen, and keyboard on an ergonomic desk; you will spend time playing with those puppies, believe me! Microsoft made significant improvements with Loadsim 2003, with the ability to "drive" many Loadsim client instances from one single console.

You can acquire these machines in several ways—for example, by renting the hardware or buying it with the objective of reusing it. There are a few benchmarking centers from major IT vendors that can be used to run these tests, but frankly I found that the most beneficial environment is the customer's premises. You can work on loaning machines to generate the workload; you can also ask the customer to obtain the machines (usually, they are low-profile servers) and then allow them to redeploy the lab hardware during the project rollout or to keep it as a validation environment.

It is also important to correctly transfer knowledge and explain what led you to a particular conclusion (e.g., you need to add four more spindles to a RAID; you don't need 4 GB of RAM, you need SSL accelerator cards for your front-end servers). Help your staff to better understand how to follow up the servers in the field, understand the workload baseline, determine the growth evolution, and plan for proper capacity increase when needed.

How Realistic Should the Environment Be?

The question of how realistic the environment should be is difficult. For example, using a "standard" LAN implementation for the load simulation client may reveal the inefficiency of the network implementation. However, this discovered bottleneck might hide others. In any case, the result of a performance benchmark should give two key indications:

- The sequence of bottlenecks encountered (network bandwidth, network adapter, storage subsystem);
- The translation of the given load into system resource utilization, which can lead to transaction cost analysis (TCA). TCA, in turn, can help in building a predictable model of the solution. It doesn't predict, however, how successful a service could be.

It is pretty much useless to run a performance test in an environment such as the server or the storage subsystems that does not represent what will actually be deployed. Don't attempt to go down that route—don't even think about it. Use the exact target configuration, including BIOS and firmware versions for the PCI adapters and additional components as you will deploy them. Performance testing can reveal very interesting data, sometimes problems or bugs in the system's components and software products, and you have a unique opportunity to get this fixed and verify the fix without feeling the warm breath of the IT director on your neck.

I found it was generally best to run a performance test as part of pilot or preproduction rollout testing. This serves two purposes:

1. You can verify that the proposed environment performs according to a certain baseline (also known as characterization) and then be able to measure any deviation as you roll in production servers.

2. You can burn in your hardware: electronic equipment has a tendency to either break during the first two weeks of their installation or run for years. This is not applicable to all components, but I've found that this rule generally applied to key infrastructure components.

Capture Data

It is fine to run performance tests for your environment, but don't forget that you have an incredible opportunity to gain experience from such an environment. For example, you can gather additional performance data that can provide good insight into the product's behavior and discover how the target platforms best address performance requirements. If you run these tests concurrently on several vendors' hardware, the data has even more value.

Too much data can kill data, and although the Windows operating system provides a first-class performance collection framework with Perfmon, you can easily be swamped with gigabytes of information to analyze. Understand, as part of the data you collect, which are key indicators of performance (latency of RPC or of disk devices, data or request rates of storage volumes) and which are those that you can collect and analyze later on for sizing purposes (for example, a rough estimate of the number of I/O operations per second per connected user).

In performance testing, it's usually a good idea to configure and dedicate a server or a power workstation to collect performance data and keep it aside for mass post-processing analysis.

One Last Word

Don't forget that you may already run an Exchange 5.5 infrastructure and that there are a lot of things to learn from such an environment. Don't hesitate to spend time analyzing message tracking logs (which give a good indication of the activity of the system), system performance counters, and message throughput to get a good feel for the existing workload. You may well find that the workload is very different from the default industry benchmark workload defined by Microsoft and OEMs. This is also known as MMB3 (for Exchange 2003) and is used for all hardware benchmarking reports listed by Microsoft. We will discuss in greater detail the synoptic of a Loadsim or ESP simulation environment further in this chapter.

The results of a performance test can serve many purposes:

- *Capacity planning*—determining whether system resources provided are adequate for the anticipated load;

- *Budget justification*—determining which vendor should be used for server rollout;

- *Systems configuration*—determining the best tuning for production systems;

- *Storage infrastructure requirement*—establishing a baseline, in a shared storage environment, that will help the SAN administration team to design a target solution and ensure that the solution delivers the expected results as you move into production;

- *Competitive positioning*—showing that a solution can handle a given number of loads and prove to be scalable and performing;

- *Integration testing*—validating a particular solution with all surrounding components and determining the impact of these external components.

Before engaging consulting resources and hardware investments, determine for which purpose the performance test has been engaged. Make sure you set expectations right to all parties, from top-level management who will receive some results to partners and employees who will participate in the benchmark.

6.2 Exchange Workload Simulation

There are two families of tools to be used with Exchange 2003. One, directly inherited from Exchange 5.5, is Microsoft Loadsim. Loadsim aims at testing and generating load for MAPI clients only (primarily Outlook, if you consider that applications that use the MAPI API can be considered clients). Because Exchange 2000 came with a significant emphasis on Internet protocols, Microsoft engineered ESP (code named Medusa), a beefed-up version of InetLoad. It is used to generate load and measure response time for Internet protocols (e.g., POP, IMAP, and HTTP). ESP can be used with Exchange 2003 and is particularly useful if you wish to stress SMTP message routing, if your deployment has an important Internet protocol flavor, such as for service providers, or if you deploy ActiveSync mobile clients.

For individual directory load simulation, you can use Loadsim, which will simulate directory lookups via MAPI (it will also exercise the DS_ACCESS component of the Exchange 2003 server), or ADTest, a specific tool that will generate and measure response time for concurrent LDAP calls to an Active Directory server (GC server or domain controller).

6.2.1 Loadsim 2003

Loadsim was developed early along with Exchange 4.0; it provides a solid tool and a de facto industry standard for simulating MAPI connections on an Exchange 2003 server. Loadsim must be carefully used because it can produce misleading results. For example, if your load simulation clients are overloaded (!), they won't simulate as many users as you might assume. Along time, and with experience building up, Microsoft improved both the tool and the documentation and practices that came with it. Always make sure you have the most recent version of Loadsim and the accompanying set of documents that describe the mode of operations of the simulation tool.

Loadsim is particularly indicated if you wish to simulate as close to reality a workload as possible. There are also certain testing scenarios (e.g., using mailboxes with a relatively large number of items in the critical folders of a mailbox) that can produce quite interesting results. We will discuss the possible scenarios later in this section. You can download Loadsim from the Microsoft Exchange Web tools page, available from: http://

www.microsoft.com/technet/prodtechnol/exchange/downloads/2003/
tools.mspx.

Key Components

You cannot just run Loadsim setup on your Exchange server and start kick-
ing simulation on the server. You have to organize a minimum environment
composed of the following items:

- *System under test (SUT)*: This is the system you wish to apply the load
  on and possibly measure the response time of (known as the *score*) as
  well as its behavior under activity. It is the server that runs Microsoft
  Exchange and that hosts the mailboxes. You may configure Loadsim
  to simulate clients to more than just one SUT. This is an interesting
  approach because it also enables you to test the interserver communication.

- *Load clients*: Typically, you will use between 500 and 600 MAPI connections per loading client. Thus, if you wish to simulate 5,000 users,
  you will need at least 10 loading clients. You must install Loadsim on
  these clients, which do not need to run a client version of the Windows operating system (e.g., Windows XP), they can also run Windows Server 2003. You should *not* install Loadsim on the Exchange
  server.

- *Monitor client*: This is a special instance of Loadsim, which typically
  simulates between 100 and 200 MAPI sessions and is used to record
  the score.

It is common to configure Loadsim clients and measure the response
time across all of the load simulator. Also, you may use server-class
machines to run Loadsim and have a slightly better ratio of simulated clients than with a standard desktop (for example, 800 MAPI clients). However, we have found that the most predictable results were generated using a
lower number of simulated clients.

When Loadsim runs, it records the response time for the various MAPI
operations done (in milliseconds) and computes a weighted average
between all those response times. The score, final indicator of the SUT
response time, is generally the 95th percentile of the weighted average.

Typical Environment

For a 5,000-user server test with Loadsim, here is the environment I would recommend:

- One or two systems under test (four or eight dual-core or hyper-threaded processors, 4-GB RAM);

- One SAN (fibre channel based, 200 GB, 4,000 I/O/s peak capacity, 256-MB cache);

- One 64-bit GC server (two processors, 4-GB RAM, local disks) or two 32-bit GC servers with 3 GB of RAM;

- Ten load simulation clients (2-GHz processors, 1-GB RAM);

- One or two servers for data capturing and analysis with 20 GB of spare space.

In fact, the number of load simulation clients will depend largely on the load profile and the type of protocol under stress. For MAPI users, Loadsim will accurately simulate up to 500 clients out of a single processor and 1 GB of RAM. For ESP, the figure is higher (2,000 clients per loading machine). A typical Loadsim system environment is shown in Figure 6.1.

Figure 6.1
Loadsim topology

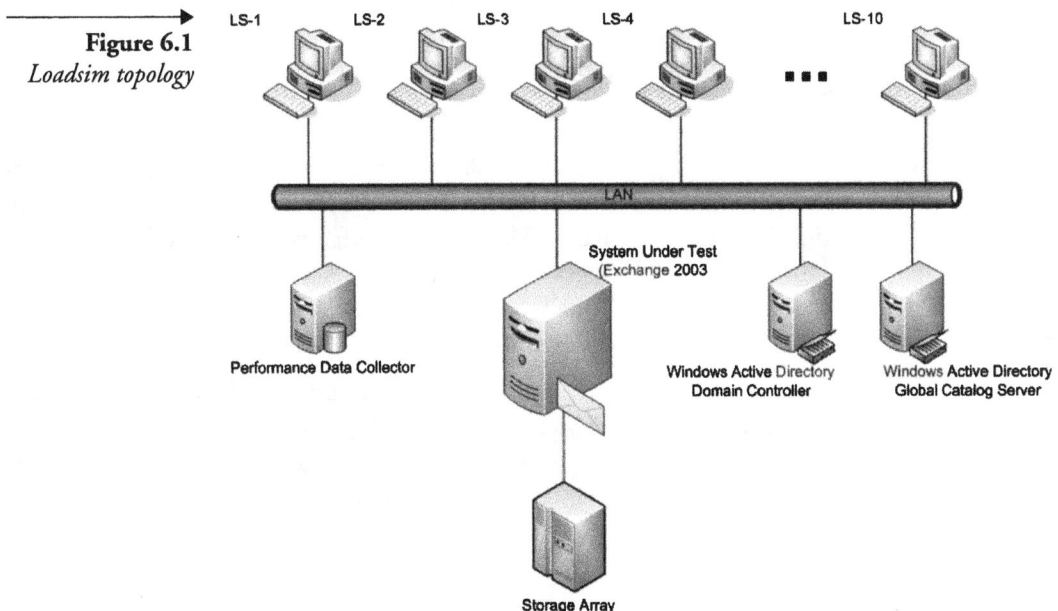

Note the presence of Loadsim clients (here we have ten clients) all connecting to the same LAN, as the two systems under test and the bridge-head servers are included in that configuration. In such an environment, we can collect performance information locally on the systems being loaded and keep track of performance reports from the Loadsim client on a single chosen client (in our case, we have a dedicated performance data collector server).

Loadsim Profile

Too often, hardware vendors and software manufacturers are aiming for the best-looking numbers. The idea is to define a standard load simulation profile and let manufacturers perform a test under defined conditions. Microsoft did some significant work and came up with a method and a standard user profile (MMB), which went through revisions for each of the releases of Exchange.

Loadsim Profile	Exchange Version	Comment
MMB	Exchange 5.5 and older	Designed after as medium a user profile workload as we could find when Exchange was introduced in the mid-1990s
MMB2	Exchange 2000	Designed to be a somewhat heavier profile, especially with larger attachments
MMB3	Exchange 2003	Designed to be heavier and implement with RPC over HTTP and search folders, functions that are only available from Exchange 2003 onward

The change of the contents of the profile was made based upon practices in the industry and also feedback from vendors that actively participate in the performance benchmarking of Microsoft Exchange. You will find that MMB3 is a "good" high-water mark for a single user workload against an Exchange server, especially useful for measuring incremental load when adding third-party solutions such as antivirus, mobility clients, and the like.

Typically, public folders are not tested in Loadsim benchmarking; however, you can enable them and tamper with the default profile to create your own. I have found that recent tools from Microsoft, such as the Exchange Profile Analyzer, are superb for scanning a typical production server and determining the usage patterns of that server.

Installing Loadsim on a Client Machine

The installation of Loadsim is very straightforward. As mentioned previously, Loadsim will use standard message files for simulating the load. You may want to add more message files to better match the environment you are running in. For instance, to create a 2-MB message, you would open Outlook, create the message, and save it as a .MSG file in the Loadsim folder (by default, C:\Program Files\LoadSim) under the name of your choice. Then, it is a matter of including this message file in the list of message files used for the load simulation, with the weight (or statistic of use) of your choice. Figure 6.2 shows the list of messages that are installed by default with LoadSim 2003.

Figure 6.2

Messages and posts used by LoadSim 2003

mcPP1Matt.msg	1,104 KB	Outlook Item	7/21/2005 6:16 AM	A
mcPP100katt.msg	127 KB	Outlook Item	7/21/2005 6:16 AM	A
mcWD2Matt.msg	2,042 KB	Outlook Item	7/21/2005 6:16 AM	A
oPf1k.msg	17 KB	Outlook Item	7/21/2005 6:16 AM	A
oPf2k.msg	21 KB	Outlook Item	7/21/2005 6:16 AM	A
oPf4k.msg	26 KB	Outlook Item	7/21/2005 6:16 AM	A
opf10kat.msg	33 KB	Outlook Item	7/21/2005 6:16 AM	A
oUps1k.msg	21 KB	Outlook Item	7/21/2005 6:16 AM	A
oUps2k.msg	25 KB	Outlook Item	7/21/2005 6:16 AM	A
oUps4k.msg	32 KB	Outlook Item	7/21/2005 6:16 AM	A
oUps10kat.msg	37 KB	Outlook Item	7/21/2005 6:16 AM	A
oUpsbmobj.msg	33 KB	Outlook Item	7/21/2005 6:16 AM	A
oUpsJApp.msg	21 KB	Outlook Item	7/21/2005 6:16 AM	A
oUpsJrnl.msg	42 KB	Outlook Item	7/21/2005 6:16 AM	A
oUpswdatt.msg	43 KB	Outlook Item	7/21/2005 6:16 AM	A
oUpsxlatt.msg	42 KB	Outlook Item	7/21/2005 6:16 AM	A
oUpsxlobj.msg	38 KB	Outlook Item	7/21/2005 6:16 AM	A

Microsoft provides several default profiles configured in LoadSim. You can view these profiles as you configure LoadSim clients workload, as shown in Figure 6.3.

To modify the set of tasks that will be executed by a particular client, you should select the Test Properties menu option and choose the button "Customize Tasks" located in the lower right corner of the dialog box, as shown in Figure 6.4.

If you modify any of the default profile, the user type will be renamed as "<custom>." You must then ensure that all clients are using a similar Loadsim configuration file for using the right profile definition. Before LoadSim 2003, you had to manually copy the files to each of the load simulation clients, but, since then, you can now use the "Remote Control" menu option, decide to take control of one client in your environment and automatically

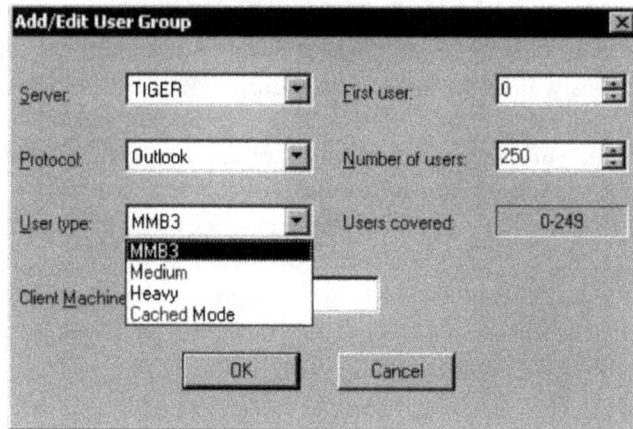

Add/Edit User Group   ⊠

Server: [TIGER   ▼]   First user: [0   ⊟]

Protocol: [Outlook   ▼]   Number of users: [250   ⊟]

User type: [MMB3   ▼]   Users covered: [0-249   ]
               ┌─────────────┐
               │ MMB3   │
               │ Medium   │
Client Machine │ Heavy   │
               │ Cached Mode │
               └─────────────┘

                    [OK]   [Cancel]

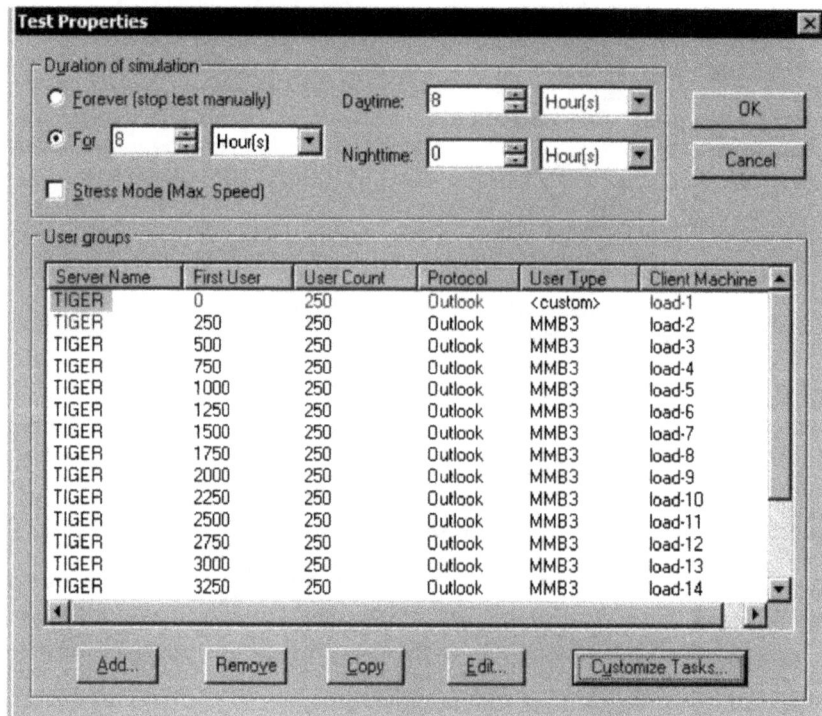

Test Properties   ⊠

┌─ Duration of simulation ───┐
│ ○ Forever (stop test manually)   Daytime: [8   ⊟] [Hour(s) ▼]   [OK]
│ ⦿ For [8   ⊟] [Hour(s) ▼]   Nighttime: [0   ⊟] [Hour(s) ▼]   [Cancel]
│ ☐ Stress Mode (Max. Speed)
└──┘

┌─ User groups ──┐

Server Name	First User	User Count	Protocol	User Type	Client Machine
TIGER	0	250	Outlook	<custom>	load-1
TIGER	250	250	Outlook	MMB3	load-2
TIGER	500	250	Outlook	MMB3	load-3
TIGER	750	250	Outlook	MMB3	load-4
TIGER	1000	250	Outlook	MMB3	load-5
TIGER	1250	250	Outlook	MMB3	load-6
TIGER	1500	250	Outlook	MMB3	load-7
TIGER	1750	250	Outlook	MMB3	load-8
TIGER	2000	250	Outlook	MMB3	load-9
TIGER	2250	250	Outlook	MMB3	load-10
TIGER	2500	250	Outlook	MMB3	load-11
TIGER	2750	250	Outlook	MMB3	load-12
TIGER	3000	250	Outlook	MMB3	load-13
TIGER	3250	250	Outlook	MMB3	load-14

    [Add..]   [Remove]   [Copy]   [Edit...]   [Customize Tasks...]

push the SIM file (LoadSim data file) to each of the clients under control
(Figure 6.5).

When using Remote Control, the clients are synchronizing their activities (such as initialization or simulation) over the network and share the

Figure 6.5
Sharing a SIM file

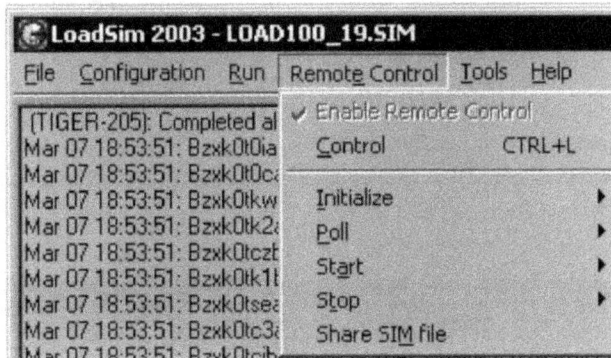

Figure 6.5
Sharing a SIM file

SIM file via a network share. Figure 6.6 shows how remote control detects and displays LoadSim clients on a simulation network.

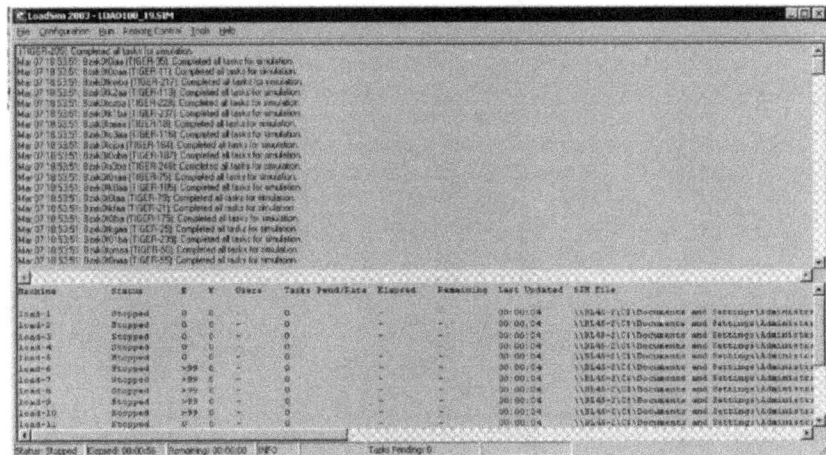

Figure 6.6
LoadSim and remote control

Loadsim Initialization

At initialization, LoadSim will attempt to detect the configuration of your organization located in the Active Directory. You may get some error messages if servers do not contain storage groups or if the storage group does not contain any databases.

You will also get similar messages if the LoadSim client is running under an account that lacks the permission to access servers or elements in already defined administrative groups. That is all right, as long as the servers that you intend to test do not belong in the initial WARNING messages. You need full Exchange Administrator permission on the administrative group that contains the servers under test.

You can decide to use either a generic account (the one under which you are logged on while running LoadSim) or a specific account with each mailbox. That last option is useful if you are running LoadSim in a production environment with an Active Directory that has implemented password-strengthening policies. Using named accounts (Figure 6.7) allows you to specify a strong password, in line with the policies defined in the Active Directory.

Figure 6.7
*Configuring
credentials with
LoadSim*

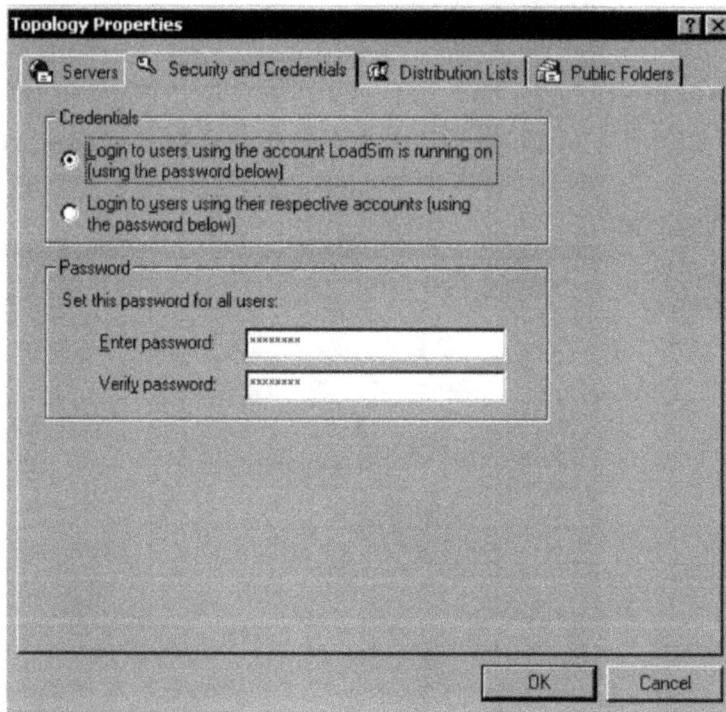

Topology Configuration

The first task to do when running LoadSim is to define the topology. Essentially, this consists of determining the servers that you intend to place your load on. To define the topology, select the Configuration menu item and then the "Topology Properties" option (see Figure 6.8).

For this property page, there are four property tabs—one for the servers, one for the security settings, one for the distribution lists, and a last one for the public folders. We will review each of these.

Figure 6.8
Topology properties

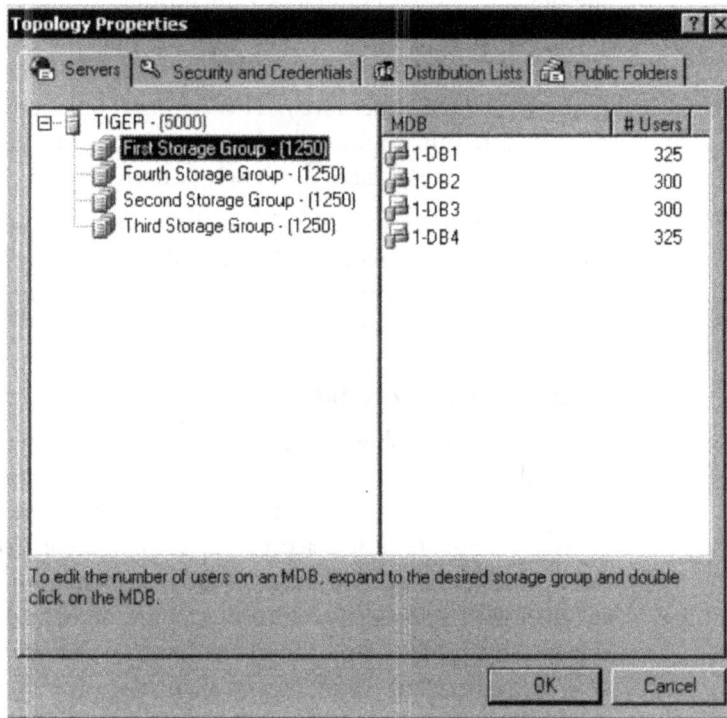

Servers Property Sheet

Here, you must define the servers that make up your load environment. By default, the complete list of servers that make up your organization is displayed. In our example on Figure 6.8, there is a single server. You can expand the server line and drill down to the database level to enter the number of users that you wish to simulate on that particular server and database (see Figure 6.9).

Figure 6.9
*Databases and
user count*

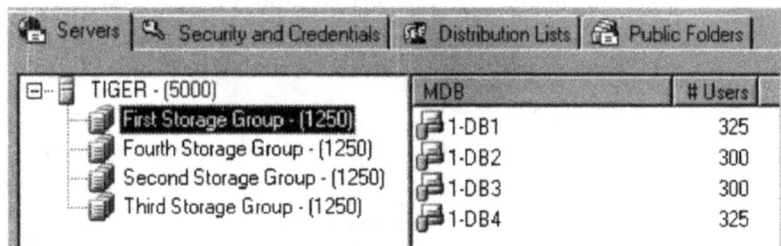

You can enter the number of users you wish to host out of a particular database by clicking on the number of users (right-hand column) and editing the field. In this example, we are hosting 325 users on the database "1-DB1" on server TIGER. As you enter the number of users for the various servers and the database, the numbers will add up at each level (storage group level, then server level). This setting is quite powerful; however, you need to determine upfront how you want users to be hosted—on one or more servers, one or more databases, or both.

I strongly recommend that you should get as close as possible to what will be eventually deployed. There is little point in testing a single database/storage group server if you plan to deploy servers with, for example, two storage groups and two databases per storage group.

Security Property Sheet

The next property sheet to complete is the security settings, and that sheet essentially defines whether each LoadSim client will use the same Windows Active Directory account or a separate one when creating the MAPI sessions (see Figure 6.7). It is acceptable to use a single account for all users (as you will see later, the first phase of the load simulation consists of "logging in" the MAPI sessions, which involves some authentication as well as placing an interesting load on the Active Directory domain controllers.) If you wish to qualify your Active Directory infrastructure for authentication performance at logon time (this is rarely done), you should look into running a separate performance-testing exercise.

Distribution Lists Properties

Don't fall into the trap of not using distribution lists (DLs). The generation of the lists is not flexible (you cannot define the actual members of the list), but you always have the opportunity to change this when importing the lists into the Active Directory (see Figure 6.10).

More important, DLs are an interesting component of the SMTP routing engine (the categorizer), and it is a mistake not to include them in your test. Note that you may want to change the maximum DL size if you are interested in doing advanced testing or if your planned infrastructure makes heavy use of DLs.

New with LoadSim 2003 (and Exchange 2003) is the ability to use dynamic distribution lists (also known as query-based distribution groups). This is indicated if you make extensive use of these lists, as the resulting LoadSim workload will involve in issuing queries to the Active Directory during message categorization.

Figure 6.10
*Configuring
distribution
lists with
LoadSim 2003*

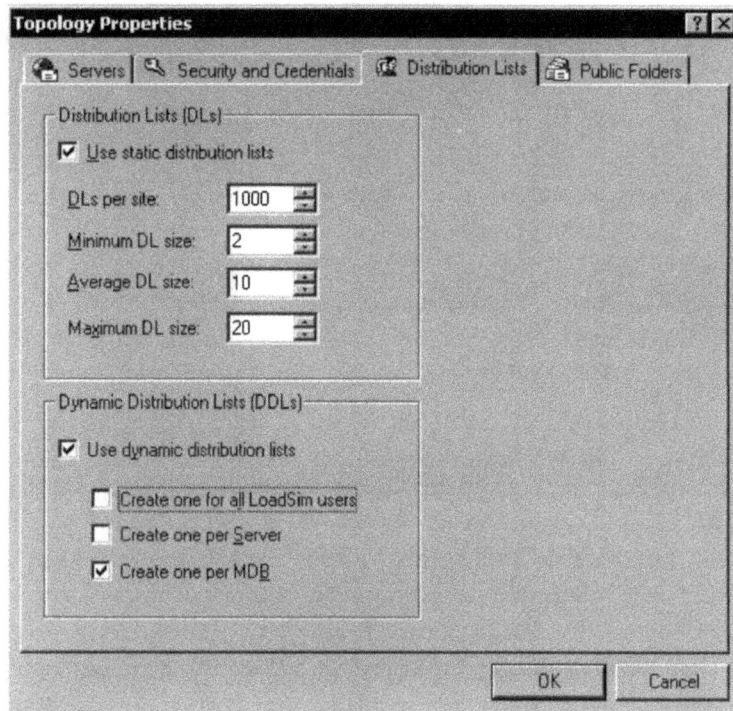

Creating the Topology

Once you have defined the topology, you should save your configuration (File > Save) to ensure that you can resume your LoadSim configuration if you should choose to interrupt the running session. The next step is to create the topology (Run > Create Topology). With LoadSim 2003, the topology creation involves creating user accounts and distribution groups in a special container.

First, a top-level container called "LoadSim Users" is created. Then, subcontainers are created for each of the servers running under the simulation (see Figure 6.11).

This is quite a practical way of separating the LoadSim users from the rest of the organization. Note that a similar feature was present in the previous release of LoadSim, which created a separate recipient container in the Exchange site. Normally, you would start off your runs by executing in a standalone environment. In this case, however, it is better to burn in your machines and do some verification of the complete setup while in production; this approach in creating accounts in containers will certainly not disrupt the production environment. It may pollute the global address list for

Figure 6.11
LoadSim OU

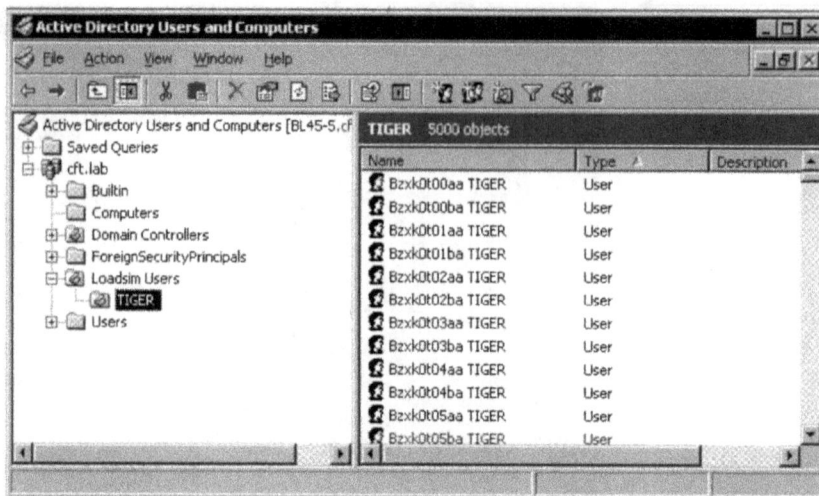

a little while, but proper warning to and education of your user base can address this issue very easily at minimal effort.

Another option, of course, is to modify the default Address List generation in Exchange 2003 to exclude the LoadSim Users container and subcontainers. User accounts are created in each server-named container, whereas distribution lists, which are global to the simulation, are created in the "LoadSim Users" container.

Configuring Public Folders

You may configure public folder initialization by using a new tab introduced with LoadSim 2003, and shown in Figure 6.12.

This setting used to be part of the user profile definition in previous versions of LoadSim. With this page, you can define the depth and contents of the MAPI public folder hierarchy. This is useful if you intend to stress test the components that access shared information—in most testing, however, we would typically concentrate on testing the Exchange mailbox attributes, as opposed to the public folders. This option remains a convenient way to load a public folder hierarchy, useful if you wish to test, for instance, replication.

Command Line Options

In order to script and automate the execution of LoadSim (which is useful when running this tool on 20 or 30 clients), there is a set of command line options, which can be listed by using the command "LoadSim /?" at the

Figure 6.12
*Configuring
public folder
initialization*

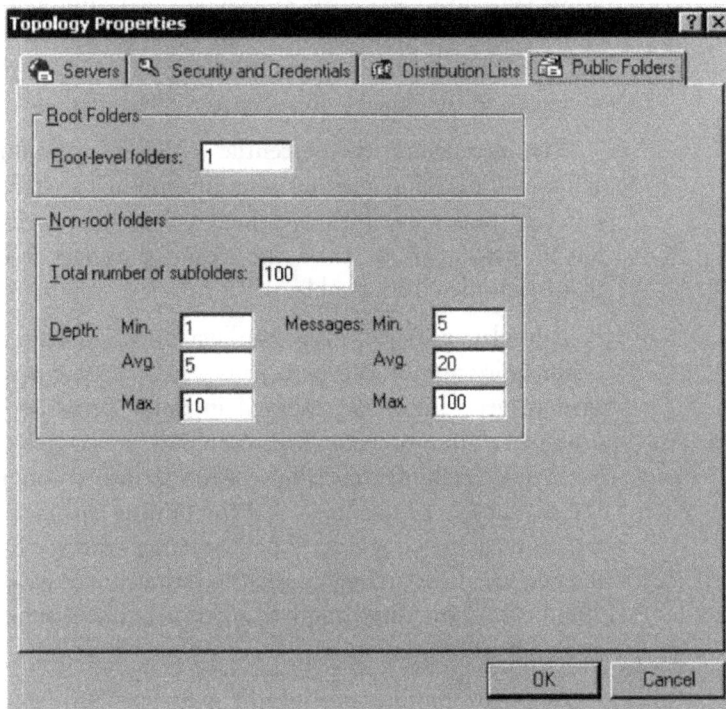

Figure 6.12
*Configuring
public folder
initialization*

DOS command prompt (provided you're in the LoadSim installation
directory)—see Figure 6.13.

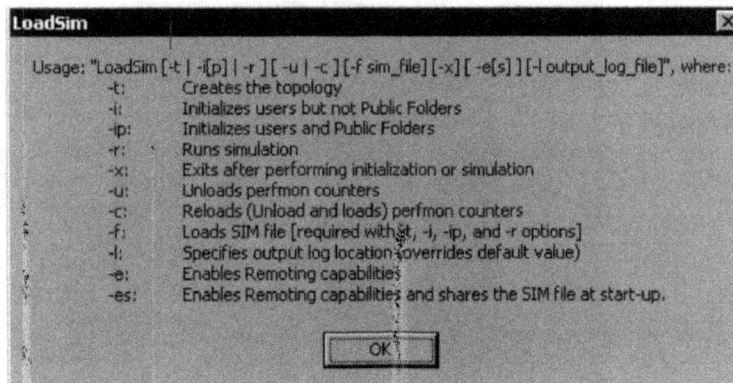

Figure 6.13
*LoadSim 2003
command
parameters*

Interpreting the Results

In a transactional world, averages don't give an indication of the responsiveness and effectiveness of a given solution. Instead, LoadSim uses the com-

bined concept of weighted average and percentiles. The weighted average aims at combining the response times for the various operations, but to a different degree. You can't really average the time it took to send a 1-MB message and the time it took to read a 1-KB message.

The idea behind the percentile is similar to producing a histogram of values and deciding whether a set of sampling is statistically significant or not. The peak value for a weighted average may well be above 4 seconds, but 95 percent of the time, the weighted average is below 1 second, and that is considered acceptable.

A similar approach can be conducted for processor time utilization. Processor utilization of 100 percent is good, because it proves that you managed to get your server engaged in doing actual work. However, if this processor utilization is too high, you may in fact lack computing resources. So, by determining that high processor utilization is possible, you can decide whether or not this is OK by putting this measurement in perspective with a large sample set. That's what percentile is for, and that is, to me, the best way to accurately measure a transactional system, such as Exchange 2003. (The same could apply to any transaction system, such as SQL Server or SharePoint Portal Server.)

To obtain performance results with LoadSim, you can navigate to the folder where LoadSim is installed and run the command lslog.exe against the most recent load simulation results file (by default, lsperf.log), as shown in Figure 6.14.

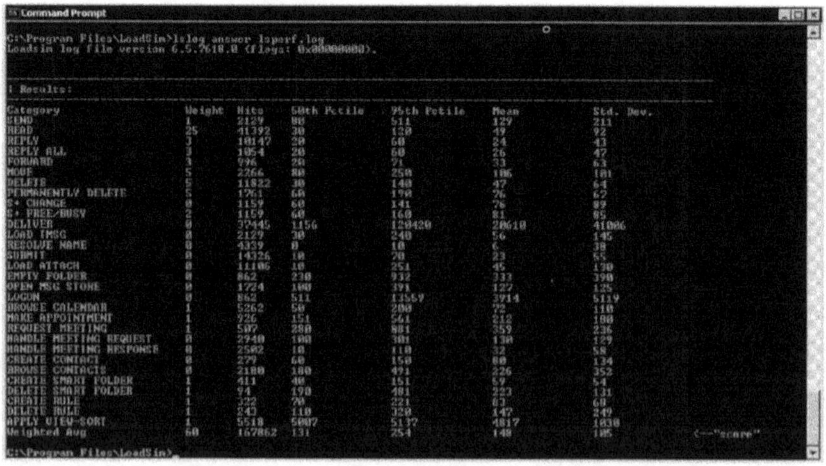

Command Prompt

C:\Program Files\LoadSim>lslog answer lsperf.log
Loadsim log file version 6.5.7618.0 (flags: 0x00000000).

| Results:

Category	Weight	Hits	50th Pctile	95th Pctile	Mean	Std. Dev.	
SEND	1	2129	80	511	129	211	
READ	25	41392	30	130	49	92	
REPLY	3	10147	20	60	24	43	
REPLY ALL	3	1054	20	60	26	47	
FORWARD	3	996	20	71	33	63	
MOVE	5	2266	80	250	106	101	
DELETE	5	11822	30	140	47	64	
PERMANENTLY DELETE	5	1761	60	190	76	62	
S+ CHANGE	0	1159	60	141	76	89	
S+ FREE/BUSY	2	1159	60	160	81	85	
DELIVER	0	37445	1156	120420	20610	41006	
LOAD IMSG	0	2129	30	240	56	145	
RESOLVE NAME	0	4339	0	10	6	38	
SUBMIT	0	14326	10	20	23	55	
LOAD ATTACH	0	11106	10	251	45	130	
EMPTY FOLDER	0	862	230	932	333	390	
OPEN MSG STORE	0	1724	100	391	127	125	
LOGON	0	862	511	13559	3914	5119	
BROWSE CALENDAR	1	5262	50	200	72	110	
MAKE APPOINTMENT	1	926	151	561	212	180	
REQUEST MEETING	1	507	280	801	359	236	
HANDLE MEETING REQUEST	0	2940	100	301	130	129	
HANDLE MEETING RESPONSE	0	2502	10	110	32	58	
CREATE CONTACT	0	279	60	150	80	134	
BROWSE CONTACTS	0	2180	180	491	226	352	
CREATE SMART FOLDER	1	411	40	151	59	54	
DELETE SMART FOLDER	1	94	190	401	223	131	
CREATE RULE	1	322	70	221	83	60	
DELETE RULE	1	243	110	320	147	249	
APPLY VIEW-SORT	1	5518	5007	5137	4817	1030	
Weighted Avg	60	167862	131	254	140	105	<--"score"

C:\Program Files\LoadSim>

Figure 6.14 *Obtaining LoadSim client performance results*

For the example shown, the score is 254, which is quite acceptable for a 5,000-user server (the norm is for the score to be below 1,000). As a further matter of verification, Microsoft provides to the hardware vendors Excel spreadsheets to which you can input key performance counters (such as the total number of messages sent and delivered), which help in making sure that the load that was applied to the server does indeed correspond to the desired load.

In Summary

There is a comprehensive documentation coming along with LoadSim that enables an experienced system administrator to configure a test and perform some simulation testing. I believe that beyond simulating users, Load-Sim carries a unique advantage because it can generate the peaks and valleys in the workload (such as the RPC or I/O workload) that you would typically not be able to get when using other tools such as Jetstress or IOmeter.

This said, to get it right, a LoadSim benchmarking environment may take as long as two full weeks of engineering and testing, setup, and possible troubleshooting. This should give you enough time to make sense of the results and get sufficient coherency in your tests such that you are certain of the workload applied to the system under test.

6.2.2 **Jetstress**

The goal of Jetstress is to benchmark the storage subsystem by means of creating one or more instances of the ESE database engine (used by the Exchange Information Store) and create baseline characterization of the storage components used in your Exchange environment.

Initially, Jetstress was delivered as a command-line tool. That command tool has been complemented by a graphical user interface (GUI) since Jetstress. The Jetstress GUI walks the system administrator through the steps of allocating logical units (Windows disks), validating the environment (e.g., using a separate drive for the transaction log files of a storage group), and running a series of performance tests aimed at the following:

- Testing the throughput and response time of a storage solution for a given (estimated) workload;

- Stress testing the storage subsystem (how fast can it be);

- Testing the throughput of the backup and recovery of Exchange.

The great advantage of Jetstress is that is does not require the server under test to be running Exchange. It does not need to be part of an existing Exchange organization or to be connected on a production network. All you need is the correct version of the Exchange database engine, a DLL file that ships with Exchange (or service packs, such as SP1 or SP2).

Installing Jetstress

Jetstress is available as a download from the Microsoft Exchange 2003 Performance tools web page, or directly from this link: http://go.microsoft.com/fwlink/?LinkId=27883.

The installation is very straightforward and places files in the Jetstress folder, under the Program Files folder on the local machine. You then need to copy the following files from the Exchange kit or from a production Exchange server, to be sure you are running the version of the database engine that you will eventually deploy:

- ese.dll;
- eseperf.dll;
- eseperf.hxx.

Comprehensive documentation is available in the Jetstress installation folder that describes the various command switches you can use with the command line edition or options you can use in the GUI. Rather than describing the documentation content, I will proceed to discuss here the key usage scenarios of Jetstress.

Running Jetstress

To get started with Jetstress, run the JetstressUI.exe file, either directly from the folder or via the shortcut installed under Programs > Exchange JetStress > JetStress 2004. After a short validation phase (shown in Figure 6.15), Jetstress will proceed to have you initialize the testing environment.

You must then step through the three property tabs shown in the main GUI. First, you define the storage environment (number of logical disks, location of files to lay down for the database), as shown in Figure 6.16.

Then you must define the Test Run information, which basically will determine the type of workload applied to the environment (Figure 6.17).

You have three types of test runs:

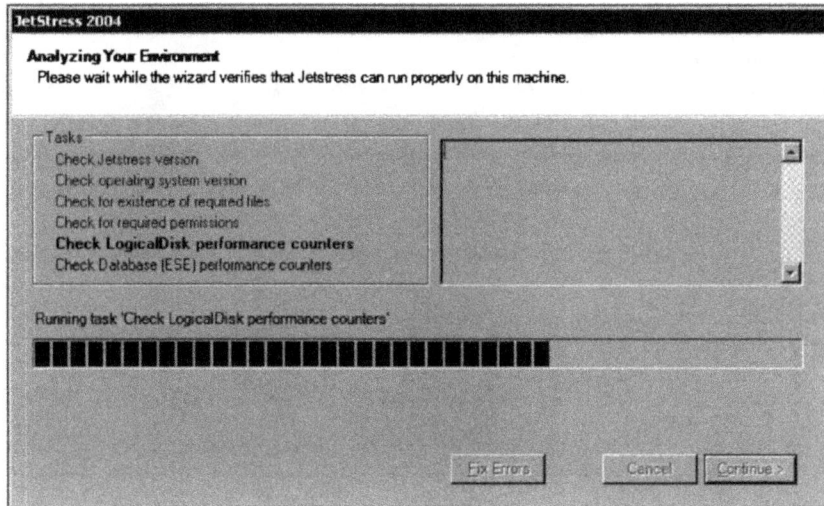

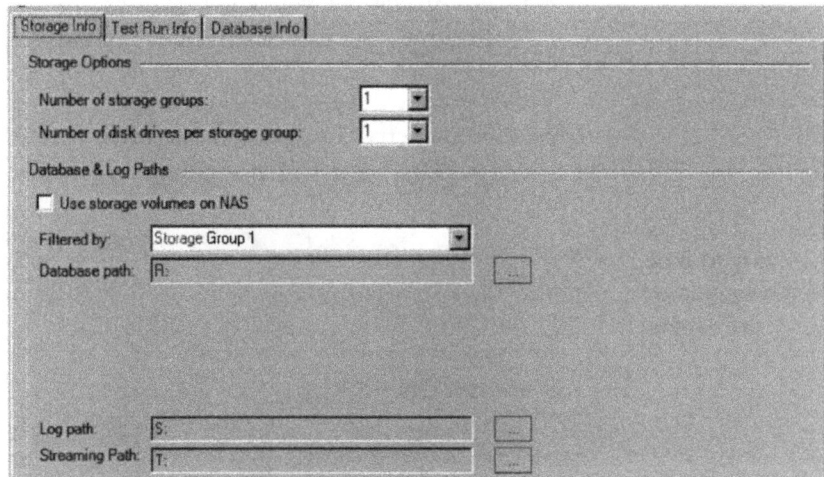

1. *Performance*: With this test, and based upon the characteristics of the database information, you can use Jetstress to determine whether your storage layout fits the requirements that would be required by a production Exchange server.

2. *Stress*: You can use this mode to stress as much as possible the storage units, something useful if you wish to establish a baseline characterization or if you wish to "burn out" your storage environment prior to production rollout.

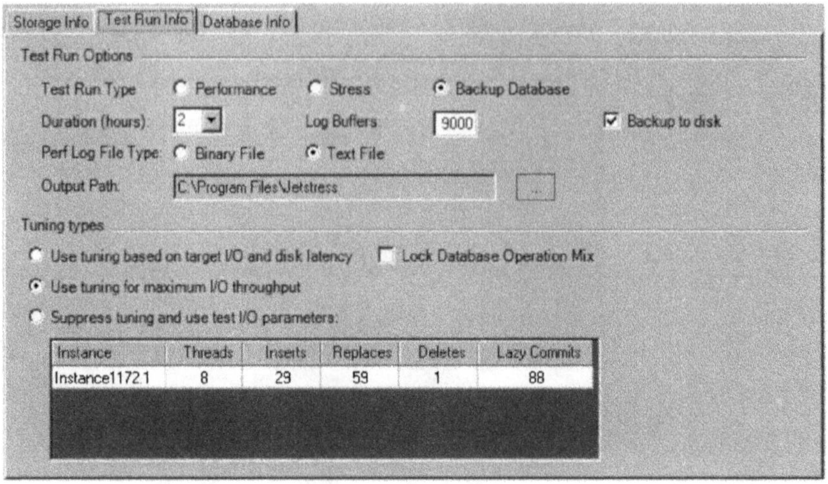

Figure 6.17
*Jetstress test run
information*

Figure 6.17
*Jetstress test run
information*

3.　　*Backup database*: In this mode, you can test backups of databases. It will quickly let you know the type of throughput you can obtain from your disk-based backup infrastructure.

The third property tab allows you to define the size of the databases and the type of workload you wish to apply to these databases (Figure 6.18).

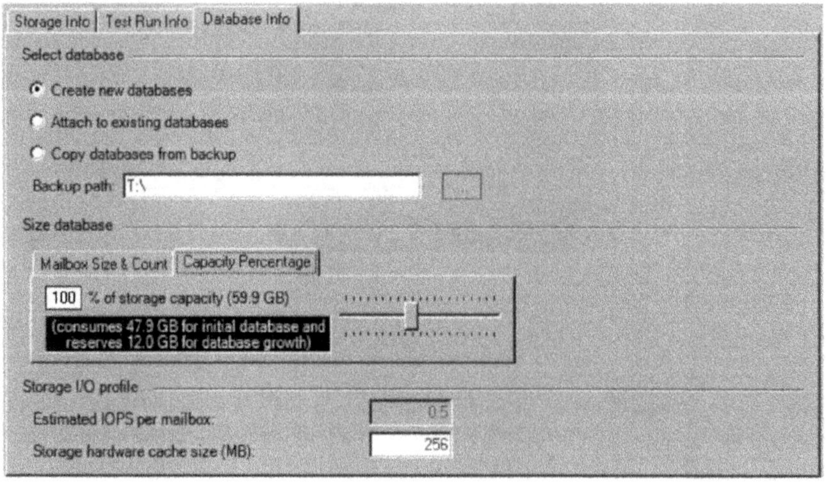

Figure 6.18
*Setting database
information*

This phase consists of creating a meaningful data set that spans across the disks that are selected for the environment and that has enough data such that the random access nature can be exercised across a large enough seek range: if you were to run Jetstress against a 2-GB database, you could potentially keep on hitting the storage controller cache, something that would not happen in production environments. The size of the target databases is typically created from the user profile that you define in the settings of the tool or from the capacity percentage that you wish to utilize. You also have the opportunity to enter the storage hardware cache size, enabling Jetstress to validate the minimum database size to be used for *cache avoidance* (i.e., testing the storage without benefiting too much from a large cache, such as those you can find in certain SAN controllers, and that can exceed 128 GB).

Reviewing Results

After each run, JetStress will generate reports that you can review and for which you can do further analysis. It is always a good idea to keep the .htm reports (see example in Figure 6.19) for further reference: if you have an unexpected performance issue with your server and narrow the problem to the storage components (because there is a high latency, for instance), you can refer back to the performance baseline and determine whether the array was stressed beyond its capabilities.

In the example shown, the total database size was 14.62 GB (which is just fine for a controller with 512-MB effective write-back cache and 1-GB read cache), spread across five databases, as shown in Figure 6.20.

Recommendations

Jetstress is a superb tool that shines with its simplicity and the data it generates. You have an opportunity to exercise your storage subsystem and obtain performance information without being proficient in specialized tools, such as IOmeter, and Windows Perfmon. I recommend that you characterize your reference storage configuration, such that you can determine, during production hours, whether the storage is responding to an expected workload.

Nonetheless, always keep in mind the GIGO rule: "garbage in, garbage out." If you enter incorrect or unrealistic input data in the tool, you will obtain results that cannot be directly exploitable. On the other hand, if you wish to stress a storage subsystem with small effort and get ballpark information on its capabilities, you will find Jetstress to be a key tool.

In shared storage environments, Jetstress is very good at generating concurrent workload. Let's consider the example in Figure 6.21.

Figure 6.19
Jetstress sample result summary

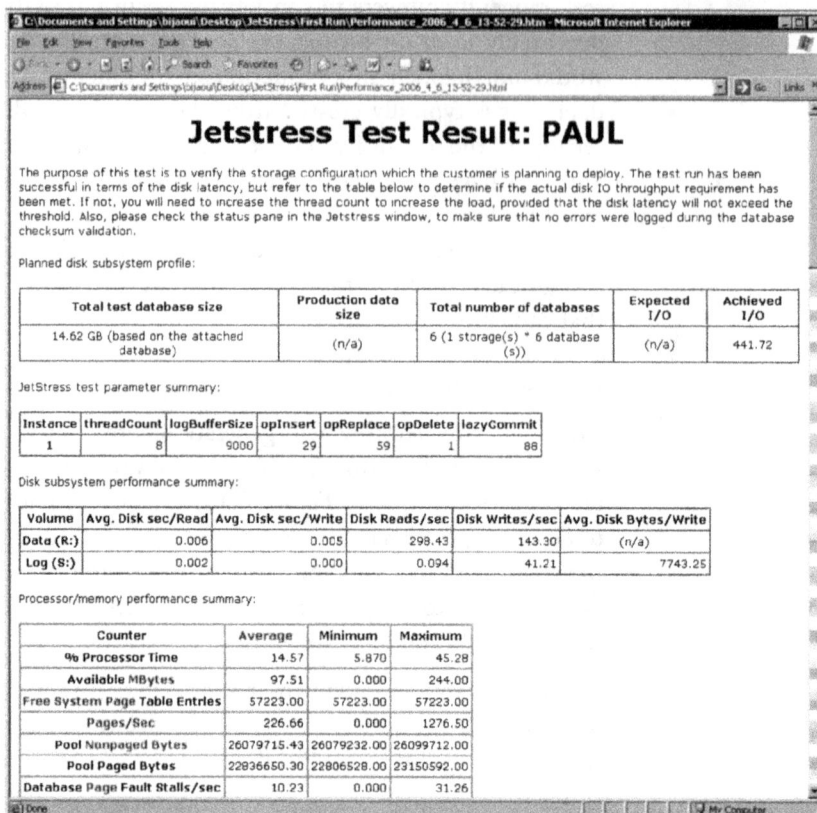

Figure 6.20
Jetstress EDB databases

It consists of three servers using a storage controller attached to a SAN. You can test each server individually or you can configure a (fairly) complex environment using Loadsim that spans across the three servers. That will give you an indication of the global capacity of the environment. At the same time, noninteractive workloads can be applied to Exchange servers, such as backup and recovery. Using Jetstress on two servers, you can perform a backup on a third server and determine the mutual impact each server has on the others. It does not necessarily represent what will happen

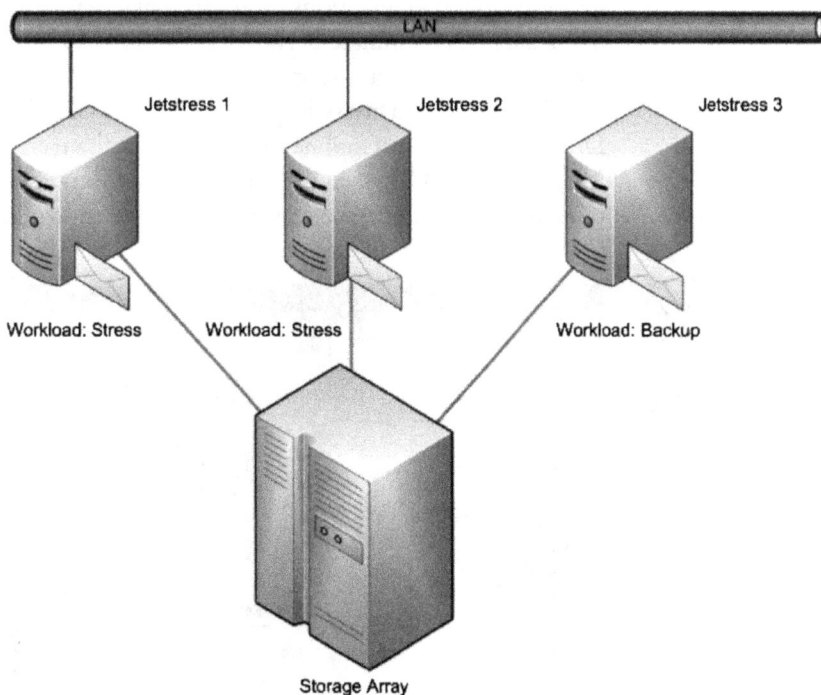

Figure 6.21
Jetstress concurrent workload

in reality (you hardly run any backup during production hours, unless you have a consolidated Exchange deployment that spans multiple time zones), but it can give a worst-case scenario and possibly outline hotspots anywhere between the servers and the back-end disks.

6.2.3 Other Tools

Exchange Stress and Performance (ESP, or Medusa)

ESP uses scripts to generate activity to an Internet protocol server, and some scripts have been defined to "mimic" the Exchange 2003 OWA or ActiveSync clients. The ESP 2003 kit that can be obtained from Microsoft (http://go.microsoft.com/fwlink/?LinkId=27881) contains sample scripts, though you will have to review them and possibly modify them to make them fit your own environment and test case.

ESP brings a great benefit compared to Loadsim in that it has a very small footprint on the machine on which it operates and enables the simulation of other protocols beside MAPI. Part of the difficulty in running Loadsim is that it can require up to 20 machines (or clients) in order to simulate 10,000 or so MAPI clients. The other part is that Loadsim only performs MAPI transactions to an Exchange server under test. ESP, on the other hand, can simulate between 1,500 and 2,000 connections per client machine and can run scripts that connect to many protocols—SMTP, LDAP, NNTP, and most importantly HTTP-DAV (also known as Web-DAV)—and the new mobile functions of Exchange 2003, such as Outlook Mobile Access (OMA) and ActiveSync. Each appears as separate modules that you can register against an ESP client, as shown in Figure 6.22.

Figure 6.22
*Registering load
simulation modules
to an ESP client*

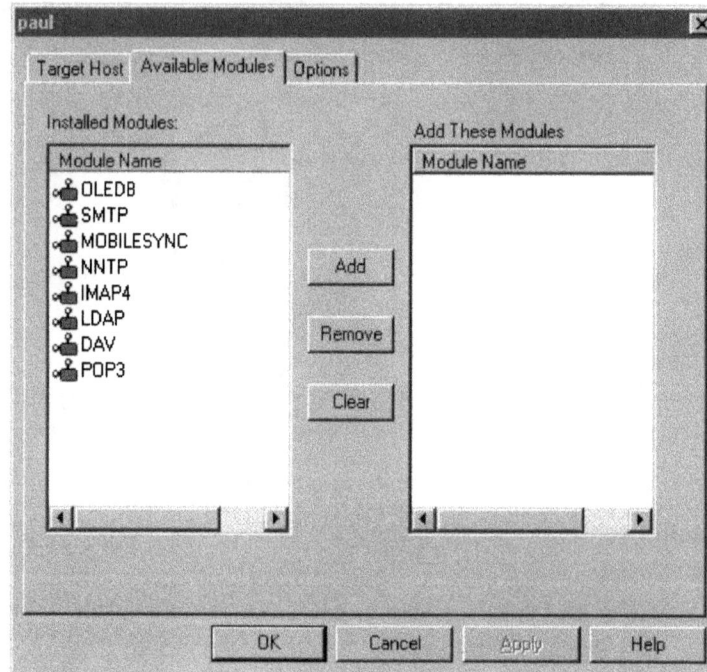

The tool in itself is not for the faint-hearted: the interface is a little bit rougher than JetStress and Loadsim.

While there is a fair dependency on the actual script content, a single client (1 GHz, 512-MB RAM) will run up to 2,000 instances of the script. If you wish to simulate additional instances, you will have to use several client machines. However, all of them can be controlled from the same main instance of ESP (what we refer to as the ESP—or Medusa—load control client).

You should configure your Active Directory servers in the same way as if you were using Loadsim: you should have at least one GC server or one domain controller and one GC server. I have found that with Windows 2000, it was better to start the environment setup and configuration with one machine for Active Directory, thereby suppressing any directory replication latency. In Windows 2003, that is not the case, as the intrasite replication is almost immediate.

Second, your client environment may be connected to a local area network or to a wide area network (WAN). It may be connected through components (e.g., routers) that will simulate the wide area network so that you can actually measure the response time of the ESP simulation as if it were running over a WAN and better determine service levels (e.g., browsing of folders, sending messages, reading messages). Finally, you can have more than one Exchange 2003 server; you can also insert front-end Exchange 2003 servers that would specialize in handling Internet protocols—either all of them or just individual protocols. If you were to test the benefit of using SSL accelerator boards, or multifunction network adapters that implement IP protocol handling (one of these functions is known as TCP offload engine, or TOE), then ESP would be the tool of choice.

As you can see, ESP doesn't keep you from setting up your environment for a test bed in the way you prefer. It depends largely on the components and services that you wish to exercise with this particular tool. As a general rule, I recommend that you run an environment as close as possible to the production environment, at least for the server class (processor type and speed), the memory quantity in each server, networking options, and storage. In Figure 6.23, we show an example of a topology that is used for measuring the efficiency of WAN accelerators spread in a simulated (it could be a real one!) WAN.

Finally, just like Loadsim or JetStress, an ESP load is also a good way to exercise and burn in the hardware and software solution and determine how well it behaves under stress.

ADTest

ADTest was developed at Microsoft to help in capacity planning and understanding stress points and thresholds in Windows Active Directory servers. Much in Exchange 2003 depends on the Active Directory; that is an area that you just can't ignore. You can get ADTest from the Microsoft Windows Server 2003 resource kit or as a direct download from Microsoft's Web site.

The hardware vendors have come up with general sizing guidelines, but do they really apply to your environment? Before doing an Exchange 2003 test, I strongly advise you to spend some time with ADTest to capture the

Figure 6.23
ESP used for simulation of WAN access to Exchange 2003 using WAN accelerators

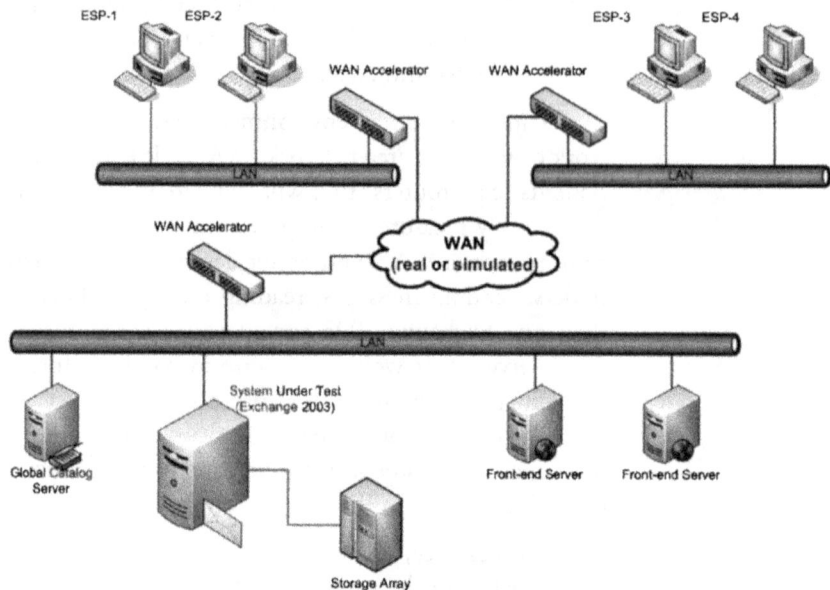

Figure 6.23
ESP used for simulation of WAN access to Exchange 2003 using WAN accelerators

behavior of the domain controller and GC you'll be placing in either your benchmark or your production environment.

The principle of ADTest is similar to that of LoadSim; one or more loading clients will perform repetitive actions that target one or more servers under test. ADTest requires Windows XP Professional or Windows Server 2003 on the loading clients. The system under test may be a domain controller (or GC server) on its own or part of a more global Active Directory forest. One advantage of testing with a deployed forest is that you can take into account the replication traffic. On the other hand, it may skew raw results (e.g., number of logons per second) if replication is occurring while a test is in progress.

ADTest has been successfully used in test and customer environments to validate the scalability of the Active Directory on 64-bit Windows environments. While they currently are the exception, in consolidated environments, 64-bit computing brings anywhere between four to six times better performance than a comparable 32-bit platform (same hardware, different boot of the operating system, 8 GB of RAM). This is primarily due to the enablement of the large memory model for the LSASS process that runs the Active Directory database engine (the LSASS Windows Service).

6.2.4 Conclusion

I view LoadSim and ESP as precise and focused tools that serve not only for stressing a server, but also for providing you with insight data about a benchmark environment and defining a baseline for your computing infrastructure. Both of these tools can determine the capacity and vertical scalability of the solution (i.e., how much it can handle). However, they do not properly address the other components that are stressed by high activity and are used by Exchange 2003, such as the Active Directory services. ADtest and JetStress have proven their usefulness in testing respectively AD servers and storage subsystems. I believe that the latter one is of crucial importance to any scaled-up environment, and JetStress should be in the toolbox of any person involved in the deployment and configuration of Exchange servers.

You will have to be very careful when properly analyzing the actual performance data in the early stage of your deployment not to rely solely upon your benchmark environment. Remember that simulation testing can bring up interesting points but does not always represent an actual user workload: an Outlook client can do many things (e.g., inbox processing rules, large item count, additional mobility clients) that a Loadsim or JetStress environment cannot simulate.

6.3   Monitoring Exchange 2003 Performance

6.3.1   Introduction

Performance monitoring in Windows 2003 has evolved from the Performance Monitor as we knew it with Windows NT 4 (and still available from the Windows 2000 resource kit) into two distinct tools:

- A system monitor, which displays current or saved performance counters information;
- Performance logs and alerts, which capture counter values and manage log files and alerts.

I value the system monitor GUI, but I still believe that post-processing tools are often required to make a proper performance analysis and assessment of a running Exchange server. Microsoft Excel can be quite handy for implementing basic statistical and mathematical functions. Further on, I will discuss a methodology to process and turn out something meaningful from several hundred megabytes of information.

The performance monitor in Windows 2003 comes with three basic features:

- Performance counters that capture into log files;
- Trace information gathering (but what do you do with this trace information?);
- Alert generation based on counter threshold, which can be utilized for triggering additional (perhaps more detailed) performance information.

I like the new monitor because it lets you concentrate on the data acquisition task and does that well, by providing data in multiple formats and by letting you schedule data acquisition (e.g., if you wanted to understand the stress put on your server during an online database defragmentation during off-peak hours). Granted, the performance counter selection dialog box hasn't changed much, and the acquisition time interval is limited to one second (just long enough). However, the monitor comes with interesting log file management features, such as the ability to stop the acquisition after a given amount of time or at a precise date/time. Sequence numbering of logfile names is also handy.

In addition to Perfmon, some tools that were in previous versions of the Windows Server resource kit are now included in the base operating system (Windows XP or Windows Server 2003). These tools allow rapid capture of performance data as well as refinement of performance data (TYPEPERF and RELOG, which we discuss later in this section).

Monitoring Exchange 2003 can be both an easy and rather complex task. It is easy because Microsoft, in both its operating systems and its applications, has always provided detailed information about the behavior of the running applications. On the other hand, it can be complex; in the process of searching for performance bottlenecks, you may be tempted to gather many performance counters, and having too much data to process can result in burying somewhat important information under irrelevant data. Too much data kills the data.

You therefore need to find a compromise that allows you to get essential data at a reasonable sampling interval. This way, you can easily report and make decisions while not overlooking essential elements, and you can have a sampling interval that does not mask peak loads, which often cause excessive queuing and bad response time. Simply put, you may design and monitor a server hosting 2,500 users, but if the CIO or one of your IT directors happens to read a message (that translates into a set of client/server protocol commands, which themselves can be expressed as a set of transactions to the messaging service) at the wrong time, the response time may be mediocre and generate a complaint that the system is slow, even though it performs adequately on an average basis.

This section provides you with both key information to collect and a methodology for interpreting information, whether it is based on 10 samples or 100,000 samples. This methodology does not mask the peak loads but puts them into perspective.

Depending on your environment, you will need to choose a representative time period of workload or a time period during which you wish to satisfy a certain workload. For example, on several occasions, I worked for companies whose largest amount of transactions were issued between 8:30 and 10:00 AM on weekday mornings, and where the largest amount of messages to transmit were issued between 3:00 and 4:30 PM on Friday afternoons. This gives an interesting perspective for what to monitor and when, and how, later, to decide whether your system architecture addresses the workload. If, in fact, it doesn't, you can determine the most appropriate components to be tuned to achieve both the workload throughput and a satisfactory transaction response time (referred to as latency in this chapter).

Many tools and products on the market address Exchange infrastructure monitoring. I usually classify them based on the number of applications and systems to monitor, the heterogeneous nature of the systems, and the level of detail requested. However, I do not believe that there is a single product that can address all the problems. It is also important to consider the existing environment and the fact that operational staffs may be used to a particular product and its interfaces and event monitoring and reporting system.

Things you should value when selecting a proper monitoring and reporting tool for Exchange 2003 largely depend on the answers to the following questions:

- Can the tool interface with other operating systems (e.g., UNIX, among others)?

- Can the tool monitor infrastructure components such as network switches, storage network switches, and controllers?

- Can the tool provide reporting functions that enable you to decide whether you have met the expected and/or committed service levels (e.g., time to deliver a message and response time to basic client operations such as reading a message)?

- Can the tool deal with a large number of objects (more than 100) scattered across a wide area network?

- Can the tool consolidate events and generate alarms that can be handled by the operational staff?

- Can the tool accurately provide both hot information (e.g., system activity during a one-hour period) and more general information (system uptime over a six-month period)?

- Can the tool interface with homegrown or other tools (e.g., integration of application-specific monitoring tools into enterprise management tools, or integration of hardware monitoring tools into enterprise or application or operating system–specific tools)?

Many products are available on the market and evolve across time. Microsoft provides Microsoft Operations Manageer (MOM). This product grew from NetIQ's technology and aims at monitoring a large number of systems (1,000 or more). I like MOM for the fact that at Microsoft, the product groups that are responsible for developing the management packs for MOM. The management pack is an application-focused component that can be used to collate reports and exploit performance and event information in the context of the application. Exchange has a pretty comprehensive management pack for MOM that can be used for real-time monitoring or more general operational monitoring and trending.

ISVs such as BMC with its Patrol product or NetIQ with AppManager have released very vertical solutions that allow drilling down a particular server or service and providing detailed information. HP has a major operational monitoring tool from the OpenView family of products, OpenView for Operations, accompanied with application-specific plug-ins (called Smart Plug In, or SPI), which allow monitoring of application-specific components and performance aspects. Table 6.4 shows a succinct comparison of the two operation management products, HP OpenView Operations for Windows and MOM.

Table 6.4 *Comparing HP OpenView and MOM*

Feature	HP OpenView	MOM
Manager-agent architecture	Yes	Yes
Built-in rules, policies, and filters	Yes	Yes
Built-in reporting	Yes	Yes
Add-on per application (Exchange and Active Directory)	Yes	Yes
Multiplatform support	Yes	No
Written by application-specific engineers	No	Yes
End-to-end management (hardware, server, network, storage, services)	Yes	No
Embedded knowledge base	Yes	Yes

In this chapter, we will cover out-of-the-box performance monitoring tools—specifically, Perfmon, from Windows. Perfmon was introduced with the very first release of Windows NT; it is really worthwhile, depending on how applications report their information and the relevance of performance counters. It is not the only solution for performance monitoring, but I found no limitations in using it to diagnose and monitor servers—other than the sheer amount of counters available, which can sometimes make it hard to diagnose performance and service level problems.

6.3.2 Performance Monitor in Windows Server

The graphic interface for viewing the performance counters is now provided as part of the System Monitor, another MMC snap-in, that can display either current system information or information captured by means of the performance log files. System Monitor has greatly improved the display of information, notably for multihour log file display. Figure 6.24 gives a snapshot of System Monitor, which you will find as "Performance" under the "Administration Tools" pull-down menu.

You can invoke the System Monitor by issuing the DOS command PERFMON. You may also utilize the NT4 Performance Monitor, which doesn't help very much in reviewing report data collected over a long period of time but allows trimming the sampling interval to less than 1 second. This last point is very important. There is always an impact when monitoring a system or an application or one of its components. For example,

Figure 6.24
*System Monitor
with Windows
Server 2003*

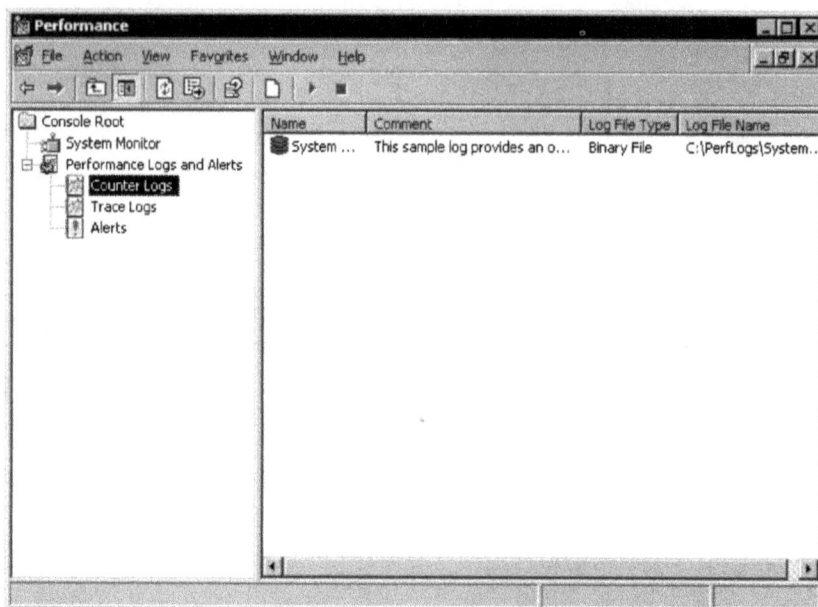

Microsoft states that enabling performance counters for physical and logical disks is usually associated with a 10 percent performance impact. This impact can be on the response time, on the overall throughput of transactions to the volume or disk, and possibly on the quantity of data transmitted back and forth between the volumes and disks to the NT I/O subsystem. Should this be really an issue? Personally, I don't think so. If you tune your environment such that you take into consideration the impact of performance monitoring, you stand yourself in a worst-case scenario that adds a small margin of operation, beneficial for production use. If you consider that your systems should not have disk counters permanently enabled for performance reasons, ask yourself, "Is it wise to run a system with such little headroom in a performance capacity?"

I personally prefer to deal with worst-case scenarios for performance analysis. Since Windows 2000, all servers now have the physical disk counters enabled by default, and this is a good thing. Logical disk counters have to be enabled manually (discussed later in this chapter).

Another question is whether you should monitor a particular counter using a 1-second sampling interval, a 15-second sampling interval, or a 15-minute sampling interval. The answer depends very much on the counter and what you wish to get out of it.

For disk counters, a sampling interval of 5 seconds is definitely appropriate. For determining the overall number of messages sent by an Exchange server or the number of active users (in the Exchange terminology), a 15-minute sampling interval is more than sufficient. You may have an appropriate sampling interval, decide on which counters to monitor, and end up with a bunch of numbers. Are they good or are they bad? The result of the sampling and reporting will not answer that question unless you have a baseline with which to work.

As described in the previous section, this baseline can be established by doing a load simulation test in which it gives a ballpark figure. The baseline can also be determined by your knowledge of the system's components. For instance, we know that 5 ms for a sequential noncached write operation is "decent" for a disk drive. It may not be optimal, but it is acceptable. For example, you may decide to enable write caching on your disk controller and go below 1 ms for similar operations, and you will know that you have realized a certain gain, one that should translate into a better performance for the overall system.

The goal of this chapter and this book is to provide you with information and experience that I have collected from many customer and real-world scenarios and baseline figures for what is good and what is not good. It is not an end in itself, since you will also need to put this data back into the perspective of your very own environment (which includes the hardware components, software operating systems and applications, and overall logical topology) and decide whether the information gathered brings value and whether it requires any particular attention.

Toolbox

The performance analysis engineer typically has a toolbox that contains a series of tools and scripts, Excel sheets, and homegrown processes that enable us to make performance analysis quite rapidly. In the last 10 years, I've been working on performance analysis in general, and for Windows and Exchange in particular. I have developed my own methods and got to meet, interact with, and exchange ideas with the most talented engineers inside and outside HP.

To be efficient in finding needles in stacks of hay, or pinpointing to a pain area within hours instead of weeks, the performance engineer for Exchange should, in my opinion, be proficient in the following tools:

- Perfmon: for both interactive and batch capture of performance data.

■ Relog: for extracting subsets of performance captures and transforming data into a manageable set (see Figure 6.25).

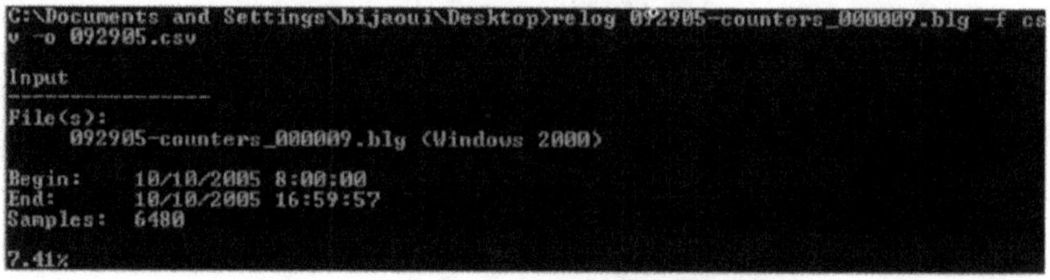

Figure 6.25
*Using relog to
convert a binary
performance data
file into a CSV file*

```
C:\Documents and Settings\bijaoui\Desktop>relog 092905-counters_000009.blg -f cs
v -o 092905.csv

Input
-----------------
File(s):
    092905-counters_000009.blg (Windows 2000)

Begin:    10/10/2005 8:00:00
End:      10/10/2005 16:59:57
Samples:  6480

7.41%
```

■ Typeperf: to quickly enable performance counter capture, such as in the midst of an event.

■ Microsoft Excel: to use mathematical functions that go above and beyond the minimum, average, and maximum calculations, such as using percentiles.

■ Charting and analysis tools: for helping you run through correlation and charting of information (HP has one, called TLVIZ, that you can obtain from searching www.hp.com—the most recent link to this tool is: http://h71000.www7.hp.com/openvms/products/t4/index.html?jumpid=reg_R1002_USEN, though it might change by the time you read this). TLVIZ was developed for analysis of comma-separated value files from OpenVMS, and the translation of Windows Perfmon CSV files into TLVIZ files is quite trivial.

Sysinternals Filemon: for figuring out what's going on a server. You can download Filemon from http://www.sysinternals.com. If you are unsure of the activity on a particular disk unit, Filemon will let you trace all I/O made to the server's file systems. Sometimes, the output of Filemon is difficult to work with, and within Microsoft support, there are some tools that allow users to parse Filemon output files and graphically present the disk activity (e.g., identifying a hotspot).

IOmeter: to assess the performance of storage units, using varying workloads (sequential or random, large or small I/O size). This is Intel's donation to the open source community. It is an I/O exerciser that is quite popular among storage specialists.

Last, but not least, Microsoft Exchange Performance Troubleshooting Analyzer: for tracing and analyzing performance problems on a server (see

Figure 6.26
Microsoft Exchange Performance Troubleshooting Analyzer

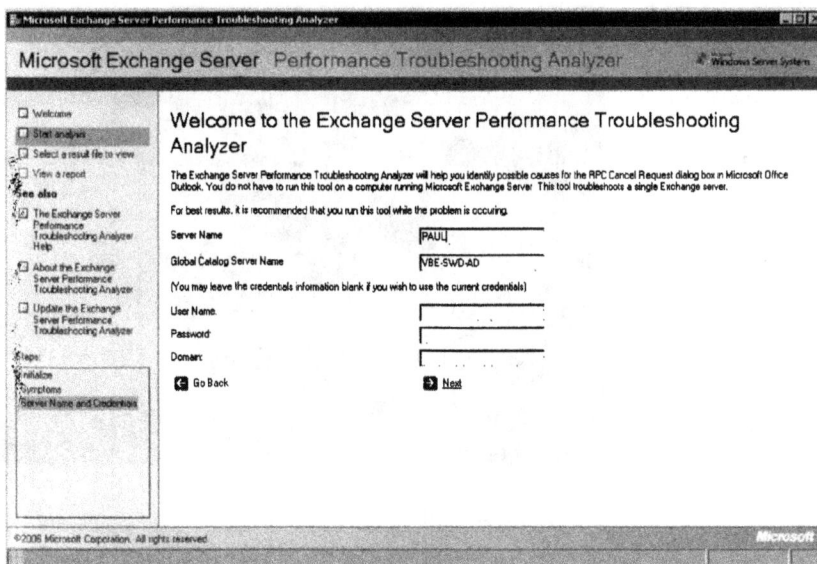

Figure 6.26). This tool is available as a free download from Microsoft Exchange tools Web site.

Prepare to allocate enough storage for your analysis; it is not uncommon to collect over 1 GB of performance data in a single working day. Sometimes, the analysis of this information will outperform common laptop environments. I have found that an old server with 2 GB or more of RAM was adequate. The disk performance is not so important, at least less so than the capacity.

In the subsequent sections of this book, I will use outputs from TLVIZ, or from "the Monkey," an underground (private use only) performance analysis tool that I could summarize as being "what Microsoft would have always wanted to turn Perfmon into." The author will recognize himself in this paragraph, and I still have a hard time finding the right words to thank him for the work he did.

6.3.3 What Would You Monitor in a Microsoft Exchange Environment?

Several areas in an Exchange 2003 environment require careful attention. First, at the system level, you should always monitor the disk subsystem. To enable disk-counter logging for logical disks, you have to utilize diskperf at the DOS command prompt (see Figure 6.27).

Figure 6.27
*Using diskperf to
enable logical
disk counters*

```
C:\>diskperf /?

DISKPERF [-Y[D!U] ! -N[D!U]] [\\computername]

 -Y  Sets the system to start all disk performance counters
     when the system is restarted.

 -YD Enables the disk performance counters for physical drives.
     when the system is restarted.
 -YU Enables the disk performance counters for logical drives
     or storage volumes when the system is restarted.
 -N  Sets the system to disable all disk performance counters
     when the system is restarted.

 -ND Disables the disk performance counters for physical drives.
 -NU Disables the disk performance counters for logical drives.
 \\computername          Is the name of the computer you want to
                         see or set disk performance counter use.
                         The computer must be a Windows 2000 system.
 NOTE: Disk performance counters are permanently enabled on
       systems beyond Windows 2000.

C:\>
```

Diskperf will enable the logical disk counters only after the system restarts, so if you plan to look into your system performance and, more specifically, your I/O subsystem performance, plan it in advance.

As with most of the parameters described here, you will need to assert the resource utilization according to the system activity (also known as *correlation*). For example, peak morning logons, online defragmentation, and content indexing are all activities that cannot really be simulated and can impact the normal operations of the Exchange 2003 server, which are to serve client requests and trade in and out mail messages.

This section describes the basic performance counters that can be obtained using PERFMON in Windows 2003. Sometimes you will find that you can use these counters directly with PERFMON and gather information in data files that can be later exploited. At other times, you can use this information as input to integrated monitoring products in order to define threshold values that can trigger alarms or to establish trends that can be used in capacity planning and overall system monitoring.

The next section provides a method for analyzing the performance data based on the use of percentiles, which is a common practice in the transactional world, of which Exchange 2003 is definitely a part.

Workload Monitoring

Workload monitoring with Exchange 2003 is a challenging task. An unmatched number of elements that relate to Exchange 2003 server activity can provide information. This is mostly done by means of a few key activity sources:

- Performance objects;
- Tracking log files;
- Number of transaction log files generated per day.

Performance objects are numerous, and trying to get them will get you to a large quantity of information to process. Subsequently, I describe methods and tools for managing this information. Tracking log files are optional, as is tracking message traffic information. They can be useful to determine message-oriented workload, regardless of the client protocol used (MAPI, IMAP, POP, HTTP-DAV, or any other).

Keeping a Scorecard of Exchange Activities

For proper workload monitoring, you should attempt to define and maintain a scorecard for Exchange activities that you can plot and visualize across a given time period. You can compare this scorecard with your baseline (established, for example and if appropriate, from a legacy Exchange activity) and determine the workload evolution.

The scorecard can vary, depending on your client profile. If you have only MAPI clients, you should concentrate on capturing information about those clients. However, if you have a mixture of MAPI, OWA (via HTTP-DAV), IMAP, POP, or even NNTP clients, remember to create the workload scorecard for each of these protocols. Fortunately, there are performance counters in Exchange 2003 to allow users to capture utilization (in terms of transaction issues) for each of the different access types.

If you intend to utilize the Exchange 2003 server by means of a custom application that utilizes CDO and ADO/OLEDB (both are object interfaces that can be used to control and interface with Exchange) to the store, it is unlikely that you will be able to trace much information from the Exchange Information Store. Make sure, however, when you design your application to take advantage, beyond simple file logging, of Windows 2000 events and performance counters. The advantage of using these two mechanisms over logging activity in flat text files is that you can take advantage of Windows 2003 enterprise management tools (first, Sysmon, Perfmon, and Event Viewer; later, MOM) or any other type of enterprise management tool that can utilize the industry-standard WBEM (Web-Based Enterprise Management) interface (implemented as WMI in Windows) to capture valuable workload information. For most of the setups, you can get away with such activity, but as you scale up and out your environment, you will find a growing need to be able to report on computing resource utilization, such as CPU and memory as well as network and storage resources.

For a good example of storage resource utilization, consider the Microsoft Exchange Profile Analyzer tool (see a sample report in Figure 6.28), which allows users to scrub a database and enumerate the mailboxes and their contents (in terms of item and folder count and size, not actual text content).

Figure 6.28
Microsoft Exchange
Profile Analyzer
sample report

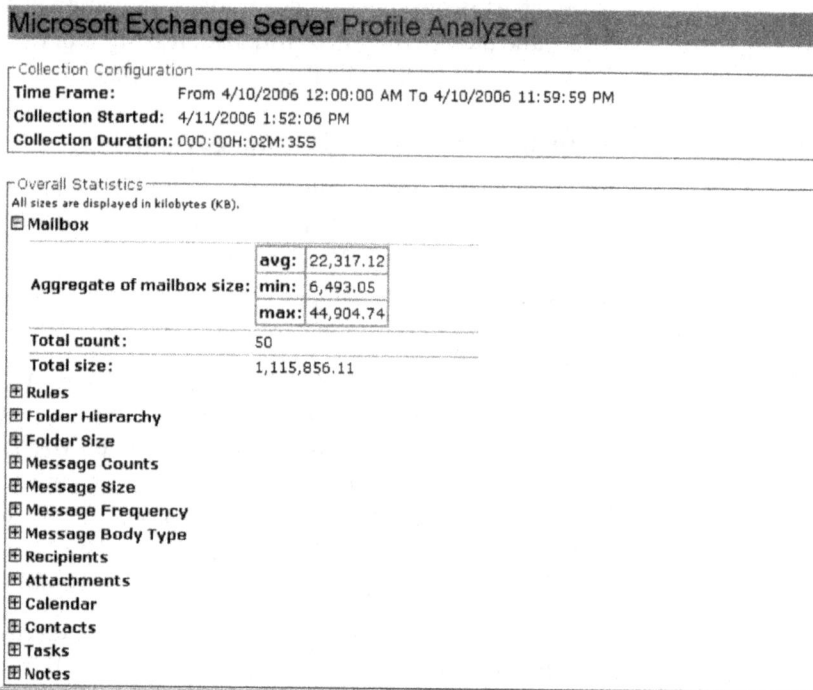

Microsoft Exchange Server Profile Analyzer

Collection Configuration
Time Frame: From 4/10/2006 12:00:00 AM To 4/10/2006 11:59:59 PM
Collection Started: 4/11/2006 1:52:06 PM
Collection Duration: 00D:00H:02M:35S

Overall Statistics
All sizes are displayed in kilobytes (KB).
⊟ Mailbox

Aggregate of mailbox size:	avg:	22,317.12
	min:	6,493.05
	max:	44,904.74
Total count:	50	
Total size:	1,115,856.11	

⊞ Rules
⊞ Folder Hierarchy
⊞ Folder Size
⊞ Message Counts
⊞ Message Size
⊞ Message Frequency
⊞ Message Body Type
⊞ Recipients
⊞ Attachments
⊞ Calendar
⊞ Contacts
⊞ Tasks
⊞ Notes

Beyond the actual utilization of the storage and the database contents, throughput (requests that can be handled per second) and latency (response time for a given transaction) are equally critical, as you let your environment grow.

Scorecard Design

A scorecard for an application activity—in our case, Microsoft Exchange 2003—should report on meaningful transactions, and, if at all possible, throughput information (transactions per second) and latency (transaction completion time). By linking (correlating) the scorecard information with the computing resource utilization (network, CPU, memory, storage), you can determine whether Microsoft Exchange 2003 makes efficient use of these resources and whether any of these resources is not meeting a satisfactory service level.

For example, if you have 1,000 transactions per second (RPC operations per second) and a high (above 80 percent) CPU utilization, you have a good indication that with this particular workload, your CPU processing capability is maxed out, so you should plan for a hardware upgrade that benefits the processing capacity of your server. For example, you can add more processors, change the processors' clock rate, or enable hyper-threading on Intel processors (if that is not already enabled).

Another way to determine the CPU utilization—and more precisely the optimal level of utilization of CPU resources—is to investigate the CPU processing queue length or the context switches per second, both of which are performance counters you can obtain on any Windows server. The scorecard should report information on meaningful period of times, or, to put it differently, you should assign a meaning to a particular time slot.

A day in the life of an Exchange 2003 server usually starts with morning logons, users starting up the Outlook client, requesting inbox contents or synchronizing the mailbox if Outlook operates in cache mode, processing mail rules that move messages around or delete them. All these operations occur during a short time period, say between 8:00 AM and 9:00 AM, depending on the opening hours of the user environment. Then you have the day's activity; activity is likely to decrease during lunch breaks and finally resume toward the end of the day when users complete their work.

Later on comes the background work, the work that is not transactional per se but that can put a severe resource demand on the Exchange 2003 server and the components it depends upon, especially the back-end storage infrastructure. These include backup jobs and system attendant maintenance tasks (online defragmentation being the main one). During the day, nonuser-related transactions, such as virus checking, mobile user connectivity links, content indexing (this is not negligible), desktop search engines, and exceptional operations such as database restore operations also occur. Note that they may or may not directly reflect upon the back-end server performance, depending on whether the Outlook client is running in cache mode or in online mode (this option is configurable from Outlook 2003 onward).

Exchange Activity

Many components of Exchange 2003 can be monitored and provide useful performance information. You first need to identify the performance objects that need to be monitored (e.g., MSExchangeIS). I discuss some of them further on in this section. Then you drill down the specific performance object *instance* and *counter* that need to be monitored.

Because Exchange comes with database-level partitioning, you will find that many objects that used to have only one instance in Exchange 5.5 (such as MSExchangeIS Private) now have several instances, and, as always, a _Total instance. I recommend, for casual monitoring, to use the _Total instance for those performance counters, unless you wish to focus on a particular database or storage group that could represent a certain user group. In a performance troubleshooting case, where we suspected a third-party mobile device management solution, we isolated all the users that had such a mobile device in a dedicated storage group, therefore allowing us to correlate the user activity with the system resource consumption (primarily storage) from that particular storage group.

In the rest of this section, we describe the performance objects and associated counters that are relevant to performance monitoring of a Microsoft Exchange 2003 server. There is some very interesting information, if you are using Outlook 2003, that comes in addition and can be exploited: indeed, as part of the MAPI protocol enhancements of Outlook 2003 and Exchange 2003, Microsoft started to introduce in-band performance reporting into the protocol: the client can report to the server its perceived response time, and the server can present this information to Perfmon (in an aggregated format) or to WMI (in a per-logon format) for determining which clients are experiencing response time problems.

For a detailed description of a given counter, you can select the Explain button when you browse the performance objects, instances, and counters on a server. Figure 6.29 gives an example of such an explanation (which is in fact relevant to the next section).

Figure 6.29
Explanation of a performance counter

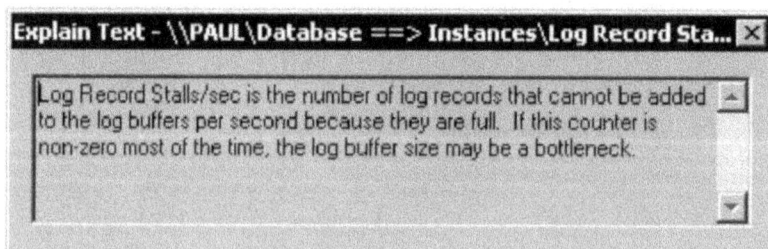

Explain Text – \\PAUL\Database ==> Instances\Log Record Sta... ✕

Log Record Stalls/sec is the number of log records that cannot be added to the log buffers per second because they are full. If this counter is non-zero most of the time, the log buffer size may be a bottleneck.

For simplicity, we will adopt the same notation as in Windows Perfmon in representing a counter. Any performance counter is tied to a performance *object* and an object *instance*. For example, the average disk writes per second of a disk is part of the physical disk performance object and applies to a particular instance (the logical unit number) of this disk.

All the performance counter information is valid for Exchange 2003 SP2. Depending upon the actual version of Exchange that you run, you may or may not have the counters available.

Database Performance Object

The database performance object has generally one instance on an Exchange 2003 server, which is the Information Store instance. For this particular instance, there is a further breakdown per storage group.

The "database" performance object focuses on the _Total instance of each "Database ==> Instance" object (Figure 6.30).

Figure 6.30
Database and database instances performance objects

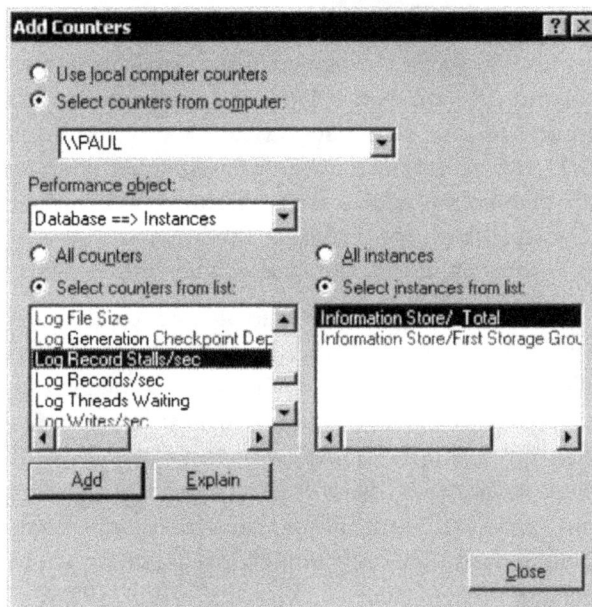

This section focuses on the "Database (Information Store)" performance object's instance, since it is the most revealing and critical for the high-performance Exchange 2003 server.

Database counters are useful to determine the stress applied on the Exchange 2003 database engine. As mentioned previously, the database cache size indicates how much system memory can be used for database operations. I would say that for a standalone server, the cache size should be more than half of the physical memory. Presented differently, you will know that your database cache size has grown to a maximum if the number of available bytes from the memory object is low (less than 10 MB). For high-end Exchange 2003 SP2 servers with 4 GB or more of RAM, the maximum database cache is approximately 900 MB (that is, 900 MB of the Information Store virtual address space are mapped directly into physical memory, and contain previously used or dirty database pages from any of the databases mounted in all the storage groups). If you have a lot of physical memory available (memory/available bytes) and the cache size is well below 900 MB, there might be an incorrect setting such as a missing /3GB boot switch in the boot.ini file or in the Active Directory (see Chapter 5 for more information about manually tuning the database cache size). You should always remember that the database cache size, shared with all the database engine instances (storage groups), is computed automatically by the DBA scheme.

While you can actually disable the DBA, I would not recommend getting near any of the tuning parameters available in the Exchange configuration stored in the Active Directory configuration naming context. These should be accessed only if you have a very specific environment (e.g., an SMP environment that requires resource partitioning) and you are using tools that do not interact with Exchange's DBA scheme—or, to put differently, using tools that Exchange 2003 has no clue about. Bluntly speaking, this is generally not a good idea for high-end servers.

The log buffers have a different function than the cache: they contain the transaction changes in progress, which have yet to be committed by the calling thread. Sizing log buffers is not something you should be doing, unless your servers have been through various versions of Exchange. Indeed, when the default 84 buffers were to be changed with Exchange 2000, as Microsoft improved the virtual memory management of the Information Store in the follow-up versions, the default with Exchange 2003 SP2 is … 9,000! In fact, it can vary from 512 to 9,000 across the previous versions of Exchange. This change in Exchange 2003 SP2 was made possible after Microsoft made improvements to the Information Store virtual address space management.

The size of the database cache and log buffers will in fact impact the following two operations:

- *Frequency of disk access for log writes.* This can be critical if you have many transactions to log (i.e., a high rate of information to be stored in the Exchange databases or a high rate of user activity), but it is not necessarily critical if the underlying disk subsystem can process log writes fast enough. Nevertheless, the less you go to the "slow" storage systems, the better your system's overall performance will be because latency is incurred less often and because fewer CPU cycles are spent in processing the I/O in the NT I/O subsystem.

- *Frequency of disk access for database reads.* A too-small database cache (trimmed automatically by the DBA because of a shortage of RAM) can cause longer response times to user transactions that require database read operations. You can therefore determine and demonstrate whether adding more RAM or changing the cache size has a good effect on the system's performance if the result is *decreased* I/O reads to the database volumes. Less read I/O means better caching, which means that the device has more capacity to handle extra load and transactions, something very desirable in a high-growth, high–throughput and transaction rate environment. Tracking this rate can be complex in a multivolume and multidatabase environment, and it requires dedicated attention for accurate reporting.

The size of the database cache will also impact the frequency of write operations to the database volume (checkpoint depth, set to 20 MB per storage group by default), but the actual response time of these write operations impacts neither the user's response time nor the message transfer, since this operation occurs in the background. However, because the database volume is receiving both reads and writes, quite understandably, fewer writes to perform means a higher transaction rate (I/O per second) available to read operations. So, while the write response time is not a valid indication of good performance, the actual number of write operations, combined with the volume capabilities—depending mainly on the controller model, the storage network, the controller cache size and fetch method, the number of disks, and the data protection level (i.e., the RAID level)—do impact on the overall volume transaction rate and data rates, which includes the read transactions, critical for user response time and system throughput.

The "Database(Information Store)\Log Writes/sec" performance counter provides the rate at which the database is writing to the log device. You will need to ensure proper write throughput if you don't wish to turn your log drive into a performance bottleneck. You should attempt to qualify your log volume(s) first. Use tools such as IOMeter (Intel's donation to the OpenSource) or JetStress to determine the data rate and the request rate of the volume. Once determined, you will know how much headroom you dispose of by checking the Log Writes/sec counter. Another related counter is the "Database(Information Store)/Log threads Waiting." On a single storage group server, this parameter will range between 0 (what you should aim for) and the number of active threads. How often it is nonzero will in fact indicate a log write performance problem—the transaction log device has trouble keeping up with the log request rate. Either the system is too loaded, or the log device is too slow. In either situation, improving the write request rate of the transaction log drive will improve not just the counter situation but also overall system performance.

Note that you should expect an initial lower performance if your database has been upgraded from a previous version of Exchange. Indeed, the upgrade from Exchange 5.5 to Exchange 2000 requires database changes, which are in fact different up to the point at which the page is actually being queried. You can determine whether there is a high rate of page conversion going on by monitoring "Database\Records Converted/sec." Normally, this rate should decrease as the Exchange 2000 database is being utilized, up to the point at which it should be close to zero. You can force the deferred database upgrade by dismounting the database, running ESEUTIL/F, and mounting the database again. Once the majority or all of your database pages are converted to the Exchange 2000/2003 format, you should expect a more decent performance, in line with your expectations.

Finally, with Exchange 2003 SP1, Microsoft has added a number of advanced performance counters that can be helpful for sizing purposes. You can now measure right off the database engine the I/O request rate (reads per second, writes per second), without necessarily having to monitor and analyze the physical disk. This is particularly useful if you wish to

- Compare storage groups' pressure on the I/O subsystem;
- Calculate IOPS per user (discussed later in this section);
- Measure the I/O workload generated by the database engine on devices where you can't measure the response time and throughput (such as a network share—not that this is something I would recommend you to do).

I prefer the database engine to report its own view of the I/O subsystem, so that you can quickly determine whether the databases are demanding too much from the storage subsystem (and, therefore, you now can see the real need for characterizing or base lining your storage subsystem).

I cover the exact counters to follow later on in a summary table, but they are found prefixed by "I/O Database" for the EDB I/O traffic and "I/O Log" for the transaction log files prefix (see Figure 6.31).

Figure 6.31
*I/O counters from
the database
performance object*

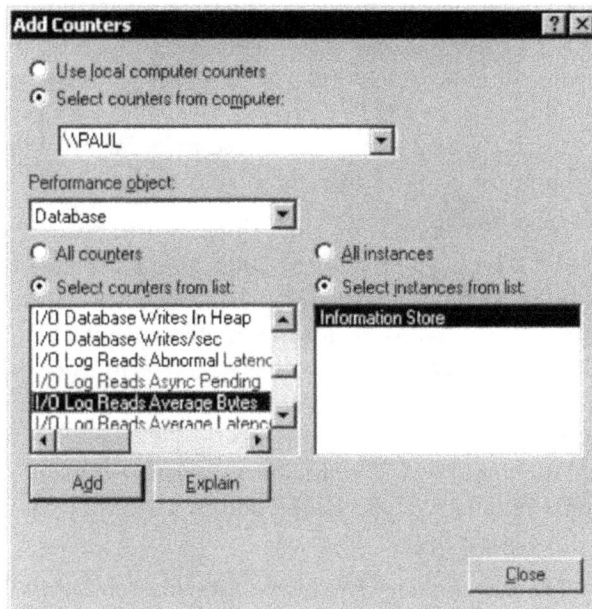

To enable the advanced performance counters for the database object, you have to create a DWORD registry value and set it to 1 in the following registry key:

```
HKLM\SYSTEM\CurrentControlSet\Services\ESE\Performance
```

SMTP Server

The SMTP server is a key component of Exchange 2003. It heavily uses the Active Directory by connecting to GCs to retrieve a user's email address and making routing decisions (known as the *categorization* process). Other queries to the Active Directory include the following:

- Distribution list expansion;

- Determining the limits for sending and receiving messages for the recipients and the originator of the message (if this applies).

You will most likely want to monitor queues in the SMTP server, as they indicate whether there is a backlog of messages waiting to be transferred. This backlog can cause a severe performance impact (delayed mail delivery) in situations in which the Exchange server is a regular mailbox server, in which it is a bridgehead server dedicated to message switching between and among the mailbox servers, or in which it connects with the "external" world (e.g., to an SMTP or X.400 backbone). As a general rule, the categorizer queue length should not exceed the value of 10, but this is a guideline, and it might be quite different in your environment.

Note that there is no such thing as a standalone process running the SMTP server. The Exchange 2003 SMTP servers (or virtual servers) are running as part of the INETINFO process. However, monitoring the INETINFO process performance object would also include information and activity about the other virtual servers. Most of the time, you will have one instance of the SMTP server object, and I recommend that you monitor the _Total instance in order to get a good view of both the inbound and outbound SMTP traffic on a particular machine. You may have additional instances if you define additional SMTP virtual servers (e.g., for traffic separation).

The key counters for this performance object are "Messages Sent/sec," which gives an idea of the total outbound throughput, and "Messages Received/sec," which covers the inbound traffic. More than anything else, these counters provide information about the traffic and message throughput capability of your server. Depending on the server's role (mailbox server, bridgehead server) and on the network and routing topology, these counters can be used as a baseline in a benchmark environment and initial deployment scenario, and they should be monitored in the long run to establish a trend for the actual message traffic occurring in and out of a particular Exchange 2003 server. In an ISP or ASP scenario where you can have multiple SMTP virtual servers possibly binding to different network interface cards and networks, you can break down the traffic per virtual server instance. Typically, the instances are called SMTP 1, SMTP 2, and so forth, and you will need to identify these instances back to the SMTP virtual server instances that can be viewed from the Exchange System Manager console. The default SMTP virtual server is always referred to as the SMTP 1 instance for the SMTP server performance object.

When you have the SMTP service running on an Exchange 2003 server, you realize that you may have many sources from which messages can be received. The performance counter "Inbound Connections Current" gives a good idea of how many SMTP connections are handled concurrently by the SMTP server component.

Once a message has been received by the SMTP mail service, it needs to be categorized for proper delivery locally or for relay to another SMTP host. The categorization performance relies very much on the Active Directory performance, and it is a good idea to actually monitor the counters prefixed by "Cat" in order to establish your baseline and define a trend. The most important one, in my opinion, is the "Categorizer Queue Length." If that queue consistently grows or never gets back to 0 or close (less than 15), you may have a categorization problem because the Active Directory service cannot satisfy the load imposed by the SMTP service.

Once the messages have been categorized, they are placed into appropriate destination queues, and, as their name suggests, it is important to track them and monitor them to avoid delays in the delivery of mail messages, either locally or remotely. The counters of importance are as follows:

- "Remote Queue Length," which describes the messages waiting to be delivered to other servers;

- "Remote Retry Queue Length," which describes messages that failed to be initially delivered and entered into a retry queue;

- "Local Queue Length," which describes the messages waiting for local delivery on the server; this queue can be a good indicator of whether or not the STORE is keeping up with the inbound traffic;

- "Local Retry Queue Length," which describes messages that had to be delivered locally, to the X.400 MTA, or to other gateways and failed to be delivered at the first attempt.

You will not come across many deployments where the SMTP server is suffering from either storage performance or CPU utilization, as this component is particularly well optimized. It is more common to face the situation where the SMTP service is getting too slow a response time from the global catalog servers.

MSExchangeIS

MSExchangeIS is a performance object that covers the entire Exchange 2003 Information Store operations. This is a good object to use to get an overall view of transaction workload, regardless of the number of storage groups and databases defined on your server.

In a pure MAPI environment (Outlook XP and preceding clients, or MAPI-based connectors), the "RPC Operations/sec" is a good counter to determine the number of requests issued by the clients. This is really a 10,000-foot view of workload demand from a client and MAPI-based connector perspective. It can, however, be useful to gather to determine trends and corresponding system resources utilization.

Other counters can be useful to determine the active user connections (e.g., MSExchangeIS\Active User Count, which describes the number of client connections that have performed an operation within the last 10 minutes). In most corporate deployments that I've seen, this value is roughly 80 percent of the actual number of connected users. Note that this counter does not include the connections issued, for example, by MAPI-based connectors. In environments where there are third-party mobility solutions that connect on the user mailbox, for retrieving messages to transmit to mobile devices, or when there is a high use of delegation (for instance, a director and his/her assistant), you may get a higher number of active users than there is of connected users (or even mailboxes). This is not a sign of bad performance, but rather of high activity that involves temporary logons to mailboxes. I like to monitor this counter, more to determine its evolution and therefore the peak and off-peak hours of utilization of an Exchange server, not necessarily draw any further meaning from it.

Accordingly, I recommend that you monitor these counters on a long-term basis to establish a baseline. Bear in mind that capturing these counters in a pure benchmark environment such as a Loadsim benchmark has little value, since the benchmark itself defines how many clients are actually connecting to the STORE process by means of MAPI RPC.

Other counters of interest with regard to the MSExchangeIS performance object are the "RPC Requests" and "RPC Averaged Latency." The "RPC Requests" counter indicates the number of RPC packets that have to be handled by the Information Store. These RPC requests are transient to the RPC server, and this counter is a good indication of queuing that occurs at the RPC server level. With Exchange 2000, the maximum number of RPC requests was 20 (number defined at the registration of the RPC service for the Information Store), and since Exchange 2000 SP2, this value has been changed to 100. Usually, that value should not go above 20–30 in MAPI online situations (i.e., those environments where the Outlook clients run in online mode). In environments where Outlook 2003 is deployed in cache mode, the value can go beyond 50 without being a real concern. The reason is that in cache mode, the Outlook 2003 client will establish more than one connection to the back-end server to synchronize the folders stored locally on the client. These MAPI operations do not keep the users waiting but might create a wind of panic at the Information Store process level. If the Information Store process is too busy to perform background synchronization, it will return a MAPI error to the Outlook client. The Outlook client will then proceed to reissue the RPC request later. To the user, this is not a problem, because the RPC connection was established in the background. You can monitor the rate of failure of background RPC calls by monitoring the "Client: RPCs Failed: Server Too Busy/sec" error rate. This counter reports the RPC errors as seen by the Outlook 2003 clients (you need to be running Outlook 2003 against Exchange 2003 to benefit from these counters, as the client-side view is carried over to the server by means of extensions to the RPC protocols that were implemented from Outlook 2003 onward).

The "RPC Averaged Latency" counter represents the averaged RPC completion time for the last 1,024 MAPI operations to the Information Store. This counter is available for all storage groups present on the system, so if you have a disk unit that is causing grief to a storage group, you may not be able to spot it at first. However, this counter is a good indication of the response time of the server. Expressed in milliseconds, a value of 50 or less generally guarantees that the server is performing fine. However, if the counter spikes above 50 too often, it may be an explanation of slow client response time. It then becomes necessary to tie the counter to system resource utilization or MAPI operations (using Microsoft ExMon) to determine the reason of the abnormally long RPC response time. Note that the response time proposed by this counter does not comprise the network components between the client and the server, so if you are experiencing networking problems, this counter will not be of great use.

MSExchangeIS Mailbox

This performance object helps you to drill down and restrict your monitoring and activity analysis to connections related to the private mailbox transactions issued to all the storage groups hosting the private mailbox database.

If you have partitioned your Exchange 2003 storage groups and database per user communities, the ability to monitor a particular instance (you have a _Total instance plus one instance for each database, regardless of which storage group they belong to) helps in determining traffic and requests to those particular databases.

Many counters provided by the performance object express a transaction rate. For example, the "Folder Opens/sec" gives an indication of how users are actually accessing their mailboxes—whether they stay within the same folder or whether they tend to use many folders for storing their information. This type of information is very helpful in a production environment, and LoadSim benchmarking gives only a restricted baseline for this counter. As we discussed previously, LoadSim does provide fairly comprehensive coverage of the very rich MAPI protocol semantics, yet it does not address operations such as rules processing or automatic message movement to folders, among other things.

With Exchange 2003 SP2, there is a new counter that is of particular interest called "Slow FindRow Rate." This counter refers to a particular MAPI operation used for searching through folders. If you have a high count of items (>5,000) in a folder, that rate may be increasing. Useful for the Microsoft support professionals, this counter is indicative of folders that have item counts that are too high, to a point where every MAPI operation against the server consumes more resources than normal. To decrease the item count in message folders, you might want to communicate to the users some processes to regularly purge the contents of their inboxes (the prime folder candidate for high item count) and otherwise define rules to purge messages automatically.

The other interesting counters that can be drawn from this performance object are those that specifically refer not to the MAPI RPC operations to the Information Store, but to other means of connecting to the Information Store. They can represent user activities, such as the HTTP-DAV series of counters. While these counters are not representing activity from clients, they are useful if you have applications that build on top the HTTP-DAV protocol.

By selecting counters such as "Message Delivered/min," "Message Submitted/ min," and "Message Sent/min," you can establish a fairly safe baseline of the inbound and outbound traffic, focused on a particular database either by selecting its instance or by selecting the _Total instance to obtain a more global view of the Information Store activity as far as message transfers are concerned.

Among all the counters provided by this performance object and among all the performance objects that are provided by Exchange 2003 and Windows 2003, I think that the "Send Queue Size" is the one to use. The sampling interval could be in the range of 5–10 seconds, but that counter is really the heartbeat of your Exchange 2000 server. If this counter goes beyond 1 percent of the connected users and if it rarely or never goes down to 0, you have a performance problem with your machine, which may not be bad as far as users' expectations are concerned but could result in sluggish performance and slow message delivery. The resulting action to correct the Send Queue Size counter can have many aspects, but in my opinion, if you walk up to an Exchange 2003 server and want to find out immediately whether or not the server is OK, *this* is the counter to monitor (you will use the _Total instance for a global view and use database-specific instances if you wish to narrow the scope of the problem). You may relate this counter to the blood pressure, heart beat, or temperature examined on any patient walking into the emergency room of a hospital. It is one of the vital signs of an Exchange server.

The "Receive Queue Size" is similar and can be used to determine the capability of the Information Store to deliver messages locally to the Exchange 2003 server databases. In my opinion, it has less importance than the Send Queue Size, but it is definitely worth looking at.

There can be many reasons why you have a Send Queue Size that grows and hardly ever shrinks. I have seen servers on which just disabling the write-back cache on the controller could cause the Send Queue Size to increase. I've seen other servers on which running out of CPU resources and the time spent in servicing kernel mode system services (Processor(_Total)\%Privileged Time) could cause such effects. Again, this indicator is key to your Exchange 2003 server performance, and its values and threshold largely depend on how fast you want your server to execute.

Previously I stated that 1 percent of connected users was a good value for the maximum value of the Send Queue Size (therefore, for 2,500 users hosted on a single server, a Send Queue Size of 25 or less is fine), but that may differ, based on your service level requirements. Trying to keep the Send Queue Size to 0 is quite unrealistic, in my opinion. Such an attempt may result in your doing very fine tuning for a long time and throwing hardware into a server infrastructure that in fact performs adequately. The notion of "good enough" should spring to mind because you will have to compromise on how much money you intend to spend on your server to provide an *acceptable* level of performance as opposed to the *best* level of performance. Probably, you can reduce the Send Queue Size average value by 10 percent with little effort (sometimes it may just be a storage controller configuration setting or a network interface card change), but reducing this value by 75 percent or more could cause you to dedicate a lot of time, effort, and hardware to get, ultimately, a result that users will not really value.

There are three performance counters in this object that do not relate directly to performance but are extremely important in establishing trends and trying to define a user profile. One is the "Single Instance Ratio," which describes the average number of references to messages in the mailbox store(s), and the other two are "Total Count of Recoverable Items" and "Total Size of Recoverable Items," which describe the quantity of information deleted by the users (therefore, taken out of their mailbox quota but still retained in the store, so that you don't have to perform a mailbox or message recovery operation). The size of this information depends a lot on user behavior and the settings of the Deleted Item Retention Period in the database property, as shown in Figure 6.32.

Figure 6.32
*Defining the
deleted items
for a database*

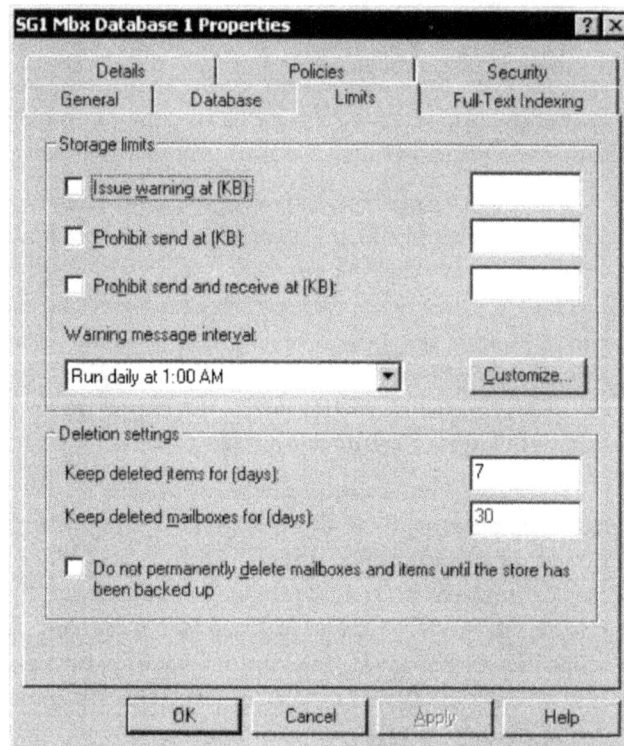

On this particular server, the deleted items in days are set to 7. This means that any items deleted by the users hosted on this database, from their deleted items folders or the result of pressing Shift+Del on their keyboard, are deleted from the mailbox, yet retained in the information store for 7 days.

The size of your database may grow artificially because you now need to keep deleted items available. In our corporate deployments, we have observed that typically, for a corporate user scenario, setting the value to 7 days would grow the database by 20 to 30 percent, to 14 days by 40 to 50 percent, and to 30 days by 100 percent. This artificial growth is typically not taken into consideration for sizing volumes, so if you do intend to change this value, you should closely monitor the "MSExchangeIS Mailbox(<database>)\Total Size of Recoverable Items," to establish a baseline and monitor the trend such that the demand for storage from the Exchange 2003 server does not go beyond what you have already planned and certainly not above 80 percent of the total volume capacity.

This is a very important point to consider. After negotiating and finally obtaining from your purchasing department approval for a 50-GB or 100-GB storage subsystem, if you have indeed overlooked this parameter and come back six months later to ask for more storage, you will be in a difficult position. (I am often in that situation with my own manager.) Certainly, resizing and expanding volumes is not necessarily a simple operation; it may sometimes involve fairly lengthy downtime, depending on your storage controller's capabilities of online volume expansion. Read the fine print carefully; some documents refer to expansion, others refer to concatenation. It makes a big difference in spindle utilization and the resulting throughput of an expanded volume as well as the backup infrastructure.

Don't forget that an often overlooked scalability feature of Exchange 2003 is the ability to set mailbox or public store policies, and these policies allow you to modify any number of database settings by means of a few mouse-clicks from your administration station. Don't forget also that if you are already running a Microsoft Exchange infrastructure based on Exchange 5.5, these counters are present and can provide you with an excellent baseline to use when you move your users to an Exchange 2003 environment.

MSExchange Web Mail

This performance object is particularly relevant if you start to roll out an out-of-the-box or a customized version of OWA. OWA, as you know, has been much improved from Exchange 2000 to Exchange 2003, and as enterprises move into an application federation model by means of Web services and the .NET infrastructure and framework, this particular component can become much more important than in the past. Most of the counters provided by this performance object can provide you with a baseline and help to determine a trend in the utilization of this particular interface.

For environments such as enterprise portals, ISP, or ASPs, this is vital data to use to perform adequate capacity planning, to determine the peak utilization period, and to perform a decent workload management job (where users are basically happy with the response time). The _Total instance is the one I would advise you to choose, although if you have a disparate Internet browser population (including Netscape browsers or "down-level" browsers), you may prefer to segregate the traffic between "IE5 and above" and "non-IE5" instances.

I would recommend a close look at these counters on any server that performs OWA functions. In the case of a front-end and back-end scenario, you should opt to monitor the front-end server and attempt to match the transaction workload with the overall systems workload (which, in the case of a front-end/back-end server architecture, will primarily be around CPU and memory utilization for rendering operations on the front-end and database access on the back-end servers).

The counters that really need attention and cover the majority of OWA deployments are as follows:

- "Authentications per sec," which expresses the number of times the underlying network services such as the Active Directory will be solicited to authenticate users;

- "Folder get contents per sec," which describes the rate of folder openings and listings per second;

- "Forms sent per sec," which describes the rate of message sent from the OWA interface (yes, OWA in Exchange 2000 uses forms for sending messages);

- "Message sends per sec," which covers similar information to "Forms sent per sec";

- "Message opens per sec," which describes the rate of messages opened by OWA clients.

To me, this particular set, sampled at or below 5 seconds, can give a good idea of the peak workload activity during the day (very important for ISPs and ASPs to be able to meet demand and provide a satisfactory end-user experience) and establish a baseline for further trend analysis. At the same time, associated resources can be monitored more closely during these peak periods, and appropriate adjustments, such as CPU and RAM increase (scale-up) or additional servers (scale-out), can be made based on real data and educated decisions. This makes knowing when to purchase additional resources fairly easy.

Epoxy

This performance object reports on the transaction rate and queues occurring in the communication layer, which sits between the INETINFO process that hosts the Exchange 2000 Internet virtual servers and the Information Store process that hosts the databases. There are typically six instances for this object: _Total and one instance per protocol handled by the Exchange 2000 storage system: DAV (for HTTP-DAV virtual servers), SMTP (for SMTP virtual servers), POP3 and IMAP4 (for client access using these two Internet standard protocols), and NNTP (for NNTP virtual serer). You may have fewer instances for this object if you have removed a particular virtual server from your Exchange 2000 server.

We will not forget here the inevitable _Total instance, which in fact has little value, because aggregating these counters together may hide some important information. Out of this object, I found that "Client Out Que Len" and "Store Out Que Len" are two very indicative counters, explaining whether either the Information Store or INETINFO (or both) are keeping up with each other's workload. An underconfigured database can cause the "Client Out Que Len" to grow without diminishing during a certain period of peak activity, indicating a particular problem with the STORE's performance.

Other Performance Objects

Aside from the previously mentioned performance objects, there are protocol-specific performance objects that provide information about the transaction workload/activity for the particular components, such as the following:

■ *MSExchangePOP3, MSExchangeIMAP4*: These two objects report on the actual protocol commands for POP3 and IMAP4, respectively. There are typically three counters for each command: Failures (reports on total number of failures since the virtual server running this protocol startup); Rates (reports on the number of commands per second); and Totals (reports on the total number of protocol commands issued).

- *MSExchangeAL*: This provides information about the address lists generation. This object does not provide real performance information per se, but indicates whether or not the address list generation is functioning properly.

- *MSExchangeDSAccess*: This is not a performance object per se, but, in fact, there are three objects related to the DS_ACCESS component of Exchange 2003—Processes, Caches, and Contexts. They basically determine whether your server is efficiently using the DS_ACCESS module, which sits on the Exchange 2003 server and is shared by all components on Microsoft Exchange 2003 that need access to the Active Directory. DS_ACCESS is certainly not to be taken lightly, especially on bridgehead servers and front-end servers in ASP/ISP-type deployments. Because it manages the relationship with the Active Directory for routing messages, for example, you could conceivably boost your message switching throughput by tuning the DS_ACCESS cache size, thereby decreasing the number of requests to the Active Directory. However, the reality is that most of the deployments do not need such modifications, and you are better off making sure that you have solid domain controllers and GCs to ensure smooth operation of your messaging infrastructure and fast message switching. With the improvements of virtual address space utilization made in Exchange 2003 SP1 and SP2, the DS_ACCESS cache size for user queries has been increased to a mere 150 MB, which enables effective caching of Active Directory entries.

Latency

Latency focuses on anything that deals with response time or that can increase the time required for an operation to complete. It can be due to a queue filling up (we will discuss queue monitoring in Exchange 2003 further on) or simply to a slow device (e.g., network link, adapter, or storage subsystem). In the first case, you have too large a throughput demand for the execution unit. In the second case, you have too high a request handling. Both can be combined and should be handled differently. In the first case, you will attempt to level the resource utilization to decrease the latency due to queuing. In the second case, there is no point in leveraging anything; you basically need to fix the unit that deals with the request.

With Microsoft Exchange, latency is unlikely to be caused directly by insufficient CPU resources, but the inability of a CPU to cope with a workload will cause operations, messages, and transactions to queue, which, in turn, will cause latency. It is also very common to see high latency at the disk drive level (storage subsystem), and there are techniques that we described in Chapter 4 for improving the response time of an I/O, usually by the means of cache memory at the controller level.

When I configure an Exchange 2003 server, prior to releasing it to production level, I exercise the system in the same way we used to drive brand new cars at reduced speeds. This was 15 years ago, and now you can take your car from the garage and start clocking the miles/kilometers. With Microsoft Exchange servers in general and their storage components in particular, it is reasonable to consider that if something is going to break down, it is likely to break down within the first two to three weeks of operation. Because this tends to limit itself to the storage components, the use of Microsoft Jetstress in performance or stress test is particularly revealing of weak storage infrastructure points. That tool has proved to be invaluable in many situations where you wish to execute a test run before going live into production and accepting production data (mailboxes).

The challenge of measuring the latency in Exchange 2003 is to determine whether you are reaching the knee of the response time curve or whether you still have a margin of operation for growth, leading you to educated decisions regarding whether you should scale up (add more users and resources on a single server) or scale out (add another two or more servers to accommodate the existing user load and possibly another user population resulting from a company acquisition or merger).

Figure 6.33 actually describes how the latency evolves with respect to the transaction rate. Observe the main curve, and note how it increases exponentially as the transaction rate grows. The response time grows exponentially, essentially as a result of queuing. As transactions queue, the time to complete the last transaction in the queue depends primarily on the queue size; of course, it increases as the queue length grows.

The strategy for dealing with latency is to obtain a similar response time between 10 percent and 90 percent of the workload; this ensures sufficient coverage of the workload and predictability. You also need to determine the inflexion point of the curve and determine after which workload or transaction rate you will decide that your system has reached saturation and has attained or exceeded a maximum acceptable limit.

There are many ways in which you can determine the latency within an Exchange 2003 messaging infrastructure. In fact, it is present a bit here, there, and everywhere within the infrastructure. I think that in terms of latency, you need first of all to determine those areas in which it is really important. To me, client response time is much more important

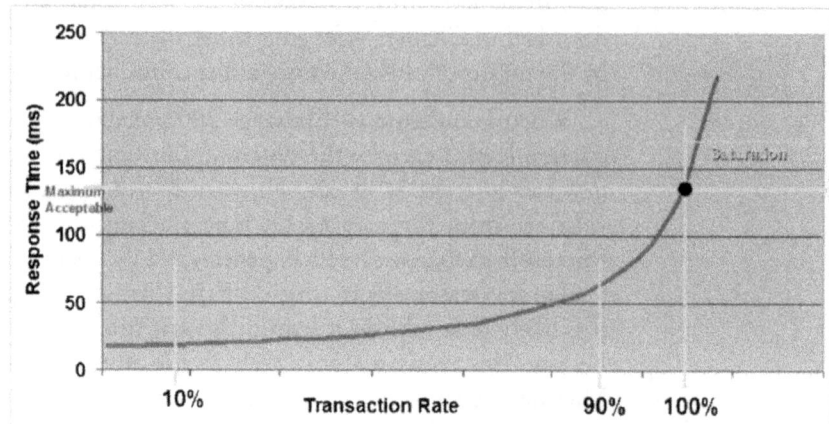

than message throughput in *most* of the cases (there are exceptions to this). Unfortunately, with Exchange 2003, you do not have access to the actual time it took to process and complete a given RPC transaction, nor do you know how important this RPC transaction is to the end-user's perceived response time.

You can measure latency with basically any Perfmon counter that can report information about seconds per <insert your favorite operation>. For storage subsystems, we can access this information by means of disk reads and writes and aggregated transfers. The relevant disk counters are described in the "Resource Utilization" section of this chapter.

For Exchange components, the latency information is easily measurable with the "MSExchangeIS\RPC Averaged Latency" performance counter. This counter reports the average latency of the last 1,024 RPC requests handled by the Information Store. You may think that 1,024 is a lot (too much), but in fact it's not. You are dealing with a *moving average* of the RPC latencies, which helps to get an overall view of the system response time. This response time is local to the server, and you may not break it down per client logon—at least not with this value. In Figure 6.34, I have plotted the RPC averaged latency, and the solid line indicates the 95th percentile (i.e., the maximum value of 95 percent of the best, or lowest, response times).

In this diagram, anything that is above 50 ms (which happens to be very close to our 95th percentile) is considered a mediocre response time, per Microsoft standards. In fact, from a client standpoint, this response time will be just fine for online mode and probably very good for cache mode because the user only gets to deal rarely with the server, except for delegated operations and public folder access (among other operations).

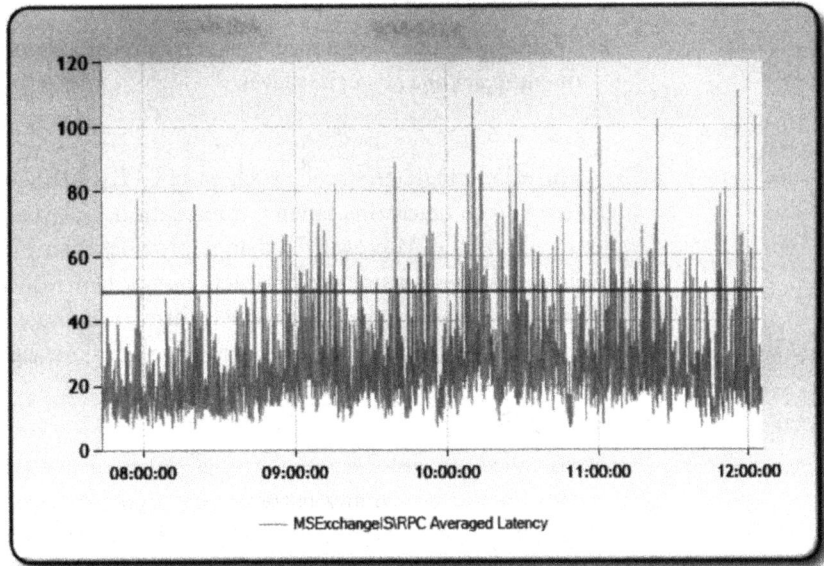

Figure 6.34
*RPC averaged
latency on
a busy server*

From a client viewpoint (and RPC clients tend to be Outlook clients, apart from a few MAPI-based applications), there are many intervening factors, such as desktop performance or network latency, that can further impact the response time of an RPC request.

MAPI latency does not always equate to disk latency; in other words, you might be in situations where the disk subsystem is the bottleneck. Whenever you have a high disk latency, you have a high MAPI latency, and this gets noticed by the end users due to the excessive presence of hour glasses or Outlook pop-up boxes that indicate that "Outlook is requesting information from the server" or similar messages. I have seen cases where the bottleneck was the CPU, and so examining and scrutinizing the disk subsystem would have been a wild goose chase. Relating the MAPI RPC latency to some system resource utilization is not obvious and requires some experience in knowing where to look for performance data in a big collection. I usually recommend starting with

- RPC average latency;
- CPU utilization;
- Overall disk latency (_Total instance of the physical performance object and sec/transfer counter);
- Per-disk/logical unit latency;

- Network latency;

- Windows Active Directory latency, which can be noted with excessive queuing at the categorizer level.

For other client protocols, such as HTTP, POP3, or IMAP4, it's more challenging to determine latency information, but you can obtain measure the queue trends. Microsoft Exchange provides queue information at many levels within and outside the product's components, such as the Epoxy layer (which sits between the Exchange Information Store and the IIS INET-INFO processes) and at the connector level (for message transfer queues).

Throughput

Often called transaction rate, throughput is measured in Exchange 2003 by monitoring how many requests, protocol commands, or messages are actually processed by the Exchange server in a given time period. Sometimes the throughput result depends on an external component—for example, the messages sent per second to a peer SMTP server *also* depends on the peer's ability to respond quickly to the workload. Nevertheless, throughput is important for calculating the workload applied to a server. When dealing with Exchange 2003 servers and Outlook 2003 clients, it is common to measure the rate of RPC operations processed by the Information Store process.

In Figure 6.35, we can view how the RPC operations per second (a rate) evolves across the working day, with peaks that can be viewed more easily if you follow the moving average curve. Here, the moving average helps to pull out a general trend from a set of samples that have a wide range in a few samples.

Assuming that this particular server is well tuned, you should attempt to record key statistics about this throughput (not average, but the 50th and 95th percentile), and keep observing the transaction rate over a long period of time (basically during the lifetime of your infrastructure).

Note that we put both the transaction and the data rates in the throughput category. I could certainly fill out pages and pages of counters with information drawn from the Windows and Exchange help files, but I prefer here to provide some key indicative counters that you should monitor and properly report on.

We have reviewed most of these counters in the previous section; they are listed in Table 6.5 based on the information that they represent. It is

Figure 6.35
*RPC operations per
second on an
Exchange 2003
SP2 server*

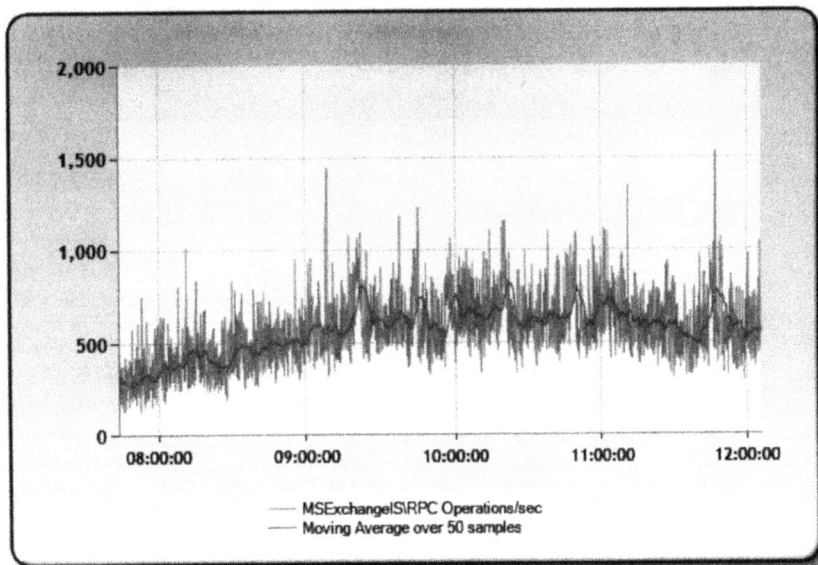

worthwhile to review these counters to really determine the transaction workload on a traditional Exchange 2003 server hosting user mailboxes. Of course, if the server is dedicated to hosting public folders, you will probably be more interested in the number of open folders per second or a similar counter than the number of active client logons or messages sent and received.

Table 6.5   *Performance Counters That Can Report on Transaction Throughput*

Performance Counter Object(Instance)\ Counter	Description
MSExchangeIS Mailbox(_Total)\Messages Sent/min	Number of messages sent by users hosted on the Exchange databases per minute (the _Total represents all the databases, but you can break down this value per database).
MSExchangeIS Mailbox(_Total)\Messages Submitted/min	Number of messages submitted by client users (or connectors) hosted on the Exchange databases per minute (the _Total represents all the data-bases, but you can break down this value per database). It does not neces-sarily represent the number of mes-sages actually *sent* from the databases.

Table 6.5   *Performance Counters That Can Report on Transaction Throughput (continued)*

Performance Counter Object(Instance)\ Counter	Description
MSExchangeIS Mailbox(_Total)\Messages Delivered/min	This counter represents the number of messages delivered to all databases per minute. You may break this down by database by selecting one or more database instances.
MSExchangeIS\RPC Operations/sec	This counter describes the rate at which RPC operations occur. On a busy server hosting 2,500 users, this counter can peak well above 1,500. The absolute value may not be relevant, as it depends upon the client version and configuration you are using (e.g., Outlook 2003, in cache or online mode)

Queues

Queues can be good indicators of performance issues. If data is not flowing smoothly between the CPUs, the RAM, the storage subsystem, and the network, the Exchange product components will start to build up queues.

You can measure some queues to get an overall feeling, and you can be more precise in monitoring certain events to be able to pinpoint the location of the problem. I found, after time, that the MSExchangeIS\RPC Requests counter was an excellent queue indicator. Figure 6.36 shows an example of a busy server.

For that particular server, we had to analyze its performance and eventually determine that

1.   We needed to get the RPC averaged latency below 50 ms for users to be satisfied;

2.   RPC requests had to be below 20 for "most" of the time.

And this is the case for that particular sample: in order to reduce the response time and improve the RPC queuing, we had to add more spindles and change the RAID of the back-end storage array.

Finally, some queues make sense in certain environments but not in others—for example, the ones you can obtain from the Epoxy performance counter have value only if you are intensively using the Internet protocols

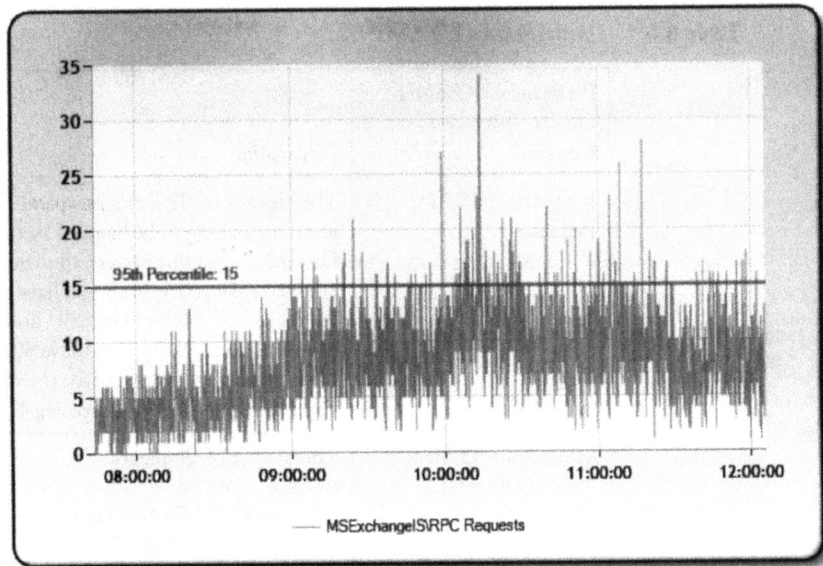

Figure 6.36
*MSExchangeIS \
RPC Requests
counter: queuing
at the RPC
server level*

on your Microsoft Exchange server. Generally speaking, queues do not have a particularly good or bad value. What is more important is the actual trend of the queue values: they should not continuously increase, and they should return back to minimal values (e.g., zero elements in a queue) frequently (every hour or so). Table 6.6 summarizes the key counters that report on queues in the Exchange 2003 product components.

Resource Utilization

In this section, we describe the performance counters that can be used to track the actual system resources utilization, which are typically the CPU resource, the memory resource, and the I/O resources, for both network and storage devices.

Processor Utilization

You can obtain a good understanding of the processor utilization by using two sets of counters. First the Processor object has a number of counters that are considered to represent the processors utilization. %Processor Time (_Total) gives a good idea of the system load. Note that it will not be abnormal that the processor time reaches 100 percent; as long as this is at peak times, it's OK. I have found that 2,500 corporate users generate, on average, 40 percent CPU utilization on a four-processor Xeon, 2.4-GHz server.

This is, however, only an indication of the processor busy state (even on a multiprocessor machine). Processor Time of 100 percent at peak is

Table 6.6 *Queue-Related Counters*

Performance Counter Object (Instance)/ Counter	Description
MSExchangeIS\RPC Requests	The number of RPC requests pending at the RPC server level and waiting to be handled by the Information Store. On well-performing servers, this counter may peak at 5 or 10, but rarely above 10. If you have a server that is under particular stress, with high CPU utilization, you will see this value go up to 20–30. Above 50, this counter indicates too high an RPC workload for the server capability; scale up or scale out, but do something ☺
MSExchangeIS Mail-box(_Total)\Send Queue Size	The mother of all queues. The counter that you should monitor if you had to choose only one. It is a very reliable indicator of the STORE performance (but not necessarily of the performance of other components, such as the SMTP virtual servers).
MSExchangeIS Mail-box(_Total)\Receive Queue Size	The number of messages waiting to be delivered by the STORE to the mailboxes. I find this counter rarely above 0, but when it is, it mostly reflects a performance issue with the STORE and its database volumes. Getting the _Total instance is appropriate for establishing a baseline, but it can be necessary to break this counter per database instance to pinpoint a particular issue (e.g., one database volume being in RAID5 reconstruct mode will show such a queue, even though it may not be present for databases hosted on other volumes).
Epoxy(<protocol>)\Client Out Que Len	The number of client requests for the particular <protocol> used. The indication of queuing at this level leads one to believe that the SMTP transport layer is operating satisfactorily but has to deal with a troubled STORE process, which may not be able to respond quickly enough to these requests. When this queue is present, you should check CPU utilization and, most important, the storage sub-system utilization.

Table 6.6 *Queue-Related Counters (continued)*

Performance Counter Object (Instance)/ Counter	Description
Epoxy(<protocol>)\ Store Out Que Len	The number of STORE requests waiting to get processed by the INETINFO corresponding virtual server running the <protocol>. This is the opposite of the previous counter; a queue present here indicates that the virtual server has problems in dealing with the workload imposed by the STORE. It could be related to a network link problem, or it may be present simply because the SMTP virtual server is running its transient mail folders out of an inappropriately configured volume.
MSExchangeIS Transport Driver\Pending Create MailMsg	This counter represents the number of items pending creation of a mail message structure to be passed to the STORE. If that number grows, it indicates that the STORE is not performing adequately.
MSExchangeIS Transport Driver\Requests Pending Transport Acks	This counter indicates the number of pending SMTP requests awaiting a protocol acknowledgment. This counter can represent the fact that a peer SMTP server is not acknowledging fast enough and can therefore be the cause of message queuing locally on the server. You should therefore determine whether the remote SMTP server has a performance problem or the network link is too slow to support the workload.

not bad, unless there are many threads or processes waiting for execution time. The counter that can be used to verify this is available from the system performance object and is called processor queue length (PQL). There is only one processor queue length, no matter how many processors you have on your machine.

The basic rule is that the queue length should not often exceed two times the number of processors on your machine. In Figure 6.37, we see how the trend of CPU utilization actually follows the RPC request rate and queues (also shown in Figure 6.35 and Figure 6.36), and queuing at the processor (using right-hand scale) starts to occur as the CPU utilization increases. This is a four-processor server, so a PQL of 8 is OK, and peaks above can be ignored if not too frequent. The 95th percentile for the data samples shown in Figure 6.37 is 6, which is fine. The average is at 0.916, which indicates how misleading an average value can be from the reality. With the introduction of multicore processors, the reference value (or guideline) may vary, and one could consider that 4 or 5 times the number of processors is fine for a dual-core server.

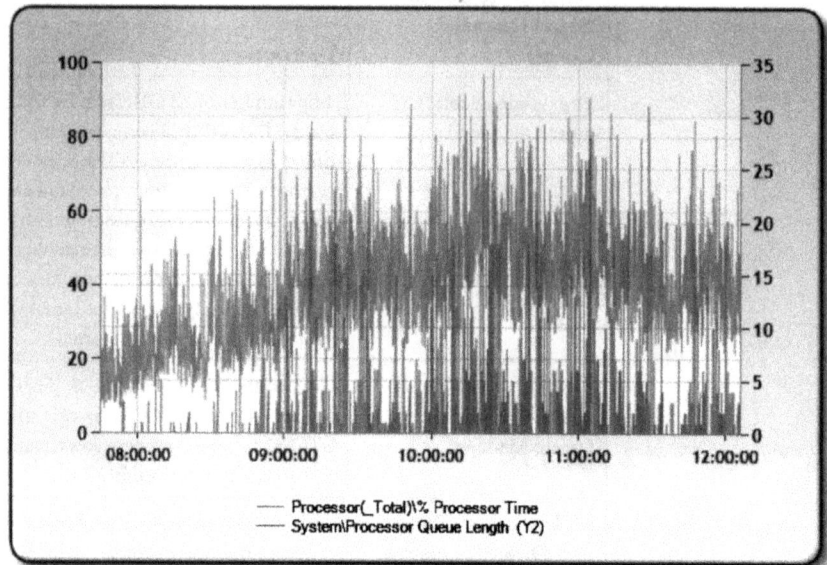

Memory Utilization

Memory is hardly an indicator of stress. Some servers will tend to use all of the memory made available, simply because it would otherwise be wasted. Depending upon the server role, 90 percent is not good (e.g., for terminal services servers), and 99 percent is OK for a database server (because that's what it's designed to do). Put additional focus on the kernel memory areas, such as the paged and nonpaged pool. Running out of them does not depend upon the quantity of RAM; however, it can be lethal when it happens (a kernel is usually clueless when it runs out of memory space and has little other option than to crash).

Exchange 2003 will adapt its use of physical and virtual memory to the activity of the system. This is the dynamic buffer allocation, implemented at the Information Store level, that controls how many buffers (for cached database pages and transaction logs) are being used by the engine. As the system gets constrained for physical and virtual memory, the DBA system will adapt the cache size, resulting in little or no paging occurring on a server. As you add more applications, however, you may encounter paging activity.

Typically, Pages Reads and Pages Writes are the two important counters to monitor: they indicate the hard page faults, which will result in a disk access. The sum of the two should not exceed 80 (roughly the limit of I/O for a single disk drive). If this is the case, you should add more physical memory to your server and possibly locate the page file on a fast drive (this is less efficient).

You can monitor the actual quantity of memory used by the database engine by checking the database parameter Database\Database Cache Size (Information Store). For example, a moderately busy Exchange 2000 server with 512 MB of RAM will show up to 300 MB of virtual memory allocated to the database cache size, while a busy Exchange 2003 server with 4 GB of RAM will allocate the full 800 MB allowed for it in the Information Store process space.

Storage Subsystem Utilization

Exchange 2003 uses a great amount of disk resources for storing and retrieving information placed in public and private information stores. How well Exchange can get access to the information from the storage sub-systems often determines the overall performance of the application. Fortunately in Windows, a lot of information can be gathered from the I/O subsystems. Ideally, you should try to isolate the disk traffic by separating the Exchange database transaction log files from the actual database files. This is strongly recommended in a production environment to provide some level of recovery (if you lose the database volume, you can still retain the log files and play them against the most recent backup).

Response Time

For disk utilization, there is really one set of counters that matter—the response time. Queue length may indicate some level of latency and business of operations, but high response times (>20 ms) will indicate whether the disk subsystem is responding satisfactorily. Beyond the actual values, you will need to understand the actual repartition of the response times reported. It is acceptable that 5 percent of the response times are above 50 ms. It is not acceptable than 15 percent or more are above 50 ms. In that case, you may hit the storage subsystem too hard and turn it into a performance bottleneck. At this point, you will need to look into other performances just as the disk queue length. The response time counters are as follows:

- _Physical disk(<instance>)\Avg. disk sec/Read;

- _Physical disk(<instance>)\Avg. disk sec/Write;

- _Physical disk(<instance>)\Avg. disk sec/Transfer.

I like to look at the "Avg. disk sec/Transfer" counter to quickly get a feel for the volume performance: a value consistently above 30 (milliseconds) calls for improvement. In Figure 6.38, the latency is fine most of the time, with a 95th percentile that is at around 17.

Figure 6.38
Average disk sec/
Transfer on a
database disk unit

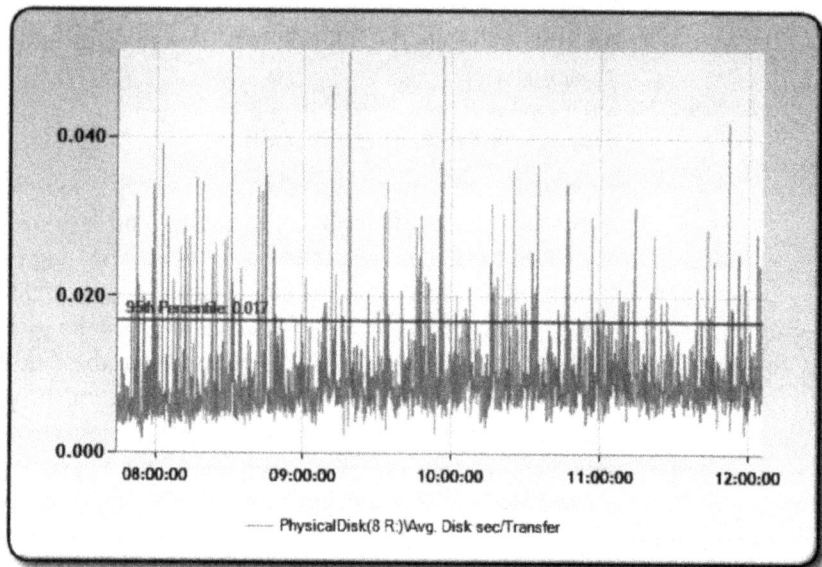

Further analysis, such as determining the efficiency of a read or write controller cache, may require you to drill down at the "Avg. disk sec/Read" and "Avg. disk sec/Write" counters. Typically, read operations should be within 15–20 ms and write operations should be below 5 ms (if you have enabled the write-back cache on your RAID controller). In Figure 6.39, we have a good example of the disk controller that does an effective job at caching write requests (consistently below 5 ms) but has trouble dealing with read requests.

If you wish to speed up your read request latency, you have little alternative than to increase the number of disks that can be used for Exchange database read operations. Because the traffic to the database volumes is very random, there is little benefit in using large cache (4 GB and above) arrays. For write requests, it is a different story: you may have some high latencies

Figure 6.39
Splitting response time between reads and writes

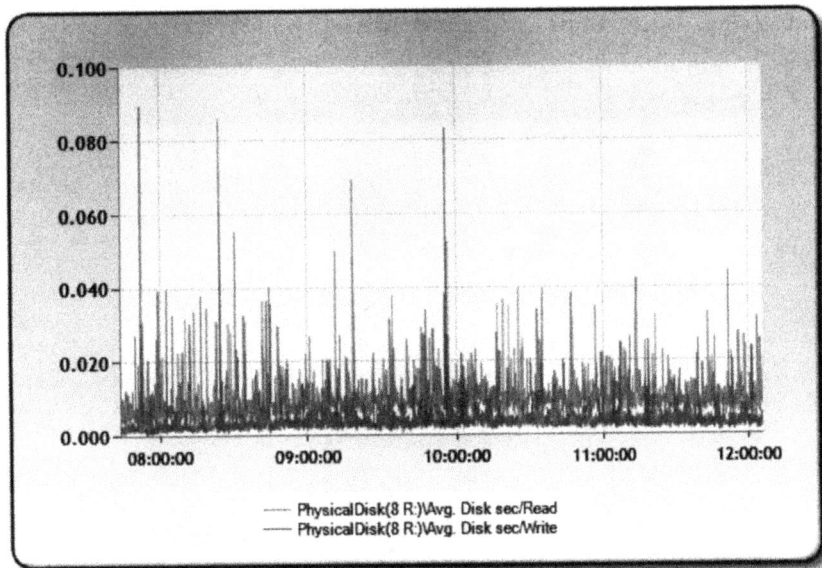

Figure 6.39
Splitting response time between reads and writes

(as shown in Figure 6.39), yet they are probably due to transient latency for cache destaging. In general, storage arrays can do an efficient job of caching a write request from the host and then proceed to free the cache memory for subsequent write operations.

Disk Queue Length

The disk queue length reports on the number of outstanding operations to a particular volume. Although Windows 2000 allows reporting separate queue lengths for read and write operations, the current aggregate value is really the one that matters. A good general rule is that there should never be more than half of the number of spindles in the queue length. If you have a 10-disk RAID volume, the queue length should be less than 5. Such a recommendation calls for capacity headroom to enable peak handlings.

You should be careful about monitoring queues on storage devices: although queues greater than the number of disk drives supporting the logical unit was once considered barely OK, with the implementation and adoption of SANs, a large disk queue length (e.g., 200) should not be of major concern because the SAN arrays have the ability to absorb these I/Os at a higher rate than traditional back-end SCSI RAID controllers. In Figure 6.40, we have a disk queue length that peaks well above 20.

Figure 6.40
*Disk queue length
for a server*

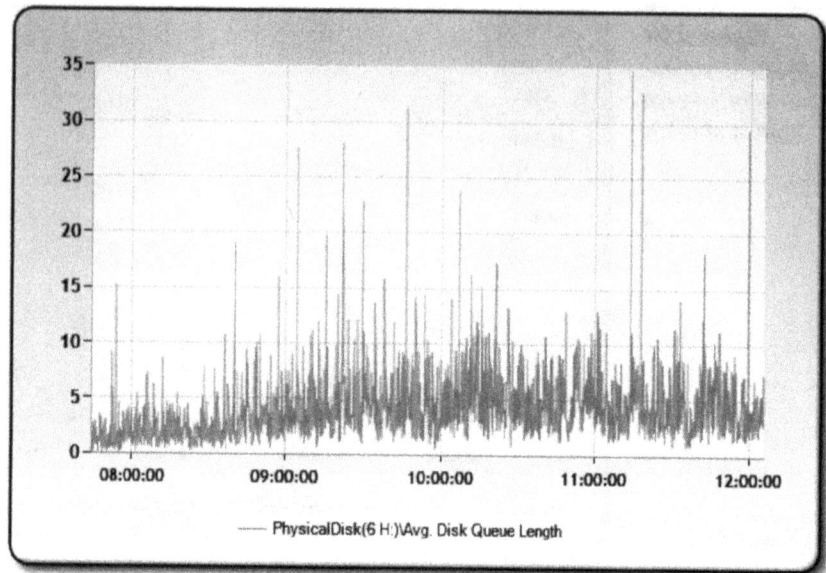

Consistently high values indicate that the volume cannot keep up with the request rate from the application, which, in turn, will generate long response times (and therefore long application response times).

In the case of the Exchange database transaction log volumes, the queue length is never greater than 1, unless you combine multiple transaction log sets on one device. This is because transaction logging is a synchronous process, which triggers a new write only after the current write has been completed. In this case, only the response time actually matters; it indicates whether the performance of the overall application is suffering from these response times. The most important indication the disk queue length gives is whether adding more disks to a subsystem will improve its performance. Actual volume performance should be qualified by the response time of the I/O operations.

Counters Summary Table

The purpose of Table 6.7 is to summarize the counters presented in the previous sections, with a suggested sampling interval and a suggested threshold that can be used for triggering actions based on threshold exception, determining the trend of activity and resource utilization, deciding which component is falling behind in satisfying the workload, and making an educated decision (based on factual data, which is always good to present to the finance department) with regard to system or component upgrades (e.g., more disks, more RAM, more CPU, new server). This type of information is useful to input into enterprise monitoring and management products, such as Microsoft's Operations Manager, HP's OpenView, or IBM's Tivoli. This table is really a summary; you should go back to the previous sections and complementary information from Microsoft that describe the performance counters in greater detail to better determine those that best fit your environment.

Table 6.7 *Summary of Counters*

Performance Object	Performance Counter and Instance	Suggested Sampling Interval	Suggested Threshold
Processor	Total/%/processor time	5 seconds or less	Less than 80 percent for 95 percent of the time.
	Percent privileged time	5 seconds or less	Less than half of the percent processor time.
System	Processor queue length	5 seconds or less	Less than two times the number of processors for more than 95 percent of the time (five times for multicore processors).
	Context switches per second	5 seconds or less	Depends on the machine architecture, but overall should be less than 80,000 on a four-way Pentium Xeon 2.5-GHz server.
Memory	Pages/sec	15 seconds or less	This counter is mentioned here because of many references in the literature about it, but it has little value on an Exchange 2003 server, since it represents both the hard page faults and the soft page faults. Do expect peak value above 500–600, but as long as you can keep the hard page faults down, you are pretty much OK.
	Page Reads/sec (hard page faults)	15 seconds or less	Less than five for 95 percent of the time.
	Page Writes/sec (hard page faults)	15 seconds or less	Less than five for 95 percent of the time.

▶

Table 6.7   *Summary of Counters (continued)*

Performance Object	Performance Counter and Instance	Suggested Sampling Interval	Suggested Threshold
Physical disk; the instance and the interpretation depends upon the type of device utilized and the type of information hosted on that device (pagefile, databases, transaction log files, MTA, and SMTP server mail folders)	Avg. Disk sec/ Write	5 seconds or less	Less than 15 ms, and if the controller is using write-back cache, it should be less than 4–5 ms for random access and less than 1 ms for sequential access.
	Avg. disk sec/ read	5 seconds or less	Less than 5 ms is considered very good, but 10–15 ms for random access is considered normal. During backup operation, the physical disk should be capable of prefetching information and the counter should read below 2 ms.
	Current disk queue length	5 seconds or less	Less than half of the number of spindles for most (95 percent) of the time—you may see peak values ranging between 50 and 150; that is OK, as long as the queue doesn't stay up too long (should be back to 0 within the next 1 or 2 seconds).
	Disk reads/ sec	5 seconds or less	Should be within your device specification (less than 120 times the number of spindles making up the volume/disk). It is important to track this value to see whether the memory caching is doing a good job and to monitor the advantage of adding more RAM, which should decrease the number of read operations to the database volumes.
	Disk writes/ sec	5 seconds or less	Should be within your device specification (less than 100 times the number of spindles making up the volume/disk) for 95 percent of the time. Going above the device specifications can cause large queues, which result in long response times.

Table 6.7   *Summary of Counters (continued)*

Performance Object	Performance Counter and Instance	Suggested Sampling Interval	Suggested Threshold
	Avg. disk bytes/transfer	5 seconds or less	Gives an indication of the data rate on the target volume. This counter is really important during backup and restore operations to determine whether you are getting good throughput in and out of the server. If you are issuing a backup to a tape drive, make sure that this counter matches or exceeds the tape drive specifications (12 MB/s for an SDLT drive, 20–30 for an LTO-3).
Epoxy	Client out queue len	Less than 5 seconds	Should be between 20 and 0 and should consistently get back to 0. The inability of the queue to rapidly return to 0 after a peak value of 15–20 indicates a performance problem with the STORE process, which cannot keep up with the load.
	Store out queue len	Less than 5 seconds	Similar comment as with Client out queue len. In this case, it would be the IIS virtual servers that have trouble with the STORE demands (such as the SMTP service failing to get message submits from the STORE process).
MSExchangeIS Mailbox	Send Queue Size	15 seconds or less	Should always return to 0 or less than 5 on large servers. On average, this value should not exceed 1 percent of the active users on the server.
	Receive Queue Size	15 seconds or less	Same as Send Queue Size.
	Folder opens/sec	5 seconds or less	Useful for baseline and trend analysis, this counter does not really express a performance issue per se.
	Message opens/sec	5 seconds or less	Ditto.

Table 6.7 *Summary of Counters (continued)*

Performance Object	Performance Counter and Instance	Suggested Sampling Interval	Suggested Threshold
Database (information store)	Log writes/sec	5 seconds or less	This is an indication counter that provides an idea of how the transaction log volumes are stressed. If this counter goes above 500 times the number of transaction log devices, you are running very close to the actual storage limit, and the transaction logging could turn into a bottleneck. You will determine whether your transaction log devices are handling the load properly by monitoring the Physical Disk(<log drive>)\Avg. sec/Write counter value and making sure it stays well below 5 ms (or 1 ms if you have enabled write-back cache, which you should anyway).
	Log threads waiting	5 seconds or less	Less than five on a busy server with many users (more than 2,000) for 80 percent to 90 percent of the time.
SMTP server	Messages sent/sec	15 seconds or less	Depends on your environment, but obviously the higher, the better.
	Messages received/sec	15 seconds or less	Ditto.
	Categorizer queue length	5 seconds or less	Should be less than five for 95 percent of the time. If it goes consistently higher, you have an Active Directory performance problem to track.
	Remote queue length	Less than 1 minute	Make sure that this queue regularly gets down to 0. If not, you may have an issue in delivering outbound mail, related to either network performance, peer SMTP server performance or availability, or both.
	Local queue length	Less than 1 minute	Should normally be at 0 and not grow over time. If it stays consistently higher than approximately 1 percent of the active users, your STORE process has a performance issue, since it cannot cope with the inbound mail traffic.

Table 6.7   *Summary of Counters (continued)*

Performance Object	Performance Counter and Instance	Suggested Sampling Interval	Suggested Threshold
MSExchangeIS	RPC operations/sec	5 seconds or less	Good baseline to monitor and to establish trends. Not uncommon to see peak values at 2,000 and above for high-performance servers.
	RPC requests	5 seconds or less	Normally below 10 for online-mode Outlook. Below 20 for Outlook in cache mode. If you have a consistent pattern that exceeds 50, you apply too high a workload to your server—scale up, scale out, but do something!

I/O per Sec and Microsoft Exchange Users

As storage is quite critical for Microsoft Exchange performance, there have been many attempts, during sizing exercises, to size not only storage per capacity (GB), but also per transaction throughput (IOPS). I am not a big fan of this particular term, so you will see this section referring to request rate (I/O per sec), transaction throughput (I/O per sec), or transfers per second (I/O per sec)—all these terms have been in practical use in the storage industry for many years, across many operating system environments and business applications.

The idea, during the storage sizing exercise, is to make sure that the volumes hosting data (databases, transaction log files, and other transient data areas) for the Microsoft Exchange application do fulfill on the throughput (I/O per sec) and response time (sec per I/O), and possibly, depending upon the storage infrastructure, the data rate (megabytes per second, sometimes expressed in gigabytes per minute or per hour).

For this sizing, we can start from known and well-defined profiles, or, better yet, figure out the user transaction rate (I/O per second per user/mailbox) based upon the existing production environment. LoadSim 2003 is a superb workload simulation tool that has continuously improved over the years; however, simulated users are just that: simulated.

In the day in the life of a Microsoft Exchange server, there are changing moments: weekends, morning peaks, weekly peaks (on the Monday if you happen to live in a country where the work week starts on a Monday), monthly peaks, and even quarterly peaks.

In your sizing exercise, you must determine whether you want to address 100 percent of the workload or just less than that. Addressing 100 percent of the workload means that no matter what day or hour it is, the storage subsystem must handle the transactional workload.

For determining, out of your production system, the existing transaction workload, you must work with Perfmon objects, where the basic rule is to bring together physical disk utilization and application level workload.

The physical disk utilization is measured using counters presented in "Physical Disk Monitoring" on page 527. The goal will be to first determine the response time and transaction throughput together.

The application workload is measured using varying counters, depending on how you wish to reuse this information. For example, you may decide to measure the number of mailboxes defined on the server. However, this measurement does not take into account the fact that mailboxes may or may not be logged in—this fact depends upon your user profile and the time of day, day of week, week of month, and so forth.

You may then decide to measure the number of users "connected" to the server. This is getting closer to the actual ratio between server activity and disk activity; however, it does not account for a few key aspects:

- Users might be connected but not active;
- A connected user might be using more than one mailbox (common in delegated environments, where assistants will access their mailboxes as well as their bosses' mailboxes);
- Outlook 2003 in cache mode might be issuing more that one connection to the server during its background synchronization process (by default, four background synchronization and one foreground connection threads are used).

To further make the distinction, you can then decide to measure the "connections" to the server. In that case, you take into account the facts that users are logged in and that a single user might have more than one connection, but you still miss the "activity" factor. Depending upon the industry you're in, the user profile and population, and the type of client, the actual number of active users (users doing "something") might be significantly different from the number of connected users, itself being different from the number of mailboxes defined on the server. Note that this activity factor largely depends upon the client protocol. With POP and IMAP users, you do not have the concept of being connected yet idle: you establish connection to the server, you synchronize your email, and that's it. The activity factor is primarily used in MAPI clients (e.g., Outlook) environments, where it is common to open the client in the morning and close it at the end of the working day, maintaining a connection between the client and the server but not necessarily using it.

For taking into account the "activity" factor from MAPI clients, the "MSExchangeIS\Active User" performance counter can be utilized: it describes the number of users who have performed a MAPI operation within the last 10 minutes.

Similarly, and probably more applicable to Outlook 2003 cache-mode environments, the "MSExchangeIS\Active Connection" counters comprises not only the users themselves, but also the additional connections to the servers, either due to the user connections or other peer server/component connections.

Which to Choose?

If you are interested in the user pattern and therefore need to have a close look, possibly down at the storage group level, I recommend using the MSExchangeIS Mailbox performance object, starting first with the _Total instance and then working it out per storage group if relevant to your objectives. Monitoring this counter will help you understand variations between the user workloads and possibly plan for more breakdowns of workloads by, for instance, confining high-workload users in their own storage groups and corresponding physical disk units.

In the "MSExchangeIS Mailbox" performance object, there are three counters that you may utilize for getting your request rate ratio:

1. Client Logons: The number of clients, including the system processes, that are currently logged on;

2. Active Client Logons: The number of clients (from the previous group) that have performed any kind of operation in the last ten minutes;

3. Peak Client Logons: The maximum number of clients connected to this storage group since it started.

For a 30,000-foot view, I find that the "MSExchangeIS\User Count" counter is "good enough." To this, you associate the "Physical Disk\Transfers per sec" and can perform a simple divide operation for determining the I/O per second per user, and possibly break down this ratio between database and transaction log disk units.

Six other counters may be used out of the "MSExchangeIS" performance object:

1.   Connection Count, Active Connection Count, and Maximum Connection Count;

2.   User Count, Active User Count, and Maximum User Count.

I have purposefully omitted the "Anonymous" series of these counters, but you might want to pick them up.

To get to the point of this section, your choice must be motivated by the intended utilization of the counter and how much of the workload you wish to address (are you really bothered with the Friday preceding the end of financial quarter close?).

In most of my performance assessments, I have been happy using the active user count from the MSExchangeIS object, but always keep in mind to relate it to the user count and the number of mailboxes defined on the server. Typically:

Active user count < user count < number of mailboxes

Sizing against the active user count enables us to take into account daily variation, found in normal production environments such as the following:

Using a simple timeline analysis tool, we display on similar scale and timeline the active connection count, the active user count, and the overall user count. This was measured on a 2,500-mailbox server.

Notice how the active connection count follows the same trend (in fact, it is simply offset by a little more than 250) compared to the active user count—and how the user count ramps up in the day. From this, you may observe several peaks and valleys: one peak sharply starting after 8:00 AM and rising at 9:00 AM, and happening again at 9:45 AM. The user activity

Node(s) : NODEA

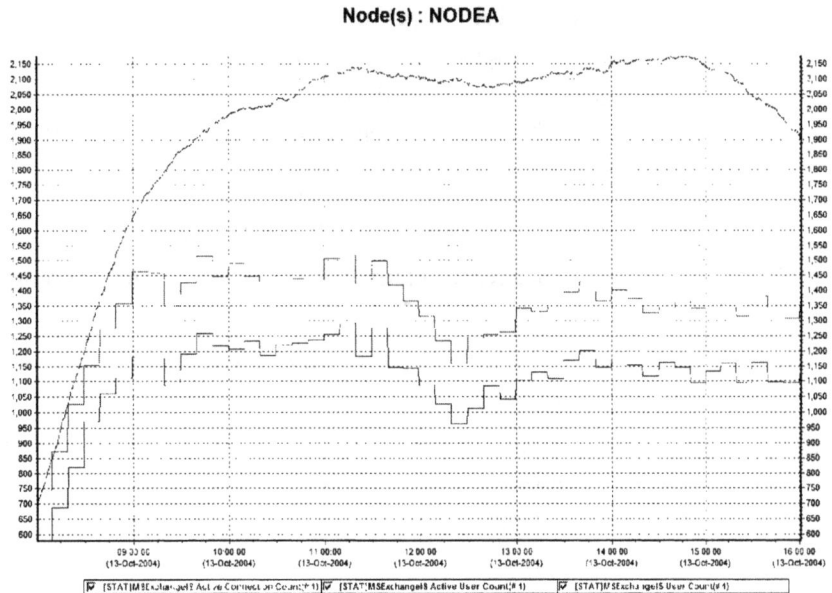

decreases during lunch time, reaches another peak at 1:45 PM, and then further stabilizes.

Note also the counter variation: we can clearly see that it only changes every 10 minutes—you do not need, therefore, to sample it at a very high rate (low interval or 5 seconds or less).

From this information, I decided to pick the "User Count" and "Active User Count" counters for determining the concurrency factor and its variation across the day. Obtaining the timeline information is important for me to focus my storage performance monitoring: unlike the active user count, which you may afford to sample every 10 minutes, Microsoft Exchange storage profiling is so brutal (large variations between low, high, and average values) that even a 5-second sampling interval is excessive (at least to me) in peak workload sizing exercises.

Physical Disk Monitoring

We discussed physical disk monitoring earlier in this chapter. The counters you must utilize depend on your sizing objectives and on the type of data held. Throughput should be measured using writes, reads, and transfers per second. The latter counter is typically the sum of both, for the given interval. Latency should be measured for reads and writes (*do not* aggregate their response time!!!) and at the smallest possible interval (this is an average counter, and in transactional workloads, "average" is your enemy).

Putting It All Together

You may take shortcuts in the procedure described next, but this varies, depending on your data set and user behavior. The basic steps for getting your I/O per second per user/mailbox are as follows:

- Monitor the user activity (10-mn interval);

- Pick a representative time slot of two hours (or more)—this is the reference time;

- Monitor the disk activity (1-second interval) during the reference time;

- Merge data together and for *each* sample, calculate the following ratios:

    - Write/sec ÷ user;
    - Read/sec ÷ user;
    - Write/sec ÷ active user;
    - Read/sec ÷ active user;
    - Active user ÷ user.

You then obtain a set of rows of calculations that include both raw data and ratios. The result is that you may view the instantaneous write and read transactions per user and active user. In fact, based on your reference time and user profile, the user versus active user ratio might be predictable enough that you only need to care about the user ratio and can dismiss the active user ratio.

From these rows, calculate the following values:

- Min;

- Max;

- Average;

- 95th percentile;

- 99th percentile.

These values will bring a sense of statistics to your data set: because addressing 100 percent of the workload (i.e., the maximum throughput ever seen during sampling) might require too many resources, you make the upfront and conscious decision that part of it (1 percent, 5 percent, or else) will exceed your environment, and you are happy with this. One percent of 2 hours is slightly more than 1 minute—maybe your users would be happy if the system was performing excellently for 2 hours with the exception of 1 minute. Maybe they wouldn't even notice.

For a production machine data set, let's have a look at the ratios and the statistical values to further illustrate the relevance for such analyses.

	User Count	Active User Count	Active User Ratio	Log I/O Rate	Database I/O Rate	Log Ratio	I/O rate per User	I/O rate per Active User	I/O DB rate per Active User
Average	1007	958	95 percent	23	159	19 percent	0.182	0.191	0.167
Min	859	834	89 percent	0	0	0 percent	0.000	0.000	0.000
Max	1078	1055	105 percent	229	1818	100 percent	1.721	1.723	1.723
95th Pcnt.	1073	1055	104 percent	61	508	55 percent	0.550	0.578	0.535
99th Pcnt.	1077	1055	105 percent	94	699	78 percent	0.779	0.812	0.752

The absolute values are of little importance in the context of this analysis (don't get upset about the active user count ratio being above 100 percent); what is more important is the difference between the average, minimum, maximum, 95th percentile, and 99th percentile values.

First, the user count indicates to us that the reference period includes a fair number of connected users that we will need to put in perspective with the actual number of mailboxes. Usually, 80 percent of the registered mailboxes have connected users in a normal work day in a corporate environment. In service provider environments, this can be as low as 10 percent. Note that the active user count is quite close to the user count, in a consistent manner: the minimum is 89 percent, the maximum is 105 percent, and the average is 95 percent: this is normal, the variation between the two counters is quite small for our sampling time (peak 2 hours of the first work day of the week).

Next, we look at the log I/O rate: this is simply the number of writes per second issued to the transaction log files area summarized for all storage groups defined on the server. The maximum value is *twice* the 99th percentile. This means that during 1 percent of the time, the I/O rate to the log area was comprised of between 94 and 229. If you were to pick the maximum value for further sizing consideration, you realize that you could significantly oversize your configuration for 99 percent of the time. For the database I/O rate, the difference between 99th percentile and the maximum is three times as much!

This back-of-the-napkin analysis (which only took a handful of minutes to make after displaying the data set) so far shows that maximum values are much larger than percentile values—it is indeed well worth dismissing 1 percent of the workload for future sizing exercises.

Finally, we look at the actual ratios and given that the user variation is not that important in the data set, the ratio would basically follow the same trend as the data rates. This time, we look at the difference between the average value and the percentile and maximum values: the overall I/O rate per user differs by a factor of almost *ten* from the maximum value. This maximum is three times more than the 99th percentile, and twice the 95th percentile, and almost *ten* times the average.

Which to trust? It depends on your environment, your workload and users, and the sampling time. We have found, in production environments and during design efforts, that using the 95th percentile gives a good "minored" peak value—which does not take into account the sudden and seldom bursts of transactions to the volumes or the frequent moments where no disk activity is present, most likely due to effective in-memory database buffering and caching.

In the previous example, our I/O per second per user is 0.550 and 0.578 per active user for the 95th percentile. Our target tuning and capacity planning will then use 0.6 I/O per second per user, well away from the 1.720 maximum and 0.182 average rates.

Logs vs. Databases

From the previous example, we did not discuss the log to database I/O ratio: this factor is interesting because in storage design, reads and writes do not necessarily have the same path. For instance, a read operation is typically not cached (because it is highly random), while a write operation is almost 100 percent cached (or should be). Also, the writes performance to the transaction log areas are synchronous, single threaded, and in the foreground of a transaction, while the writes to the database are performed in the background, independent (almost) of the user activity. The 100 ms for write latency to the database drives is far better than the 5 ms of write latency to the transaction log areas. Furthermore, the write throughput to the logs, because it is sequential and synchronous, directly depends upon the latency: the higher the latency, the fewer the writes per second to the logs, and therefore if you focus your attention only on the writes per second, you might think "my log traffic is not very high" and not spend the focus you should to fix a potential problem.

As part of I/O traffic analysis, we often see quotes about the read/write ratio (3:1 is quite common), but this ratio (3 reads for 1 write) does not comprise the write operations to the transaction logging. See the following table (which is a subset of the previous table):

	User Count	Log I/O Rate	Database I/O Rate	Log Ratio	I/O Rate per User
Average	1007	23	159	19 percent	0.182
Min	859	0	0	0 percent	0.000
Max	1078	229	1818	100 percent	1.721
95th Pcnt.	1073	61	508	55 percent	0.550
99th Pcnt.	1077	94	699	78 percent	0.779

Our log/database ratio is 55 percent for 95 percent of the time, and, on average, 19 percent—this value indicates that there are moments where more than half of the write operations were issued to the transaction log drives but in a fairly small quantity: 61 is the 95th percentile for the write throughput. Ten percent is generally used, but it is worthwhile to look at your own systems, and beyond this possibly identify systems where you have more writes than others (the most common and typical case is when journaling is enabled on a server).

Other Approaches

From its technical publications and communications about Microsoft Exchange, Microsoft does have a similar way of computing I/O rates per users (IOPS in Microsoft literature). The simple formula can be expressed as:

IOPS/mailbox = (average disk transfer/sec) ÷ (number of mailboxes)

In most environments (remember, 90 percent of Microsoft Exchange deployments are in the SMB space, with less than 1,000 users per server), this formula will work well. However, in atypical environments, such as 5,000-

user servers or service providers, you will want to get closer to the numbers and figure out how you may "oversubscribe" your environment while preserving a good service for "most" of the time ("most" = percentage of time/operations that will be satisfactorily serviced by the storage subsystem).

In Summary

With this method, we have reviewed how to sample counter information, quickly identify a reference time period using timeline analysis, and then use simple mathematical formulas (with Microsoft Excel) for simple (yet not simplistic) statistical analysis.

You might want to automate this information reporting if you wish to perform baseline analysis and possibly report on excessive server utilization—as a matter of fact, the data presented here was taken from a customer case where eventually a faulty add-on to the Outlook client was identified as being the root cause of an excessive storage request rate. We could identify the norm (baseline) for the request rate, further sample on several servers, and bring the data together.

At the same time, you will want to be somewhat careful about these calculations: the request rate per user depends on many factors: the type of the client and eventually the version of Microsoft Exchange. In Exchange 2003 SP1 and further, efforts were made to "flatten" the request rate for the database volumes, resulting in a less spiky workload, less inactivity, and less rush: the result is that peak-based analysis can be affected and yielded to smaller peak I/O ratios.

The consequences can be quite significant if you intend to use the I/O ratios for storage sizing exercises—a 20 percent or 50 percent difference directly (linear) impacts the cost of acquisition for such storage infrastructures!!!

6.3.4   Reporting Performance Results

This section focuses on how to best interpret and report performance information. There will be times when a time-based graphic is of value; which sampling interval to use depends largely on the type of counter being used. For example, if you monitor the Send Queue Size for the MSExchange\IS Mailbox, a sampling of 1 minute is enough. On the other hand, if you focus your attention on the disk counters, an interval of 5 seconds is necessary.

On the Use of Percentiles and Moving Averages

Percentiles give a much better view of the repartition of the various values in a series, as opposed to peaks and averages. They allow us to understand the proportion or determine the importance of peak values versus minimum common values. I have found that customers prefer assertions like "CPU utilization was below 60 percent for 80 percent of the time" rather than "CPU average utilization is 33 percent."

Furthermore, you will find it quite expensive to build a system that handles 100 percent of the load. Generally, 5 percent is considered acceptable for decreased or nonoptimal performance. For example, Microsoft uses the 95th percentile of all the transaction performance readings during a load simulation as an indicator of whether or not the system performed OK.

Figure 6.41 is an example of sampled response time for a database volume taken during production hours of a *very* busy server.

Figure 6.41
Sampled response time for a database volume

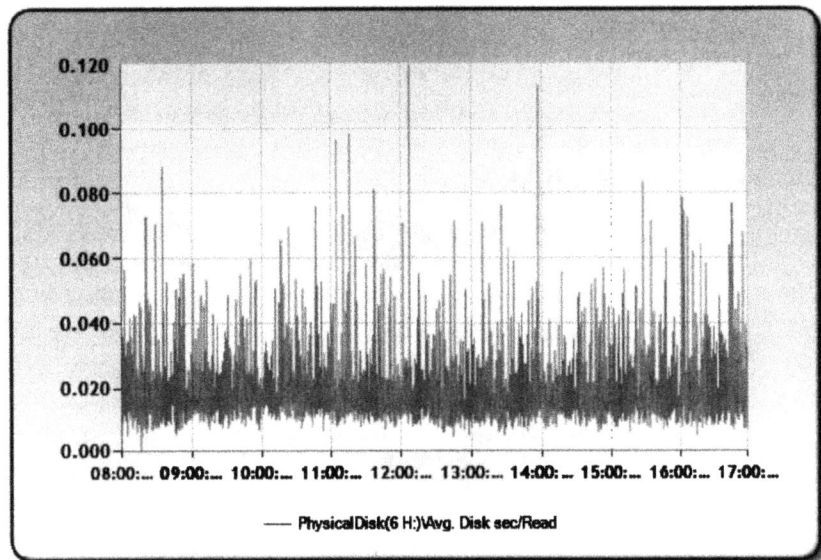

As you can observe, there is a fair amount of operations above 20 ms. In fact, that server is not producing great response times, and the users of that machine do complain about performance. Still, it's hard to really quantify and determine relative values.

If, instead of bluntly reporting on the actual values, you proceed to sort them by arranging them by order of percentile (5th percentile, 10th percentile, and so forth), you can get a much clearer view of the proportion information in Figure 6.42.

At this point, peak values still appear, but they are of a lesser importance—what is really important is to determine the acceptable response

Figure 6.42
Response time distribution

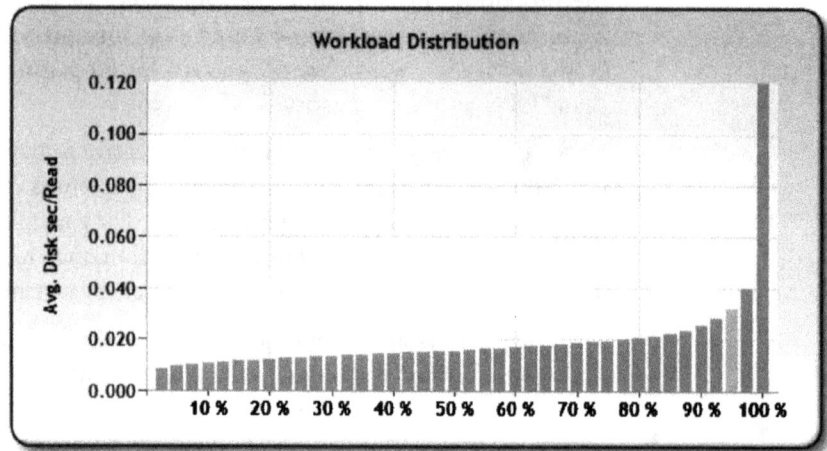

time (20 ms for instance) and figure out that "only" 80 percent of the operations are satisfying to this performance criteria. In fact, 20 percent of the time, the disk is not producing a good response time, and in a day, 20 percent of the time is a *lot*.

There are many ways to plot diagrams and percentile information, and there are no great tools freely available on the market. You may develop some simple Excel spreadsheets that gather percentile figures and allow you to make quick decisions regarding your server performance analysis and troubleshooting. I certainly had the opportunity to develop one. I saw a colleague of mine, Christophe Dubois, enhance it and grow it up, and eventually share the results with the technical community. This is the bit of "intellectual property" I cannot transmit via a book (but I can by email ☺).

Moving averages, on the other hand, are useful if you wish to measure the duration of a peak. A moving average is calculated over a defined number of samples. If your moving average reaches above 10 (for example), you have certain evidence of the duration of a particular peak of throughput or response time. In Figure 6.43, I have added a moving average. It does not really express the same information as the percentile.

When my percentile data indicated that 20 percent of my samples were of bad response time (i.e., above 20 ms), the moving average navigates between 20 ms but erases (way too much in my opinion) the peak values, which can be to the detriment of performance problem detection.

I think moving averages are useful to detect spikes over a short period of time, but they fall short of global performance analysis across a day of work. They are appropriate for threshold and event alarming—percentiles are

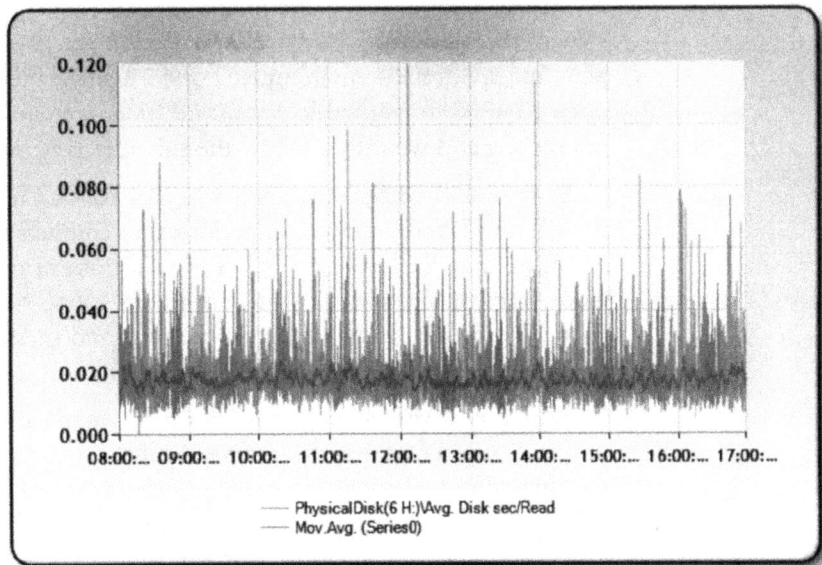

Figure 6.43
Using a moving average to a data sample

more appropriate for dealing with the overall timeline of a performance capture/analysis.

6.4   In Summary

Performance monitoring and system tuning is not very far from being an art, and it would be very presumptuous of me to say that I am a master of this particular art. Great artistic work, in my opinion, is typically a combination of talent (often a gift) and know-how. I hope that with the information provided here, you have enough know-how to check and monitor your Exchange messaging network performance, and I trust you will have the talent to interpret and fine-tune the data. I cannot, unfortunately, transmit any kind of talent, but I hope to provide you with best practices that can be helpful as you do your day-to-day job.

Among the key things to remember, I would like to mention the following: do not hesitate to equip your messaging infrastructure with vertical and complete monitoring solutions. They will let you sleep peacefully and take care of properly interfacing a complex messaging environment with operational support staff by providing events and associated actions that can help the system run smoothly and address problems before the users are even aware of them (this is a nice goal to have for complex and distributed system monitoring). Vertical solutions aim at drilling down a particular application and providing an intelligent way to interpret the data and report events and activity. Complete monitoring solutions provide a 30,000-foot view of the computing infrastructure and *federate* the many operating systems and application environments under a single viewpoint of reporting, often required in large-scale computing environments that require 24 × 7 monitoring and typically a follow-the-sun operating model.

Be critical of whatever counter you monitor and how you interpret the data. You will find hundreds of performance counters on a Windows 2003 Server running Exchange 2003, but with just one or two counters, you can quickly determine whether your machine is falling behind or providing a good service level, from user response time and message throughput and background activities perspectives.

With this, I wish you a great performance monitoring of your Exchange servers. You will find that this activity can be extremely rewarding both personally and to your organization if you can draw conclusions that help in reducing your IT infrastructure costs and provide a better service to your user communities. Remember that you should strive for a balanced infrastructure, especially regarding your servers and storage configurations, and, where you can, use acceptable budgets to satisfy to a certain service level. Throwing CPU and RAM into a box do not help if your storage component is falling behind.

Knowing that a server is not performing adequately is fine, and it is very important to address before your users complain. Knowing *why* the server is not performing up to your standards is better. Knowing how to improve your server performance is the best approach.

Without a sound analysis and comprehension of Microsoft Exchange 2003 performance and monitoring, you don't stand a chance of achieving these three points.

7

Best Practices

7.1 Best Practices

In this final chapter, I want to share with you some actual server configurations and give a real-world context for the elements of theory that were covered earlier in this book. There is no doubt that technology will continue to evolve, some components at the rate of Moore's law (e.g., CPU and RAM) and others at a probable slower pace (e.g., disks, WAN bandwidth). In the meantime, Microsoft continuously improves its product and technology offerings, bridging a smaller and smaller gap between what the products can offer off the shelf and the solution that customers actually need. As the technology increases on the application, hardware, and operating system fronts, server design best practices may evolve. Consequently, you should make use of the suggestions offered here with an understanding of how they are formulated. That way, you can better judge whether they apply in your environment as technology moves forward, hopefully, for the better.

Within HP, we have developed a fair number of best practices. They are considered "best" because they result from the mental work involved in designing the most complex Exchange messaging solutions imaginable. Combined with the best practices defined by Microsoft for operating their products, which are easily auditable by using the Exchange Best Practice Analyzer (ExBPA), you eventually reduce risks in the deployment of Exchange and augment the predictability of the solution put in place, no matter the scale.

In this chapter, we review the configuration guidelines for Windows Server 2003, bearing in mind that much will depend on your own implementation guidelines and Windows server deployment policies. These are hints; you are not necessarily forced to adhere to or agree with the approach, but I hope that they can properly serve your environment and your current and future Exchange networks.

7.1.1 The Exchange Best Practice Analyzer

The ExBPA is a superb tool from Microsoft. It can audit the Exchange environment, make sure that the servers are configured according to evolving best practices, and greatly diminish the uncertainties of a deployment (see Figure 7.1). I'm not going to review this tool in detail herein, or provide potential best practices that would conflict with those of Microsoft. Suffice it to say, at this point, that best practices evolve, and that running a single audit is fine to define the baseline of your environment, but it is also important to regularly run ExBPA and keep track of the changes.

Figure 7.1
ExBPA in action

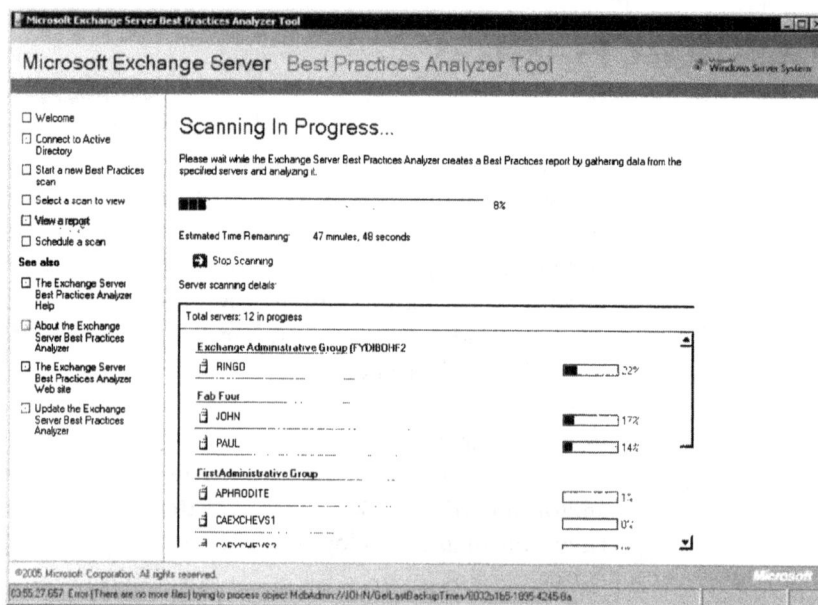

The tool alone is not going to solve your configuration and change management problems, but it definitely contributes to improving and perfecting the integrity of the Exchange server network.

If you have a particularly large environment (more than 20 Microsoft Exchange servers spread in a wide area network), ExBPA may take some time to execute. Once completed, ExBPA will display a status icon for all the servers found in the Exchange organization (this is done by looking up the Windows Active Directory and auditing the configuration remotely, without requiring an agent to be installed on each server of the network), as shown in Figure 7.2.

Exchange Administrative Group (FYDIBOHF2
RINGO
Completed
Fab Four
JOHN
Completed
PAUL
Completed
First Administrative Group
APHRODITE
Completed
CAEXCHEVS1
Completed

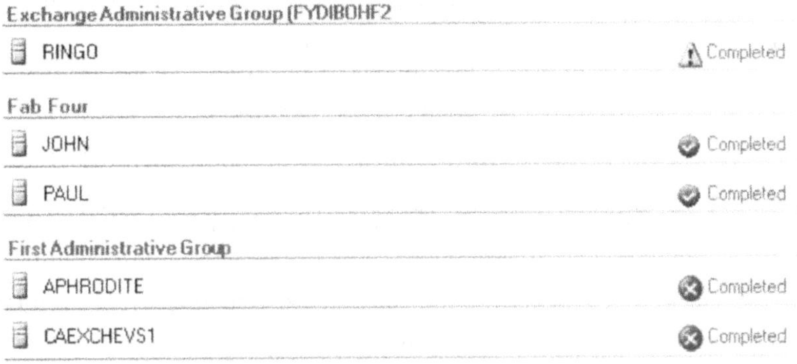

Figure 7.2 *ExBPA status information after a scan*

Once you have done a scan, you may review a report about it, which will list all issues found, as well as provide a detailed report of the scan. One feature I found interesting is the nondefault setting of the Server environment. In Figure 7.3, there is an example of the results of a scan and view of accessing the local help file of ExBPA for obtaining more information about the report.

Microsoft Exchange Server Best Practices Analy
View Best Practices Report
Non-Default Settings
Disk timeout is not set at default
HKLM\System\CurrentControlS

Figure 7.3 *Listing nondefault settings in ExBPA*

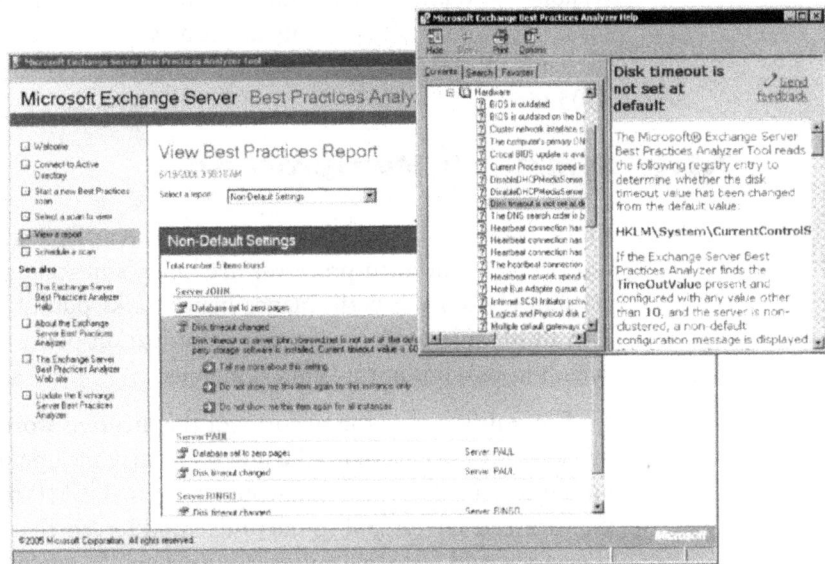

You should check more information about ExBPA on http://www.microsoft.com/exchange. This is a freebie from Microsoft that is well worth the use: not only will you find potential issues in your environment, but you will also learn many configuration tips for your environment.

Just like best practices, an ExBPA scan is not an end in itself. It should be one of the key tools for operating your Exchange environment, especially if you have many servers and possibly many administrators. The single-seat view of the environment, running in an agentless mode (with sufficient Windows Active Directory permissions, still) is priceless!

7.2   Configuration Guidelines for Windows 2003

The Windows 2003 operating system is quite complex when it comes to tuning and to defining configuration settings. I deliberately do not address certain Windows 2003 server configuration options, such as security settings or network services. Frankly, a similar sized book could be dedicated just to Windows Group Policy Objects and to the art of hardening the security of a Windows server, something that has been vastly improved with the Windows 2003 server release. In fact, I really encourage you to consult the various sources of information—from Microsoft but also from other companies or organizations. For example, the U.S. National Security Agency provides a series of security configuration guides that can be used on various versions of Windows and other operating systems (http://www.nsa.gov/snac). This chapter also contains my views on configuring a scalable Exchange 2003 messaging network composed of—obviously—Windows 2003 servers.

7.2.1   Symmetric Multiprocessing

I have found, during performance testing, that Exchange 2003 was taking real advantage of quad-processor machines, still scaling to eight processors (as shown from the performance benchmarks published by Microsoft on http://www.microsoft.com/exchange/evaluation/performance/default.mspx), but not in a linear manner.

The reality is that the majority of the incurred workloads are addressed by quad-processor systems; the processors may include more than one computing core (as found in dual-core processors). SMP really brings value to the back-end servers and to the bridgehead servers that must issue protocol conversion and real-time antivirus scanning. Therefore, I would highly recommend you to aim high (overconfigure your server) if you have plans to place an additional workload on your Exchange 2003 server beyond simple mailbox access.

Examples of additional workloads include:

- Implementation of content indexing: Content indexing can be a real CPU killer. Between 20 percent and 40 percent of additional CPU usage should be considered if you plan to implement content indexing locally on an Exchange 2003 server, and 60 percent during initial database crawling and indexing.

- Use of journaling: Copying each message sent and received on an Exchange server typically generates incremental workload, estimated to be between 15 percent and 30 percent of additional workload. In high-end environments, you might even decide to dedicate servers to be recipients of content and envelope journaling, as made available in Exchange 2003.

- Implementation of business process applications: Exchange 2003 lends well to automatic processing of information as it arrives on a particular server, by providing access to synchronous and asynchronous event sinks. Most of the preliminary characterization of Exchange 2003 in customer projects has dealt with simple configurations of Exchange. It would make sense, after assessing the performance characterization of Exchange, to stress and benchmark the server under the production environment, including the registration of antivirus products and custom-made, if applicable, event sinks.

- Increasing use of Internet protocols: These are being used as opposed to MAPI for accessing the information store.

- Mobile devices: The use of third-party mobile devices requires an intermediate component that can synchronize the contents of a mailbox with the mobile device.

In choosing the server model, you should investigate the expandability features of the server, even if you consider four processors to be sufficient for your workload (implemented on single or dual-core die). The majority of customers embracing a new Exchange 2003 infrastructure typically employ new hardware components, with the precise intention of not needing to modify it later on (at least for 18 to 24 months). Some customers even deploy with the firm intention of not touching the server components (no change in processors, RAM, bus, and the like) for the next 36 months. A lot depends on the depreciation model employed by the company and the projected lifetime of the server.

In choosing a server model, aim for one that can expand, that adopts advanced redundancy concepts (e.g., redundant memory banks, processor hot swap), that can be later supported by the Windows operating system, and that requires relatively small maintenance.

Above all, however, choose a unique server model for each family of Exchange servers you intend to deploy, and either scale up or scale down the number of processors, depending on the estimated current and future workloads. It is much simpler to deal with one single BIOS update across many servers, than several updates for several server models. In fact, in their attempts to reduce their total cost of ownership, many customers go that route and find it advantageous.

My recommendations for SMP machines are as follows:

- Front-end servers: Two physical processors max (L2 256 KB min), dual-core preferred, hyper-threading enabled;

- Back-end servers: Eight physical processors max (sweet spot is at four dual-core processors), L2 at 2 MB max, 1 MB OK;

- Journaling servers: Two physical processors, dual-core, L2 at 1 MB;

- Bridgehead servers: Two physical processors max (L2 at 1 MB max). Interestingly enough, bridgehead servers are a potential target for high CPU consumption resulting from add-on products such as real-time antivirus protection, anti-SPAM software, message conversion, and possibly content scanning.

In all situations, it is better to aim for the highest clock speed, since it can also affect the front-side bus (system bus) throughput. Many transfers actually occur to disk; therefore, there is little chance for system bus contention with machines that have four or fewer processors.

7.2.2 Memory Sizing

The memory sizing for an Exchange 2003 SP2 server depends primarily on its role as well as on other applications that could be running on the same server and possibly in dire need of RAM; physical memory access is always better than paged-out virtual memory access.

For pure Exchange 2003 servers (i.e., those that run Exchange, antivirus, and monitoring products), the breakdown for optimal memory sizing is as follows:

- Back-end server—4 GB max;

- Front-end server—2 GB max (depends on protocol);

- Bridgehead server—2 GB max.

You may tempted to add more RAM to your server if you observe the quantity of physical memory available on a running production Exchange server. The fact is that Exchange implements the DBA scheme described earlier in this book and will attempt to use as much RAM as it can until the system is stressed. Typically, you will have approximately 5 MB of physical RAM available on an Exchange server. If there is demand from other applications (for example, growing their working set), Exchange will trim its database cache and working set size to let other applications benefit from the RAM.

Exchange may not be the only application on the server, and 4 GB of RAM will be well utilized by virtue of other applications' demands on large-scale servers. I would hesitate to load a server with more than 4 GB of RAM, unless you are running an application that is AWE-aware. One of these applications could very well be an SQL Server or an I/O cache tool that can insert a filter driver in the NT I/O subsystem and proceed to do caching in the upper memory, above 4 GB.

On the use of the /3GB switch, you will see recommendations to enable this boot switch if your server is equipped with more than (and not inclusive of) 1 GB of RAM. This is certainly appropriate for maximizing the Information Store database cache that is created in the process virtual address space. This setting also has the effect of "starving" the kernel from its 2 GB address space down to 1 GB. This can be undesirable if your Exchange 2003 server will place heavy demand on the Windows NT kernel structures, such as file handles and file cache.

You should not use the /3GB switch if you deploy servers that primarily use the streaming store interface to Exchange, which is the case for all Internet protocol communication with the Exchange 2003 server. This will be at the expense of creating a large cache for the main database pages, which will result in more frequent read accesses to the database as opposed to caching database pages in memory. You should therefore carefully monitor your disk subsystem's performance to make sure that the level of read requests—and, most important, the response time of the read requests to the database volumes—do not exceed an acceptable value (<20 ms in general, and a queue length less than half the number of drives making up the volume, regardless of the RAID level being utilized).

7.2.3 Logical Drive Partitions

Partitioning and planning your storage space is a double-edged sword: you may get great flexibility in designing your logical and hardware partitions, but you run the risk of locking yourself up for future growth.

Personally, I like large partitions with one-to-one mapping to physical drives. This allows for clearly isolating the I/O traffic, which helps in both characterization and performance tuning. Still, not all servers can afford to have four or five volumes minimum to host the various components that can make up an Exchange 2003 server—back-end, front-end, or bridge-head server. In this section, I offer some suggestions for partition name, label, and utilization. We will see, depending on the physical server model and associated subsystem, how we can map these onto physical drives.

To start, let's remain at a logical level and review the fundamental reasons for the logical disk arrangement. Table 7.1 shows a sample logical drive arrangement. Because of the generalized support of mount points for mapping disk partitions in the NT I/O namespace, I use the term "drive path" as opposed to the too-restrictive term "drive letter." I recommend about 8 GB for the logical partition that holds the operating system and the core product binaries. Generally, you should include Exchange 2003 in that set of core product binaries, but there are exceptions to that rule, depending on the server role in the Exchange topology.

Table 7.1 *Sample drive layout for a Microsoft Exchange Mailbox Server*

Drive Path	Size	Label	Content
C:\	16 GB	System	Operating system and binaries
C:\Logs	4 GB	Logs	Event and IIS logs
Z:\	8 GB	Swap	Pagefile and system dump
I:\, J:\, K:\, L:\	20 GB	Logs-1, Logs-2, Logs-3, and Logs-4	Transaction log files for storage groups 1, 2, 3, and 4
N:\, O:\, P:\, Q:\	100 GB	Database-1, Database-2, Database-3, and Database-4	Database files for storage groups 1, 2, 3, and 4

The "C:\Logs" partition of 4 GB is reserved to store the IIS and event log files. Locating these files in a particular partition will prevent your server from being down as a result of a denial-of-service attack, which has the aim of filling up your system drive and preventing the system from operating correctly. This shouldn't prevent you from having a solid garbage collection policy on your servers for these event and application logs.

The Z: partition is for the pagefile and solely for the page file. You may need to reserve some space on the boot partition for the location of the memory dump, but Z: is suggested for holding the page file to better understand the growth of the pagefile—and, most important, its usage.

The drive units are then chosen, in sequence for logs and then for the databases. I do not recommend using individual partitions for each storage group database, as it will unnecessarily waste disk space due to the necessity to avoid unexpected drive fill-up.

Mount Points

You may wonder about the significance of using Windows 2003 mount points instead of using drive letters. Mount points are a way in Windows Server to get to a volume or partition without assigning a drive letter to it: the partition appears as a folder (Figure 7.4 shows how to create the mount point) underneath an existing volume folder hierarchy (Figure 7.5).

Figure 7.4
Defining a mount point for a disk volume

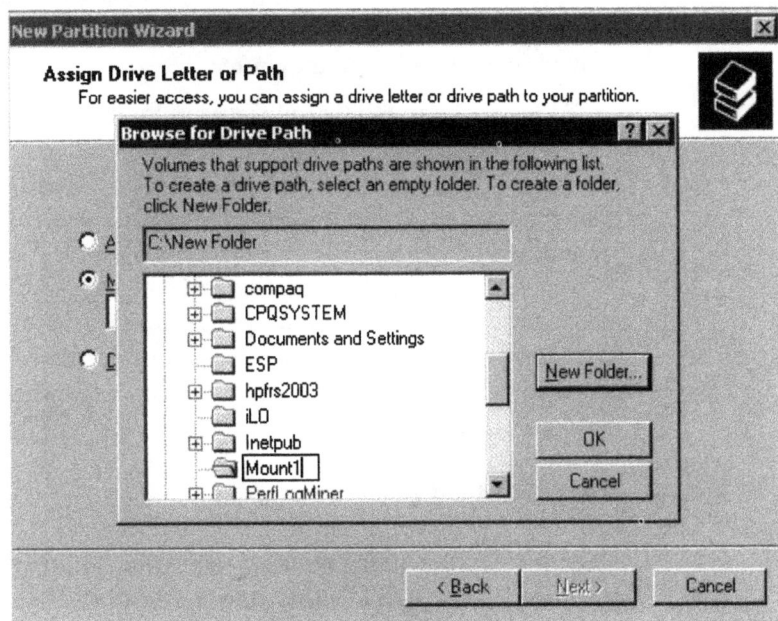

Figure 7.5
A mount point in the root folder of C:\ drive

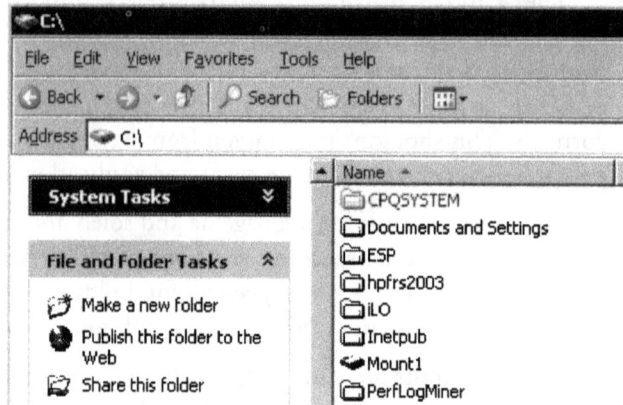

I certainly find mount points to be very useful and largely support using them to simplify operations and reduce the number of drive letters used in a server. To counter this view is the fact that not all administrators are fully aware of and comfortable with mount points (which, in fact, consist simply of plugging a logical partition in a folder structure) and may be "annoyed" by such an arrangement.

With Windows Server 2003, mount points are also supported in clustered environments. You do not have to map physical volumes and logical partitions by means of letters if you wish to have them used by the cluster resource manager. This is a great benefit, typically required in 8-node clustered environments, where any physical volume must be uniquely represented across all nodes of the cluster.

Using a mount point is only relevant for mapping a disk partition in the NT I/O namespace. In other words, there is no performance impact, but there is a dependency created between the parent partition and the mounted partition. If the parent drive is not available, the mount points hooked off this parent drive become unavailable—you may or may not accept such a dependency. It has become common, in Exchange server deployments that utilize mount points, to use a drive letter for the transaction log partition and a mount point in the root folder for the database disks. If the log volume becomes unavailable, the databases would not be used anyway by the Exchange database engine.

7.2.4   Physical Drives

Requirements for Exchange 2003 concerning the physical drives can vary, depending on the server's role. As a general rule, the more disks you have, the better performance you will obtain (and, of course, the more capacity in size terms). On the other hand, there are few opportunities for a server hosting a small user population (e.g., 100 users) to have many spindles, let alone the fact that some servers have their own constraints for built-in storage. Indeed, if you are planning to use a pedestal server, you are not likely to have space for more than six or eight drives. You may actually host other files and applications on that particular server, and it would be very unwise to have an external storage cabinet linked by SCSI or optical fiber cables. If you do need an external storage bay (with or without an embarked RAID controller), I strongly suggest you choose a rack model, where cables are properly attached to the cabinet and do not run the risk of someone pulling them out inadvertently (this has happened). Inevitably, for production servers, you will want to use one form of redundancy or another.

There are three forms available on the market, two of which are widely known and implemented:

- RAID5: Distributed parity across a stripe set. This is by far the most popular RAID level, yet it is not the most efficient for write operations. Still, it gives the best return on investment for capacity (gigabyte) purposes.

- RAID0+1: Stripe of mirrors (sometimes mirrors of stripes). More expensive on a dollar per gigabyte basis than RAID5, but it is cheaper to implement than RAID5 if transaction throughput is a concern.

- RAID6 (also known as advanced data guarding): Double distributed parity. We see some implementations of this, including HP's latest PCI-Express RAID controllers and StorageWorks XP arrays. The big advantage of RAID6 over RAID5 is its ability to cope with a second disk failure during the reconstruction phase resulting from a first disk failure in the member set. The big disadvantage is that the cost of generating and synchronizing two parity elements is even larger than with RAID5. I would generally not recommend it for Exchange databases (and certainly not for transaction log files) unless the data access pattern is "mostly" read (as in a data mining environment).

Drive level redundancy is certainly a given, but there are other forms of redundancy related to storage, such as the controllers themselves. If you opt for a PCI RAID controller, bear in mind that you can build redundancy at the disk level, but the controller itself is a single point of failure (and so is its cache memory). Some RAID controllers, even those embarked on the mother of servers, do have the ability to transfer the memory board of the controller without losing the content, thereby dealing with a controller hardware failure without losing information and transactions in progress.

For configuring the volumes themselves, and especially when determining the size of these volumes, always plan for the maximum database size (including an estimated deleted items retention space) and choose to fill your drives at 75 percent maximum of the actual capacity that they will provide. If you obtain large volumes (in gigabytes) because you had to assemble many spindles to satisfy the planned transaction rate, you may well have a fill of 50 percent or less, and that is all right. There is a moment where you will need to decide whether you size for request rate (I/O per second) or capacity (gigabytes). In the former case, you will have unneeded space but retain the necessary performance.

You should be careful not to build too-large volumes that could result in both long rebuild times if a disk were to fail or long restore times if the entire volume is made unavailable. Most deployments use volumes well under 200 GB. Of course, this may vary and may be gated by the actual requirements in terms of capacity handling of the storage subsystem as well as the resulting backup and restore infrastructure that is needed to get back into operating mode if a disaster-sized problem (i.e., loss of the entire server) were to occur.

I described a good deal of this technology earlier in this book, so I won't expand on it here. Instead, I would recommend that you build balanced servers, which combine appropriately the needed performance, reliability, and cost features.

7.3   Configuration Guidelines for Exchange 2003 Servers

This section contains actual server configurations that I recommend for running Exchange 2003. There are, of course, several models, and there can be at least one or two orders of magnitude of price differences between any two configurations of this set. Price differences are not necessarily due to the capacity of the server but more to the ability to handle growing workloads while maintaining high availability.

7.3.1   Back-End Servers

Back-end servers regroup the category of servers hosting user information such as mailboxes and public folders, including both MAPI public folders and additional public folders built from separate hierarchies. They also comprise Exchange journaling servers, when dedicated to this particular function.

Back-end servers are prime candidates for Windows 2003 clustering because they contain information that, with the exception of MAPI public folders, cannot be replicated and is therefore unique within the Exchange organization. User mailboxes are stored in a single place in a Microsoft Exchange network (i.e., in the mailbox database, accessed by the Exchange Information Store process), and they may not be activated on another server. That server, hosting user mailboxes, better be up and running, and delivering satisfactorily on performance requirements, both while users access the server for their regular work and for any management tasks that need to be achieved within a defined time period (e.g., running a backup at night, or recovering databases within, say, 2 hours).

Everything you can do to protect, proactively monitor, and maintain this server will be work that is both well regarded and well rewarded. That said, there are some guidelines that you should follow in building your server. These guidelines depend primarily on the user load factor and the quantity of data "owned" by the server. It is quite difficult to provide a ballpark figure for the number of spindles needed for hosting a group of databases without knowing the type of user profiles and the resulting workload generated.

The configuration is provided as tables, each of which contains the configuration for the core elements of a Windows server: CPU, memory, network I/O devices, and storage I/O devices. The indications given are minimum values; you may, of course, top these resources with additional elements as you desire, depending on the application set on the machine. These configurations primarily aim at sizing for MAPI clients. When using other protocols, such as IMAP and POP, the numbers can vary quite a lot (typically, you may scale up to 20,000 mailboxes using such protocols, with similar processor and disk requirements).

As you can observe, the 200-user server in Table 7.2 provides quite a lot of capacity, yet might require bigger drives for the database files if the user mailbox quota is to be above 500 MB. For a small server (with a low number of users), you really need to keep a separation of the Exchange database and transaction log files. Two hundred users are unlikely to saturate a 2-disk RAID1 mirror for the database files. The transaction logging should not exceed 20 to 30 I/O per second; thus, it is OK to co-locate the transaction log files on the system disk, for which there should be little activity if the server is primarily running Microsoft Exchange.

Table 7.2 *200-User Back-End Server*

Resource	Description		
CPU	Single or dual-core Intel Xeon 2.8 GHz AMD Opteron 1.8 GHz		
	L2 cache 512 KB or 1 MB		
Memory	1-GB RAM		
Network	1 × 100 Mb/s NIC		
Storage: internal, on-board, or PCI RAID controller	RAID1 (2 × 72 GB)	C: (8 GB)	Operating system and all products binaries
		D: (2 GB)	IIS and event logs
		Z: (4 GB)	Pagefile
		L: (8 GB)	Exchange transaction log files
	RAID1 (2 × 72 or 146 GB)	N: (100 GB max)	Exchange database files
	Tape drive	Built-in SDLT or LTO, or network backup	

For a 500-user server, as shown in Table 7.3, you must bring consideration to the back-end storage request rate capacity (I/O per second): you will need at minimum 4 disks to deal with the anticipated I/O demand from Exchange to the databases. The transaction logging becomes heavier and might even require being on separate disks, if the users are particularly heavy (sending more than 50 messages and receiving more than 150 messages per day).

Table 7.3 *500-User Back-End Server*

Resource	Description
CPU	2 × single or dual-core Intel Xeon 2.8 GHz AMD Opteron 1.8 GHz
	L2 cache 512 KB or 1 MB
Memory	2-GB RAM
Network	1 × 100 Mb/s NIC

Table 7.3   *500-User Back-End Server (continued)*

Resource	Description		
Storage: internal, on-board, or PCI RAID controller, external storage controller	RAID1 (2 × 72 GB)	C: (8 GB)	Operating system and all products binaries
		D: (2 GB)	IIS and event logs
		Z: (4 GB)	Pagefile
	RAID1 (2 × 72 GB)	K: (12 GB)	Exchange transaction log files for storage group 1
		L: (12 GB)	Transaction log files for storage group 2
	RAID5 (4 × 72 GB or 146 GB SAS)	N: (150 GB max)	Exchange database files for storage group 1
		O: (150 GB max)	Exchange database files for storage group 2
	Tape drive	SuperDLT, LTO-3, or network backup/robotics/backup to disk	

The configuration in Table 7.3 requires a total of 8 disks, which is not a common server configuration with locally attached storage, unless you use an expansion bay. If you have a server that can host up to 6 high-performance disks (15-krpm SCSI), you may consider co-hosting the transaction log files' partitions on the same mirror hosting the operating system. For 500 users, the number of disks for the database volumes will range between 3 and 4, depending on the user demand; you may of course benchmark your environment, but I recommend that you use 4 disks in RAID5 (RAID0+1 is OK, too, if you do not need the space), and refrain from using only 3 disks. Note that if you use RAID5, you should make sure that the disk controller has a battery backed-up write cache (even if you disable write caching: the RAID5 parity update operation needs to be atomic, and using a battery backed-up controller is one of the best ways to ensure this atomicity and avoid having to go through a volume reconstruction phase that would be detrimental to the server performance and availability).

The configuration shown in Table 7.3 suggests the use of two storage groups, which would help to grow the environment without the burden of large files. It is not mandatory to deploy more than one storage group, but since Exchange 2003 SP1, the overhead of virtual memory utilization has been largely diminished when using several storage groups, and this enables you to parallelize certain activities, such as databases backup and recovery.

The maximum partition sizes I suggest depend largely upon the backup and recovery capabilities. With the advent of high-speed tape libraries and virtual tape libraries, the backup throughput is largely augmented and may address small recovery times with large data quantities (in excess of 150 GB).

The 1,000-user back-end server greatly resembles the 500-user server, with the exception of two additional volumes for a second storage group transaction log file set and databases. I would say that this type of configuration could be taking advantage of externally attached storage, either directly by the means of UltraSCSI buses or networked (fibre channel SAN or IP SAN using iSCSI). Then, you should consider using clusters for such a large environment, which helps to reduce the duration of planned maintenance and addresses server failure issues.

I personally like to keep a single database below 250 users—this diminishes the maximum database size (if you have the same mailbox quota for all users) and the transaction rate to that particular database file set (transaction logs and property and streaming stores). You may very well decide to scale up (and, in fact, you have to scale up when hosting many more users per server), but with Exchange 2003 SP2, you should take advantage of the low overhead of database engine instances (storage groups) and create the four of them (the maximum number allowed) before adding more databases to a storage group.

The configuration shown in Table 7.4 for 1,000 users proposes the use of relatively small drives (72 GB and 146 GB) because these are known to produce good performance with a high rotation speed (15 krpm maximum). However, depending upon your deployment, you might use larger drives (300 GB) at a reduced rotation speed (10 krpm). In that case, add two drives or more to the RAID sets for the databases, which helps to make up for the reduced performance (and you'll get extra capacity!).

Table 7.4   *1,000-User Back-End Server*

Resource	Description
CPU	2 × single or dual-core Intel Xeon 2.8 GHz AMD Opteron 1.8 GHz
	L2 cache 1 MB
Memory	3-GB or 4-GB RAM

Table 7.4 *1,000-User Back-End Server (continued)*

Resource	Description		
Network	1 × 100 Mb/s NIC		
Storage: internal, on-board, or PCI RAID controller, external storage controller	RAID1 (2 × 72 GB)	C: (8 GB)	Operating system and all products binaries
		D: (2 GB)	IIS and event logs
		Z: (4 GB)	Pagefile
	RAID1 (2 × 72 GB)	I: (30 GB)	Exchange transaction log files for storage group 1
		J: (30 GB)	Transaction log files for storage group 2
	RAID1 (2 × 72GB)	K: (30 GB)	Exchange transaction log files for storage group 3
		L: (30 GB)	Transaction log files for storage group 4
	RAID5 (8 × 72 GB or 146 GB) or RAID0+1 (6 × 72 or 146 GB)	N: (150 GB max)	Exchange database files for storage group 1
		O: (150 GB max)	Exchange database files for storage group 2
	RAID5 (8×72GB or 146GB) or RAID0+1 (6 × 72 or 146 GB)	P: (150 GB max)	Exchange database files for storage group 3
		Q: (150 GB max)	Exchange database files for storage group 4
	RAID5 (6 × 72 or 146 GB)	R: (no max)	Disk staging area for backups and use with the recovery storage group
	Tape drive	Built-in SDLT or LTO, or network backup—consider dual tape drives for increasing the backup and recovery speed. Disk-based backup is also good for performance: use RAID5 sets of SATA drives (high capacity and "good enough" performance).	

The backup of such a server may be done to local tape or disks. In the latter case, you may consider the use of ATA disks (SATA or FATA), which provide greater capacity than SCSI drives at a lower cost. I would rather recommend you use high-performance and highly reliable SCSI drives for the production data and ATA disks for backup data, which is not accessed very often and is accessed in a different way (sequential) than online databases. It is also a great spot for temporarily hosting databases when using the Exchange 2003 recovery storage group.

For a 3,000-user server, as shown in Table 7.5, we basically add databases and scale up the database disk unit size by adding more disks to the RAID5 or RAID0+1 sets. It becomes appropriate, at that point, to dedicate a drive pair to each transaction log set (one per storage group). Remember, however, that this is not mandatory—all you require from the back-end storage subsystem is fast write response time. In running Jetstress qualification tests, you will be able to ensure such a fast response time, regardless of the sharing or dedication of drive units to the transaction log files.

Table 7.5   *3,000-User Back-End Server with SAN Storage*

Resource	Description		
CPU	2 × dual-core Intel Xeon 2.8 GHz AMD Opteron 1.8 GHz or 4 × single-core Intel Xeon		
	L2 cache 1MB		
Memory	4-GB RAM		
Network	2 × 100 Mb/s NIC minimum		
Storage: internal, on-board, or PCI RAID controller for system disk	RAID1 (2×72GB)	C: (8 GB)	Operating system and all products binaries
		D: (2 GB)	IIS and event logs
		Z: (4 GB)	Pagefile

Table 7.5 *3,000-User Back-End Server with SAN Storage (continued)*

Resource	Description		
Network storage controller for logs and databases	RAID1 (2 × 72 GB)	I: (70 GB)	Exchange transaction log files for storage group 1
	RAID1 (2 × 72 GB)	J: (70 GB)	Transaction log files for storage group 2
	RAID1 (2 × 72 GB)	K: (70 GB)	Exchange transaction log files for storage group 3
	RAID1 (2 × 72 GB)	L: (30 GB)	Transaction log files for storage group 4
	RAID5 (8 × 72 GB or 146 GB) or RAID0+1 (6 × 72 or 146 GB)	N: (150 GB max)	Exchange database files for storage group 1 temp area SMTP mailroot folder
		O: (150 GB max)	Exchange database files for storage group 2
	RAID5 (8 × 72 GB or 146 GB) or RAID0+1 (6 × 72 or 146 GB)	P: (150 GB max)	Exchange database files for storage group 3
		Q: (150 GB max)	Exchange database files for storage group 4
	RAID5 (6 × 72 or 146 GB)	R: (no max)	Disk staging area for backups and use with the recovery storage group
	Tape drive	Built-in SDLT or LTO, or network backup—consider dual tape drives for increasing the backup and recovery speed. Disk-based backup is also good for performance: use RAID5 sets of SATA drives (high capacity and "good enough" performance). Consider VSSs for fast recovery of the databases.	

With Exchange 2003 SP2 and Windows Server 2003 SP1, the maximum number of users varies, but generally, it's considered safe to stop at 3,500 users. Past that number, in cases of high concurrency (4,500 users connected and above) and utilization of many connections per client, as with Outlook 2003 in cache mode, there can be a kernel memory pool depletion (consumption for security tokens) that can result in failure to connect and, ultimately, system crashes. This is basically where Microsoft Exchange reaches the architectural limits of the 32-bit version of Windows Server 2003, and only by Exchange 2007 and Windows Server 2003 on x64 machines (therefore running in 64-bit mode, with a 64-bit address space) will we be able to scale up servers and host more users. Exchange

2007 comes with many other features that enable such a scale-up (more storage groups per server)—but here, we're hitting a hard rock and need to scale out for stability reasons.

In the case of non-MAPI clients, you should be able to scale up the environment, especially if you are running as a service provider with a relatively low concurrency rate (we have seen servers supporting in excess of 125,000 mailboxes, but with a low concurrency rate and using POP3 protocol).

7.3.2   Front-End Servers

Front-end servers typically require different resources than back-end servers, especially at the storage level. They are prime candidates for 1 U–type servers that have a small footprint in a computer rack and can easily scale out (by adding more machines). Because you can efficiently use network load balancing with front-end servers, something you can't do with back-end servers, you can omit some of the traditional availability features, such as hot-plug drives and memory modules, and scale out the number of servers in your environment. Don't neglect the more recent features introduced with Exchange 2003 SP1 and SP2, such as ActiveSync and OWA spellchecker; they can consume resources on the front-end servers, possibly in the ratio that we typically recommend (one front-end server for four back-end servers).

Table 7.6   *Typical Front-End Server for Client Access*

Resource	Description
CPU	Dual-core Intel Xeon 2.8 GHz or AMD Opteron 1.8 GHz
	Dual processor optional
	L2 cache 1 MB
Memory	2-GB RAM
Network	2 × 100 Mb/s NIC

➤

Table 7.6   *Typical Front-End Server for Client Access (continued)*

Resource	Description		
Storage: internal, on-board, or PCI RAID controller	RAID1 (2 × 72 GB)	C: (8 GB)	Operating system and all products binaries
		D: (2 GB)	IIS and event logs
		Z: (4 GB)	Pagefile
		L: (8 GB)	Exchange transaction log files
	RAID1 (2 × 72 or 146 GB)	N: (100 GB max)	Exchange database files

Bridgehead Servers

Bridgehead servers include SMTP relay hosts in service provider environment functions as well as acting as message switches in the realm of a single Exchange 2003 organization with multiple routing groups. The challenge with bridgehead servers—and in fact, with any server that will intensively use SMTP message routing, now predominant in Exchange networks—lies with the storage support to be provided by the NTFS-based queues utilized by the routing component.

You also need to keep in mind that this type of server will need local, intermediate Exchange store capabilities for the MAPI-based connectors, as well as hefty CPU processing capabilities for antivirus real-time scanning and message conversion if needed. Therefore, I would suggest emphasizing the scale-up capabilities of the machine (start with two processors and allow it to scale up to as many as four processors), rather than emphasizing the physical RAM, disabling the /3GB boot switch (even if there is more than 1 GB of RAM), and tuning the server to max out the NT I/O subsystem cache, as shown in Figure 7.6. To reach to the performance options of the server, select the properties of the computer in the start menu, or use the System applet in the Control Panel.

This recommendation holds true for all Exchange servers' roles except back-end mailbox servers (which will need all the memory available for the database engines); see Table 7.7.

7.3.3   Sample Scale-Up and Scale-Out Configurations

In this particular section, I would like to present some actual scale-up and scale-out configurations that should be considered for Windows 2003 clus-

Figure 7.6
*Maximizing the
system cache on a
bridgehead server*

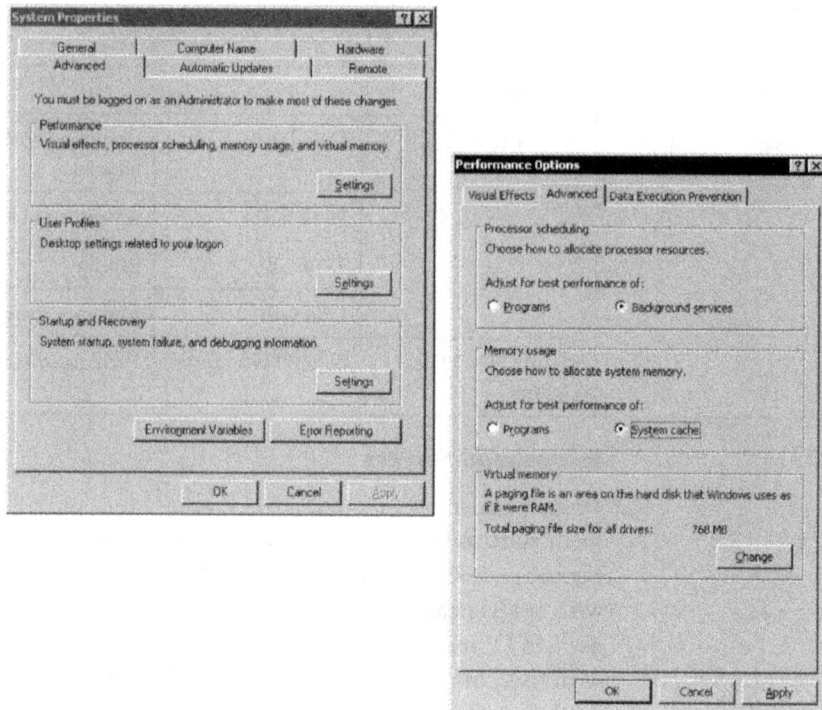

Table 7.7   *Bridgehead server configuration*

Resource	Description		
CPU	Dual-core Intel Xeon 2.8GHz or AMD Opteron 1.8GHz Dual processor optional		
	L2 Cache 1MB		
Memory	2GB RAM		
Network	2 × 100Mbps NIC		
Storage Internal, on-board, or PCI RAID controller	RAID1 (2×72GB)	C: (8GB)	Operating system and all products binaries
		D: (2GB)	IIS and event logs
		Z: (4GB)	Pagefile
		L: (8GB)	Exchange transaction log files
	RAID1 (4×72 or 146GB)	N: (100GB max)	Exchange Database Files and SMTP mailroot

ters or service-provider environments. We actually touched base on some aspects in the previous chapters of this book, and I hope that these can serve as reference points for you.

7.3.4   Data Center

The enterprise data center really aims at hosting, in the most secure and available manner, the largest number of users in a single location. Typically, these data centers have a secondary, not-so-distant (15-km or so) site, which contains an exact replica of the production environment, or at minimum enough computing resources to restart after a site failure. Computing operations can be switched to this recovery site in case a major disaster occurs in the main production data center.

Let's have a look first at the overall picture shown in Figure 7.7.

Figure 7.7
*Data center
topology for
Exchange 2003*

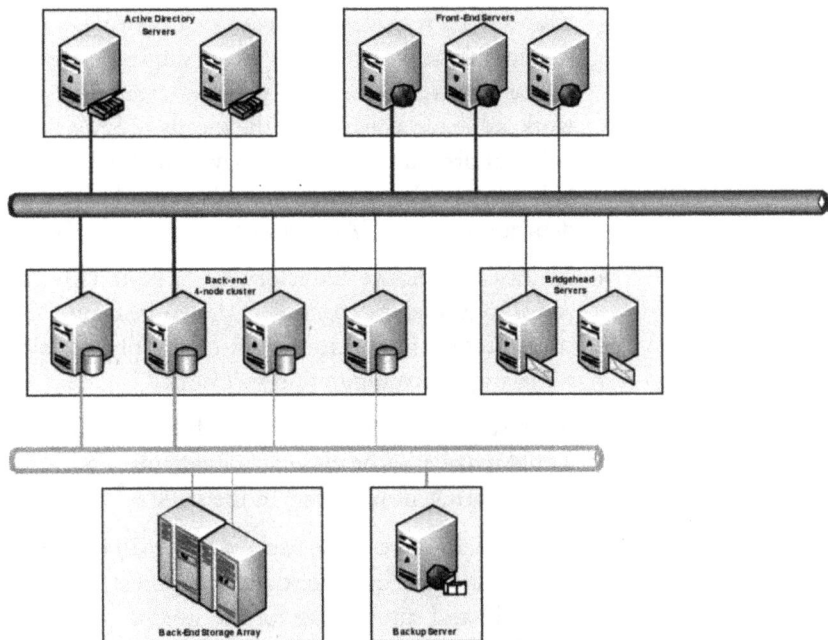

As you can see, the data center in question is in fact composed of key central elements (e.g., the mailbox store servers, which we refer to as the back-end servers), but it also has surrounding servers. This may be considered going backward in a server consolidation scenario (i.e., having additional servers around a core of a few main back-end servers), but in fact it's not. It is crucial to understand the dependence that Exchange 2003 has on surrounding network services such as Active Directory and DNS.

The main elements of this data center are as follows:

- Four back-end servers in a clustered environment (three nodes are active and one is passive).

- A supporting SAN that holds the private and public stores utilized by the back-end servers. The SAN, in itself, does not need to hold Active Directory information. Because the Active Directory works on the basis of a multimaster replicated environment, the loss of a volume holding the NTDS.DIT Active Directory database can be addressed by rebuilding the volume and recreating the domain controller or global catalog. Note that this can take a significant amount of time if you deal with a large (>1,000,000 entries) directory. Note that all connections within the storage area network are duplicated. Indeed, it wouldn't be reasonable to create single points of failure in that particular infrastructure. The volumes created in the storage area network are made available by the means of SAN RAID controllers. The volumes are built in such a way that if a back-end SAN controller fails entirely, the volumes are still available. This approach may vary, depending on the SAN vendor.

- At least two Active Directory GCs. Note that Exchange also needs access to a domain controller (shown in Figure 7.7) for retrieving its configuration information, but connecting to either of the GCs for retrieving the configuration will suffice.

- At least two bridgehead servers for outbound communications. It would make a lot of sense to actually place both the back-end servers and the bridgehead servers in the same routing group.

- One backup server. The backup server (in fact, it is common to use a series of servers for redundancy purposes) is necessary to connect to the SAN and run backup for the storage network. We are not showing the tape or disk media used for the backups in this diagram in Figure 7.7. In fact, this can vary greatly, depending on your backup strategy and current operations. I have seen many customers that have already deployed a fibre channel–based SAN for running their backups. Rather than worrying about the possible interoperability issues with the database storage area network, all they do is add an additional adapter in the servers to be backed, which connects to the SAN backup. This, in fact, is creating SAN islands, but it's OK for the time being, until all SANs of the world (or at least those in your data center) unite!

■ Front-end servers that are used for primarily Internet protocols. MAPI clients would connect directly to the back-end servers, but since the introduction of RPC over HTTP, it becomes interesting to use front-end servers to act as RPC proxies (this is in fact the recommended approach from Microsoft). Therefore, you create a level of "independence" between the Outlook client and the back-end servers, where the MAPI client connects to the back-end servers via an intermediate server.

7.3.5 Replicated Data Center

Once you have deployed in a data center, you will probably be interested in deploying Microsoft Exchange in a redundant manner—there are some limitations to how fast you can run your servers and how high you can scale them, depending upon the storage replication technology used between the two data centers (Figure 7.8).

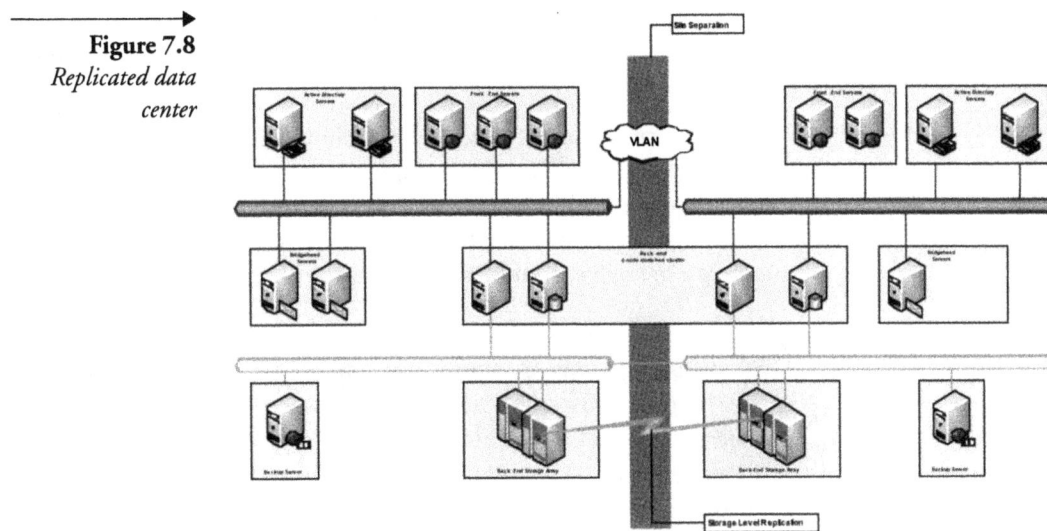

Figure 7.8
Replicated data center

In such an environment, the replication between the two storage networks is rather crucial, ensuring that any change done on the left side of the topology gets timeline replicated to the remote end and then acknowledged to the local so operations can continue.

In this diagram, you noticed that all nodes of the cluster are not active. In fact, each node in the 4-node stretched cluster can be either passive or active (represented by the little database icon tagged on the server symbol).

A virtual LAN connects each site—the VLAN is required to enable the cluster keep-alive traffic between *all* nodes of the clusters (located in either data center). In addition, it must have a latency of less than 500ms: that is the time-out limit used for intra-cluster node communication. If exceeded, the node will be considered out of reach and considered offline. Usually, network administrators are not too happy to configure VLAN across long distances. But all nodes in a Windows cluster have to be in the same subnet, a restriction that is likely to be taken away with the next major release of Windows, currently code named Longhorn. That version is the basis for the Windows Vista operating system that will come out in early 2007.

Because there are production servers on both sites, it becomes necessary to duplicate infrastructure components of the data center for Exchange, such as front-end servers and backup servers. They do not necessarily have to be the same number because the network unavailability of any of them may fall back to the "other" site—but it's better than nothing.

Although this is not something related to the scale-out or scale-up of an exchange environment, I would like to come back to the stretched cluster components of that diagram in Figure 7.9.

In such an environment, you have the opportunity to perform local failovers that do not simply involve storage components from one machine to another. This is particularly useful if you wish to apply a simple service pack or run some planned maintenance on an active server. Then, if you perform a remote failover, you have two opportunities:

1.   Accessing the storage components remotely from Site B to Site A: this is really OK if the sites are only meters apart (500m or so) and can provide sufficient bandwidth with a reduced latency. This is something we typically find in data centers with a failover site within a campus or perhaps a metropolitan area.

2.   Accessing the storage locally in Site B: then you need to perform a storage failover if the intersite link is not fast enough—this is often the case.

So, depending upon the site geographical characteristics, you will have to complement the Site A service failover with a Site A (to Site B) storage

Figure 7.9
*Failing over locally
or remotely*

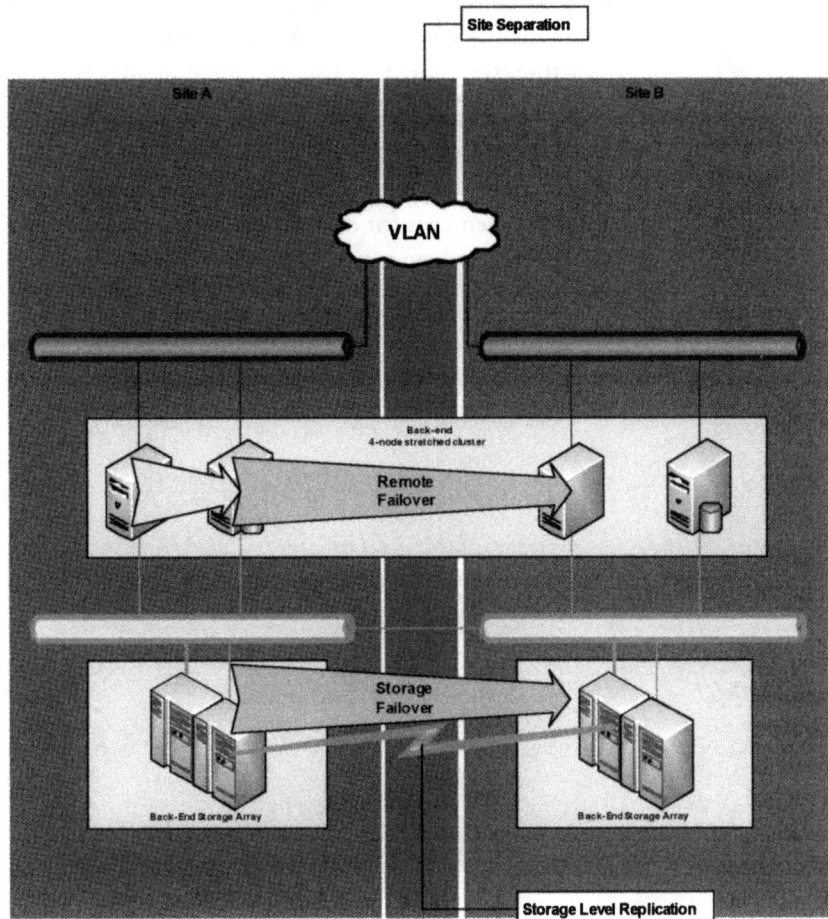

failover. This tends to be relatively complex, depending on how dedicated or aware your storage administration team is about the Exchange "peculiarities."

7.4 In Summary

In the previous section, we have seen how servers would need to be configured for most of the roles and how data centers should be equipped in terms of functions. The actual implementation and sizing of each of the components is largely dependent on the work that these servers will have to do. In general, you can scale up most servers, in terms of processors and storage capacity. The *storage* replication features when operating in multiple data centers are *necessary* because, typically, you will want some form of redundancy—scaling that redundancy is probably the area where you will need to spend the most time. Fortunately, there are sizing tools and stress tools (such as Microsoft's JetStress) that can be used to verify that the infrastructure components deliver upon requirements.

So, no matter what type of components, back-end storage arrays, or interconnects you will be employing, you should, for maximizing the predictability of your deployment, ensure that you properly formulate your requirements for each of the components, and especially the storage subsystem, and even *more* especially if you have a replication topology to deal with.

With this, I hope that you have found in this book enough hints on how to get to a scaled-up environment and how to add more machines/servers for scaling-out the environment.

Index

www.ingramcontent.com/pod-product-compliance
Lightning Source LLC
Chambersburg PA
CBHW060941210326
41598CB00031B/4690